RUNNING
on a mind
ЯEWIRED

"I can relate to the horrific self-induced, drug-addicted lifestyle that Jennifer led, as I survived my own thirteen-year drug addiction. I believe that we can overcome addiction once we determine we are doing so for ourselves and are willing to put the same effort into discovering a new life as we did into destroying our previous one. Traditional ways of attaining sobriety do not work for all of us, and therefore I applaud Jennifer for showcasing the benefits of running as her way of sustaining her sobriety and dealing with her medical condition."

—**Todd Crandell**, professional counselor, licensed
   chemical dependency counselor, and founder,
   Racing for Recovery (www.RacingforRecovery.com)

R U N N I N G
on a mind
ЯEWIRED

a memoir

To Kelsey,
Thank you for your support!
Cherish life & keep listening
for the lessons.
Shine On!
NC

NATE
~~JENNIFER~~
CANNON

SoulBalance
Press

SoulBalance Press, Minneapolis, MN
For more information, go to: www.runningrewired.com

ISBN 13: 978-0-9839448-2-9
e-book ISBN: 978-0-9839448-6-7

Cover design by Brad Norr. Photography by Vanessa Cannon.
Book production by Trio Bookworks, Minneapolis.

Printed in the United States of America
15 14 13 12 11   1 2 3 4 5

For my mom, who never lost faith in me

For Krissy, for being the most amazing woman in the world

And for anyone who never gave up on me—
or who won't give up on themselves

Contents

Contents

PART TWO

Foreword

Life is a journey that comes with expectations and dreams. Jennifer Cannon should have lived an accomplished life filled with athletic and academic achievements. Instead, a perfect storm of anxiety, depression, injuries, addiction, and alcoholism derailed her journey. In her formative years, Jennifer waged one battle after another with her inner demons. Many of my friends have fought these same battles, and way too many have been lost along the way to drugs and alcohol. But Jennifer is a survivor. This book chronicles her journey through the highs of athletic and academic achievements, which were overcome by the lows of depression, the spiraling abyss of drug addiction, the scars of serious physical injuries, and the dark, lonely depths of alcoholism. Jennifer bravely allows us to travel the long road with her as she struggles to become the person she desperately knows she has to be to regain control of her life. She overcomes seemingly insurmountable hurdles, and yet her struggles are not behind her, as the perilous odyssey gave her one ironic and cruel souvenir: dystonia.

Dystonia is a battle one cannot win, for there is no cure. It is a fight that can only be endured and persevered. Jennifer and I and possibly another three hundred thousand Americans are now on this journey of life, in which no one is given a map or a weather forecast. We never know what tomorrow will bring; we must be ready for whatever dystonia delivers. Unlike her earlier struggles against addiction and alcoholism, Jennifer now faces an opponent she knows she can't defeat, but she also knows she can't let dystonia win and take away the life she has built. Those of us with dystonia are playing for a tie every day; we have to keep getting up off the floor.

Jennifer's unrelenting determination, along with her courage in sharing her life with the world, is an inspiration to me and everyone who has dystonia. With her every step in training and racing, Jennifer carries along the hopes of all who face the challenges of not one but two or more chronic diseases. Like dystonia, there is no cure for either addiction or depression. There are only physical and emotional trials to be faced every day with hope, optimism, love, and determination to aid us. After having faced so much adversity, Jennifer still has the courage, resilience, and fortitude to carry on her fight for the rest of her life.

I met Jennifer a few weeks before the 2010 Twin Cities Marathon. I was impressed by this young woman's determination to not only complete a daunting task for a second time but also tell the world her personal story. The mere fact you are holding this book is evidence of her spirit and dauntless resolve. During the race I was glued to my computer for news, and later I waited on pins and needles to hear that her book would be published. I received wonderful news on both counts. Jennifer finished both her second Twin Cities Marathon and her book—a testament to her struggles that also honors everyone who stood by her.

In every triumph over adversity, no one is ever alone. At every juncture of her journey, Jennifer has been fortunate to have had a loving support system. Everyone who has helped her along her journey has my sympathy and admiration. Having been on both sides of this fence, I know the challenges they faced with tough love. Krissy has admirably and unconditionally joined Jennifer in her continuing struggle against dystonia, a disease that is as tenacious and unforgiving as addiction. Knowing you are not alone does not make the journey easier; it just makes it worthwhile.

I am proud and honored to introduce Jennifer's intrepid and compelling story about her continuing struggle for a quality of life we all deserve. To Jennifer and everyone on a similar journey: fight on, for you are never alone. We are all with you, and together we are stronger.

—Noel Valero
Founder, American Dystonia Society

PART ONE

Breathe

I'm fighting to open my eyes, fighting to stay conscious. I'm coming to, but don't know where I am. Visions of a hockey rink are running through my mind. I'm skating down the ice with wind rushing my face, flying toward the silhouette of a net illuminated in white. I hear the roar of a crowd. It gets louder and louder until I take a shot and then *bang*—I get pulled off to the right and up toward a bright light.

Now I'm back at center ice. The sequence repeats. I'm skating down the ice toward the net, with the wind, the roar, the shot. There's that bang, then the pull. And I'm back at center ice. Again. Repeat. Each time I get pulled, I get pulled a little further. Each time I hear the bang, it gets a little louder.

A wall separating the bleachers from the ice stops my path. I never cross that line. I only get pulled so far before *bang*—I get spit right back.

My EYES SPRANG open. My body heaved backwards. I gasped deeply for air. My eyes started to close. My head smashed to the floor.

I pried my lids open. My whole upper body heaved backwards once more.

Something was wrong. But what?

At some point I figured it out: I had to breathe. If I didn't, I was going to die. Or maybe I already had.

I was coming to when my vision became blinded by a sea of red. Perhaps it was the blood soaking my face. Or maybe it was just the color my mind chose to create in the moment. It didn't really matter. All I knew was that something was wrong. Terribly wrong.

The rhythmical thud I kept hearing grew louder and louder. Eventually it echoed loudly enough inside my head to awaken my consciousness.

I was taking what could've been my last gasp when my left hand guided itself to the back of my neck. Fighting to loosen the noose strangling my airway, I summoned my last bit of strength and—by the grace of some power greater than I—managed to unknot the remaining portion of the cord and loosen it from my neck.

The blood flow quickly resumed, sending throbbing pulses through my upper body as it crept back through my system to exchange between my heart and my brain. At last I could take in air, the precious oxygen I so desperately needed.

I lay curled up awkwardly on my right side, arms pinned tightly against my chest. Panting heavily, I tried to collect my thoughts and retrieve my breath. Sweat poured from my body. My head was pounding. My vision was still blurred. Where was I? What happened? How did I end up on a bathroom floor in a pool of blood with a cord wrapped around my neck?

Gradually I realized what I'd done: I'd tried to hang myself.

I'd almost succeeded. But—worse—I'd failed.

Remembering that I was locked in a psychiatric ward, I frantically started working to conceal my actions. I had to cover up the mess I'd made before anyone could find out what I'd done. I was already committed by a court for crack addiction after hitting my own mom. How much lower could I get?

How pathetic to not even be able to kill yourself, I thought. *What a failure you are.* It was yet another thing I couldn't do well enough to be successful at—one more thing I couldn't get right.

I tore off my new sweatshirt, which bore the name of the college I was set to attend in just a few months, and tried to wipe up the blood covering the floor. It was a futile effort. The bitter tang of blood trickled down the back of my throat as I reached a hand to my face. It was gushing in a stream from my right eye to the floor.

Why was I so bloody, anyway? I had to see for myself just how bad this was. Struggling through the dizziness and intense pressure barreling down on my head, I managed to stand up and stumble over to the mirror.

I PROPPED MYSELF on the counter as I stared into my own eyes. I couldn't believe what I was seeing in my reflection. A wide gash intersecting my right eyebrow oozed blood. My right eye was bloodshot and becoming increasingly swollen. My nose, caked with dried blood, was taking on a pinkish tint. It also looked to be a bit crooked.

A thin red line circled my neck, drawing a clear mark where the cord had been wrapped. The multicolored hue spreading outside the ring was turning darker by the second.

I was going to have a hard time covering this up.

Holding out hope I could come up with some other explanation for the situation, I attempted to conceal the remnants of my make-shift noose. I was still holding in my hand one half of the electrical cord, the half that had remained wrapped tightly around my neck after it snapped. The other half was still wedged into the top of the shower door, where I had secured it before kicking the wastebasket out from under my feet. Unfortunately, the shower door had locked when I closed it, and now there was no way of removing the piece of the cord still trapped there.

Panic stricken, I stood helpless in the middle of the bathroom, looking around me. There was blood everywhere: on my body, my clothes, the floor, the walls, the toilet, the shower, and the wastebasket. It even covered the note on the counter. It only made matters worse that the cord was still stuck. Though I was a pretty good liar at the time, I couldn't construct any sort of explanation for it all. I was going to have to be honest. It didn't help that I was starting to feel light-headed.

I stumbled through the doorway and out into the hall, head down. I didn't take two steps before I ran into the psych ward nurse, who was on her way to see me.

I was on suicide watch and knew I was being checked on every fifteen minutes. It really wasn't her fault I'd tried to do myself in on her shift, though. I was determined to kill myself that night. The lamp with the electrical cord should have never been left in that psych ward room. But the fact that I used the cord from that lamp, and not a bed sheet is probably what saved my life.

I wasn't out of the woods yet, though. I was becoming very weak.

The nurse's eyes darted back and forth between the cord in my hand and the blood pouring from my right eye. "Oh my God," she said. "What did you do?"

I was feeling fainter by the moment, and my hoarse voice drifted to a whisper. "I, uh . . . well, I tried . . . I tried to kill myself."

"Oh my God!" She shouted down the long corridor, "We need assistance down here, immediately!" A second nurse rushed in our direction, pushing a wheelchair.

I softly collapsed into it before drifting out of consciousness.

SUCCESS RUNS IN my family. Almost as strongly as chemical dependency does.

In the early twentieth century, my great-great-grandfather established Cannon Mills, which would become the largest textile company in the world. He had five sons, according to *Time* magazine, "four of them given to jollity and excesses, one given to sober industry." He would will his textile mills to his "sober youngest son."

My great-grandpa was that sober one. He led Cannon Mills to the height of success in the mid-twentieth century but still couldn't undo his genetics. My dad was also an alcoholic. He took off when I was just two, leaving behind a wife and four young kids. I didn't communicate with him much while I was growing up, but I inherited his genetic potential, for both success and self-destruction.

I never set out to become an addict or an alcoholic. I never wanted to destroy my life, damage my brain, or come so close to killing myself that I'd wake up strangling on a psych ward floor. Quite the contrary: I fought to resist my genes. I fought to drink socially and use drugs experimentally, as other kids seemed to be able to do. I never wanted to get hooked.

But I did. And in the end I was the only one who could save me from myself.

I'd love to say that life after drugs and alcohol is easy. Chemical dependency isn't always as simple as going to rehab and coming out fixed, though. Nor are head injuries and concussions things you can safely play through.

Sometimes the damage is permanent. But you have to keep running.

1

Smoked

Hockey was my first high. The ice is where I first learned to take a hit.

Growing up as a tomboy in western Iowa in the mid-1980s, I had no choice but to hang with the boys in order to do the things I wanted. And more than anything, I wanted to play ice hockey.

There was no girls' hockey in Iowa back then. There weren't even any girls in the league. From the time I started skating at eight years old, it was just me and the boys—just the way I wanted it. And as the only girl on the team, I learned to always get back up on my feet, no matter how plastered I got.

It's a lesson I'd carry with me throughout my chemical dependency: to never let the effects show. However dazed I felt, I learned from a young age that no matter what happened, you never stay down after taking a hit, you never let the pain show, and you always get back up to your feet.

Maybe it was the influence of my two older brothers that pushed me to get involved in boys' activities at such a young age. Or maybe it's just the way I am. Long before I ever had to admit to being an addict and an alcoholic, I had to accept the fact that I was a tomboy. From the time I chose the boys' Big Wheel on the preschool playground, I made my personal preferences clear, too. I didn't like the things the other girls liked.

I didn't like the color pink, the pretty glittery lace on the handlebars of girls' bikes, or even the fact that the other girls were using them. Wearing my blue Oshkosh B'gosh overalls, I wanted to go over to the black Big Wheels and park myself on one of those instead. So that's exactly what I did.

I spent most summers of my youth with a mouth full of dirt, riding bikes and playing Little League baseball. But when school was in session, I couldn't spend long afternoons hanging out with the boys. I had to play after-school sports with the girls. Of course, I would have preferred to have registered for the boys' teams, but in the case of basketball and soccer, I didn't have that option.

I was only in second grade when, at the end of the school day on an early fall afternoon, a stack of brochures was handed out to the class. I sat in the back row, waiting for the light blue handout to reach me. I noticed immediately that the girls in class were uninterested in the material. They each took one glance at the brochure, put it down, and turned to their nearest friend to talk about something unrelated. The flyer reached my desk just as one of my bike-riding friends leaned over and said to me, "Maybe you should play."

I looked down at the brochure in my hand. "Youth Hockey Association," it read.

My male friends had already been playing hockey for a couple years. I had spent my winters taking ice skating lessons but then playing basketball with the girls. And now here it was, in big black letters: "Boys and Girls Welcome."

MY MOM WASN'T taken with the idea. Hockey involved expensive equipment, early morning practices, and weekend travel. It all sounded so inconvenient that she hadn't even let my two older brothers play. But I had a leg up on them. I already knew how to ice skate, and I wasn't about to take no for an answer. In the face of my incessant nagging, she finally folded. Thus began my love affair for a sport that would save my life.

As the years went by, though, I discovered that my size and gender worked to my disadvantage. I was one of very few girls playing hockey in the state of Iowa, and I drew attention from players and parents alike wherever I went to skate.

WHEN THE BOYS started checking at the age of twelve, I started to get hit. At that young age, I could still hold my own, and I grew adept at using my agility and quickness to get out of some sticky situations. But as the boys got older, they got bigger.

I, on the other hand, did not. As an adult, I'm only five feet two, so you can imagine how I was dwarfed in size when the boys started to hit their growth spurts.

With my long brown ponytail flowing from the back of my helmet, I was hard to miss. And to the boys on the other teams, that ponytail looked like a bull's-eye on my back. Every chance they could, they took a run at me just to let me know that they were stronger than me and that I was out there playing their game.

My coaches encouraged me to put my hair up in my helmet, but I wouldn't do it. The players and parents all saw me walk into the arena with my bag. They knew there was a girl on the team before I ever set foot on the ice. Putting my hair up wouldn't have made a bit of difference. Besides, I was proud to be holding my own with the boys, even if I was getting smoked so hard during weekend tournaments that it hurt to breathe on Monday mornings.

I'd already sustained two concussions when I was encouraged to try the goaltending position at age fourteen. I enjoyed the transition. But after I tore my meniscus and needed surgery on my left knee, I pushed against the urgings of all the parents and sought desperately to move back to my position as a forward.

My mom grew increasingly uncomfortable with the idea. She took me up to Minnesota, where I tried out for an elite girls' team. I made the roster and played two seasons as a member of both a boys' team in Iowa and a girls' team in Minnesota. But making the five-hour trek to and from Minneapolis every weekend was both exhausting and expensive.

If I was going to keep playing in high school, I was going to have to keep playing with the boys.

THROUGHOUT MY YOUTH, whenever I wasn't skating on ice, I was skating on Rollerblades. Either way, I always had a hockey stick in hand. I'd strap on my skates, grab my stick, and head out the long driveway to the quiet cul-de-sac where I could shoot the puck at the net I had set up. The older I got, the less often the boys came over to play, and by the time I was twelve, I was frequently skating alone.

I really didn't mind. It was the one place I preferred to be all by myself. It was exactly where I wanted to be. I'd spend hours skating, shooting pucks at the blue mesh of that steel-piped net. It was like my own private sanctuary.

Hockey was the one thing I craved, and getting my hockey fix was all I needed to get through the day.

ON ONE PARTICULARLY sultry summer day, I pulled on my thick black gloves and stepped out into the sunshine, smiling.

I practiced for one hour, then two, then three. Visions and fantasies of Olympic gold medals streamed through my mind as I brushed the sweat from my brow. *I just need to feel that breeze brush my skin once more. Just one more time around, then I'll go in.*

I pulled the puck back on my stick and circled toward the net, picking up my skates and propelling myself toward it at full throttle. One stride left, then a second to the right, I pushed full speed ahead, feeling the breeze rush by. One breath in, one breath out—I pushed the air through my lungs to keep pace with my strides. I faked to the left, then back to the right. I took a shot . . . I roofed it.

There it was, my very first high.

I DREADED LEAVING the warmth of the summer sun to go back to school each fall. I didn't mind the school work; I was an outstanding student. It was the social scenes that were a challenge. And each year, I found the transition more difficult.

In the fall of seventh grade, it all came to a head. Not only was hockey getting more physical, but I was also finding myself pushed out of my social circles. Despite being short and boyish, I was still popular enough to be elected to student council. Everybody—the brains, the preppies, the athletes, the outcasts— liked me. But nobody wanted to be close enough to be a good friend anymore. The boys had started to look at the girls differently, and vice versa. I, the hard-core tomboy, was caught somewhere in the middle.

Having once been the go-between for the boys and the girls, I found it disheartening to suddenly be on the outside. The conditions were set for my first mental health crisis.

On an early December day, I left sewing class to attend a student council meeting. The next morning, the teacher, Mrs. Davis, opened the period by calling me up to the front of the class. It was an unusual request. Students weren't usually called on to come up front.

I hesitated and then rose from my seat and made my way to the front of the room. I stopped next to the teacher's desk, bowed my head, and peered over my right shoulder to look out at the classroom. All eyes were on me.

I looked up at Mrs. Davis, her piercing stare exaggerated by the frames of her thick black glasses. She looked at me with absolute scorn.

"Jennifer, would you please explain to the class why you got up and left yesterday without permission?"

My stomach dropped. I'd never been scolded by a teacher in front of a class before. In fact, I realized as I stood there blushing, I'd never been scolded by a teacher at all. I'd never even been in trouble before. I was usually the one setting the bar for grades and proper behavior.

My face started to feel hot; I knew I was turning red. The class started to chuckle. I had no response for the teacher's question. I shifted my weight back and forth, staring at the cracks in the tile floor.

"Ummm. I . . . I left to go to a student council meeting. I'm sorry."

"Did you get permission to go to the meeting?"

"No. I guess I didn't," I said, twisting my shoe on the tile.

"Well, do you think that's the kind of behavior that sets a good example for the rest of the class, Jennifer? To just up and leave without asking permission?"

"No, I guess it's not."

She turned to the class. "Okay, then. Hopefully we've all learned a lesson here. Ask permission before leaving the classroom." She sent another scolding look my direction. "You may be seated."

I took my place and tried to let the incident go, but I couldn't. My heart was still racing and my stomach still turning. My face was still bright red.

I couldn't take the embarrassment anymore. I had to get out of there.

I pushed my chair back, stood up, and bolted out of the room—without permission.

After a stop at the bathroom, I rushed to the school's front reception area. "I need to call my mom," I said.

"Why?" the receptionist asked.

I tried to explain but started to cry instead. "Please, just let me call my mom."

She dialed the number.

The next day I refused to go to school. And then the next. And the next.

I didn't return for four months.

Each morning my mom would roust me from bed and nudge me to get moving. I'd make my way to the bathroom, shower, and perhaps down a bowl of cereal. And then the anxiety would start in.

As the time to leave for school grew closer, I'd feel the inner tension build. My heart would start racing, my palms would get sweaty, my face would get flushed, and before I knew it, I was curled up on the floor in a ball, crying my twelve-year-old eyes out.

My mom would put her hand on my shoulder. "What's the matter, sweetie?"

"I can't go in there, Mom. I just can't do it."

I really couldn't. I didn't have it in me to walk the lonely corridors of a middle school filled to the brim with seemingly happy tweens. Most days I just couldn't bring myself to get in our minivan. If I did, then I couldn't bring myself to actually get out once we got to school.

My mom sent me to a psychiatrist, who put me on Prozac and called me depressed. Every week I'd sit on a couch and talk to a psychologist about how I was feeling. But I still wouldn't return to school.

Finally, after weeks of phoned-in absences and minimal improvement, I was put in an intensive day program for adolescents. I was the only one there for depression. Most of the kids were delinquents. When the Branch Davidians' compound burned to the ground on April 19, 1993, my peers were thrilled by the smoke and flames. I tried to stick to arts and crafts time and attended to my papier-mâché.

I learned very little from my peers during my six weeks of treatment—except how to use drugs and where to score them. We all went to class together, met with counselors, and had group together, but for the most part I stuck to myself. Still, I made some progress and won my first battle with clinical depression.

By May I was back in class part-time, ready for the summer sun. But things were never the same. I no longer fit in nor was I on student council. I was still too much a boy to be a girl, too much a girl to be a boy. And now I had a mysterious and lengthy absence that the other kids seemed to wonder about.

Hockey increasingly became my escape, my socialization, and, most importantly, my vision for my future in college.

By fifteen, I was playing boys' high school hockey, taking hit after hit, and always getting up to my feet. I was a tough girl ready to take on any guy in the league.

Then, without warning, everything changed.

2

Dislocated Dream

I couldn't move. I thought I was paralyzed. A wicked rush of uncertainty and fear overcame me. Tried as I might to orchestrate the instructions to make my muscles move, my legs and arms simply wouldn't budge. The crisp sound of skate blades cutting into the ice whirled through my ears. The whistle hadn't yet been blown, and play was still going on. I lay motionless, staring through my face mask at the cool surface beneath me.

A frantic voice erupted from my core: "Oh my God! I can't move! I can't *move!*"

I was stricken with panic. I was just fifteen years old, but I'd never been so scared in my whole life. I was absolutely certain I'd broken my neck.

I took great pride in having gotten up from some pretty serious hits over the course of my hockey career, but immediately I knew this one felt different. I'd been hit from behind and thrown head first into the boards. I can still recall quite vividly the moments leading up to impact: I turned my head to the left and put my right arm up over my face, to shield myself from the blow. It was an instinctive response. I wondered if I hadn't protected myself well enough, though.

As soon as I returned to consciousness, I knew something was wrong.

I feared my cries for help were falling on deaf ears until the shrieking sound of a whistle interrupted my pleas. The noise of skate blades quickly vanished, replaced by an eerie silence. Amid the whispers, the shuffling sound of shoes grew louder. The team's trainers were rushing in my direction. A tingling sensation started to creep through my legs, a sign that my brain was communicating with my limbs. It'd be years before I'd be able to appreciate the importance of such sensations.

Out of the corner of my eye, I could see a pair of brown loafers coming toward me. "Don't move. Just stay still," a voice said.

A man knelt down next to me.

"Where does it hurt?" he asked. Worry was evident in his tone.

"Everywhere," I said. "I can't move."

"You can't *move*? At all?"

"No."

He paused before continuing. "Uh—okay. You're gonna be okay. Can you wiggle your toes?"

"I don't think so. I . . . I can't move. Nothing will move."

"Give it another try."

I tried again. This time the message got through. I wiggled my toes and bent my knees, exploring the full range of movements my lower limbs were capable of in that position. The bottom half of my body, at least, still seemed to be functional and intact.

Cautious applause swept through the audience. While my movement was a good sign, I wasn't in the clear just yet. There was still the matter of my upper body. Contorted off to the side with my right cheek angled toward the ice, I still couldn't move my right arm, which was bent at the elbow and locked awkwardly over my head. In fact, attempting to move it at all elicited the most excruciating pain I'd ever experienced.

Suddenly, I was on the verge of crying. I did my best to choke back my tears. But with sensation returning, my body and brain were figuring out that something was seriously wrong.

I pulled my knees up to my stomach to prop myself up. Doing so forced my shoulder joint to move. Pain pulsed through my every cell. But slowly, and with the aid of two trainers, I sat up and coaxed my arm into a more normal resting position.

"Do you think you can get up on your feet?" the trainer asked.

I nodded. My determination to always get up after a hit still shone through. With the help of a lift on my left side, I rose to my feet and skated off the ice. A skate blade kicked against the inside of the players' bench, hockey sticks banged on the ice, and hands clapped. But while the support from the fans and players was reassuring, it couldn't change what was happening. The game would go on without me, and I wasn't coming back anytime soon.

I was really hurt, and I knew it.

THERE WERE ONLY two real locker rooms at the old Sioux City Auditorium, and as the only girl on the team, I'd grown accustomed to dressing separately in a curtained-off portion of the stage area at the end of the rink. I climbed the few stairs to get off the ice and reached my destination backstage, where I quickly embraced the opportunity to sit down.

I was in a world of pain, and I felt stupid. All the parents had told me this would happen. They all said if I kept playing hockey with the boys, I'd get seriously hurt. Now I had.

Whom better to share the moment with but my ever-supporting mom, who'd been in the stands. She'd been watching through her video camera and didn't initially realize it was me. As soon as she did, she rushed backstage. Now she could only stand and watch helplessly as the search for answers unfolded.

The trainers tugged at my right arm, trying to move it without causing me pain. After a few long minutes, they were able to remove my jersey and shoulder pads. They could see I had an injury to my right shoulder that required immediate attention by a doctor. With the help of an Ace bandage, they wrapped me up mummy style, attaching multiple ice packs to my right shoulder girdle. They offered to call an ambulance, but since the rink was just a dozen or so blocks from the hospital where my mom worked as a social worker, she drove me to the ER herself.

The ride felt unusually rough. My shoulder and right arm seemed to absorb the impact of each pebble and pothole. Though the discomfort made it feel like an eternity, we arrived without incident just a few minutes later.

Once settled in an ER room, the nurses took some information, asked some questions, and shined a few lights in my eyes. Every second seemed to drag on. I was growing impatient and wished nothing more but for them to get down to business and treat my medical emergency. I was ready to scream from the pain I was in, and they needed to know my middle name? *Just stick to the important stuff, please.*

Eventually they removed the ice packs and bandages.

"Okay, we'll need you to take your shirt off, too," the nurse said.

Together, we tried. I had moved my arm only a few inches when I screamed. Something wasn't right.

"Alright, I guess we're just gonna have to cut it off," she said.

"What—my arm?"

"No, the shirt, of course." She stared at me quizzically.

Scissors in hand, the nurse cut apart my shirt. It wasn't much of a loss; just an undershirt. But with my skin visible, I was finally able to look down and see my arm. The deformity was gruesome and obvious. My whole shoulder joint looked out of place. A huge lump protruded from the top of my arm, stretching the skin out so far it appeared shiny.

"Holy crap," I said, reeling with shock. "Look!" I pointed down to my shoulder.

My mom looked down at my arm and drew her hands up over her face. "What is that?"

The nurse took one look and tossed out her opinion. "Jennifer, we need to do an X-ray on your arm to see if your shoulder is dislocated."

I agreed hesitantly. What else could I do? Object? In retrospect, perhaps I should have. The X-rays involved forcing my arm into otherwise natural positions that were, at the time, excruciating. Once they were complete, I was wheeled back into the ER, exhausted and sweaty.

My mom and I waited in the small exam room. Every moment that passed brought the pain to a new level. After what felt like an eternity, a man wearing a white coat entered and offered me his left hand. His firm handshake felt a fitting match for his stocky build and husky voice.

"I'm Dr. Armstrong," he said. "I've got your X-ray here. Looks like you've got a dislocated shoulder." He held up the film to illustrate. "We need to put that back in place right away."

I had no idea what putting it "back in place" involved; all I knew was that the pain was becoming unbearable. I'd never even heard of a shoulder dislocation before, so I had no idea how serious of an injury it actually is. I wondered how it differed from a separation, which was the only kind of shoulder injury I'd ever heard of.

It's a common misperception that they're the same, but they're actually very different injuries. A separation involves the collarbone separating from the shoulder blade. A dislocation means the arm bone has come completely out of the shoulder socket.

Aside from the pain, the mental disconnect that sets in when your brain realizes what's happening is almost intolerable. Your brain knows something isn't right, so the signals to the limb start to get crossed. It all comes together to generate a deep, gnawing sensation—a painful alarm that disrupts your equilibrium.

"Okay," I said. "Do whatcha gotta do. Just—please—make this stop." I couldn't help but bite my lip as I squirmed in the small bed, riddled by anxiety.

"Well, we'll give you a little medicine so you won't feel much of anything," Dr. Armstrong said. His words struck me. Not feeling anything sounded pretty good. He made a few notes on his chart before looking up at me again. "You know, I was at your game tonight."

"What? You were?"

"Yeah, we just moved to town here, and my boy plays hockey. I've seen you play. You're pretty good. That was a nasty hit you took tonight, though." He paused. "You've got quite a serious injury here, but you're lucky you didn't do more damage than you did. We'll get some Versed goin' and then get you fixed up."

That night in the hospital, I got one of the first clues I might have a tendency toward addiction. I enjoyed the Versed just a little too much.

Awhile after I was given the medication, Dr. Armstrong returned to observe what my mom had already witnessed: I was high as a kite. Glassy-eyed and goofy grinned, I lay staring off at the wall, laughing intermittently at nothing even remotely funny.

I'd just sustained the most painful injury of my life, and my whole hockey career was hanging in the balance, but for a moment, just one moment, I got away from it. I escaped. And though it wasn't my first time being inebriated, it was the first time I remember putting it together that I could use chemicals to get away from whatever it was I was feeling. The realization was empowering, almost intoxicating.

The doctor seemed taken aback by my reaction but remarked only briefly on my markedly changed behavior before getting down to business. He explained he'd be "reducing" my shoulder, which is the technical term for putting a dislocated shoulder back in its socket. This procedure requires the arm to be moved and twisted until it pops back in. Whatever he had in mind, I didn't really care. I was off in my own little world. My mom agreed to the procedure on my behalf, and Dr. Armstrong got to work. I was feeling a bit restless, lying there flat on my back on the hospital gurney. He assured me there was nothing to worry about.

"Just relax," he said.

He grabbed a hold of my feet, adjusted my body alignment to ensure proper placement of my shoulder joint, and took hold of my right arm with his own. With a quick tug, he yanked and then twisted the limb. An audible pop echoed through the room as the joint snapped back into its proper place.

Relief swept over me. The unbearable internal itchiness disappeared. The pain subsided. The mental disconnect resolved. I hadn't even realized how intense it had all become until it was alleviated. With the joint returned to its proper place, I could not only breathe easily again but also hear more from the doctor about when I could get back on the ice.

"Well, Jennifer," he said, jotting down some notes, "I'm sorry to say that you might have a difficult time ahead of you. With your age, you're at very high risk of dislocating this shoulder again." (In fact, the medical literature suggests that approximately 90 percent of individuals under age eighteen who sustain a shoulder dislocation will go on to dislocate it a second time.)

He continued on with the good news. "You'll need to keep this arm immobilized for a couple weeks, and then we'll work you into a sling."

The difference between an immobilizer and a sling is night and day. Unlike a sling, an immobilizer functions to keep your entire arm from moving even the slightest bit. It wraps around your body at your midsection and has two straps: one in front, one at the side. The smaller strap sits at the bicep level and keeps your arm at your side. The second strap rests in front of the body and holds your forearm against your belly. You have to wear it at all times, including while you sleep, and it is quite an annoying little contraption.

"After all that," he said, "we'll get you going on some intensive physical therapy. I don't want you playing hockey for awhile, though."

"How long is awhile?"

"At least six to eight weeks—if things go well."

Instantly I started to cry. I'd fought back the tears through all the pain. At the time, I wasn't much for crying. But this was horrible news. I'd never been out of hockey that long, and it was all happening at the wrong time.

I played during the week and on most weekends in a high school boys' league, but I was also the assistant captain on the girls' team up in Minnesota. I was supposed to be headed to Saskatchewan with the girls in just a few weeks. I'd been looking forward to that trip all season.

To make matters worse, the hockey season was in full stride. Six to eight weeks off the ice would effectively end my sophomore season, which is vitally important for college recruitment. Colleges out east and up in Minnesota had been recruiting me, and playing college hockey was the biggest goal I'd set for my future. Suddenly, my dreams were shattered.

AFTER THE INJURY, everything changed. I could no longer head to the hockey rink to escape. With my prospects of playing collegiate hockey just as violently dislocated as my shoulder, my world, it seemed, was crashing down all around me. Unable to practice, I found it far too difficult to even set foot in the rink. When I finally did get back on my skates six weeks after the injury, my shoulder slipped right back out of its socket again—not once, but multiple times.

It was fast becoming a problem, one that Dr. Armstrong repeatedly recommended surgery for, but which I repeatedly declined.

I didn't want a big scar running from my neck to my armpit. I didn't want to be put under. And I didn't want to go through any more rehab. I'd been through all that with my knee.

I grew depressed. Without hockey, I not only lost direction with respect to my goals and ambitions for the future but had nothing to fill my time after school or on the weekends. Pretty soon I was spending more time drinking. I also started to hang out with a crowd that liked to smoke weed.

It wasn't long before I found myself sitting across a coffee table from a dealer chopping up lines of meth. Under the pressure of the moment, I did a few.

A few weeks later, I found myself trying cocaine.

From the moment it hit my nose, I knew I liked it way too much. I bought a gram on the spot. I took it home, did a few lines, put it away, got it back out, did a few more, put it away, got it back out. Finally, I hid it from myself in the closet. A half hour later, I dug it back out. It just kept calling me.

By the end of the night, I'd used the whole gram. It wasn't long before I was hooked.

My depression deepened. The more it did, the more I withdrew from hockey and school. The more I withdrew, the more I used. The more I used, the more depressed I got.

By the middle of my senior year, I was barely functioning. To top it off, I hadn't yet made a decision on college.

I was attempting to prepare myself for a life far different in just a few months, but my addiction was out of control. My mom was growing more suspicious about my behavior; she would sometimes catch me at home in the middle of the day, skipping class. "I forgot something," I'd tell her. All of a sudden, for the first time ever, I was "forgetting" something once a week, skipping class to go home and do a few lines.

I was also withdrawing hundreds of dollars from the emergency credit card she'd given me. When she discovered what I was doing, she took the card from me. At first I resorted to using my paycheck, selling my CDs, and other more respectable ways of acquiring cash, but as my addiction escalated, those methods didn't cover my expenses anymore.

I had to start stealing—even if that meant right out of my own mom's purse.

On a balmy February night, I took her credit card and went on a binge. I withdrew $400, purchased an eight-ball of coke and an ounce of weed, and returned home to my bedroom to use.

In all my eager anticipation, I neglected to put the card back.

The following evening, my boyfriend, Mike, came to my house. Blond haired and blue-eyed, Mike was the hard-working son of two Gulf War veterans. He didn't care for drugs and had grown increasingly uncomfortable with my unquenchable interest in all things drug related. When we had met over a year earlier, I hadn't had any interest in that stuff. But as time had gone on, the culture had lured me in ever deeper. He had little idea how serious my addiction had become, but knew I was developing a problem with coke.

He pleaded with me to stop. I told him I would. But I couldn't.

We sat together at the kitchen table, watching television. My mom sat in her usual spot at the built-in desk on the other side of the peninsula intersecting the dining room.

The phone rang, and I looked over from my seat near the TV as she picked it up. I tried not to listen in but was consumed by the sudden realization that I'd forgotten to replace her credit card. I'd seen her empty her purse and shuffle through it. She seemed to be looking for something.

I put two and two together and took a hard swallow. Then my worst fear came true: she was on the phone with the credit card company, reporting a lost card. I started to fidget in my seat as I leaned one ear closer to hear. It wouldn't be necessary. She screamed.

"What? What do you mean?"

I looked at Mike. He looked at me. I looked away. As I stared off unfocused, with my ears at attention, I heard the words that shook my world.

"I want whoever did this to be put behind bars."

My stomach sank. I bolted from the kitchen to the other end of the house, slammed the door to my bedroom, crashed onto the bed, and pulled a pillow over my head. All my life my mom had supported me. She encouraged me to follow my heart and believe that I can do anything I put my mind to. She was my biggest supporter. I'd betrayed her on the deepest of levels.

The shame was overwhelming.

After Mike left, I wrote a letter explaining to my mom exactly what I had done and why.

I couldn't bring myself to hand it to her, though. I had to have Mike give it to her the following night. She read it and immediately told me to pack my bags. The next day, we drove to South Dakota, where I checked into an inpatient chemical dependency program.

It would be the first of my many failed rehab attempts.

3

Detoxic

The picture of Jesus in the lobby greeted me with leering eyes. It should've been enough to alert me I was in the wrong place.

The lighting, the atmosphere, the setting all felt terribly depressing and dark. It was almost as if the building harbored unspeakable secrets about the events that had unfolded under its roof. But I didn't have any choice other than to behave and be patient.

After checking in and touring the facility, I lay back down on the bed in my small detox room. The springs squeaked under me as I sank down into the grooves of the old, thin mattress. The pasty white sheets, reeking of bleach, fit with the institutional décor of the drab room.

I looked up at the fluorescent ceiling light, which buzzed incessantly. A shadow streaked by as voices echoed in the hallway. I shot a glance toward the window in the door. A knock rapped against it as it swung open.

"Hi Jennifer. How are you feeling?" a voice said. Before I had a chance to answer, a woman in white scrubs entered. "I'm the nurse on duty. We'll let you settle down and get some rest here in a little while, but first we've got to get your vitals and have you meet with an otolaryngologist."

"A what?" I sat up in bed.

"An ENT—an ear, nose, and throat doctor."

"What do I need one of those for?" I fidgeted with the sheets, restless and agitated. Cocaine withdrawal will do that to you.

"Well, you've complained of some nose troubles associated with your cocaine use, so you need to have that examined. Can you come with me now, please?"

"Sure."

She led me around the corner, through the back of the nurses' station, and to a small examination area. "Have a seat," she said. I sat down in the sunken, squishy chair. "On the examination table, please."

I switched seats as a tall, wiry man with glasses entered and extended a hand to greet me. He introduced himself as an ear, nose, and throat doctor.

After grilling me about my cocaine consumption, he stuck a light in my ear, had me open up and say "Ahh," and then finally looked up my nose. He removed the light, flipped it off, and looked at me. "Well, you've got some damage to your septum," he said. "It's inflamed and scabbed, primarily on the right side. That can't be very comfortable. Does it hurt or bleed?"

"A little," I said. "I've been snorting through my left nostril a lot more lately because my right one gets so plugged up. It burns to snort through it anymore. And when I blow my nose, it scabs and peels. That's when it bleeds."

"Well, it's not too late. This can still heal. But you're at a stage where if you keep using, you risk permanent damage to your septum." He put the cap back on his scope. "It's good you're here to get yourself clean."

I stared down at my dangling feet and tapped my fingers against the table. "Yeah, maybe so."

The doctor left, and the nurse returned. She escorted me back to the nurses' area and continued with the exam.

"Open up," she said.

She shoved a thermometer in my mouth, reached up and grabbed the blood pressure cuff, and ripped the Velcro apart. "Okay, we're just gonna get your vitals here quick, and if it all checks out, we'll get you some medication. After that, you should be able to rest."

Rest. It sounded good. It had eluded me for months. Still, I wondered what magic pills they thought were going to save me from the restlessness that was starting to overtake my body.

"Interesting. Your pulse and blood pressure are both on the low side of normal," she said, hanging the cuff back on the wall, "but we'll go ahead and get you started on some meds."

She slid a small paper cup with two pills in it in my direction, then set down a cup of water next to it. I examined the pills.

"What are these?"

She picked one up and rolled it between her fingers. "This one is Ativan," she said. "It'll help you with your anxiety. And this one," she said, exchanging pills, "is Valium. It too will help with the anxiety, but it will also help you get some sleep."

I looked up at her, perplexed. I certainly knew what Valium was, and I'd heard of Ativan. I'd never taken either, but knew they were both mind-altering substances and both addictive.

It seemed illogical. I was in treatment to get off drugs, and here they were introducing me to new ones. I had half a mind to ask about their rationale for treating my addiction by pushing highly abused substances my direction, but my inner addict quickly squashed that train of thought.

Just shut up, Jen, I thought. *They're giving you free drugs!*

I picked up the cup, threw back the pills, and gulped them down with a big swig of water. I set the cup back on the desk and stacked the pill cup inside.

"Now," the nurse said, "you're free to go get some rest."

Three times a day for the next three days, that's exactly what I got.

My head grew heavy as I made the slow trek back to the detox room. I closed the door behind me and rubbed my fingers along my temples. There was no need to flip on a light. It was practically dark in the room but still bright enough to disturb my eyes. All I wanted was sleep. I hadn't had a good night's sleep in months.

I'd lost close to thirty pounds and stopped having periods. I was ghostly pale, ghastly thin, and in dire need of both rest and proper nutrition.

I changed into the gown the nurse instructed me to wear, peeled back the thin blanket, curled up in a ball, and tucked myself in. The bleach in the coarse white sheets singed the hairs in my nose. I twisted and contorted, but nothing felt right.

I reached around and patted the pillow resting under my head. It was thick, firm, and too large for my small neck. It also felt unlike most pillows. I peeked underneath the pillowcase and saw why. It was covered in rubbery plastic. So too was the mattress.

Did they think I was gonna wet the bed? I wasn't some kind of freak. What was this?

This felt so institutional. So uncomfortable. So degrading.

I stared up at the ceiling. The room started to spin. I closed my eyes and let the pills take hold.

WHEN I AWOKE, I was soaked in sweat. The blanket and sheet, interwoven between my legs, were twisted about, ripped from their corners. The sheet beneath me was sopping. So was my gown.

I threw the blankets off and sat up. Within seconds I grew chilled. Teeth chattering, I curled back under the covers in the fetal position.

A moment later, I was sweating again. Almost feverish. My internal thermostat was on the fritz.

I squirmed to find a dry spot, but there was none. Just when I thought I might have to expose myself to the cold to get up and get help, a knock on the door interrupted my distress. "How ya doin' Jennifer?"

"I'm miserable," I said. "I'm freezing. I keep getting too hot, then I get so cold. I got the sheets all sweaty, and now they're all wet. I'm just miserable."

I peeked out from under the corner of the bed sheet. The nurse stood by the door, tapping a finger against the door frame. "Well, you can get some more meds in a few hours. Are you up for some food? It's almost time for dinner."

"Actually, I'd like some dry sheets. And some clothes. What did you do with my clothes?" They were gone.

She chuckled and folded her arms. "Well, we can get you some dry sheets. But we'll have you wear the gown until you get out of detox. Those are the rules."

"Seriously?" I fell back onto the bed. "This is unbelievable! I want a cigarette. I want my clothes. And I want to wear those clothes while I go have that cigarette."

She forced a smiled. "Well, we're gonna have to check on that. I don't think that program rules allow you to smoke because you're only seventeen."

"Big deal! I'm on the adult unit, and I'll be eighteen in less than four months. Come on, I'm coming off coke here. I'm not asking for a line. I just want a cigarette."

She headed toward the door. "We'll see. I'll check on it and get you some sheets."

In an instant sweat was pouring from my body again. It was as if my body couldn't expel the toxins fast enough.

Then, unexpectedly, a foreign sensation set in. Pressure started to build behind my eyes. My lip started to quiver, and a tear fell. Then a second. Within moments, they were falling from my eyes like rain.

I was gripped by a flood of emotion unlike anything I'd felt in years. The tears had been pent up for far too long, and now, in the absence of my mind-numbing drug of choice, the emotional pain was all coming out at once.

"Jesus. What the fuck is wrong with me?" I folded my hands over my face and curled back up into a ball on the bed.

I drifted back off to sleep, tears and all.

"Jennifer," a voice said, "I've got some fresh sheets for you here. And you've been given permission to smoke, so you can—"

My eyelids shot open. "I have? Where do I go?" I sprang up in bed.

"Well, you'll have to go to the patient lounge. We're really not supposed to allow this since you're seventeen and all, but apparently your mom and the director are both fine with it. So here ya go."

She handed me my smokes, my precious security blanket. I adjusted my hospital gown and marched out the door and down the hallway to the small smoking lounge. I lit up a menthol and sat down next to a middle-aged blonde woman taking drags off a Virginia Slim.

Half an hour later she was seated beside my bed, holding my hand while I bawled my eyes out. She was just another patient—but she was an older, wiser patient who had been through all this treatment stuff before. Even though her drug was alcohol, not cocaine, it didn't matter. She listened to me and, most importantly, let me cry.

All I could think about was how badly I wanted to be using. I could taste the coke on my tongue, feel it in the back of my throat. My need for a fix came out in one big, teary-eyed, emotional mess. I was a basket case, plain and simple.

By the time my new friend had left the room, I'd created a puddle of tears and drool on the corner of the bed and given myself quite a headache. Thankfully, it was time for more pills. It was also time for the lights to go out on my first night in detox.

It was much easier to knock me out and let me sleep than to try to help me while the cocaine worked its way out of my body. For the next three days I was ordered to stay in my small detox room, away from the other patients. My only companion was my buddy next door, Doug.

Doug was stuck in detox, just like me. But he was in a much different place in life. He'd developed cirrhosis of the liver from alcoholism. Not only was his skin green, but his eyes were completely yellow. I'd never seen anything like it.

He'd gotten much sicker since he'd checked in. So much so that a nurse had to help him to the restroom. Even then, I heard, it wasn't a pretty scene in there.

I was in a world of hurt, but I was in a much better place than my new friend. Indeed, in life, no matter how sick you get, there's always someone sicker.

Doug knew he was going to die. He just wanted to die a sober man.

A few days into my stay, he disappeared. A few days after that, we got word he had passed.

Meeting Doug was my first real lesson on death and addiction. Here was this man who, had he not thrown himself into a bottle of booze, would still be alive and breathing. Instead, his chemical use killed him. Alcoholism is slow suicide.

I was determined to avoid such a fate. Even if detox was miserable, I'd never let myself end up like Doug. I'd never let my addiction get that bad.

At the same time, though, I wanted to run from the reality of my own illness. I wanted to hide from the world. I didn't want anyone to see me so pale, so sick, so addicted.

COMING OFF COCAINE that first time remains the most miserable experience of my life.

I was paranoid, withdrawn, sullen, and sleepy. I shook, I sweat, I swore. But in the end, after seventy-two hours of being supremely doped up, I was allowed to join the general population. I was looking anything but wholesome to my new acquaintances, though.

"I've seen you down there in detox. You looked like the fucking anti-Christ when you came in!" The woman smiled, threw out a hand, and introduced herself as Sandra. We fast became friends. She was just a year older than me and had gotten in over her head with meth. Despite that, she said she still had a lot of experimenting she wanted to do. Much as I did.

We tried not to, but we ended up, somehow, always feeding each other's inner addicts. We made each other want to use. Whether it was rolling up gum wrappers and passing them back and forth like a joint, or drawing out lines of lemonade mix on the table, we were always goofing off. And it always had something to do with drugs.

True, we weren't model treatment center clients. But when the Friday before St. Patrick's Day rolled around, we weren't the ones talking about green beer and rehashing the good old days, either. We weren't drinkers. So rather than partake in the optional group session offered to combat the added temptation brought on by the holiday, Sandra and I opted for individual piano lessons from Carl, a male counselor just six months out of prison.

When the hour of my lesson arrived, I sat down on the piano bench. I tapped at a few keys and played the first few notes to Beethoven's "Für Elise" as Carl closed the door. I'd taken piano lessons for many years growing up. I hoped that if I got back into piano, it would give me something to do with my fingers other than fondle drugs. I looked forward to rekindling my lost passion for playing.

Carl sat down next to me. Too close.

He flipped open a booklet of music. I inched to my left to give myself space. He got up, grabbed a different booklet, and sat back down, again *right* next to me. I tried to wiggle away again, but he wouldn't have it.

"Piano requires that I be able to see your hands and guide them," he said, applying his hand to my thigh. His palm slid slowly up my leg.

I leaped up from the bench. "I don't want this lesson anymore," I said, crossing my arms. "You're sick, man."

I headed straight out the door.

I hurried to Sandra's room, where I closed the door behind me and propped my weight up against it for added security. There were no locks on the doors to keep the riffraff out. We were addicts—we *were* the riffraff.

I looked at Sandra, who was sitting on her bed. She'd had a piano lesson just before me. As soon as we looked at each other, we knew. We'd gone through the same thing.

By the time we were done exchanging stories, we decided we had to say something to someone.

Unfortunately, there were no high-ranking staffers around on that Friday afternoon. So we agreed we would tell the nurse.

Together we marched to the nurses' station and sat down to chat with the RN on duty. The wooden legs of the old schoolhouse chair scraped across the tile as she inched forward toward the desk. "What's the problem, girls?" she asked in a husky voice.

Sandra and I darted glances at one another. We took turns explaining our stories before agreeing in unison, "He should be fired."

The nurse leaned back and folded her arms. She seemed stunned but not necessarily surprised by the facts. She shook her head. "He knows he's not supposed to be alone with females," she said. Clearly, this wasn't the first time he had done something like this.

"I want him fired," I said again. "This needs to be dealt with."

"Well, we'll see what happens." She stood up and put her palms on the desk assertively. "I'll pass along your complaint to my supervisors. Thanks, ladies."

MORNING CAME, BUT nothing felt the same. The air was filled with tension, and I got the distinct sense that I had something to do with it.

At mid-morning I met with my counselor, who encouraged me to talk about the event with Carl in group. So that's what I did.

But when group was over and word got out to the others about what had happened, I discovered that Sandra had been told to be quiet. I was the only one making allegations, and I had apparently just started some big-league gossip. Even though my own counselor had encouraged me to share what had happened, doing so had caused an uproar among the clients.

Suddenly I became public enemy number one. None of the other clients wanted to be seen near me. And nobody—client or staff—wanted to do anything to help me.

At the end of the day I retreated to my room to sleep the night away.

When I rolled out of bed on Sunday morning, another visiting day had commenced. The zombie-like drones who moped around the facility all week long started to come to life.

I wasn't expecting any visitors. My mom and Mike had come up to visit me the week before and I knew they weren't going to drive up again so soon. I decided to give my mom a ring and punched in the numbers.

"Mom! Hey, it's me," I said, twiddling the dangling phone cord between my fingers.

Silence poured from the other end of the line.

I held the receiver out in front of me and examined it, seeking confirmation we hadn't been disconnected.

"Mom?" I said again as I pinned it back to my ear. "Are you there? What's wrong?"

A muffled sigh cut through the tension. "I just don't know what to do with you," she said, voice trembling.

"What? What do you mean? I'm fine. I mean, I'm okay. Or, well, I'll *be* okay. This is just a weird place. And weird things are happening."

"Yeah, that's what I hear."

"What do you mean? What's going on?"

"I think you know," she said. "We're on the way out the door to come up there right now. We'll be there about noon. I just really don't want to talk about this over the phone. We'll talk when we get there."

"You're coming to visit? That's great!"

"Well, don't get too excited. We're not coming to visit," she said. "We're coming up to meet with some people."

I furrowed my brow. "About what?"

"You know," she said.

Truly, I didn't. I had no idea what would require her to drive up and attend a meeting on a Sunday morning.

Confused, I hung up the receiver and made my way to the patient lounge to wait.

Three hours later, she arrived. She went straight to a closed-door meeting with staff, to which I was not invited. Then she came to the patient lounge. Together we sat down at a table. She seemed very upset.

"Well, are your bags packed?" she said.

"No. Why?"

"I thought they told you all this before I got here. They want you to leave. You're being involuntarily excused from this treatment facility, and they want you gone, right now."

"What?" I threw my hands down on the table, rattling the Dr. Pepper can atop it. "For what?"

"Because," she said, "they say you broke into a counselor's office last night."

"Oh my god! You're kidding, right? Mom, I never did any such thing!"

I forced in a few deep breaths to try to calm my racing heart.

"Who said I did this?"

"I just talked to the director, who explained it all. I don't know who this Carl is, but he filed a report and told her that you broke into his office last night."

"What? No way. That's the counselor who put his hands on Sandra and me during piano lessons. He's lying, Mom!"

My foot rattled beneath the table as my anger began to reach a boiling point. This was unbelievable. As the shock set in, I immediately went on the defensive. Rightly so, too. I did some pretty awful things while on drugs, but there are two things I never did: I never stole from my friends, and I never broke in anywhere or vandalized anyone else's property.

I pleaded with my mom to hear me out and believe me. I brushed a tear from my eye and reached my hand out across the table, waiting for her to take hold of it. "Mom, seriously. This is the guy who put his hands on me. The piano man. Please, Mom, you gotta believe me: *I didn't do this.* Don't believe them. I swear on my life I didn't do this."

I'm still not sure whether she believed me. I was a pretty untrustworthy character. But I was in treatment, where I was supposed to be practicing honesty and learning how to be more respectful to both myself and others. That's what I thought I was doing by coming clean about what happened with creepy Carl. Instead of greeting my complaints receptively, though, the treatment center staff conspired against me to protect themselves.

As the fucked-up coke addict—the one in treatment for lying and stealing—I couldn't get anyone on my side. I had zero credibility, and nobody, it seemed, trusted me. Not even my own mom.

I was so far down on the totem pole of life that I couldn't even be honest without being accused of doing wrong.

My mom heard me out, but maintained her skepticism. "You should just pack up your bags," she said, pulling a tissue from her purse. "They want you to leave here as soon as possible."

I retreated to my room and packed up my things. The only person I wanted to talk to before leaving was Sandra. I wondered if she too had been accused of something outrageous.

Duffle bag zipped, I headed out the door and down the hallway to find her. She was chatting with her parents in her room and didn't look too happy. "We've gotta talk," I said. "Excuse us." I smiled at her parents politely.

"I'll be right back," she told them.

We hurried down the hall and stood in an isolated entranceway. She told me she already knew I was being kicked out of treatment. But she wasn't being asked to leave.

"Why aren't you saying anything then?" I asked. "You know Carl's lying."

"Yeah, but Jen, I'll get kicked out too if I put up any more of a fight on this. I have to stick this out. I can't get kicked out, or I'll end up in jail. You know that."

"Yeah, I know." We were both fighting back tears.

"They're just using you as an example, Jen. To get the rest of us to shut up. It's not fair to you. I know you didn't do this. But I can't risk the consequences here."

"So you're just gonna let them shut you up like this? You're gonna be a part of their lies and cover up?"

"No, Jen. I'm just doing what I gotta do. I hope you understand."

She reached out for a hug. I hugged her back.

"We'll keep in touch, though, okay?"

I nodded.

As I TRUDGED out to the parking lot, a cold breeze pierced my lungs. I set my duffle bag on the pavement and lit up a cigarette, waiting for my mom. Staring at the ground, I kicked at the hardened snow with my shoe.

I heard the sound of footsteps behind me. I looked up as they stopped, expecting to see yet another authority figure who would, no doubt, criticize my behavior.

Instead, I saw my big brother John. He'd accompanied my mom on the trip but had been waiting in the van the whole time she'd been inside.

Three years older than I, John was the closest thing I had to a positive male influence growing up.

He stopped, sighed, and tucked his hands into his coat pockets.

I picked my head up from staring at the ground and, with all the honesty I could muster, looked him in the eyes. The tears quickly welled up. "John, I know I've done some horrible things here lately," I said, "but you gotta believe me, I didn't do this. I didn't break into any office." I rubbed the sleeve of my sweatshirt across my teary eyes. "I swear, John. I didn't do this. Please, please believe me."

I expected him to doubt me, reject my story, and label me a liar. Instead, he reached out his arms, squeezed me in a bear hug, and lifted me up off the ground. My arms clung tightly around his neck.

He ran a hand through my hair. "Shhh, I know," he said. "I know. I know you didn't do this. I believe you. It'll be okay. We'll figure something out. We just gotta get you some help someplace else."

My tears evaporated as I clung to his embrace. I sniffled and tried to speak in response. "Thank you," I finally managed to say. "That means a lot to me."

He set me back down and let go of his hug. After tossing my duffle bag over his shoulder, he reached out a hand. I grabbed it tightly, and we walked across the lot to the van, where our mom sat waiting, watching the scene unfold.

John opened the sliding door, and I got in. As the door slammed shut, the engine turned over. The Creed song "My Own Prison" rang out from the radio. It seemed a fitting melody for the moment.

4

Revolving Rehab

I returned home with good intentions. But I still had cocaine hidden in my bedroom closet.

So the very same night I got home, I used it. All of it. I just couldn't resist the temptation. The following day, after I'd spent the night sniffing up lines, my mom announced that I'd be headed to the Twin Cities for my second rehab. This time I wouldn't be headed to some small, faith-based program in the middle of South Dakota, though. Instead I was going to the young adults' program at Hazelden, the granddaddy of all drug rehab programs.

I don't recall much about the brief period of time between South Dakota and Hazelden. I spent roughly a week to ten days at home before Hazelden could take me in. During that time, I did very little but use. The way I figured, I was just gonna get shipped off again, so I might as well get as fucked up as possible before I had to leave.

Even if I had tried my hardest to avoid my old playgrounds and playmates, I'm not sure I could've succeeded at staying clean. I had little to keep myself occupied.

My high school had allowed me to bypass the second semester of my senior year so I could focus my attention on getting my life back on track. I was already finished with the core requirements for graduation, so it wasn't like they bent the rules for me all that much, but it was still a nice gesture.

I also had a pretty good history of good behavior on my side. All three of my older siblings were model, straight-A students. So was I, until I became addicted to drugs. The school knew what kind of student I was before addiction set in and understood that my drug problem had become quite serious. They agreed with my mom that my health needed to be my first priority.

Suddenly, my physical and emotional well-being became much more important than my final semester of high school. The administration told my mom to help me get my life together and not to worry about whether or not I could graduate with my class.

So, worry I didn't. Get healthy? That's another matter.

Rather than focusing on keeping my nose clean, I worked on finding new ways of getting fucked up without using my nose. I still wanted cocaine; meth just wasn't the same. I tried shooting up but didn't care for it. So I did something I said I'd never do.

I smoked crack.

It was more than just a step in the wrong direction. It was an instant addiction.

Coke addicts are coke addicts, through and through. If it's the drug your brain is wired to be addicted to, then it's the drug you will seek out to use. And use it you will, until it kills you.

In fact, in laboratory settings, mice will continue to press a lever to self-administer cocaine until they overdose and die. Once they taste it, they can't stop. There is no restraint, no control. From the moment it hits your brain, cocaine can enslave you to its commands. You can taste it on your tongue, that bittersweet love, even when it's nowhere around. I had to have it. So I smoked it—all day long.

I wasn't ready to help myself yet. So I gave in to its every call. I was young, overly confident that I wouldn't face consequences for my actions, and altogether too stubborn to listen to the things people were telling me about the severity of my illness.

Today I think back on the time I entered Hazelden, and I simply draw a blank. I don't remember anything about talking to them on the phone, the ride up there, or leaving behind my precious cocaine, in whatever form. All I remember is feeling helpless to stop my life from unraveling.

At least I had one thing to look forward to: college. I'd made a decision. I'd sent in my acceptance letter to Gustavus Adolphus College in St. Peter, Minnesota, and filed it in my mind under the tags "future," "life," and "purpose."

Not only was college going to get me away from everything in Sioux City, but it was to be the payoff for all the torment I'd put myself through in my years of playing hockey. I'd wanted to play college hockey since I went to my first camp at age twelve. But my shoulder dislocation set my goal way back. I was never able to get back to the level I was playing at before the injury.

Despite my mounting troubles, both with my body and with my brain, I continued to be recruited by some schools, including Gustavus. I loved the school, the campus, and especially the rink. I was really looking forward to playing for Gustavus's women's hockey team, and nobody was going to take that goal away from me.

After my weeklong-plus bender, I packed up my bags and hopped back inside my mom's minivan. We arrived at a sprawling facility outside Minneapolis five hours later. I had fallen in love with the Twin Cities while playing hockey there in high school. Checking in for a stint at one of the most well-known drug rehab facilities in the world, right in the middle of my senior year in high school, wasn't exactly the triumphant return to the area I'd had in mind.

As it was, I found myself parking my duffle bag on another small, sunken mattress, in another sterile detox wing. The similarities ended there, though. This was no run-down, one-story building from the 1970s with a flat roof and archaic feel. This was a sprawling lodge nestled in rolling hills on acres of private land. This was the rehab Ritz. Even the grounds, so luscious and meticulously maintained, felt rich.

Before I ever arrived at the door, I could feel it in the air. I didn't belong.

I walked through the automatic front doors into the spacious lobby. A thin woman with blonde hair and bright red lipstick threw out a hand to greet me.

"Hi there. You must be Jennifer," she said, shaking my hand vigorously.

"Yup, sure am." I stared down at my shoes.

She turned to my mom. "So that must make you Paula then?"

They engaged in some chitchat as I rubbed my now sore arm. I didn't like this greeter. She was too happy. Sporting high heels and a knee-length skirt, she was wearing relatively revealing clothes for business attire. She struck me as a bit superficial, overly boisterous for my taste.

Coming off my experience in South Dakota, I was disappointed by my first impression of the staff.

After I said good-bye to my mom and dropped my bag off in the detox wing, my new escort led me through the maze of a building to tour the facility. Immediately it hit me how different it felt. This didn't look like tough living at all. This place felt more like an upscale lodge than a rehab facility.

The lighting provided a warm ambiance, while the high ceilings in the foyer created an open, airy space perfect for a patient lounge. I gazed up at the ceiling as she led me around a corner. She opened the door to a patient room, and I poked my head inside. "Four people share a room, including a bathroom, and you're all responsible for keeping it clean," she said. "You'll have chores that you'll be assigned."

"Is there a balcony in every room?" I asked, pointing to a sliding door at the other end of the room.

"Yes. There is." She backed out of the room and leaned against the open door.

"Sweet."

We started down another long hallway and headed toward the opposite side of the building. After passing through a double set of doors, she stopped. "This is the cafeteria," she said, motioning to the room around us. "And these," she said, pointing to the people occupying the chairs, "are the patients."

I looked over the twenty or so small dining tables seating my new peers and noted several pairs of eyes darting in my direction. They could tell I was new.

We walked back out to the hall. "You'll get to meet the others shortly. Right now we've got some medical testing you'll need done." We started back down the hall just as a young male patient walked toward us.

My escort stopped to chat, and once more I tuned out the conversation.

"Jennifer?"

"Huh?"

"Jennifer, this is Matt. He's been here for a few weeks and will be in your group. His counselor is Amber, too."

"Hi Jennifer," the boy said. "So what's your D.O.C.?"

"My what? You mean my drug of choice?"

"Yeah. I'm Matt. I'm an addict-alcoholic. But my D.O.C. is heroin. What's yours?"

"Cocaine," I said.

"Oooh, yeah. Coke is nasty. You snortin', bootin', or smokin'?"

"Mostly snortin'. Been smoking lately, though." I looked down at my feet, ashamed. My drug of choice was perceived to be much less glamorous than his. Crackheads, unlike junkies, get no respect. Some people see heroin as chic. But you can't find any glamour in being addicted to crack—not one bit. As soon as you admit to being a crackhead, even other addicts start looking down their noses at you.

"Alright, well, thanks Matt. It was good to see you," the escort said. She put her hand on my shoulder and started us back down the hallway. I wondered what Matt's angle was—I hadn't been able to figure him out. Fast I'd discover the truth.

Rehab, for many seventeen- to twenty-year-olds, is nothing more than a competition to see who is worse than who. And the goal is, always, to be the worst. It's a competition driven by sick and twisted thinking. And the sicker and more twisted you can get without becoming crazy, the cooler you are. It's tough to get clean at seventeen—addiction and drugs are seen as glamorous. It's hard not to fall into thinking things like, "my addiction is worse than yours" or "I've done more kinds of drugs than you." It's like being regarded as cool in college because you can drink other people under the table—it's just how many people in that age group think.

AFTER TESTING, PAPERWORK, and more introductions, I grabbed some dinner and headed for the detox wing to settle down. By lights out, I was starting to crave pretty badly.

As I tucked myself in under the sheets of the small bed, though, I found myself far less anxious than I had been during my first detox, which was surprising since Hazelden wasn't dosing me up with anti-anxiety medication. Still, my internal restlessness mounted.

I put my head down to a now-familiar, rubber-covered pillow but struggled to close my eyes. With the lights off, the room felt enveloped by a thick darkness. My eyelids fluttered, popping back open every few seconds. I stared out at the pitch black and then flopped over on my side, readjusted my pillow, and tried again to drift off to sleep. A bright light infiltrated my eyelids, creating a reddish tint as I peered out straight ahead.

In an instant, my lids popped wide open. I was drawn to the gap under the door. The bright fluorescent fixtures in the hallway illuminated the inch of space, allowing in just enough light to be distracting.

A thin white line pierced the blackness of the room. I rolled off to my left, then back to my right. Every time it caught my eye, all I could think of was cocaine. The numbness, the rush of the high. The way it feels creeping up your nose, sliding down your throat. The unforgettable way it melts into the pores of your fingers when you touch it. That bitter taste it leaves behind.

My thoughts spiraled. I wanted to reach out and touch it, feel it, taste it.

Sweat began to bead on my forehead. I pulled my legs out from under the covers and threw them overtop, but it was too late. The withdrawal was setting in. I already knew I was going to have to get through this crash without the aid of replacement drugs, but now I'd also have to do it with a white line staring me in the eyes, teasing me.

I flipped over on my belly and threw a pillow over my head. *Oh my God*, I thought, *just shoot me.*

A BANG ON the door of the dark room let me know that morning had arrived. "Rise and shine!" a voice said. A woman walked in and drew open the shades as I sat up, groggy. There would be no sleeping off the withdrawal this time. This time, I was supposed to get on with the game and get going on rehab.

It was also time to start being what many people who use drugs stop being: accountable. I was fine with the cleaning and chores, fine with being held accountable for my behavior. But Hazelden took things to an extreme.

Within a week, I was ready to run.

I've never been so unhappy in any place in my entire life.

By the first weekend of treatment, I was planning my escape. My counselors had already started talking about aftercare, and they had some very concrete plans. Not only did those plans exclude any kind of return to Sioux City, but they involved shipping me off to stay in a halfway house in some other region of the country. More specifically, the counselors started talking about sending me to Houston or New Orleans for as long as six months, immediately after my twenty-eight-day inpatient stay.

It sounded horrible. I knew no one in either of those towns. To this day I can't understand how they thought it was going to help me to ship me off to stay in a halfway house with a bunch of other addicts in a rough part of some city I'd never even been to before. All I could do was think about how much crack I was gonna smoke once I found hookups in a large city like Houston.

In a way, getting shipped off to live on my own sounded appealing—it would give me a great opportunity to get fucked up. On the other hand, I had big plans for my life. Getting shipped off for six months would mean being in aftercare until October. I was scheduled to start at Gustavus in September.

College, I tried to explain, was going to get me away from my using playground in Sioux City. But for all the plans and goals I had set up for my future, they still didn't believe me. They assumed I wanted to attend college for no other reason than to drink and use. Their assumptions angered me.

They would not accept geographical relocation in the form of a college education as a justifiable reason to bypass aftercare. Shipping their clients off to the nether regions of the country, away from their friends and family, seemed to be their protocol. And they weren't about to bend their own rules.

I wondered why they were so adamant about shipping me off. As we settled in for visiting day on Sunday, March 29, 1998, I raised the question with my mom and Mike. They had driven up in the morning, and by noon we were settling down to discuss how the treatment was going. I had little positive to say. I was unhappy with the program and its plans for me, and both my mom and Mike could sense I was growing increasingly uneasy with my environment.

Perhaps it was the energy in the air that had me all riled up. Sirens and severe thunderstorm warnings sounded early during our visiting time. Instead of being free to mill about the acres of campus, we—along with all the other families—were ushered single file down the stairs to duck for cover in the basement.

Huddled together in the windowless interior of a rec area, we had little to do but chat. Three chairs surrounding a table sat empty near the Ping-Pong table in the corner. We passed the sofas and chairs near the TV in the main area of the room to go sit down. Mike shuffled the deck of cards atop the table while my mom watched.

"We stopped at Gustavus on the way up here," she said.

"You did?"

"Yeah, Mike wanted to see it."

I looked up at Mike and smiled. "What'd you think?"

"It was nice," he said, in his usually polite fashion.

I couldn't agree more. It was beautiful. And that campus was my future.

After a few games of cards, the all clear on the tornado warning was given. It was mid-afternoon and also way past visiting hours. We made our way upstairs and headed for the door, where we exchanged hugs and said our good-byes. I stood inside the doors and waved, watching them do the same as they opened their car doors out in the parking lot. They were leaving, headed back to Iowa. I was settling in for three more weeks of rehab and, more immediately, dinner and group therapy.

After rinsing off my dinner tray, I headed toward the lounge. It was group night, and tonight was a Big Book reading. We each took turns reading a paragraph aloud to the group. I stared down at the page and lost myself in the drone of the voices regurgitating the words.

Suddenly I felt a tap on my shoulder. I jumped in my chair, startled. A twenty-something man stood over me with a pink piece of paper in his hand, extending it in my direction. I looked up at him, grabbed the paper, and unfolded it without saying a word. "You have a phone call," it read. The messenger leaned down and whispered, "You can take it in your counselor's office."

The readings kept on as the other patients jostled in their seats nervously, watching me and the scene. "Right now?" I said.

"Yes. It's an emergency."

My heart skipped. I dropped my Big Book to the ground and pushed myself up and out of the sunken chair.

"This way," he said.

Up the spiral staircase and around the corner, we arrived at Amber's empty office, where the lights were on. Stepping inside, I could see that the phone resting on the desk was off its hook.

"Here?" I pointed at the phone.

"Yeah, you should just be able to pick it up."

I did just that. "Hello?" The voice on the other end concerned me even more.

"Jennifer!" it said.

"Mom?"

"Yeah."

"What's going on? They said this was an emergency? Are you okay?"

"Well, you're not gonna believe this . . ."

"What? I'm not going to believe what? What's going on?"

"We're being detoured around St. Peter."

"For what? Why?"

"We were just driving, and when we got here, the police had the interstate blocked off. I asked the officer what was going on, and he said there was a tornado. They detoured us around the city. The tornado went right through town!"

I sat silent on the other end of the receiver. I didn't even know what to say. Finally I managed to spit out some words. "Oh my God. Are you—are you driving right now?"

"Yeah," she said. "It's pitch black out here. I have no idea where we even are!"

"Oh my God! Mom, you should be paying attention to the road. Are you on your car phone?"

True enough, she had one of those precursors to a cell phone: a car phone that plugged into the lighter.

"Yeah, thank God for this thing, huh?" It cut out on the other end.

"Mom, you shouldn't be driving while talking on the phone in a storm," I said. "Put Mike on. Do you have a map? Where did you get detoured to?" I pulled the counselor's chair from the desk and sat down.

"I don't know. We'll figure it out. We're dodging tornados, though. The trooper said there's been over a dozen in the state so far today."

"Holy shit! Mom, you should just find a bridge and park under it or something until this all settles down. That's scary!"

"We'll be fine," she said, "just as soon as we get out of this blackness and back on a recognizable road, we'll be fine."

I shook my head, remembering that sometimes there is no dissuading my mom.

"Was St. Peter in bad shape?"

"Uh, well, actually, it sounds like it was. We couldn't see much. But the officer said there was a lot of damage to campus." She paused before continuing. "It sounds like it's pretty much been leveled."

The words stung. She said "leveled." And she didn't mean just any campus. She meant *my* campus. My future home. The place I'd committed the next four years of my life to. The news, much like the tornado, was devastating.

The school I'd just decided to enroll at was no longer even functional. All of a sudden my future felt entirely uncertain.

I propped my elbows up on the desk. The tears kept building beneath the force of my fingers as I rubbed them along my eyes. "No. There's no way. You can't be serious." I shook my head. "That's my school. My future. And you're saying it's gone? This can't be."

The scratchy sounds of our intermittent reception filled the line. "I'm afraid it is," she said after a moment of hesitation.

"Well, I'm . . . oh man. I guess—I don't know. I'm just glad you're okay. That's good news."

"Yeah, we're fine. We'll be fine, sweetie. I just had to call and tell you because that was one of the craziest things I've ever experienced. We just drove through that town and that campus six hours ago. And now, here it is, gone! Just . . . gone!"

So, too, was my sense of stability. I hung up the phone not any less anxious than when I picked it up. I got to my feet. There was nothing to look forward to anymore. The vivid mental imagery I'd been carrying around of the campus that was going to get me away from my problems was suddenly murky.

My mental health seemed to sink into the floor beneath me as I stood, shaken by the shock. Once I collected my senses, I walked back out the door and headed straight for the smoking patio. I lit up a smoke and sat down alone with my thoughts. Everything I worked for had been destroyed. Suddenly I had no interest in treatment anymore.

I just wanted to get out and get fucked up.

My inner tension only mounted over the coming days. Safely back home in Sioux City, my mom wasn't about to just let me bluff my way through treatment so I could come right back home to a room full of drugs. On Hazelden's cue, she searched my room, top to bottom. And she found all my hiding spots.

4/8/98
My life is over. Everything came down. She found my
pot, my pipes, everything. She said she found some

rock cocaine too, which I don't remember. God, why
is this happening? I can't fucking deal with this shit
now. It's just too much. First Gustavus. Now this. I
gotta get outta here.

Indeed, it felt like the end of the world. And truly, I didn't remember leaving any crack stashed. If I would have had crack, I would've
smoked it—every last bit, until it was all gone. And then I would've
scraped the pipe to try and get more.

No, it couldn't have been crack she found. More likely, it was
meth—my fallback drug when I couldn't find an immediate fix.
Unlike any form of coke, I could put meth down and leave it alone
for a day or two. Crack? No way.

It wasn't even so much the fact that she had found my drugs that
bothered me. It was that she had blatantly violated my privacy and
invaded my room. She'd never done that before in my life. But she
knew I was in serious trouble, and along with Hazelden, both of my
brothers were pushing her to take action. She took it, and it pissed
me off. I didn't want to stick around rehab another day. And I sure
didn't want to get shipped off to aftercare.

Suddenly it occurred to me. I knew people in the Twin Cities—
people who liked drugs.

Just a few hours after being scolded by my counselor for engaging in addict behavior *prior* to coming to rehab by leaving drugs in
my room back home, I walked to the pay phone and picked up the
receiver. It wouldn't take long for me to find a potential exit.

I reached Lisa, an old hockey teammate who, like me, fell into the
drug scene. I hadn't talked to her in two years, but her thick Minnesota accent was still the same, and so too, I discovered, were her
interests.

She was drunk when she picked up the phone and unhappy to
hear I was stuck in drug rehab just twenty miles from her house. I sat
down on the stool in front of the phone and explained my situation.

"Want me to come get ya?" she asked. Her offer was unexpected.

"No shit? You'd do that?"

"Yeah, I don't care. I can be there in, like, half an hour."

Immediately I felt conflicted. I didn't know if I should be so bold
as to actually *leave* rehab. What would happen if I did? I jiggled my
foot and tried to collect my thoughts.

I had to be cool.

"I, uh, yeah. Yeah, that sounds good," I said. "I'll just get my things together and meet you out front in about thirty minutes."

We hung up the phone. "Oh shit," I said aloud. "What did I just do?"

I made the long walk back to my room. I didn't have much time to think. If I was gonna go, I had to go. I paced back and forth, fidgeting with the string on my black hoodie.

I reached under the bed, grabbed my duffel bag, and made a quick decision. I heaved my clothes and belongings inside and zipped it up, pausing in the mirror as I walked to the door. I took a hard look at my reflection before turning convincingly toward the exit.

As promised, half an hour later, Lisa was parked out in front of the main door. The staff had their eyes on her. I marched to the lobby with my duffle bag draped over my shoulder and headed straight toward the sliding doors. I didn't care who saw me go. I'd made the decision to get out. And besides, I was there voluntarily.

Two steps from the door, a voice barked from behind me. "I wouldn't do that!" it said.

I stopped in my tracks and spun around. Standing behind me next to the front desk were three counselors. The man, standing in between the two women, stepped forward in my direction. "If you get in that car and leave," he said, folding his arms in front of him, "we'll have you arrested."

"Excuse me?" I dropped my bag to the ground. "For what? I'm not here on any order. I can leave when I want."

"You're seventeen. You've been placed in our care by your parents."

"By my *mom*, asshole. My dad doesn't know a thing about me."

Stunned by the transition, he hesitated. "Okay, well, whatever your circumstances are, I don't know, but you're here because your— your mom—has put you here."

I shifted my weight and put my hands on my hips, glaring at him standing there all smug in his corduroys and loafers. Who the hell was this guy? Just some night-shift counselor who didn't give a fuck about me or my life. He's probably had his own addiction issues. And who knows, maybe he had just got out of prison, too.

Still listening intently, I glared at the man barking threats and did my best to appear intimidating.

He continued: "If you leave in that vehicle, we'll be forced to have you picked up. Not only will you get hauled off to juvey, but your friend there will be arrested and charged with kidnapping. Are you sure you want to do that to her?" He pointed to Lisa and her rusted, raucous old car.

"Are you fucking kidding me?"

"We've got the license plate. We can just call it in and have you picked up. It's pretty easy, actually."

"This is fucking crazy! I'm here on my own free will. I'm two months shy of eighteen, and you're gonna treat me like a fucking kid? Fuck you. I *should* just leave."

"Well, you're free to do so," he said. "But you should think really hard about whether it's gonna be worth it in the end."

"So basically what you're saying is I'm stuck here?"

"Yup. Pretty much."

I couldn't argue anymore. I kicked my duffle bag and threw up my hands. "Fine. Fine! I give up. You win."

A few deep breaths later, the storm settled. We discussed things in a more civilized fashion, and they gave me permission to talk with Lisa about what was happening. I walked out to the front and hopped in her car. Just as she reached to put the car in drive, I stopped her and explained that, as much as I didn't want to, I had to stay put—at least for the time being.

Once I was back inside, my anger resurfaced as I watched her pull away from the facility. How dare these people. They claimed to want to help me but threatened to punish me if I didn't obey. They inferred that my mom had entrusted them with my health and well-being, but yet they were blaming me for being a drug addict and having drugs in my room back home. Isn't that why my mom put me in their care? Because I was unable to stop using drugs?

It started to feel as though they wanted me to fail at rehab. They kept pushing my buttons. And the more they told me to stay, the more I wanted to leave. The more they blamed me for my addiction, the more I wanted to get fucked up. The more they pushed, the more I pulled.

The pressure inside was mounting by the moment. I retreated to my room to calm myself. I threw my duffle bag back on the burgundy bedspread and ran my hands through my hair, pacing. I couldn't escape the anxiety or anger. I had no chemicals to calm me, no loud music to lose myself in. There was no punching bag to help me handle my rage nor anybody to talk to. Hell, I couldn't even scream without being in violation of the rules. What the hell was I supposed to do with this rage creating such urgency inside me?

I stopped at my dresser, opened the door to the armoire, and draped my arms over the top of the door. My heavy breathing labored as my chest expanded in and out. Nothing at all was helping me. There was no escape from how I was feeling.

Bam. Bam. One. Two. *Bam.* Three. *Bam.* Four.

I backed up from the armoire, having drilled my right fist into it repeatedly, at full strength. It was all I could think to do. Hit something. Get it out. Let go of the rage.

I looked down at my bloodied knuckles and raised my hand to examine it. My entire fist was swelling up and starting to throb. I held my right hand in my left and paced around the room once more, letting the pain soak in like a necessary, self-inflicted punishment.

With my rage defused, the boiling simmered. I took a seat on my bed and tried to collect my thoughts.

> 4/8/98   10:45 pm
> Oh, boy, what a day. An old hockey friend came to
> get me. I almost left with her, but if I would've I'd be
> in jail right now. I could just really give a shit about
> my life right now. I'm much more miserable here in
> sobriety than I ever was when I was using. I can't
> fucking wait to get out of here and get high.

One week later, I'd get my wish. I phoned Lisa again. And again she came to see me. This time, though, she arrived during appropriate visiting hours, carrying the half gram of meth she agreed to bring. Rather than coming in and risk being recognized, she parked in the back parking lot. Against all boundaries and rules, I walked out to the visitor parking area and met her at her car. She got out, we hugged, and made the exchange as discreetly as possible.

With each passing second I grew more paranoid that one of the other patients had seen me step away from the permitted areas and venture to the parking lot. I knew there was no time for chitchat.

We finished up the exchange and said our good-byes. I turned back to the building, eyes darting left to right in search of potential witnesses.

The coast, it appeared, was clear.

Stealthily I retreated back through the lodge to the bathroom of my room. I was growing ever more anxious. All I wanted was to get high. Buying meth while in rehab wasn't exactly what I'd had in mind, but it's what had happened. And I had, in my possession, a decent amount to snort up. Without a razor blade or mirror, I improvised and used my driver's license to chop it up on my notebook. Line by line, up my nose it went. Ten minutes later, I was rubbing my fingers on the bag trying to get one last taste.

It only took a few hours for word to spread. Another patient had seen me and reported me. By the time I went to dinner, the counselors knew I'd gotten something in the parking lot. So too did most of my peers.

They watched me closely as I sat down to force in some food, growing ever higher by the moment. I could feel the stares as the beads of sweat built up on my brow, a single drop trickling slowly down the bridge of my nose. The meth was working. The room was spinning. The food tasted like cardboard. Maybe I was just paranoid, but nobody seemed to want to talk to me or get near me.

I sat alone at my table and put my head in my hands. My ruse wasn't working. My anxiety was mounting. I had to get out of the cafeteria.

I shoved my chair back, stood up, and tossed my food in the garbage. After rinsing my tray and stacking my plates, I marched out the side door and straight to my room. I didn't make it halfway before a counselor stopped me.

4/14/98

Lisa came to visit today. She brought a half-gram of crank with her, which I quickly snorted up in the bathroom. I was so paranoid someone saw me get it from her. Someone did, and now I've been asked to exit my second treatment in two months. I'll spend tonight in isolation, in the detox wing, and tomorrow evening I'll be hopping on an overnight bus back to Sioux City.

Although I was unaware of it at the time, my mom completely objected. She wanted to drive up to get me, but they denied her requests. Hazelden wanted me out the door as soon as possible, and they wanted to teach me a lesson.

Some lesson.

4/15/98

It's 1:10 am, and I'm on a bench waiting for my bus here in beautiful Des Moines, Iowa. I've had a great trip, until now. No, it isn't too bad, it's probably something I'll never experience again, but who knows where I'll end up now. Two girls are outside selling themselves. I hope I never get to that point.

The journey from Minneapolis to Des Moines was eventful to say the least. I've been treated like a freak. Two guys, one in front of me, and one next to me, asked me whether I was alright. They said I was really jittery. I told them I've been up for 48 hours on meth and that I'm really fucked up. I don't even remember the last time I was this high. What a place to enjoy it. The dude, what's he called, the conductor, came around and was checking tickets. Half the bus doesn't speak English so it took a long time. I think everybody can smell the weed on me. Maybe I'm just paranoid because of the crank in my system and lack of sleep.

This dude from Omaha had a bag and I could smell it. It's strange though, I almost knew he was hold-ing before we even left Minneapolis. I knew that paper I kept in my wallet would come in handy. Shit I'm wasted. If I could only get some sleeping pills. I'm approaching 48 hours up straight. I see everyone on this bus as no good losers. The funny thing is, they all look at me as a freak because I'm fucked up on drugs. Maybe I should take a look at that.

4:30 am

My final bus from Omaha has arrived. The guy and girl in front of me were talking the whole way. He was saying how he was gonna beat my white ass to a bloody red pulp. I must have hallucinated or something. I kept hearing this other guy say "smoke, snort, smoke, snort" etc. and then, "she's staring at you." He was telling the chick right in front of me about how he would go about beating my ass. It's either that or I must've been really tripping. I didn't sleep a wink the whole way here. But I made an ass out of myself in the North Omaha bus station in the middle of the night. It's safe to say I didn't fit in.

Around 6 AM, my mom picked me up at the bus station in Sioux City. Somehow I made it home in one piece, which seemed to surprise both of us. She spent all that night worried sick about my safety. I spent the night fucked up.

I realize I was in the wrong when I used drugs while in drug rehab, and I take responsibility for my behavior. I shouldn't have used. But isn't that exactly why I was in rehab in the first place? Because I couldn't quit using drugs when I was supposed to?

Hazelden realized they couldn't help me. They didn't ask me to leave nicely, though. They endangered my safety. I still have to wonder where the liability would've been if I had been raped, kidnapped, or killed on that ride home.

Two WEEKS BEFORE forcing me to leave, they wouldn't let me walk out the door. I was under their care, they said. Since I was a minor, they said I was their liability and responsibility. But as soon I used, they didn't seem to care at all about their responsibilities as my guardian. They gave up on me.

It was the worst possible thing they could've done for my mental health and addiction.

5

Hung Out to Dry

As soon as she got word of my dismissal from Hazelden, my mom tried to arrange for me to start an outpatient program in Sioux City. Her plan was to have me attend that until she could send me off for a third try at inpatient treatment once I turned eighteen in June. But because of my age, and since I'd already been kicked out of two programs, no place was willing to take me until then—not even on an outpatient basis.

Ironic, isn't it? I got kicked out of drug treatment for doing drugs, and then I couldn't find another rehab to take me because I couldn't quit using drugs. It still seems a bit backwards. Chemical dependency programs are supposed to help people who are unable to quit using drugs. It must be a sad testament to the severity of your condition when you can't even find a rehab program that will take you.

As it was, I found myself right back in my using environment, where I still had a lot of connections to the drugs I still wanted to use.

It didn't make my family happy, but I sure wasn't complaining. It was great to be back home. I could be with Mike again, and we were all set to graduate at the end of May. Amid all the chaos, there were actually a lot of positive things happening. But I was also still a practicing drug addict, and my mom knew it.

She set up a series of drug tests for me up at Park, one of the two hospitals in town. There was very little she could do to help me at that point, but she did her best to at least try and keep tabs on what I was up to.

She also instructed me to find a job. I didn't mind working. After all, it gave me money to buy drugs.

I got a gig at a bakery, working early morning shifts. I'd finish up my workday by noon or 1 PM, run out for my fix, and return home to use all afternoon long. I had the house all to myself while my mom was at work, so I could pretty much get loaded without any worries on that front. All I had to do was not look nervous when she got home. It was easier said than done.

> 5/14/98   6 pm
> I'm gonna be real busy the next couple weeks. I've got an honors assembly to attend, 80 billion open houses, graduation, not to mention work. I'm not doing a damn thing about any of it. I don't know how my mom will react when she gets the results from most recent U.A. [urinary analysis] either.
>
> When I'm using coke, it's all I think about, all I care about, all I want. As long as I have some coke, I can make it through the day. It's when I don't have it that I run into problems. I'm a total bitch. Nobody can stop me from getting that next fix. I can feel it already. Cocaine has me again. Not only does coke have me, but crack is consuming me.
>
> I'm right back in the depths of my addiction now, and this time I'm smoking crack. That's fantastic. I've only been out of coke a few hours, but I'm already searching for my next fix. Tomorrow. Tomorrow. I have to wait until tomorrow. I'll call first thing in the morning to get a $50 rock. That should help. I can't even sit still tonight. I've got to pull myself together.

I made it through prom, went to a few open houses, and held down my new job. On the surface I might've appeared functional. But underneath I was unraveling.

My behavior grew more erratic, and when I failed the first of my mom-imposed drug tests, it was the final straw. She took the keys to my truck—my getaway vehicle—and said she couldn't have me living under her roof any longer. She did what she had to do: she kicked me out of the house.

Thankfully, Mike's parents agreed to let me stay at their place until I could get my feet on the ground. Though I couldn't foresee myself shacking up there for long, it was a welcome gesture. There was no more meddling family to interrupt my drug usage.

It wasn't as much fun as I hoped it would be, to have so much freedom to use, but it was working out well—at least until the day before the honors assembly, when I realized I'd left my cap and gown at my mom's house. Graduation wasn't for another few days, but I was supposed to wear the ensemble to the assembly the next morning.

I knew I had to move fast.

I devised a plan to sneak into the house at a time that I thought my mom would not be there. I'd get what I needed, maybe grab a few other things I wanted, then get out.

I ran the plan by Mike, who, seeing no alternative to the situation, agreed to the idea. A few hours later, we were pulling up to the house in his diesel truck. It was not a silent approach. We inched up the long driveway and parked in front of the double-door garage. I hopped out, pulled a single house key from my pocket, and opened the door to the garage. My truck was in there, but my mom's car wasn't.

It looked like the coast was clear.

I tiptoed through the main level toward my bedroom. Something told me I wasn't the only one home. I listened to the sound of my breath and reminded myself it was just the crack making me paranoid.

My uneasiness intensified as I made my way to the far end of the house and arrived at my bedroom, tucked in the corner. With my internal sense of urgency growing greater by the moment, I rifled through my bedroom closet to gather what I needed.

With cap and gown in one hand and a duffle bag half packed with mismatched clothes in the other, I turned toward the doorway to make my exit. As soon as I spun around, I froze in my tracks. Standing in the doorway, with arms folded, was my mom.

Where did she come from? I hadn't been in that house for more than a minute or two when she found me.

She took a few slow steps in my direction.

"What are you doing here?" she asked.

Still stunned to see her standing there, I tried to explain.

"I needed to get my cap and gown." I motioned to the robe draped over my left shoulder. "For the honors assembly tomorrow."

"Well, you are not welcome in this house, and you know that. How did you even get in here? I took your keys. Did you break a window or something?"

"No! I absolutely did not. I had an extra key. The one you used to leave out for the painters."

She shook her head. "I don't even know what to do with you anymore. I do not want you in my house! Period. You aren't welcome here while you're using drugs. Now give me that key." She reached out a hand. I pulled the key from my pocket and threw it at her feet.

She glared at me, eyes tight as slits.

"Pick that up," she said, pointing to her feet.

"Pick it up yourself. It's your fucking house. Your fucking key. *You* pick it up."

"Why are you acting this way? I did not raise you to be this disrespectful." She reached down and picked up the key. "As far as I'm concerned, you just broke into my house. You're not welcome to live under my roof any longer. Not while you're using."

I could feel my heart wrench. That house was the only place I'd ever known as home, and I was downright hurt I'd had to sneak into it like a thief.

The emotion and intensity of the crack rushing through my system pushed my heart rate higher.

"Well, good. Fine. I don't even want to be here anyway. I'll never come back again. Okay?" The tears welled up. "This'll be the last time you'll ever see me. I'm leaving. Right now."

I picked up my duffle bag, started past her, and headed toward the garage. She followed right on my heels. The argument worked its way to the entryway, where we continued to exchange verbal blows.

I rifled through the junk drawers in the entry room in search of the keys to my truck; the same set of keys she had taken from me a few weeks earlier. They had to be there somewhere, but drawer after drawer I was coming up empty.

I slammed one closed and pounded my fists on the counter, turning around to scream directly at her. "God damn it! What the fuck did you do with my car keys? Give me my keys back so I can get the fuck out of here!"

"No. I'm not giving you those keys," she said. "That's *my* truck, not yours. I'm not letting you have it."

"Your truck? I'm the one who makes the payments on it. It's not yours. It's mine."

We stood toe to toe, just steps from the garage, where the truck sat idle.

A knock on the door interrupted our stare-down. It was Mike. He'd been waiting out in the driveway but must've seen my mom pull up. What was supposed to be a quick trip inside was taking much longer than he expected.

He stood outside the screen door, eyebrows raised, shrugging his shoulders. "What's going on?"

I picked up my duffle bag and marched out the door. "Come on, Mike, let's go. Let's just get the fuck out of here." I made it halfway through the garage when I heard a voice behind me.

"Mike," my mom said, "please don't listen to her. Don't let her leave. She needs help."

I dropped my bag once more and spun around, struck by her words. "Mike, I'm fucking serious. Get in the truck right now, and get me the fuck away from here!" His lips quivered as he wiped a tear from his eye with his sleeve. My mom has told me I started threatening him at that point, but I don't recall doing that. My psychological state was in complete collapse.

Whether it was the drugs, the circumstances, or a combination, I just couldn't handle the frustration and panic I was feeling. Everything was out of control—and out of *my* control. Coming down off crack, it all just served to fuel my rage.

I'd come to the house for a legitimate reason and was trying to get in and out as quickly as possible. She was the one who had kicked me out. She said she didn't want me there. Why wouldn't she just let me leave?

I walked back inside the house. Mike followed, carrying my getaway bag.

The argument between my mom and me became more heated as my impatience grew more urgent. My emotional control was unraveling by the second. I pulled a deep breath in and pushed it out, clenching my fists and my teeth, but there was nowhere to put the stress, nothing I could do. My efforts to cool down were failing. Pretty soon I was in an all-out rage.

I picked up the duffle bag and hurled it through the entryway window, screaming at the top of my lungs. After a loud crash I turned to my mom and got right up in her face. She tried to grab my arm. I pulled it away.

Then I did something I never in my wildest dreams imagined I could do: I hit my mom in the face.

I didn't just slap her, either. I hit her hard.

In retreat from the blow, she reached up and put one hand to her cheek. I backed up, drawing both hands over my gaping jaw. Out of the corner of my eye, I could see John rushing toward me.

He'd come home from college and had been in the house the whole time. I had no idea he had been sleeping downstairs. When he heard all the commotion, he came up to see what was going on. As soon as he did, he saw me hit Mom. He walked through the kitchen and rushed toward me with intent.

He reached out to grab hold of my arm. A rush of adrenaline flooded me. I fought back, wrestling my way out of his grip, putting him to the floor before he could push me away.

"Jesus Christ," he said, as he stood up. "What the fuck are you on?" He brushed himself off; the collar of his shirt completely stretched out.

"Oh my God, John," said my mom. "She's completely out of control. Just call the police!"

Rather than try to fight with me while I was in an intoxicated rage, he retreated to the phone. I stormed out of the house to the driveway, hollering back at Mike, who stood at a standstill in the garage. My mom approached him.

"Mike, come on! Let's go before the cops get here! I have to get out of here now!"

He heard my every word, but he wouldn't budge. He stood silent in the garage, sobbing, staring at the ground. Mom put an arm around his shoulder.

Out in the driveway, I lit up a cigarette and paced. Taking deep drag after deep drag, I quickly finished it and lit up another.

"I can't believe this!" I said, throwing the still burning butt in the direction of my mom, Mike, and now John. "I outta just fucking kill all three of you! You're ruining my life here! You go ahead and call the cops. I don't fucking care anymore. You'll be sorry, though. Just you wait! You'll see. You'll pay for this!"

I searched my brain to try and formulate an escape plan, but there was no place to run. I had no vehicle. No ride. No control over anything that was happening. I could take off on foot, but where would I go?

Before I could plan any further, two cop cars pulled up in the driveway. An officer stepped out of one.

"That's her," my mom said, pointing to me.

The officer took one step toward me, and I took off. I wasn't in the best of shape, and he caught me just a few steps later. I initially resisted but fast realized there was no sense fighting. No matter what I did, it was still going to end with me in cuffs.

He tightened the handcuffs around my wrists and forced me head first into the back seat of his patrol car. The door slammed shut behind me.

My anger fast dissolved into regret and remorse. But I wasn't about to shut my mouth. I wasn't finished with my tirade yet. I still had a few choice words for my mom, John, and even Mike, who stood in the driveway, talking with the two officers.

"I'm gonna fucking kill all of you! You think you can just lock me up like this? All I did was come back here for my cap and gown, and you're gonna fucking lock me up? You'll be sorry. All of you will be sorry!"

The tears built up behind my eyes. I curled up in a ball and flopped over lengthwise on the backseat, drooling on the seat as the lingering rage switched rapidly to a deep sense of self-hatred and sadness. It was an emotional pain unrivaled by any of my prior bouts of clinical depression. It felt completely different. This time, it felt chemical. And surely, the chemicals in my brain were on the fritz.

A moment later the driver's door opened.

"Well, Ms. Cannon," said the officer as he took a seat, "your mom and brother both want to go ahead with filing charges against you. You're going to be facing two counts of assault. So I'm sorry to say it, but we're gonna have to take you into custody now."

I sat up, lifted my shoulder, and wiped my nose on my sweat-soaked shirt. "What does that mean? Am I being charged as an adult or what? Where are you taking me?"

"Well, you're not quite eighteen yet, so we'll have to transport you to Juvenile Detention. It'll be up to the courts to decide whether to charge you as an adult."

Whether it was as an adult or a juvenile, I was suddenly in unfamiliar territory. I'd never been in the back of a police car before, let alone taken into custody.

With the crack still filtering out of my system, I was overwhelmed with emotion. The bittersweet taste of that all-alluring drug trickled down the back of my throat like a hallucinatory tease. The withdrawal that was setting in only amplified my agitation.

We navigated our way through the city and arrived at the JD center downtown. After getting booked and strip-searched, I was allowed to put my own clothes back on and escorted to a small confinement cell, a white-walled, windowless cubicle with a cement bench along one wall.

"Okay, well, this is where my job ends," the arresting officer said. "You'll be held here until a determination is made about where to take you."

"How long will that be?" I asked.

"I don't know. It depends."

The officer pulled the door half closed behind him and walked into the cell. He sat down next to me on the hard, cold bench.

"You've got a lot of potential," he said. "And you're just throwing it away. You've got a very loving family there, and they care a lot about you. I hope you can find the strength to fight for yourself."

I nodded in agreement, unable to utter a word. He stood up and walked to the door.

"Good luck to you," he said.

The door slammed shut, and an eerie silence set in. Time dragged on. Without a clock, I quickly became disoriented. There was no sunlight to gauge the hour by. No fresh air to breathe. There was nobody who would bail me out.

It was just me, all alone with my thoughts, locked in a cell, completely on my own.

For six hours, I sat in the small, silent cell without food, water, or a toilet. It made no difference. I was too dehydrated to need to pee, too high to want food.

All I could think about was crack. My behavior. My mom. My graduation. My situation.

I couldn't believe I was in JD. I was no delinquent. Or was I? I knew I had a serious problem. And I knew I was throwing my life away. But did I deserve to be in juvey? This wasn't how I had my life planned out at all.

I tried to make do with what I was given. I curled up on the bench, shivering from cold sweats, trying desperately to think of something—anything—positive.

A knock on the door broke the waves of my depressive thoughts. A man with a tie poked his head in the room.

"Jennifer?" he said.

"Yeah?"

"Hi, I'm Rick. I'm a probation officer with the county. I've got some orders here for you."

I sat up, listening intently.

"We're going to be transporting you to your doctor's office for a routine physical now."

"A physical? Why? I'm probably not gonna be playing any hockey anytime soon."

"Well, you've been consuming a lot of drugs lately. We just want to make sure everything is okay, physically."

I insisted I was fine, but it was one of many times in my life in which I had no say in the matter.

Cuffed once again, I made the trek back to the backseat of a squad car. Though we were headed in the same general direction as my pediatrician's office, it's not where we arrived. Instead, we went to Park Hospital. And I wasn't taken to any clinic area for a physical. I was taken to the fifth-floor psychiatric ward for an evaluation. Supposedly this was also a drug detox unit, but the clientele looked to be seriously mentally ill. These people were not in because they were drug addicts.

Maybe I had no idea how sick I was. Maybe I did need to be locked up in a psych ward, not incarcerated in a detention facility. Maybe I was in a place where I could finally get the help I needed.

Or maybe not.

I was committed to this locked ward with a lady who was absolutely convinced I was trying to kill her with radio and television. She thought she was a witch, galloping down the hallway on a make-believe broom and making cackling noises. I was a crack addict, not a schizophrenic. My behavior may not have been the most wholesome, but I didn't belong there. Did I?

Either way, it was only an evaluation. If I could pass the eval, maybe I could still get out right away. It seemed logical, but it wouldn't work that way.

I'd been court committed, by my mom and John, for being a danger to myself and others. I wasn't going anywhere for quite awhile.

Despite being served the commitment papers, in addition to criminal charges, I was still unable to grasp the magnitude of the situation. Only when they took my shoes and gave me the next day's meal options did the reality of it all start to kick in.

After I was checked into the ward, a medical doctor came to "evaluate" me. It came as no surprise to hear that I was just fine physically. But pretty soon it was going to be the psychiatrist's turn to tell me whether or not I was okay psychologically. That exam would be a little more difficult to pass.

There were only five days until my graduation. I had to hang onto my belief that I would be out of the ward in forty-eight if not seventy-two hours. Even my psychiatrist, Dr. Schmidt, agreed I probably would be. After all, I was only there for an "evaluation."

Even so, it would still require the collective approval of the courts, the doctors, and my mom for me to go anywhere, including the honors assembly the following morning.

I stayed on my best behavior for the night, and thankfully, they let me attend. I returned to the hospital afterwards and prepared for the evening's visit with Dr. Schmidt.

It'd been over a day since I'd been admitted, but I was unhappy to be back in the ward in a hospital gown. I was ready to get the hell out of there.

With the drugs still filtering out of my system, though, I was still unstable. I was locked up, pissed off, and crashing not only off crack cocaine but also cigarettes. Because I was two weeks shy of eighteen, I was unable to sign a release for myself to go smoke. I know cigarettes are bad for you, but coming off crack cold turkey is hard enough. Why escalate that anxiety further by depriving someone of their nicotine fix? It just doesn't seem right.

I was, on the whole, feeling pretty miserable. I paced back and forth in my small, private room, anxious for the evening's meeting. A psychiatrist—just one psychiatrist—held my fate squarely in his hands. And he knew the severity of my depression. He'd seen me battle through my first round of clinical depression at age twelve. He knew I had a lot of issues, but he wasn't about to cut me a break. Or even hear my side of the story.

A nurse poked her head in my room and cleared her throat. "Jennifer?"

I spun around from my spot at the window, staring out the safety-reinforced glass to the ground five stories below. "Your mom and brother are here. Dr. Schmidt is meeting with them now. I've got some clothes here for you. Can you change into these and then come with me?"

"Sure."

We walked down the hall, around the corner, and through the doors of a conference room. Already seated at the table were John, my mom, and Dr. Schmidt.

I took a seat and started fidgeting with the threads sticking out from the ripped knee on my flannel pants. It wasn't doing much to quell my anxiety. They started talking to me but made it clear they weren't about to let me speak. I was apparently only there to hear my family discuss my mental health with a shrink, without being able to provide my own two cents.

The meeting started off badly and only got worse. They were discussing plans to keep me locked up for quite awhile, without any sort of pass to get me to my graduation ceremony. I tried to interject but was told to be quiet. I pleaded with them to hear me out.

"All I want is to attend my high school graduation," I said. "I don't care how long you keep me here; I just want to graduate with my class."

"Well, Jennifer," Dr. Schmidt said, leaning back in his chair, "I don't think that's gonna be happening. You're not going anywhere for awhile now. You've demonstrated that you are a danger to yourself and others and you need to be here; you need to know that there are consequences for your behavior."

"Consequences? I'm already locked up, aren't I? It's not going to help me at all if you punish me this way. Why won't you believe me? I just want to go to my graduation! I worked really hard in school. I was a straight-A student!"

Dr. Schmidt shook his head as if I were the most tragic, pathetic client he'd ever had to deal with. He turned back to my mom and continued on with the discussion of my mental health.

Their unwillingness to listen to me pushed my agitation to yet another level. It was all getting to be too much. I couldn't take the emotional chaos anymore. I tuned out the conversation. I had to plan an escape, think about something else.

My eyes were drawn to the disheveled appearance of the room. It seemed to be just as disordered and chaotic as me. In the corner sat a moving box piled up with old books, outdated literature on mental illness, and a folded stack of faded, yellowed pillowcases.

On the opposite side of the room was an old bookshelf. I tapped my shoeless foot anxiously against the floor as I stared dead ahead at it, intentionally ignoring the conversation going on around me. The shelves were empty, save for a few aged pamphlets with ripped corners on the bottom shelf. The fluorescent lighting, illuminating the dust covering the top of the bookshelf, buzzed overhead.

I couldn't even hear the conversation anymore. The buzz of the lights, the ringing in my ears, and my own breathing drowned out the voices. I stared at the middle shelf wide-eyed, unblinking, grinding my teeth. I looked down at the table, but was quickly drawn back to the bookshelf. An old, institutional-looking lamp rested on the top, unplugged. The cord was wound around the base, with the plug draped over the front edge.

My thoughts started to spin. *Why is there a lamp in here? There's fluorescent lighting. There's no need for a lamp.* The buzz drilled into my head as I stared at the lamp and the attached cord.

For the first time, I started to look at the items in the room as tools for potential suicide. My thinking spiraled before I was jarred back to reality.

"Jennifer likes to write," my mom said. Her words made me perk up my ears. "I've got some of her journals and poetry here, and I've highlighted some things. As you can see, she's been writing more and more about death, depression, and drugs."

I threw my hands down and leaned forward over the table.

"What the fuck, Mom? You went through my shit? And stole my words? You know my words are my life! How dare you betray me like that!"

I was absolutely fuming.

She pushed the stack of notebooks in Dr. Schmidt's direction. He flipped through them, shot me a tragic look, and concluded the meeting.

I wasn't going anywhere. I was ordered back to my room, to sit down, behave, and shut up. I moped back to my space feeling utterly hopeless. Dr. Schmidt went off to chart my status:

5/21/1998

Diagnosis

Axis I: Polychemical dependency including crack, amphetamines, marijuana. Major depression, severe, recurrent, without psychotic features.

Axis II: Atypical personality with dependent features.

Axis III: No acute medical problems.

Axis IV: Psychosocial stressors.

      1.   Unresolved issues with parents including both mother and father.

      2.   She is quite a bright young lady who I think harbors and maintains a large level of anger.

Axis V: GAF score at the present time is 15.

Plan

I truly believe this lady is a lady who has a dangerous addiction. She is drug seeking. She is willing to bargain and negotiate in order to maintain her drug addiction.

I highly recommend that we try to get a chemical dependency evaluation set up for her. While she is outpatient, she cannot continue to not use chemicals and drugs, and at this point I will recommend an inpatient residential type of setting for her chemical dependency treatment.

The patient does have a history of depression, and I think it is going to be very important to look at treating that, titrating her medications to an effective antidepressant dosage.

With the shrink out of the way, I was free to talk privately with my mom about graduation, the journals, and the whole general mess we were in, but the conversation went just as poorly as the meeting did. I could do nothing but cry, and when I did manage to speak, nothing came out but the wrong words. The emotional pain setting in from the withdrawal was becoming almost unbearable.

Shivering and sweaty, I pulled up the sleeves of my Gustavus sweatshirt and sat down on the corner of the bed, sobbing uncontrollably.

I was growing remorseful for what I had done to my mom. I longed for her to hug me, hold me, tell me it would be alright. I needed her to understand that it was the drugs that made me behave the way I did; it wasn't me.

But she wouldn't give me a hug. She wouldn't sit down on the bed with me. She just stood there, arms folded, silent, and guarded. I pleaded with her to stay with me, to talk to me, but she had had enough. She wasn't going to stick around to hear anymore of my bullshit. Instead, she walked out the door and walked away. It remains the only time I can remember when my mom would not hug me or let me cry on her shoulder.

Just when I needed her the most, she left. Just as my father had.

I WAS NOT only crashing but feeling utterly abandoned. I was a prisoner of the law, the hospital, my family, addiction, and depression. Everything was unraveling. My life, I quickly decided, was over.

I paced, I cried, I yelled into my pillow. I punched the wall and kicked the door. I did everything I could think to do to dispel the emotional upheaval ransacking my core. I wasn't offered any medication for the withdrawals nor anyone to talk to. But every fifteen minutes, a nurse poked her head in, looked at me, and then closed the door without saying a word. It was my fifteen-minute suicide watch; she was checking in just to make sure I hadn't killed myself yet.

Each time she poked her head in, the more I thought about dying.

I was growing exhausted from lack of restful sleep and from trying to calm my fury. Maybe if I wrote, I could get a little clarity. I grabbed the notebook and pen I'd requested, pulled over the tray table, and sat down on the bed.

With my thoughts reeling, I put the pen to paper and began writing a note, addressed to no one in particular. In it, I explained that I couldn't live without drugs. Nor could I comprehend that I would miss my high school graduation because I was locked up in a psych ward for crack addiction, with criminal charges pending. It all seemed so outrageous.

I was sure I had nothing more to live for.

I put my pen down, folded my arms behind my head, and took in a few deep breaths. As I sat I noticed a lamp on the dresser on the opposite side of the room. It was very similar to the one that caught my attention in the conference room, and there was no way it was supposed to be in my room.

When I was checked in, all potentially self-injurious items had been taken from me. That included my shoes and belt, both of which seemed to suggest the potential for hanging.

The lamp in the conference room had also made me think of hanging.

Struck by the presence of the lamp, I started to think seriously about killing myself. I looked down in surprise to see that the two letters I had been writing, one to my friend Jess and one to Mike, were both effectively suicide notes.

There it was, written right on the page: suicide. It was the only answer.

5/21/98

Jess,

Hey there. I'm not real sure where to begin. My life is just completely fucked up these days. I guess Mike told you that I ended up in JDC yesterday. Well, it gets better. I'm at Park right now, in detox. I'm here on court commit from my mom. They made a major exception this morning by letting me go to the Honors Assembly. It had to be cleared with the courts and my admitting doctor. The repercussions from this are going to be very long lasting. I'm going to be on probation, have community service, and be court ordered to wherever they decide to send me. My court date is, get this, on May 26th. What a way to graduate, huh?

I fucked up everything, again. I'm not real sure what's happening in my life anymore. All I know is that I can't get much lower than where I'm at. You probably don't know this, but I've been smoking a lot of crack. I think it just pushed me off the deep end.

I'm on the 5th floor of Park, which is drug detox/ psych ward. I'm in a locked facility (a nuthouse) on court order. I'm the only one here in drug detox, so all the other patients are nutcases! This place is making me crazier than

I already am! The patients here talk to themselves and pee their pants. I'm not kidding.

I'm in a little white room with a hospital bed. Everything is safety reinforced so we can't harm ourselves. They took my shoes, jewelry, belt, make-up, everything. I was hauled here from JDC by a cop, with cuffs. This is absolutely crazy. I never thought I'd end up like this. I don't even know if it's all worth it anymore.

The psychiatrist should be here within a couple hours. He holds the key to my near future. Whatever he decides to do with me I'll have to do. I'm praying to God he will not send me away again, at least until after graduation. I don't want to be shipped off again. I can't stand it. I'm wasting so much of my life going through treatment. I'm ready to just give up. I'm just sitting here crying. That's all I've been doing since I got here.

I just got my court papers and I may not be able to graduate. It says in the papers that I will be escorted from here by the cops to my hearing on the 26th. The hearing is at 11:30 am, which means I would miss the graduation rehearsal, and therefore, the graduation. If I miss my graduation because I'm in a nuthouse, my life will be over. I couldn't live with myself if that happened. I'm a basket case. What the hell is wrong with me? Why can't I see what I'm doing to myself? I'm gonna be on a leash for the rest of my life. Sometimes I think it would be better if I was dead. I don't care anymore. I need, and want to go back to counseling. I want to keep my job and live at home and be with Mike. But, I don't want to get sent away again. Not now, not ever. My mom told me today that if I use anything when I get out of here she'll send me somewhere for a lot longer than 30 days.

I can't do this. Drugs are my life, my identity, my love. I don't know how to live without using. If I end up in this nuthouse until Tuesday and miss my graduation, I'm leaving. I'll go to Minneapolis and disappear for awhile. I just won't be able to go on if I can't graduate. All I can do is cry. This is 18 years of emotional pain coming out all at once. I've run from

> my problems since I was born—stuffing the pain by using
> drugs and putting a smile on my face. I've stuffed the pain
> for so long now that it's too hard to deal with. It's too over-
> whelming for me. I just want to run again, use my drugs
> and not have to feel anything but HIGH.

Everything that was happening was a sign of what I was supposed to do. There was no turning back anymore.

I got up and, with trance-like ambition, walked to the lamp, unplugged it, and methodically removed the cord from the lamp base. I walked to the bed, tore the letter to Mike from the notebook, and walked in to the narrow, tile-floored bathroom carrying nothing but the cord, the note, and a pen. I signed the letter and set the pen and note on the counter.

Then I got down to business. I planned my death.

I stood in the bathroom, observing my surroundings. With the door behind me and the shower to my left, I panned right to the toilet, complete with a call button and handicap rails, then to the sink straight ahead of me. The large mirror above it reflected the image of an unkempt, disheveled, and pale young woman—one whose eyes I couldn't force myself to connect with.

There had to be a way to get this done, to get rid of this pain.

I clutched the cord in my hand as I looked around. The nurse would be coming back any minute. As soon as she left again, I'd have to get moving if I wanted to succeed. I had to do it right.

Beneath the sink, my eyes were drawn toward a beige, plastic wastebasket.

A knock on the door to the room startled me. I pushed the bathroom door closed and quickly sat down on the toilet to pee. The stream trickled as a voice asked, "Jennifer, is everything okay?"

"Yeah, I'm fine. Just going to the bathroom." I finished up and, while the toilet flushed, walked to the sink and turned on the faucet. I put the cord, pen, and note inside the wastebasket before opening the door. The nurse, two steps inside the room, looked at me suspiciously.

"Everything's alright?" she asked.

"Yeah," I said again. "I'm fine. Just had to pee."

"Okay, well, dinner will be in about an hour. I'll be checking on you every fifteen minutes until then."

"Whatever." I retreated to my bed and curled up under the covers. Nothing further to say, she backed out of the room, closing the door behind her.

Now was my time to act.

I bolted to my feet and returned to the bathroom.

I retrieved the note, cord, and pen from the wastebasket. I put the note and pen back on the counter, next to the sink.

Cord in hand, I placed the wastebasket upside down in front of the shower door. I stepped up onto it. I closed the sturdy, full-length, metal shower door on one end of the cord. Then I tied a makeshift noose around my neck with the other end of the cord. I stood on the wastebasket, looked down, and saw the end of my life just one small step away.

In my mind I could see only the positive side of death. Not only would I escape from myself, but more than that, it seemed like a pleasant ending for everyone. In the grand scheme of things, my family and friends would be better off with me gone. Life was just too much, and all I was doing anymore was hurting those I loved.

I inched a small step forward, hesitated a moment, and took one last hard swallow before finally kicking the wastebasket out from under my feet.

Then I dropped.

As my weight hung from the cord, the ligature squeezed ever tighter around my neck. I wiggled my dangling feet as the pressure started to build up in my head. Another second passed in what felt like an eternity. Then the light turned to darkness.

6

Still Breathing

The bright light in my eyes led me to think I really had died after all. I looked up into it and then off to the side. There I saw my mom, Mike, and John.

As I stared up at them, I thought perhaps they were crying because they were seeing my dead body. Was I, in fact, seeing them from my own perspective after I died? I really didn't know.

An unfamiliar male voice snapped my consciousness back to attention. "You really should have died tonight. You're very lucky to be alive."

A man kneeled over the bed and looked at me, awaiting a response.

The front of my neck, including my throat, was very sore, but I managed to force out scratchy sounds to construct the necessary words. "You mean I'm alive? I'm still breathing?"

"Yes, but you should consider yourself very lucky to even be here talking to us."

"I'm alive," I said. "I almost died. I mean, it *felt* like I died. I *thought* I died." The ER nurses applied a cervical collar to my neck and took my vitals while the doctors and my family stood over me, shocked. "Maybe I *did* die."

"Can you tell me what year it is?" a nurse asked.

"It's 1998. May. 1998. I'm supposed to graduate from high school in five days."

"Follow this light with your eyes," she said. I complied.

"Stick out your tongue." She kept barking orders at me. I didn't want these nurses in my face. I didn't want to talk about what hurt or what happened. I just wanted to talk to my family and tell them what I had seen.

"My throat hurts," I said.

"Well, you just tried to hang yourself—that's probably why. Now stick out your tongue." I did as I was told.

"Are you in pain?"

"I don't know. My neck hurts, and I have a headache. My legs are tingling."

She looked up at the other nurses, each moving at a frantic pace, and said a few words I didn't understand. After a brief exchange, she leaned back over me.

"Well, it looks like your cervical spine X-ray came back okay. So we're just going to keep you in the cervical collar for a little while and keep an eye on your vitals." Believing that the staff knew how to handle such a situation, I followed along with the rest of the tests. After a few more needle pokes and lights in the eyes, I could get back to explaining to my family and the doctors what really happened.

"I had this vision," I said. "I was playing hockey. And I had a breakaway. I skated down the ice to the net, and then I heard this rushing roar, like the crowd was cheering louder. When I got to the net and took a shot, the puck went in. Then there was this bang, and I got swept off to the right, up toward a light. Then I was back at center ice, skating toward the net again. Every time I went down the ice, the roar got louder, and I got pulled further toward the light. But there was this thud, this bang. Maybe it was my head hitting the ground. I know I was gasping for air and trying to breathe. I saw myself lying there, from above."

The doctor looked at me with intense interest, as if he were attempting to extract some sort of medical explanation from the things I was saying. He rephrased his earlier statement: "You came very near to death tonight, Jennifer. You're very lucky to be alive."

I knew I was. And I also knew there was a reason I had survived. There was a reason I'd had such an elaborate near-death experience involving hockey. And there was a reason the rink looked so familiar.

It was the rink at Gustavus—uniquely identifiable because it has a wall separating the ice surface from the bleachers above. Though the details were murky, they were clear enough. It was a rink I'd never stepped a skate on before but was awaiting my arrival in the fall. It was, I quickly decided, my brain's way of telling me that it wasn't my time to go yet. My work here on earth was not yet done.

The next thing I knew, I was back upstairs in the psych ward. This time, I wasn't in a private room but in an open observation room, directly across the hall from the nurses' station. There would be no more private rooms or peeing alone. Now I would need a nurse to accompany me even to do that. Any further attempts at hurting myself would land me in a straightjacket and the rubber room next door. But even if I did behave myself, how was I going to get out in time for my high school graduation?

MY FATE WAS still in the hands of the psychiatrists and the courts, and I hadn't done myself any favors by trying to off myself. I couldn't help but wonder if I even wanted to go to graduation looking so awful. I didn't care how embarrassing it would be, though. I wanted to go. I had been a very good student and had earned the right to graduate with my class. Graduating from high school is one of life's major milestones, and I wanted to be a part of it, no matter how I looked.

I was in pretty rough shape. I slept very little on the night of my suicide attempt, tossing and turning in search of a comfortable position. When I did doze off, I was jarred awake at random, often because of intense neck pain. Despite getting just a few hours of consistent sleep, I found myself wide awake by breakfast time. The cervical collar, I discovered, had been removed sometime during the night.

The smell of coffee awakened my senses.

I flipped the covers off, sat up in bed, and turned my head to see what was for breakfast. Electric shocks zinged through my neck. Not only did my head ache terribly, but my neck was painfully rigid. It only made my head pound worse to move or turn it. Feeling a bit nauseated, I slowly stood up. Pinning my gown closed on my backside, I started toward the bathroom. My seemingly innocuous action commanded attention from the nurses' station.

"Where do you think you're going?" a voice said. A nurse scurried my direction.

I stopped, let go of the gown, and turned around to greet her. "I'm going to the bathroom. Where do you think I'm going?"

"Well, one of us will have to accompany you so you don't try to hurt yourself again." She put her hands on her hips.

She said it as if I made a habit of this sort of thing. I stared at her, shocked.

"Are you serious?"

"Yes, I'm absolutely serious." She folded her arms. I put my guard up. Something felt different from the day before, though. I felt unusually compliant and passive. I didn't feel like fighting. Still, I couldn't shake the attitude entirely.

"Well, come on in then. Enjoy the show." I motioned her to follow my lead. Pinning my gown closed again, I headed toward the safety-reinforced bathroom. With each step, my body sent me a message that something else hurt—badly. Apart from the more obvious injuries to my head and neck, I had also rolled my ankle in my fall and so was literally in pain from head to toe. I was also emotionally and physically exhausted. Even though it was only breakfast time, I knew it was gonna be a long day. At least, I thought optimistically, I was alive to see it.

> 5/22/98   9:30 am
> What an eventful 24 hours. I almost died last night. I tried to kill myself. I took a serious, impulsive action which nearly cost me my own life. Isn't that what I wanted? If I wanted to die, would I have fought so hard to keep breathing? Would I have experienced the near-death visions I did? Why do I not remember anything after? Would I be dead if the cord hadn't snapped? In the grand scheme of things, I believe someone or something was watching over me. My mom told me tonight "I honestly believe there are guardian angels watching over you."
>
> I really wanted to die. But subconsciously, I don't think I would have pried myself off that floor if at least a part of me didn't want to live. I fought with every ounce of energy in me to be able to live. Now I must decide—if I feel as if I want to live—why have I been killing myself slowly by using drugs? What efforts am I willing to go to in order to really live again? What is it I'm fighting for? Am I willing to let people help me in order to fully recover from my

addiction? As I lie here in the observation room of a
psych ward, I ask myself continuously, what do I have
to do, and what am I willing to do to save my own life
and realize where I can go?

I walked in and took a seat on the toilet. The layout was identical
to the bathroom down the hall where I'd attempted to end my life.

I hurriedly took care of business and stepped over to the sink.
Still preoccupied with the awkwardness of the moment, I lathered
up, scrubbed, flipped off the faucet, and reached for a towel. As I
grabbed it, I caught a glimpse of my reflection out of the corner
of my eye. I paused, backtracked, and looked slowly up into the
fluorescent-lit mirror.

I didn't even recognize the person staring back at me.

If I thought I looked horrific immediately after the attempt, I
resembled the walking dead now. It was as if I'd applied makeup to
wear to a Halloween costume party. The sewn-up gash over my right
eye, held together by thirteen stitches, was the least of my concerns.
It was the swelling and bruising that made me look so dead. It was
everywhere on my upper body, too. I had bruises in places I didn't
know could get bruised; I was puffy in places that don't normally
ever get puffy.

My blue lump of a nose looked smashed in. There were contu-
sions on the front and sides of my head, including opposite the side
I had been banging on the floor. I also had two black eyes, one of
which was completely bloodshot. The left eye looked better off than
the right, which had puffed up significantly overnight. It was now so
swollen it was trying to close on its own.

I stood and stared at my reflection, trying to absorb the shock.
Jaw already slightly agape, I opened my mouth. My tongue was sore.
Though it felt a bit weighed down, I was still able to lift it up and
stick it out. It didn't look quite right. The cuts and scrapes made me
wonder if I had bitten it while I was gasping for air. That logic didn't
seem to be able to explain why it was so swollen and purple, though.
Like my shiners, the bruising inside my mouth seemed to be the
result of blood pooling in the wrong places. Even the insides of my
cheeks, I could see, were swollen and bruised.

I closed my mouth and shifted my gaze into my own eyes, thoroughly disgusted with myself. They quickly diverted and drifted downwards to focus on my neck.

It was encircled by a deep purple ring. There were splotchy red and purple spots visible under my chin and along my jawline. Combined with the yellowish and bluish streaks, they made me look as if I were either doing a movie scene or in need of a toe tag. It was straight out of a horror film, but altogether too real.

Nobody should have such patterns of markings and bruising and still be alive. These were things that a forensic pathologist would be accustomed to seeing.

I had no idea I was still at risk of ending up in the morgue, either. I've since learned that people have died from complications *days* after the initial trauma of a hanging event. Likewise, survivors of near-hangings are at both immediate and delayed risk for a number of neurological and physiological complications, from seizures to pulmonary edema to stroke. I have no idea whether the doctors knew I was still at risk of such a fate. After all, how many cases like mine had they seen? Very few, I'm sure.

Even if I was presenting with a relatively rare injury, the hospital could've handled my case better. The only diagnostic test they performed in the ER was an X-ray of the cervical spine, which has been shown by researchers to be a test of questionable value for the injury I was presenting with. They were looking for broken bones and fractures when the medical literature says they weren't going to find any. Self-inflicted hangings don't typically cause the "hangman's fracture" associated with judicial hangings.

It used to be that when people were executed via hanging, they were dropped from a significant height. The weight of the fall would cause the neck to fracture in a specific spot, which was thought to lead to instant death. Though not impossible, it's exceedingly rare for an individual who has attempted suicide via hanging to present with a fracture or break in the neck. It's further unlikely that a basic X-ray would've caught the more dangerous problems that could've been ruled out via a CT scan or MRI. It's not the bones at risk in suicidal hanging; it's the brain, the airway, the venous structures, and the soft tissues.

My case wasn't just a simple hanging, either. It was three injuries rolled into one, and any one of them could've proved fatal. After hanging myself, I fell face first into the ground. That, together with banging my head against it, repeatedly, caused me to sustain an injury described in my case notes as "blunt force cranial trauma." That should've been investigated more thoroughly. I developed a goose egg on the opposite side of my head from the impact, which suggests that my brain hit the floor, rattled, and hit up against my skull on the opposite side of my head. That is, by definition, a brain injury.

The way I had that cord wrapped around my neck also lent itself to severe strangulation. I had no idea how to make a slipknot or tie a noose. I just wrapped the cord as tightly around my neck as I could, multiple times, then tied a knot in place. I remember I wedged two fingers underneath the cord so I could still breathe while I got myself all ready to drop. It was wrapped tightly enough around my neck that it could've rendered me unconscious even if I hadn't kicked the wastebasket out from underneath me to suspend myself. The full weight of my body falling on it could've only tightened it further.

It would've been a totally different ball game if, when the cord snapped and I fell to the floor, the cord had loosened from my neck. It did not. And it was likely completely strangling both my oxygen and my blood flow.

"Hypoxic brain injury" occurs when there is insufficient oxygen supply to the brain. When the oxygen is cut off completely, it's termed an "anoxic brain injury." Though they're commonly used interchangeably, that subtle difference does exist.

The ligature mark I presented with is described in the ER flow charts and in subsequent doctor's notes as "circumferential." This type of ligature mark is seen when there's been complete obstruction of the neck that, in turn, causes severe brain anoxia. It's a mark more typically found among people who don't survive hangings. The fact that I presented to the ER with a mark around the circumference of my neck seems to suggest that my oxygen, like those less fortunate than I, had been completely cut off.

When the force of the suspension in a hanging, or the pressure applied in strangulation, is great enough so as to completely cut off the oxygen supply, significant brain damage is likely to occur very quickly. Some medical experts believe this asphyxia is likely the actual cause of death in suicidal hangings.

Much less force is required to interrupt blood flow through the neck than is needed to obstruct the oxygen through the windpipe. The cessation of blood flow through the neck leads to cerebral ischemia, which other medical experts believe to be the actual cause of death. Some researchers suggest that survivors of hangings must only have suffered incomplete obstruction of blood flow because, while irreversible brain damage occurs within five to six minutes of complete cessation of cerebral blood flow, people who have been hanging for upwards of thirty minutes have obtained complete recovery.

There's no way I would've made it thirty minutes. I don't think I would've made it out alive after five. I'm not an ER doctor or a pathologist. I'm a survivor. And it just seems logical to me that the tighter the ligature, the less likely there is to be adequate blood flow, and the more quickly the blood will be congested in the brain. The same would seem true with respect to oxygen.

If my oxygen was completely cut off, as the ligature mark suggested, then so too was my blood flow. The bruising that resulted is accurately described in my medical records as "blood settling from trauma" and is evidence that blood was indeed rapidly congesting in my brain.

Despite the frequency with which suicidal hangings occur, the mechanism of death is still not well understood by the medical community. Most researchers do agree, however, that those who survive have probably suffered from a mixed ischemic-hypoxic brain injury, rather than either injury alone. Whether through oxygen deprivation, the interruption or congestion of blood flow, or a combination, both hanging and severe strangulation cause the body and brain diffuse and devastating injuries. Because of the multifaceted nature of the cerebral insult, researchers suggest that hanging injuries may, in fact, represent one of the most difficult pathologies of cerebral hypoxia to treat.

It's HARDLY MAINSTREAM news, but people do survive hangings. The fact is, though, most don't. Hanging is now the second most common method of suicide behind firearms. It's a violent, frequently fatal means to an end. Though it used to be a more preferred method of suicide among men, it has, in recent years, been occurring more frequently among women. Regardless of sex, substance abuse and psychiatric illness frequently play a role.

There are people who have hanged for a lot longer than I and survived. In general, though, with straightforward suicidal hangings, the cutoff seems to be about five minutes. Any longer and you either die or have significant brain damage.

Nobody has any idea how long I was hanging, how long I was unconscious, or how long I was gasping after I crashed to the floor. My guess is that the whole ordeal lasted just short of two minutes. A recent study of filmed hangings showed that deep respiratory attempts start at approximately twenty-two seconds of suspension and cease at approximately two minutes. In those two minutes of time, the body loses consciousness, convulses, assumes certain bodily postures, and, finally, loses all muscle tone.

I was still gasping when I came to, lying on the right side of my rib cage, on my stomach. With my legs fully extended, I had my arms drawn up toward my chest, fists clenched. This position, which has been observed to occur after about one minute of hanging, is a sign the brain is being damaged.

With each gasp for air I threw my head violently backwards, which caused me to arch my back and extend my whole upper body off the ground. Abnormal posturing similar to this is seen in response to an anoxic brain injury and has also been observed to occur in nonfatal hangings.

After each gasp, I slammed my head back into the hard tile. It's an absolute miracle I was able to move my left hand to the back of my neck, let alone utilize the dexterity and nimbleness it required of my fingers to remove that knotted cord. My muscles had become as rigid as a board—an ominous sign from the brain under such life-threatening circumstances.

I still can't say whether I actually died, physiologically speaking. I'll never know for sure what happened. But I do believe that my elaborate near-death experience functioned to protect me. The incredibly vivid imagery and sensory information I received caused me to have what the near-death experience researchers would classify as a deep "core experience."

I could feel the warmth and welcome emanating from the light. It felt so inviting. I wanted to let go and be pulled in, to cross over to the other side. With each gasp, I got pulled closer to the light and closer to crossing that boundary.

In my case, the boundary was the wall beneath the bleachers at the side of the Gustavus hockey rink. If I had crossed that separation, I would've crossed the point of no return and not been able to come back.

The force pulling me grew harder and harder to fight. But somewhere in the chaos of the moment, the message got through: it wasn't my time to go yet. So rather than embrace the light that was sucking me ever nearer, I fought to breathe, to come back to life.

I consider myself extremely lucky to still be alive and alert. I don't think I would've made it at all if I hadn't woken up when I did.

I'm one of the lucky ones. I didn't require ventilation, resuscitation, or intubation. I was never in a coma. I did not pass go; I just went straight to meet my maker. I was right there, on my last breath. I saw the other side. I was down to my last gasp. I should be dead. For some reason, though, all these years later, I am still alive as a soul in this body.

I'M ALSO CONVINCED that the hospital staff's main goal in the aftermath of my foiled suicide attempt was to cover their asses. Apart from their failure to run the proper tests and their negligence in leaving a lamp in my room, my mom also remembers that when she left the hospital right before my attempt, she told the nurses I was very angry, impulsive, and needed to be watched closely.

She flat out told them I was at high risk of killing myself. They told her they would take good care of me.

Sure they checked on me, but only once every fifteen minutes. That's a long time when you're talking about suicide, especially when it only takes a few minutes to kill yourself.

Of course, in the aftermath of the event, they had every reason to be concerned about their liability. But rather than performing the proper precautionary tests, which could have ruled out any possibility of a life-threatening head injury, or even considering that the attempt could still kill me after the fact, they seemed far more concerned with downplaying what had occurred. They also wanted to make damn sure I couldn't do anything else to harm myself. That meant that instead of getting quality follow-up care from a medical standpoint, I was going to be watched over every second by a psych ward nurse.

They did have a pediatric doctor stop by once a day to check on me. But if something had gone wrong, I don't think I could've convinced the psych nurses, or the doctors, that I needed help. I complained of numbness and tingling in my right ear, which became bruised a few days after the attempt. Rather than send in a neurologist to look at me, though, they sent in a pediatric doctor, who shined a light in my ear and determined I was fine.

Unless blood had been pouring from my every orifice, I'm pretty sure they would have dismissed any subsequent complaints I made and told me to shut up and behave. They likely would have said I was just feigning the complaint to get to the ER because I was planning some sort of escape or attempting to obtain drugs.

Nothing could've been further from the truth. I don't complain of physical maladies unless there's a problem. And I wasn't messing around when I put that cord around my neck. I wanted to die. I had a clear expectation of death. There was no denying the severity of my circumstances or the attempt. The psychiatrist's notes reflect that.

With impeccable timing, Dr. Schmidt went out of town for Memorial Day, just days after my attempt. The psychiatrist filling in for him, Dr. Patrick, details in his notes from May 23 the "very serious," "near lethal" suicide attempt. He describes me as "a kid who has had a lot of difficulties since she was a preteen" and goes on to write: "It has really been next to impossible for anybody to assist her because she has been so clouded in her thinking with her drug usage. Hopefully, she will be involved in some treatment modality that will restrict her access to drugs so that we can treat her underlying depression, and increase the probability that she would have a much more functional life."

Apparently, the seriousness of my situation meant I shouldn't be allowed to attend my high school graduation. Neither of the two treating psychiatrists had any intention of letting me out to attend the ceremony, which was fast approaching. They wanted to increase the likelihood I'd have a functional life, yet they were attempting to deprive me of a rite of passage.

They said I was unable to meet "the requirements" the school had "set up." It was completely inaccurate. I had permission from the school to graduate with my class. It's not like I was asking to crash the ceremony—I was on the list.

At first my mom agreed I shouldn't be allowed to attend. But I begged her to understand that I had no sinister motives for wanting to go. I wasn't looking to score drugs or escape from the psych ward. I just wanted to graduate. At some point she got it. She started to realize I could be forever scarred by the fact that I missed my high school graduation because I was locked up on court committal. She also understood how important it was to me. Suddenly she became my biggest supporter, imploring the doctors to let me attend.

She couldn't change anything, though. I was still there on court committal, which meant I had to get approval from the courts. That approval would come only if the doctors agreed it was in my best interest to go. They didn't seem to think it was and didn't seem to want to be convinced otherwise.

5/25   4:10 pm
This day has gone by terribly slow. I'm feeling just about every emotion I can, yet I feel nothing at all. I'm really beginning to get nervous about tomorrow. It seems almost like I'm having a bad dream or something. I'm really ready to get out of here. Dr. Patrick just got here, so my fate will be dealt to me soon. I'm anxiously awaiting the decision of my "superiors" regarding my life. They don't care about me, though, they don't even know me. "They" now hold my future. How fair is that? The crazy lady is screaming again. The other crazy lady (the one who walks the halls and glares) keeps turning off the lights in the tv room when I'm in there. The screaming crazy lady yelled at me earlier and said "she thinks she's god!" Yup, that's it. I think I'm god—sure. I'm beginning to approach insanity myself I think. Tomorrow is the day of my graduation and I will have to live the rest of my

life knowing I spent it in a psych hospital. Boy that
sure does make me feel good about myself. If they
keep me here any longer than tomorrow—I'm gonna
end up like the screaming crazy lady down the hall.
I'm going nuts in here. I want to go outside. I'm just
getting more and more nervous by the minute.

It was all getting to be too much. All I wanted was a definitive answer from someone. It started to feel as if people were keeping secrets from me, intentionally not telling me what they knew.
Maybe they were keeping me in the dark to test me, to see how I
would react. Angered by what I perceived as persecutory treatment,
I spent much of the day on the phone, seeking reassurance from my
mom. She said the same thing the psychiatrists did: I'd just have to
wait until the hearing.

I tossed and turned. The night dragged on forever. But, finally,
the moment of truth arrived. I had no idea what to expect.

I woke up bright and early and, for the first time since the attempt,
was able to put on my own clothes. I reveled in the luxury before
taking a spot on the corner of the bed. I lay back, taking in the gravity of the moment.

Laughter exploded from the nurses' station across the hallway. It
grew louder.

"Yeah, she's right in here," a voice said. I sat up in bed. A woman
knocked on the frame of the always open door and poked her head
inside. It was one of the nurses, still smiling from what was apparently a comical conversation.

"Okay, Jennifer," she said. "The officers are here to take you to the
hearing now."

I stood up. She backed out of the door, allowing an officer in full
uniform to step in her place. He wasn't taking any chances with me,
either. He immediately cuffed me and grabbed a hold of my right
arm. He didn't let go the whole way downstairs. We walked out
through the main entrance of the hospital, drawing stares from waiting patients and curious staff alike. Out in the parking lot, another
officer sat waiting, sitting idly in the front seat of a squad car.

With the beams of warm sun shining down, I drew in a deep
breath of the fresh spring air. It was the first time I'd been outside in

days—and the first time since I'd almost died. Everything looked, and felt, different. The skies seemed brighter. The sun seemed warmer. Life, it seemed, was sprouting up all around me.

Then reality sucked me back in. "Watch your head," the officer said. He nudged me inside the car. I looked ahead through the bars of the cage and quickly bowed my head.

I stared out the window as we made the short trek downtown, observing closely the pedestrian traffic as we passed through some of the neighborhoods I was accustomed to buying drugs in. After passing through the rougher parts of town, we arrived at the courthouse.

The car rolled to a stop, just outside the front steps of the building. The officers made their exits from the vehicle and opened up the back door.

"Ready to go, Ms. Cannon?"

"As ready as I'll ever be," I said. I swung around and put a foot to the cement. With that, a hand grabbed hold of my right arm and pulled me up and out of the car.

The two officers, one on each side, escorted me through the main level of the courthouse. We wound through the marble-floored hallways before descending the stairs to the basement.

Junkies and nutcases like me get sent away, locked up, and sentenced in the dungeon-like courtrooms on the lowest level, not in any of the fancier courtrooms upstairs. Those are reserved for the more highfalutin criminals, ones who, no doubt, had done something to get themselves on the news. I was no politician or mass murderer. I was merely a mentally ill drug addict with a court commitment. I certainly wasn't commanding any media coverage.

A row of small courtrooms lined the poorly lit, circular lobby at the bottom of the stairs. "We'll wait here. Your attorney should be out to greet you shortly," one of the officers assured me. I sat quietly on a bench between the courtrooms, but I couldn't help but feel out of place surrounded by attorneys and officers in uniform.

Soon enough, a woman who didn't look much older than I approached me and introduced herself as my court-appointed attorney. I immediately had my doubts that she cared at all about my fate. She assured me she'd do everything in her power to recommend that I be allowed to attend the ceremony. When we finally entered the courtroom, though, she did very little to advocate on my behalf. I sat silent. Not by choice, either.

The attorney, I was told, was my voice. She was there to speak on my behalf. She fumbled through her notes, collected her "umms," and began to speak. But not a single word about my graduation ceremony came out. In fact, she uttered few words beyond "yes sir, your honor." She didn't even *try* to speak up for me.

I did my best to negotiate my nerves and manage my anger. She wrapped up a most ineloquent appeal and, after only a minute or two of speaking, rested her case. The judge peered over the tops of his reading glasses, eyes directly on me. He then turned the case over to the county's attorney.

On the opposite side of the courtroom, another female attorney in a blue suit took the floor. She stood up from the small wooden table, tapping her long, painted nails against it. "Your honor, may I approach the bench?"

The judge nodded. She walked up and handed him a stack of documents—no doubt, all about me. He thumbed through them as she turned around. The tap of her high heels echoed through the room as she walked back and forth.

"Your honor, as you can see from the documents, Ms. Cannon has a very serious chemical dependency problem and is in great need of current psychiatric care. She was escorted to the psychiatric ward on May 20 following a confrontation with her mother and brother. She assaulted both of them and threatened their lives. The following day, while on fifteen-minute watch, she attempted suicide by hanging."

She stopped and turned toward the bench.

"Your honor, Ms. Cannon has demonstrated both suicidal and homicidal behavior in recent days. Based upon her behavior and history, I highly recommend that she remain on court commitment in the psychiatric unit until which time she can be transported to another residential treatment facility for chemical dependency treatment."

She didn't stop there. She went on about how I was a menace to society, still very much a danger to myself and to others, and demanded that the court not allow me to set foot outside the psychiatric ward until I could get sent off to inpatient drug treatment again.

It was like a dagger to my heart. I put my head in my hands.

This woman had never spent one minute talking to me. She didn't know me. How could she be standing up there making such sweeping assertions about my character?

Sadly, I've discovered that when you're a ward of the state, mentally ill, and addicted to drugs, the words of the authority figures around you carry more weight than your own. No matter what I said or did, I just couldn't be heard. Nobody believed me that the graduation ceremony meant so much to me. Everybody just thought I wanted to go use drugs. Truth is, I didn't even *use* drugs with the kids graduating from my high school.

I was a crackhead. I smoked crack with dropouts and lowlifes, not my classmates. I certainly didn't buy it from them, either. It didn't matter what I said, though; nobody was listening. It was a double-edged sword: Neither the doctors nor the courts would hear me out about anything rational I had to say. But I guarantee that if I had stood up on the table, clucked like a chicken, and screamed, "I'm going to kill all of you!" they would have heard my every word.

Everything seemed to be out of my control. And according to the psychiatrist's notes, control was one my biggest issues.

On the day of the hearing, it was charted that: "This is a lady who has real difficulties with impulsivity and when things seemingly are getting 'out of control' around her or when she gets the sense of loss of control is when it often times leads to very impulsive and sometimes dangerous and threatening behavior." How true.

Before I even knew it, the hearing was over. The attorneys spoke, the judge listened, and the gavel got thrown down. I wasn't going anywhere. I was ordered back to the ward, to sit quietly and mind my behavior until the court could send me off to treatment.

I was in shock. People started to mill about and exit the room. An officer tugged at my elbow and instructed me to get up from my seat.

"Time to get goin'," he said. I wasn't ready to budge. I needed a minute. This was my worst fear coming true.

"Let's go. We've gotta get you back to the ward now," the officer said again. He tugged again at my elbow and nudged me to my feet. He led me back out through a maze to exit the courthouse via a back entrance.

Tears started to well up as we walked the last long stretch of hallway. My thoughts spiraled in a whirlwind of negativity, and pretty soon I was getting sucked into thoughts of death again. I had come so close to dying, and I was trying so desperately to turn over a new leaf. The suicide attempt had changed me. The near-death experience gave me a purpose in the world. I knew I was still alive for a reason. But there I was, thinking about killing myself once more. I thought it was all over. I'd fucked up my life, permanently, and it would never be the same.

I started losing control of my emotions.

Step after step, the officer's keys jingled. Hanging my head, I looked up at the officer's belt. His keys clanked against a pair of handcuffs. Next to those handcuffs rested a gun. The officer, walking two steps ahead of me, was much taller than me. His gun sat just an arm's reach away. I looked at it longingly.

What if I grabbed it, shot him, went on a rampage, and shot myself? Why not? What do I have to lose? I started fantasizing about the news headlines that would circulate the world about me and my evil deeds. Then sanity broke through. I realized what I was thinking was just plain crazy. It didn't matter in the moment, though. I was ready to grab and start shooting.

Instead, for one of the first times I can remember, I resisted my impulses and respected authority. I put my head back down, sulked the rest of the walk back to the car, and returned dejectedly back to my psych ward observation room.

THAT AFTERNOON, SOMETHING changed. I don't know what. I have no recollection of how the circumstances got altered so drastically. All I remember is that my emotional well-being took a turn for the worse. Then, for some unknown reason and in some unknown fashion, I got the clearance I needed to go to graduation.

It was confusing. The psychiatrist wrote in his notes prior to the hearing that he was willing to let me out of the ward on a pass so I could attend the ceremony. Despite that fact, the court denied my request to go. Either the judge only received the psychiatrist's recommendation after the hearing and changed his decision, or he changed his mind independently and decided I could go after all. Whatever the reason for the change, I was the last to know.

I don't remember getting word that I was being allowed to go. I don't recall putting on my clothes or getting my cap and gown from my mom. I don't even recall the ride downtown.

But I remember the Auditorium. The same building where I learned to skate and where I grew up playing hockey was now the site of my rite of passage.

Sporting my red gown with its red and blue tassel, I walked up to greet one of the staff, who instructed me where to go. I snuck my way into the mix without drawing much attention—at least initially. The other three hundred fifty students were already lined up in the hallway when I took my designated spot.

To my left was a girl I didn't know well but who looked very pregnant with what I believe was her third kid. To my right was a young man I'd been in many advanced placement classes with. I did my best to blend into the scenery but noticed a few heads bobbing up and down, peeking around bodies, turning my direction. It felt like people were talking about me. But I wasn't on drugs anymore. I wasn't being paranoid. My presence, not to mention my appearance, was generating a lot of buzz.

I didn't care what they thought when they looked at me. I just wanted to walk in, hear my name, get my diploma, and be done with it all. It wasn't going to be so easy, though. I wasn't going to get through it without a few questions first.

Dan, on my right, was one of those kids who would ask you anything. The injuries to my face and neck apparently demanded some kind of an answer. For what seemed to be an eternity, he grilled me with questions. Eventually I got tired of telling him it was none of his business, so I told him I'd been in a car crash and hit my head on the dashboard. He bought it but didn't seem entirely convinced.

"How did you get that mark around your neck then?" he asked, pointing.

"Must've been the seat belt," I said.

He seemed skeptical, but I stuck to my guns. I'd had enough.

"Please, Dan, just shut up. Stop asking me questions." He smirked, turned around, and started talking to someone else.

I resumed my protective posture, propped up against the cold, cement wall.

When the moment finally came, I was greeted with another shocked response. I entered the auditorium from one side while a classmate I had worked with, been in classes with, and partied with was coming toward me from the opposite direction. We were to meet in the middle and walk down the aisle together to our rows. Instead, when we met in the middle, I was greeted with a wide-eyed, jaw-dropped, and straight-to-the-point question.

"Oh my God. What happened to you?"

I started to give an explanation but didn't get very far before changing my mind. "Car accident," I said.

The truth about my injury—and about the circumstances of my life—was, I was fast discovering, something I was deeply embarrassed about.

I GREW MORE and more nervous as the ceremony unfolded. Eventually, it was my turn to walk across the stage.

"Jennifer Cannon," a voice said, with deliberate enunciation. A few lonely claps could be heard, no doubt coming from where my mom and John were sitting. I walked up and greeted the principal, who stood waiting for me, hand outstretched.

"Congratulations," he said.

For the first time in weeks, perhaps months, a genuine smile crept across my face. "Thank you."

I returned to my seat for the rest of the ceremony. Once we moved our tassels and tossed our hats, the ceremony ended—altogether too soon.

After snapping a few reluctant pictures, bruised face and neck and all, my mom and John hauled me back to the psych ward. We stopped to pick up some frozen yogurt on the way. My celebratory treat, I guess. After that, I don't really remember much of anything. But I must've behaved because I got released just five days later.

Finally I was free.

7

Cracked

As soon as I got out of the ward, I went right back to smoking crack. I didn't stop until the day I left for college.

In early June, my mom did me a big favor and dropped the assault charges against me. It wasn't to go easy on me; it was to spare me from having a criminal assault conviction on my record. The court was going to charge me as an adult, and since she didn't want to destroy the rest of my life, she dropped the charges. That, in turn, stopped the court from intervening any further in my treatment.

Her plan still was for me to go off to treatment again, but since I was eighteen and a legal adult, she didn't have as much authority to send me anymore. I wasn't in any state to accept any help, either. I was still trying to kill myself with chemicals and there was absolutely nothing she could do to save me.

I really didn't take much time to feel, think, or even be cognizant of my surroundings during the period immediately following my suicide attempt. Nor did I really give my brain any time to heal following the hanging. They never told me I had suffered a brain injury, but there's no denying that I sustained one.

Convulsions are common occurrences during suicidal hangings. I'll never know if I had a seizure during my suicide attempt, but it would certainly make sense.

Crack also lowers the seizure threshold. Everyone's brain has a breaking point, and anyone can have a seizure if their brain gets pushed far enough. Cocaine, in any form, not only lowers that threshold but has also been known to directly cause seizures.

Regardless of whether I had an actual convulsion while unconscious, the head injuries alone were jarring enough to my brain to lower my own personal seizure threshold. In other words, the injury made my brain more vulnerable to suffer from seizures in the future.

The last thing it needed right after my suicide attempt was more crack.

AT THE TIME, I didn't know anything about head injuries, seizures, or seizure thresholds. I likened my head injury to one of my more minor hockey concussions. Only years later would I discover that it was much more serious.

Rather than attempt to care for myself and my health following the event, I promptly went out and relapsed—hard, on the worst drug I could've possibly put in my body. Perhaps if I had known that I had done damage to my brain, I would've thought twice before putting cocaine in my system again.

As it was, I didn't know anything was wrong, nor did I realize that smoking crack was any more dangerous than it had been prior to the attempt. But, after the attempt, weird things started happening when I would smoke—things that hadn't happened before.

My limbs would stiffen, and I would start shaking. I'd lose consciousness and wake up on the floor.

Usually I was alone in my bathroom, with the shower running, music blaring, and a crack pipe in hand.

At the time, my bathroom was my only truly private space. My mom might've been able to remove my bedroom door, but she couldn't take the door off my bathroom. So whenever she was home, it's where I used.

The wall-to-wall mirror over the marble-top counter stalked me while I was in there. I avoided looking at myself as much as possible. I was drawn, sickly thin, and, even though it was summer, extremely pale. It wasn't a flattering picture. When my eyes did connect, I quickly looked away at the shower or the toilet reflected from the opposite side of the room.

My mom had removed the lock from the door, but I discovered that opening the drawer right inside the door functioned just as well, perhaps better. I can only imagine her panic and despair if she had ever called on me in the bathroom and I didn't answer. She surely would have tried to get in. But the drawer would have stopped her. And I would have been unconscious on the floor.

More than once, that's precisely where I woke up.

Each night I'd flip on the shower, sit down with my rock, hunch over the counter, and break off a hit. I'd fill up the pipe, light it up, and hold it. I'd take hit after hit, growing increasingly paranoid that my mom might be getting suspicious of me.

After letting the water run for ten or fifteen minutes, I'd jump in the shower for three. Then I'd get out, dry off, throw on some clothes, and pretend to be doing something. I'd turn on the blow dryer and let it run while I'd light up a big hit. I'd open and close drawers, flip water on and off, blow my nose—anything to make noise. You know: just in case she had her ear to the other side of the bathroom door.

After planting my paraphernalia inside a towel at the back of a drawer, I'd retreat to my bedroom to write. With my mom's bedroom just across the hallway, I was far too paranoid to try and smoke anything in my doorless bedroom while she was still awake.

Instead, I'd run to the bathroom every fifteen minutes to take one more hit. Once she'd gone to bed, I'd stay up all night smoking in my bedroom. I wouldn't stop until I had smoked every last bit.

On nights when I would actually go to sleep, I'd keep a butcher knife by my side and a baseball bat on the floor next to the bed. Most nights I slept very little, others not at all.

We lived in a very quiet neighborhood where there was hardly any traffic. But frequently during my restless sleep, I'd be startled by the sound of a car. Usually it was around 4:30 AM. Slowly but surely, the rumble of a muffler would grow louder. Then headlights would pass by outside the window.

Somebody, I was convinced, was after me. I'd grab the knife, hop out of bed, and peer through the corner of the curtain, spying on whoever was out there. Whoever was driving around the neighborhood at that hour surely must have been there to get me.

My paranoia grew so intense one night that I went into my mom's bedroom and woke her up to tell her what was going on.

The paper, she assured me, gets delivered every morning.

The summer of 1998 is, on the whole, a massive blur these days. I was still working mornings at the bakery. I actually enjoyed the gig, too. It was perfect for my thriving addiction. I not only had the house to myself in the afternoons, but I could also use that free time to buy drugs. That way, I could avoid late night deals and go and meet my guys downtown in the light of day, when it was much less conspicuous.

On any given day, I'd go to work early in the morning, on very little sleep, smoking crack in the bathroom during my break periods. Then, after my shift, I'd pawn some CDs, video games, old sports equipment, or whatever else I could get my hands on, stop downtown to pick up some more rock, and then go back home to start the cycle all over again.

My mom knew I was using all that summer. She tells me she worried every single day that she'd come home and find me dead of an overdose. It remains a stark reminder of just how dangerous a game I was playing with my life.

My poor mom. I was just too far gone to even be reached. There was absolutely nothing she could do but hope I didn't die.

Whether it was right or not, I was still not welcome at any of the inpatient treatments she had in mind, despite the fact that I was eighteen. My reputation, it seemed, was preceding me. So she allowed me to stay at home while I attempted to fight my addiction on an outpatient basis in the evenings. The hope was that I could stick it out until fall and then get my shit together when I went off to college.

I went along with the show, but treatment was nothing more than a ruse. Going for only a few hours at night, just four days a week, wasn't going to stop me from using.

I probably could've fought a little harder to help myself that summer. Or at the very least, spent the time and freedom afforded me by focusing on my sobriety instead of getting fucked up. I had the support to stay clean, and the outpatient program turned out to be decent enough, but I just wasn't ready to quit.

I was smoking upwards of $200 of rock cocaine each day, racking up debts with my dealers and using Mike's urine to get me through the treatment program. When he left for basic training in mid-July, it only sent me deeper into the abyss.

In his absence, I had no one to hold on to. Even though he was unhappy that I was fucking up my life so badly, he still loved me with all his heart. He was really worried about leaving me alone. I, in turn, needed him in my life at that moment, to be there with me while I battled my demons. His presence couldn't save me, but his physical absence sure didn't help me, either.

In the end it wasn't his going away that got me in trouble in rehab, though.

A few weeks before his departure, my counselor went out of town on vacation. A different counselor stepped in to collect my urine sample. Her methods differed a bit, and I could no longer pull off one of my patented piss exchange moves.

Unlike my usual counselor, this lady didn't turn her back on me. Instead, she sat outside the room in a chair, which had a mirror facing right into the bathroom.

I went in by myself and thought the coast was clear, until she instructed me to leave the door open. I got ready to squat over the toilet. I planned to do what I always did and retrieve the pill bottle filled with clean urine from the hand warmer in my pocket. Then I'd open it up and dump it into the cup provided, while making it look and sound like I had really peed in the cup. All this with someone in the same room, back turned. But my plan wouldn't work on this lady. From my spot at the toilet, I looked up into the mirror and could see her sitting outside the room watching me. If I could see her, then she could see me. She was watching my every move. I got nervous. I panicked. And I peed in the cup.

Positive for cocaine, amphetamines, and marijuana. No more outpatient rehab. A third treatment program asked me to leave.

My mom was at a loss. So was Mike. He was heading off for six months away and was scared I'd stop loving him while he was gone. He proposed to me before he left, and we talked seriously about marriage. But just a few weeks shy of his leaving, I was in no position to be thinking about walking down the aisle. I was lucky just to be breathing.

I was throwing my life away, and my debt was mounting rapidly. I was working thirty hours a week, but it wasn't enough to feed my habit anymore. It didn't seem to matter what I did, I could never come up with enough cash to support my ever worsening crack addiction. I was stealing thousands from my mom and pawning our family possessions. I pawned most of my own stuff and even sold the expensive set of golf clubs my father had sent me when I was four-teen. They only got used a handful of times, but they fetched me about $350. It all went up in smoke over just a couple of days. I was running out of options.

Pretty soon, I knew I'd have to pay up.

When I first started smoking crack, I was merely substituting for an absence of cocaine. I had a steady dealer for powder, but my guy could only get his hands on crack sporadically. As I started craving it more, I began venturing into downtown on my own. Out there by myself, I was able to buy rock from a few different guys I'd met on the street. None of them were particularly reliable, though. Fre-quently they were all out, so I found myself driving around down-town searching elsewhere, anywhere. But as my habit grew greater, I started to adjust the timing of my trips downtown so as to suit the schedules of my two semi-reliable dealers. (Another advantage to buying during the daylight is that there's less competition for what becomes a limited amount of product by nightfall.)

The guys I was buying from at the time were "runners"—the term for low-level drug dealers who deal directly to customers on the street. Usually they work on behalf of other, higher-up dealers. They take the job out of economic necessity, make very little profit, but are, in actuality, the ones in the most danger of being arrested. Working on the streets, dealing rock cocaine directly to customers, is a dangerous way to make ends meet. So too, it turns out, is buy-ing from them.

The runners I was buying from could see I was bringing them a steady supply of cash every day. That was great, but it also meant I was wiping them out of their supply too quickly. It's much more lucrative for runners to sell smaller quantities to a greater number of customers, and usually they can each only get so much from their supplier on any given day. Not only was I costing these guys money, but they were having to give me all their day's supply of rock, too. So it made sense that eventually they'd send me to the next guy up the ladder and bypass my business altogether.

That's when they introduced me to Franklin, a forty-three-year-old career criminal. I knew his name, and I knew he was the highest-level dealer around, but I didn't know he'd been expecting me.

He'd heard about who I was and told his cronies he wanted to meet me.

I waited with one of his runners, outside the run-down building where he kept an apartment. A gold low-rider Monte Carlo, complete with tinted windows, a fuzzy steering wheel, and dice hanging from the rearview mirror, pulled up and parked right in front of me. Out stepped a middle-aged man wearing polyester and a gold chain, with a protruding belly that jutted out over his gold-buckled belt.

Prior to coming to Sioux City, Franklin had been a pimp in Chicago. I don't know if he had any legitimate reasons for coming to Sioux City, but he ended up a mid- to upper-level cocaine dealer. A big cheese. The main man. And as soon as he stepped out of the car, he was ready to work with me.

"Well, well," he said, looking me up and down. "You must be Jennifer. It's so nice to finally meet you." He took two steps closer to me, reaching out to tuck my hair behind my ear. "Would you like to come upstairs with me, sweetheart?"

"Yeah," I said reluctantly. "I'd like that."

BEING THE CHARMING guy he was, he offered me some free coke right from the get go. Straight from a briefcase full of the same. I'd never seen so much coke—or crack—in my life. He'd buy in quantity, keep some in powder form, and rock the rest up. Turning powder cocaine into rock cocaine involves baking soda, a glass jar, a pot of water, a stove, and a lot of cocaine. Done right, you get "good" rock. Done poorly, you get baking soda flavor, less of a high, and an inferior product.

Franklin was good at this. He knew what he was doing, and he had his system. I learned fast.

I'd arrive at his small apartment downtown, park out front or in back, walk in past the cameras in the hallways—which I had heard had been planted by the FBI because they had Franklin under surveillance—and head upstairs. There I'd take a left and knock. This was an old building with just a couple apartment units. I always felt like I looked suspicious walking up to the door.

A peep hole would open up. A lock would unlatch. Then another. And then a third. I'd walk in and take a seat in the kitchen at the small, heavy folding table. The lock would latch. Then another. Then the third. He'd put down his gun and pop open the briefcase on the table. From it he'd pull out a baggie filled with cocaine. He'd spoon out a small amount and line it up on the table. I'd snort it up while he rocked up a batch of crack.

He wasn't dealing peanuts. He had plenty of product to tease, entice, and peddle while he worked on accomplishing his new goal: scoring with me.

What started as a free twenty rock led to a free fifty rock. I couldn't keep up with his advances. I smiled back, in the name of maintaining my addiction, but this was interpreted as flirtation and didn't sit well with him. He let me know he was starting to feel like I was leading him on. I assured him I was not, but he was giving me free rock cocaine with the understanding that I would "pay him back" either in cash or by doing him sexual favors.

I wanted to pay him back in cash, but he started pressuring me more and more to make the repayment sexual in nature. At some point, my habit grew so great that I could no longer keep up with the costs. I didn't have enough money—or access to enough money—to cover my habit for a day, let alone repay him for all the "free" rock he had provided me with. I was taking the bait he was offering to me every time—hook, line, and sinker. And pretty soon, it came time to pay up.

I was thousands in debt before he started putting his hands on me, so I didn't object when he did. At first I only let him stroke my hair, but as weeks passed, I allowed him to fondle my breasts, feel my legs, and touch me in between them. I let him kiss my lips and stick his tongue right down my throat. Still, whenever he touched me for more than a second, I would back away. Each time he advanced, I retreated. And I kept declining the invitations for sex.

Frustrated by my reluctance to sleep with him, Franklin made me an offer: a free eight-ball of rock for five minutes of sex, all debts forgiven. It was an enticing proposal, one I couldn't see myself saying no to.

By the end of July, the summertime heat was sweltering. The air bouncing off the scorching downtown sidewalks seemed to be rippling. Mike was gone, and I was at the end of my rope. I was spending almost all my time smoking crack and was seeing Franklin multiple times a day, but never with quite enough money. He just kept feeding me drugs and offering the proposal.

The longer I held out, the more scared I became. I knew he was a convicted felon with a history of violence. I observed cautiously his closet full of guns, which included loads of ammo, rifles, pistols, and even an AK-47. Wherever he went, he kept a .38 at his waist. I was never worried he would hurt me. On the contrary, he was quite protective of me. I felt safe in downtown because I knew I had him on my side. Everybody knew not to fuck with me, but they also knew me as one of his "girls." That not only made me off limits for anyone else to sell to, but also implied that I was one of his sexual conquests. At one point, he pistol-whipped one of his runners in the alley behind his apartment because he tried to deal to another female customer Franklin had started selling directly to.

He was in charge of the neighborhood and not the kind of guy you wanted on your bad side. I was growing fearful he might try to hurt me or force me into sex if I didn't give him what he wanted. So finally, after weeks of badgering, mounting debts, and groping reminders, I folded.

"Fine," I said. "I'll sleep with you."

As soon as I spoke the words, he steered the conversation to a discussion of details. He had a girlfriend who could walk in on us there at his apartment in the old house, so he didn't want to do it there. He was also under heavy police surveillance, and the apartment building where I was accustomed to meeting him was growing more and more suspicious. He was, as he and his cronies put it, "hot." So, he said, I should get out of his apartment and meet him at a certain motel where he kept a room. He pulled a key from his pocket and dangled it in front of me. Suddenly I realized he wanted to do it the very same night I agreed to it.

I'd been thinking we would set the appointment for some date in the future. That I could at least get some rock, get out of his apartment, and *think* about this whole indecent proposal before ever conceding my body outright. But that wasn't what he had in mind. There was to be no cooling-off period, no time to think about what I was doing. I had agreed to do it, and now I was being expected to follow through. He dropped the key into my outstretched hand, pushed me toward the door, and instructed me to meet him at the motel in half an hour.

I walked through the parking lot back to my truck. A working vehicle provided me with a means of escape. *I don't have to go*, I told myself. *I don't have to do this.* I sat in my S-10, staring at the motel key in my hand. Sweat squeezed from my skin as the heat overtook the cab. *I can't not go, though. He's expecting me.*

And I was completely and utterly dependent on him. I had to go—for my addiction's sake.

I turned on the car, resolving to follow through on the commitment I'd made. The motel was less than a mile away, and I arrived at my destination before I even had a chance to back out. I slowed and made the right-hand turn into the lot. Perched over the entrance stood a half-functional sign, with what few light bulbs that were left blinking intermittently the motel name and the word "Vacancies."

I turned the truck off and stared down at the keys in my lap. My hands were trembling. I wasn't high. I wasn't crashing. I was scared to death. There was still time to get out of this.

The humid, muggy night created a stagnate thickness in the air. It was suffocating, and I couldn't find any clarity.

I had to either take off or go to the room. Either way, I had to make a decision. I was growing more paranoid by the moment about what I perceived as the presence of surveillance or police in the area. Paranoia—and the police—were the last things I needed. Not wanting to arouse suspicion any longer, I threw open the door and hopped out.

The doors to the motel rooms lined the two long corridors of the single-story building, which intersected in the middle at what appeared to be the management office. I walked the few steps to the room, turned the key in the lock, and pushed the door open. An ominous creak gave way to pitch blackness. A musty smell overwhelmed my senses. Unable to locate a light switch, I fumbled through the darkness toward the bed to find a lamp. I found one on the nightstand, flipped it on, and took a spot seated at the edge of the bed. I looked around to observe what kind of room I'd gotten myself into.

It felt disheveled and unkempt. Plastered-on striped wallpaper peeled from the pasty white walls. The thin flowery bedspread I was seated on oozed filth—only partially because of the stains. I couldn't help but wonder when it had last been washed. Much the same could be said of the long, shag-style, burnt orange carpet, which didn't look any younger than twenty years old.

What was I doing in this nasty motel room? This was crazy. I had to get out.

I looked over at the nightstand to the phone. Maybe I could call Jess. She'd been my best friend since we were freshmen, and she had been devastated to watch addiction take its toll on me. She supported me after my suicide attempt and knew I was in deep with crack.

She picked up the call. "Hello?"

"Jess! Holy shit. I'm at this motel, and Franklin gave me the key, and he's gonna be here in a few minutes, and I don't know what to do cuz I'm in serious debt and I'm in serious trouble with this crack shit, and if I sleep with him . . . I can get out of my debt if I just sleep with him. But I don't know if it's worth it. I don't know what the fuck to do."

"Oh my God, Jen, please, just get out of there—now! Just leave. Just walk out the—"

"If I left, what would I do with the key?"

"Just leave it in the door or something. Just get out of there! You can't do this. What if he has some sort of disease? Oh my God, Jen, just get out! You don't have to go through with this!"

I sat hunched over on the edge of the dingy bedspread, the tapping of my foot rattling the phone receiver pressed to my ear.

"I don't know. I might have to do this. I don't know what else to do. If I back out now, he's gonna be really mad. What if he forces me into sex? Or comes after me and tries to hurt me or steal my stuff? I'm just coming apart here, Jess. This is fucking crazy. I'm pretty much screwed here. I think I have to do this."

Jess's patience ran out. She'd put up with my addiction for years and was at a point where she didn't know what she could possibly say or do for me anymore. No matter what she said, she knew I would most likely do whatever my addiction told me to do. She was sick of it.

"Look, I don't think you should do this. I'm saying that as your best friend, Jen. I can't make your decisions for you, but please, I'm begging you: Don't do this. Do not sleep with this guy. You'll regret it forever."

She let out a sigh. "It's your life and your body, though. You do what you think is best. I don't know what else to say."

"Listen, Jess, I—"

I jumped, startled by a rattling noise. I looked to the door and saw the doorknob moving.

"Shit, I gotta go."

I hung up just as the door swung open. Cool, calm, and collected, Franklin took two steps in, closing the door softly behind him. He approached me and set a very large crack rock on the nightstand next to where I sat.

"That's yours when we're through," he said. "I'll bring your debt down, too."

"Wait, that's not what you said before. You said it would be erased."

"Yeah, well. We'll see how this goes. Maybe we can do this again and work it down that way."

"No way, I'm not doing this again. This is it."

He smirked, thinking otherwise.

"You will be wearing a condom, right?"

He paced the room in slow motion, tugging at his belt. I could see he was already aroused.

"No. No. I don't believe in condoms. It goes against my religion."

"Excuse me?"

How on earth could a former pimp and active crack dealer have religious values concerning sex? This was all very new to me. And his opposition to condoms threw a whole new spin on the idea of having sex with this man.

"I don't wear condoms for religious purposes," he said. "I absolutely will not wear one just for *you*, either. I don't have any diseases."

"You don't?"

"No."

"Have you been tested?"

He shook his head. "Look, woman, I'm ready to go here, and I'm gonna take my pants off now. So you should do the same. You don't have your period, do you?"

I froze. "Uh, no. No, I just finished it a few days ago."

I was staring at the orange shag carpet again. I looked up. Standing in front of me was this man, wearing nothing but black knee-high socks, boxers, and a tank top.

"Good. I wouldn't want to do this tonight if you were still bleeding. That's in violation of my religious practices."

He stripped off his tank top and reached down for his socks.

"Are you gonna take off your pants, or do you want me to do it for you?"

His boxers dropped to the ground. So too did my jaw.

He was enormous.

"I'll . . . I'll get them. Can I leave my shirt on?" I asked, trying not to stare.

"I don't care. I just want your pussy."

I kicked my shoes off and unzipped my jeans. "I can't get pregnant. You promised me you'd pull out. You said you would from the start, so please. I'll do this, but I just can't have you—"

"I won't. I'd love to have you carry a part of me someday, but right now I just want to fuck you."

I knew that's what he wanted. But I just couldn't handle the idea of getting knocked up by my crack dealer.

"Okay, okay." I stood up, slid my pants off, and sat back down on the corner of the bed with my legs crossed. He took two steps toward me, stopping with his penis just inches from my face. "Come on, I can't get at you in that spot. I'm ready to go here, and you're just messin' around. You can only lead a man on for so long. Now lie back. I promise I'll be gentle."

He was taking on a much rougher persona than usual. I didn't believe him.

"Look, I'm really having some reservations about this. I don't know if I feel comfor—"

"Woman, I swear! You're the most expensive whore I've ever had. I'm losing money just being here right now, and I'm putting more money down on your body than I have for any woman, ever. You should be sucking my cock and fucking me, thanking me for being so generous. Now lay back and spread your legs if you want your fucking rock!"

Franklin had never called me a whore before. He'd never even yelled at me. I'd clearly pissed him off.

There was no getting out of this anymore. I had to lie down. I took a hard swallow and braced myself. I inched back on the dirty bedspread, rested flat on my back, bent up my knees, spread my legs, and closed my eyes.

Pain gripped me. I bit my lip to keep from screaming. He didn't follow through on his promise to be gentle.

He fucked me. Hard.

With my eyes fixed on the ceiling, my body rocked back and forth to his pounding rhythm. After a few minutes he slowed down and looked up.

"Take off your shirt," he said.

I started to remove it when he took hold and stripped it from my head and arms. He reached around and unclasped my bra.

"Wrap your legs around me."

I did as I was told.

He barked these sexual instructions in such a way that I felt obligated to obey his commands. With my legs wrapped around him, he seemed content to fuck me for awhile.

As I stared up, I focused in on the patterns and shapes of the brownish water spots and stains on the popcorn-contoured ceiling. I couldn't bear to think about what was happening. I had to think about something, anything else. Every second seemed to last forever. I could only stare so long. Eventually it grew so physically uncomfortable that I couldn't fight it anymore.

I decided to fuck him back. For a moment I embraced my role and became his whore. I wanted him to get off of me as soon as possible. In an instant, I flipped the switch. I went from docile to domineering. I spanked his ass, talked dirty, and thrust my body right back at his. In a quick minute, he was ready to shoot. He let out a soft moan, backed out, grabbed a hold of his cock, and made a beeline for the bathroom. A few strokes later, he was cumming in the toilet.

I sat up breathless, shaking from head to toe. I bounced to my feet, retrieving my clothes from the foot of the bed.

I zipped my jeans and reached for my bra as he shouted. "God damn you, you fucking whore! You said you were done with your period! I've got your filthy blood on me. I can't believe this!"

I threw my T-shirt on as he trailed off, ranting about how having sex with a woman who is menstruating is in violation of something in the Bible. Not being well-versed in the Good Book, I had no idea what he was talking about. I stood silent, not sure what to say. I watched him grab a towel and wipe off his dick, which had apparently been made dirty by my body.

"I'm sorry," I said.

I apologized for something that was not my fault and that I had no control over. I'd been honest with him about the timing of my period. As far as I was concerned, I was done for the month. He, on the other hand, had been very rough with me. It's entirely possible that he *made* me bleed and then blamed me for it. In the moment, though, as the whore, I took the blame and apologized for my filthy behavior.

The realization of it all was enough to make me need a hit. I turned to the nightstand, grabbed my eight-ball, and headed straight out the door.

I hadn't even made it to the car before it struck me how disgusting I felt. I felt disrespected, degraded, and dirty. *How dare he blame me for bleeding, and how stupid, too. So what about him? What the fuck did I just do? Did I just give myself HIV? Hepatitis? What did I just do to myself?*

I'd just violated my every core value and moral. I'd sold my body for drugs. I'd become a dirty, filthy crackwhore. In that moment, I realized how dangerous my game of Russian roulette had become. But there was no time for deep contemplation or analysis of potential behavior modification. I needed to get home.

I needed to smoke some rock.

I DRAW THE hit and hold it. The high sets in. The pressure in my head intensifies by the moment. A tingling sensation crawls up through my legs, then through my midsection, and finally down my arms to the tips of my fingers.

Colors start to flash. A yellow-brownish hue creeps through my sight, drawing over my eyes like a shade. Shimmering sparkles dance through my vision. My head grows weak.

As I lie propped up against the base of the tub, my chin falls to my chest. My upper body begins to tremble. Slight at first, it escalates. A slight tremor evolves into a vigorous shaking. My arms stiffen. Still breathless, shaking, I can't let go of the hit.

Hands clenching the lighter in one hand, the pipe in the other, I try to force an exaggerated exhale. It's too late. The crack's hit my brain, and there's nothing I can do anymore.

The lights go out. I wake up on my side, curled up on the floor.

The sound of the shower filters through the Everclear song filling the air. Drenched in sweat, my head is pulsing, throbbing, pressing like a fist squeezing a balloon. My tongue feels tender and bitten. I push myself up to my feet but don't immediately recognize my surroundings.

The song is still repeating. The shower is still running. I look up into the mirror, at the scarred face of a female body—which, I realize, belongs to me.

What the fuck just happened? I'm stuck—in this rut, in this bathroom, with this sickness.

In the months after my suicide attempt, crack started giving me seizures. At the time I didn't know that's what they were. Nor did I know I was destroying my brain. But it was sending out grave warnings—quit, or you die.

Just when I got in too deep, I escaped.

8

Escape Artist

By the time I left Sioux City at the end of August, I was an absolute disaster. I was gaunt and disheveled, pale and self-mutilated. I had absolutely nothing left in the tank. I'd given it all to my addiction.

Franklin got arrested just a few weeks after the night at the motel. But other dealers happily filled in for his absence. I'd started frequenting flop houses and met a few folks to use with—people who knew other higher-level crack dealers. They were still competing for my business—calling my mom's house—long after I'd left town. I'd developed a reputation. Dealers knew I was hooked, and they were seeking me out.

I just couldn't keep going on the way I was. Nor could I keep frying my brain. I'd started taking a liking to black-tar heroin and, after Franklin got arrested, started smoking it along with crack. It was only intensifying the seizures that had started to overrun my body.

I had to get away from that town, the people, and all the drugs it contained before it killed me. Thankfully, I had Gustavus to escape to.

My goal since my youth had been to play college hockey, and Gustavus was where I'd have a chance to do that. It was also going to save me from my addiction. I couldn't have been happier to head to St. Peter. I had loved the campus, especially the rink—long before it appeared in my near-death experience. That only helped strengthen the bond.

I wanted nothing more than to move to campus, get my life under control, and prove myself, both as a college hockey player and as a student. It wasn't going to be that easy, though.

So much had changed between the time of the tornado and when I arrived as a freshman that fall. Much like a trip we would've made to Minneapolis a few years earlier, my mom and I packed up her minivan and set out for the open road. Except this time, I was battling withdrawals. And this time I had more than just a few clothes and my hockey bag; I had everything I needed to start living on my own.

We took a left off the main highway and headed toward the hill. Perched atop was my new home. As soon as we arrived, I knew I was out of my element. The campus looked nothing like it had before, when we last saw it in March. It was now essentially a construction zone.

As we crept closer to the brick-lined entrance at the foot of the hill, I was struck by the devastation in the heart of the town. Trees were missing, blue tarps covered the roofs of homes, and the buildings composing the front façade of the campus seemed almost unrecognizable. Thankfully, some comfortable familiarities remained. The rink had been untouched in the storm, and the freshman dorm only had some windows blown out. At least those things, I thought, were going to be essentially the same.

Student greeters, decked out in black and gold, cheered our approaching vehicle as we arrived at the bottom of the hill. We slowed to a stop to meet them at the main school entrance.

"Welcome to Gustavus!" a voice said.

My mom rolled down the window. A blond-haired, blue-eyed girl handed her a map and a T-shirt that read "Rebuilding a Better Gustavus." My mom turned and handed the items to me as a Green Day ballad rang out from a stereo the students had set up in the grass, appropriately crooning lyrics about having the time of your life.

"Norelius Hall is up on the top of the hill on your right," the girl said, pointing. "You can head up there to get checked in. Go Gusties!"

We pulled away as the students resumed their cheering and drove up the steep hill before coming to a stop in front of the freshman dorm. I hopped out of the car and lit up a smoke, gazing up first to the dorm, then across the parking lot to the rink and the adjacent construction. I couldn't help but wonder how I ended up there, on that hill, on that campus, after everything I'd been through. It was so devastatingly different from the way it had been just a year before, much like me.

Despite my desperate condition, I arrived on campus that fall anticipating that I'd be able to succeed both in the classroom and on the ice. Like the other freshmen, I had to learn the ropes during my first few weeks on campus. But unlike the other kids, I was coming off crack. Getting off the most stigmatized drug in our culture in the environment of a small liberal arts college is a lonely endeavor.

I quit crack cold turkey.

I left it and all my paraphernalia behind when I went to Gustavus. But college is not detox or the psych ward. I couldn't just lie in bed for a week. Struggling just to get to class, I began to rely more and more heavily on beer to get me through each day.

Drinking not only seemed to help me think less about coke and how much I wanted to use but also seemed to be a way to fit in. Most college kids drink. And alcohol, I knew from my high school days, was something that could help alleviate some of that social awkwardness I'd battled since I was twelve.

Right off the bat, my drinking abilities won me some friends to party with. But I soon realized that none of the kids I was meeting were drinking the way I was. They went out on the weekends, and even if they did occasionally drink to excess, they drank during times it was socially appropriate to do so. They didn't drink at noon, before class, the night before a big exam, or by themselves. They didn't stay up all night, every night, drowning in a bottle.

Within a week of arriving on campus, that's exactly what I was doing.

Not only did beer make it easier for me to interact with people, it also made it easier to deal with my crack withdrawal and mounting depression. My brain had been fried in the past few months, and now here I was changing all the chemicals I was pouring on the pan.

The alcohol, the crack, the situation. It all came together to push me into an emotional and spiritual spiral. Without my drug of choice, I turned to the only drug that was scarier—the one that had cost me my dad. Despite the sedative effects of all the alcohol, I still couldn't sleep. I was accustomed to sleeping during the day and staying up at night. Unable to correct this dysfunctional pattern, I frequently drank beer and wrote until the sun came up.

I wasn't writing anything for school, either. I was writing to myself.

I knew my psyche was in turmoil. I knew where I was but didn't know how I got there or how to make it work. I tried hard to excel with what little I had going for me at the time. I wanted to succeed at Gustavus more than anything in the world. I didn't want to fail. But my soul was in chaos. And it kept calling me to write, so that's what I did.

Nothing else, except beer perhaps, seemed important. I wrote all night, every night, crying in my beer, listening to music. The numbness provided to me by a year of cocaine use was wearing off, and I simply couldn't stop the onslaught of emotions overtaking me. My whole world had been flipped upside down in the past year. But somehow, someway, I had gotten to exactly where I wanted to be. I was at college, with the hockey season approaching.

And yet all I could seem to do was ponder the meaning of life and my own existence in it. I desperately needed to make some kind of sense of my near-death experience. Why did I see the Gustavus rink? Why did I live? Why was I not in a coma or suffering from significant brain damage? Why was it so vivid in my mental imagery when I had gaps in my memory both before and after the event? At the time, I had little idea of the aftereffects of a near-death experience. All I knew was that I'd experienced something as close to death as I ever imagined I could come, but for some reason, I was still alive.

I needed to figure out what had happened to me, why, and what it meant with respect to that hockey rink across the parking lot. I needed to be at Gustavus. I had needed to get away from the drugs, the town I was in, everything and everyone I knew. But I wasn't ready to be in college—not yet.

As my soul spun around during the first weeks of my freshman year, I did a lot of LSD on top of the drinking. The acid seemed to help me negotiate the spiritual mess I was feeling. But it sure didn't help me make it to class.

Whenever I was able to get there, I still couldn't pay attention. And it wasn't because I wasn't trying. Or even because I was using. Whether I was drunk, stoned, tripping, or on coke, I'd always made school a top priority. It's part of the reason I got hooked on coke to begin with; it helped me stay up and study for absurdly long hours. But this felt different. This felt like a struggle. I just couldn't get myself to focus or retain what I was reading. It was unlike anything I'd ever experienced in school before. Drugs had never affected my grades before. Why now? Was I not smart enough anymore? What had happened?

How was I supposed to hold it all together?

> 10/19/98   3 am
> I'm so fiending out for coke. I had one of those lovely little explosions of cocaine in my brain just a little while ago. I'm like, at my wit's end. What am I gonna do? All I care about right now is feeding my addiction. Just a little cocaine.
>
> I don't know what it is, but after about three weeks off that stuff, I go into withdrawal. I don't know what's wrong with me. I usually have withdrawals for about two days after coming off and then it's mostly psychological. This isn't just psychological.
>
> I'm sitting alone in the computer laboratory at 3 am, shaking from head to toe. I don't know, it's all fucked up. It's like I get a little outburst of coke every now and then and I can taste it. I can literally taste it, and it's driving me insane. I can't take this anymore. I think I'm gonna go nuts. Right now, I would just kill for about ten beers, or an 8-ball of coke.
>
> I'm seriously getting madder by the second. I don't think my conversation with my mom helped much, either. She kept telling me that if I was in Sioux City I'd still be using coke and heroin. Yeah, so, maybe I would be. I wish I were! I'm just totally a basket case. What the hell am I supposed to do about this whole situation? I can't sleep, I know, because I tried that earlier. I'm all out of weed, so I don't have that option. I couldn't get any cocaine if my life depended on it, and my beer is gone. I have absolutely no mood altering chemicals to alter my mind.

> All I see, hear, smell, and taste is coke. Beautiful coke, nothing but some coke. I'm really, really hurting here. What am I gonna do with myself? Who's up at 3 am that I can go to? Hmmmm . . . Nobody! Imagine that, nobody is up at 3 am. All I can think about is all those late nights I spent doing cocaine from dusk till dawn. How am I gonna be able to function when I can't think of anything but cocaine? I can't. School, hockey, everything seems so unimportant to me right now.

The more I craved coke, the more I drank to numb the pain. For the first six weeks of school, I was only able to make it to class sporadically. I tried to keep current on the assignments, but no matter how hard I tried, I just couldn't keep up. It wasn't long before I was failing school altogether, risking my entire hockey career and academic future in the process.

And my drinking problem was starting to get ugly.

I OPENED MY eyes, and found myself draped over the edge of my lofted bed. The alcohol had come right back up, and it was all over my hockey equipment.

The hockey season was just getting started in mid-October, so we didn't yet have a locker room. It's an NCAA rule. You can't have the locker room open or have on-ice practice with the coaches before a certain date.

Until that date, teams practice by themselves, off campus, in sessions led by the captains of the team. These so-called captain's practices come along just before tryouts, which start as soon as NCAA permits the season to start.

I returned to my dorm room one night after a captain's practice and lugged my sweat-laden bag up four long flights of stairs. As usual, I scattered my wet equipment on my half of the dorm room floor.

This must've really irritated my roommate, Alix, but if it did, she didn't let on. Born and raised in the Twin Cities, Alix and I got along pretty well, primarily because we both liked to drink and smoke. But unlike Alix, I was quickly turning into an alcoholic, one with an affinity for beer. On this particular night, I was out of my drink of choice and so had to substitute with a bottle of rum.

I got settled in for my nightly drinking, swigging off the bottle on an empty and dehydrated stomach. After adding some pot and pizza to the mix, I was pretty well loaded up. So, too, was Alix, who had joined me. Soon enough, though, she did what most normal people would've done. She quit drinking and went to sleep.

As usual, I stayed up for just a little more.

Once the room started spinning, I decided to call it a night. I climbed the ladder to my lofted bed, flipped on the TV, and started up an episode of *The Simpsons* to help me drift off to sleep. I hadn't yet realized I'd created a perfect recipe for an unexpected onslaught of vomit. I found that out at around 3 AM, when I bolted straight up in bed, half-unconscious, and hurled. I puked all over my bed and the floor and soaked my already damp, musty-scented hockey equipment.

Still drunk, I looked down over the loft at the mess I'd made. Nobody was gonna clean this up for me. I knew I'd have to do it myself. I sat up, thumping my head against the ceiling, and flopped back to the pillow. The room sucked me into a whirlpool.

The spinning accelerated. I sat back up but couldn't avoid gagging once more.

The blue light beaming from the television illuminated the room in a soft glow. I looked across the room to Alix, still sound asleep in her own loft. Panic overtook me as I worried about what she'd think if she woke up.

I had to clean this up pronto. More than that, I had to get myself together. I was supposed to be getting off crack and going to class, not drinking myself stupid and puking all over my dorm room. This was my shot at a better life. And I was just throwing it all away.

THAT'S WHEN I met her.

She caught my eye the moment I saw her, and like magnets we just connected. She was on the hockey team. Her name was Amy. And I don't know what it was, but there was something special about her. My mind and body began rushing to life when our eyes first met.

She literally took my breath away.

There were a few girls on the team I was starting to connect with, but not in the way I connected with her. Problems were plentiful, though. Chemical dependency aside, I was trying to maintain a long-distance relationship with Mike. Plus, this was a conservative college, and I had no idea what her background was like. I needed to find out, though, because I just had to get to know her. It didn't take long before I realized that she wanted to know me, too. Suddenly I had a dilemma. I had a serious boyfriend, but a serious crush on a girl.

With her long dark hair, piercing eyes, and seductive smile, she was the most beautiful creature I had ever been blessed to see. She'd look in my eyes, I'd smile, and I swear I could feel my soul light up.

We started talking, and it was as if we'd known each other forever. We each wanted to know everything about the other and fast became best friends. It wasn't long before she was sharing her darkest secrets with me, and I was sharing mine with her. After all, she was asking all the right questions.

She was the first person to ask me questions about my near-death experience. The first person I talked to about it. And the first one who held me while I poured my heart out, shook to my core, and relived the moment.

I was flattered that she was so intrigued by me. Unlike most people I'd been conversing with in 1998, she thought everything I'd been going through was really cool. She was fascinated by the craziness of my drug-addicted, mentally ill life. I desperately needed someone to embrace that part of me, and she seemed to have a deep wont to do just that. Even though she seemed unusually curious about drugs, she really seemed to care about me and what they had done to me. It all came together to make her that much more attractive. I could see in her eyes that she was feeling the chemistry, too. Our seemingly casual conversations became increasingly flirtatious, and the intensity between us grew more electric each day.

I just had to wait for the right time to make my move.

It came on one of those crisp November evenings in Minnesota where you don't really need a coat but should probably bring one anyway. Either way, your nose is still gonna get cold.

November is my least favorite month of the year. The sun is going down earlier; it's getting colder; everything is shriveling up and dying. On this night, like most others, I would've just as soon stayed in and gotten drunk alone. Instead, I agreed to head out to a movie with some teammates.

A few hours before we were set to leave, I knelt down over the mini-fridge to see what goodies I had in store. Inside, row after row of Rolling Rock. I flipped off the bottle top and tipped it up, a perfect way to kick off the party. Or something like that.

Even if I wasn't doing so hot on the addiction front, I was trying my best not to let it show. I gulped down a few bottles as I kept an eye on the clock. Once the time arrived and I felt the confidence factor rise sufficiently, I grabbed a hoodie, stumbled out of the dorm, and hopped into a waiting car full of girls.

I wasn't looking forward to the prospect of being without alcohol for the rest of the night.

We arrived at the movie theater on the main road just a few minutes later. Everyone piled back out of the vehicle and headed toward the theater. The last one out of the car, I lagged behind the group.

Standing near the entrance was a second group of girls. I was pleased to see Amy among them. She spotted me, grinned, and headed my direction.

"Hey, I didn't expect to see you here," she said.

A smile swept away my usually tough expression. "Well, I'm glad I came."

Indeed I was.

WE ALL FILED into the theater and got settled. Amy and I sat down next to one another and huddled up closely side by side, sipping off the airplane-sized bottles of liquor she snuck into the theater.

It wasn't beer, but at least it was something.

The alcohol nearly succeeded in making *A Night at the Roxbury* funny. But more than that, it gave us an excuse to be close. After the show, we gathered with the group and all milled about in the parking lot before collectively deciding to go for a milkshake. It might be a 1950s thing to do, but at least it was a wholesome activity. There's not much to do in the small town of St. Peter. There's not much there but a state mental hospital and an elite liberal arts college. It makes for an eclectic population.

This was a weekend, though, so I could've just as easily been out partying at a frat or something. It's probably a good thing I was there at the restaurant, nursing a triple-thick. More than I craved any chemical, though, I just wanted to be wherever Amy was going.

When we all finally returned to campus sometime after 11 PM, I wasn't ready to call it a night. Amy wasn't either.

We had been dropped off like a herd outside the freshman dorm, but Amy, a sophomore, lived across campus. Since she was so close to my place, I just had to ask.

"Do you want to come over for a drink or a smoke?"

I flicked the ash off my cigarette and took a deep drag. She turned my way. I could tell from her subtle smirk that we were on the same page.

"Sure," she said.

WE MADE THE long walk up to the fourth floor, where I was pleased to find I had the room to myself.

"Make yourself comfortable," I said, walking over to the desk to sit down. I started to roll a joint but quickly got distracted. Much to my surprise, she'd sat down on the rug rather than on a chair. And there she sat silent, simply smiling at me. That half-cocked smirk crept back over me. I couldn't stop looking at her.

I turned in my chair to face her and leaned forward on my arms. Our eyes locked. That weird smile that only she seemed to be able to elicit became fixed onto my expression.

We gazed at one another. "Would you like to kiss me right now?" I finally asked.

Her eyes flooded with fear and excitement. She'd never kissed a girl before and had been taught in school that homosexuality was a sin. After a moment's hesitation, she nodded yes.

I motioned her closer.

When I opened my eyes a few moments later, I was looking deep into hers. The alluring glow I saw there felt so hauntingly comfortable, the unfamiliar emotion that swept over me so genuinely pure. I smiled. My heart fluttered. This woman, I quickly concluded, must be my angel.

Even though we'd been flirting for awhile, I wasn't expecting our first kiss to hit me so hard. All of my rigorously constructed defense mechanisms came crashing down in an instant. For the first time in a long time, I was actually *feeling* something. And this felt unlike any kiss I'd ever had before. This wasn't just a kiss. Or just a drunk kiss from a pretty girl. This wasn't drugs fucking with my perceptions of my feelings. This felt real. It felt like my soul finding a mate. And it felt better than any chemical I'd ever had.

Suddenly I welcomed my second chance to breathe. I was reminded of the beauty of life and love and knew in that moment I was still alive for a reason.

There was still a lot of life here on earth left for me to experience.

We fell hard and fast in love. It doesn't matter how incredibly fucked up I was. It was love. It was real. And she would change my life forever.

9

Resolving to Rehab

I lost my footing when I fell head over heels—both in school and on the rink.

I don't even remember being told that I was no longer welcome on the hockey team. I'd made it through the rigors of tryouts and through the first few weeks of practice. But I felt off balance on my skates in a way I never had before. Never mind the fact that my shoulder had gotten so weak and unstable that it was popping out during my sleep.

Still, despite my struggles, I'd made the team. In fact, I was the top recruit, so I got first pick of a locker, first dibs on equipment, and first choice of number. But I wasn't really in any condition to be playing hockey.

I only got to play in one game before the coach put his foot down. Between my smoking, shoulder injury, poor grades, and the drinking problem the administration had made him aware of, it didn't take long before he'd had enough.

I'd have to get my feet on the ground if I ever wanted strap on my skates again—and not just from the coach's perspective, either. If I didn't pick up my grades, and soon, I was going to lose my NCAA eligibility altogether.

The dire messages from professors regarding my repeated absences were growing more urgent. But no matter how serious they got, I still remained unaccounted for. I was still mired in the mess of my sickness. But this time, I knew I needed to get some help, and I'd started to let the people I was becoming friends with in on my little secret.

Molly and Diana were two such people. They were both on the hockey team and were both, in a word, wholesome. They seemed real and stable, and unlike my other friends who partied, they didn't drink much. They didn't smoke, do drugs, or go out and have sex with random people. They were normal people walking the normal line that most normal people walk. I liked that because I needed that. But as hard as they tried to understand what I was going through, they couldn't quite comprehend the idea of having such an overwhelming desire to drink or use.

Amy did. She was showing interest in drugs and its culture much the way I had in high school. She seemed to understand what I was battling.

Each night after midnight, we'd exchange emails. But as the hours passed, I'd grow increasingly intoxicated. We'd either flirt, or I'd get overly emotional and want to talk. Either way, one of us would end up going to the other's dorm.

I was doing everything I could to hang on, but was reaching the end of my rope.

I stumbled my way across campus to her dorm late one night. Her roommate, also a hockey player, was home. And since almost everyone on the team, except Molly and Diana, was in the dark about Amy and me having a relationship, we planned to meet up in a little room we called simply "the yellow room." It was nothing more than a small square room with an ironing board and yellow walls. It was always open, always empty, and the perfect place for Amy and me to sit and talk.

We took a seat propped up along the wall and snuggled up close. I looked down at the floor and sighed. "Look," I said. "I have a lot on my mind tonight."

She knew I was failing my classes and supposed to be meeting with the dean of students and the school psychologist the next day.

"What if I have to leave school because I'm failing out? I don't know what's gonna happen to me. Or if I'll even be here next semester."

She locked her arm around mine and laid her head on my shoulder. She stayed perfectly silent, clinging to me tightly. The stillness in the air amplified my emotions as I let down my walls and started to cry.

"Everything's gonna be alright, Jen," she said. "I promise you it will."

I lost myself there in her warm embrace. I believed her.

Time escaped us as we clung tightly to one another and every lasting second of our secret, forbidden romance. Finally, she unlocked our hold to cover a yawn. I didn't want us to part but offered to get out of her way for the night. It was close to 3 AM, and she had a lot going on the next day.

Before I could leave, though, I wanted to get something ready to smoke on the walk back. "Do you mind if I roll a joint first?" I asked.

"No," she said. "Not at all."

I pulled a bag of weed and some papers from my pocket. "If they ship me off tomorrow, I might not be able to smoke again for a while," I said.

She watched me—deliberately, intently. I pulled a paper from the packet. Just as I did, she asked a question I was completely unprepared for.

"Will you teach me how to roll a joint?"

My heart hit the floor.

It was hard enough to accept that I was failing out of school because of what my chemical dependency was doing to me. I couldn't stomach the idea of getting my girlfriend caught up in drugs, too. I was seeing her own tendencies toward addiction, and I wanted desperately to protect her from it.

But since I was going to roll it anyway, with or without her sitting next to me, I proceeded reluctantly to demonstrate.

The instruction turned into a discussion of all things related to drugs. How to use them. How to prepare them. What they feel like. She fired away, holding nothing back, posing question after question.

My nerves grew irritated. The last thing I wanted to be talking about the night before my big meeting was what cocaine tastes like or how it makes you feel.

I licked the paper to seal my newly rolled joint, shoved it in my cigarette packet, and stood up, ready to go. Amy detected my frustration. "Are you okay? Are you mad at me? Why are you mad at me?"

"I'm not mad, Amy. I'm just . . . disappointed, I guess. I don't want you to get into this stuff. Drugs and chemicals, I mean."

She furrowed her brow, unaware that her questions were not only poorly timed but also terribly worrying for me.

I said good-bye, turned around, and walked out the door.

It was late, but I wasn't tired, and now I was pissed off at my girl-friend, too. So, since it was already close to 3 AM, I did what any good practicing addict or alcoholic would do: I stayed up all night and got supremely loaded.

After I knocked back a handful more beers, light started to break through the window. The sun was starting to come up, and my eyes were growing heavy. I crawled up on my loft and curled up in a ball.

A KNOCK ON the door jarred me from my slumber. I sprang up, sweat-dampened mop of hair covering half my face. The bright sun pouring through the shade pierced my lids before I could pry them open.

"Jennifer Cannon," a voice said. More words were spoken. Some-one was talking about me outside the room. The squawk of a radio barked out a response.

Now I was awake. "Who's talkin' about me out there?"

I looked at the clock. 1:52.

Shit. I'd overslept and missed the meeting.

I pushed the covers back as the doorknob rattled. In walked Alix, with a police officer right behind her. She sat down at her desk and promptly opened a book. He looked around the room then up to the loft at me.

"Ms. Cannon?" he said.

"Yeah?"

"I need you to come with me. Right now." He put his hands on his hips. "There've been some concerns about your whereabouts. Can you step down from the loft, please?"

I started toward the ladder, but paused. "I'd like to change my clothes first, if it'd be okay."

"Fine," he said. "Just make it quick."

He stepped out of the room and shut the door behind him, leav-ing in his wake an awkward silence. I thought Alix was going to wake me before the meeting. Not that it was her responsibility to do so, but we'd discussed the meeting and all its potential ramifica-tions. She agreed to help me out.

Though the tension in the air grew thicker by the moment, I chose not to say a thing. It wasn't her fault. I was the one who couldn't get my drunk ass out of bed in time for a 1:30 meeting. The only person I had to be mad at was myself.

I threw on some fresh clothes and walked out the door without saying a word. "Ready?" the officer asked.

"Yup."

"I don't need to cuff you or anything, right? You aren't gonna try and run on me?"

I had to chuckle. "No, I'll behave. Thanks, though."

We walked down the four flights and out front to his squad car. I plopped down in the backseat.

"Where we headed?"

I'd figured out long ago how this worked. The more tolerance for the unknown I could demonstrate, the better off I'd be. I'd lost control over my life, so others were taking control of it for me. I no longer had any say in what was happening. I had to just roll with the punches.

"To the counseling office," he said.

I couldn't help but laugh. It was, literally, across the parking lot from my dorm. It would've been just as easy to walk, but instead I got front-door service, rolling up to the student union, in the heart of campus, in a police car. The dozen or so students who watched me get out of the backseat must have wondered what was up.

I, on the other hand, knew exactly what was up. Since I'd missed the meeting over at the dean's office, I was meeting up with just the psychologist. It wasn't my first time meeting Julie. I'd been in to talk to her quite a lot in the previous few weeks, but I could never follow through when I'd give her my word that I wouldn't drink. I always drank, even when I said I hadn't. I'm sure she knew it. She had me all figured out.

The officer led me right up to her office door and knocked. She answered. I bowed my head.

"She was fine," the officer said. "Just sleeping. No trouble getting her over here."

"Great. Thanks." Julie nodded and motioned me in, holding the door open as the officer nudged me through the open frame. I landed on the couch—my usual spot—and folded my arms over my chest. I tried to be cool, but was very much on edge.

Julie sat down across from me. "So . . . what happened?"

I shrugged my shoulders, choking back the strain building up behind my eyes.

"We waited for you. And your mom was waiting on the phone." I turned and looked out the window. "Have you called her?"

"No, I haven't talked to her in a few days," I said.

"I think you should call her. She's very upset. When you didn't show up, I think she feared you might've tried to hurt yourself. I've already let her know you're okay. I called her just as soon as the officer paged to let me know they found you. But she needs to hear from you right now, not me."

"I was just sleeping. I didn't do anything to hurt myself."

"I know, but I think you should call her," she said again.

Twenty minutes later, after shedding a boatload of tears, I hung up the phone. I felt horrible for causing my mom so much stress. She was absolutely certain they were going to find me hanging in the basement of my dorm. To this day she says she's never worried more about my safety than she did that afternoon.

Once the tears dried, Julie opened the door. An Gustavus security officer and two St. Peter police officers stood up from their seats. They'd been waiting to escort me to the hospital for some much needed rest.

I followed them back out through the student union and to the waiting squad car. Students again stopped to stare as the back door opened up. Julie sat down beside me.

Back to the ward I went, escorted this time not only by police but also by my psychologist. I was headed to a hospital in Mankato, just south of St. Peter. Even though I was in a different state, headed to a hospital with a different name, once we arrived, it all looked the same. It had the same sterile flavor, the same white walls and floors, and the same veiled pages floating through the intercom system.

After checking in, I said good-bye to Julie and the officers and followed my new escort, a nurse in white.

We arrived on the third floor, where the psychiatric ward sat adjacent to the inpatient chemical dependency unit. The units looked a little different from the rest of the hospital. The floors were carpeted, and the walls were papered; much the way the mental health units looked in other hospitals I'd been in. Together they occupied much of one floor of the hospital.

I wasn't being taken to the chemical dependency wing, though. I was headed for the observation room in the psych ward. According to Julie, I needed to be there because I was showing signs that I was a danger to myself. Even my mom was worried that I might've succeeded in getting the job done that very day.

But it was the email I'd sent to Diana a few weeks before that'd raised the alarm to a new level:

11/19/98   4:34 am

Hey, yeah, I kind of did get caught drinking tonight. The dorm head and my RA talked to me a little while ago. I'm getting three violations, so that sucks.

I'm so depressed. I don't know what to do with myself. I have a Geology test at 1:30, so hopefully I can get up. I feel like hell, emotionally. I just want to get out of this school— now. I love it here, but I just can't do it. I guess I need to go home and fuck up some more. I'm just so sad, and so angry. I don't know what to do with these emotions. If I didn't think I'd get in trouble for it, I'd put my fist through the fucking wall.

God, I just want to get out of here. I can't stand this. I never thought it would get this bad. What should I do? I can't quit crying, and I am seriously on the verge of taking my own life. I just wish I could die. I think I'm to be an example to others, and I must do that through death. Am I really sick, or what? As I sit here pondering my existence, I wonder what will really happen to me. Unless I get really impulsive again, I won't have the guts to commit suicide. I wish I had the guts to try it again. Because if I did try it again, I would not fail. I would die. I wish I would.

I guess I don't know how to deal with all this emotion. What can I do? I have no chemicals to cover myself from my feelings, and I can't deal with it. I'm so frustrated. If you have some time on Thursday, please come see me. I'd really like to talk to you. (And I won't be wasted, I promise.) Something's got to give. I just hope it's not me who is giving up.

No, I wasn't giving up. Far from it. I was preparing myself for battle. Even if everything was slipping through my hands, I wasn't going down without a fight.

Ever since that first round of depression knocked me flat at age twelve, I'd pushed away help. I didn't want it then, I have a hard time accepting it now, and I was fortunate to have been so compliant for a brief period of time in between. If I hadn't found that piece of compliance, I don't think I'd be alive.

During that in-between period, which started in or around November 1998, I did something I'd never done before—I asked others to help me help myself.

It's a good thing I did, too. I'd sunk so low I was discussing suicide again. But Diana wasn't about to keep it to herself. She forwarded my email to Julie, who sent it to the drug and alcohol education department, which sent it to my dorm's head resident, who sent it to my RA. Then they all talked about it with my mom.

I was the last to find out the email had been circulated. In fact, I didn't find out about it until a few weeks later, after I'd overslept and missed my all-important meeting with the dean.

I could've been angry at Diana for violating my confidentiality and betraying my trust. But she was special. I knew she cared about me and had nothing but my best interests in mind. She could see I needed professional help. And for the first time, so could I.

INSTEAD OF PREPARING for finals, I set out on a mission: to get through rehab.

I woke up in yet another white-walled room, gown pulled down over one shoulder. Tugging to adjust my attire, I sat up and crossed my legs underneath me. A yawn escaped as I stared around the room and took in my surroundings.

It looked just like all the other detox and psych ward observation rooms I'd been in. Four white walls. A camera mounted in the corner. One small bed with safety reinforcements. This room differed in just one respect from the others. This one had its own bathroom. What a luxury.

After I napped my way through dinner, a knock on the door awoke me.

"Jennifer, you have some guests here," a nurse said and left.

I pushed my mop of hair out of my face and put it up in a ponytail. In walked Amy, Molly, and Diana.

Pale, disheveled, and drawn, I slid back down and pulled the covers up over my gown, shrinking in embarrassment.

Amy offered me some clothes, which I quickly accepted. After switching out my gown for a sweatshirt and some flannels, I headed toward the patient rec area to meet my visitors looking a little more respectable.

I sat down at a table where Amy, Diana, and Molly were all tending to a puzzle. I picked up an edge piece and rolled it between my fingers, turning to look at an older man strapped to a wheelchair in the corner of the room. He stared wide-eyed at the TV, which blared loudly. I couldn't tell whether he was actually watching what was on or simply staring off into space as a result of being medicated. Either way, the block sitting on his tray dissuaded me from adjusting the volume.

I tuned out the drone of the news anchors and turned back to my friends.

"So," I said, tapping the puzzle piece on the table, "here we are."

They looked at me and then at one other. An awkward silence loomed. It was the middle of the hockey season. Two weeks before finals. And the three people I'd grown closest to over the previous semester were putting together a puzzle while visiting me in the looney bin.

I couldn't help but feel like a burden. "Well, I know this isn't how you want to see me. But thanks for coming. I really do appreciate it."

Molly and Diana looked at one another. "We're just glad you're getting some help," Diana finally said. "Have you talked with the school about your options?"

"No, I don't know what's gonna happen yet. Julie escorted me here, but I haven't talked to her since—"

"Ahem." A nurse cleared her throat and approached the table. "Hi girls. What's goin' on here?"

I looked around, confused. "What do you mean? We're visiting. These are my visitors." I motioned around me to my friends.

"Well, that's fine. But I'm talkin' about your clothes. Where'd you get those?"

"They brought them for me. Comfy clothes sounded much better than a hospital gown." I smiled sheepishly.

"Well, that's strictly against the rules," she said. "Everything brought in by visitors is supposed to be checked in at the front desk. Did you gals check in at front?"

"Yeah, we did." Amy quickly answered. "They have a whole bag up there they're going through. I just grabbed a pair of pants and a shirt for her."

I looked up at the nurse, as if to confirm that what Amy was saying was the truth. She hadn't tried to sneak me in any drugs or booze or anything else incriminating.

"Well, I'm sorry," the nurse said, "but we're gonna have to take those clothes from you. We need to have you wearing a hospital gown right now because you're on suicide watch. And apparently you have a history of a suicide attempt, too?"

Whoa. Hold up. I wasn't feeling this. So what if I had a history of a suicide attempt? I wasn't even in remotely the same situation as I was back in May. I wasn't nearly as impulsive. Nor was I in the same hospital or even in the same state. How could my reputation be preceding me?

I understand now that they were just doing what they needed to do keep me alive. I probably didn't deserve clothes. Even if I wasn't feeling as if I were going to act on my suicidal thoughts, I was still extremely depressed. And I was also crashing again. That combination had nearly proved fatal for me in the past. I can't blame the hospital a bit for watching me like a hawk and ensuring that I didn't do anything to endanger my safety. At least they cared enough about me to do that.

I thought to bark back and argue but I knew it was in my best interest to simply comply. I was no longer a belligerent crack addict with a bad attitude and little to lose. I'd made it to college, I had gotten off crack, but still I failed.

I failed to avoid becoming an alcoholic. I failed to monitor my mental health until I got in too deep. I failed to accomplish my goal of playing college hockey. I failed to complete one single semester of college.

I had to get my shit together. Not because anyone else told me to, but because, for the first time, I recognized that I alone was throwing my life away and that nobody else was going to fix it for me but me.

It had to stop. I had to start taking my disease seriously and do everything in my power to stand up to it.

At the nurse's request, I retreated to my room to don a gown. After switching up my ensemble, I no longer felt all that social. Diana and Molly milled in the hallway as Amy joined me in the room.

As I curled up in bed, she pulled up a chair alongside me. She produced several pages of paper.

"I just feel so bad about this," she said, staring down at them. "You disappeared, and I couldn't find you all day. I got so worried." She crinkled the corners of the papers in her hands. "I just hope you can forgive me."

"For what, exactly?"

"For my insensitivity last night. I wrote you several emails to tell you how sorry I am. But you didn't respond. I couldn't find you all day. I called everyone, but you were gone. I even emailed Jess. You probably have, like, ten emails from me waiting for you. But here," she said, extending a few pieces of paper my direction, "I printed them off. This is what I was trying to say."

I grabbed hold of the pages, each containing a separate, printed email. At the top of each, the header. In the body of one, one phrase: "I'm sorry." It repeated. Over and over again.

"I didn't write it that many times, by the way. I pasted it. Pretty neat, huh?"

I nodded, smiling as I skimmed the remaining emails. I could see she felt absolutely horrible for what had happened. And I sure didn't do much to ease her mind when I ran off and wasn't heard from.

I had sent her an email after my late-night departure the previous evening. In it I let her know why it bothered me that she had played twenty questions with me about drugs and my addiction on a night when my entire education and hockey career were on the line. She really had hurt my feelings. But I know she hadn't meant to. She was just fascinated by addiction. She was also in shock. She couldn't believe that I might actually be removed from school. Neither could I.

As I read her apologies, I couldn't help but let my emotional defenses break down. She was tugging at my heartstrings. I wiped a tear from my eye as I absorbed her words. My thoughts shifted from suspicion to appreciation. I couldn't believe that someone—anyone—could care so much about me. After all the places and all the people who had pushed me away in the course of my addiction, it felt too good to be true.

I reached out, grabbed hold of her hand, and clenched it with my own. Even though she'd come into my life when I was at my worst, she loved me. Correction: she more than loved me. She said that, with me, she felt complete. And I felt precisely the same way.

With all the weight of my history barreling down on me, I looked deep in her eyes. "I love you more than anything in the world," I said. "I'm gonna do everything I can to get myself better."

Whether it was for her or for myself, in that moment I turned a corner. I decided, for the first time, to try and get clean and sober.

PERHAPS MY MOTIVATION was misdirected. I wanted to get well. But I was not in a place where I was able to stop drinking. Cocaine? Crack? Yes, I wanted to put that all behind me. But was I really ready to give up alcohol? It was a legal drug, not like crack, which could've cost me a felony just for possession alone. And plus, I was in college. It was almost *expected* that I drink.

I liked to drink, and so did Amy—a lot. She was also excited about the prospect of us tripping on LSD together. That sounded like a lot of fun. I loved to trip but had grown accustomed to doing it solo. With all that going on, I wasn't yet convinced that complete and absolute sobriety was for me.

I was feeling terribly conflicted and even more confused. On the one hand, I was ready to quit using cocaine in any form. On the other, I wasn't ready to quit drinking. On the one hand, I had a girlfriend I would have given my life for and I was prepared to get well for. On the other, even though she wanted me to get away from cocaine, she didn't seem to want me to get *too* far from the drug scene or from a bottle.

As the days went by my resolve evolved. Even if there were appealing aspects to drinking and using, for everything my addiction had already cost me, I needed to give rehab my best shot. I couldn't control what was going to happen once I got out. I just needed to stay there, follow the steps, and take it one day at a time.

I didn't *have* to stay sober once I got out. It was my choice. If I wanted to drink once I got out, I could. But each day I woke up in the hospital, I found myself increasingly grateful to wake up clear-headed. And I wanted to keep it that way once I got out. But as the days passed, it became apparent to my counselor that I was lacking in the support department, particularly at home.

Completing the full twenty-eight days of treatment would've meant spending Christmas in the hospital. But after just eighteen days, my insurance coverage ran out. Just two days shy of Christmas, I was allowed to graduate. There was just one condition put on my release: that I not return home to Sioux City.

I agreed. So too did Amy's family. They agreed to take me in for Christmas break. It was the kindest gesture I could've hoped for. And a welcome way to get closer to Amy.

For the first time in my life, I spent Christmas away from my family. Instead, I spent it perfectly sober, wrapped tightly in the arms of the woman I was falling deeply in love with.

10

Relapse and Remorse

Christmas break ended almost before it got started. Just a few days after New Year's, Amy and I packed up our bags and headed back to campus for J-term. With only one class to look forward to during January, it was a great way to ease back into student life and academic expectations.

As Amy sped off to her dorm, I threw my duffle bag over my bad shoulder and turned around to stare up at the four-story brick building sprawling out in front of me. I couldn't help but reminisce. I'd been away from campus for thirty-one days, and I'd spent every waking minute of that time completely clean and sober.

I felt great. But I was also scared of the temptations that being back on campus would bring.

The frigid Minnesota air seeped through my clothes, pinching my skin. I drew in a deep breath, watching it draw patterns in the air right before me as I exhaled. It was time to get back to school. Time to get this college thing right.

Backpack on, duffle bag hanging on my hip, I made my way to the doors. Four miserable flights later, I plucked my key from my pocket and turned the knob, dropping myself and my bags into a heap in the center of the room.

Alix wasn't back yet. Her side of the room was spotless, organized, and clean. Usually my half of the room looked the same. But today it was a mess. My bed was unmade. My clothes and belongings were tossed about. People had obviously moved things to find my clothes when I got escorted from school. But clearly, nobody had made it a point to search my room the way my mom had.

I pulled my chair away from my computer and settled down at my desk. My hockey bag beneath it took up most of my leg room. I turned on my computer and scooched my chair up to the desk. The bag underneath needed to go. I moved my chair back again, but my foot slipped.

Clink. I'd kicked the bag.

It made a noise—a noise unlike anything normally found in a hockey bag. Struck by the sound, I paused, and kicked at it again.

Clink.

Couldn't be. Could it? Was that *glass* I was hearing? It sounded like it. In fact, it could be nothing else. I leaned over, ripped open the pocket on the side of the bag, and reached inside. It was unmistakable: the rough edged cap, the long smooth neck, the shape of the bottle. It was beer. And there were four of them. I fished through the compartment and removed each one, then ripped open the bag to search for others.

No luck. I'd hidden four beers, right there inside my own hockey bag. I can't understand why. It was almost like self-inflicted punishment. Hiding any number of beers was enough to set me up for a relapse. But four is like torture. It's just enough to get a little tipsy but not enough to get drunk. It's just enough to whet your alcoholic appetite but not enough to quench your thirst.

I don't remember when or why I put those four beers in my hockey bag. But a month later and a month sober, there they were. Mine for the taking.

I set the bottles on the rug and stared at them. I thought to pour them out. But after a moment of hesitation, I instead transferred them to the fridge, making myself froth with anticipation. I was starting to taste it.

The minutes dragged on as I contemplated my forthcoming sips. It seemed inevitable that I was going to drink. It was just too big of a temptation to resist. I didn't want to slip. But I wanted those beers.

I reached in, popped the cap, and took a ferocious swig. One by one, down they went. When the forty-eight ounces were up, they were up. Did I need to get more? Did I want to? How could I? I wasn't twenty-one, and all the liquor stores were closed.

As the night progressed, I ducked outside repeatedly to smoke. It seemed the only thing I could do to distract myself from the incomplete nature of my buzz. I wasn't as trashed as I wanted to be. I was still halfway coherent. But more than that, I'd let my addiction loose again, and now it was talking in my ear.

I paced the small landing space at the side entrance of the dorm. *You can't get anymore tonight,* I told myself. *Besides, what the hell are you doing? You just blew your sobriety!* I sucked my cigarette down to the filter and tossed the butt to the ground, smearing it with my shoe. "Enough," I said aloud. "This is it, Jen. Don't let this happen again."

It was the first of many times I'd make such a promise to myself. "This is it!" Or: "This is the last time!" Or even: "Never again!" I'd implore myself to stop my behavior, turn my life around, and walk the line.

The problem was I wasn't ready. I was still too far seduced by chemicals to let them go entirely.

I marched up the four flights back to my dorm room, parked myself at my computer, and typed an email to Amy, confessing to the drinking.

"I'm sorry," I wrote. "I promise this is the last time."

It wasn't. Not even close.

I TRIED, BUT I just couldn't stay sober. Within a few weeks of the start of class, I was back to drinking most nights of the week. I wasn't about to let the people in my aftercare program know that, though.

I was doing pretty well, as far as I was concerned. As long as the alcohol didn't interfere with my life anymore, what was the big deal? Everybody drinks in college. And besides, my biggest enemy was, I was still convinced, crack. *That* was the drug that had tried to kill me. The biggest thing I could do to avoid crack—or cocaine in any form—was to avoid being in Sioux City.

When Mike came back from basic training, I had no choice but to be honest with him and break things off. It wasn't easy. I loved him. But I was head over heels with Amy, and I knew I could no longer be happy with him.

I had very few reasons to go back to Iowa. But my mom still lived there, and of course I wanted to visit her. I worried about her, taking care of the house all by herself.

It only made my troubles focusing in the classroom that much worse. When I started up a full load of classes for the spring, Julie sent me for testing. I was diagnosed with ADHD.

I'd never had trouble in the classroom prior to arriving at Gustavus. It made me wonder what had changed in my brain. I was having trouble retaining what I was reading. But with accommodated testing and an Adderall prescription, my grades started to climb.

I'd settled into a nice groove when spring break rolled around, and I went home to Sioux City. Amy decided to come back with me. It was my first time back in months—and the first time I'd invited Amy to my home.

It only took one night before I got a phone call. A buddy of mine from high school gave me a ring. She wondered if I could hook her up with some coke.

I couldn't say no. She had a fake ID.

After picking up some beer, she, Amy, and I rolled through downtown to my old stomping grounds, pulling up to the back entrance of a rundown apartment complex.

"I'll just run in and grab it, if that's okay," I said.

Objections were raised. Neither of them wanted to stay in the car. So they came in with me.

Huge mistake. Three white girls in a crackhouse doesn't work. Especially when one of them is wearing brand-name clothes and looking very sheepish.

The female dealer in charge of the house was none too happy to see I'd brought company. She instructed her cronies to search Amy. I stood by and watched as two rather large men patted down my girlfriend. I felt horrible for the trauma I was putting her through.

When it was all said and done, I walked out the door with some rock. I shoved the four rocks, separately packaged, into my pocket and waited for the scolding. As soon as Amy and I got dropped off at my mom's house, it came. Amy was pissed—and rightly so. Not only had I just endangered her safety by bringing her to a crackhouse, I'd purchased the one drug that everyone seemed to agree I needed to stay away from.

We didn't make it halfway through the garage before she grabbed hold of my arm and stopped me.

"Jen, you aren't gonna smoke that, are you?"

I glared at her, silent. I wasn't really sure. I wanted to, but I didn't want to. I wanted to stay true to my goal: stay away from cocaine.

But it felt too late now, just like the beer in the bag. Once I put those bottles in the fridge, it was too late to turn back. Once I gave the dealers my money and put the rocks in my pocket, the slip was underway. Wasn't it?

I couldn't just throw away $80.

I looked down at the ground and then back up at Amy.

"Jen, answer me. You aren't gonna smoke that, are you?"

A switch flipped. Suddenly, nothing mattered more than the crack in my pocket. Not the beer in my hand. Not my mom's worries. Not my sobriety. Not Amy.

Even though I hadn't even smoked it yet, all I could see, taste, smell, and feel was cocaine. I suddenly didn't care whom I hurt. I just needed to be alone so I could use my drugs in private. And Amy was getting in my way again.

"Yeah, ya know, I actually was. I bought it; it's in my pocket; I might as well get fucked up."

She looked at me as if I'd just transformed into a monster.

"Jen, you can't smoke that. It's crack! Think of what it's done to you already. If you smoke it, you're just gonna want more. Please, please don't do this."

I took a step toward the door. She grabbed my arm once more. "Jen, I'm serious. If you smoke that, I'm leaving. You hear me? I won't stand for this."

My indecision was turning to anger. It was my money, my brain. It wasn't her place to tell me what to do.

"Amy, if you say a word to my mom about this, I swear to God I'll fucking kill you. I don't give a shit what you do. You wanna leave? Leave. I don't give a shit."

I turned, headed through the front door, said hi to my mom seated in her usual spot in the kitchen, and headed straight back to my bathroom. I pulled the drawer out to lock myself in. Two seconds later, the knob turned, and the door crashed into the drawer, blocking it from opening—just as I knew it would.

The hairbrush in the fully extended drawer rattled as the pounding continued. I pulled my pipe from my pocket and broke off a hit of rock.

"Jen," I could hear on the other side of the door, "please." Her voice was breaking. "I'm begging you. Please don't do this. It could kill you!"

It was too late now. I was too far in. My inner addict was running the show. Jen was gone.

"Fuck off, Amy. Just leave me alone. I'm gonna do what I'm gonna do, and there's nothing you can do to stop me."

We exchanged a few more verbal blows.

"Fine," she said. "I'm not putting up with this. I'm outta here. You're on your own."

She walked away.

Silence blanketed the room. She'd sounded serious.

Torn between love and addiction, I hesitated, reaching first for the door, then for the radio. I turned it on, then the shower, and lit my Bic. I held it to the rock and watched it start to melt. My mouth watered as I put the pipe to my lips. The rush of the hit took hold, and thirty seconds later, I came back to reality, amped and on edge.

One hit is never enough. But this time, I had to keep smoking. If I didn't smoke it all, I might not get another chance. Amy might tell my mom.

Smoking $80 of rock in one sitting, after months away, is not a wise move. I knew it was dangerous. So I thought maybe I could hide some and just *say* I smoked it all. That sounded like a better plan. But if I didn't smoke it all and held onto some for the next day, then I'd have to smoke it the next day. And if I smoked it the next day, then I'd surely want more.

The situation grew stickier by the moment, but with each hit I grew closer to a decision. With just a $20 rock left, I decided to call it quits.

I was high, and my body was remembering. My heart wanted to beat out of my chest. Sweat beaded on my forehead as the pressure inside my head intensified. My brain was starting to feel electric. I knew I needed to stop or else risk giving myself one of those episodes where I'd wake up on the floor.

Besides, I needed to stop because I felt like shit for the way I'd talked to Amy. She didn't deserve that. She was only trying to help me.

After a quick shower, I hid the pipe and remaining rock inside a hand towel, concealed in the back of a drawer. When I finally made it next door to my room, Amy was standing by my bed, packing a bag.

I stood silent, unable to hold still. She darted me a scolding look. "Well?" she finally asked.

"Well what?"

"Did you smoke it?"

"Yeah, I did, actually. Every last bit of it."

"Was it worth it?

"Whaddya mean?"

"Was it worth it? The high, I mean. I hope so, cuz it's gonna cost you. I'm leaving first thing in the morning. I don't want to be around you while you're using that drug."

She piled her clothes into the bag she'd just unpacked earlier that day. I watched, dumbstruck.

My anger and anxiety melted into a puddle of remorse. I stared at her profile, watching her expression. The same eyes I connected with so well now looked flooded by disappointment. I could see I'd let her down. I walked two steps closer and sat on the bed.

The chemical cascade of the crack in my brain was underway. The agitation stirred me. I rubbed my knees, propped up on the bed frame, and tried to slow down. But everything felt like it was going so fast. I was high, anxious, and emotionally numb.

With crack, just as soon as you get high, you come down. And with the comedown is an onslaught of emotion—the magnitude of which was only amplified by the fact that, for the past year, I'd put an overwhelming number of chemicals in my brain, then injured it, then flooded it again.

Here I was once more, high on crack, slightly drunk, still recovering from a brain injury, and attempting to articulate the mess of emotions hitting me. I wiped the sweat from my brow and dried my cheeks as my body began to tremble.

"Look, this isn't at all how I wanted this trip to go," I finally said. "I didn't even want to smoke the shit." She stopped packing and sat down. I ran my fingers through my hair and sighed.

"It's gone now, though. I wish I hadn't done that." She stayed guarded, quiet. "I don't know. You saw how it happened. It just *finds* me when I'm here. It's like I can't get away from it. I'm sorry. But please—just know I'm trying. I'm trying to get better."

I put my head back in my hands and started to sob. She hesitated for what felt like an eternity before putting a hand on my back. "I know you are, Jen," she said. "I know you are." She reached her arms around me and squeezed.

Though we talked much of the night, I arose the next morning still feeling the effects of the rock. I could feel the restlessness in my core and the jitteriness in my movements. I could hear it whispering in my ear. I could taste it on my tongue.

I'd told Amy there was none left. That I'd smoked it all. But I knew right where it was. And it was calling for me.

I couldn't help but finish it off during my morning shower. And just as I expected, smoking the last $20 rock left me wanting more.

I had a perfect plan.

"I've gotta run to the bank," I told Amy. "I'm gonna run out to the mall and grab that Everlast CD, too."

Feet tucked under her, she sat curled up in the oversized chair in the corner of the living room, studying. She was glowing in the mid-day sunshine pouring through the large front windows. My heart wrenched as I looked at her. She looked so beautiful.

I'd brought her into my home because I wanted to share my whole life with her. I didn't want to be lying to her, especially not to cover my addiction again. It panged me. I wanted to stop being that person.

But I had to do what I had to do. And what my addiction told me I had to do was smoke some rock. With permission from my mom, I hopped in my truck and headed to the bank. Afterwards, I made a trek to the mall and then, on the way back, downtown.

It might've only been noon, but the crackhouses were open for business. I was in and out so fast, my mom seemed surprised by the quickness of my return.

"That didn't take you long," she said, as I walked back through the kitchen with my new goods.

"Nope," I said. "I'm gonna go check out this CD now."

I made my way toward the bedroom, stopping in the living room once more. Amy was still sitting in her corner spot.

"You're back already?" she asked. "My gosh, I've still got so much to do. I'm gonna be at this for another few hours."

Perfect.

"That's fine. I got the CD!" I held it up as proof. "I'm gonna go give it a listen."

I had a CD player connected to a pretty sweet speaker system in my room. Music had always been a sort of therapy for me as a youth and had become even more of a passion as I grew older. I was excited to hear what the former front man of House of Pain had to sing about.

I inserted the CD, opened up the lyric book, and pulled a rock from my pocket. I had my bedroom door back, thankfully, but I still didn't have a lock. With each hit, I grew a little more paranoid.

I turned the music up louder, but not so loud that I couldn't hear footsteps coming. Ears at attention, I took in the tunes only between hits. A guitar strummed, a voice sang, and out poured "Ends," a song about addiction and the price people pay when they get hooked.

I lit up another hit and held it. Then a second. The lyrics pierced me—they were too on point. I couldn't listen anymore.

I was getting too paranoid to even keep smoking in the bedroom, so I made a trip to the bathroom. Fifteen minutes later, a second. Within an hour, I'd smoked up $60 of my $100 in rock. I had to stop. I was getting that shaky electric feeling.

Headed back to school in just a few short days, I desperately didn't want to deal with the crash again. I was already growing so agitated that I was sure my mom or Amy would notice my change in behavior. It was making me restless and twitchy. I didn't like the feeling. I didn't want to be high. At all.

In that moment, I knew I wanted to quit. Forever.

I never wanted to smoke that shit ever again. I had $40 left, but who cared? It had to stop. Right there. I made a decision. I took in one last hit. A big one. I held it. And I let go. That was it. No more. I was ending it.

I walked out to the living room and told Amy exactly what I'd been up to.

"I don't want to smoke the rest of this shit," I said, handing over the last two rocks. "I don't want to smoke this shit ever again. I want this gone."

She seemed stunned. She told me to tell my mom or else she'd do it for me.

I could've chickened out. I could've had her tell Mom. But for the first time I wanted to take responsibility and tell her myself. My chemical dependency was a serious problem, and Mom knew it. Instead of keeping secrets any longer, I wanted to keep my mom on my side so I didn't have to battle my demons alone.

It was a tough admission to make. But when it was over, I knew it was over.

I was done smoking crack.

11

Getting Up (and Passing Out)

Though I was committed to stopping the cycle of relapsing on cocaine—in any form—as soon as I got back to campus, I was back to drinking every night to the point of blacking out. My relationship with Amy grew tumultuous as the alcohol began to change me.

But I made it through the spring semester, and in the end, I did alright. I got good grades taking a three-class load and made it through aftercare, all the while doing my very best impersonation of a sober person.

But the more comfortable I got in my role as a functional alcoholic, the more I was able to drink and still maintain. Amy pleaded with me to slow down and moderate, but as my tolerance continued to increase, I needed more to get the same buzz. Perhaps it was only a matter of time until I hit the floor.

Or maybe something was really wrong. Whatever started happening, it was knocking me out right quick. I started to pass out.

I don't mean falling asleep on the couch drunk. I don't mean fainting. I've never once fainted from the site of blood or heat or anything else. With these incidents there was no warning. It was just me collapsing.

Almost everyone's experienced light-headedness when standing up suddenly. It's an act we take for granted, but maintaining equilibrium as you stand is actually a very delicate process. If you stand up too quick, your body usually gives you a warning. You might feel a pressure in your head or get slightly dizzy. Your systems try to correct things so you stay upright and conscious. Usually the body does a fine job.

Whatever had started malfunctioning in my body, though, it was giving me no warning. It also seemed to hit hardest while I was drinking. I'd stand up, take a few steps, pass out, and wake up on the floor, often bloodied and bruised. But just like in hockey, I always got up on my feet and brushed myself off.

Of course the episodes didn't seem quite normal, but I figured that—much like my nightly recurrence of drenching sweats that reeked of vinegar—they must've had something to do with the amount of alcohol I was drinking. So that meant it was *my* problem and *my* problem alone.

Nobody—not even Amy—needed to know about these episodes. Since I drank the hardest when I was alone, they were initially pretty easy to hide.

But after spending much of the summer living in the Twin Cities, taking summer classes, and trying in vain to maintain sobriety, I returned to Sioux City for a few weeks in August. There, back in my old stomping grounds, I had an even harder time staying sober even one night a week. I concealed my drinking from my mom by drinking not so much that she would notice, but enough to get emotionally numb.

It was a perpetual practice in moderation and balance, the very thing my alcoholism rebelled against. But I really had no choice. If I drank the way I wanted, she'd hear me slur. If I didn't drink enough to get numb, I'd grow agitated and irritable. Even though I was drinking every day, I was still, on the whole, drinking less than I had been at school. Which is why it surprised me so much to wake up on the floor.

We had been watching TV, sitting at the kitchen table. I'd kicked back, at most, one or two beers—hardly enough for me to get any sort of buzz. The credits rolled on *America's Most Wanted*. Mom got up from her seat and walked away from the table, toward another room.

Ready for another brew, I too got up. I didn't take but two steps before the lights went out. Everything went black.

The next thing I knew, I was curled in a fetal position on my side, our two dogs licking my face. I sat up and leaned back against the cabinet to collect myself, but my vision felt blurred. A voice interrupted my confusion.

"Jennifer! Are you okay?"

I smeared a sleeve across my face to wipe away the drool and dog slobber. In a quick second, I bounced up to my feet.

The voice continued. "Are you okay?" it asked again.

Doing my best to minimize any hint of physical discomfort, I adjusted my clothes and brushed myself off. My breathing, slightly hollow, forced my brain and body to continue their line of communication. I had to snap back to reality, but I couldn't quite speak yet.

My mom was standing in front of me, silent. She waved a hand in front of my face and snapped her fingers. "Jennifer, answer me! Are you okay?"

I stared, vacant, fumbling for an explanation. "I'm fine," I said. "Just fine."

I was doing my best to downplay the severity of what had just occurred, but my mom wasn't having it. Whatever had just happened, she knew it was far from normal. On the contrary, it was alarming. She looked scared, almost panicked.

I had to reassure her. "Mom, I'm fine, really. It's fine. Just please—"

"I was walking toward the dining room and heard a thud. I turned around, and you were on the ground, unconscious. What the hell just happened to you? Do you feel okay? Do you need to go to the hospital?"

"No! I'm fine. This just . . . happens sometimes. Sometimes I just pass out. It's no big thing. I'm fine. Really."

The dogs still nervously awaited confirmation regarding my condition, nudging my hands with their noses.

I kneeled down to the ground and sat in between them, rubbing their heads and patting their backs. I looked up at my mom, still standing in front of me, shaking her head. She seemed shell-shocked.

"It's alright, Mom. Really. I'm fine now. I don't need to go to the hospital."

"Well, if you're not going to the hospital, then you're going to the doctor."

And that was a point on which she would not bend.

A week later, after a visit to a cardiologist, I got strapped in for what was to be a battery of tests. After a failed sleep test botched by my own insomnia, I donned a gown and lay flat on my back on a hospital bed. Once the tech smeared an adequate amount of goop across the sensors on my chest, cold electrodes were rubbed along my rib cage over the area where my heart is.

This test, an echocardiogram, involved a tech holding a wand to my chest, with a machine right next to me. The machine looked like an old boxy computer from the 1980s, with a black screen, green letters, and nothing more. Only this was much more sophisticated.

I looked up at my heart, beating away. It brought a smile to my face.

"So can you tell me what I'm looking at here? Obviously it's my heart, but—"

"Well, we're doing an ultrasound," she said. "Here you can see the different chambers of your heart."

She pointed at the screen and explained what the different chambers do. I just couldn't get over the fact that there, looking back at me, was my own beating heart.

I stared at the blobby mass: living proof that I was still alive and breathing. The rhythmic pulsing bored into my brain. My fears were starting to get to me. After everything I'd put my heart through, it was still ticking. The question was, was it still working right?

After the echocardiogram came a treadmill test. And after that it was time to get glued in for the final exam. A number of electrodes were stuck to my chest, all of which were attached to a Holter monitor, which records the signals coming from the electrodes. It's pretty much an EKG on the go.

Once I was glued in, they sent me home.

For three days, I went everywhere with my electrical getup and oversized fanny pack. And when it was all said and done, the verdict was in: my heart was fine. Instead, they said, my blood pressure was dropping when I was standing up. This phenomenon, called orthostatic hypotension, might be what was causing me to collapse unconscious.

I tried to heed their advice and make an effort to stand up more slowly. They even suggested I eat more salt.

I collapsed less often when getting up from a seated position. But when I was already standing, when I'd taken more than a few steps, when I thought I was in complete control of my symptoms and orientation, I still woke up on the floor. And I had no answer for why it happened.

Heart in check, I went back to school.

12

Ice Dreams

I hunkered down and got ready for a full load of classes, bound and determined to get myself back in good academic standing.

But when hockey season rolled around in October, I was still NCAA ineligible. I couldn't even practice, let alone play. I was in contact with the new coach, an older, pudgy man with a splotchy complexion. Coach Dix didn't seem to be a friend to my fight to get myself back in gear. I knew from the get-go that I was on the outskirts of his plan for the team.

For that reason, as the hockey season got underway, I tried to make myself scarcely seen. I avoided games, didn't watch practice, and generally stayed away from most of the players. Every now and then, though, I'd walk into the rink when it was empty and stare at the ice. I'd smell the air, brush the cool, smooth surface with the tips of my fingers, and remember the tingle of the wind on my skin as I skated.

I always felt a subtly weird presence at the rink at Gustavus. The place just felt special. Perhaps because it looks and feels like the rink that appeared in my near-death experience. Correction: the rink at Gustavus *is* the rink in my near-death experience.

At the time of my near-death, I'd never stepped foot on the ice surface before. But in my vision I skated down the ice and got pulled up and to the right, toward a light. Each time it replayed, I got closer and closer to that light. There's a door in the Gustavus rink at precisely where that light was. When that door is open, it takes on the appearance of a bright light. It's strikingly similar.

All I wanted was to play college hockey. That's it—nothing more. I didn't need to be a star or score any goals. I just wanted to be a part of the team—to put the jersey on and skate a few shifts. To accomplish the goal I'd set for myself at age twelve.

It seemed like a lot of red tape to cut. There were so many hoops to jump through to be made re-eligible for NCAA competition, it was almost too overwhelming. But when it got right down to it, college hockey was what I wanted more than anything in the world. I vowed to myself I'd make a comeback.

After dancing all the right moves and earning straight As for the fall semester, I got clearance to get back on the ice midseason. It was an exciting opportunity. But with my still rampant drinking problem and a smoking habit, I was no poster child for personal fitness. I was hardly in shape.

It didn't take me long to discover I wasn't skating quite up to par. Whether it was my shoulder, chemical dependency, or the head injury that came right in the middle of it all, I was no longer the skater I used to be. I was one step behind everyone else. It was embarrassing. But I held out for the opportunity to see a little ice time in a game.

I trudged my way through a particularly grueling practice when Coach called us all over to the players' bench for a talk.

I put one knee on the ice like the other players and propped myself up on my stick.

"Alright, ladies, listen up," he said, as we caught our collective breaths.

"Nice work out there tonight. Way to skate hard. But as we're finding out, we can't do much without a second goalie. Since Erin transferred, Beth is our only hope. We really do need someone to be our backup goalie."

A few of the girls, outstanding players as forwards, had given it a shot during the week. But nobody was capable of skating in the equipment, let alone stopping pucks coming at them at high rates of speed. They certainly weren't enjoying it.

It was almost tragic. This was one of the best women's hockey teams in the state. But we only had one goalie?

The girls stared at the ice in awkward silence.

Coach let out a final request. "If there's anyone else here who has experience at goalie or even just wants to give it a try, please, *please* volunteer now."

I stared down at my skates and cut the ice with the outside of the blade, then shot a look up over at Molly, standing just a few feet away from me.

I wasn't sure whether to say anything. In my near-death experience, I was skating down the ice, not standing in the net. And growing up, playing goalie had caused me all kinds of knee problems.

Coach continued. "You'll probably never see any ice time or play in any games, but you'd get to dress for every game, and you'd really be taking one for the team."

The way he put it, he made it sound so honorable.

"Any volunteers?"

The only person on the team who knew that I'd played goalie was Molly. Amy had decided not to play that season, and Diana had transferred. Molly and I exchanged glances as the other skaters avoided eye contact with the coach. It felt as if they were waiting for me to say something.

A force inside me implored me to speak up before it was too late. Just as the silence grew uncomfortable, I did.

"I'll give it a try," I said. The words blurted from my mouth before I realized I'd spoken them aloud. Heads turned in my direction. "I'm not any good or anything, but I played a season of goalie back when I was fourteen. I could sit on the bench."

Collectively, the team stirred in excitement. I looked up at Coach Dix, who, for the first time, smiled at me.

"Thanks, Cannon," he said. "Get here early for practice tomorrow so we can fit you with some gear. Alright ladies, that's it. See ya tomorrow."

Coach turned and skated off the ice as the players rose to their feet and did the same.

Molly rubbed a glove on my head as we skated toward the bench. "Wow, Jen. I'm surprised you said anything."

"Yeah," I said. "Me too."

THE NEXT DAY, I arrived early at the rink. After fishing out some properly fitted gear, I strapped on the goal pads, donned a glove and mask, and headed toward the ice. I was, as usual, the last one out there.

As soon as I emerged from the locker room, I could hear the chuckles start up. They were laughing at me. Not in a mean way, but just because it was such a ridiculous idea. Me? A college goalie?

I was surely gonna make a fool of myself. I stood at the door to the ice uncertain of my decision. After much hesitation, I put one blade on the ice and promptly fell flat on my face. I'd apparently not secured the loose strap on the bottom of my pad. It was just one of the many things about being a goalie that I'd completely forgotten.

The laughter subsided as I stood up and brushed myself off. Strap secured, I attempted to make my way to the net. Skating with goal pads on is different from skating as a forward. After a few strides, my body remembered, much the way you remember how to ride a bike.

Stretched out and geared up, I made my way to the net, the same net that had appeared in my near-death experience. I stood in front, posing as a real live goalie.

My nervousness grew so intense I could feel myself shaking under my layers of equipment. Though my anxiety was invisible to others, standing there all alone in front of that net with every eye in the rink on me, I felt I was under a spotlight.

One by one, the players approached and shot the puck. At first very softly.

They saw I was stopping them, so they picked up the pace. Pretty soon, I was starting to hear some "oohs" and "aahs." I wasn't expected to step into my first practice as a goalie in roughly five years and perform anything better than poorly.

But shot after shot I was making save after save. It was surprising not only Coach Dix and my teammates but me. Soon they were coming at me full speed ahead, holding nothing back.

And still I stopped their shots. I was in some sort of a zone, and the players were becoming mightily impressed. During the ensuing drill, our captain rounded a corner on open ice and barreled her way in my direction. I skated out a few feet, stopped, and slowly crept backwards as she approached. She got just inside the blue line when, in one swift motion, she threw her stick backwards and then slapped it to the ground.

The shot she unfurled catapulted above my left hand. With my left leg kicked out to the side, I reached up with my oversize mitt and snagged the puck out of midair.

A collective silence fell on the players lining the boards on either side of me as they watched in amazement. I stood back up, dropped the puck to the ground, and smiled. The boards rattled as the players banged their sticks in approval.

A host of cheers from my teammates echoed through the arena. "Yay Cannon!"

Nobody could see the smile under my mask, so I let it shine. I was back, playing the game that had given me so much with what came out of nowhere: the talent of a gifted goaltender. Within a matter of weeks, I was starting every game. And carrying the team on my back.

I WAS ON top of my game when the playoffs approached. We were in a tight race for first place, and it was all coming down to the final game of the regular season. I was so happy that my mom, John, and Amy were all going to be there to see the highlight of my career.

It was a tight game in front of a packed crowd. In a teeter-totter match, we exchanged goals, but my team headed into the third period up by one.

Shot after shot, I denied the opposition. And as the final seconds ticked down, I watched anxiously from my spot in front of the net. I shot a glance over to the bench at my teammates, then up to the stands at my mom. It all seemed surreal. I couldn't believe what was happening. With each second that ticked down, I tapped my stick on the ice.

"6, 5, 4, . . ." the crowd counted down.

"I can't believe this is happening to me," I said aloud. "3, 2, 1—oh my God!" I threw my arms up over my head and looked up to the sky. A smile burst from my soul as I shouted.

A mob of teammates rushed in my direction. The goalie playing backup, whose position I had essentially stolen, was the first to greet me. Never resentful of my presence, she threw her arms around me, grabbed hold of my face mask, and shook it.

"How's that feel, Cannon? Yeah!"

I rubbed my glove on her bandana as she skated away. One by one the other teammates lined up to greet and congratulate me.

It was unbelievable—the moment I'd dreamed of all my life. After celebrating and changing, we all made our way back out to the lobby.

I set my bag down next to Amy. She looked at me and smiled.

"Nice work out there!" she said.

An official from the game stopped by. "Great game out there, goalie. That was fun to watch."

The father of one of my teammates overheard and agreed. "Yeah, nice work, Jen. Well done."

It was all so unfamiliar; I couldn't help but gush a little. I took each compliment and responded graciously, smiling all the while. I couldn't believe I was the star of the big game. I chugged from my water bottle and took in the moment.

"Ms. Cannon?" a voice asked.

I spun around, twisting the cap back on the water.

A man in a hat, not much taller than I am, reached out a hand and introduced himself.

"I'm a reporter with *Let's Play Hockey*," he said.

Let's Play Hockey is a publication that covers all things hockey in the state of Minnesota, from the youngest age groups to college to the pros. It's where you turn to find your state rankings and stats and to read up on who is going to be the next big thing.

If your name makes *Let's Play Hockey*, you are doing well. And here a reporter wanted to talk to me, individually, to collect a few quotes for a piece he was writing up. It was the thrill of a lifetime.

And it was over practically before it began. I returned to my spot along the boards, where Amy was waiting. "This is unbelievable," I said, shaking my head. The high I was riding rivaled any drug. Nothing, it seemed, could bring me down.

I shot a quick glance up at the ceiling to remind myself how far I'd come since that night on the psych ward. Everything in my life was falling into place. I had straight As and a girlfriend I was passionately in love with, and now I was the star of the hockey team to boot. This was almost too good to be true.

"Have you seen my mom or John?" I asked Amy. "I figured they'd be over here by now."

I took another swig of water. She nodded her head and tightened her lips.

"Yeah, I, I think they're still up in the stands. I, umm . . . I don't think your mom is doing so well."

Her comment caught me off guard. "What? What do you mean?"

I looked up to the stands. What I saw shattered my world.

My mom was clinging onto John, who was helping her down the stairs. The expression on her face spoke of a pain I'd never seen her express before.

My smile dropped as I faded into a vacant numbness. I stood staring, shocked, my bubble of happiness deflating. Amid the people and the crowds and the pats on the back, the sound of the Zamboni vanished. The conversations faded to a whisper. I became frozen, and all I could do was stare.

By March, she couldn't walk. Hockey was over. And I drank evermore, trying my best to numb the pain of whatever was happening to her.

Bottle by my side, I spent the rest of the spring semester dreading with anticipation the idea of going back to my mom's house for the summer. My siblings, all in their twenties, were scattered about the country, focused on their lives and careers. Since I was the youngest and still in college, much of the responsibility fell squarely on my shoulders.

Once I was finished with finals, I packed up my car and headed back home, but not without worry for my own well-being. After all, it had been my geographical relocation and avoidance of my own hometown that helped me keep my nose clean from coke and crack for almost a year. Now, I had to go back home to my using environment in order to take care of my mom.

It was a scary prospect, but I wasn't about to bail out on my mom when she needed me. She stuck by my side when no other parent alive would have. I owed it to her to be there for her.

13

Caretaker's Ball

I bolted awake.

A voice was screaming my name. My mental reflexes, a bit slow from the alcohol still pumping through my system, jumped to attention. My fight-or-flight response kicked into overdrive. There it was again.

"Jennifer! Help me!"

I hopped to my feet and ran across the hall.

My mom, lying on her back in bed, hugged her leg tightly with both arms.

"Oh my God, Mom. I didn't hear you! What should I do? What *can* I do? What do you want me to do?" I started to reach for a pillow to prop under her leg.

"No, don't do that," she said.

"Okay. I won't." I withdrew my hands. "What's going on? What's wrong?" She was in so much pain she could hardly speak.

"Just call an ambulance. My hip is out."

"It's out? You mean it's dislocated?"

"Yes, it's out of its socket. Just call an ambulance. Now!"

"Oh my God. We'll get you fixed up, Mom. I know this has to hurt. Just hold on. Hang in there."

She'd had her hip replaced because her bone had died. It developed osteoarthritis so badly that the bone in her hip joint became necrotic and had to be replaced. Now she was on the mend.

But every night I'd help her to bed. She'd sit on the edge of the bed, I'd grab hold of both her ankles, and together we'd lift and spin. Once on the bed, she'd lie back to get her head and neck comfortable. I'd then grab an A-shaped foam wedge and strap in her legs, two straps on each side. The device prevented her from crossing her legs in any way. Hips are most prone to dislocate when they get crossed, and this contraption was supposed to help her refrain from that instinct to roll your legs and cross them while sleeping.

It didn't work. She dislocated it anyway. And I knew exactly how much pain she was in.

In what would become the first in a series of 911 calls, I picked up the phone and dialed for an ambulance. They arrived without sirens—along with a fire truck—a few minutes later. After barricading the dogs in the kitchen, I ran to the front door to let them in.

"She's this way," I said, leading them back to her room. They followed behind, but their movements seemed to be in slow motion. Or maybe I was just in a panic.

All I wanted was for them to hurry up and get her on the gurney and get her to the hospital. I stood by the bed, biting a nail, watching a handful of large men manhandle my mom. After several minutes of excruciating screams, they successfully transferred her to a stretcher. Once settled, she reached over, grabbed a hold of my hand, and squeezed.

"You'll take care of the animals and meet me up at the hospital?"

"Yeah, yeah, I can do that," I said. "Or do you want me to ride in the ambulance?"

"No. Stay and get the dogs taken care of. Then just drive up. You'll need a car to leave again. I'll be fine until you get there."

A paramedic fastened a final strap before turning to me. "We're ready to go," he said.

I let go of her hand, ran out to the front hall, and threw open the door. A few seconds later, I turned over the ignition to her minivan and opened up the garage door. Sitting idle in the driver's seat, I looked out the rearview mirror to the ambulance behind me. It was still parked in the driveway. What could be the hold up?

I lit up a smoke, foot firmly on the brake.

When the vehicle finally turned down the driveway, it didn't have its lights on and was crawling at a snail's pace.

Following anxiously on their bumper, I pulled a second cigarette from my pack and lit it with the one I was finishing. This was no time to be thinking about my own health. My mom was in pain. And it hurt just to watch.

I later learned that they'd gone slow to avoid hitting a bump at a high speed, which could have caused her significant pain or even jarred the hip further out of place. At the time it seemed wrong, though.

I knew what a dislocation felt like. I knew she was in torturous pain and discomfort. I only wanted them to treat it like the emergency it was. It didn't matter what I said or did, though; they were going to get her there, admit her, anesthetize her, and relocate the hip on their timetable, not mine. It was a harsh reality in the field of medicine that didn't sit well with me.

By THE TIME she got out of the hospital the next day, I'd made a number of trips back and forth between home and the hospital. I'd also taken advantage of the empty house and taken in plenty of beer. I didn't, however, use my time to go downtown and smoke any crack. I had too much going for me to sink so low again.

I had duties and responsibilities. I was an adult. I couldn't be doing that shit anymore. Instead, drinking myself under the table seemed much safer.

Unfortunately, the stress of the summer would just keep mounting, and the more it did, the more I'd pour. Apart from her hip, my mom had been warned by the doctors that her neck was in such bad shape she was at risk of paralysis. They had been advising her for months to have her vertebrae fused as soon as possible. Just six weeks after her first hip replacement, surgeons drilled through her throat to insert screws in her neck bones.

Much the way I had six weeks prior, I sat patiently in the waiting room on the morning of the surgery, awaiting word on her outcome. This time, though, I had John by my side.

Once the all clear was given, we were pointed toward a room upstairs where she would be staying. I walked in, flipped on the light, and drew open a shade. After plopping my backpack on the ground, I pulled out a notebook and pen to jot down some thoughts.

7/18/00   5:15 pm
I'm on the 6th floor of Park Hospital, one floor above where I nearly died a little over two years ago. Today,

I'm the visitor. My mom's the patient. Her surgery is over but this hasn't been easy. Somehow, through all this, I've abstained from cocaine. The dealers keep pestering me, and the cravings still exist, but I believe I'm worth more than a rock.

Right now, all my mom is trying to do is eat. So far she's only been able to handle a sip of grape juice and a Percocet.

I couldn't get over the irony. I was sitting in the same hospital, just one floor above where I had almost died. I'd been admitted because of my drug addiction; now my mom had been admitted and given drugs that are addictive.

In just two short years, the roles had completely reversed. I was no longer the patient. My mom needed my help. Just a few days later, John left town, and she was released. She returned home with a slew of painkillers in her purse and me as her only caretaker.

I GOT USED to my routine as full-time home health aide. During the day, I'd handle getting groceries, cooking meals, and taking care of the animals while my mom rested. At night, I'd drink, try to be social, cook some dinner, and, after helping her into bed, get completely tanked.

I didn't mind the routine, but it took its toll on my ability to moderate my alcohol intake. Every night I drank. Every night I hid it from her. And every night, after she drifted off to a painkiller-induced sleep, I tapped her painkiller supply and stole an Ambien, a Vicodin, or an OxyContin.

As long as I wasn't smoking crack, I didn't care what rainbow assortment of drugs I was ingesting. Anything, I discovered, was better than feeling the pain of seeing my mom this way. Each time I looked at her, the pain in her eyes drove a dagger through my soul. But after everything she'd done to be there for me throughout my cocaine addiction, helping her was the least I could do.

Just ten days after her operation, we settled in the kitchen to take in what seemed to be a relaxed summer morning. I took up a spot at her computer and started surfing the internet. At the time, her online access was via a dialup connection.

"Don't stay on there too long," she said. "I'm expecting some phone calls here this morning."

"I won't. I'll be off in five minutes."

I shot a glance at the clock: 11:30 AM. I clicked on a link, watching the page load pixel by pixel, when an uneasiness enveloped me.

It hadn't even been five minutes, but I closed the browser, disconnected from the internet, and returned to the desktop. Just as I set the mouse down, the phone rang.

"Is this Jennifer?" A female voice cracked on the other end.

"Yeah."

"Jennifer, please give your mom this message as soon as possible. I'm calling because, well . . . I'm the hospice nurse, and I'm here with your grandma. She doesn't have a pulse or a heartbeat. We've got an ambulance on the way. We're doing everything we can for her right now."

My stomach sank. The nurse continued.

"Please let your mom know what's going on. The ambulance should be here any minute."

I spun the cord of the phone between my fingers. "Okay, I'll let her know. Are you taking her to Park?"

"Yeah. Is your mom around? Do you want to meet us up there?"

I could tell the woman was a bit shaken. Her voice was trembling.

"Yeah, she's right here." I glanced over at her, sitting at the table. "I'll let her know, and we'll meet you up there as soon as possible."

I hung up the receiver, drawing in a deep breath. This wasn't going to be easy news to deliver. I took the few steps toward my mom and kneeled down in front of her.

I took hold of her hand. "Mom?" I said. "That was the hospice nurse." I squeezed. "They're taking Nanny to the ER at Park. She doesn't have a pulse or a heartbeat."

Immediately she drew her hand away. "Oh my God," she said. Although she had been spending half her time in a wheelchair, half using a cane, she propped herself up to her feet and started without either.

"What do you need to do before we go?" I asked. I grabbed hold of her cane and gave it to her.

"Oh my God," she repeated again. "Just put the dogs out and get ready to go," she said. "I need to put on some different clothes." She limped off toward the bedroom.

I headed out for a smoke. A short while later, I started up the engine, helped her into the car, and started off on the altogether too familiar route to the hospital.

My grandmother had been pronounced dead on arrival.

Two years after nearly losing her own daughter in that same ER, my mom lost her mother instead. I held her hand as she stared down at the body, doing my best to be a pillar of support instead of the burden I'd once been.

Over the coming days, family filtered in. For the first time in years, my entire family was brought together. And together, they united around alcohol.

Since I was an alcoholic, and they all knew it, I was not expected to partake in any of their reindeer games. It only made me sneak and hide beer that much more.

Thankfully, Amy came to Sioux City to be with me during the ordeal. She too could see how crazy the situation had become.

8/3/00

Sometimes you have to run. Everything is falling apart at once. My mom has dislocated her newly replaced hip twice in the past two days. The first dislocation came at 3 am on the day of her mom's funeral, the second came at 11 pm the same night. It's been less than 24 hours since returning from the hospital; the very hospital where my grandma died, and the very same hospital I nearly lost my own life.

I've sat and watched my family drink for the past four days. I've been drinking alone. After all, I can't drink with them, so I might as well get tanked in private. They say I should be able to stay sober throughout this ordeal despite the temptation of beer in the fridge. I know I can't control other people's actions, but it's hard enough to be here in Sioux City. For my siblings to waltz in at such a difficult time and turn right to alcohol is more than I can handle.

I'm being blamed for distancing myself from them in recent days. Isn't that what I'm supposed to do? Am I doing something wrong? Am I running from my problems, or am I running for my benefit? Am I doing this only for my own good, rather than for the good of everyone else? I don't know. All I know is that no matter what I do, I can't seem to do anything right in the eyes of my family.

14

The Deepest Cut

The dominos were ready. All they needed was a nudge.

By the end of August, I was more than ready to get back to my other life at Gustavus. I spent much of the summer at the hospital. Being in that building, and even in Sioux City, was starting to make my skin crawl, and I wanted nothing more than to leave it all behind.

When time came to pack up the car and actually go, though, I had to physically force myself to leave. I felt horrible leaving my mom behind, all alone at home. I was suffocating under the weight of the thought that I was abandoning her in her time of need.

I couldn't let it stop me, though. I was getting on with my life and moving up in the world. I had broken free of my crack addiction and was escaping the city that was strangling me. I couldn't put college on hold and live at home—in my using environment—to take care of my mom.

Amy was waiting for me at our very own dorm room. I was the returning starting goalie, all-conference on the academic team. I had gotten straight As three semesters in a row and was growing accustomed to seeing my name on the Dean's List. My life, at Gustavus at least, was nearly perfect.

Or so it seemed.

Back in March, after the hockey season had wrapped up, I had sat down with the coach for my post-season individual meeting. I'd gotten a distinct sense from him then that he still didn't like or trust me, mostly because of my addiction. He had told me he couldn't look forward to the next season with me the way he could with other players because I had to take it "day by day." Despite the fact that

I'd been his go-to goalie—the answer to his goaltender dilemma—my performance and commitment to the team still couldn't erase my history.

Coach Dix hadn't recruited me. He'd stepped in at the beginning of my sophomore season and taken over the team. He knew me only as the highly touted recruit who had turned out to be a bust. The one who not only smoked and had an addiction problem, but whose shoulder was shot. The one the previous coach had kicked off the team, and who had been NCAA ineligible because of her academic difficulties.

True enough, when Coach Dix first met me, he had little reason to trust me. But I had worked really hard to change that during my sophomore season. I proved I could be not only a reliable, hard-working skater but also a respected figure in the locker room. I wouldn't call myself a leader, but my actions on the ice and my attitude off it spoke volumes. Freshman year, I had run my mouth, carried a bad attitude, and skated with half-assed effort. More than one girl on the team remarked on how amazing of a transformation I'd made since then. It was as if I'd become a whole new person.

My teammates had noticed. I'd earned their respect. It was rewarding to be able to help the team win some games. At times I'd stood on my head.

I also played through dislocation after dislocation, even though I really shouldn't have done so. More than once I popped my shoulder out and, with Coach's encouragement, went back out and picked up a hockey stick the very next day. The pain seemed worth it at the time. After all, as he said, the whole team was depending on me. So, too, I thought, was he.

I at least figured he would have noticed the caliber of my performance on the ice and appreciated it for what it was worth. I hoped that he would praise me for my change in attitude and compliment me on the progress I'd made. But by the time I took a seat in his office that March afternoon, all my hard work had been forgotten. Nothing I'd done even mattered.

Still, I arrived on campus in the fall with great anticipation for what awaited on the ice. All eyes were on me as the returning starting goalie. But much to my surprise, when the season got started, I discovered I'd lost an edge.

I wasn't making the saves I'd made the previous season and was being outshined in early-season practices led by the captains of the team. There weren't any coaches present at those sessions, but it didn't ease my mind to look around and see that I was competing against not one, not two, but three other goalies.

I only knew one of them. One was a junior transfer student. The third a skilled freshman recruit. One of us, I feared, would have to go.

If the too-many-goaltenders situation wasn't enough to distract me, here was Amy barreling down on a breakaway, coming straight at me.

Though she hadn't played since she was a sophomore, she wanted to get back on the ice for her senior year. I couldn't tell her not to. But aside from the fact that she was busy applying to schools and preparing for her future life as a doctor, I thought it would make things awkward to have her around. It did.

Amy and I had come out to the team the previous season, when I was the star goalie. Everyone loves you when you're a star, so it was the perfect time for it. But I wasn't expecting Amy to return to the team in the fall. Suddenly, she wouldn't be in the stands watching me. We'd be in the locker room and on the ice together.

During my brief stint on the team as a freshman, I had skated out as a forward—on a line with Amy and Diana. But now that I was a goalie, I was facing Amy one-on-one, multiple times during a practice. She was trying to score on me in a way I never wanted her to.

Even during scrimmages, when she was on the opposite team, we were still teammates. But we were also way too competitive with each other to go toe to toe in anything. Especially on the ice.

Every time she scored on me, I felt deflated. Beaten. Broken. Because she was always just that much better than I was. No matter what I did, she always wanted to prove she could do it a little better. Hockey was no exception.

After awhile, the presence of Amy and three other goalies on the ice really started to warp my sense of potential. I was getting down on myself while on the ice, and drinking myself stupid every night after practice didn't help my performance either. I skated horribly during tryouts, and when it was all said and done, it happened.

I got cut.

And I was the only player on the team to *be* cut.

I found out before the coach ever told me—by process of elimination. He let us know he planned to keep three goalies. When the moment of truth came, one by one, we were called into the equipment room to talk to him.

First the skaters. Then the goalies.

When the third goalie came out smiling, I knew my time with the team was up. I was the odd one out. He'd cut me without even having to face me to say it. It pissed me off. And I would not go gently. First, I had to rage.

Gustavus had been the light at the end of the tunnel. My vision of being at Gustavus, playing hockey at Gustavus, may have played a role in saving my life. Hockey was my first love. My first drug. My very first high. It'd been the driving force in nearly every decision I'd made in my life for over a decade, and here this man was taking from me my ability to enjoy it any longer. Hockey was the only reason I was really even at Gustavus. It's all that ever mattered to me.

Sitting alone in the locker spot that was once my own cubby, I rocked gently back and forth, grinding my hands together like stones. Sweat beaded up on my forehead as my chest grew heavy, gnawing with ache. It felt like I'd been stabbed, my heart ripped from the slit of the wound. The deepest cut of all was starting to sting, right where it hurt the most.

It was just a few short steps to the small side room where hockey equipment and a skate sharpening machine were stored. Coach was waiting for me there. But I needed to calm down first.

My soul felt fragile and battered. The cut opened me up, and there was no place to contain my fury anymore. I could either leave without saying a word or let my rage unleash.

I made my decision. I hopped to my feet, marched the few steps to his makeshift office, and glared. He said nothing.

I asked for an explanation but choked up as I uttered the words. Like a wounded animal, I couldn't let him see I was hurt. I pinched back the emotion and slammed down the stoicism. Talking politely got me nowhere. Every excuse he offered seemed like just that: an excuse.

His reasons for cutting me, and only me, made no sense. It was, I will always be convinced, a personal attack. After all, if you were a collegiate coach, and you had to agree to let the NCAA randomly drug test your athletes, would you want someone with a serious chemical dependency problem on your team? Not likely.

But after everything I'd done, all the progress I'd made, how hard I'd worked, he could at least have treated me like an equal of everyone else. He'd made up his mind, though. It would be in my best interest if I no longer played hockey on his team. It would be, he later told the team, "good for me" to be cut.

Hockey was my world. I fail to understand how singling me out and cutting me could've possibly been good for me. I failed to understand then, and I fail to understand now. But it didn't matter what I said. I was off the team.

Since I had nothing left to lose, I let him have it. I yelled and screamed, called him names, and when I finally walked back out to the locker room, it was dead silent. You could hear a pin drop.

I stopped in the middle of the fluorescent-lit room and gazed around, absorbing what I knew would be my last view of the newly remodeled locker room. The other players milled around and looked at the floor, trying their best to avoid eye contact with me. Nobody wanted to say a thing.

Nobody wanted to come to my defense or say something to the coach. Why not? How could this be happening? Why was I, the returning starting goalie, the only one cleaning out her bag and giving back her equipment?

It all seemed so personal, so unfair. I couldn't stand it.

In my solitude, I began separating out my own equipment from that of the school. I decided the school's property meant about as much to me as I apparently did to them: nothing at all. And since I meant so little to Coach, I decided to let the whole team know exactly what I thought of him.

I stood up from my spot in the cubby and started barking rants. The expletives and goalie pads flew. My anger hit a pinnacle, and it was all coming out. First a "fuck you," then a glove. An "asshole" and a flying mask. A stick, "up your ass." I was fuming.

Once it was out of my system, relief swept over me. Panting heavily, I stood silent, looking at the mess I'd made around me. Wide-eyed stares shot my direction.

I zipped my bag shut, threw it over my bad shoulder, and picked up my sticks. As I marched out of the locker room, I ran my hand across the row of sticks along the wall. One by one they crashed to the floor.

"Fuck this! Just fuck all of this!" I kicked up my heels, clearing my feet of the fallen debris, and made my way through the dim lobby toward the exit.

The cold wind struck a stinging blow. I hunkered down, wet-headed and bare-handed, to head back to my dorm room. My thoughts quivered under the weight of my reality. I picked up the pace, but the tears started to stream, freezing on my face.

I couldn't be seen. What if someone I knew saw me crying, walking away from the hockey rink with my bag and stick in hand? Why, they would surely wonder, was I taking my bag away from the rink? I was the starting goalie and the season had just started. There would be only one explanation to a casual observer.

Somewhere between the rink and the dorm room, the tears dried up. In their wake, I grew numb.

I arrived back at the dorm room, where Amy was waiting for me to return. She'd decided not to play after all, quitting halfway through the week of tryouts. True to form, she hung around just long enough to throw me off my game, and then she split. Even though she was no longer a part of the team, she knew the schedule. She knew it was a special night, so she treated it as such.

I walked in and was immediately struck by her provocative positioning on the futon. She was showing me some leg, wearing just the top half of the silky blue pajamas I loved so much. I dropped my bag off my shoulder and threw my stick down on top of it. I looked her up and down and then at the items on the table by her side.

On the coffee table was a to-go box from a restaurant. I walked over and flipped open the lid to peek at its contents. Inside was my favorite meal: pancakes with extra syrup.

Next to the box rested a twelve-pack of Miller Lite. My other favorite meal.

"How'd the tryout go?" she asked.

I knelt down to inspect the pancakes. She looked at my bag, oblivious to the misfortune I'd just encountered.

"Horrible," I said, closing the box.

"Why? What happened?"

The words wouldn't come. I was still in so much shock I couldn't say it. I ran my hands through my hair and got to my feet, pacing the room in silence before finally spitting it out.

"I got cut."

"What? You got cut? You can't be serious."

"I'm dead serious. I got cut. And I was the only one who got cut." I choked back the tears, fixated on the twelve-pack staring back at me from the table. The beer—my addiction—was calling me to find solace in it.

I continued on, rambling about how it all shook out. "I can't believe this! My whole hockey career is over!" I trailed off, then pounded my fist against the wall and paced furiously throughout the room.

Finally I snatched up a beer and popped it open. I gulped down a large swig before wiping the dribbles from my chin. As I set it back on the table, foam poured from the top. I was already drinking way too fast and knew it. But I didn't care. Everything had been lost. As far as I was concerned, the world had ended.

Nothing else mattered. Nothing, of course, except getting fucked up.

"I'm getting tanked tonight," I said. "I'm gonna get so drunk, I don't want to feel a fucking thing."

She stared at me, brow furrowed.

I just wanted to numb the pain, to make reality go away. The last thing I needed was to drown my sorrows in alcohol, but the realization wasn't enough to stop me.

I sat down on the couch and held my head between my knees. The tears pushed up again. I pushed back. Time for another swig. Just as I reached for a bottle, Amy draped her leg over my lap and put an arm around me.

"It'll be okay, Jen," she said, stroking my hair. "You'll be okay without hockey. You've got me here. And look, I got you your favorite things! Beer and pancakes! Maybe we can just have a nice quiet evening here the two of us. You know *I'll* make you feel better."

She traced her finger up my thigh, pulled me close, and planted on me one of those soft, sweet kisses that leave you begging for more.

I fell into her embrace and let reality escape.

UNFORTUNATELY, THE NIGHT I got cut from the hockey team was one of the few that semester when Amy and I actually got along. We lived in a double room, capable of housing up to four roommates. But for some reason we got a big room all to ourselves.

It's a good thing there was a door dividing the two rooms. We needed it. We moved in as optimistic little lovebirds in early September, but by October we were at each other's throats. It didn't help that, in the weeks after getting cut, I sank headlong into a deep depression. I'd hole up in the back room with my mini-fridge, drinking and smoking myself into oblivion all night long. It was the only way I knew how to cope.

Unfortunately, the alcohol I was drinking to escape from my troubles was also widening the rift tearing Amy and me apart. She was struggling with moderating her own intake. I was no longer moderating at all. I was out of control. Since she was twenty-one and I wasn't, I was also reliant on her to feed my addiction. At times, she was my enabler. At others, my savior. But in both cases, I knew it.

I also knew that, no matter what she said or did, underneath her intrigue and lust for addiction, she didn't want me to die from the disease. She wanted me to get well, just not while I was with her. She couldn't help me get better, either, because doing so would've meant she'd have to get better herself.

So after awhile, instead of picking me up when I'd fall down, she started to point the finger. She blamed my addiction for everything wrong with our relationship, letting me know just how incredibly fucked up I was. Then she'd buy me beer.

We'd get drunk, fight, forgive, and fuck, and then the next day do it all over again.

I got sick of the dysfunction. On November 19, our two-year anniversary, I finally said the words: "We're through. It's over. We're done."

I wished she hadn't heard me so loud and clear. I changed my mind just a few days later and wanted to try and work it out, but she wasn't having it. She wouldn't take me back.

In the days immediately after our breakup, I did my best to avoid her. I'd already set up camp in the back room of our ground-level dorm suite. One afternoon, after my 3:30 class, I stopped by the cafeteria, picked up some pasta, and headed back to the room for the night.

I had beer. I had books. I had dinner. It was all I needed to get me through.

Amy had been off at the library studying for the MCAT, which she was preparing to take in just a few weeks. By the time she got home around dinner time, I was already tanked, drunk on an empty stomach.

Somewhere along the course of my addiction, I had stopped eating right. I hadn't eaten well before I got hooked on drugs or became a drunk, but the disordered patterns were heightened amid my chemical dependency. Alcohol had calories, and those calories, I knew, were making me gain weight. Likewise, drinking on an empty stomach accelerated intoxication. So for a number of reasons, as my alcoholism progressed, I drank more and ate less. This night was no different.

Shooting blank stares at the criminology book on my lap, I twirled my fork, picking at the box of cold spaghetti and marinara sitting beside me on the floor. After swallowing a few more unsavory bites, I closed up the box and reached for another beer—a much more appetizing dinner.

I grabbed hold of the box and put a hand on the bed, pushing myself up to my feet. Two steps later, I reached the dresser. I set the box down but couldn't let go of my grip. Locked in a semi-extended position, my whole arm began to shake. I clenched onto the box even more tightly as the trembling intensified.

Mustering all my strength, I tried desperately to release my grip and get myself safely down to the floor, but it was too late. The communication between my brain and body had been disrupted. A kaleidoscope of colors flashed before my eyes, the curtain closed, and life faded to black.

The next thing I knew, I heard a voice.

"Jen! Oh my gosh. Jen!"

I pushed opened my eyes. Intermittent slaps stung my face to jar me awake. I was conscious and not dreaming. The voice continued. "Jen, are you alright?"

The sting of another slap.

"Jen. Seriously. There's blood all over, and you're, like, foaming at the mouth! What happened? You've got to get to a hospital!"

The blurriness dissipated.

Curled up in the fetal position, I rolled over on my back and looked up in the direction of the voice, right into Amy's eyes. She was down on her knees next to me, eyes full, shaking from head to toe.

I couldn't stay down. I had to get up.

"What? What are you talking about? I'm fine," I said, sitting up.

"You're fine? You collapsed, and you're foaming at the mouth, and you're fine? You need to go to the hospital!" Her voice was trembling. She was really worried.

I understood her concern for my health, but I wasn't hers to care about anymore. And I wasn't having any more hospital visits. My patience quickly ran short.

"Look, I said I'm fine!"

I adjusted my shirt, stripping a spaghetti noodle from my shoulder and another from my pants. The pasta painted the dresser, floor, and me. I looked like a fool, embarrassing myself in front of my ex-girlfriend. Every defense mechanism I had kicked into overdrive.

Why was she in here anyway? I got to my feet and brushed myself off. My nose dripped once more as the dried blood caked up beneath my nostrils. I wiped it with my sleeve. She stared at me and my disheveled condition, shaking her head.

"I heard a thud earlier. But I thought you were just throwing beer bottles again."

"Throwing beer bottles? Are you serious?" I took a step toward her and stood toe to toe.

"Jen, if I'd known you collapsed, I would've come in here sooner."

She would have, too. I knew she still cared about my health and well-being. But, I couldn't handle that thought. I still had the most intense feelings for her, and the idea of her having any feelings at all for me sent shockwaves through my soul.

We stood silent for a moment, staring at one another. Glaring at one another. The air grew thick.

I cut the silence.

"Whatever, I don't care. Just leave!" I said. "Just leave." I motioned to the door and turned away, kneeling down in front of the fridge. I pulled a fresh beer from the shelf, cracked it open, tipped the bottle up, and took a big gulp. Then another.

She stood stationary, hands on her hips, watching my every move.

"Just leave? You want me to just leave? Jen, this was really traumatic for me!"

"Traumatic for *you*? This was traumatic for *you*?"

Finding me unconscious on the floor had to be terribly traumatic. But it was the timing of her remark that was so poor. It upset me.

"Yes, Jen. This was traumatic for *me*." She sneered and sighed, watching me down another big gulp before firing back.

"Wow," she said. "You really are sick. Really, really sick. You need help. You just collapsed here, and now you're drinking again already. And look at how fast you're drinking! My God!" I smeared my forearm across my lips as the bottle frothed over. "You need help. Serious help. And I'm sorry, but I can't be the one to help you. I can't even be around you anymore."

She turned, walked through the door, and slammed it behind her.

"Cheers," I said.

I sat down with my bottle and opened up a notebook.

It was official. I'd not only lost hockey but the love of my life, too. I couldn't bear the idea of being stuck on that campus for another two years. My time at Gustavus was well spent, but it was over.

I was unraveling, and I had to get out. It couldn't wait until the end of the year or even the semester. I had to get out now.

15

Snapped

As the brisk late November nights ushered in reminders of the long, cold season ahead, things took a turn for the worse. I tried to carry on, but nothing was working. Amy was asking me to go places and inviting my help on school work. She suggested that if we were mature about it, we could be friends. But my heart was breaking every time I looked at her, and I couldn't stand that we were still living together. We didn't really have any other options until the semester ended, though.

After a few weeks of trying to be cordial, things bubbled over. We got in a fight. I don't remember specifically what sparked it. We could fight about anything. But the argument between us escalated. And I was drunk to boot. At some point, I grabbed her. She grabbed me back. I wouldn't let go. We ended up on the ground. And in the ensuing scuffle, I struck her.

I'm not sure what came over me. I was quite drunk, and when alcohol gets in my system, something in me changes. I no longer think—or behave—rationally. In a moment of clarity, I realized what I'd done. I quickly backed up off her, stood up, and started to pace.

I couldn't believe what I'd done. I'd hit a woman.

Not just any woman—my partner. I loved her more than I had ever imagined I could love someone. I'd fallen too hard for her: when our time together finally ran out, I couldn't handle the idea of living life without her. Now I had not only lost her but physically abused her.

She got to her feet and walked straight to the mirror to check her face.

"I'm leaving," she said, thumbing at her eyeliner. "When I come back, I want you gone. You should pack up the rest of your things."

I looked around the room at the half-filled boxes. "Haven't you forgotten something? I don't have anywhere to go! We're stuck here together until the end of the semester."

She chomped right back. "No, we're not. I'm not living with you another day. I want you out of here when I come back." She pulled her car keys from her pocket.

"Well, when are you coming back?"

A jingle interrupted the silence. "I'm going to Molly's for the night," she said. Then out the door she went. A poster fell from the wall and hung, dangling from a corner, as she slammed the door behind her. I stood alone in the middle of the dorm room, staring at it as it swung to a stop.

Her words were the straw that broke the camel's back. Not only had I lost the love of my life, but now she was turning to my most supportive, non-using friend for a shoulder to cry on. About me and my behavior no less.

Molly was a good friend to both Amy and me. She knew first-hand the fiery nature of our relationship. I couldn't believe Amy was running to her. Even though she was Amy's friend, too, it still stung. With Diana having transferred after freshman year, and Alix after sophomore year, that left Amy and Molly as my closest support systems. All of a sudden, I had lost both of them.

I'd lost everything. The energy inside me grew more explosive by the second.

I reached inside Amy's dresser and snatched up the bottle of Vicodin I knew she had tucked away in there. After popping open a bottle of her wine, I threw back a couple of pills and tossed the pill bottle in my backpack. It was mine now.

Clenching the wine in my hand, I paced the length of the two rooms, drinking furiously. My clothes clung to my body as a chemical sweat began to seep from my pores.

My emotions were set to explode. I needed to hit something. So I hit myself. I ran my hands through my hair and took another deep breath before punching with full force the wall separating the two rooms.

The pain pulsed through my hand.

Nothing seemed to be able to calm me down. Not lashing out. Not deep breathing. Not pot. Not cigarettes. Not pills. And certainly not alcohol.

Something had to give. I was losing my grip.

I looked around at the mostly bare walls separating what we'd shared from what was now only hers. What posters and pictures that remained belonged to her, not me. Interspersed with the few remaining photos of us that hung on the wall were pictures of celebrities and models she thought were hot. It always hurt me that she found it necessary to stare at other women's bodies when we were living together and in a serious relationship. I tore them in half. One by one, the pictures of us got destroyed, too. It was history. We were through. And I was done being nice.

I had two years of frustration to vent. Our relationship, I quickly decided, was the worst thing to ever happen to me. I'd given her every part of me, heart and soul, and she had broken me in half. She had spent two years both consoling and enabling me, seemingly seeking out the same disease that had almost killed me. Now that disease had cost us our relationship.

So she didn't need that Buckcherry CD she'd bought after I told her how much that song "Lit Up" bothered me. She had sung about loving cocaine, knowing full well what it'd done to my life. I ripped it from her CD tower and snapped it in half. She didn't need the bottle of Vicodin or the other bottles of wine she had in the room, either.

After polishing off one bottle, I popped the cork on the next and hurled the empty at the wall, half strewn with the remnants of pictures of scantily clad women whose bodies she had apparently adored more than mine. The bottle shattered as I started reaching for her wine glasses. One by one they hit the wall and crashed to the floor. By the fourth, I was throwing as hard as I could.

I picked up another and hurled it. It shattered into tiny shards just as I screamed. I threw my shoulder right out of its socket. It stopped me in my tracks. I stood frozen, hunched over in the middle of the room, clinging to my arm, which I pinned to my belly. I cringed as I maneuvered the limb gently in front of me. A moment later it slid back into place.

The floor began to spin under the drain of my pain, anger, and intoxication.

I wanted out—of that room, of St. Peter, of my body and my own skin. Out of the world of chaos I was living in. In times like that, when I just can't stand myself or my situation, my brain starts to consider plan B. That plan is, of course, to kill myself.

It was all I could do to keep from grabbing hold of the bed sheet. It was calling me, urging me to end it all. All I had to do was wrap one end around my neck and tie the other end to the ladder of the loft. I didn't need to drop or be fully suspended. I knew better than to try using an electrical cord. I knew how to hang myself now.

And if I tried it again, I vowed to myself, I would not fail. I lit up another cigarette and paved a path amid the broken glass and boxes, pacing back and forth between the rooms. Contemplating suicide.

Sometimes, for reasons I don't understand, suicide seems the most logical answer to a problem. Sometimes, especially when my life is in crisis, it seems like the only option.

I talked myself out of it. I couldn't justify killing myself to get away from reality. I knew I had been kept alive for a reason the first time I tried. I had gotten the message: it wasn't my place to decide when it was my time to go. Why try to force it again?

I couldn't stomach the thought of leaving behind those I loved, either. I still can't. I had seen firsthand how painfully real my attempt at suicide had been for my family and loved ones. Plus, if I did kill myself on the heels of breaking up with Amy, it would destroy not only her but Molly. And in some weird Holden Caulfield kind of way, I didn't see committing suicide on campus at a small liberal arts college to be the best way to go out anyway. People would talk. I just couldn't do it.

But how the fuck else could I stop feeling the way I was feeling? Where could I go? What could I do other than drink? I had nowhere to go. Nobody sober to turn to. It all served to remind me of how desperately lonely I was. I'd lost hockey, the love of my life, and now my best friend, too. Things just kept getting worse. I felt trapped. All the while my mom was sick at home, unable to work or walk.

It didn't seem real. I wanted to run. The anger and sadness melted together in an intoxicated blend of shock. After a few more swigs and a smoke, the shock shifted to rage—at Amy, for everything that happened between us.

In a mad frenzy, I let loose once more, thrashing about the room, taking aim at whatever might have offended me over the course of our relationship. I was selectively cautious in what items to destroy, though. Instead of destroying her computer, I poured wine on her keyboard tray. Instead of smashing her TV, I broke her DVDs. I didn't do a significant amount of damage. But I did destroy some of her property as well as the school's.

When all was said and done, the room was a pigsty, and I was exhausted. Wine dripped from her desk. Broken glasses and CDs lined the floor. Holes decorated the walls, along with ripped corners of pictures, random bits of tape, and red wine stains. The mirror above the dresser, cracked and broken, was written on with my blood: "Bitch."

I stared at my reflection, callous and broken, as if I'd just realized I'd murdered my own family.

I hadn't destroyed anything terribly valuable. But I had hit her where it hurt, and I had sent her a message. Perhaps too strong of one. I needed to flee the scene.

I called Alix, who agreed to let me come stay with her at her place in the Cities for the night. That wouldn't, of course, work for the semester, but at least it was something. I gathered together enough clothes and essentials to get me through the weekend and prepared to walk out the door. Before going, though, I decided to let Molly know what was going on.

It was stupid to call. I should have just left. But in my drunken stupor, I decided to rage, thereby letting my ex-girlfriend know what I'd done and what my plans were. My fingers punched the keys without my full awareness. Molly picked up.

"Molly."

"Yeah?"

"Is Amy over there?"

"Yeah, but I don't think she wants to talk to y—"

"I don't want to talk to her, either. You just tell that bitch I destroyed her shit, so now I'm leaving. She won't have to talk to me ever again." I ranted on about Amy and her character for a few moments before hanging up. I threw the phone to the ground with my now sore, freshly loosened shoulder.

It was time to go. I marched out the door with my alcohol, clothes, and toiletries, intent on driving the eighty miles from St. Peter to Minneapolis while both drunk and high. My loneliness and desperation only made the walk across campus that much colder.

I tossed my bags in the backseat of my hand-me-down Civic, once John's, and tossed my backpack onto the passenger seat. I pulled a beer from the bag, popped it open, and flipped over the engine. The gas gauge was close to empty. I'd have to fill up soon. I reached around, fished through my pockets and bags for my wallet, but grew panicked as I discovered it was nowhere to be found.

Then it dawned on me. I'd left it back in the dorm room, on the dresser.

I had no choice but to go get it. I wasn't gonna get very far on a nearly empty tank with no money. Since I was going to be quick, I pulled up to the dorm room, parked in a loading zone, and put the hazard lights on. As I threw the driver's door shut, I caught a glimpse of what looked like Amy's car parked out front. I craned my neck to get a better view when a Campus Security car pulled right up next to me.

I wasn't about to stick around to find out why.

I dashed inside the basement-level door and took a right hand turn around the corner. Past the bathroom and the other dorm rooms, at the far end of the long hallway, I could see the door to my dorm room standing wide open. I hadn't been the one to leave it that way. I bolted down the hallway past the bathroom, where I could hear a shower running. Perhaps, I hoped, it was Amy. Maybe all the damage had freaked her out, and she had to jump in the shower.

The idea instantly seemed ridiculous.

As I slid into a stop at the door frame and peeked inside, I found out just how wrong I was. She and Molly were standing in the middle of the dorm room, gaping at the damage. This wasn't good. They looked at me. I looked at them.

It was on.

My mind jumped into overdrive. The security car outside was probably coming to see the room, since Molly and Amy had probably called about it. I was in serious trouble. I hopped over a box and dodged broken glass to get to the back room, snatched my wallet from the dresser, and took off back toward the open door.

I slowed to take a few parting shots at Amy before leaving the room. Just as I turned the corner, I ran straight into a security officer.

"Excuse me," I said, sidestepping around him. I started coyly toward the exit, heart thumping.

Behind me, a knock on the door frame was followed by a male voice.

"Excuse me, ladies. Safety and Security. Got a call about a—"

It was quickly interrupted by a voice I knew much better: Amy's.

"It's her! Don't let her get away!" she said.

I set into a full-on sprint as I approached the corner closest to the exit. Grabbing hold of the wall, I wheeled myself around the corner and darted toward the doors, ready to hop in my car waiting just a few feet outside. I reached the glass door entrance but was stopped dead in my tracks. A second officer was blocking the doorway in front of me.

Frozen, we each stood at a standstill. After an awkward moment of eye-locked silence, he reached out to grab my arm. I kicked him between the legs, and he let out a yelp. I hopped up over his out-stretched knee to squeeze past him, but he grabbed hold of my feet and pulled me to the ground. A St. Peter police officer joined in and took my arms. Within a few quick seconds they had me hog-tied.

The game was over. Still I kept resisting. I wiggled and squirmed, but try as I might, I could make no Houdini-like escape.

The seriousness of the situation settled in as the handcuffs gripped my wrists. I bit back the tears. This was already a disaster. But like a runaway train, I couldn't stop the momentum of my emotion.

Unleashed from my mouth came every insult and derogatory remark I could come up with. Insults and threats hurled down the hallway aimed directly at the woman I'd loved so deeply and who was now being consoled by none other than my best friend. Though I don't remember saying it, I apparently threatened to kill Amy.

True to my state, I blacked out soon after. I vaguely recall waking up in a police car, twisted and contorted, face smooshed to the seat, unable to wipe the drool dribbling down my cheek with anything other than my shoulder. I sat up, struck by the darkness of the roads around me. We weren't in the city anymore.

"Where we headed?" I asked.

The officer in the passenger seat spun around to look at me. "To detox," he said.

"Where's detox? How long have I been sleeping?"

"It's in New Ulm, still about twenty miles away. You haven't been out that long. You should just go back to sleep."

That's exactly what I did.

Apparently, before passing out in the police car, I'd spent a few hours in jail. I was cited for underage consumption. I don't remember being at the jail at all, but that's where the records say officers first transported me. Thankfully, in the end, I was only charged with what amounts to a minor citation, instead of assault on an officer, resisting arrest, or some other crime. After all, I did kick the Safety and Security guy in the family jewels. Only after receiving the citation was I transported to county detox, thirty plus miles from St. Peter.

Some hard-core alcoholics and addicts come through the doors of the county detox facilities. I don't know about other places, but in rural Minnesota most people are in for alcohol. In this case, the clientele was mostly older gentlemen with yellowed skin and ghastly faces that haunted you even when you looked away.

I didn't exactly fit in. But it's where I needed to be.

After a night in the observation room, with only a gown, I was content to sleep the day away. They had me on such lockdown that I couldn't even have a pencil. I couldn't write. I had nothing to read. All I could do was lie there in bed across the hall from the nurses' station, just where I'd been so many times before.

After breakfast, I piled on the thin wool blankets and snuggled back up under the covers. Just as I drifted off to sleep, a knock startled me awake.

"Jennifer, you've got a phone call from Gustavus." A woman with a husky voice stood in the doorway, waiting for me to respond.

I sat up, dangled my feet off the edge of the bed, and pushed myself up, wondering what was to become of me next.

The nurse escorted me around the corner and motioned me down a separate hallway with a row of offices. "Second door on the right," she said. I took the few steps and looked inside. A lady seated behind a desk looked up, smiled, and offered me the receiver positioned up against her ear.

On the other end was Julie. She was calling to inform me that I wasn't welcome back at Gustavus anytime soon. First, I'd have to have a hearing with the disciplinary board, and then I'd have to follow through on what they recommended. Most certainly they'd recommend chemical dependency treatment, so if I got started on that right away, that might make a good impression on them.

In the meantime, I was to stay off and away from campus. If I needed to be on campus, it would require an escort. And last but not least, I was to stay away from and avoid all contact with Amy. She was scared of me and considering a restraining order.

Twirling the phone cord between my fingers, I stood silent, staring at the floor.

This was the worst news possible.

I was being made out to be some kind of monster. And I'd just been suspended from college—indefinitely.

AFTER SPENDING THREE days holed up in a tiny observation room with nothing more than a worn-out mattress and oversized gown, I was ready for a change. Not just of clothes, but of scenery. And that's exactly what I got.

Bright and early on my third day of detox, a nurse called my name. A car had arrived to take me away, she said. She handed over a wadded pile of clothes, the same clothes I'd been wearing the night I was brought in. I threw them on without hesitation. Though slightly unclean, they felt extraordinarily comfortable. I didn't care that they were dirty. They were mine.

Equally as exciting as clothes was the prospect of getting out of the drunk tank and on with my life. But the car that pulled up to haul me away had arrived with intent. Where on earth was I being taken to next?

I said good-bye to my detox room and headed across the hall, where a nurse was waiting for me, along with my escort.

"Well, Ms. Cannon," the nurse said. "I think everything's in order. Good luck to you."

She handed over a stack of intake and citation paperwork. I rolled them up like a newspaper and tapped them nervously in my hands.

"Ready to go?" A thin blonde woman with stringy hair approached me, keys in hand.

"Yeah," I said. "Just get me outta here."

Though my destination was still a mystery, any place had to be better than detox.

I followed the woman down the vaguely familiar front hallway. The heavy front door creaked open like a casket to expose the sunlight outside. I cringed, squinting to adjust to the brightness. For the first time in days, I took in a breath of fresh air. The brisk cold slapped my lungs and escaped in a cloud as I exhaled. Warm sunshine poured from the clear blue sky, sinking into my skin, making the fabric of my black hoodie feel warm to the touch.

I stopped, took a deep breath, and looked up at the sky. My escort stood silent next to me, watching me for a moment as I absorbed my surroundings.

"We gotta get movin'," she said.

I dropped my arms to my side, put my head back down, and followed her silently to the car. "So, uh. Where are you taking me?" I asked. She opened up the back door.

"To the hospital in Mankato," she said.

"Seriously? Why? Says who?"

"That's just what the orders say."

"Well, who are you, and why are you escorting me?"

"I'm an escort. This is my job—to drive this route." She closed the door after I got in and hopped up front, turning over the engine on the beat-up old Bonneville. Muffler rumbling, we pulled out onto the empty county road.

The silence grew awkward. "Wow," I finally said. "Sounds like you've got a horrible job. Dealing with fuck-ups like me all day long."

She chuckled.

"It's not so bad," she said. "It'll be a little while here, about half an hour, so you can take a nap or something if you want."

"No thanks," I said. "I've been sleeping for three days straight." I got the picture, though. She wasn't in the mood to talk.

I propped my head up against the window and stared out at the lifeless farmland, barren and snow-caked. Mile after mile, the desolate fields told stories of the seasons before, when life teemed and flourished. Now everything had died, shriveled up, and wilted away. The vacant fields, so meticulously tended to and cared for when they were thriving, were now exposed and lonely, forced to endure the harsh winter all alone.

My head fixed to the window pane, I stared out, lost inside. The car suddenly came to a stop. I picked my heavy head up and looked around me.

I knew right where we were. It all looked hauntingly familiar.

The same beige brick building where I'd spent so many hours trying to get myself together was now once again to be my home. I knew the process and already knew my next question. I'd seen my cigarettes sitting up front with my escort, on her passenger seat.

"Can I have a smoke before I head in? I won't be able to get one for several days again now." I knew the drill.

She turned and looked at me as if she should scold me. "Well, I really shouldn't let you," she said. I looked down to my feet and kicked at the snow. "But, okay, if you make it quick and don't get me in trouble."

"I'll be fast," I said. "And I won't."

She handed over the plastic baggy with my smokes and lighter.

"Just take one," she said. I did as told, lit up, and put the goods back in the bag. Without a coat, hat, or gloves, the cold quickly drowned out the warmth of the sunbeams. Though I was excited to be outside, and smoking, I was ready to be back indoors.

I drew in a puff, blew it out, and then drew in another. The menthol crystallized. A large red cherry burned precariously at the end of the fast-disappearing cigarette. It'd been three days since my last smoke, and before I even got to enjoy it, it was over.

My top half began to wobble. I knelt down slowly and held my head between my legs while snuffing out the butt. It was a great decoy for what was an awkward neurological moment.

I rose to my feet and attempted to remain steady. Equilibrium askew, my head amplified my breathing like a seashell. A black shade enveloped my peripheral vision, and my face grew numb. That electrical feeling was starting to overtake me. I put one foot in front of the other and walked casually toward the door with my escort at my side, trying to conceal my disorientation.

A few hours later, I woke up in yet another hospital bed, in the same wing of the same hospital I was stuck in two years before. Somehow I knew it was coming. I knew I'd fall apart again. But I never thought I'd lose everything.

What the fuck was wrong with me? Why couldn't I get the message? This was my fifth stint in rehab and the second time in this program. When I'd been in the first time, I'd gotten my shit together. Or at least I'd tried.

But here I was, right back in the same place. Only this time, I'd have to go it alone, without Gustavus, or Amy, on my side.

Once more, and with what little I had going for me, I hunkered down inside the confines of my own mind and tried to find the strength to pull through.

> 12/3/00   12 am
> It's Saturday night, and I'm back in the hospital, after spending the last few days in detox. The fall has not treated me very well. I was cut from the hockey team. I lost my girlfriend on our two-year anniversary. I started going downhill. Then I got suspended from college. I knew I'd end up back here in the hospital, I knew it. I was on a downward spiral, I just wish I could've held out a few more weeks and made it through the semester. But, I'm alive. I am alive and I want to live again. I want to be sober. I want to stop destroying my life.

Truly I did. I just didn't know how.

Ten days into inpatient treatment, I was asked to leave. Another student from Gustavus was on the unit, and the administration didn't want us interacting. Since my insurance was about to run out anyway, I was asked to pack my bags. My departure was win-win for everyone except me. For me, it was just another place I wasn't welcome.

I was no longer welcome on the campus of the college that had been my lifesaving vision of the future. I was no longer welcome in the arms of the woman who had helped save my soul. Nor at the only rehab I'd actually ever been able to succeed at. I had nowhere to go but back home to the town I had tried so desperately to escape.

16

Unbearable

My resident advisor did what the administration asked and came and picked me up from the hospital. She brought me back to Gustavus so I could pack some things under her supervision. I would then be asked to leave.

We pulled back up the hill of the campus under the dark backdrop of a new moon. It was frigidly cold. I was still without gloves or a hat but now had two coats.

Nicole had brought one for me. An innocent Lutheran girl from small-town Minnesota, she was nice enough, but I don't think she'd ever dealt with someone like me.

She dropped me off at my car, which had been parked in the back of a lot at the far end of campus.

"I'll drop you here, and then you can park up by the back door of the dorm." She handed me my keys. "Just stop by my room when you're finished up!"

I smiled reluctantly and stepped out into the brisk wind. She started off and headed back to her dorm.

Once the engine thawed, I headed across campus to the exact same spot I'd last seen my car: at the back door, just around the corner from my ground-floor dorm room.

I retraced the footsteps of my falling out as I packed up several loads of things. It was arranged that Amy wouldn't be there. But the hour was growing late, and there was no way I was gonna be able to transport everything in one shot.

I'd have to arrange to get the rest of my stuff some other time. For now, I just needed to get on the road. It was getting late, and I had to drive three and a half hours back to Sioux City.

I topped off the pile in the backseat with the last few hanging clothes from my closet, closed the car up, locked it, and started toward the dorm to hand over my keys. I was reaching out for the handle to the entrance when I looked back. Glowing under the streetlight overhead sat the car. It looked lopsided.

I walked around the front to get a closer look. It *was* lopsided. The front passenger tire was completely flat. I couldn't believe my luck.

It was close to 7 PM, and Amy was about to be back at the dorm. I had to let Nicole know what was happening.

She offered me a phone book to call for a tow truck. "It'll be an hour," they said.

I no longer had a room, so I had no choice but to sit in Nicole's room and be patient. So I waited on her couch, growing more awkward as the time dragged on.

She sat in the other room and studied. I played with the zipper on my jacket.

I perked up as the door knocked and swung open.

In walked Amy.

"Nicole," she said, "I just wanted to let—" She stopped, looked at me, disengaged, and marched straight past me to the back room of the double dorm room, similar to the one we'd shared.

Just a minute later the phone rang. The tow truck had arrived.

After unpacking everything to give the driver access to the spare, I repacked everything into the Civic once more.

"You're not gonna wanna drive on that spare all the way to Iowa," the driver said. "There's a tire store down in Mankato that's open late, though. You should be able to get a new set down there without too much trouble."

After handing over my keys to Nicole, I said a final good-bye to both her and the campus and hopped inside the car. With emotion packed just as tightly as my vehicle, I put the car in drive and headed down the hill. One final time, spare tire and all.

One more time, in Mankato, I unpacked. With my stuff strewn about the shop, the mechanics replaced my tire. They even helped me load my car back up.

It was after 9, but finally I was ready to hit the road. I pulled out to a four-way stop. Straight ahead, just across the street, were the neon-illuminated words "Liquor Store."

The sign blinked, beckoning me to come closer. Instead of taking a right, I went straight.

They were still open. I parked out front and waited for someone who looked like they might help me out. It didn't take long before I found someone. Five minutes later, I was diving into a case.

I'd only been away from beer for ten days or so. My tolerance was, I thought, still pretty high. I didn't like to drive drunk, though. It made me very nervous.

I threw back a single can, lit up a smoke, and fastened up to settle in for the long drive. Two hours later, ninety miles from home, my phone rang.

It was my mom.

"Where are you?" she asked.

"Worthington," I said. "I'll be there in under two hours."

"Well, I don't know what to do here. The dogs got out of the yard."

"Uh-oh." She was in no condition to be out chasing them around.

"It's below zero out. I managed to get in the car and drive around to look for them. Rebel came back on his own, but I can't find Bear anywhere. He's missing!"

I clenched the steering wheel as a semi roared past me in the opposite direction.

"Oh boy," I said. "That's not good." I paused. "He'll come back, Mom. Don't worry."

"He's been gone for hours, Jen. It's so cold. How long will you be? Can you look for him?"

"Yeah, I will. I'll be there as quick as I can."

I again offered my reassurances. We hung up.

I threw the phone to the floor, reached in my duffle bag, grabbed a beer, popped it open, and picked up the speed. I couldn't refrain any longer from numbing the pain. It's a good thing I was heading back home.

My mom needed me.

ONE BY ONE, I downed can after can. By the time I took the exit off the interstate and made it to our neighborhood, I'd put back a six pack. Still, I felt barely buzzed, and my stress was mounting.

Just a few blocks from the house, at the bottom of a snow-covered hill, I slowed to a crawl. I could hear a dog barking. I stopped the car and poked my head outside. It sounded familiar.

"Bear?" I said.

A response barked.

"Bear-bear?"

Another bark.

It sounded like him. It responded like him. It had to be him.

I closed the car door behind me and traipsed through the snow in my low-top shoes, inching closer to the sound. I opened up the gate in a chain-link fence and walked into somebody's backyard.

Curled up in a ball against the back fence lay a dog, whimpering. Under the darkness of the new moon, I couldn't make out the animal until just a few steps away. As I got closer, I could see it was Bear.

No wonder he couldn't get home. He'd fallen over a retaining wall. He was completely fenced in—and frozen. Shivering and whimpering, he laid curled up, unwilling to stand.

"Come on, Bear," I said. "Let's go."

A Norwegian elkhound, Bear loved to roll around and play in the snow. His utter refusal to stand concerned me. His frosted coat, caked with miniature icicles, shivered under the cold. I grabbed a hold of his choke chain and pulled him to his feet, but he fell right back to the ground.

"Come on, Bear," I said. "Let's go home and get you warm." I tried again, but he wouldn't budge.

Since he weighed over sixty pounds, I didn't see any other option than to coax him along. But it was clear he wasn't having it. He needed some help. So I made a decision. In one fell swoop, I reached down and scooped him up in my arms.

"Alright, big guy. Here we go."

I picked up one leg and lifted it out of the snow before plunking it down and lifting the other. Step by step, I inched my way back to the street. Somehow we made it to the car. After rearranging my luggage, I freed up the passenger seat, picked Bear up once more, and set him inside. The ice from his coat melted into my seats as the distinct smell of wet dog permeated the car. Thankfully we were just a few blocks from our destination. I inched up the long driveway to the house and turned the car off in the garage.

"We made it, Bear," I said. "We're home. Safe and sound."

He panted, smiling. Thawed and relieved, I let him out of the front seat. He stood idle, wagging his tail. I threw my backpack over my shoulder, pulled my key from my pocket, and opened the front door. Bear made a beeline for my mom, sitting at her computer desk, and jumped up to lick her face.

"You made it!" she said. "And you found Bear!"

"Yeah, I did."

I put my backpack down and kneeled. We hugged.

"I'm glad I'm here."

I WAS, BUT I was also scared. I had no idea what I was gonna do. I just knew I wasn't going to give up on school.

I was still devastated over everything I'd lost the semester before. As the holidays led to New Year's, my depression worsened. I was absolutely heartbroken. According to Molly, though, Amy was moving on. So I tried to move on. But for the first time since I was sixteen, I found myself single. And it all came at such a crazy time. Alcohol seemed to be the only thing that could console me.

My mom's left hip hadn't gotten any better, either. She'd continued to dislocate it, despite all of the interventions that had been made—much the way I'd continued to drink, despite my mounting number of rehab attempts.

In the process of compensating for her left hip, she'd trashed her right one. She was in a world of hurt by the time I got back home, unable to walk, sit, or lie down without excruciating pain. Seeing her suffer every night took an emotional toll on me. She downed painkillers; I downed beers.

In early January she had her right hip replaced. The same week, I started rehab number six: an outpatient program at Riverview, the hospital on the other end of town from Park.

I was holding the fort down at home, checking in with my mom at Park during the afternoon, then spending the evening at Riverview. I moved from one hospital to the other, balancing my role as both caretaker and patient.

ROAMING THE LONELY corridors of the downtown hospital, I couldn't help but think of my mom's struggles. She'd worked for many years as a social worker at Riverview. It was also where I was taken the night of my shoulder dislocation. Now, after so many years away, I was back for my own health once more.

Three nights a week, I hopped in my car, drove downtown past the crack houses, and pulled up to the hospital lot. Up on the sixth floor, I'd spit out all the answers and give all the correct responses. Playing the rehab game was becoming old hat. I really was trying to work the steps and trying to follow the program. I was trying to stay sober, but everything was so crazy, I couldn't do it. So instead, every night after treatment, I drank, stayed up all night, and wrote my pain away, often laying my head down when the sun came up. It was a cycle I couldn't seem to stop.

I'd be up checking on my mom until 3 or 4 AM, begging her to get up and head to bed. But the painkillers would have already knocked her out. I'd leave her to sleep at the kitchen table, retreat to my room, and down more alcohol. She slept in most days, so I had no obligations in the morning hours. As long as I was there to help her in the afternoon, and as long as I kept up with treatment in the evenings, I was doing all that I needed to get by. It just wasn't enough to keep me sober. I couldn't let the treatment program know that, though. I had too much on the line to share with them my struggles to abstain from alcohol.

Gustavus decided I needed to do a number of things if I ever wished to enroll in classes there again. One of those things was to graduate from chemical dependency treatment and maintain sobriety. I wasn't sure I wanted to jump through so many hoops to go back to a place that had so many memories, but I wanted to have the option. So I needed to get through treatment.

The chemical dependency program at Riverview wasn't all that different from any other program. I knew how it worked. The philosophy was the same; the end of group prayers were the same; the whole thing was the same. I went over the same history and described the same life stories.

Then a month into the program, I talked about my brush with death. A bearded man in plaid normally slouched low in his chair perked up to listen. He sat across from me in the circle and listened intently as I described how I did it. He heard me say that my experience had given me a purpose in life. He talked about how he was trying to find his.

A week later, he hanged himself.

His death loomed over me like a dark cloud. We talked about it in group, but nothing felt the same. It was the first time anyone I'd been in treatment with had committed suicide. I couldn't help but feel like I'd somehow given him the idea to do it. Perhaps if I hadn't discussed my own attempt at ending my life, he would have still been alive.

I tried not to let it nag at me, but as the days went on, it grew more and more difficult for me to maintain my composure. My drinking was getting out of hand. No amount of alcohol seemed able to quench my thirst. My guilt was tearing at me. I needed something else to get me by.

17

Busted

The red and blue lights flashed in my rearview mirror. Panic set in. I grabbed the beer from the cup holder, rolled down the window, and heaved it to the street. Reaching over toward the passenger side, I shoved the other empty cans under the seat.

I needed to stop. But the two guys in the backseat I'd been smoking crack with had other ideas. They both had warrants.

"Don't stop!" yelled the one with the gold tooth.

I kept pressing the gas pedal. One block, then the next.

"Just get to Nebraska!" yelled the other in the bandana. The border was just a mile away. "They can't follow us there!"

My thoughts churned as I sped along. The sirens rang. A second police car joined the chase. What the hell was I doing? This was crazy. I was running from the cops.

Another block blurred by. I gripped the wheel, looked in the rearview, and picked my foot up off the gas, slammed on the brakes, yanked the car over to the side of the road, and screeched to a halt. From the backseat, threats hurled my direction.

"You fucking bitch! I outta fuckin' kill you!"

"Fuckin' white ass hos, man. Can't trust 'em."

I put my hands up. "I'm sorry, guys," I said. "I can't do this. I can't run from the cops."

A flashlight shone in from behind the car. I rolled down the window, squinting as the light reflected into my eyes. The clomping of the officer's shoes grew louder and then stopped.

"License and registration, please," the officer said, shining the light at me.

He looked around the vehicle with his flashlight, first to the beer can on the passenger side of the floor, then to my two companions in the backseat. I produced the items.

"How much have you had to drink tonight, Ms. Cannon?"

I stayed silent for a moment before mumbling. "I . . . I don't know."

"Step out of the car, please," he said.

I did as told.

A female officer grabbed hold of my arm as I put a foot to the pavement and escorted me to the front of the vehicle.

"Hands on the hood," she said. "Spread 'em." She patted me down.

"You have the right to remain silent. Anything you say . . ."

I dropped my head to my chest. She grabbed hold of my other arm and pinned them together behind my back as she finished reading my rights.

"Have you got any dope in the car?" she asked.

My stomach dropped. I'd come downtown under the premise of looking for weed. But I'd ended up smoking crack with the two guys I didn't know sitting in my backseat.

I had set myself up for a relapse. I'd gone downtown, right into the heart of crack country, and sought out just the right spot. I had been asking for weed. But I was really looking for rock. And I found it.

I'd been so proud of myself for staying away from it. But I was really struggling. Alcohol just wasn't cutting it anymore. I'd found these two guys, picked them up, and dropped them off at an apartment building where they told me they could hook me up with some rock. It was a low-lying, two-story brick building with a single, faintly lit front entrance. There was no other lighting in the parking lot whatsoever.

I sat outside with my bandana buddy while gold tooth went inside. He lit up a hit of crack. It melted and crackled the way that gives it its name. I sat in the driver's seat, listening to him smoke it. My mouth started to water. The taste of it in the air dripped with memories. It flooded me with cravings.

"Yo, can I get a hit of that?" I turned to ask.

He nodded and loaded one up. "I've only got a couple more, though." I looked out at the dark, dilapidated building. It had been two years since I'd last held a crack pipe.

He nudged my shoulder. "Here," he said.

I grabbed the pipe, reclined my seat, held up a lighter, and lit up the flame. It started to melt.

I never wanted to see that damn drug again. There's just something about it, though. It's that lure. Once it gets you, it never lets go. You might stop using, but your brain and your body never forget. It only takes a second for that switch to get flipped, and suddenly you're right back in that same place in your head.

I put the pipe to my lips, drew in the fumes, held the hit, and let the high take hold. I faded out.

"Yo, gimme my pipe back."

I snapped back to reality and handed back the pipe. He loaded up another hit.

I reached over and grabbed the near empty beer in between the seats, sucking down the last drops. It was the last beer I'd brought. I lit up a smoke as my anxiety swelled.

"What could be taking so long?" I finally asked. Gold tooth had been gone a long time.

"Man, I don't know."

I flicked cigarette ash out the window and took a drag. In the shadow of the dim light near the entrance appeared the silhouette of a person, running in my direction.

I sat up. "What the hell?"

"Just go! Just go!" a voice said.

A few strides closer, I made out who it was. It was gold tooth. He was charging toward my car. He opened the back door, threw himself inside, and slammed it shut. "Just go! Get out of here!"

I put the key in the ignition and turned it over. Adrenaline rushing, I threw it in drive and put my foot to the gas.

"What the hell just happened?" I asked, looking in the rearview mirror. "Who were you running from?" Past the row of bushes lining the road, I turned out of the lot onto a major one-way running through the heart of downtown, heading off in the direction of Nebraska.

"The cops," he said.

Red and blue lights then followed.

Now the question was, did I have any dope? I didn't have any rock. Neither did my partners in crime. They'd swallowed what was left.

But I did have some weed. Enough for about a single joint. I didn't want to confess to it. So I stayed silent.

"Ms. Cannon, if you don't tell us about any dope you might have in the vehicle, right now, we'll charge you with a felony when we find it later."

That didn't sound good. Being convicted of marijuana possession would mean losing my financial aid for college. But a felony would be even worse. Maybe it would be best to come clean. "Alright, yeah, I've got a little bit of weed in that CD case on the floor," I said. The officers immediately searched for it.

I bowed my head and fought back the tears. "Please, don't charge me for that," I said. "I'll . . . I'll lose my financial aid. And I'm supposed to go to law school."

"Not now you aren't!" A male officer stepped in and grabbed hold of my arm. "It's these clowns you were hangin' out with that got you in trouble. Now you're not going anywhere but jail."

It was only a few blocks away, not even far enough to warrant a drive. He walked me, cuffed and tipsy, to the police station and performed the sobriety tests I'd refused to take on the spot.

I was hoping my alcohol levels might go down a little if I stalled. But it didn't work. I was still over the limit and charged with a DUI.

I arrived at the booking area spent and defeated. A stocky female officer performed an invasive strip search and then put me in front of a Plexiglas window. A male officer not much older than myself sat on the other side, at a computer.

After I forked over the earring I was wearing at the top of my left ear, as well as my wallet, shoes, and all other similar items, he started in with some questioning—my name, age, address, criminal history, etc. I responded and complied. Then the questioning took a more personal turn.

"What is your sexual orientation?"

"I don't think that's any of your business," I said.

"Well, we need to have an answer for our records. Do you identify as homosexual, heterosexual, or bisexual?"

"I shouldn't have to answer that."

"Ms. Cannon, we need a response."

"Fine, man. You wanna know? I'm a lesbian, alright. But I like dick. Put that in your records. What the hell does that have to do with my criminal charges? What are my criminal charges anyway?"

He continued on to press more about my psychological history. I was growing agitated.

"Have you ever hurt yourself or attempted suicide?"

I looked up and stared blankly. I didn't know what to say. This was getting awfully intrusive. But I didn't want to lie to the cops.

"Yes. As a matter of fact, I have," I said.

"Are you considering suicide right now?"

"No, I am not, thanks."

"Are you on medication for emotional instability?"

"Yes. But, once again, what does this have to do with what I'm being charged with?"

I don't advocate lying to the police, but I wish I hadn't told them about my history. There is just no right answer to any of these questions. If you admit to having a history of a suicide attempt, suicidal thoughts—or even if you're just being treated for depression—you're bound to be deemed a danger to yourself. Either you lie, or you get subjected to worse treatment by being put on suicide watch. In jail, that means being thrown into isolation and put under strict observation. It's a no-win situation.

"Okay, Ms. Cannon," the officer behind the glass finally said. "We've got your charges here. You're being charged with the following misdemeanor crimes." I held my breath. "Operating a motor vehicle while intoxicated, possession of a controlled substance, possession of drug paraphernalia, possession of marijuana, and reckless driving. You are also being charged with felony assault on a police officer."

I nearly wet my pants. "A felony? You're charging me with a felony?"

Every emotion in my soul exploded like a volcano blowing its top. Anger, frustration, confusion, and helplessness. All the things that made me want to kill myself back in '98 were creeping up on me again.

I had to defuse, but this was bad news. And there was absolutely nothing I could do about it.

The female strip search officer chuckled. "Good, we're gettin' ya on the felony." She seemed to be getting some sick thrill out of my troubles. She hadn't even been there. She didn't know what happened. *I* didn't even know what happened.

"Why am I being charged with that? What did I do to assault any officer?"

The Plexiglas officer turned around to talk to two other officers in the back of the booking area. Once finished he returned to the glass.

"Apparently you tried to run over an officer with the front right side of your car while exiting the parking lot. So you're being charged with assault on a peace officer with a deadly weapon."

I was stunned. I did no such thing. I never saw any officer.

"Your bond is set at $14,300, and you're allowed one phone call."

I stepped away from the glass and over to the phones. I had to call my mom and let her know where I was. She was back home, worried and waiting. I'd told her I'd gone to an Alcoholics Anonymous meeting. But I'd been gone for hours. Surely she was worried.

I dialed her number.

"Mom?"

"Jennifer, where are you?"

"I'm . . ." I pinched back the tears. "I'm in jail."

"What?" She screamed. "You're in jail?"

"Yeah. I got arrested. For drunk driving. And that's not all. They say I tried to run over a police officer with my car, but I never saw him, Mom. I swear. I never tried to hit any officer. I don't know what to do. They're charging me with a felony."

She sat silent on the other end.

"My bond is $14,300."

"Oh my God."

"I know. I think we need to call a bail bondsman." I flipped through the list of numbers on the wall next to the phone. "There's a list here."

"Alright, one minute, Ms. Cannon," the strip search officer said.

"Are bail bondsmen open twenty-four hours?" my mom asked.

I turned to the officer and repeated the question.

"Yes, they are," she said. She went on to explain that, because it was a Friday night, court would be held in the booking area rather than a courtroom in the morning.

I looked at her, surprised. "Really? That seems kinda shady."

"We can keep you 'til Monday if you'd prefer." She took one step closer to me.

"That's quite alright," I said. I started to read off a number to my mom when the officer reached for the phone.

"Just a second," I said, "I'm trying to read these numbers." Click. Dial tone. She hung up the phone. I slammed the receiver down.

"Hey, that wasn't cool. I was trying to get the bond situation figured out." I was practically shouting at her.

My mom warned me on the phone not to piss off the police. Unfortunately, I usually have to learn things the hard way.

"Time's up," she said. "It's time to go to your cell."

"You mean you decided my time was up. You just hung up the phone on me." I was getting feisty. "It woulda taken me thirty seconds."

"It's time to go to your cell now," she said again, grabbing hold of my arm.

"Fine. Take me to a fucking cell then." The switch had been flipped. I was no longer thinking—or acting—in any sort of rational way.

Together with another female officer, she led me like a dog on a leash from the booking area to the cell block. We didn't go far, but I unleashed loads of unflattering remarks. We took a right-hand turn into the first cell on the block. They marched me straight to the back of it.

"On your knees."

I did as told and started to kneel. Pushing on the small of my back, they forced me face first into the concrete floor. I slammed my forehead square into the ground.

"Turn your head to the right," she said.

With my head pinned to the concrete, two more officers joined the fray, tugging at my legs.

"Keep your head turned," they ordered. I squirmed, unsure what they were doing. It took me a moment to realize that they were attempting to remove my pants. Without use of my arms, I lay with my head cocked and locked awkwardly into a forced position, and they went after my shirt. With each tug, the pain shot through my shoulder and right arm as they contorted my body into awkward positions to remove the garment.

"Stop fighting," one of the officers said.

"I'm not! I'm just laying here."

Really, I wasn't fighting at all. I was as limp as I could be, but it's tough not to move when three officers are pulling in three different directions. My shoulder was really starting to feel it.

"Listen, I've dislocated my right shoulder a number of times. Please be careful. You're gonna pop it out of its socket."

"That's not my problem," the strip search officer said.

"It will be when I have to go the hospital!"

She either didn't hear me or didn't care because she kept on forcing it. A moment later, they succeeded in stripping me of my shirt. They'd already taken my bra and underwear, so I was completely naked. They even took my socks. An officer threw a crumpled up paper wad in my direction.

"Now stay there and shut up," she said.

I looked up from my position on the concrete slab and watched the two female officers exit the cell. The male officers stood behind them and observed. The strip search officer shot me one last smile, grabbed a hold of the thick, rust-tinged door, and slammed it closed like a coffin on my dreams.

I reached to my toes to retrieve my paper blanket and tried to cover myself up. Huddling beneath the thin layer of coverage, I looked around to absorb my surroundings. Suddenly I felt like the world's worst criminal. The cell seemed so uncivilized, so inhumane.

There was no toilet—just a drain in the middle of the room. There was no bed—just a concrete slab. I sat on it and stared out at a thick steel door with a small window in it, rather than at bars. Surrounded by cement walls, the one to my left had three or four small windows. I stood up to see what was out there. I looked out to the booking area at the officers lounging.

Shivering and naked, I felt exposed to the entire world. Like an animal at the zoo, caged and on display. I huddled back in the corner, trying my best to keep my body warm and covered. But with every move, my paper blanket ripped apart. Pretty soon, I was left with nothing but bits and pieces. I aligned the remnants in effort to cover my most vulnerable areas, but it was a futile effort.

The concrete, so cold and coarse, started to numb my skin. I tried to think about something else. But there was nothing to do, no way I was gonna sleep. I'd smoked crack and was not only high but uncomfortable.

Minutes passed in what felt like hours. An occasional knock rapped on the windows to the booking area. I'd look up to see an officer waving and smiling at me. Every time I looked up, it seemed like another male officer was peering through the windows at little naked me.

Time dragged on, and as my paper blanket continued to be shredded apart, I finally knocked on the window and asked for a new one. I was told I would only get one blanket. I had no choice but to accept that.

I was just trying not to think about how bad I had to pee. It was unavoidable, though, that the beer would flush through me. In humiliating fashion I squatted over the drain, hoping no one would look at me in the process. I tore off a corner of my precious paper blanket to use as toilet paper, but had no way to dispose of it, let alone wash my hands.

I sat back down on the concrete slab, knees drawn up to my chest. I tried to close my eyes but couldn't quite fall asleep.

Occasionally, throughout the night, I rearranged my paper towel pieces in deliberate fashion to conceal my vulnerable areas. But the small piece I'd placed underneath me was far from a cushion for my bony butt. I couldn't sit anymore, so I paced the cell. For awhile, I ran in place to generate heat.

Whatever I attempted to do to keep myself warm and sane that night, the morning couldn't have arrived soon enough. I sat propped in the corner, head on my knees.

The creak of the cell door commanded my attention. A female officer stepped inside.

"Cannon?" she asked.

"Yes?"

"A bondsman is here to get you." She tossed an orange jumpsuit at me. "Put that on."

I welcomed the covering.

"Come with me." I followed her out and back around to the front of the booking area. In the hallway leading back to where inmates were not allowed, I noticed a stack of real blankets.

"Wow," I said, "so you do have real ones."

"Yup, we sure do."

They'd had me on suicide watch. In all likelihood, I'd not been given a real blanket because they feared I would use it to hang myself with. After all, I did confess to a history of a suicide attempt by hanging. Still, was my history, or my big mouth, cause enough to put me on display without so much as a working toilet?

If anything, it made me feel like even more of a nutcase than I was already made out to be. Being holed up naked, in isolation, on display, with nothing more than a paper towel to cover your body, does not do much for your mental health.

The officer led me around the corner to a small room reserved for fingerprinting and mug shots. I've never seen my mug shot, but I imagine I look like a real celebrity, disheveled and bruised after a sleepless night of humiliation.

After I applied my thumbprint to a sheet of paper, we walked into an adjacent room where the bondsman awaited. He finished up his paperwork and started to go over it with me. I signed the necessary documents and was given a sack with my clothes in it. I thought I was home free, but not before one last surprise.

The female officer who'd been escorting me returned to the room. "So you came in here without any shoes on last night?" she said.

"What? No. I had shoes."

"Well, they're not back there." I peeked inside my sack to find my pants and T-shirt. Not only were my shoes missing, but so was my sweatshirt.

I tried to stay cool. I described my shoes and explained that I'd given my shoes to the guy behind the Plexiglas when I got booked. She seemed to doubt my recollection of the previous night's events or of my shoes.

I was feeling a bit insulted but refrained from getting riled up. She could see I was being serious and so agreed to check with a few people. She returned and again said they could not be found. I insisted she look again. The bondsman and I continued to discuss paperwork. Eventually the female officer returned, carrying with her a bag containing my shoes and sweatshirt.

I still have to wonder: if they can lose someone's shoes in a matter of one night, then what else are they losing? Finally, I was free to put my clothes back on. I've never been more excited to throw on a dirty outfit.

Charges and release paperwork in hand, I walked with the bondsman to his office a block away. My mom was there waiting. The look in her eyes was fiercely scolding. I hung my head in shame.

I knew I was throwing my life away.

4/14/2001
I got arrested. Damn it.
   I tried so damn hard to get my life straightened
out, but now I'm really sinking. I'm lucky I haven't

been arrested on drug charges before. I guess it was only a matter of time before I got nailed. It could be worse, I could've had crack on me. It's hard to look at the bright side right now, though. These charges will have serious ramifications on my future. They say in treatment that the definition of insanity is doing the same thing over and over and expecting different results. I never expected these particular results, but I know it's insane for me to keep using chemicals.

This disease is killing me. It nearly killed me before, and now it seems like it's killing me slowly. It's stripping me of my freedom, my integrity, and my future. I know I can go to college, maintain my grades, and still manage to drink and use. But, the consequences of my drinking and using on my college education go beyond the classroom.

I'm so scared that I won't ever be able to go to law school with these charges that are pending. I'm so scared that, with drug charges, I won't be able to afford college at all because I'll lose my financial aid. I'm scared that this disease is gonna kill me before I have the opportunity to exhibit the potential everyone says I have. What does it matter if I can get straight As in college if I keep throwing my life away like this?

I'm trying to think of this as a wake-up call. I always used my lack of consequences (never being arrested as an adult that is) as an excuse to continue on with my same old behaviors. It made it easier for me to think about all the times I got away with things. It's only a crime if you get caught, right? Well, I got caught at Gustavus, and I'm still paying. Now, I pay the price for my most recent actions. Maybe it's just what I need to get my ass back on track.

I'll be 21 in June and I've been extremely scared of that. I often think that if I don't take a good hard look at my drinking by the time I turn 21, there's nothing on earth that could stop me. Maybe this is God's way of telling me to get my shit together before I die from this disease.

I'm not sure what the consequences of this are gonna be. I know my mom can't afford to hire a lawyer for me, so I'll be talking to a public defender. I don't know whether I should tell Gustavus about this. I don't know if I'll be able to go to school there, or anywhere, in the fall. I don't know if I'll be facing jail time, or whether, because I'm a first time offender, they'll be lenient with me.

Given the number of treatments I've already been through, though, who knows whether they'll want to give me another chance. They may just decide I'm a menace to society and beyond help. I don't know what to think right now. I don't know. I just don't know anything. I don't know what all of this means for my future. I just feel lost.

I'd already graduated from rehab.

I was in aftercare but going in just once a week. It obviously wasn't enough to keep me sober. I'd still gotten busted.

The drinking was starting to catch up to me on a physical level, too. I was starting to look puffy and red. And every morning I was waking up in a pool of vinegar-tainted sweat, a pure chemical odor. My body was doing everything it could to rid itself of the toxins, but the more I drank, the more I sweated. And the more I passed out. I assumed that, too, was from the alcohol. But as the episodes got more frequent, it got harder to conceal.

One night, I reached up to get a cup out of the cupboard and woke up on the floor, having bitten right through my lip. It was hard to hide the damage from my mom, as I'd scarred myself pretty severely.

"I tripped over the dog," I told her.

A few days later, I used the same excuse for my fat lip at rehab. Whether they bought it or not, nobody seemed to care. There were more pressing matters to attend to.

A seventeen-year-old boy named Ethan, just a few days shy of his own high school graduation, had hanged himself—three years to the day after I had attempted to end my own life. He was the second member of my treatment group to commit suicide. The second to hang himself. And he too had heard me talk about my attempt. His death caused my guilt to magnify. It was more than I could take.

I had to get out of Sioux City if it was the last thing I did. Unfortunately, I still had some pretty serious criminal charges pending. The days blurred together as I spent regular mornings visiting my public defender and afternoons taking care of my mom.

I couldn't go back to aftercare, not after Ethan's death. I dropped out, and in June I turned twenty-one. No longer did I need to ask others to buy alcohol for me. No longer did I have to lie and tell the cashier I'd forgotten my ID. I was free to drink as much as I pleased. But it was clear to everyone, including myself, that the environment wasn't conducive to my sobriety.

THANKFULLY, I'D PLANNED my escape. I'd applied to the University of Minnesota in the spring and been accepted. I was set to enroll in the fall. In July, I was offered a plea deal. They dropped the felony and marijuana possession; I pled guilty to the DUI and reckless driving. I couldn't have been happier.

I lost my license, was given two years of probation, and was ordered to pay fines and fees, complete a drunk driving class, and follow through on the recommendations of a substance abuse evaluation. But for everything I was gonna have to do to get my license back and my life on track, at least my jail sentence got suspended. I wouldn't have to serve any time.

I'd been spared a lifetime of trouble by having the felony assault on a police officer charge dropped. I would've faced many more obstacles in going back to school had the pot charge stuck, too. My pudgy, balding probation officer knew it. He could see I had a lot of potential and encouraged me to leave Iowa to finish my college degree.

With a heavy heart, at the end of August, I packed my bags. It was time to say good-bye to Sioux City, my childhood home, and my mom.

18

Escape Artist, Take 2

The day started off with a bang.

I'd arrived in Minneapolis intent on completing my college education, but I hadn't yet found an apartment. So John said I could stay with him in Uptown until I found a place of my own. The old grey-brick apartment building stood like a fortress on a hilltop corner where prestigious historic homes and previously upscale apartments blended together in a diverse array of housing that catered mostly to yuppies and grad students. I certainly couldn't afford a place in that neighborhood. I was just grateful to have a place to crash.

The squeal of an alarm clock jarred me awake on the morning of September 11. I was accustomed to waking up to an empty room; John is the kind of guy who gets up before dawn and is hard at work before the sun even peeks up from the horizon. On this morning, though, I knew he wasn't on campus in his corner office of the astronomy building. He was at a conference in Baltimore.

I could've just gone back to sleep. But I'd come to Minneapolis to succeed, not to piss my life away. I rolled over and looked at the alarm clock pounding my ear drums. Rather than give in to the temptation to hit snooze, I turned it off, rolled out of bed, planted a toothbrush in my mouth, and flipped on the shower.

Once I'd spit, rinsed, lathered, and zipped, I walked back out into the living area and flipped on the news. You never know about Minnesota weather. My belly grumbled and called me to the kitchen for a bowl of cereal. I walked away from the television set and pulled a box of Raisin Bran from the cupboard.

The voices on television seemed animated, almost panicked. I returned to the living room and stared at the screen. The monotonous drone of usually bored news anchors spewing previously written drivel had been replaced by unprompted dialogue. I'd have to wait awhile to hear any kind of weather report; the news had suddenly taken center stage. It didn't seem real. I stared at the television.

The talk of the 1993 subway bombing made me think they were discussing something altogether in the past. But I'd never seen footage of smoke pouring from the top of the World Trade Center before. This didn't look like stock file footage. This looked live.

I changed the channel to be sure. There it was again. It wasn't just on ABC. It was on NBC, CBS, and every other channel, too. I rubbed my eyes and looked back once more. It was still there.

This wasn't old. This was real. Live. And absolutely mind boggling.

Minutes passed before I moved. I turned away, scrambled to find my books, and threw my bag over my shoulder before returning to my spot in front of the television.

With smoke billowing from the roof of the North Tower, the second plane crashed. My jaw dropped. I looked down to the corner of the TV. It was 8:03. I needed to get on the bus to get to class, news or no news.

I arrived on campus where the classroom was abuzz. The professor acknowledged the historic nature of the day, then got down to business. After class, so did I. It was close to lunch time—time to start drinking. I holed up at a restaurant with my notebook and pen, downing pint after pint as I watched the nonstop, heart wrenching coverage on television. America, they all said, was under attack. I couldn't help but wonder if John, out in a government building in Baltimore, was safe.

By the time my lunch had come and gone, I'd put away a few brews and was feeling nicely numbed. I felt an itch to keep moving, though. I had class in the afternoon and still had a lot of loose ends to tie up with respect to declaring my major, getting enrolled in the honors programs, getting accommodated testing for the ADHD they'd diagnosed me with at Gustavus—the list went on and on.

The University of Minnesota is known for not closing or canceling classes even when it's 20 below zero outside. Why on earth would they shut down for something happening thousands of miles away?

Turns out they had. Even though the university and its offices stayed open, all classes were cancelled, and the campus had gone from buzzing to somber in a matter of hours.

Rather than go back to Uptown, where I would surely just sit and get loaded, I spent the afternoon bouncing from office to office, filling out forms, dropping off others, and requesting even more. Each place I went, I was greeted with the same messages: "Classes are cancelled." "You're about the only person on campus doing anything productive this afternoon." "You've heard the news, haven't you?"

"Of course," I said. But I was determined to stay on the ball and work toward my degree. It didn't matter whether I was drunk or what the date was, I was going to jump through hoops and cut red tape until I accomplished my goal and got through college.

I just had to hurry up so I could get back to drinking. I wasn't quite ready for self-improvement just yet. And like millions of other Americans, I felt justified in having a stiff drink on the night of the terrorist attacks.

When the night was all over, I was headed home from a bar, drunk and driving without a license. Somehow I made it back to John's apartment in Uptown without hurting anyone or causing any accidents. Such an accomplishment deserved another cigarette. Since I couldn't smoke inside John's apartment, it was going to be the last one for the night.

I parked, kicked the seat back, cracked the window open, bumped up the volume on some tunes, and lit up. One drag later, time vanished.

A knock startled me awake. My eyes opened to the stunning glare of a bright light as I pried my head from the window. I propped myself up in my seat, bass beating my ears. The music was still on, and it was loud.

The light traced around the interior of the vehicle, then back to my eyes, effectively blinding me. I squinted as I held an arm up to shield myself from the assault. I could make out the silhouette of a man outside the door.

"Minneapolis Police. Roll down your window, please."

My stomach dropped.

I looked down at the console in front of me and observed that, not only were the keys still in the ignition, the car was still on. I turned down the volume on the stereo and rolled down the window.

"License and registration, please," the officer said.

Anxiety swirled. I was in big trouble.

"I . . . I . . . I've got my Iowa ID, but I don't exactly have a license," I said. I reached to retrieve the proper paperwork from the glove box. "But here's the vehicle registration."

I handed the items to the officer, who maneuvered his light throughout the car once more. The unmistakable odor of stale beer wafted toward the open window.

"How much have you had to drink tonight, Ms. Cannon?"

I knew there was no right answer to this question. It was the same question I'd been asked in Iowa. I stared down at my lap and put my hands up over my face, rubbing my fingers with my eyes. *This can't be happening*, I thought. *I'm so screwed.*

After a moment of hesitation, I confessed to the drinking but nothing more. "I don't remember," I said. "I was drinking with some friends. We were watching the news. I came out for a smoke. I must've fallen asleep."

The officer shone his light in my eyes and glared at me, skeptical.

"Step out of the car, please," he said. He reached in and opened the door for me.

I set my left foot on the ground, then the right. I was barefoot. "Let me just get my sandals here on the floor," I said. I reached down to the ground.

The lock of a gun stopped me in my tracks. "Do not reach to the floor," he said. "Keep your hands where I can see them. Step out of the vehicle, *now*."

He pointed his gun at me as I stepped from the vehicle, hands up.

A second officer grabbed hold of my arms, pinned them behind me, and locked me in handcuffs. This was becoming altogether too familiar of a position.

I shot a quick glance up to the sky as if pleading with some higher power for help. After a quick pat-down, I was escorted to the rear of the police car. On the bright side, at least this time I wasn't getting boxed in or carrying crack dealers in my backseat.

That might've been something of an improvement. But I'd taken a step backwards, too. It looked as if I'd been driving a car, and I clearly didn't have a license.

The loose, frayed leather let out a squishing sigh as I plopped down on the back seat of the vehicle. The officers took their seats up front. A female voice chirped across a radio scanner while a dizzying array of bright lights on the dashboard blinked on and off in red and green.

I stared at the front dash through the caged steel, gnawing on my bottom lip.

Finally, a question. "So why is your Iowa license suspended?" the driver side officer asked. He spun around to talk with me.

"Because I got arrested and charged with a DUI in April."

"And now you're here in Minnesota driving drunk again? Without a license?"

"I wasn't driving," I said. "I've been here drinking in my brother's apartment all night. I just didn't feel comfortable standing outside to smoke late at night, so I went to the car. I only turned it on cuz I was cold. But I didn't drive anywhere. I'm drunk, yes, but I didn't drive. I'm sorry I fell asleep with the music on so loud."

"Well, that's why the neighbors called us. Because of a noise disturbance. We weren't expecting to find *this*, though."

I inched up to the front edge of the seat. "Listen. I moved up here to go back to college. I've only been here a few weeks. I'm trying so hard to get my life together. I've been through several rehabs, and I know I'm an alcoholic. I know I need to get sober. I just don't need any more trouble with the law, though. I'm already on probation. Please. I'm a good kid. That DUI was my first arrest."

The officers looked at one another for a moment. The passenger-side officer tapped his pen against his clipboard. "Well, you're about to get your second," he said.

"Please, guys. I'm begging you—don't do this." The emotion started to squeeze my voice.

"We have enough here to charge you with driving while intoxicated as well as operating without a license. That's not to mention the noise violation."

"My brother's at a conference in Baltimore right now. I've been worried about him all day because of the terrorist attacks. I shouldn't have gotten drunk tonight. And I shouldn't have fallen asleep in the car. I'm really sorry. This has just been . . . such a tough day. For everyone. Please, please, please don't arrest me tonight. I swear on my life you'll never see me again if you let me go."

For a second time, the officers communicated via unspoken eye contact. They seemed to be on the same page. "Alright, relax," the passenger-side officer said. "We're just gonna write you up for operating without a license. We'll still have to impound your car, though."

"Oh my God, thank you," I said. "That's fine if you need to do that. Fine."

Headlights approached. "There's the tow truck now." The passenger-side officer hopped out.

The tension grew thick. I was too scared to say anything at all. With the officer in the driver's seat still scribbling, I inched myself back and rested my head. This guy didn't seem quite as sure about me. I stared up at the ceiling, hoping he wouldn't change his mind about what to write me up for.

A moment later, the thinner, younger officer plopped back down on the passenger side.

"Here," the driver said, offering up a piece of paper. "This is your citation."

He explained what I needed to do to resolve the ticket and also to deal with the impound. Once finished, he lectured me on drunk driving, then got out of his vehicle. The back door to the police car swung open, and he ordered me to get out. I gladly complied.

"You've got your ticket. Make sure you get that taken care of. And get yourself together. I don't want to see you again, you hear me?" He removed the key from the lock of the handcuffs.

I nodded affirmatively. "Yes sir."

"Alright then. We're letting you go." He started back to the car, turning around one last time. "Be good," he said.

I stepped up to the sidewalk and watched them pull away. I reached into my pocket, pulled out a smoke, and lit it up. That was a close call.

I knelt down, tapping the filter of the cigarette. Something didn't feel right. It wasn't just that the cops were still parked down the street.

I was barefoot. My sandals, I remembered, were still on the floor of the car. But, hey, at least they were safe. I had other shoes upstairs. It was time to call it a night.

I shoved my lighter in the front pocket of my jeans and headed for the front door. Under the buzzing glow of the entrance light, I fished for my keys. They weren't in the left pocket. Or the right. They weren't in the back. They were nowhere to be found. I patted myself down again, frantically turning my pockets inside out. Still

I came up empty. Scanning my brain, it dawned on me. They were attached to my car key, still in the ignition of the car.

I was completely locked out.

Down the street, I could see the taillights of the police car, still parked along the road just a few blocks away. I turned and set into an all-out sprint. Stride after stride, I pounded the balls of my bare feet to the pavement, pebbles pressing into the skin. The car was pulling away from the curb.

Arms waving, I put one foot in front of the other and chased the cops. Perhaps cops are unaccustomed to having someone chase them instead of the other way around. I shouted but couldn't grab their attention.

The harder I ran, the further they got. They gained ground until, finally, they disappeared. Deflated and defeated, I slowed to a stop, putting my hands up to my head. "God damn it," I said, panting to catch my breath. "What the fuck am I gonna do now?"

I was stranded. In the middle of the night. In the city I called home. With no phone, no keys, and no shoes. *At least*, I thought, *I have cigarettes.*

I lit up another and headed toward the lights illuminating the Uptown area. Perhaps I could find a phone. Maybe Molly would come pick me up and take me to the impound lot. If she wouldn't help me out, then I was gonna be shit out of luck. Nobody else I knew would be sober.

Thankfully, she agreed. I sat down and leaned against the wall outside a twenty-four-hour restaurant, folded my arms over my knees, and put my head down to rest. By the time Molly arrived, the sun had come up. She looked none too happy to see me so disheveled or to be bailing me out yet again. Thankfully, though, she wasn't bailing me out of jail.

I deserved a second DUI that night. Instead, I got a break. I got my car impounded and a citation for operating a vehicle with a suspended license. It was a small price to pay compared to the toll my alcoholism was starting to take on my life—and my body.

19

Bottled Up

It's not like I was enjoying my life as a drunk. I was trying desperately to get away from it. But after moving into an efficiency apartment off campus, I quickly hit the bar scene. Still, I settled into a productive groove at school, and when the hockey season rolled around, I decided to join the club team.

The first practice, slated for late on a Thursday in early November, couldn't have arrived soon enough. I'd been bottled up in my musty old apartment since early afternoon, drinking. I had an urge to get out. But by the time 8:30 arrived, I was in no position to be heading to the rink, especially when I'd have to lug a twenty-pound hockey bag onto a city bus to get there.

Tanked and feeling far less than agile on my feet, I questioned how I'd fare on two tiny skate blades. But, despite my state, I couldn't miss out on the opportunity to join the team.

I dragged my bag out from the closet and threw two sticks down on top of it. Grabbing my bottle of Miller Lite, always nearby, I gulped down the last swig before setting it next to the sink. The clock on the oven read 8:37.

I flipped open my pocket bus schedule to confirm it. I'd missed the last chance bus. There was no other choice but to drive. Drunk. Without a license. Rain and all.

I didn't like driving drunk. Every time I did it, I feared I was going to hurt someone. I didn't worry so much about myself, but I thought constantly about what a true lowlife it made me to be out tooling around intoxicated—yet again. I loathed myself. I was also starting to hate the feeling of drinking too much. But my tolerance was so high, it took a lot to push me from okay to too far. This night I'd had too much, and it had to come out.

I made a pit stop in the bathroom, took off my shirt, hunched over the toilet, and stuck a finger down my throat. Once, then twice. I puked until I'd puked up all the liquid left in my stomach. I brushed my teeth, bundled up, and headed out the door.

Drops pelted my windshield as I squinted out through the fog-soaked streets ahead of me. I reached over and flipped off the radio. The squeak of the wipers crooned a lonely tune. Turn by turn, I weaved the streets of downtown Minneapolis, eventually arriving at campus.

I knew University Avenue like the back of my hand. I first played hockey at the rink at the U when I was fourteen years old. A few years later, I found myself accidentally driving the wrong way down the one-way while searching for a shortcut to my dealer's house. I'd been on the road countless times since and knew which way not to go now. The trouble would be finding anyplace close to the rink to park.

After settling on a lot a few blocks from the side entrance, I wedged my old green Civic between two trucks, threw the vehicle into park, and flipped off the lights.

I'd made it, safe and sound, without hurting anyone. As a bonus, it only took me half as long as the bus would have. So I reckoned that meant there was time to drink more. I reached into my bag, plucked out a Miller Lite, and popped the cap. A few swigs later, I tucked the empty bottle under my seat.

Stepping out into the rain, I threw my bag over my shoulder and fished my two sticks from the backseat. By the time I pressed the walk light on the street corner, I was drenched, my bag waterlogged.

Relieved of the pelting by the comforts of the indoors, I wound down to the basement level of the arena. A girl about my age walked past. To my right, the door to a locker room sat wide open. She appeared to have come from that direction. I figured that was probably where I needed to be.

I started and then stopped, collecting myself before walking in. Much like an actor, I needed to prepare. To me, the team locker room was, in and of itself, a sort of stage. It required a certain performance to fit in.

I was always quiet in the locker room. I kept to myself. But this was a new team and a whole new set of people, so I had to at least try not to look like a depressed alcoholic. As I turned the corner, I was struck by the informal environment. I walked in, and nobody even noticed. I knew I was in the right place.

Finally, I could drop my bag to the floor. As I did, the feeling in my fingertips rushed back down my arm, spreading a wave of tingling through my hand. I shook it off as I parked down on the bench.

I wasn't telling anyone about my goalie history. I just wanted to skate, so I got myself ready to go. First I put on the shorts, then the garter belt, the shin guards and straps, the long socks over my shin guards, and the hockey pants, or "breezers." Then the skates, shoulder pads, elbow pads, and finally, the jersey.

Like clockwork I completed the routine I'd performed hundreds of times before. I pulled my jersey over my head and sat down on the bench with my helmet in my hands, waiting for the signal to get ready.

The giggly voices of my new teammates surrounded me. They all seemed to either know each other or be socially vivacious. I was already on the outside—and drunk to boot. None of them were drunk.

I started to wonder if I'd made the right decision. What if I couldn't even skate when I got out there? I might have been able to put on my equipment without thinking about it, but what about play? I hadn't skated as a forward for over two years.

I'd skated many open hockey sessions back in Sioux City while drunk, but that was as a goalie. Playing forward was different. I'm not as agile as a forward as I am as a goalie.

I tugged at the chin strap of my helmet. A voice interrupted my silent concern.

"Hey!" it said.

A girl plopped down next to me. I looked up at her. With a piercing below her bottom lip and another in her nose, she looked at me silent, grinning ear to ear. I couldn't help but smile back—or be distracted by her hair. She had, of all things, dreadlocks.

I'd never seen such a hairstyle on a white, college-aged woman before. It suddenly made her very intriguing.

"Did you go to Gustavus?" she asked, pointing at my jersey.

I looked down at my white top. "Yeah . . . yeah, I did."

"When were you there?"

"'98 until last year."

"Really? Do you know Diana Connor?"

A huge smile swept across my face. "I love Diana!"

"We played hockey and went to high school together," she said. "We've been friends since middle school."

I shook my head. "Wow. It's a small world. We played together briefly freshman year at Gustavus and got to be pretty good friends." We sat silent, absorbing the coincidence.

I couldn't believe it. Here was this girl I'd never even met before, and of all people, she'd been friends with Diana, the one who had, in essence, helped me get the help I needed during the fall of my freshman year. Diana wasn't at Gustavus long, but she had a huge influence on my life during that short period of time. I missed keeping in touch with her.

I shook my head as I smiled. "Do you still talk to her?"

"Yeah, we just talked the other week."

I nodded. "Cool."

"I'm Krissy, by the way," she said.

"Jen." We shook hands.

"Nice to meet you."

She bounced to her feet. "I'm sure we'll chat some more later." I nodded, picked my helmet back up, and started twiddling with the chin straps again.

"Alright, ladies," a voice said. "Let's all gather around and say our introductions. We've got some newbies in the room."

Sure enough, much of the team was already acquainted. One by one, the girls went around and introduced themselves. Apart from her name, year in school, and major, each person described her hockey history: how many years she had played, where, and for whom.

I sat quietly in the corner opposite Krissy, mentally preparing for my mini-speech, as the girls each took their turns. When the time arrived, I introduced myself and my history, glossing over, of course, those details that were either unflattering or unnecessary. All these girls needed to know was that I was still studying and still playing hockey.

My speech wound down, and the players shuffled. They seemed collectively excited. I could see it all over their faces what they were thinking. *She must be good.* But it just wasn't true.

As usual, I had more hockey experience than most people in the room. Not only had I skated longer than the majority of them, but I had also played on some elite teams. But much the way having three older siblings who all earned straight As set me up for great expectations before I ever entered a classroom, my rehashing of my hockey history set a bar. Before I even stepped on the ice with my team, I could sense it. They expected big things from me. Little did they know that my credentials looked far more impressive on paper than in reality. I was on the downward slope of my hockey career.

By the end of the first practice, it was confirmed. I'd lost my edge. I was drunk, out of shape, and flat out slow. I tried to stay positive about it. I was keeping up with the activity that once fueled my soul, and perhaps, even more important, I was also meeting some new people.

Still, I was only able to make it to practice sporadically. Whenever I was less than too far trashed, I'd lug my big ol' hockey bag to the car and drive drunk to the rink for some late-night ice time. Usually my game was subpar, and I was half in the tank. But at least it got me out doing something other than drinking.

One night in late November, after yet another late practice, I walked out of the arena with a few teammates, including Krissy. I zipped up my big red Columbia jacket as we walked out the front doors. Bag on my back, stick in hand, I walked hunched over, staring at the snowy pavement beneath my feet as my pals around me engaged in conversation about a party. Krissy turned to me.

"Hey, you're gonna come, right, Jen?"

I wasn't actually expecting to be invited to any party. I was more prepared to hear about it, not get invited, then go home, and get pickled on my own tab, in the privacy of my apartment. I preferred to drink alone.

I was surprised to be invited, but I couldn't risk making an ass out of myself at some party. I'd been in that situation too many times.

"Nah, that's okay," I said, looking at Krissy. "I don't think I'll make it. Thanks, though."

I gave a nod to confirm my decision.

"Good night, everybody." Veering off from the group, I headed toward my car. Krissy followed.

"Do you have plans? You should come," she said.

"No, no. I really don't think that's a good idea," I said again. "Me, parties—bad things tend to happen."

She pressed the issue, not taking no for an answer. Finally, I folded.

After several hours of drinking, it was time to call it a night. I was in no position to be driving, though, and Krissy knew it. She ordered me to the couch and instructed me to get comfortable.

Already asleep on the foldout sofa was Crystal, another teammate, a more straight-edged sort who had only taken in a few wine coolers before calling it quits. She awoke to see me crawl in bed next to her, then rolled over the other way.

Within just a few minutes, the noise dwindled. The last of the partygoers drifted out the doorway as Krissy locked the doors. Her roommate disappeared to her room. Without all the people to create warmth, the temperature started to drop. Krissy had mentioned that their heater didn't work so well. I was starting to understand what she meant when she said she threw parties to create heat.

Shivering under the thin blanket, I pulled up the sheets. Krissy walked by.

"Cold, isn't it?" she said. "I'm really sorry."

"It's a little chilly. But I'll be fine."

Crystal sprang up in bed. "Well, I want an extra blanket. I'm cold."

Krissy looked around her for a remedy to the problem. "Umm . . . I don't have any more blankets, I don't think." She reached for the pile of coats. "But here, I'll throw these over you." Jackets in hand, she draped one over my sleeping partner and then came around to my side.

"Thanks for tucking me in," Crystal said, laughing.

Krissy tossed my jacket over me and pulled it up under my chin. I smiled. "Now it's just my nose that'll be cold."

Standing over me, Krissy smiled and leaned in closer. I looked up at her. Our lips met, and we kissed.

It surprised us both. It was an accident. To this day, Krissy swears she leaned in to kiss my cold nose. I swear she aimed for my lips. Either way, accidental or not, we kissed.

Krissy backed up, looked at me, then Crystal, then back to me. "Whoa," she said. "Uh . . ."

"Ugh. Just get a room, would ya?" Crystal threw a pillow over her head and flopped over to the other side. I sat silently, unsure what the hell had just transpired. Krissy stood at the foot of the bed, seemingly wondering the same. "Well . . . uh, good night," she said. She disappeared into her bedroom.

After the kiss, we decided to spend more time at my place, where we had a heater. We also started dating. There was only one problem: she was leaving the country in just a few weeks for seven months.

Somehow, through the holidays, the frigid winter, and the thaw of the spring, I waited. I'm not sure how. I was a drunk. I could've ended up in anyone else's bed or with anyone else in mine. Instead, for the first time in my life, I stayed faithful. Tried and true. I waited for her.

It actually worked out well. I could stay at home and focus on getting inebriated, rather than trying to find some kind of affection at the bar to make my nights feel less lonely. In her absence, I drank even more, studied just enough, and took on only as many hours as a cashier and stocker at the grocery store up the street as I needed in order to keep the bills paid and my tummy full of beer.

I was being afforded a fresh start at a new school in a city I loved. I could've spent more time focusing on career paths and internships. Instead, I thought more about how to conceal my intoxication when arriving drunk at work at 4 PM.

Sometimes, I couldn't conceal it entirely. Of course I brushed my teeth and chewed gum before ever setting foot in the workplace, and luckily, never once did anyone call me out or accuse me of being inebriated. But the problem was apparent in my psychology. If I was scheduled 4 to 8, I'd drink about six beers before walking the few blocks over to the store. If I drank any more than five or six, I feared I'd start to slur, stumble, and perhaps blow my cover.

That was nowhere near sufficient for my needs, though. I needed twelve to sixteen a day to get my fill. It constituted most of my diet. Drinking six and walking away from the case for four hours to lose my buzz was not my idea of a good time. In fact, it sounded downright horrible.

My agitation often caused my attitude to suffer on the job. I didn't want to be there. Period. I wanted to be home drinking. Sometimes I'd arrange for just that. Whether I was making up some sort of plumbing emergency or simply reporting that I didn't feel well, I'd always find a way to get back to my apartment sooner than I was scheduled to. Even if it meant sprinting the three blocks back to my efficiency during my break period to chug down a beer or two, brush my teeth, and haul ass back to work thirty minutes later.

It was growing to be quite a problem. On the nights I wasn't scheduled to work, I'd either stay home alone and drink or go to the bar with Alix and her friends. Even they were getting tired of my antics, though.

Every time I opened my mouth, I seemed to be sticking my foot it in it. There was nothing anybody could do to stop me from drinking myself stupid anymore. I was living on my own, with all the freedom to get fucked up that I wanted. As long as I paid my bills and kept my grades up, nobody was going to stop me from continuing in my ways.

Cocaine took everything from me very quickly. Alcohol just slowly sucked the life out of my veins. I didn't falter. I still functioned. I made the Dean's List, paid my rent, and spent every other waking hour getting hammered. It was starting to take its toll on me physically. Some days beer was my only meal. I'd scheduled my classes between 10 and 2, not too early, not too late. As soon as I'd get home, I'd crack a brew. If I was running low, I'd order more to be delivered to my door from the liquor store down the street.

More often than not, I'd find myself tanked by 6 PM. Sometimes to such a degree I couldn't stand it. I absolutely felt sick and nauseous. But no matter how much beer I drank, I'd lost my puking reflex. My body just learned to keep taking it unless I forced it back out. The saddest part is that, even after all that, I'd drink more. Sometimes with the taste of toothpaste still swimming along my tongue.

I'd lost all ability to even remotely monitor my alcohol intake. I was no longer trying to control it. I was trying to get as far from reality as possible by getting as fucked up as I could get. The more fucked up I got, the worse I felt. The worse I felt, especially about myself, the more I wanted to get fucked up. It's that vicious cycle of addiction that's so hard to stop.

20

Moping at Mayo

There had to be some kind of explanation, something other than lupus or mixed connective tissue disease. Even if one of those things was, in part, responsible for the deterioration in her health, how could it possibly be causing all of the dislocations?

At the urging of her hip surgeon, my mom made a trip to the Mayo Clinic in Rochester. I joined her and quickly became a regular at the local bars. I was twenty-two years old—old enough to get drunk but too young to be the closest thing my mom had to a caretaker. It was becoming unbearable to see her so sick, and now even the best doctors in the world didn't know why.

Her initial visit was supposed to be nothing more than a consultation with an orthopedic surgeon. She met with him, and he looked at her X-rays from home, instructing her to come back in two weeks, when he could perform revision surgery. But first he wanted her to get a set of X-rays done.

By the time Mayo finished wheeling her around and conducting tests, they had no choice but to admit her. Not only was her hip dislocated at the time of the X-ray, but her entire pelvic bone was shattered—so much so that they couldn't even put her hip back in its socket. There was no denying the fact that she had been in some serious pain. How she put up with *that* much pain, I'll never understand.

The seriousness of the situation came as a surprise to us all. In good conscience, the Mayo Clinic couldn't let her go. They had to not only fix her hip and her shattered pelvis but figure out why on earth her hip replacement had gone so horribly wrong.

I was trying to keep up with school and keep it together, bouncing back and forth between Rochester and the Twin Cities. It was easier said than done.

> 11/23/02   11 pm
> I'm at the bar again. Man, this sucks. My poor mom.
> It's been a rough day. No homework done, nothing
> productive. I just bopped in and out of her room all
> day, trying to keep my head on straight. This whole
> circumstance is fucked up. This bartender is good to
> me, though. I just wish I was sitting in a bar for fun
> and not because my mom is seriously ill in the Mayo
> Clinic. I guess because of my own disease, I shouldn't
> be in a bar at all. But it would be hard to go out to
> dinner and not be in a place where I could get drunk.
> Not that I eat anyway. I hate this. My mom is sick and
> all I have to get my mind off things is alcohol.

I sat in the corner, downing pints, scribbling my frustrations in my notebook. Two hours later, at closing time, it was time to head out. The bartender had been bringing my pints to the table, and it had been a good while since I last stood up.

I struck up some internal dialogue to convince myself I was sure enough on foot to stand up and walk without drawing unwanted attention. First, I had to plan my route. Navigating the hallway and getting to the bathroom seemed much more negotiable than the maze of chairs separating me from the front door. I decided to hit the ladies' room and collect myself before my departure.

As soon as I arose, I felt the intoxication set in. The room spun. I tried to be cool. Hands propped on the table, I pushed myself upright and flexed my knees to grip the wobbling floor beneath my feet. One foot in front of the other, I staggered to the bathroom.

By the time I walked out, a half hour had passed. I'd called Krissy. I'm not sure why I called her from the bathroom, nor do I remember what I said, but I'd made her very angry. And why not? I was supposed to have called her much earlier. Instead I called her drunk as a skunk at 1 AM, unruly and as disrespectful as could be. She was back home at our apartment by herself, worried about me and my safety.

There was no reason for me to be such a bitch. I hung up on her, stormed out of the bar, and headed back to the hotel just a block away. I lit up a smoke and stumbled to my destination before I ever had a chance to finish it. After snuffing it out, I pulled my key from my pocket and headed right to the elevator, then straight to my room.

The green light lit up. I pushed down the door handle and leaned forward. Tripping over the ottoman, I threw a hand up to brace myself on the protrusion of wall separating the sleeping area from the living area. My eyes melted into the flowery pattern on the bedspread.

I let go and crashed forward, flat on my face.

A LOUD SERIES of knocks rattled me awake.

Bang. Bang. Bang. "Housekeeping!"

I opened my eyes, shielding them from the slivered beam of sun slicing through the shades. Three more pounds on the door. "I'm still sleeping. Come back later," I said. The voice silenced.

Hand drawn to my face, I wiped the streaks of drool from my chin and cheek, rolled over on my back, and sat up. I was still wearing my coat. My pants, cold and damp, were sticking to my skin. What had happened? Had I gotten night sweats on the lower half of my body?

I got up to my feet and removed my jacket. The bottom of it felt wet, just like my pants. As I marched my cold, soggy self to the bathroom, a wafting scent of urine twisted my nose hairs.

That confirmed it: my drunk ass had wet the bed. It's the only time anything like that ever happened. But I can only wonder how high my blood alcohol level must have been. It was embarrassing, but, in retrospect, I know it was a sign of my disease. My alcoholism was becoming very serious. I was no longer eating. I was just drinking—as much as I could, as quickly as I could—to avoid feeling anything at all.

The longer my mom stayed at Mayo, the more I drank. Thankfully, my sister, Chris, ten years older than I and a veterinarian, came to the rescue. She flew in from Detroit and stayed by our mom's side for weeks. Her help couldn't have been more appreciated. I needed to return to Minneapolis for class. John was also busy studying the week before Thanksgiving. With Chris down in Rochester, we could tie up our loose ends before heading down to be with her for the holiday. All together, me, John, Chris, and Krissy spent Thanksgiving by my mom's side, with Mom dazed and confused from the morphine drip and me drunk as a skunk.

The holiday weekend came and went, and the hospital had performed every test in the book. There was just no explanation for what was happening to her. When it was all said and done, she got her hip and her pelvis fixed, but no answers as to what was causing her progressive problems.

I returned to Minneapolis, unsure of how to help her or myself. For another year, I sank. Krissy held on as I spiraled ever deeper into the abyss of my alcoholism. Amy even came back into my life. In all our drunkenness, we ended up hooking up.

I knew if I didn't get my act together, I was going to lose the best thing I ever had going for me. Krissy delivered an ultimatum: get sober, or it's over.

21

A Sober Decision

I was starting to loathe myself.

I was also starting to feel like a victim. I'd grown tired of fight-clubbing with my addiction. No matter how hard I fought back, it always seemed to win. It was kicking my ass.

After escaping crack, I'd told everyone during my college years that I'd never make it to thirty. I was sure everything would catch up with me, and I was starting to wonder when. My future I perceived to be nothing more than an unavoidable reality as a lifelong drug addict and alcoholic. Addiction was a part of me—haunting, controlling, owning me. It was only a matter of time before it killed me.

I couldn't stand to have it inside me anymore. I grew increasingly frustrated that I was seemingly "stuck" in this world, living the life I was, in the body I was in. Addiction was destroying every aspect of my being. It was always going to be with me. Or, was it?

Slowly, my thinking started to shift. I wondered why I had to keep living such a life. Why did I have to keep thinking like a victim? Why did I have to be such a sorry addict? I was sick of it.

I'd destroyed my life and my family's life, and I'd become a burden on the friends who'd supported me. I was tired of being the jackass who made rude remarks while fall down drunk, sick of getting drunk again the next day in part to try and forget about what I thought I remembered about the night before. I was just plain sick and tired of feeling so sick and tired.

All my anger turned inward. I'd really screwed up my life. I'd turned into a disrespectful asshole. I'd pushed away the people closest to me and become a sullen, withdrawn, bitter woman with a beer belly, one whose pale skin hadn't seen a tan for years.

I hated myself, and I couldn't take it anymore. I couldn't stand the idea of being an addict or alcoholic for the rest of my life. I didn't want to be the person I'd become. I was just about ready to give a middle finger to life and try again to rid myself from the world when it hit me: I had the power to change.

I didn't, I realized, have to live that way at all. I didn't have to be a practicing alcoholic or drug addict. I could change that. In fact, I was good enough at it that I didn't have to "practice" it at all anymore. And if I could change that, then I could change the decisions I made each day. I could change the way I looked at myself. And I could change how I looked at the fact that I was still living and breathing. It was a powerful discovery.

I no longer had to look at drugs and alcohol as something delicious and sensual that I'd somehow be missing out on if I didn't partake in them. What good had drugs and alcohol done for me other than destroy every area of my life? What would I be missing if they were gone?

For the first time, I answered the questions convincingly to myself: *nothing.* I would be missing absolutely nothing if I silenced my addiction. I wouldn't be depriving myself of anything. I would, on the contrary, be freeing myself to live a healthy life.

As my internal conversations with my addiction started to grow more heated in January 2004, I grew even angrier. This time, though, something felt different. I wasn't angry at myself, my family, or my behavior while intoxicated. I wasn't beating myself up or allowing my addiction to seduce me. I was just flat out angry at my disease—for everything it had done to me.

Finally, I made a decision. I decided to get more than sober. I decided to get well.

On a balmy 20-degree Monday in February 2004, I voluntarily embarked upon my eighth rehab—an outpatient program at a hospital near our apartment.

The odds were stacked against me. The counselors expressed doubt about my ability to stay sober on an outpatient level. They were also concerned about whether I could safely quit drinking, given the amount I'd been taking in. I declined inpatient treatment, explaining that I'd have better success if I maintained contact with the outside world while trying to stay sober. If I went inpatient, I'd most likely just get out, not be able to handle the temptation of bars and liquor stores, give in, and get drunk. I needed to get sober in spite of triggers rather than while secluded from them.

"We'll give it a try," they said. I don't think they believed the desperation in my fight.

I wasn't about to fail again. I was ready to change. I'd made the decision to turn my life around, and there was nothing that was gonna stop me.

First things first, though: I needed to get the alcohol out of my system.

IN THE HEART of winter, Krissy started up my old battered Honda, escorted me the few miles to the nearby hospital, and dropped me off for my first night of treatment. It was also my first night sober in years.

"You're gonna make it, Jen," she said, coming to a stop outside the front door of the behavioral health building on campus. "I believe in you."

I took a final drag off my smoke and snuffed it out in the ashtray. "Thanks, sweetie," I said. I grabbed hold of her hand and looked her in the eyes. "I'm ready to fight it this time."

Once upstairs, I got settled in with my group in a square, stuffy office filled with twelve chairs and the counselor Karen's desk. A single desk lamp lit the room as darkness started to fall on the early evening.

In a circle of chairs once more, all I could think was how badly I wanted out. I didn't want to be sitting there, hearing stories about alcohol. I was the only one in the group with any illegal drug history. I felt out of place surrounded by older patients whose consequences for their addictions seemed far fewer than mine.

"Hi. My name's Tom, and I'm an alcoholic."

"Hi Tom."

Another story.

The clock ticked audibly during the moments of silence accompanying the storytelling. I tuned out the words, but every tick of the second hand drilled into my brain.

Tick, tock, tick, tock.

I was already jumping in my skin; hearing someone else cry about beer wasn't helping my agitation in the slightest. Tom continued.

I started humming a tune in my head, but his words were making their way to my ears anyway.

That chemical sweat started to seep from my skin once more. I took a deep breath and tried to relax. But I couldn't stop the anxiety. Maybe I did need to be inpatient. This was no place for me.

I inched forward on my chair, propped my forearms on my thighs, and hung my head, tapping my foot against the leg of the chair. I looked down at my hands clasped in front of me. I was still shaking.

The subtle tremor radiating through my hands and fingertips gnawed at my sense of inner equilibrium. I could feel myself trembling, and it looked as if it was visible. I tried to make it stop but couldn't. I retreated on my seat, leaned back, withdrew my hands, and folded my arms in front of me. I couldn't let it show.

At the end of the night, Karen, a middle-aged woman shorter than I am, pulled me aside. Stale coffee and cigarette smoke lingered in the air as the other clients filtered toward the exits. "So how are you feeling tonight, physically?" she asked. She took off her glasses and wiped them with her shirt.

"I'm doin' alright," I said, tucking my still shaky palms in my pockets.

"Really?"

"Yeah. I guess I feel a little shaky, but that doesn't surprise me. I'll be okay." I leaned up against the wall to steady myself.

She watched before giving me a look of concern. "If that gets any worse, you'll need to go to the hospital. You could go into seizures from alcohol withdrawal."

"Oh, no. I'm fine. I'll be fine."

"Jennifer, I'm serious. Alcohol is a dangerous drug. It's very important that you get medical help if you're experiencing severe withdrawals."

She paused.

"Can you make me a promise that you'll get to the hospital if things get any worse?"

She had no idea yet how deeply I despised hospitals. I would just as soon drink to fix it than check into the hospital.

Deflated, I conceded. "Okay, if things get really bad, I'll go to the hospital."

I assured her that I'd be fine, that I had Krissy by my side to help should any serious withdrawal issues arise. With that, we said our good-byes. But as I walked off to battle my first night without alcohol, I could feel the skepticism in the air. She seemed to be worried about more than just my potential for seizures; she seemed to doubt whether I'd even come back for a second day. With the taste of beer tricking and tantalizing my taste buds, I was starting to wonder myself.

A wicked cold wind blasted my body as I passed through the revolving doors to make my way outside. Sitting out in the parking lot was Krissy, waiting to escort me home.

She'd stay by my side for the rest of the night, holding me tight as the shakes blistered me. She was on a mission to get sober with me. Even though alcohol wasn't causing her any troubles, she wanted to support me fully. It's a rare level of support to receive, and I embraced it.

Once I'd smoked a sufficient number of cigarettes, I curled up in bed to try to sleep. Krissy curled up right next to me, vowing to stay awake just as long as I did.

My eyes closed. I tossed and turned, kicking off the covers when my internal thermostat turned up and huddling back underneath when the shivering set in. No matter what I did, though, I couldn't find any balance. I was too hot, too cold, too uncomfortable to sleep. The numbers on the clock kept changing. I tossed about, twisting with the sheets as I rolled over. I was starting to smell the alcohol in my sweat. The subtle drone of the heating system, normally so easily ignored, rattled my eardrums. I pulled the pillow over my head and rolled over once more.

Finally, after what felt like hours, I shot straight up in bed, pushed the covers off, and sighed, exasperated.

"Can we turn the temperature down?"

I looked over at Krissy, half asleep next to me, trying her mightiest to stay awake and alert until whatever time I had drifted off soundly. She would've had to wait all night. It didn't matter the temperature in the room; my body was at war, and it wasn't about to let me rest yet.

I stepped out on the porch into the subzero temps and lit up a smoke. It was gonna be a long night.

THE NEXT EVENING at group, I was greeted with the same questions about the severity of my shaking.

"I'm okay," I kept saying. I was. I was far more concerned about when it would stop than if it would get worse. Day three wasn't much different. The shakiness was sticking around, but at least it was steady in its severity.

Thursday, however, turned out to be a whole different day. I was growing more and more uncomfortable in my skin. I made it to treatment. I talked about how I felt. I knew I had to be close to getting beyond the physical part of the detox process.

It was my head that was messing with me, though.

Krissy dropped me off, but she wasn't able to pick me up. She had to work. And since I'd announced to the group that I still hadn't gotten my license back after my 2001 arrest, I figured that pulling away in a vehicle would be an ill-advised move. Besides, it was just a few blocks over to the mall, where I could catch a bus straight back to the apartment. Save for my drunk driving to the rink, I'd gotten used to taking the bus in my three years without a license. It seemed like a much more sensible option.

Once group finished up and we said our good-byes for the weekend, I headed for the door. Trudging through the snow, I made my way through the blustery lot and huddled inside a barely heated bus shelter. I had fifteen minutes to wait.

I took a seat on the frozen bench, zipped up my jacket, and tucked my nose into the warm pocket created by the collar. The feeling started to return to my face as I peered out across the parking lot at the dusty waves of snow whipping in the brisk wind. It didn't look so inviting. Across the street, a neon sign flashed one word: liquor.

I'd worked up some heat walking through the snow and wind, but now I was losing it. I needed to move. Fifteen minutes is a long time to kill. It's also just enough time to pick up a twelve-pack.

I didn't want to do it. I didn't want to give in. But before I could even stop myself, I was up on my feet and on my way to the liquor store. Pretty soon I was closer to the store than the shelter.

The wind rushed my face, brushing harsh strokes across my exposed ears as I trudged across the lot. My addiction was governing my actions, and I felt helpless to stop what I knew was a bad decision. I was operating on autopilot.

Ka-ching. I made the purchase, clutched the paper bag, and rushed back to the bus stop, twelve cans of Miller Lite in hand. I started to grow paranoid. What if somebody from my treatment group saw me with this mysterious paper bag? Who cared about them? What the fuck was I doing? This wasn't what I wanted at all.

Just as my body heat started to fade, the bus arrived. I grabbed hold of my sack, took a seat near the back, and leaned up against the glass. As I stared out at the city passing by, hand propped on the twelve-pack in the seat next to me, time seemed to slow.

Like a movie montage in which happy couples appear in every direction, alcohol seemed to follow me. A liquor store or bar sat at every street corner. The condensation glowed on the bottles on the billboards. A rider walked to the back of the bus dragging the smell of beer with him. The entire ride home, my addiction was calling me. It was trying to seduce me again.

I yanked on the lever to call for a stop. The backdoor opened, and I dashed outside, straight down the block toward my empty apartment. The door slammed shut. Like a starving animal I tore open the twelve-pack and fished out a can. I cracked it open, raised it to my lips, and then, without taking a single sip, pushed it away and set it on the coffee table.

My heart raced just as fast as my mind as I stood, paralyzed by my actions.

2/12/04   8:34 pm

After three days sober, almost four, and four days of treatment, I bought beer. I have one open in front of me, staring at me. I'm staring back. I'm smelling it, feeling the can, everything but drinking it. Do I want to do this?

Fuck. I had a drink, now what? It tastes so good, but do I want to do this? I'm shaking with fear and disappointment, but also anticipation. This is the first night since starting outpatient that Krissy hasn't been home with me. It's hard to be alone while try-ing not to drink. This treatment hasn't been the best but goddamn it, I should be able to do this! What the fuck is wrong with me? Why do I keep running back to this terrible drug? It fell in love with me and I fell in love with it. Does it taste as good as I recall? No,

not really. Funny, my brain just told me that might be
because I'm drinking cans, not bottles. Bullshit. It has
me. But, physically, if I've learned anything in the last
three days, it's that I can handle the withdrawal. It's
all in my head now. My head is what's telling me to
drink now.

I'm smart, but I have to learn to outthink my brain
with my heart. I know that when I put my heart into
something, I can achieve it.

So I had a little set back tonight. I'll be damned if
I'm gonna let that stop me. 4½ beers now. Do I feel
any better? No, not at all. I feel like I fucked up again.
I can't stay sober for more than four days?

Oh yes I can. Oh yes I can. Oh. Yes. I. Can. Just
watch me.

I was scarcely tipsy, but I'd had enough. I was done—the love
affair was over. It stopped right there.

I picked up the half-full can still sitting on the coffee table, took
it to the kitchen, and dumped it down the drain. With the taste of
beer still on my lips, I vowed never to give into its call again. One by
one, I dumped the remaining cans, rinsed them out, and returned
them to their place in the twelve-pack. Once they were all empty,
I marched them downstairs to the recycle bin. Down they went.
Never to return again.

I'd made up my mind. If I could quit crack, then I could quit
drinking, and finally I was ready to give it up for good.

My index finger traced along the pasty brown and yellow wallpaper as I marched down the hallway toward my apartment. My chest
started to puff up as I unexpectedly developed an urge to cry. I flung
open the door and leaned up against it as it closed behind me.

I slid down the door like the tears on my cheeks, melting into a
puddle on the floor. With my head in my hands, I started to sob. The
silence in the air felt magnified. Just as I started to fall apart, I looked
up, right at Krissy. She kneeled down in front of me, offered me her
hand, and helped me to my feet. I let go and fell apart in her arms.

I didn't have to fight anymore. I had a supportive partner who
would stay sober with me and help me. And most importantly, I
had the desire to help myself. It was over. I was confronting my

addiction and there was no turning back anymore. For the first time in my life, I decided to devote myself wholly and completely to my sobriety. And for the first time, I had the support to actually follow through on it.

It was February 12, 2004. I haven't had a sip since.

I DON'T GO to Alcoholics Anonymous, Narcotics Anonymous, or any twelve-step groups. The program works for a lot of people, and I have nothing against it. But it's not my thing. When I got sober, I made a decision to move forward, not live in the past.

I just live my life, and I live it on my terms. I'm certainly not perfect. Like most true addicts, I still sometimes gaze longingly over at my addiction as it stands in the shadows, whispering my name and calling me to rejoin it. But I know that, underneath it all, the seductive whispers are complete and absolute lies.

My disease only wants to drag me down. I know it's always there, ready to tease and flirt with me. I respect it for its power and remind myself why I can't give into its calls again. Addiction tried to kill me, and it almost succeeded. I can't trust it anymore. In the end, it's up to me to decide whether or not I want to let it back in my life.

In the early weeks of my sobriety, I felt pretty miserable, both physically and emotionally. Those episodes had started to come back—the ones where I'd lose consciousness and wake up on the floor. I was sure they'd go away. I just needed to do something to quiet the energy pent up inside me. Then it occurred to me: before addiction destroyed my life, I'd been an athlete.

Exercise seemed like a great way to not only start feeling better about myself and my body but tap into that lost athlete inside. In the basement of our apartment building, right next to the pool, was a gym, complete with a treadmill and other workout equipment. I ventured daily to the basement to swim a few laps or lift a few weights. Exertion seemed to help me deal with the anxiety riddling my newly sober body.

Then, one day, for no particular reason, I got on the treadmill. I'd never liked running. In fact, as a hockey player, I avoided it as much as possible. But I also knew it was a good way to get a workout.

At first the treadmill was merely a barometer for my fitness. If I could run a mile, I reckoned, then I must be in pretty good shape. During my first few attempts, I was only able to jog about a quarter mile before needing to stop. At twenty-three and with five years of beer jiggling around my belly, I was far from an athlete anymore.

BUT AFTER SIX weeks of daily exercise and eating right, and without the fifteen hundred or so calories a day I was consuming in alcohol, the weight started to drip off. I could fit more comfortably in my old jeans and was slipping happily into a whole new external shell. I peered out from inside my brand new skin, feeling healthier and more refreshed than I'd ever felt before.

By the end of March, the spring sun was melting the winter snow-pack. The thaw was also bringing on a serious case of cabin fever. I'd been cooped up inside that apartment, dusty and tarnished by the leftover aroma of stale beer, all winter long. In that time, I'd gotten myself together. I had to put school on hold again to do it, but I'd finally succeeded in getting sober.

And I'd started to fall in love with running.

I dug out my running shoes from the closet and sat down to lace them up. I walked out the door and jogged the half dozen blocks to the pathways along Lake Calhoun. It was gorgeous out. Life, nature, and the beauty of it all commanded me to pay attention. I took a deep breath in and held it for a moment while listening to a songbird in the distance. The laughter of kids passing on their bikes provided a second melodic line.

I'd lost myself in the moment. But, in that moment, I found myself. And, for the first time in my life, I found myself at peace. Everything was in its place.

I WENT BACK to school.

Finally, I'd jumped through the hoops and cut all the red tape. I finished up that last class and completed my college degree.

After graduating, I enrolled in a post-baccalaureate paralegal program to become more employable. I breezed through the program and in early 2006 got a job at a law firm, working on behalf of people who'd been discriminated against in the workplace. It seemed like a perfect fit for me, the champion of the underdog.

I also kept running. In fact, running was becoming such a part of my life that I decided to run a race. Not just any race but a half marathon: 13.1 miles.

I AWOKE ON the morning of the race, lit up a smoke, and walked outside to gauge the weather conditions. I nearly choked on the thickness in the air. It wasn't in my cigarette but in the hazy sky. It was as humid and heavy as I'd ever felt air to be. To make matters worse, it was also 75 degrees. For running conditions, it was oppressive.

Nevertheless, I followed the herd and headed toward the starting line. When the gun went off, I sprinted forward. The miles blurred by. The first few were easy. Then each mile became more difficult than the one before. I pushed myself until I could push no more.

Finally, it all got to be too much. I stopped, put my hands on my knees, and hung my head. The salty flavor of sweat singed the back of my throat as I stood under the scorching sun, panting fiercely in the muggy air. I picked up my heavy head and put my arms on top of it. One foot in front of the other, I could only settle back into a slow walking pace.

I'd hit mile 11 of my first half marathon and my Jell-o–like legs simply wouldn't go anymore. They were threatening to buckle right underneath me. I was ready to curl up on the side of the road until whatever time someone came to scrape me off the pavement. I was roadkill.

Suddenly, an unfamiliar female voice shouted at me, "Don't stop! You've come too far to quit now!"

I absorbed the remark and walked a few more steps, hands on my hips. I wasn't convinced. The fried food permeating the air caused my stomach to flip-flop. I had nothing left in the tank.

The voice came back. "Don't give up! You're almost there! You can do this!"

The sun pressed down on my exhausted and dehydrated body. Who was this lady? She didn't know me or how I felt. I was ready to collapse, and here she was playing the role of personal cheerleader.

I looked over at her. She was an everyday woman in running shorts with a sleek build, sunglasses, and a green visor. She could've been anyone's mom or sister. Now she was walking by my side, screaming in my ear to let me know just how strongly she believed in me.

She offered me a cup of water. I raised it up and dumped it over my head, wiping the cool drops from my brow with my forearm.

"Thanks," I said, smiling.

I dropped the cup and picked up my pace to jogging speed. As I trotted off, I realized that she understood exactly how I was feeling.

She might not have been walking in my shoes, but she was by my side supporting me, and she knew I could pull through it.

At one point in time, nobody believed in me. Everyone expected me to fail; expected me to stay sick. I'd proved them wrong.

She was right, though. I *could* finish this race, and I *could* reach my goal. If I could battle through the darkest depths of depression and a deadly addiction, and come out the other side a better, stronger person, then I could surely run two more miles.

I'd come too far in my two years of sobriety to quit now. I was earning back trust. People were starting to believe in me again. I loved my job and had just bought a home with Krissy. My mom's hip problems turned out to be the result of faulty implants, and she was getting stronger. I'd even started to develop a relationship with my dad.

I'd come out victorious. I was exactly where I wanted to be: on top of the world.

I pressed on, for half a mile, then a mile, then two. With more than two years of sobriety behind me, I crossed the finish line of my first half marathon feeling like I was in a fairy tale.

I THOUGHT I'D escaped my past, that I'd gotten off scot-free. I had done my time and made my amends and could breathe easy again. There was nothing more for me to feel guilty or sorry about, no reason to live in fear that the other shoe was about to drop.

But then, just as the leaves turned in the fall of 2006, it did. My body finally got my attention. It had been alerting me for years that something was wrong. Yes, I had those occasional spells when I'd wake up on the floor, wondering how I got there. But they were rare enough to ignore. It was when the pain set in that I could no longer shove my body's problems all under the rug.

PART TWO

22

Weight on My Shoulders

I thought it was my shoulder and nothing more. After all the dislocations, both partial and complete, I could feel my body starting to rebel. That couldn't explain why I'd started having trouble swallowing of course, but I chalked that little issue up to the half-a-pack-a-day smoking habit and nothing more.

The general doc I'd seen about it sent me out the door with an antidepressant, Cymbalta, designed to work on depression-related pain. Perhaps then, that's all this was: depression.

It started as a dull ache, right around my shoulder joint. Usually, it only bothered me while at work, where I sat at a desk forty hours a week at a computer station without a keyboard tray. It wasn't the best setup for anyone, but I wasn't getting much sympathy from my employer, either. Out of necessity, I purchased my own workstation accommodations, including a keyboard tray. I asked them to install it, but they refused. I returned the tray and tried working with a low-back cushion, foot rest, wrist rest, and neck rest. One by one, my remedies failed.

I'd been working in pain for over a year when, finally, I broke down and purchased a pricey Herman Miller chair, right out of my own pocket. Unlike the chairs in the office, it didn't cause me to cry in pain. It was an expensive solution, but it seemed to be worth it.

The firm refused to offer me any accommodations beyond finding me a different chair within the office. At the time I understood. They were taking on big defense lawyers and sending every penny out the door. The only time they made money was when they won a case. They were willing to risk every last penny to get that big payout in the end, so there was no room for them to be buying fancy, ergonomically designed office supplies. We, as employees, were expected to take one for the good of the team.

I had no idea where this was coming from, though, this unbearable and gnawing ache that was taking over my upper body. It never used to bother me to sit in the office chair provided. It was a relatively decent chair. Why, all of a sudden, could I not sit without hurting so badly? Why, I also wondered, did it seem to help to slouch?

With my body sunk low, I could not only prop up my upper back and neck, but also position myself a little differently, in a way that allowed my shoulder blades to splay out and roll forward. It relieved the immediate pain, but it's a horrible posture. It's an abnormal posture; and, even when seated in a chair that didn't make me hurt, I couldn't stop doing it. I tried to sit up straight, hold my shoulders back, and behave like a professional in the workplace. Within minutes, I was involuntarily slouching back down again.

By the time the summer heat hit, I couldn't hold up my own body anymore. It was mind-boggling. The new chair helped, but I was still in a world of hurt. My whole right arm was getting intermittently numb and tingly. It also felt hot and swollen. I had to get my shoulder checked on.

For the first time in seven years, I scheduled a visit with an orthopedic surgeon. After everything my mom and I had been through, both individually and together, the orthopedic office was the last place I wanted to go. But there seemed to be no other explanation. My arm was shot because of my shoulder joint. At least, that's what I thought.

A sports orthopedic specialist who worked a lot with athletes, Dr. Solomon had a different opinion. He didn't think there was a single muscle working right in my shoulder. After seeing the severity of the muscle dysfunction, he recommended a round of physical therapy to address weakness and imbalance. He also ordered an MRI of my shoulder, which showed the expected damage. There's the torn cartilage, known as a Bankart lesion, which can be surgically repaired. But there's another lesion called a Hill-Sachs lesion, which cannot.

A Hill-Sachs lesion forms when a person dislocates a shoulder multiple times. It causes a compression fracture in the ball of the arm that looks like a dent or a chip. It's not an issue unless it becomes large, but the more you dislocate it, the larger it gets. I didn't even have a Hill-Sachs lesion when I last had my shoulder imaged in 1999, and that test came after about five dislocations. I had roughly four more after that.

Dr. Solomon ordered some PT, which I followed through on for the next six weeks. He also wrote a letter to my employer and ordered them to provide me an ergonomic evaluation.

I returned to Dr. Solomon's office, having been given my two weeks' notice. I'd given the letter to my employer but never got any evaluation. Instead, I got the complete runaround. Then I got let go. It may or may not have had something to do with the letter, but the timing sure seemed odd. Either way, it left me out of a job, two weeks before Christmas, with only two weeks of severance—right when America's economy was on the verge of collapse.

Workers' comp. Unemployment. These are not friendly terms. I didn't know what to do. That job had been my pride and joy. I had worked damn hard to get to my life together, and when I lost that job, I lost more than just my financial security. I lost my psychological security as well.

I couldn't believe I'd actually gotten a job working at a place where I could stand up for the little guy and help those who'd been wronged. If people hadn't supported and helped me, I wouldn't have made it. I wanted to return the favor and be there to help others. Doing so, I discovered, helped me to find strength in everything I myself had been through. I thought I'd found my place—a place where I could help some people, where I never thought I'd have to worry about being treated poorly myself.

Instead, I spent the morning of my last day of work at Dr. Solomon's office. He was running late as usual. I sat idle in the fluorescent-lit exam room, arms folded, legs crossed, kicking my dangling left foot nervously in the air. I was growing impatient.

When the door finally opened, he'd already heard about my job predicament from his assistant and was none too happy.

For me it was all too much to think about. The day was hard enough as it was. I didn't want to be discussing job-related matters with the doctor while not in the office on my last day of work. I just wanted to know what he recommended for my arm.

"Can't you just fix this surgically?" I asked. "They told me over and over when I was younger to have it fixed."

"No," he said. He couldn't do that. He knew I had the structural issues but said they weren't enough to account for my other symptoms. For those, he thought, I needed to see a neck doctor.

So what problems I thought were confined to my shoulder were, according to the shoulder doctor, not related to my shoulder at all. Since Dr. Solomon could do nothing more for me until my apparent neck issues were resolved, I quickly followed up on his referral—even if the very idea of talking about my history of a neck injury was enough to make me want to run for the hills.

The neck doctor he referred me to was a physiatrist, or a doctor of physical medicine. Dr. Johnson uses invasive, nonsurgical approaches to treat neck problems. I went over all the facts of my history with his assistant, Anita. Much to my chagrin, I had to regurgitate the details of how I had injured my neck while so gloriously failing to off myself—to a woman my own age.

Once we finished up, she left and returned with Dr. Johnson. He entered, introduced himself, and said nothing further to me. He spoke to Anita as he looked at me and inspected my posture. She sat at the small built-in desk and took some notes.

"Sit up on the exam table here for me please," he said, pushing his glasses up his nose. With the tip of his shoe, he pulled a small step stool out from underneath the table. I stepped up on it and parked myself down on the paper sheet covering the exam table.

"Great. Now just sit as you would normally sit."

I assumed my usual posture.

He cocked his head, held his index finger to his chin, and tapped. "Hmm." He walked around to my right and observed me. Then around to my left to do the same. I started to grow anxious. I darted my eyes back and forth between the floor and the doctor, who was watching my every movement like a hawk.

He folded his arms and walked back to stand directly in front of me. "I see what you mean. There's a difference there." He said a few more words to Anita, shook my hand, and left the room, leaving me oblivious to whatever it was he had been observing. It felt inhumane, as if he were regarding me not as a patient or a human, but as a lab rat he was analyzing.

In the end, he referred me to a neurologist and prescribed more physical therapy. But his first recommendation? Drugs.

Not knowing really what else to do, I went along with it. He thought I could benefit from a facet joint injection, so that's what I agreed to have done. It wasn't without hesitation, though. Anita phoned me to let me know about the recommendation, so I had the opportunity to ask some questions, namely, what drugs were in the injection. More than one ended with the suffix "caine."

She assured me it was a perfectly safe procedure that they could do at one of their own facilities. It would, however, require that I be anesthetized.

Having shared everything I could with the doctor and his assistant about my history of blacking out, passing out, and overall intolerance to medication, I had to believe that they were taking those variables into consideration. And perhaps they were. Even still, my body didn't respond well to the anesthesia. I had no idea anything was even amiss when I was carted back to the observation area.

Either my blood pressure or pulse had dropped, but thankfully, whichever it was, the other had stayed level. So, for that reason, I apparently averted some unknown catastrophe—or potentially, just a minor glitch. Either way, it was all too close for comfort. And another one of those weird physiological responses that people with near-death experiences seem more prone to.

I wasn't about to get all caught up in thinking about that, though. All I wanted was pain relief. Instead, I got sick. For the first time in my sobriety, I vomited—not even an hour after leaving the outpatient facility. For the next week, I stayed glued to the couch. Every muscle in my body hurt, and I felt like hell. The shot offered me no relief, and I wasn't about to repeat it.

Instead, I started thinking more closely about the recommendation that I see a neurologist. The very idea of seeing a brain doctor was enough to make my head spin. But maybe that's why I needed to see one to begin with. I'd certainly experienced some unusual things. It was also the third time I'd been referred to one. Twice before, I'd refused. I was just too scared. But this time I knew I needed to go.

I scheduled the appointment and tried not to look back. As the day got closer, my anxiety grew. Something inside me told me to be careful with what I was about to unearth.

Pretty soon the morning arrived. I awoke and set out to do something I'd successfully avoided doing for ten years: visit a neurologist.

Not just any neurologist, either, a neurologist whose name was on the clinic I was going to. I figured the fact that his last name was on the stationery gave him some sort of credibility. I'm sure my logic was astray, though. The fact that my family's last name is on towels in millions of homes doesn't command me any respect whatsoever.

Recently unemployed, in pain, and chronically depressed, I parked my behind down in a rigid wooden chair in a cramped exam room on a frigid February morning. Krissy sat across from me. Patiently we waited. And waited.

After what felt like an eternity, I got up and walked over to the window, looking right out at our old apartment.

"Wow," I said. "You can see our old place from here."

Nothing good had happened since I'd left that apartment and bought a house. I turned away and looked down at the desk next to my wooden chair, catching a glimpse of the notes the nurse had left. Hunched over with eyes on the scribbles on the desk, I tried to glean from the numbers what my major malfunction was. I heard a knock and jumped, startled.

An older man with a band of white hair frowned at me as he entered. Without uttering a word, he extended his hand. I shook it firmly as he introduced himself.

"I'm Dr. Benson."

I figured he already knew my name. "Nice to meet you," I said.

The absence of any reply was telling. He wasn't interested in hearing about the things I'd been experiencing. In fact, he thought I was altogether in the wrong place.

After going over my history and symptoms he performed a neurological exam. Once that was complete, I returned once more to the small wooden chair next to the desk. He sat down next to me. We discussed more thoroughly what tests I'd had done, my psychiatric and addiction history, and my recent job loss.

"It's all been very . . . depressing." Krissy offered me a tissue as my emotional control started to slip.

He leaned back, tossed the pen to the desk, and folded his arms in front of himself. "Well," he said, "I think you're in the wrong place."

"Excuse me?"

"You're in the wrong place. You need a psychiatrist, not a neurologist."

"I already see a psychiatrist."

"Good. Keep going."

"Well, even she agrees I need to be seeing a neurologist. This is the third time I've been referred."

"Well, you have some psychiatric problems, but I don't think you have any neurological issues I can help you with, nor do I think you've ever had a seizure. But because you have this apparent history of syncope, I can order some blood work, a brain MRI, and EEG to rule some things out. Would that make you feel better?"

I glared, somewhat shocked. "Yes," I said. "It would."

"Are you sure you want to go through with that right now?"

I nodded. "Yeah. I need to figure this out."

An EEG, or electroencephalogram, measures the electrical activity in the brain. It's most widely used in the diagnosis of seizure disorders. A routine, standard EEG lasts about twenty to forty minutes, plus the time it takes to attach multiple electrodes to your head. It's uncomfortable and unattractive, but it serves a purpose.

The patterns of waves that show up on an EEG can confirm an epilepsy diagnosis. Or at least it can in theory. In reality, only very rarely does a standard-length, routine EEG capture any kind of abnormal brain waves, let alone capture a real, live seizure. As a result, people who suffer from seizures are often forced to undergo lengthy hospitalizations in order for the activity to be captured on an EEG and therefore localized. Even people with severe epilepsy often have normal results on standard EEGs.

Armed with such knowledge, I figured I had little to fear. Even if I'd suffered from seizures in the past, odds were that any abnormalities in my brain were going to be conspicuously absent from my brain wave test. I'd get the normal result back (and of course a normal MRI, too) and be able to rule out any neurological illnesses causing my as of yet unresolved shoulder pain.

That would be wonderful. But, on the flip side, if my tests came back normal, then it would seem to support Dr. Benson's theory that nothing was neurologically wrong with me. I knew that wasn't the case.

In the days between the tests and the follow-up appointment, my anxiety stewed. There *was* something wrong with my brain, and I *knew* it. I held my breath as I awaited word as to whether the tests knew it, too.

WHEN TIME CAME for me to return to Dr. Benson's office to discuss the results, I took a seat and a hard swallow.

Krissy had to be at work and couldn't be with me. I sat alone in the same small, sterile clinic room, tapping my foot rhythmically against the same wooden chair. After I'd been waiting for what felt like hours, a woman entered and introduced herself as Dr. Benson's nurse.

Unlike Dr. Benson, she seemed interested, attentive, and, unfortunately, concerned by my situation.

"Well," she said. I stared. With her bright red suit and bleach blonde hair, she looked like anything but a nurse. She crossed her legs and cleared her throat before continuing. "Your blood work came back normal."

"That's good."

"Yes, it is. But there were some abnormalities on both the MRI and the EEG. To be honest, we're kind of surprised. These sorts of EEG abnormalities don't usually show up on a standard-length test. We usually have to do sleep-deprived tests or else have the person go home with the electrodes for a few days, for an ambulatory EEG, in order to find abnormal seizure activity."

She shuffled through my file as the words seeped into my brain. She pulled the report and started to talk about the various types of seizures and what sort she thought I was having. I grabbed onto the words as she hurled them at me. I wanted to duck and dodge, but they kept sinking in.

"It says they're arising from the left temporal region," she finally said. "That coincides with the abnormalities we found on the MRI."

I stared at her quizzically. "I . . . Hold on here. I don't think I understand. What does this all mean? All this EEG stuff?"

She put the paper on her lap and nodded before folding her hands in front of her.

She looked up and right at me, holding her stare. "It means you have epilepsy."

I PULLED BACK from my position leaning on my elbows. As I slouched down in my seat, the world outside muted and slowed, like a bullet scene in a movie. The words hit me just as hard.

"What does this have to do with what's on the MRI?"

"Well, there were a few areas of hyperintensity that showed up—most likely, in your case, from previous brain injury or trauma. It doesn't look like MS, though, so you can take solace in that." She smiled, her bright red lipstick giving way to a bleached set of pearly whites. "You are staying clean and sober, right?"

"What?" Her questioning caught me off guard. "Yeah. I've been sober for over four years now—off coke longer."

"Well, that's good. The best thing you can do is keep it that way. You've most likely had some pretty serious seizures in the past. If you start drinking or using cocaine or crack again, you're likely to start having more serious seizures again."

Numb, I nodded.

"And since you're not losing consciousness, you won't have to report anything to the DMV right now."

"Right now?"

"Well, seizures arising from the temporal lobe are called partial seizures, and they can be either simple or complex. Simple partial seizures don't cause loss of consciousness. Complex partial do. You're having some aspects of complex partial because you're blacking out. But it's only for a second. If you start losing consciousness for any longer, we'll ask you to report it to the DMV."

I shook my head. "This is unbelievable. This is precisely what I didn't want to get myself into."

"I know, dear. This is a difficult diagnosis for me to hand out, too." She paused and frowned, as if she felt sorry for me. "Are you still seeing your psychiatrist?"

"Yeah. She actually started me on Zoloft since I was last in."

"Okay, good. You can keep on with that. The epilepsy needs to be medicated too, though. It might surprise you to know that the location of your seizure activity often creates emotional symptoms, particularly depression and anger outbursts."

"Really? I struggle with those things."

"Well, you can take some reassurance in knowing that some of what you feel is not your personality; it's your brain waves. For that reason we'd like you to keep your psychiatrist in the loop on this and vice versa."

She turned to look down at the desk. "Dr. Benson wanted you to start on some Insanix, so I'm gonna go ahead and write that up."

She posed several questions, including whether I ever planned to have children, before doling out the script. In retrospect, I probably should've been scared off by the questioning alone. But I was in too much shock to know what to think.

I snapped back to reality as she handed over a plastic bag. "Here you are."

I grabbed hold and got up to my feet. She opened the door and stood back to let me go first. Together we walked to the front desk, where we stopped.

"Well, Ms. Cannon," she said, extending a hand, "I'm sorry to deliver this diagnosis today, but I assure you we're here to help in whatever way we can."

I tried my best to believe it.

I JUST NEVER expected to walk out the door with such a definitive diagnosis. Even if I had been preparing mentally for the diagnosis itself, I had in no way anticipated hearing that I needed to be medicated for it.

It was all coming out of left field. What did this have to do with the pain I was experiencing? Maybe this explained some of my symptoms—and some things that had happened many years earlier—but what did this have to do with the pain?

I walked out the door, clenching the handles of the bag, which suddenly seemed to summarize my life. In it were five weeks of a trial of medication, a prescription, and an appointment reminder for my next visit, six weeks out.

I braced against the February wind, drew in a deep breath, and pushed it out, losing myself in the thought that, once again, in some sick, weird way, my life completely revolved around drugs.

23

Out of Rhythm

Something was wrong. I had a seizure—or something like it—the morning after the first day I took the medication.

It was all downhill from there. The internal rocking sensation coupled with the unsteadiness of the ground around me made me feel like I was on a boat. By the time I upped the dose at the end of the first week, I called to complain of a headache.

"It's too early for that," they said.

With each passing day, the pressure in my head grew greater. I couldn't read. I couldn't follow the puck while watching hockey. I couldn't even run. Everything felt wrong. I called again. I was told to titrate my dose upwards in the prescribed increments. So like a good little patient, after two weeks, I upped the dose again. The pressure in my head only intensified.

By the end of the third week, I could no longer function. Every time I stood up, the pressure barreled down. Each time I turned my head, the crawling sensations seeped through the veins in my neck. The physical sensations, not to mention the emotional instability, were becoming unbearable. Despite my pleas, my requests for help fell on deaf ears.

"Just keep taking your meds, Jennifer," they said.

So I did. But when it came time for me to increase the dosage once more, I finally put my foot down.

I'd heard a voice in my head. It wasn't one of those normal hallucinations that you might have just as you fall asleep. This was a real, actual voice in my head. "Temptress," it said.

I knew exactly whom it was alluding to: Amy. The last time I'd seen her was seven months earlier, at Molly's wedding. Seeing her again after all that time only confirmed to me how unhealthy our relationship had been. It frightens me to think that, in the craziest of states, I received the sanest of messages. Some people are like addictions. They try to seduce you, to keep you sick.

After the voice, I decided to cut back on meds. A wise move, I do believe. After all, I'd never heard a voice in my head before. People take pills to make voices go away, not the other way around.

Knowing that stopping anti-epileptics cold turkey can be lethal, I cut back my dose. I felt better. Two days later, I tapered back again, confident that I was making the right move getting the drug out of my system. I felt much less likely to pass out or fall to the ground with a full blown seizure. But the skipping in my chest persisted. I could feel my heart missing beats and my chest getting tighter, as if a boa constrictor was wrapping itself around my midsection, crushing my rib cage.

I told Krissy my chest hurt. She made every effort to assure I stayed horizontal as much as possible and played her best role as caretaker. It was the sweetest gesture she could've made. But there was nothing she or I could do to combat what the medication was doing to me. My eyes wanted to pop out. My head wanted to pop off. There was no way to escape the pressure in my head and chest. The internal sense of urgency grew.

Krissy went downstairs for a bowl of ice cream. I wasn't feeling up for the descent. But a few moments after she departed the room, I changed my mind. I didn't want to be alone.

I got up, walked down the stairs, and headed toward the kitchen. She stood on the opposite side of the room, scooping up mint chocolate chip. I pulled a chair from the table and sat, putting my head down like a third grader during quiet time.

"Nothing's right," I said. "I don't feel right—in my chest or my head or anything."

She looked at me, ice cream scoop in hand. "Think some ice cream might help?"

Krissy is eternally optimistic.

"I dunno. I hope so."

I picked my head up from its spot resting on my folded arms and rose to my feet. I made my way to the opposite side of the kitchen, shaking my hands out.

"I don't know what's wrong with me," I said. "I'm just so uncomfortable inside." My inner restlessness would not abate. It was becoming more intense by the moment. I bounced up on my toes, stretched my neck, and shook out my hands once more.

"I don't know what to do," I said again. I put my hands up over my eyes. "I just feel like something's gonna pop."

Just as I said the words, everything went black.

"Jen?" A sting slapped my face. "Jen? Are you okay?"

I peered out from my barely open eyes through foggy lenses. Kneeling down next to me was Krissy, trembling from head to toe.

"Jen," she said again. "Answer me. Are you okay?"

Cheek to the floor, I tried to get my bearings, but nothing made sense. "What . . . what happened?"

"You just collapsed. You were talking and you just, collapsed."

Sweat began pouring from my skin, soaking my shirt in seconds. I'd hit the floor many times before, but never once had that happened. And never had I felt so weak and unwell after coming to.

"Your eyes were wide open, but you weren't there. Are you okay?"

I could feel my temperature rising, my heart skipping underneath. I propped myself up against the kitchen cabinet. Head in my hands, I couldn't catch my breath. My stomach was throbbing. Sweat was pooling around me. Something wasn't right.

Everything felt so weak, so blurry. I struggled to fight against the weight of my eyelids. Something inside told me not to let them close again.

"Jen, what's going on?" Krissy finally asked. "Say something. What can I do for you? What do you need?"

"I . . .," I'd never said it before. The words, feeling so foreign, finally fell out. "I think I need to go to the hospital."

Krissy nodded. "Okay. You want me to call 911? Or take you?"

"Just—I need to go to the hospital," I said again. "Call 911."

Krissy scrambled to find her phone. I tried not to give into the urge to close my eyes. My clothes stuck to my skin as I arched my back against the cabinet. My chest heaved under the pressure of the disequilibrium.

I had to get up. I took a deep breath, gathered myself, and with all my strength tried to push myself to my feet, but I couldn't do it.

I tried again. Again I failed. For the first time in my life, I couldn't get up after collapsing.

But I couldn't stay idle. Krissy helped me to my feet, but I nearly collapsed again as we made our way toward the bathroom. I was intent on removing my contacts before being hauled away, only to discover I wasn't wearing them. I was just seeing double.

On my knees, elbows on the sink, I propped myself up but still couldn't get to my feet on my own. The pressure inside felt so very wrong.

Krissy, on the phone with the 911 operator, tried to pass along information about how I was doing while simultaneously gathering the necessary medical records and putting the cat away.

A few minutes later, the paramedics arrived. An older man escorted me to the couch, put an oxygen mask on me, and searched for a pulse.

He was struggling to find one.

I was struggling to stay conscious.

"You might've collapsed because your heart was going too slow," he said. "It still is. I understand you have epilepsy, too? You could've also had a seizure in there."

They loaded me onto a gurney, put me in the ambulance, and headed off for the hospital.

My fears swirled. I was also coming out of my skin.

It took awhile to tap any of my veins for an IV. It was running, but it was doing me no good. I was still so restless I was thrashing.

A thirty-something, blonde-haired doctor came in to check on me. She discussed the possibility that I might've had a brain or abdominal hemorrhage. She wanted to rule those out immediately.

Both the brain CT scan and abdominal sonogram came back normal. The EKG, the equivalent of an EEG of the heart, showed a marked bradycardia, or slow heart rate. In fact, my heart was only beating forty beats a minute when I arrived. I was a runner, and regular exercise can lower the pulse. But my heart rate had never been below fifty. The EKG also showed an arrhythmia. But was it enough to make me collapse the way I had?

The ER doctor returned and asked a few more questions before shaking her head. "I really have no answer as to what happened to you tonight," she said. "All the tests came back okay, so we're gonna go ahead and discharge you. But I strongly encourage you to follow up with both your neurologist and a cardiologist."

I returned home with a syncope diagnosis, the same diagnosis I'd received in 1999. I didn't buy it, though. I wanted to get some answers. But first I had to get off the Insanix. Even though my dose was down to a more tolerable level, the fact that I collapsed the same day I cut back more quickly led me to think that the medication was still capable of messing with my system if I were to just up and stop. So I kept cutting back, but even more slowly, waiting patiently for my return visit to Dr. Benson.

It wasn't easy. My electrical rhythm was out of whack. My heart continued to skip. The tightness inside my chest gripped me like a vice. I was nearly expecting to hit the floor again. And if I did, I was pretty sure I wouldn't wake up. Thankfully, I avoided such a catastrophe.

I arrived at Dr. Benson's office for my follow-up five days later and Insanix-free. But it was all I could do to keep the steam from pouring from my ears. I'd tried to tell his nurse just how crazy that Insanix was making me feel. I tried to tell them I was having the worst headache of my life and that my heart wasn't beating right. But despite the fact that I'd never before complained of headaches—or pain for that matter—the nurses at the clinic ignored my concerns. It was not something I could let roll off my back.

BACK IN THE same wooden chair, I was hardly able to contain my rage. Dr. Benson entered, looking just as smug as before.

"So I hear you've been having some more troubles," he said, taking a seat at the desk.

"Yeah, I am. I collapsed. And I'm angry about it. I don't think your clinic handled this well. I don't know what just happened to me, but I tried to tell your nurses something wasn't right."

He immediately went on the defensive. He had no idea why I collapsed, and he straight up admitted it. Then he pointed the finger back at me, labeling me "emotionally labile" and "too complicated" for his clinic. He suggested I follow up not only with my psychiatrist but also with the doctors at the epilepsy clinic in order to determine what the next step should be.

I was none too happy about the idea. Before I could go check into some epilepsy clinic, though, I first headed back to see my psychiatrist. I've always had a hard time trusting psychiatrists, but Dr. Wentworth made it even more difficult. I'd only been seen three or four times when my life came apart.

She'd pushed a few different antidepressants on me, but each one resulted in such significant night sweats that I had to change the sheets at 4:30 AM. "You're running out of options," she'd told me before she'd started me back on Zoloft.

It was the Zoloft that had made the Insanix situation so much more complicated. I had tried to do as I'd been told. She was to monitor the Zoloft, Dr. Benson the Insanix. But at some point during the Insanix ordeal, I'd complained to Dr. Wentworth about the problems. "Talk to your neurologist," she'd said.

Now that I was off the Insanix and pissed off about what it had done to me, I wanted to let Dr. Wentworth know what was going on.

I arrived at her office for my appointment, just a week after seeing Dr. Benson. With her knee-high boots, short skirt, and loose-fitting top, she looked straight out of the 1980s. She sat down in her oversized leather chair and crossed her legs, staring right down her nose at me.

I leaned forward on my elbows and produced a stack of documents. I explained the voice in my head, the trip to the ER, the follow-up with the neurologist, and the fact that I had appointments scheduled with both the epilepsy clinic and the cardiologist the following week.

"I'm not happy," I said. "I'm gonna be straight honest." I rolled the papers up and tapped them in my hands. "This drug really messed with me. I've got all the ER paperwork here if you want to look at it." I held out the documents for her. She grabbed them, thumbed through them, and set them down on the desk.

"We'll have a copy made out front after we're done." She picked up her coffee, took a sip, and set it down. "So are you still taking the Adderall?"

"No. I didn't want to add it on top of the Insanix and Zoloft. Then we agreed I should stop the Zoloft, but I . . . no, I didn't take it much. I don't really want to take it now, either. It seems to make me sweat funny."

"What do you mean?"

"I'm sweating funny. Like, profusely on my right but not at all on my left. It seems worse when I take Adderall. Do you know why?"

She looked at me as if I'd just told her I was a leper. "No, I have no idea. You'll have to ask your neurologist about that one."

"I *have* talked to a neurologist about it—Dr. Benson. But he said I'm too complicated. I won't be speaking to him again, but fine, I guess I'll ask a different one." I looked down at the floor and shook my head. "I guess I just don't respond well to medication anymore."

She picked up her mug once more, kicked one leg over the other, and stirred her beverage, silent.

"Look, I've got all this research here that says Insanix can cause something called metabolic acidosis. I know I hit the floor because of that medication, and I still don't know if it did permanent damage to my heart."

Drops splashed from her cup as she slammed it to the desk. She sat forward on her thighs, narrowed her eyes, and pierced me with a stare.

"Are you on drugs?" she asked. "You're not behaving like yourself."

I leaned back, folded my arms, and sneered. I couldn't believe what I was hearing. I sat back up again, agitated. "No, I am not on drugs. I resent that you would even suggest that."

"Well, are your friends noticing any differences in you? You're awfully paranoid about this Insanix."

"Because it almost killed me!"

I was getting furious. This drug had caused more side effects than any chemical I'd ever ingested in my life, and here my own psychiatrist was accusing me of being on drugs because I was concerned about my health after collapsing?

She wasn't listening to me. At least crack dealers showed some sense of concern for my well-being. They warned me about the dangers of the drug they were selling. Some psychiatrists, on the other hand, will minimize the dangers of the drugs they tell you to take. Then when you have problems, they deny the drug was to blame. Crack dealers *see* what the drug does to you, and they tell you it's the drug that's doing it to you. Then they tell you to quit, even though quitting would mean losing you as a customer.

I'D HAD ENOUGH. I wanted to get up and walk out. But how?

I'd first seen a psychiatrist when I was twelve. I rebelled, and security was called. At seventeen and eighteen, I was escorted in cuffs to the ward against my will. Then, at twenty, I got introduced to the criminal justice system and was again forced to sit compliantly in a shrink's office. For most of my life, I was told to sit still, behave, and respect authority.

Since getting sober, though, that respect had blended into submission. In my recovery, I walk the line. But I fear that if I stray from it just an inch, as any normal person would do, I'll get in trouble for doing something wrong. It's a terrible fear that leads me to take more than my fair share of abuse before standing up for myself. Before getting sober, whenever I would try to assert myself, I got too aggressive. It was more like acting out. Now, as a sober adult, acting on my own free will, how was I supposed to know when to stand up for myself? And how was I supposed to do that?

"It didn't almost kill you," Dr. Wentworth said. "You're blowing this out of proportion. What are you doing? Are you even looking for work?"

"No, I told you: I've been writing a book. And besides, I don't even know what just happened to me. The last two months have destroyed me, and I still have more doctors to visit. I'm not blowing this out of proportion at all. That drug did something to me that no drug has ever done. It made my heart beat funny, and I couldn't sweat. I couldn't even exercise and—"

"Well, maybe you're just out of shape."

"Oh, no, no, I don't think that's the case. I run. I thrive on living a healthy lifestyle, including exercise and proper nutrition."

"You run? How many miles a week are you running?"

I put my head in my hands. I knew right away what she was getting at. She was trying to see if I was exercising obsessively, restricting my calories, or otherwise practicing disordered eating.

She'd already accused me of being on drugs and out of shape. Now she was going to accuse me of an eating disorder, too? In the few months I'd been seeing her, I had talked about the fact that, when I'd gotten sober, I'd started running in moderation and eating healthy. I also discussed with her that it was painful to work and that I was writing a book.

If she couldn't keep that much straight, then how on earth was she fit to be telling me how to govern my mental and physical health? It was all getting to be too ridiculous. Why was I putting up with this? What was keeping me in that chair?

I'd been pushed around and manipulated and used long enough. I had to stand up for myself. So that's precisely what I did. "I'm sorry," I finally said. "I really don't need this. Thanks for all your help."

Documents in hand, I collected myself and, for the first time in my life, stood up and freely walked out on a psychiatrist.

Just two days later, I walked into an epilepsy clinic—a place I never thought I'd be stepping foot in. But really I had no choice. Dr. Benson took the results of my first EEG, and my response to Insanix, as a collective indication that I was actively having seizures. Not only that, but he thought the fact that I had lost consciousness on Insanix also meant I was ineligible to drive. Most states have laws governing whether people with epilepsy are allowed to drive a car. Generally speaking, if a person with epilepsy has a type of seizure that causes them to lose consciousness, odds are they aren't allowed to operate a vehicle. Dr. Benson didn't think I was legal to drive, and he put that in his notes.

I'd already lost my job. Now my license was in jeopardy, too. It all seemed so crazy.

On the bright side, it forced me to follow through on an appointment with The Epilepsy Experts, a place where they seem to treat their patients instead of pushing pills. They seek to use the minimum amount of medication necessary. Their goal, above all else, is no seizures, no side effects. As weird as it sounded in my own head, it sounded like exactly where I needed to be.

This time I wasn't headed in for a standard thirty-eight-minute EEG. Instead I was going to be glued in for three long hours. I was dreading the idea of having those itchy electrodes stuck to my head for so long.

I arrived at the clinic encased by tunnel vision. It was a clear spring morning, but in my mind there was no weather, no birds, no traffic. It was just me and my brain, headed to the clinic, hands gripped to the steering wheel.

Once I arrived, I handed over the stacks of paperwork they'd sent me to fill out and took a seat in the lobby. Just as I slouched and propped my head up on my palm, a short blonde woman opened a door and called my name.

She smiled as she escorted me down a narrow hallway with exam rooms on either side. "I hear it's beautiful out there today," she said.

I nodded and smiled, unable to think about anything other than what I was getting into.

Together with a second tech, she glued twenty-six electrodes to my skull, two more to my heart, and then sent me into a dim room with a hospital bed.

"Just go ahead and lie down," she said.

Mindful of the ropes of wire extending behind me like a ponytail, I laid down on the lumpy bed. I fished them out from behind my head as the light went out.

"Don't worry about the wires," the woman's voice said, from over an intercom. "Just try to relax."

Easier said than done. Up in the corner a camera watched my every move, even in the dark. They could see when I had my eyes opened or closed; they could see everything I was doing.

For the next three hours, the voice barked instructions at me. I opened and closed my eyes and responded to instructions, all the while tossing and turning, electrodes pinching my skin. Relaxing, it seemed, would be impossible.

A part of the test requires you to stare at a strobe light, eyes wide open, as it flashes. After what amounts to a visit to the discotheque, you're ordered to hyperventilate for five minutes. Then they expect you to go to sleep.

Like the strobe light, hyperventilation has been known to provoke seizures in people with certain forms of epilepsy. True enough, epilepsy is not a catchall term; not all seizures are the same.

When someone falls to the ground, loses consciousness, and shakes, such an episode is called a generalized seizure, formerly known as a grand mal. This is only one type. Some people have seizures that don't involve loss of consciousness. These are called simple partial. Others have complex partial seizures, which do cause you to lose consciousness, but not to shake. These types of seizures may involve a sequence of behaviors, such as staring off and picking at one's T-shirt. They are not what people usually think of when they think of seizures.

In a generalized seizure, the entire brain goes haywire. In partial seizures, it's only one area of the brain. Most commonly, seizures arise from abnormalities in the temporal lobe. This form of epilepsy, known as temporal lobe epilepsy, is the most common form among adults. It was temporal lobes that were giving me a tendency toward seizures.

My three-hour EEG came back abnormal, just as the first one did. The same afternoon, I met with Dr. Ramos, who delivered the news. Her white coat, long black hair, and warm smile gave her an elegant and sophisticated appeal.

She looked down over her wire-rimmed glasses, pulled out a seat, and sat down across from me at a table. She informed me that the EEG showed "unequivocal epileptiform abnormalities." Such patterns she described as "suggestive" but not "diagnostic" of a seizure disorder. It's about as close as you can come to having epilepsy show up on EEG without having an actual seizure during the test.

Few conditions in the world carry the stigma epilepsy does. People often inappropriately associate it with mental illness and developmental disability, even though few people with epilepsy have those conditions. I desperately wanted to avoid being diagnosed with epilepsy, out of the fear of being rejected by my friends, family, insurance, and the DMV. I didn't want to lose my license. I wasn't voluntarily seeking help for any sort of seizure issue. I went to the neurologist to figure out why I was in so much pain. So far, nobody had been able to tell me.

MY BRAS HAD started fitting funny. When I would move my right arm, my whole bra would move with it. It drove me crazy. The strap would ride way up my neck on one side and be pushed off my shoulder on the other. It had little to do with fit. I switched to ones I could clasp in front, which helped, but only marginally. The best remedy I've found is a sports bra, but it has to be cut just right, and it's not always practical.

Around the same time, I started sweating unevenly. My left side would sweat normally, but my right armpit would be absolutely dripping. It seemed to be tied into my pain. With time, this sweating progressed to my entire shoulder region on the right side. When I sweated, I had difficulty lifting my arm, and it would start to feel swollen. It was as though I was lopsided. I felt pulled down on the right side.

The more I tried to use my right arm, the more it hurt. The more I hurt, the more I sweated. I didn't even want to feel clothing up against my skin. I blamed it all on my shoulder problems—until the pain spread to my neck.

By the time I sat down to talk to Dr. Ramos, I was in a world of hurt. Whatever it was, I'd have to just put up with the pain until I resolved the epilepsy issue. The Epilepsy Experts weren't going to just look at my brain waves, diagnosis me with a seizure disorder, and throw drugs at me, though. They were going to make sure I was experiencing symptoms that warranted being medicated.

After hearing me out about the Insanix, the light-headedness on standing, the episodes on crack, and the collapsing while drunk, Dr. Ramos agreed. She didn't think anything I was actively experiencing were seizures. But there was no doubt I'd experienced them in the past.

She instructed me to return if I began having symptoms more typical of seizures arising from the left temporal lobe. For example, if I should ever walk into a room and not remember how I got there or if I repeated the same word for about two minutes.

Nothing like that had ever happened. But weird things *were* happening to me. They'd been happening since I attempted suicide. It started with the crack in the bathroom, led to the passing out while in college, and then after all the alcoholism, it came back to the surface. Those episodes on crack—and those I experienced in the months immediately after getting sober—really were seizures.

But I didn't tell Dr. Ramos that the episodes were still happening every now and again. I was trying my hardest to be as minimal in my disclosure as possible so as to avoid being deemed in need of medication, and I didn't want to lose my privilege to drive.

I had been without my license for three years after my DUI. Once I got sober, I had to jump through hoops between states to get myself cleared to even take the test in Minnesota, and still I had to show that I had completed chemical dependency treatment.

That's why I was without a license for so long. I would've had to have stopped drinking and get through rehab, and I wasn't ready to do that. Getting my license back, after completing rehab and staying sober, was like getting my license for the first time—but even more thrilling. I'd come to realize that driving is a privilege, not a right. Having earned the privilege again, I wasn't about to do anything to jeopardize it—even if that meant overlooking those once-a-year episodes in which I shook.

These little brain storms were rare enough to ignore. All I wanted to know was what the fuck was happening to me. Perhaps Dr. Ramos could get to the bottom of it.

"Hop up on this table here, and we'll do a neurological exam," she said.

I got seated as she put a tongue depressor up to my face. "Say ah."

I opened up. "There are so many other medications that would be better options for you than Insanix." She disposed of the depressor, pulled out a hammer, and began testing my reflexes. "You're already so slight of figure, and it's one of the few anti-epileptics that can cause weight loss." She stopped to look up in my eyes. "It can also make your hair fall out." I raised my eyebrows. "There are a number of other more appropriate medications."

We went on to talk more about the incident that caused me to collapse. She suggested "metabolic acidosis" might have been setting in—the same horrible condition I'd mentioned to Dr. Wentworth in which the body's pH system gets out of whack. Apparently it can be fatal, and it's also a potential side effect of Insanix.

Indeed, she agreed that Insanix would have been the last drug she would have prescribed for me, particularly at such a high dose. Her tone and description led me to think that the drug was nothing to mess around with.

I'd never given much credence to the idea that prescriptions were as dangerous as illegal drugs, but Insanix changed my mind. Unlike even crack cocaine, it pushed my brain to the point of psychosis. It led to a disruption in the coordination between my heart and brain I'd never before experienced. Thankfully, once I got off the medication, the headaches, heart skipping, and all other indications that something was wrong subsided.

I was starting to feel stronger. I also walked out of the epilepsy clinic without a prescription—but still no closer to an answer.

24

Listening to My Body

I've learned to listen to my body. It knows. It remembers everything it's been through.

The reminders are there, pumping through my veins. In the unevenness of the blood flow. In my neck, when I turn my head to the right and receive an electrical shock through my entire upper body. In the rigid but delicate side of my throat, where the pain pulses through my stressed muscles and nerves. Reminders are in my brain, too, crawling through my white matter like a spider.

I'm often asked about my scar. Sometimes it's almost invisible, but from some angles it dominates my profile. It does not detract from my beauty but rather enhances it. If it hadn't made its mark, so eloquently woven in the fabric of my skin, I would no longer be here on this earth. It is the marker of my existence, the reason I'm alive. It represents my struggles, my suicide, my life.

The swelling and bruising faded. The broken blood vessels healed. But scars never fade. They stick with you forever—and sometimes, so do consequences.

I listened to my body. I got healthy, started treating it right. Still, it came apart. The damage had already been done. Never did I think that my health would become such an issue at such a young age. Never did I think I'd have to fear for the health of my brain.

For everything I was losing, though, I couldn't forget what I'd been through. Even if my stability was being shaken by a job loss and the onset of a chronic health condition, I had to take comfort in the fact that I'd survived everything I'd been through so far—including the crazy collapse on Insanix.

The cardiologist took a look at my ten-year-old heart test results and quickly determined I wouldn't benefit from a pacemaker. I had a subtle arrhythmia, but he assured me my heart was pumping just fine. The medication I was taking did cause my heart to slow, but unless I started passing out and collapsing again, everything should be okay. I took his word for it and tried to move on.

It was hard to know what move to make next, though. All I knew for sure was that I wanted to be as far away from doctors as possible. I wanted to jump ship, forget that I ever opened up that can of worms, get my life back to normal.

I did my best. I got back to work. But within just a few days of being back in a 9 to 5, I knew I was in trouble. A miserable ache had set into the right side of my jaw—the same side I had repeatedly banged against the floor during my suicide attempt. First, just my jaw would feel hot, hard, and swollen. Then the discomfort would begin to spread. It seeped through my neck, creeping down toward my right shoulder, then from my shoulder to my hand. Pretty soon, my clothing was twisted and contorted, and so was I. The muscles in my neck got hard as a rock—so hard that Krissy jumped back and said "eww" the first time she felt it.

Then there was my arm. Using it to manipulate the computer mouse had become painful. First, my armpit would drip sweat. Then the clothing against my skin would itch with such intensity that I'd fantasize ripping my shirt off like the Hulk. Even wearing a bra was enough to trigger pain and discomfort. With each passing moment I grew more miserable.

The pain was a process, and it all started by the simple act of sitting in a chair. I knew, before I ever sat down at the beginning of the day, that it would eventually start. And once it did, I could do nothing to stop it.

I dreaded going to work more each day. I was exhausted and beaten down, fighting against some beast that had overtaken my body. The idea of being confined to a chair was growing to be unbearable. The anticipation became almost as bad as the suffering itself. Nevertheless, I had no choice but to park my ass down.

Nobody understood why I was having such difficulties, and neither did I. But I had to figure it out.

So back to the doctors I went. First to Dr. Solomon, then back to Dr. Johnson, then to more physical therapy. What started as an aggressive regimen of exercises designed to treat my shoulder and rotator cuff muscles was scaled back to a more gentle set of exercises involving my neck. When those proved too difficult, they got scaled back to a set of exercises requiring that I do nothing but move my eyes and think. Every day, I unfailingly performed the prescribed exercises at home.

I pushed, pulled, pressed, and turned. I fought the pull of my muscles as they continued to battle against my will to stand up straight and hold my head up. By early 2009, I knew I was losing the fight. Sporting a cervical collar to support my floppy head, I frequently found myself lying over the exercise ball, tears dripping from my eyes. The physical therapy wasn't working. And the pain in my muscles just kept getting worse.

I had no idea what my options were, and I foresaw a future filled with nothing but prescription painkiller addiction, a shoulder joint replacement, and disability.

A new job, with fewer hours sitting and more hours standing at a counter, did little to help. My neck had become so tight and painful that I wanted to simply flop my head down to my chest. I began wrapping a scarf around my neck in order to function. It was becoming all I could do just to get out of bed in the morning and force myself into the office every day.

I DECIDED TO revisit some records. I looked back and reviewed all of my doctors' notes. Perhaps there was another option. Dr. Johnson had recommended Botox, a drug that is most often associated with wrinkles. I didn't understand why. And after that awful facet joint injection, I wasn't about to agree to get shot up with any more drugs—especially not the world's most powerful neurotoxin.

Hidden in the back of his notes from early 2008 were his impressions of my condition. "Torticollis," he wrote. He never uttered the word to me directly. I had no idea what the term meant.

A quick internet search led me to the answer. Torticollis is a term often used to refer to babies who have what's called wryneck, in which their necks are twisted to one side. But torticollis in adults is not the same. It's a neurological condition, closely related to Parkinson's, known as a movement disorder. Spasmodic torticollis is also known as cervical dystonia. In people with dystonia, the neurological mechanism that makes muscles relax when they're not in use does not function properly. The result is involuntary muscle spasms and contractions that lead to abnormal, often painful postures. I'd never heard of such a thing before.

Dystonia literally means "abnormal muscle tone," but a more accurate descriptor might be abnormal muscle posturing. It can strike almost any muscle in the body. It can be genetic, or it can be caused by brain injury, peripheral trauma, medications, or toxins. It can also be idiopathic: having no known cause. Whatever sparks it, it can destroy people's lives and deprive them of the freedom to move, talk, walk, and run.

Some people have dystonia in muscles throughout their bodies. They have generalized dystonia. For others, it's focal and only affects one area of the body. Mine was most visible in my neck.

I'd never heard of dystonia before. I researched it at length to better understand what it was Dr. Johnson thought I had. When I looked at pictures of people with dystonia, I saw folks who were twisted and contorted, and many had to use wheelchairs. I didn't look like them—or at least I didn't think I did.

I had no idea whether his assessment of torticollis was accurate, or if he was just looking to poke me with more drugs. But as time went on, the pain persisted—and more and more, the symptoms actually seemed to fit. Dr. Solomon had been right all along: he said from the start that something much bigger than a torn labrum in my shoulder joint was causing my problems. It was also still unclear whether any of the pain, numbness, or tingling I was experiencing was related to epilepsy. And until I figured that out, no one was going to touch me with a ten-foot pole, let alone a needle. So back to the epilepsy clinic I went.

IT WAS THE last place I wanted to go. I'd gone over all the head rushes, the light-headedness, the episodes on crack, the episodes while drinking. But I hadn't discussed with Dr. Ramos those episodes that had persisted since I had gotten sober. Nor had I mentioned the other symptoms that had gotten worse. Mostly it was the pain, but there were other things, too.

There was that black spot in my right eye that had popped up right when all these other symptoms had. The eye doctor called it a floater and attributed it to the injury I'd sustained during the suicide attempt. Then there were those floating objects in my vision, squiggly lines and so forth, which I had no explanation for.

My biggest issue wasn't my visual complaints, though. It was an inability to retain what I'd been reading. I'd first noticed it at Gustavus. It was actually my chief complaint when I was sent for ADHD testing in college. But they never tested my memory, only my attention.

I returned to meet with Dr. Ramos. Mature and educated in her appearance, she always offered her undivided attention. Since I'd last seen her, I'd taught myself to use a mouse with my left hand. The progressive nature of my symptoms elicited genuine concern from her.

"My shoulder is still bothering me, too," I said. "I've been back to see Dr. Solomon and have done all kinds of physical therapy. Dr. Johnson recommended Botox for my neck, which scares me, but Dr. Solomon won't fix my shoulder surgically until my neck is all figured out. In the meantime, neither of them are sure epilepsy isn't an issue here, either."

"Well, it's possible," she said. "You could be having some what we call subclinical seizures; those could cause you to have lapses in your thinking. Let me just see here." She paused as she flipped through my folder. "You had a brain MRI, right?"

"Yeah, a little over a year ago."

"Okay, well, I think we should do another and also a longer EEG. You've had the thirty-eight-minute and the three-hour, and they've both come back abnormal. But so far, we've not found any seizures. I think we should run it for forty-eight hours to see what we get."

I readily agreed. It wasn't going to be easy to negotiate, though. Since losing the job I loved so much in December 2007, I'd been nothing more than a traveling temp. After months of looking, I got a part-time job working at a newspaper. Then, six weeks later, a full-time paralegal job opened up. I took it, too. Suddenly, I had a fifty-hour work week, working two jobs at once. Neither offered paid time off.

So when I needed to take time off so I could sit at home for days with electrodes glued to my head, it was easier said than done. I worked it all out, though, and was relieved to have three whole days away from miserable office chairs.

More than anything, though, I just wished I had cut my hair. It was grown out at the time, and its length made the EEG application process much more difficult. This wasn't the same glue as before, either. This was stickier, heavier glue designed to cement the electrodes to their location for a period longer than just thirty-eight minutes or a few hours. This was serious stuff.

A female tech braided my hair into tiny strands, while a male tech applied the glue and twenty-six electrodes. She quickly finished up braiding and left the room. An hour later the less experienced tech got done with the gluing. He summoned his colleague for her approval.

She stood in front of me and tapped her chin with her pointer. "Several of them will need to be adjusted," she said.

They applied nail polish remover to each electrode, then repositioned them one by one, slapping more glue to the correct locations. What should have taken a half hour or an hour took two. When it was all done, they put a surgeon's cap on my stiff and weighted head.

"Okay, this is your pack," the male tech said, handing me a purse-size black bag. I took hold of the handle and cupped the bundle of wires sticking out of the unzipped corner of the top. Guiding the bag over my head and across my shoulder, I realized that the wires were again attached like a ponytail to the back of my head. It was going to be a long couple of days.

By the end of the first night, I wanted to rip the two electrodes attached to my forehead right the hell off. They itched miserably.

I tried to look on the bright side. At least I could spend the time at home and not in a hospital. I just had to go in once a day to have the electrodes checked. That meant slopping on more glue. By the time I got the things off on the third day, I felt like I was wearing a cement helmet—as if I didn't have enough difficulty holding my head up already.

After all that, it was time for a brain MRI—my second. At least this time I knew what to expect. Brain MRIs require your head to be strapped down inside a cage-like contraption, similar to something they might put Hannibal Lecter in. It's quite uncomfortable and appears very medieval. I certainly felt like I was being tortured.

My return visit to the clinic heralded both some welcome and some unwelcome news. On the bright side, I didn't have a brain tumor, which had been Dr. Ramos's main concern. But my MRI came back showing a few more spots than the first one had. Thankfully, the difference in number turned out to be because the second machine had much better resolution than the first one and so caught more things. It wasn't because of any changes in my brain. Even so, Dr. Ramos explained, the spots were most likely the aftereffects of previous trauma—probably the lack of oxygen during my suicide attempt.

There were four or five of them scattered throughout my brain. Otherwise, she thought there was nothing too serious—nothing more than some "mild to moderate diffuse cortical atrophy." In other words, my brain had wasted away. It had literally shrunk in size—most likely, Dr. Ramos explained, as a result of my alcoholism and head injuries. It matched up well with the verbal memory deficit documented on the neuropsych testing.

The ambulatory EEG also came back abnormal, showing some "fairly frequent" abnormalities. Dr. Ramos furrowed her brow. "Your whole brain kinda slows down, which is . . . somewhat unusual," she said. I nodded. "This too may be reflective of anoxic damage from your suicide attempt, or damage resulting from the alcoholism." I kept nodding. "There were some sharply contoured waves in your left temporal lobe again as well." She looked down at her notes before continuing. "This most likely reflects a greater seizure tendency, meaning that your brain is more prone to seizures than the normal adult brain. This would make sense, since you began experiencing what were likely seizures soon after your suicide attempt. There were no seizures during the test, though. I was almost hoping we would find something, to explain your memory complaints. If the slowing lasted any longer, then we would call it a seizure, and we could try some medication in a small dose. But as it is, I think this is all part of a more permanent, structural problem, related to your past head injuries and chemical dependency."

In other words, the tests showed I have brain damage.

It all led her to conclude that I had sustained an anoxic brain injury during my suicide attempt and possibly also a traumatic brain injury—anoxic from the lack of oxygen, traumatic from the fall. And it all made my brain more vulnerable to seizures, forever.

It all seemed to fit. I sat silent, shocked.

Dr. Ramos looked at me. "If the memory issues *are* related to these more permanent problems, they won't be helped by medication. This may just be something you'll have to adjust to and . . . uh . . . live with."

"Live with?"

"Yes. You may actually want to reconsider your educational and vocational plans based on these results. These are some pretty significant impairments, and I would worry about all the memory work required to be successful in a graduate school environment."

Stunned, I kept on nodding, taking the news the way I would a hit in hockey. Even though I was braced for the blow, it still hurt. All I could do now was to try my best not to let it faze me.

Indeed, for the past few years, lots of everyday tasks had gotten more difficult, things that weren't difficult for me before. In the workplace, I couldn't figure out how to work the copier or transfer a call. Instructions didn't help. Diagrams didn't, either. And being shown how wasn't enough to get it to sink in. Likewise, those times when my thinking felt scattered had become much more frequent.

I gathered my thoughts and prepared for the difficult discussion about what this meant for my pain.

"The physiatrist I saw, Dr. Johnson, he diagnosed me with something called torticollis." I looked down at my nervous hands. "I guess it's also called cervical dystonia. It was never treated, though. And my shoulder doctor, Dr. Solomon, won't touch my shoulder in surgery until I can tell him what these symptoms are on the right side of my body. So if it's not seizures causing my pain and these other weird things, do you think dystonia might explain some of what I'm experiencing? He recommended Botox injections."

She observed my posture and head positioning, much the way Dr. Johnson had a year earlier. "Do you mind if I feel your neck?"

"No, not at all."

She stood up, came around to where I was seated, and put two fingers to my neck, touching it lightly.

After a moment of massaging the front right side of my neck, Dr. Ramos returned to her seat. "Well, dystonia would certainly make sense," she said. "I suggest you seek treatment for that. You could get some relief from Botox."

Finally, the magical words I'd been waiting to hear. My problems weren't being caused by seizures; they were being caused by dystonia. And it had become a real pain in the neck.

25

Back to Campus

I'd wanted to go back to school.

But after meeting with Dr. Ramos, everything changed. She wished me luck and sent me on my way, leaving me to process the fact that my neurology was probably not going to allow me to pursue any further education. It was a tough pill to swallow.

I was still working two jobs. The economy was collapsing, and our home had lost a quarter of its value, but we still owed a mortgage payment every month, and the medical bills were starting to roll in. I had to keep fighting through the pain.

The last thing I was going to do was take unpaid time off so I could go pay someone to listen to me talk. I'd grown accustomed to living in emotional pain. It was the chronic, physical variety that had become intolerable. More than anything else, I needed to find a doctor who could figure out what was going on with me neurologically. It certainly wasn't Dr. Johnson. But even if I didn't trust him, he'd clearly seen something wasn't right—something that both he and Dr. Ramos suggested could be treated.

Meanwhile, each day it grew harder to work through the discomfort. Of course I couldn't have my special chair in both jobs. It made more sense to bring the chair into the full-time job. But that meant that three nights a week, I was expected to do something most people wouldn't think twice about—sit in a normal chair.

My Herman Miller chair helped the pain in between my shoulder blades, but not even it could help my neck pain or hand issues anymore. Nor could it correct my postural issues. The very act of sitting had grown to be too much. Sitting in a normal chair was no longer an option.

At my part-time job, I was expected to sit in a standard chair for four hours per shift, but I could only make it through three. I appealed to my supervisor for assistance in finding a new chair, but my requests fell on deaf ears. Perhaps the fact that I was in my twenties and apparently healthy gave employers more room to ignore me. Perhaps they doubted that I had anything remotely constituting a disability, despite what I said about a history of shoulder and neck injuries.

Having never needed accommodations in a workplace before, I didn't know how to go about informing an employer of a disability. If there was a proper way to go about it, I'd evidently gone at it all wrong. I could've gotten a letter from one of my doctors, but I didn't want to lose another job because I'd handed over a doctor's letter, especially when I was still trying to find a doctor who knew much about what I was battling.

I decided to call my insurance company. "I need a list of doctors who specialize in dystonia," I said.

The operator on the other line wasn't familiar. "I'm sorry. In what?"

"Dystonia."

"Uh, okay. Can you spell that?"

Eventually I got off the phone with a name and a phone number.

Dr. Robert Lewis at the University of Minnesota. The same school where I'd finished my degree and drank myself stupid was now the home of my new brain doctor. Still, I was excited for the appointment. I was finally going to see a doctor who knew something about my condition—or at least the condition I was pretty sure I had.

Dystonia is so rare and little understood that my primary doctor had never even heard of it. I called her office to request a formal referral to see Dr. Lewis. After leaving a message for her nurse, I received a call back.

"Uh, hi, Jennifer," the voice in the message said. "We received your message regarding the need for a referral. The doctor would be happy to write you one. She just needs to know what your diagnosis is."

Frustrated, I called back and was able to speak with the nurse herself. "It says here that you need to see a podiatrist," she said.

"No. I don't need a foot doctor. I need to see either a movement disorder neurologist or a *physiatrist*, which is also called a doctor of physical medicine."

"Oh, I see." Her silence seemed soaked with confusion. "So what is your diagnosis, then? It says here dist—uh, distone—"

"Dystonia. Dis – tone – eee – uhh."

"Okay, well, the doctor just needs to know what the diagnosis is."

"That is the diagnosis. It's a neurological disorder."

If my own primary doctor had never heard of it, was it any wonder I'd not yet received any treatment for it?

In March 2009, nearly five years after graduating from college, I went back to campus. It wasn't the triumphant return I'd envisioned. I was hoping to return for grad school, not because of the onset of an incurable neurological illness.

I bypassed the law school and the Social Science Tower, and strategically avoided looking at the various bars and restaurants lining the East Bank of campus where I'd spent so much time as an undergrad.

Instead I went to the University Medical Center, a building I'd never set foot in but knew to be the end of the line when it comes to treating disease and illness. University doctors are the best of the best. But could I really have such a complicated or serious case that I needed to be seeing this sort of super-elite brain doctor?

I parked myself in the waiting room, anxious to find out. A short, middle-aged man with blond hair and glasses called my name. From his resemblance to the picture online, he looked to be the doctor. Odd—no doctor had ever come out to the waiting room to get me himself.

After having me step on a scale, he escorted me to an exam room.

"Have a seat. We're just gonna take your blood pressure and pulse first." I sat quietly as he cuffed the crux of my elbow and placed a thermometer in my mouth.

A moment later he removed them and scribbled a few notes.

"So," he finally said, dropping his pen to the paper on the small desk, "what brings you in to see me today?"

I took a deep breath and looked down at my feet. He wheeled his seat to the center of the room, so to be looking at me straight on.

"Uh, well," I said. "I think I might have dystonia."

He seemed surprised I'd already drawn such a conclusion. "What makes you think that?"

"Well," I said, pulling a note from my stack of records, "Dr. Johnson diagnosed me with something called torticollis. He wanted to do Botox injections last year, but I never got them. Then the epilepsy doctor also thought my problems might be related to dystonia."

"Are you in pain?" he asked.

"Yeah. This is—this is actually pretty miserable."

He nodded. "Do your muscles feel like they tug or pull?"

"Yeah, ya know, I guess they do. They feel like they're pulling me down, or forward actually—and to the right. I want to drop my head to my chest. It's like holding myself up against gravity is way harder than it should be."

He sat back, crossed one leg over the other, and cupped his chin with his hand, observing my posture. "Well," he said, "you're too young to be dealing with an idiopathic case of torticollis. That's a condition that typically hits people who are a little older, in their forties or fifties. You're way too young for it. If we're dealing with dystonia, then there would have to be a secondary cause. An injury or something. Have you suffered any trauma or injuries?"

With that, I spit out the entirety of my history. Everything from the shoulder dislocation to the suicide attempt, the head injuries to addiction. He listened—warmly, intently, nonjudgmentally. After hearing my lengthy and complicated explanation, he shined a few lights in my eyes, asked me to repeat words, watched me walk down the hall, and asked about my lifestyle and living situation.

We went over my records. He took a look at my brain MRI and EEG reports. We discussed my brain waves and the epilepsy diagnosis, brain damage and seizure tendencies. Then we homed in on my symptoms. Again, once I opened my mouth, everything came out. The pain, the discomfort, the uneven sweating, the lopsided feelings, the difference in the way my clothes fit, and the inability to sit up in a chair. I complained, and he listened. He actually *listened*.

For the first time, a doctor seemed to really care. He didn't throw up his hands and try to push me off on another guy. He didn't tell me I was "too complicated" or pigeonhole me into the easiest diagnosis. He heard me out. And what he heard apparently was enough to confirm his impression.

"Usually I like to run a few tests before I go forth with Botox treatment. But you've been through enough already. You didn't try out the Botox before, when you were seeing Dr. Johnson. Are you open to trying it out now?"

I inched forward on my seat, excited by the possibility of getting some actual pain relief. "Yes, I am. I'm more than willing."

"Okay," he said. "We can get that scheduled. You should call your insurance company first, though. They're usually pretty good about covering Botox injections when it's under a dystonia diagnosis, but you should call to be sure. The injections are very expensive if not covered."

I nodded. "Yeah, I'll check on that before scheduling anything." I took up my typical posture, head cocked, staring down at the floor.

"Do you have any questions for me?" he asked.

I could think of none. I'd spit it all out. "No, not right now."

Seated at my level, he rolled his stool closer to me and reached out a hand. I did the same. He gave me a firm handshake and looked me in the eyes. "Thanks for coming to see me today," he said. His sincerity felt genuine.

I'd landed. And I knew in that moment that I'd landed in precisely the right place.

Two weeks later, I returned to the clinic for treatment—to get poked with needles repeatedly.

I took up a spot in a low, sunken chair in the waiting room. Soon a nurse came to greet me. After the standard weight, blood pressure, and temperature check, she escorted me to a cramped exam room. A moment later Dr. Lewis entered, carrying with him a square, boxlike machine. Attached to it was a needle.

"Nice to see you again," he said as he sat down. "You talked to your insurance?"

"Yeah, yeah I did. They assured me it would be covered."

"Good. Do you have any questions right away?"

"Nope, I don't think so."

"Okay." He pushed the box closer to me. "Well, this is the machine. It has an EMG, or an electromyogram, built into it that will allow me to listen to the electrical activity in your muscles. So what I'm gonna do is I'm going to use the attached needle here"—he held up the large, filled syringe—"to target a few different muscles, and we'll take a listen. It's all loaded up with Botox, so we can inject any muscles that are giving you trouble. Can you pull your chair up so I can get behind you?"

"Sure."

Chair pulled forward, Dr. Lewis walked around me, needle in hand, intently observing my movements and posture. I could feel myself growing more self-conscious by the moment. A brain doctor— one who specializes in observing people's unconscious movements and behaviors—was watching my every position. The way I held my hands and positioned my arms, how I carried my head on my body and turned it. The more I thought about the fact that he was watching me, the more unnatural being natural seemed. Just as I started to feel awkward, he stopped.

"Okay, I think we'll try this muscle first. The *levator scapulae.*"

"The what?"

"We call it the 'levator.' You have two, one on each side. They elevate your shoulder blades." He leaned around to look at me. "Are you ready? You're gonna feel a poke now."

"I'm as ready as I'll ever be."

He inserted the needle into the side of my neck. I felt a stab as the skin broke, a sensation much like getting a booster shot. He moved the needle to ensure proper location within the muscle tissue. As he did, static and scratching erupted from the EMG machine. It sounded like a radio tuned to the wrong frequency.

"Wow," he said, shaking his head. "Hear that? That's the sound of your muscle. It's supposed to be relaxed right now. When it's relaxed, it doesn't make any noise. I know there's something going on there in your muscles now because I can hear it."

"So my neck muscle shouldn't be making any noise right now?"

"Right. In most people, if I sat them in that chair and stuck this needle in their muscles, that machine would stay completely silent."

With each poke, the machine rustled. After about a dozen or so shots, ranging from up near my skull to the middle of my side, he finished up.

The dystonia was much more widespread than I'd ever imagined. It was not only in my neck, but in my jaw, shoulder, back, and rib cage, too. It was also in my tongue, but he couldn't do anything about that. Botox in the tongue can cause serious trouble swallowing.

"I think that's a good enough dose. It's as much as I feel comfortable injecting on the first round. Let's go with that and see how you do."

He stood up from his stool, disposed of the needle, and washed his hands.

"You might want to take a second to look in the mirror before you go," he said. "You look, uh, you kinda look like you've been attacked. You've got a few spots of blood there." He walked to the sink, grabbed a tissue, and handed it to me. "I always feel so bad, putting my patients through so much pain. How ya doin'? You okay?"

"Yeah, I'm fine," I said, blotting the blood. "Great, really. I just hope this helps."

"Well, please do let us know how you're doing. Give us a call in a few weeks, okay?" He gave me another firm, honest handshake. "Thanks for coming in today."

With that, it was over.

I stood up, walked to the mirror, dabbed the remaining bloody spots from my jaw and neck, and went about my way, loaded up on Botox—the most powerful neurotoxin in the world—and the last drug on earth I ever thought I'd be injecting.

THE RELIEF FROM the constant contraction in my muscles was almost instantaneous. Within a few hours the web-like tautness along my windpipe seemed to loosen. The pull to look down at the ground also lessened. And the gnawing pain in my neck, jaw, and shoulder began to fade. It was as if the needles had popped my muscles, letting the tension out like air from a tire.

It was an absolute miracle. I felt so good that I went home, put on my running shoes, and headed out for a mid-afternoon run around the lake. Usually I run in the morning, when I feel best. But I needed to get outdoors, stand up, expand my lungs, and run—as hard and fast as I could. I took off, breathing in the crisp early spring air and feeling the life in my lungs.

I marveled at the miracles of medicine as I sat and ate dinner with far less difficulty swallowing. It's not a cure—Botox needs to be repeated every three months—but at least, for a little while, I was feeling some relief.

For the first time in a few years, I fell asleep pain free.

As SOON AS I awoke, though, I discovered the freedom was fleeting.

Flat on my back, I stared up at the ceiling, frightened. I tried to pick up my head, but I failed. I sent the signals from my brain to my neck once more, telling it to lift. But the message wasn't getting through. My muscles were paralyzed.

I picked up my hand and put it behind my head, lifting it up with me as I swung my feet to the floor and stood. Pressure swept upward toward my head as a searing pain settled in. The muscles at the base of my skull screamed.

For the next two weeks my head pounded constantly, and I had to wear a cervical collar just to keep my head off my chest.

The weakness diminished with time, but my head still hurt. My tongue still sat off in between my teeth on the right, and the pain in my shoulder wasn't gone, either. But at least the tautness and contraction in my neck muscles had lessened.

I was starting to feel better. I still couldn't sit up in a chair without pain and posture problems, but at least I could stand straight, hold my head up, breathe deep, and run.

For the first time since my brain got sick, I could run without pain, difficulty, and discomfort. The right side of my rib cage no longer burned when I breathed in. My neck wasn't going into spasms, and I no longer felt lopsided, leaning way off to my right.

I was alive again. I felt motivated, inspired. Like nothing in the world could stop me. For all the things I was losing and could no longer do, I was not about to give up on the activity that had been my saving grace in sobriety. I might not be the fastest runner in the world, or the most mechanically efficient, but running breathes life into my soul.

I've clung tightly to my ability to run, to do what has come so naturally to humans for so long. Even if I am slow, neurologically impaired, and fighting through pain with every stride, I don't care. All my life I've proved people wrong when they said I couldn't do something. They said I couldn't play hockey with the boys. They said I couldn't get sober in outpatient treatment. They said I'd never finish my degree.

Nobody ever told me I couldn't run a marathon. But as soon as I mentioned it, people started to doubt me. They never thought I'd be able to make it. They worried something bad might happen if I tried to push myself and my muscles to such an extreme.

Fueled by the intoxicating fumes of feeling a little better, I kept getting drawn toward the registration page on the Twin Cities Marathon website. I heard and understood the naysayers and their concerns. But I kept wanting to prove them wrong.

Running a marathon seemed like the next logical step. Since getting sober in 2004, I'd run a few 5Ks, 10Ks, and even a few half marathons. But for as much as I had always wanted to run a full marathon, I wasn't sure I could actually make it 26.2 miles. And that was before my health fell apart.

With the onset of a chronic health condition at such a young age, and with being told by numerous doctors that I had a difficult future ahead of me, a marathon seemed impossible—yet another goal I'd never be able to accomplish.

I wasn't giving into such self-defeating thoughts, though. I was tired of letting my past prevent me from doing the things I wanted to do with my life. Even if there wasn't anyone in the world who expected me to be able to run 26.2 miles, I was determined to give it my best shot.

On a beautiful spring day in April, I went to the Twin Cities Marathon website, entered my information, pressed enter, and paid money to torture myself for the next four months.

RUNNING IS MORE than just a test of your will and self-discipline. It's like a drug in that it can get you high. But when you discover its benefits and start to respect it for its intensity, it doesn't become an addiction. It becomes a way of life.

If I ran every day, I'd run my body into the ground. I don't exercise compulsively. I haven't replaced my addiction to chemicals with running. I've learned to enjoy running in moderation because it's something I want to enjoy for as long as I can.

Sure, there are some days I want to run but don't because it's my day off. I'm flexible with my schedule but try to stick to three runs a week. Likewise there are days, especially when my dystonia is flaring up or my depression is dragging me down, that I have to force myself out the door. But what motivates me to get out there is that I know I'll feel better once I get going. Not only will the vigorous exercise force my overactive muscles to relax for a while once I'm done, but I'll also be riding as intense of a high as I've ever experienced.

The longer you sit around in a dark room, staying idle, the harder it is to drag yourself out of the cycle. Much like with addiction or depression, at some point you have to grab the reins and take hold of your life. That means taking responsibility for yourself and your behavior. If you don't at least try to make healthy decisions and choices, it will become harder and harder to stop making poor ones.

The longer I stayed mired in my addiction, the easier it became to stay there. The more I've committed myself to a healthy lifestyle and sobriety, the easier it's become to maintain. The same can be said for running. The more disciplined I am about getting in a few quality runs each week, the easier it is to get myself out the door for the next one, even on the days when I don't feel like doing it.

In fact, when I don't get my run in, I feel it. I have an urge there. It's a good urge, like the urge to pee when your bladder is full or to eat when you're hungry. My craving to run is healthy. It's my body talking to me, and I've learned to listen.

It tells me that if I can get even just a mile or two in, then I've won. I've invigorated my heart and my brain, and set life cascading into motion within my body. Each stride, each breath, feels like a practice in maintaining a balanced, healthy life.

Running is like taking life and breathing it all in. For a significant period of time back in 1998, I couldn't breathe, couldn't get oxygen. Today, I thrive on feeling it flow freely through my lungs.

Mile after mile, I discovered, that's exactly what I was in for when I registered myself for a marathon. Three days a week I was going to be taking in a whole lot of strides, breathing in a whole lot of life.

SINCE IT WAS my first marathon, I followed a beginner's training program. I was already comfortable running a considerable distance, but at some point I got out of that comfort zone.

Each Sunday I increased the distance of my long run. Pretty soon I was up to fourteen miles, further than I'd ever run before.

The day of the fourteen-miler fell on a wicked muggy day, when breathing in the air felt like inhaling pea soup. Anybody, not just people with my history of smoking, would have struggled on that hot August day. During the final few miles of the run, the thoughts of giving up set in. But I couldn't do that. I pushed myself through and finished.

But I wasn't confident I could repeat the task. I was hurting much of the following week, mostly at the front of my right hip. Knowing bad hips run in the family, I was reluctant to drive my legs into the ground anymore. Thankfully, I had an extra week to heal before my next long run.

When the day came, I was eager to lace up my shoes. Perfect running conditions were calling me. So out the door I went for sixteen miles.

Krissy rode alongside me on her bike, offering up water and orange slices. I approached another runner who looked familiar. She turned out to be an old hockey friend who was also training to run the Twin Cities Marathon. She and I won a state championship together back when I was fourteen and full of potential. Seeing her again after all those years, in that circumstance, made me feel as if my life had come full circle. She'd known me as an athlete, before addiction derailed my life. Now here I was, a health nut, succeeding despite neurological problems in the wake of my chemical dependency.

That awareness pushed me through the last three very painful miles. It was farther than I'd ever run before. I knew I was pushing my body, and my dystonia, to the absolute limit. But no matter how much my muscles pulled, no matter how hard it got for me to stay standing straight up and breathing properly, I wasn't going to give up.

I'd set a goal for myself. I was gonna run a marathon, and nothing was going to stop me. No matter how much it hurt on a dystonia level, I wasn't going to quit. Or so I told myself.

After my sixteen-mile jaunt, though, I started to feel a different kind of pain—the type of pain that runs from your hip all the way to the outside of your knee. That part of your body is called your iliotibial band, and it can be the bane of a runner's existence. When it gets tight and flares up, it makes it nearly impossible to run. The more you run through it, the worse the injury gets. The remedy is to rest, ice, and elevate it. The alternative is a chronic injury, one that could jeopardize not only my ability to run a marathon but my ability to run injury-free forever.

It's one thing to push yourself through pain. It's a completely different thing to push through injury. I had to rest. But I only had one week before my next long run, 18 miles. All I had to do was make it through that and then a 20-miler, and I'd be set. Most marathoners train up to 20 miles for a 26.2-mile race on the idea that their fitness and adrenaline will carry them to the finish line. I was banking on it.

Ice pack strapped to my knee, I took a spot on the couch.

26

Running for My Life

I made it through the eighteen-miler. But halfway through the twenty, I had to stop. I couldn't run safely through the injury any longer. And if I did, there was no way I'd make it to the starting line in three weeks.

On the bright side, at least I had three weeks. When running a marathon, it's important to taper back your mileage as you get closer to the race. My training plan, like most, gave me three weeks of tapering.

It feels weird to scale back as the race gets closer. You worry that you'll be out of shape by the time the big day rolls around. But if you've trained properly, then you're already in the shape you need to be in three weeks prior to the event. The grueling nature of the race needs to be respected. Those last three weeks are better spent resting and recovering from your training than pounding yourself into the ground. Thankfully, those weeks also allow injuries to heal.

It occurred to me that I wouldn't be able to recover from it as well if I were still smoking.

Quitting smoking is not easy. It's a tough habit to kick. But at some point in every addiction, you have to put everything you have into the decision to quit. Whatever gratification you're getting out of it isn't enough to offset the problems it's causing. At some point, my desire to run and live and inhale life outweighed my desire to smoke a cigarette.

No matter how deeply addicted you are, you also have to believe that you will not fail when you set out to accomplish your goal. You have to believe that you can stop, that you can change. Alcoholics Anonymous teaches that willpower will keep you sick. I disagree. I believe it helps you finally get well. Of course, nobody's will is strong enough to control an addiction. But when you're ready to get well, at some point you have to employ willpower.

I'D BEEN SMOKE-FREE for almost a year. As I contemplated this, an awkward sensation overcame me. Something I don't usually feel. It felt good. I was proud of myself.

After twelve plus years of smoking, I'd quit cold turkey, on my first try, and not had a single puff since. The realization provided me with internal confirmation that I could accomplish any goal I put my mind to. If I could quit smoking, then I could run a marathon.

I knew I was ready.

The Friday night before the race, I picked up my runner's packet. Such packets typically include your race bib and a small chip that you place on your shoe, which times you from the moment you cross the start line to the time you finish.

The Twin Cities Marathon draws over ten thousand runners every year. If you aren't up near the front when the gun goes off, it can be a good ten minutes before your feet actually cross the start line. That's the benefit of chip timers. They keep track of your own unique race data.

Chip and race bib in hand, I spent Saturday anxiously anticipating Sunday's race. The hours dragged by.

It's never easy to sleep the night before a big race, but I dozed off soundly without trouble and awoke on a mission. I'd come so far. And now it was time to get to work. To show the world just what a recovering crack addict, alcoholic, neurologically impaired person can accomplish.

After a frantic morning spent worrying and wondering what it was that I was forgetting, Krissy and I finally got out the door. A few blocks from home, I realized it was my winter hat, which I'd need for the cool temperatures. We dashed back to the house to grab it and headed out toward the Metrodome in downtown Minneapolis, the site of the starting line.

Being late for a race is never a good idea. Though the gun hadn't gone off yet, the crowd had been established. I was at the back of the pack. There was no way I'd be able to run my normal pace, given my placement in the mass of people. I tried to push my way forward but found most people unwilling to accommodate the requests of a lonely, single runner looking to move up in the pack.

I stepped up on my tiptoes to get a glimpse of the scene. I was so far back, I couldn't even see the starting line or hear when the gun went off. But eventually, the mob started to move forward.

The sound of cowbells clanging rang through the air as we inched toward the start. Encouraging cheers came from all sides. "Go, runners! This is it! This is the race! Give it everything you've got!" The sounds of thunder sticks and drums surrounded us.

What had started as a walking pace was evolving now into a slow jog. I wiggled my way to the side of the course and inched my way forward. Up ahead, I could see the starting line. At a slower pace than I would've hoped for, I approached it. My foot crossed the mat, and with that step I set off on my marathon journey.

Even if it had been ten minutes since the gun had gone off, I didn't care. I wasn't racing anyone. Not even myself. I was merely on the course to accomplish a goal: to do something I never in my wildest dreams would have thought I could accomplish. After everything I'd pushed myself through in life, this was my reward. To show the world that, no matter how the odds are stacked against you, when you put your mind to a goal, nothing can stop you.

The first mile was a treat. Meandering through the streets of downtown Minneapolis at 8 AM on a Sunday morning, I found it hard to believe that the streets could hold so many people, all of them cheering and motivating us to keep putting one foot in front of the other. Mile after mile, they were there. And every single one of them was there to support me. What more motivation could you need?

Before I even knew it, I was approaching the half marathon point. It was just a few miles ahead when the pain in my iliotibial band started to flare up. I picked up my right leg, but with each stride it seemed to grow heavier. By mile 12, I was growing concerned as to whether I'd make it to the end of the race. No matter how bad it hurt, I was going to keep pressing on, though. This was the moment I'd worked so hard to accomplish. I wasn't about to give up.

I knew that Krissy awaited me at the halfway point, at a spot very close to where I live and train. I held onto the thought for inspiration. If I could make it to my home, then I could make it to the finish line in St. Paul.

Thinking about running home, to the halfway point, made the length of the race feel more manageable. One step at a time, I pushed forward, thinking more about the smaller goal of making it halfway. It was working. It was taking my mind off my knee.

When I finally rounded the southeast corner of the lake, to approach where Krissy was waiting, I wasn't feeling the pain at all. I could see her up in the distance, holding the bright neon sign we thought to be so defining of the occasion.

"You're Crazy!" it read. Sure enough, that's precisely how I felt. Some chuckles could be heard from the runners on my sides as we got closer to the sign.

As soon as I reached Krissy, I came to a stop. It was my intermission. My rest.

I sat down in the grass and propped my head up, elbows on my knees. "Wow," I said, panting. "This is it. I'm running a marathon, and I'm halfway there! But I wish I could just stop here and go home. I'm so tired already."

Krissy unscrewed the cap from a sports drink. "You're doing great, Jen. You look fantastic." She nudged me with her arm. "Here, drink some of this. Do you want an orange? A banana? Fig Newton?"

I downed a few careful swallows, ever mindful of my difficulties with that activity. "I'm okay, actually. I think I just want to change my hat. It's soaked." Krissy fished my baseball cap from her shoulder bag. I removed my sopping wet winter hat, threw the dry cap on in place of it, and bounced to my feet.

"Alright, I think I'm ready!" I said. "I'll see you at mile 17?"

"Yup. I'll be there. Keep up the good work!"

I started off toward the next mile marker as Krissy shouted one last encouragement. "You're awesome, Jen! You can do this!"

I couldn't help but look back over my shoulder and smile. "I know I can."

I rounded the northeast corner of the lake, where the course connects to a parkway. The narrower roadway made for much tighter conditions. Suddenly, runners were in much closer proximity. It couldn't generate enough body heat to keep me warm, though.

Along with my winter hat, I'd also left with Krissy the light jacket I'd been wearing over my long sleeve T-shirt. It was soaking wet, and I'd been growing too warm for the 50 degree temperatures. But, without it, I was fast becoming chilled. Dystonia can make you very sensitive to temperature changes.

By mile 15, the nagging pain in my iliotibial band was starting to burn. I couldn't let it stop me, though. I had to press on. Turn by turn, stride after stride, breath by breath, I kept inching my way closer to my goal.

At mile 17, I greeted Krissy a second time. "My hip is really hurting," I said as I slowed for a quick drink.

"Uh-oh. That's not good." She handed over a bottle containing the electrolytes my body was craving. I took a swig.

Just as quickly as I stopped, I was ready to go again. "It's okay," I said. "I'm not quitting until I can't pick this leg up at all."

Krissy smirked, knowing full well my stubborn nature. "Alright, well, make sure you keep listening to your body, okay?"

I smiled. "You know I will. That's what I do best." I handed off the sports drink and darted off, picking up my pace. "See you at mile 21!"

Mile 18 turned to 19. Each step seemed to be getting heavier on my right leg. The dystonia, which was starting to get aggravated by the grueling nature of the endurance test I was putting my body through, was only exacerbating my imbalance. With each step, I fought against my body's inclination to lean to my right. Step by step, the pull grew greater. Step by step, I kept fighting back. I wasn't going to let my condition stop me from finishing the race.

Another mile down, I rounded the corner and crossed a bridge over the Mississippi, officially marking my arrival in St. Paul. I was approaching mile 20, a distance in the marathon at which many runners have been known to hit "the wall."

I knew my body needed fuel. I'd been keeping myself well hydrated and taken in a good amount of carbohydrates, but I needed to load up one last time.

It's vital to know how to fuel yourself when running a marathon. With time and attention, you begin to learn what your body is craving and why. By mile 20, my body was begging for carbohydrates.

I retrieved my last chewy block from my pouch but would have to wait until the next hydration station to get a glass of Powerade. I slowed to a walk as I chomped on the gumdrop-like chew. It's not recommended to take them without water, and my mouth was already parched. But in this instance I had no choice but to force it down dry. I needed it to help propel me up the steepest hill on the course, between miles 20 and 22. Those also happen to be the most demanding miles of the marathon, on both the body and the mind.

Surely I wasn't the only runner on the course whose legs were growing exceptionally heavy. But I picked them up and settled back into a slow trot as the weighted, achy sensation in my feet spread up into my calves.

My legs were out of their comfort zone. I'd reached that point in the race where I was beyond any distance I'd ever trained for. From this point forward, I would need to rely on my fitness and adrenaline to propel me through.

Stride by stride, I considered my position, my body, and my ability to push through the last six miles. Picking up my right leg, I corrected my posture to adjust myself back to center, forever compensating for the pull of the dystonia.

As I wrestled internally against my condition, suddenly it occurred to me. The pain in my hip and knee, the pain I most worried would jeopardize my ability to finish the race, was gone. It had vanished entirely.

I couldn't believe it. I trekked up the hill, plowing my way forward, fearful with each step that the momentary reprieve would cease. It did not. For whatever reason, it simply disappeared. Maybe the overall fatigue and exhaustion settling into my legs was drowning out everything else. Whatever it was, I didn't care. All I knew was that I could pick up my leg and plant it without wondering whether my knee was going to buckle.

I drove further up the hill. Close to the top, I saw a mile marker and a Powerade station. Not only had I found the electrolytes I needed, but I was close to conquering the largest hill on the course. If I could make it to the top, it would be all downhill from there.

Step by step I continued to climb, and at mile 22, I reached the top.

But my body was starting to rebel against everything I was putting it through. Without my winter hat, my ears had started to go numb from the cold. I was deeply chilled. There were runners out there in T-shirts, but I've never been able to go out in short sleeves in

50-degree weather. In addition to all of my other problems, the brain doctors tell me I have some autonomic dysfunction. That means that my body can't always regulate things like heart rate, blood pressure, and body temperature all that well. And being cold is one of the worst aggravators for dystonia.

Now, approaching mile 23, I was starting to wonder whether the stress and impact of the race were going to be too much for my body.

I was growing ever colder by the moment. The chilled sensation creeping through my cells was causing my neck muscles to spasm.

I raised my shoulders in response to the pulsing pain at the back of my head. Pins and needles stabbed my palms and fingers, while electric shocks zinged through the back of my right hand. Spots started circling through my vision. My hearing became hollow, and my head began to ring. And for the first time in my life, I started to feel pain radiating from the bones in my neck, not just from my muscles.

Thank goodness it was time for another stop to meet Krissy. I ran right by her as we started down the long, flat, tree-lined stretch that takes the runners to the finish line at the State Capitol.

With the benefit of a bike, though, she caught right back up to me. "Jen! Hey!"

Her voice barely registered with me as I pressed on, lost in my ambition. Out of the corner of my eye, though, I caught a glimpse of her and slowed to a walk.

I pulled the bud of my headphones from my left ear and walked to the side of the course. "Thank God you're here," I said. "My neck hurts. And my whole face is numb. I've got these pins and needles in my hands, and this electrical shock keeps zinging the back of my right hand. Some of this feels unlike anything I've ever felt. I don't know if I can do this much longer."

Krissy shot me a look of great concern. "You've come too far to give up now. I mean, do you think you can keep going?"

"Yeah, yeah. I think I can. I'm not gonna quit."

"No, you're gonna do this, Jen. I'll meet you at mile 25, okay?"

"25? No way! We're not even to 23!"

"Okay, okay. I won't go that far. Do you want me to bike alongside you?"

"No, no. Go ahead. Up to 24. How's that?"

"Sounds good."

Krissy took off, steering through the flocks of people lining each side of the street. The crowds were growing thicker with each mile. The constant clank of cowbells and noisemakers was now interspersed with the sounds of marching bands, guitars, and amplified radio stations. The constant cheers and encouragement pushed me to keep picking up my lead feet.

It couldn't help me adjust my temperature, though. I pressed on through my chills. Even with mile marker 23 now behind me, 24 still seemed so far away. I tried to lose myself in my music, to get high on the moment. But the distance I had yet to conquer was starting to feel insurmountable.

My neck was as rigid as a board. I desperately needed to address my temperature problem. With each step, I seemed to lose more of my core body heat. Pretty soon, I was so cold that I couldn't hold my head up. I hunched down and forward, trying to protect myself from heat loss the way you would in a cold January wind. But the posture I was adapting wasn't voluntary in the slightest.

Without Krissy by my side, I was starting to doubt myself. Everyone else around me looked just as tired as I was, but they probably weren't battling the uncertainties of a body that had been beaten, broken, and battered the way mine had. They might not have been running through what I was, but I reminded myself that the race wasn't easy for anyone. I was surely not the only one out there running against the odds, either. If the other people around me could keep pressing on, then so could I.

After fighting my way through mile 23, I got another glimpse of Krissy. I slowed up as I approached her, losing more time to idleness. It didn't matter. What was important wasn't the time on the clock, but my own goal: making it to the finish line in one piece.

I was starting to feel very shaky. It's that shakiness that's caused me to have both seizures and syncopal episodes. I know the feeling well, and it's something I dread.

My thoughts started to spin. Though I was still feeling well fueled and hydrated, I wondered whether I was pushing myself too hard, too far. A pulsing pressure weighed my head down. I fought against the pull to drop it to my chest. When I picked it back up, dizziness and light-headedness set in once more.

"I'm starting to feel like I'm just gonna pass out or something," I told Krissy. "I don't want to collapse or something here."

She hopped off her bike and pushed it alongside her as we walked along the edge of the course. "You're gonna be okay. You've come so far, Jen. I can't believe you're doing so great. You can do this!"

"I'm not so sure," I said. "I'm so cold. My legs are so heavy, and I think I might pass out if I don't lie down."

"You're cold? You look cold, actually. Your lips are blue. Here." She stopped and stripped off her black fleece. "Do you want this?"

"No, no. You've just got a T-shirt on. You'll get so cold if I take that. Do you have my jacket?"

"It's sopping wet, Jen. It'll be cold. Just, here, take this." She shoved the fleece my direction.

I threw it on and zipped it up to hug my neck. It was already warm.

"Do you want something to drink or anything?" Krissy asked.

"No." I adjusted my sleeves. "I'm okay. Thank you. This is—this is going to make all the difference in the world." I started to pick up my pace and settled back into a jog. "Just, whatever you do, just stay by my side. This is just—I don't know what this is. This is just too hard on my body."

"But you're gonna do this! Just keep going!"

"Yeah," I said. "I'm gonna do this. I'm gonna *do this*."

With a warm, dry jacket, my core started to warm up. My neck muscles began to loosen. And suddenly, I got a second wind.

But during mile 24, my legs turned to Jell-o. My neck turned back to stone. My body pulled to the right. And with each step, my legs tugged at me with more urgency, instructing me to stop.

I didn't listen. Even though every step seemed to intensify the dystonia, I pressed on.

Mile marker 25 was visible in the distance ahead of me. So was Krissy. "John and Vanessa are just up ahead at the bridge!" she said. I knew my brother and his wife were going to be there at the race, but I hadn't known where.

"What bridge? The one at the finish?"

"Yeah, just up ahead."

"You're kidding, right? I've still got a mile and a half to go, and you tell me they're *just* up ahead?" She had no idea what sort of misery I was in. When you've already gone over twenty-four miles, and you're fighting your body's wish to do nothing more than stop, going another mile and a half can seem almost impossible. They were not *just* up ahead. They were over a mile away.

A MILE I had yet to conquer. Fueled by the frustration of the moment, I pushed myself another quarter mile, passing the mile 25 marker; 1.5 miles was now down to 1.2. Then down to 1.

My neck and legs were orchestrating a rebellion. They were in absolute defiance of my continued efforts to press on. But there was no injury screaming at me, no pain that felt like bad pain. It was just me and body, fighting a battle, together but apart. My mind was telling me to do one thing, my body telling me to do another—much like dystonia.

I wasn't about to give up on myself. I wasn't about to stop fighting for my goal, no matter if my body was begging me stop. This was a time for me to push through—to respect and listen to my body, to appreciate its limitations, but to never give up. I had to keep believing I could conquer this.

Internally I wrestled with the demons of my past. My history, my wrongdoings, my mistakes, and my amends all saturated my memory in the moment. With less than one mile left, I was sure I'd make it. The only question was how long it would take to drag myself across the finish line. The final mile seemed to go on forever.

I slowed to another stop and hung my head. Krissy hopped off her bike. "You're so close now, Jen. Don't stop."

"I'm just dying here," I said. "This is—this is miserable. I'm never doing this again. Hear me? I'm running this race and then never ever again. This is just too hard on me, with all my muscle and neurological problems. I just—I just can't do this."

"You *are* doing it! You're almost there! Just around this corner is the Capitol."

"Really? This is the final turn?"

"Yeah, right up here. Don't give up! Keep going! I'll see you at the finish line!"

Too tired to articulate a response, I smiled and settled back into the middle of the road. I pressed on, anxiously anticipating the final turn.

I had run the last few miles of this course in a ten-mile race a few years before. I knew what the final turn was like. It was one of the best highs I'd ever experienced.

I began losing myself in thoughts of the finish line as a middle-aged woman approached me. Her sky blue T-shirt matched her bright, cheery disposition. She put an arm on my shoulder. "Have you run this race before?" she said.

"No," I said, wiping away a tear. "This is my first marathon." I was lacking the strength and orientation to explain that I'd run the end of the course, though.

"It's amazing. The fans will bring you home."

I knew they would, too.

My neck, forever tugging at me, pulled me to stare at the ground. Looking down at my feet as they lumbered forward, I forced myself to pick up my head and look to my left. I was at the cathedral at the top of the hill.

Below, a sea of people. The homestretch. And in the distance, the finish line.

Stride for stride with my new pal, we each picked up the pace, descending the final hill to the finish. The adrenaline kicked in, the endorphins started pumping, and suddenly, the pain vanished. There was no heaviness in my legs, no muscle pulling in my neck, no pins and needles in my arms.

We headed down the hill. A smile crept over my face as I plowed through the final steps of the race. This was it. This is what I worked so hard for. This was the high that I'd been seeking. I was aiming at the finish line, flying on my feet at top speed.

The State Capitol building, up ahead in the distance, was getting closer with each stride. The home stretch was right here and now. All around me, cheers. A sea of people on both sides of the road roared in approval, fueling my high.

Up to my right, I could see John and hear his voice. "Yeah! Way to go, Jen! That's my little sister there!"

I approached, riding a grin stretching ear to ear. "Oh. My. God!" I screamed. "I just ran a marathon! I can't believe this! I can't believe I just did this!"

I reached out an arm, gave John a high five, and threw my arms overhead in triumph.

I trotted off to the finish line, riding a high better than that of any drug I've ever done. It was like running on air, and it propelled me the final few steps.

Finally, I crossed the line. I finished a marathon.

It hardly seemed real. I slowed to a walk as the blood immediately started to pool up in my legs. My thoughts spun as my life flashed before my eyes.

I ALMOST DIED. I was accused of running over a police officer, kicked out of college, told that I was too far gone to ever be saved. And despite it all, I triumphed. I overcame. I fought back from the brink of death and got myself well. Even if my body is forever scarred by what I put it through, I conquered my demons. I survived my suicide, beat my addiction, and pushed through dystonia to conquer one of the ultimate tests of human endurance.

It was, in a sense, a confirmation that I am still very much alive in this world, that there is a lot of life left here on Earth for me to live, and that despite everything I've put my brain and body through, I am still here in this body, living this life, for a reason.

I am still breathing.

EPILOGUE

Rewired

All any of us have is today. None of us is guaranteed a tomorrow. So we should all make it a point to live in the moment.

I've lost quite a few friends to addiction and mental illness. A few died. Some stopped calling. Others I stopped calling back.

Back when I was in the throes of addiction, my friends tolerated me but didn't put up with my shit. They were there for me when I needed them but called me out when I stepped over the line. I appreciated that. But somewhere along the way, people stopped caring about what I was going through and started expecting me to get the hell out of it. It was a slow transition, but once it hit, it stuck. Slowly but surely, my friends—and my family—got sick of my being sick. And so did I. So I made a decision to change, and I never looked back.

But some things about brain injuries and chemical dependency you just can't move through. I can't take it back. My life happened.

According to my movement disorder neurologist, I've "rewired" my brain via my head injuries and chemical dependency. I'll never be the same again. I have a team of doctors at the University of Minnesota now, where I'm a regular. I've spent much of the first thirty years of my life in therapy or rehab of one form or another. I have to believe that things can only get better from here.

The truth is, life is what you make it. And I didn't get anywhere using drugs or drinking. I didn't get creative or productive. I didn't make friends. I just got dumb. I got fucked up to get away from reality. So now, all these years later, I might get so far away from reality that I lose touch with it entirely.

The course with repetitive head trauma can be hard to predict, my doc says. It scares me a lot that we even have to discuss it.

Despite my efforts to stave it off, the dystonia has spread into my abdominals, making running even more of a challenge. I still receive Botox injections every three months and battle the weakness and side effects that accompany it, but I hold out hope that I'll live to see a cure for a poorly understood disorder. I also continue to run.

The dystonia, in my case, is a symptom of my injuries and may well be connected to my brain-wave abnormalities. Most people with dystonia don't experience the sweating and limb pain I do. Between my repeat dislocations and suicide attempt, I sustained an injury to the brachial plexus—the bundle of nerves that runs from your neck to your arms. Thus I experience both nerve pain and symptoms, in addition to the muscle pain and symptoms from the dystonia.

It's all put me at such high risk of surgical complications that I've been encouraged not to have my shoulder repaired. I've also been advised to stay away from psychiatric medications, including antidepressants. I guess I really am complicated after all. But I couldn't be more grateful to have the best doctors in the country monitoring my condition.

Addiction and depression will always be a part of me. So too will the neurological consequences of my history.

Sometimes I wonder who I would've been if I had quit playing hockey when the boys started checking. Or if I had never tried drugs or drank. Sometimes I can't believe I went through all that and that I came through it alive. There was a "me" before, and there is a "me" now. But the two people are in no way the same. They merely inhabit the same skin.

I lost who I was when I lost the best years of my life. But I've learned more about addiction in my sobriety than I ever did while using. I think back on my using years every day, and though I am many years sober, I always have to remember I'm just one slip away from a great big fall. Still, it's a heck of a position to be in—to be a person with a history of mental illness and chemical dependency, living in chronic pain. I used drugs and drank to escape emotional pain; now I live in chronic physical pain and so have to take drugs.

I have to be both very responsible and very careful.

I'm prescribed medications that not only are psychologically addictive but can cause physiological dependence and severe side effects, including suicidal thoughts and depression. I reluctantly take these meds, but only as needed. They make me feel drunk, and they have a detrimental impact on my self-esteem.

I've also used marijuana to mange my pain. Not only do I believe it to be a safer and more natural alternative to pharmaceuticals, it has also proven superior at alleviating my pain and discomfort. Even the government agrees that marijuana has medicinal value for my conditions. I've used it only in moderation, only within my home, and only at the end of the day. But just as I don't want to rely on pills, I don't want to rely on marijuana to manage my pain, either. At some point, you have to pick your battles.

I can't do anything to make dystonia go away. I can't change my behavior or my thinking and put my condition in remission. Unless there's a cure, I'll spend every minute of the rest of my life battling the pain and discomfort of dystonia and nerve pain.

Despite all the consequences I've been left with, I've been forever transformed by what I've endured. It's an empowering moment when you can look back and realize that you've not just survived what you've been through, but thrived. You've not just recovered, but discovered.

You can conquer what you put your mind to. Adversity *can* shape you, and you *can* come through the other side a stronger person. But you don't have to go through hell— or face near-death—to be able to appreciate life. You just have to listen for the lessons. So today and every day going forward, I'll make it a point to appreciate every step, and every breath, I'm still able to take.

I hope you will, too.

Sources Consulted

Adams, Nick. "Near Hanging." *Emergency Medicine* 11, no. 1 (March 1999): 17–21(5).

Diesing, T. Scott, and Eelco F. M. Wijdicks. "Arc de Cercle and Dysautonomia from Anoxic Injury." *Movement Disorders* 21, no. 6 (2006): 868–69.

Kaki, Abdullah. "Airway and Respiratory Management Following Non-Lethal Hanging." *Canadian Journal of Anesthesia* 44, no. 4 (1997): 445–50.

"Law: *Reynolds v. Reynolds.*" *Time*, January 23, 1933, http://www .time.com/time/magazine/article/0,9171,744981,00.html.

Matsuyama, Takeshi, Kazuo Okuchi, Tadahiko Seki, and Yoshi-nori Murao. "Prognostic Factors in Hanging Injuries." *American Journal of Emergency Medicine* 22, no. 3 (May 2004): 207–10.

"National Suicide Statistics at a Glance: Percentage of Suicides, by Age Group, Sex and Mechanism, United States, 2002–2006." Centers for Disease Control and Prevention. September 30, 2009. http://www.cdc.gov/ViolencePrevention/suicide/statistics/ mechanism02.html.

Sauvageau, Anny. "Agonal Sequences in Four Filmed Hangings: Analysis of Respiratory and Movement Responses to Asphyxia by Hanging." *Journal of Forensic Science* 54, no. 1 (January 2009): 192–94.

Acknowledgments

This book was a project thirteen years in the making. My suicide attempt in 1998 left me with the message to write it. For nearly ten years I assembled bits and pieces, prepared drafts, and preserved documents and journal entries. In the fall of 2008 I was finally able to start telling the story. It would take three more long years to write and publish this book, but it would have never come to fruition without Krissy's unwavering support. Through thick and thin, she stood by my side as I relived each and every moment captured in this book and poured my heart out onto these pages.

I owe tremendous thanks to her and her family; to my mom, John, and Chris; and to Tina, Heather, and Brian for their encouraging words and feedback and for at times playing the role of my personal book therapist.

Thanks to Scott Edelstein and Mary Jean Port for their input and guidance in the creative formation of this book; to Beth Wright, Ann Delgehausen, and Zan Ceeley of Trio Bookworks for their time and attention to the production of this project; to Brad Norr for his creative insights and outstanding cover design; and to Vanessa Cannon for her exceptional photography.

I'd also like to thank all those who supported me throughout this journey, including everyone in my dystonia family. To my health care providers, for their patience and compassion in helping me manage and treat my conditions, and anyone else who inspired me to make changes in my life: thank you.

To learn more about dystonia, please visit www.dystonia.us. To learn more about me, including my races and upcoming speaking events, please contact me via my website: www.runningrewired.com.

This book is dedicated to my grandmother, Claudia Brewer Strite, whose stories about the Mississippi Chinese stay with me. It is also dedicated to Conor Brownell, Meredith Brus, Sam Brus, and Bridget Brownell in hopes that those of us who occupy the space between my grandmother's life and their adulthoods will pass on to them a more peaceful world.

Contents

Illustrations

Acknowledgments

This book has crystallized out of the fourteen years of research, writing, and speaking that I have done since finishing my first book in 1993. In those years, I have benefited from the numerous friendships and professional exchanges that contributed to this book. I would like to thank my friend and colleague Michael Cosmopoulos for urging me to go ahead and write it as well as for his support of my professional career in general. I would like to thank my mother, Claudia Strite Brownell, for editing and commenting on drafts. As always, she is my harshest critic and most reliable supporter. I also thank Laurie and Tag Strite for providing a peaceful paradise for me to escape work and finish writing.

My trips to China between 2002 and 2006 and my archival research at the Olympic Studies Center in Lausanne, Switzerland, were funded by fellowships from the Center for International Studies and a Research Award from the University of Missouri, St. Louis. The primary purpose of the funding was to translate *He Zhenliang and China's Olympic Dream* into English. I am honored to have had the opportunity to work with He Zhenliang and Liang Lijuan on this project and learned a great deal from their decades of experience in sport diplomacy. Philippe Blanchard and Nuria Puig of the Olympic Studies Center of the International Olympic Committee (IOC) in Lausanne introduced me to many of the practical problems for the Olympic Movement discussed in this book and facilitated my access to the IOC archives. I am grateful to Ren Hai for intellectual exchange as well as for providing me with office space and making arrangements for me at the Beijing Sport University and the State Sports General Administration. I am also grateful to his students, Wang Fang, Qiu Xue, and Qiu Xiaohui, who facilitated my research.

This book utilizes portions of some previously published articles and chapters, which are acknowledged at the start of the chapters. Most of the manuscript is drawn from invited lectures and conference papers that I have delivered over the past fourteen years. For those invitations, I am grateful to Miquel de Moragas and Kostas Georgiadis for the International Symposium on "Television and the Olympic Games: Cultural Exchanges and the Understanding of Olympic Values" at the International Olympic Academy, Olympia, Greece (1993); John Bale and Olof Moen for the International Conference on "The Stadium and the City" at the University of Gothenburg, Sweden (1993) and again for the International conference on "Citius, Altius, Fortius: Social Scientific and Humanistic Studies of Athletics" in Gothenburg (1998); Mayfair Yang for the International Conference on "Mass Media, Gender Formation, and Public Sphere/Public Culture: Mainland China, Hong Kong, Taiwan" at the University of California, Santa Barbara (1995); Liu Xin and Yeh Wen-hsin for an invitation to talk at the Institute of East Asian Studies, University of California, Berkeley (1996); Chuck Korr for the panel discussion on "The Whole World Was Watching: The 1996 Olympics and the Politics of Television" at the Center for the Humanities and the Center for International Studies, University of Missouri, St. Louis (1997); Wayne Wilson for the conference on "Doping and Elite Sport" at the LA84 Foundation, Los Angeles (1998); Judy Polumbaum for the international seminar on "Sport and Cultural Distinctiveness" at the University of Iowa (1999); Doug Hartmann and Mary Jo Kane for the panel discussion on "Images of Women, Sexuality and Nationalism: What's (Olympic) Sport Got to Do with It?" at the Tucker Center for Research on Girls and Women in Sport, University of Minnesota (2000); John Bale for the International Seminar on "Post-Olympism? Questioning Sport in the Twenty-First Century" at the University of Aarhus, Denmark (2002); Michael Cosmopoulos and the Greek Studies Program for the International Conference on "The Olympic Dream: Past, Present and Future of the Olympics" at the University of Missouri, St. Louis (2003); Andreas Niehaus for the invitation to talk at the East Asian Institute, University of Cologne, Cologne, Germany (2003); Prasenjit Duara for the Workshop on "The World in Asia, Asia in the World" at the University of Chicago (2003); Otto Schantz for the invitation to talk at the University of Koblenz-Landau, Germany (2004); Bob Edelman for the conference on "Globalization and Sport in Historical Context" at the University of California, San Diego (2005); Jens Andersen for the "Play the Game" Conference on "Governance in Sport: The Good, the Bad and the Ugly," Copenhagen, Denmark (2005); Haun Saussy for an invitation to talk at the Center for East Asian Studies at Yale University (2006); Steve Jackson and Steve Haigh for the 41st Otago Foreign Policy School Conference on "Sport and Foreign Policy in a Globalizing World" at the University of Otago, Dunedin, New Zealand (2006); Gerald Kenyon for the 9th World Leisure Congress, Hangzhou, China (2006); Philippe Blanchard and Nuria Puig for the 5th World Forum on Sport, Education and Culture, organized by the IOC's Commission on Culture and Olympic Education, in Beijing, China (2006); Monroe Price for the Workshops on "Communications and the Beijing Olympics" at the Annenberg School of Communication, University of Pennsylvania and the Communications University of China, Beijing, China (2006); Xu Xin and the Princeton-Harvard China and the World Program for an invitation to talk at Princeton University (2006); and Kostas Georgiadis for the 2nd World Congress on Sport Management at the University of the Peloponnese, Sparta, Greece (2007).

I also owe a debt to Sylvia Yu, who provided me with videotapes, helped me track media coverage of Chinese sports, and saved me much time and effort with her encyclopedic knowledge.

I have tried to write a book about the human side of the Beijing Olympic Games, and indeed the book itself was the result of human networks and support.

Note on Names and Translations

In this book, Chinese names are presented in the order in which Chinese people speak them—family name first, personal name second. The pinyin spelling system, which is used by the People's Republic of China, is generally used except in those cases where names are more commonly known by another spelling. Taiwanese names are spelled in the Wade-Giles system, which is preferred there.

All translations into English from Chinese and German were done by the author unless otherwise noted.

Introduction

What the Olympic Games Mean to China

In 2008, the Olympic Games will be hosted by the least westernized nation in the world to yet host them. It will be only the third time the Olympic Summer Games have been held outside the West, and it will be the greatest-ever meeting of East and West in peacetime. Surely this should be a moment to celebrate the interconnected global culture of the twenty-first century, but there has been a consistently negative reaction in the West centered around criticism of China's human rights record. When Beijing won the bid and it was shown live on Chinese television, tens of thousands of people took to the streets to celebrate. Why aren't we celebrating in the West?

Newspaper editorials that surrounded Beijing's Olympic bid in 2001 revealed the hostility toward the bid in the West: "China Doesn't Deserve the Olympics," "Unwelcome Bid from Beijing," "Olympics Tied Up in Chinese Puzzle," and others. During the bid process in 2001, multiple petitions were sent to Chinese leaders, the International Olympic Committee (IOC), multiple national governments, and human rights groups. Fax machines and e-mail inboxes were flooded with so many messages about Tibet and the religious sect Falun Gong that some had to be shut down. The U.S. Congress debated a resolution of opposition to the bid but finally did not pass it; the European Parliament passed a motion of opposition. As the opening ceremony on August 8, 2008, approached, the coverage appeared to have become even more negative. The ever-popular stereotype of China's sports boarding school system as organized child abuse produced headlines such as "Beware the March of China's Sinister Super-Race Champions," and coverage of a book on National Basketball Association star Yao Ming included the headline "NBA Star Was Bred to Push China Plan." In May 2007, actress Mia Farrow spearheaded an attack on China's support of the government of Sudan in which she labeled the Beijing Olympics the "genocide games."

People in the developed Western countries seem fixated on the question of whether the Olympic Games will change China. Will they improve China's human rights record? Will they open up China more to the outside world? As defined by the IOC, which awards the Olympic Games to the host city, the Olympics are supposed to be an occasion for cultural exchange and the improvement of international understanding, part of a movement for world peace through sport—the "Olympic Movement." The assumption in the West seems to be that any cultural exchange with China should be a one-way exchange in which China learns from the West, not a two-way dialogue. Chinese people hope that the West can learn something from China through the Olympic Games, but will it?

WHY IS THE WEST SO CONCERNED ABOUT CHANGING CHINA? PART I—THE MYTH OF THE MONOLITHIC COMMUNIST PARTY

Why is the West so concerned about changing China? One answer to this question should be fairly clear. In what used to be called "the free world," there is a deep mistrust of communism left from the Cold War. China's central government is still largely a one-party system with nonelected leaders, although the economy is no longer a state-planned socialist economy, elections have been implemented at various levels of government, and the National People's Congress and the People's Political Consultative Conference no longer automatically rubber-stamp party decisions. The stereotype of a monolithic Communist Party that is using the Olympic Games as a propaganda tool to prop up its regime doesn't hold up to scrutiny. Few critics seem to have noticed that the main public symbols have been designed by artists who have been much admired in the West for their opposition to the orthodox party ideology.

Ai Weiwei, "bad boy nihilist, and the man who collaborated with a Swiss company to design the Olympic stadium,"[1] is the son of China's most famous modern poet, Ai Qing. After establishing a career as a revolutionary poet extolling the Communist Party, Ai Qing was denounced in the antirightist campaign of 1957, then sent to Xinjiang for labor reform during the Cultural Revolution and prohibited from publishing for twenty-one years until his rehabilitation in 1978. His son Ai Weiwei grew up in Xinjiang and later produced works such as the photographic series "Finger," which depicts a human hand "giving the finger" to great monuments of state around the world, including the White House and Tiananmen Square.[2] The symbolism of the Olympic Stadium will be discussed in chapter 3.

The opening and closing ceremonies will be choreographed by Zhang Yimou, the director of films that have won international acclaim.[3] His father was a major under General Chiang Kai-shek, Zhang had done farming and manual labor for seven years during the Cultural Revolution, and a trend of stubborn antiestablishmentarianism runs through much of his work. Although the film that initially won him international acclaim, *Red Sorghum*, had been popular in China, many of his later films were not well received and were popularly criticized for catering to the Western appetite for exotic Chinese stereotypes as well as for their historical inaccuracies, both of which, it was argued, meant that they were not truly "Chinese." These criticisms would resurface with respect to the "Eight Minute" segment that he choreographed for Beijing's spot in the closing ceremony of the 2004 Athens Olympic Games (see chapter 7). This popular discontent culminated in an official ban against showing *Raise the Red Lantern* (1991) and *To Live* (1994). Although in the interim *The Story of Qiu Ju* (1993) had been well received in China, Zhang developed a reputation in the West as "banned in China," which contributed to his popularity outside China. The image of the "dissident filmmaker" was never completely accurate—even while it still existed, I saw him acting as one of the judges at the 1995 Elite Look Supermodel Contest in Beijing, which was supported by the central government and attended by high officials from the textile industry.

He Zhenliang, the IOC member in China (since 1981) and China's senior sports diplomat, was one of the architects of the guiding slogan of the Beijing Olympics, "One World, One Dream." Yet he knows as well as anyone what it is like to be in a situation of "one bed, two dreams" (a colloquial Chinese saying) because he is a bridge between the Chinese government and the IOC. His lifetime membership in the IOC has assured him a political security over the past twenty-six years that his compatriots have lacked. Sometimes this resulted in political conflicts inside China.[4] When the Central Committee voted to bid for the 2008 Olympic Games in November 1998, He Zhenliang, who had retired from his official posts in the State Sports General Administration four years earlier when he reached the age limit of sixty-five, was not notified of it or asked to take part in the bid, apparently at the direction of the Sports Administration. A meeting with Vice Premier Li Lanqing at the end of November brought his plight to Li's attention and gained his support. Still, when CCTV aired a program on the bid on January 13, 1999, interviews with him had been all but edited out of the program at the request of the Sports Administration, whose leaders seemingly did not understand that IOC members are critical in mobilizing support within the IOC. When high-level supporters within the Beijing Municipal government formally proposed to the Sports Administration that they should utilize He Zhenliang in the bid, a key leader reportedly refused and replied, "Isn't he Chinese? He has to vote for Beijing." Meanwhile, He's status within the IOC rose during the crisis of the Salt Lake City Olympic scandal, and in June 1999 he was unanimously reelected to the Executive Board. The Chinese Central Committee "adjusted" the leadership of the Sports Administration in April 2000, and Yuan Weimin replaced Wu Shaozu as the director. This eased He's difficulties, and in September he was named as an adviser and member of the Executive Board of the Beijing Organizing Committee for the Games of the XXIX Olympiad (BOCOG). However, in April 2003, the French sporting newspaper *l'Equipe* reported that He Zhenliang had been prevented from running for the IOC Executive Board again by his government (which, in this case, would have meant the Sports Administration) so that IOC member Yu Zaiqing could run in his place.[5] The IOC reacted by spurning Yu in this election, although he was later elected in 2004 since it is generally regarded as a good thing to have an Executive Board member from the host city of the upcoming Olympics. He Zhenliang has not been reelected to the Executive Board since.

In sum, it is not accurate to think that all the top leaders of the Chinese Communist Party and of the government are of one mind, so that there is a uniform plan to exploit the Olympic Games as a propaganda tool. Three of the major symbols of the Games—the stadium, the opening ceremony, and the main slogan—were shaped by freethinking Chinese who have often clashed with party-liners and government officials. And these are just three of the more prominent examples. In reality there is no unified Communist Party and central government. There are factions and ferment everywhere, and if these three examples are significant, the freethinkers are winning the conflicts over shaping the meanings of the Olympic Games.

WHY IS THE WEST SO CONCERNED ABOUT CHANGING CHINA? PART II— IMPERIALIST AND COLONIALIST ARROGANCE

A second answer is that there is a certain residual arrogance from the age of colonialism and imperialism. The West considers that the rest of the world should be like the West, and there is a lack of understanding of China. China is actually a rather well-run country with a level of social order that is truly remarkable for such a populous nation, which has undergone such turbulent changes in the past decades. It is still a developing country in which 60 percent of the population makes its living from agriculture. I live inside the city limits of St. Louis, Missouri, which has one of the highest per capita crime rates in the United States. In my neighborhood, we often hear gunshots at night, and occasionally the police helicopters have flown over my neighborhood and shined their spotlights into my backyard, looking for some criminal on the run. I feel safer in Beijing, which has a population of 15 million people, than I do in my own home in St. Louis, which has a population of 3 million. My Chinese friends complain that social order is not what it used to be in Beijing and express concern when I leave the gates of the Beijing Sport University. I tell them, "I am an American. Do you think I'm afraid of the crime in Beijing?"

Chinese people have seen tremendous improvement in their standard of living and their human rights since the end of the Cultural Revolution in 1976 and the beginning of the era of reform. During the Cultural Revolution, most urbanites who are now fifty years of age or older endured forced relocation to the countryside or to low-level manual labor, and many of them endured beatings, attacks, and imprisonment. Only fifteen years ago, people were still assigned lifetime jobs by the state, and it was very difficult to change jobs. Housing went along with the job. A person's marriage had to be approved by his boss. Major consumer goods and food items were rationed and could not be bought freely on the market. Today, Chinese people can choose their own jobs and buy their own houses and cars. They can marry the person whom they want to marry. They can purchase any product and eat any food that they can afford. Human rights improve along with development, and one Chinese response to critics is to argue that the right to equitable economic development is a fundamental human right. Chinese people who have thought about human rights consider them as part of a historical process. They think the situation in China was very bad thirty years ago. It is much better now, and they have faith that it will continue to get better in the future.

One of the three themes of the Beijing 2008 Olympic Games is intended to present an image of China to the world as a nation that cares about its people. The theme is the *renwen Aoyun*, translated as the "people's Olympics" or the "humanistic Olympics." The other two themes are the "high-tech Olympics" and the "green Olympics." *Renwen* is difficult to translate into English here. Normally the translation for the academic word "humanities," it is formed of the characters for *ren*, "human," and *wen*, "writing, literary pursuits, culture." When it was bidding for the Olympic Games in 2001, the Beijing Olympic Games Bid Committee (BOBICO) emphasized that a central characteristic of Chinese culture is the importance it places on human beings, a tradition as strong and as ancient as the Western humanism that undergirds the philosophy of Olympism. *Beijing 2008*, a book that tells the story of Beijing's bid, contains a section titled "Humanistic Olympics: With Humankind as the

Root, Emphasize the Spread of Universal Love."[6] It argues that Chinese humanism is characterized by the value placed on human life and action in this world. Humans are considered neither dominant over nor subordinate to heaven and nature but equals. One of the strategic reasons for the choice of this theme was to counteract the accusations of the lack of human rights in China with an image of a people-centered Olympic Games. But its main function is domestic: it provides the orientation for the intense focus on the training and cultivation of the next generation of Chinese people through "Olympic Education."[7] In that sense, it will be a "people's Olympics" on a scale never seen before. Chapter 7 will discuss this further.

CHINA, THE OLYMPIC GAMES, AND ME

This book tries to tell a human story of the 100-year history that led up to the 2008 Beijing Olympics. Because it is a people story, I cannot remove myself from the picture. I am an American human being who has been encountering Chinese human beings through sport for more than two decades. My interest in China dated back to the childhood stories told to me by my maternal grandmother, Claudia Brewer Strite, who was born in Mississippi in 1906. Her father, Earl Leroy Brewer, was a lawyer who, in 1922, tried perhaps the first civil rights case before the U.S. Supreme Court, *Brown v. the State of Mississippi*.[8] He was also governor of Mississippi from 1912 to 1916. There was a large population of Chinese immigrants in Mississippi; they arrived building railroads, and they stayed to open laundries and small shops. In those days of harsh racism, they occupied an uneasy middle ground between white and black. Recognizing their vulnerability, they organized the Mississippi Chinese Association and sought a fair-minded lawyer who would not cheat them. They selected my great-grandfather, and he represented them in court for many years. Every Christmas, representatives of the association would arrive bearing gifts at the front door of the home in Clarksdale where my grandmother grew up. My grandmother might well have been the only person in Mississippi who grew up loving lychee nuts, a fondness that lasted her entire life. When I became interested in China, she gave me a woven silk tapestry that she had kept for over sixty years.

I was a member of the first generation of American female athletes to benefit from the sports opportunities created by the passage of Title IX in 1972. I took advantage of the opportunities opened up to me and competed at the national level in track and field in the United States from 1978 to 1990. I participated in the pentathlon in the inaugural 1978 National Sports Festival (later the name was changed to the U.S. Olympic Festival), winning a bronze medal. I still remember the rhetoric about competition with the Soviet Union that surrounded the event, which was an attempt to imitate the Soviet Spartakiades by creating a national multisport competition. At that time there was no World Championship in athletics, and the most important international meet every year was the U.S.–U.S.S.R. Dual Track Meet. I qualified for the teams to compete against the Soviets in 1979 and 1982 and thus personally experienced the days when a Soviet athlete would accost you in the dorm hallway when the chaperones were not looking and drag you into a dorm room in order to trade her vodka, caviar, or a "CCCP" uniform for your blue jeans. When I entered the University of Virginia in 1978, I was a member of the second class of women that had received athletic scholarships. I had personally experienced the integration of girls and women into the U.S. sports system and the Cold War pursuit of Olympic supremacy.

My event was the pentathlon and, after two more events were added in 1981, the heptathlon. I had been a high school state champion and a Division I collegiate all-American, had been nationally ranked as high as seventh, competed internationally, and took part in the 1980 and 1984 Olympic Trials. Since I had been a child, I had always dreamed of making the U.S. Olympic team, but the closest I would come was a seventh-place finish in the 1980 Olympic Trials pentathlon. No Americans went to the Olympics that year, however—those were the Moscow Olympic Games boycotted by President Jimmy Carter. The Olympic Trials were depressing because we already knew that no one would be going to Moscow. There was heated discussion about the U.S. government's sudden interest in sports, which was regarded with a measure of bitterness since in those days all Olympic athletes were nominally "amateurs," and except for a handful of celebrities, most of us were supported either by university scholarships or by part-time jobs as waitresses, postmen, or other menial work. It was a system that was reaching its breaking point at that time since the international rivalries of the Cold War had pushed the levels of top competition in track and field so high that one really needed to train full time to reach them. Athletes in the Soviet Union and other socialist countries were state supported, and there was discussion that this might be a better system than the U.S. system. What, we asked, gave our government, which never gave us any financial support, the right to turn around and prevent us from fulfilling the dream of participating in the Olympic Games, for which we had sacrificed so much? This was the time at which my interest in socialist sport was sparked. (Later, as I came to understand the system better, I realized that I would never have been able to start as a national-class athlete and end as a university professor if I had been a socialist athlete tracked into the sports school system, which was separate from and academically inferior to the regular universities.)

In 1979, the People's Republic of China (PRC) had just opened up to U.S. social scientists who wished to do research there. The antirightist campaigns of the 1950s and the Cultural Revolution of 1966–1976 had been periods of political attacks on intellectuals within China and isolation from the international academic community outside China. From the 1950s to the 1980s, anthropologists who wished to study "China" had been forced to do their fieldwork in Taiwan, Hong Kong, and Singapore and among overseas Chinese. Sino–U.S. diplomatic relations were restored in 1979. The U.S. and Chinese governments established an exchange program that was administered on the U.S. side by an organization called the Committee on Scholarly Communication with the PRC. This organization, which was under the auspices of the National Academy of Sciences, was the single channel by which U.S. citizens could obtain official permission to carry out doctoral research in China until the late 1980s. The first class of grantees went to China in 1979, the same year in which the PRC was readmitted to the IOC after a twenty-one-year absence. Exchanges between the United States and China were restored in the realms of the mind and of the body. During 1987–1988 I would spend a year doing dissertation research at the Beijing Institute of Physical Education (now the Beijing Sport University) supported by a CSC grant.

Because China supported the Moscow boycott, its first reappearance at the Olympic Summer Games was at the 1984 Games in Los Angeles. Xu Haifeng won China's very first Olympic gold medal, and China finally "broke the big duck egg" (the record of zero medals) that it had maintained since it participated in its first Olympic Games. Coincidentally, that had also been in Los Angeles in 1932. I attended some of the track-and-field events, followed the news coverage of China, and eventually wrote two master's theses on Chinese sports. In those days there was almost no published work in English (or German, which I also speak) on Chinese sports, and writing two master's theses with almost no information except that gleaned from Chinese government propaganda and American newspapers involved a creative use of data.

I arrived at Beijing University in the fall of 1985 to study Chinese. Immediately after my arrival, I approached the head coach of the track team, Gong Lei, to inquire about joining the team. Thus I stepped into the middle of a situation that I only later came to understand. As it happened, the second National College Games were scheduled for the spring of 1986. These games were a symbolic marker of a major social change that had begun with the era of reform in 1978. National games echoed the class ideology of the party-state. The first National Soldiers' Games took place in 1952, the first National Minorities Games in 1953, and the first National Workers' Games in 1955. The first Chinese National Games had taken place in 1959. These games marked the groups favored by the central government: soldiers, workers, eth-

nic minorities, and "the Chinese people." Intellectuals were not one of the favored groups until the first National College Games in 1982. In preparation
for the 1986 Games, colleges nationwide had begun recruiting top athletes by
lowering their admission standards and in some cases waiving the admission
requirements. Beijing University, as the top liberal arts university in the nation, refused to give anything but minor concessions to athletes, and as a result the Physical Education Division was panicked that Beijing University
teams would do poorly in the Beijing City and National games, causing the
university to "lose face." And then I appeared on the scene—a legitimate student who was capable of winning multiple medals and setting multiple
records at the National Games (records as well as medals were rewarded with
points toward the team championship).

Foreign students and visiting professors at Beijing University were housed
in the "foreign ghetto," the Shaoyuan dormitory complex on the western edge
of the university, which backed up against the wall that encircled the entire
university campus—walls and supervised gates being a standard architectural
feature at all "work units." Any Chinese student who wanted to visit a foreign
student in his or her dormitory had to register at the front door. After a few
visits, it was likely that his or her class supervisor would pay a visit to ask
about why he or she had visited a foreigner and to discourage further visits.
Chinese female students who visited foreign male students were monitored
more strictly than the other way around, which gave me a bit more freedom
as a foreign female. Foreign students took classes along with other foreign
students, which made it difficult to meet Chinese people. Relationships between Chinese and foreigners were regarded with suspicion, and I knew both
Chinese and Western friends who were detained for "self-criticism" at the local police station.

I am often asked whether I encountered a lot of restrictions in my research
and life in China. The answer is no. Perhaps it was because sport opened so
many doors, but I think that is not actually the reason. I found Chinese people to be very friendly and Chinese society to be very open. If one has the
guanxi (social connections), then obstacles melt away because of mutual trust
and even affection that has been established over a long time.

Since I trained every day with my teammates, I had a way of meeting
Chinese students and a reason to engage in daily interaction with them. My
Chinese-language skills quickly surpassed those of my classmates. I joined
my teammates in their own dormitories for conversations in the evenings after practice, and I often ate with them in their own cafeterias, where the food
was quite poor compared to that offered to foreigners—but considerably
cheaper. I hung out with my teammates and coaches during the intramural and
the Beijing City track meets, where I was the only foreigner among several

Figure I.1. The author with two competitors in the 1986 Beijing City College Track and Field Invitational. At 1.70 meters (5 feet, 7 inches), she was shorter than most of her competitors, who had been selected for the heptathlon because of their height.

hundred Chinese. I spent time at the Beijing City Team Center and the National Team Center in Beijing. These team centers were regarded as part of the national defense system, and foreigners were not allowed to enter them at will. However, I was able to enter either as an athlete or with the introduction of my coaches.

AN AMERICAN EXPERIENCE OF "COMMUNIST DISCIPLINE"

Based on my performance in the Beijing City collegiate track-and-field meet, I was selected to represent Beijing City at the 1986 National College Games. In preparation for those games, I joined my teammates for a two-and-a-half month training camp, which was held at the Beijing Institute of Aeronautics and Aviation. Because of the defense research carried out there, this institute did not allow foreigners to pass through its gates. I had to use a small gate in the back wall to come and go since the gatekeepers there had been notified about me. I, eight coaches, and twenty-eight teammates—one of whom was another American, James Thomas—lived in a small dormitory building and observed the military-style discipline that was common on Chinese sports teams through the 1990s. We had regular "political study sessions" in which we reviewed the guiding slogan of the Games ("Civilization, Unity, Learning, Vigorous Progress") and our assignment ("increase knowledge, improve friendship, receive education") and practiced singing the official meet anthem. Every other morning after our 6:20 A.M. roll call, we walked to the sports field to practice our technique for the Parade of Athletes in the opening ceremony. We were to shout slogans in time with our goose steps as we passed the reviewing stand where the high officials sat.

"Train the body!" This was shouted out by our march leader, followed by a response by the rest of us. Our responses were the following:

Study diligently!
Bravely scale the peaks!
Carry out the Four Modernizations!
Defend the Nation!

Our performance was considered technically difficult because it entailed cradling flowers in one arm, shouting slogans, and unfurling banners, all while goose-stepping. I had to learn goose-stepping for the first time, which

Figure I.2.   A university team marching in the opening ceremony of the 1988 Beijing City College Track and Field Meet. Photo by Susan Brownell.

provided a good source of amusement to my teammates, who had been drilled in it since grade school.

Although I did receive some concessions as a foreigner, on the whole I was held to the same disciplinary standards as a Chinese athlete. Like most Americans raised during the Cold War, I had preexisting notions about authoritarian, militarized, "communist discipline." Before I experienced it, I assumed this "communist discipline" to be antithetical to the "democratic" regimes of a "free" society. I expected that my Chinese teammates would follow the rules of the Big Red Machine like the automatons that they were often stereotyped to be. During the training camp, however, I soon noticed that I was perhaps the most disciplined athlete on the team. I obeyed the rules more strictly than most of my teammates. They consistently violated the rules when they felt they had more important things to do. They were also quite cynical. The main problem with the regime of discipline was boredom. As my roommate complained to me, it seemed like all we did was sleep, eat, train, and sleep again. The main sanctions were criticism and the threat of a negative entry in their dossiers, but my teammates felt confident that a good performance in the meet would override criticism and did not seem to take the threat seriously. Not being Chinese, I did not fear a negative entry in my dossier—and so I asked myself, "Why am I obeying these rules?" I reluctantly concluded that I was obeying them because they were familiar to me. Obeying the rules seemed to be more habitual for me than for my teammates. I had lived this life before in the United States.

The experience was most similar to a girls' sailing camp I attended one summer at the age of sixteen. This camp also had morning roll calls, curfews, sanitation checks, a talent show, and inspirational singing after lunch and dinner. It was not until I returned to the United States that my mother reminded me that this camp was run by the YMCA, and I finally put together the pieces of the puzzle. The YMCA had introduced Western sports into China at the turn of the twentieth century. What I thought of as "communist" sports discipline was actually what the YMCA's Muscular Christian disciplinary techniques had evolved into after half a century in China.

In sum, my experience of "communist" sport discipline forced me to acknowledge that the dichotomy between "communist" and "democratic" discipline was a mirage and that, if anything, I was more of an automaton than my Chinese teammates. When I arrived in Beijing, I had hardly shed my roots as a conservative, small-town southern girl who grew up in the Blue Ridge Mountains of Virginia. But China challenged the categories I took for granted. Ever since realizing that American society had made me more "disciplined" than my Chinese teammates, I have asked myself, "Who is really more 'free' after all?"

In the end, I fulfilled my duty. I won the heptathlon, and I ran on two silver-medal relay teams. Beijing's women placed second overall, and I was given a spirit award (a "spiritual civilization athlete" award). A magazine article captured my double identity well when it quoted me as responding, "To use the American formula, I want to say, 'Thank you.' To use the Chinese formula, I want to say, 'I still haven't done enough!'"[9]

CHINA'S OLYMPIC DREAM AND ME

Sport made possible this convergence of my life history with Sino–U.S. relations: sports diplomacy happened to receive a great deal of government attention in China, and I happened to arrive at Beijing University in the year of the second National College Games. I have traveled a long journey since then. I wrote a book based on my first years of experience in China,[10] and I became a university professor.

While I was in Beijing in 1996, Dong Erzhi found me. He was the son of Dong Shouyi, one of the three IOC members in China when the PRC was established and the only one to remain in mainland China after the revolution. When he was twenty-two, Dong Erzhi had been labeled a "rightist" while his father was at the IOC Session in Sofia. He was sentenced to labor reform that involved gathering stones on a mountainside and carrying them on his back to be crushed into gravel. His father was attacked shortly after that, even as he was exchanging the heated letters with IOC President Avery Brundage (recounted in chapter 5) that led to China's withdrawal from the IOC in 1958. Dong Erzhi ended up doing twenty years of "labor reform" and developed lung disease from breathing the stone dust. He found me in 1996, when he was very insistent despite his ill health. He must have known that I was one of the few persons in the world who was in a position to write his father's story in English. Half a year later, I received a brief fax at the University of Missouri informing me that he had died. I had acquired a book about Dong Shouyi by chance in a bookstore in 1995 but did not realize until 2006 that the second author of the book (which was written under a pen name) was Dong Erzhi, and I suddenly better understood his insistent attitude eleven years earlier.[11] He had become dedicated to writing his father's story after finally being rehabilitated in the mid-1970s. In turn, he was carrying on his father's desire to record this history, which Premier Zhou Enlai had enjoined him to do after the premier had arranged his transfer back to Beijing in 1972 following two years of labor reform at a cadre school in the countryside. Dong had been prolific until his death in 1978—one year short of seeing the PRC readmitted to the IOC.

In 2000, I became a member of the seven-member Research Council of the IOC's Olympic Studies Center in Lausanne, a committee charged with selecting recipients of postgraduate grants and facilitating relationships with the academic world. At my first meeting, I had the opportunity to sit next to He Zhenliang at dinner. Mr. He is the IOC member in China, China's senior sports diplomat, and the person ultimately responsible for the success of Beijing's bid for the Olympic Games—known in China as "Mr. Olympics."

As the Beijing Olympic Games approached, I felt the need to tell the world the story of China's 100-year relationship with the Olympic Movement from the Chinese point of view, a viewpoint that was not then reflected in any English-language publications. I felt that this story should be available to journalists, scholars, and fans before the Olympic Games. In 2002, I scheduled a meeting in Beijing with He Zhenliang to discuss this idea. As it happened, while doing my usual circuit of the bookstores the day before the meeting, I found a copy of his biography, written by his wife Liang Lijuan. When I started reading it in my hotel room, I was pleasantly surprised: I did not know that it was possible in China for a high official to write such a candid, personal account. It was not necessary for me to do all the research necessary to write a book about China's relationship with the IOC—it had already been written based on sources I could never access, and all I had to do

Figure I.3.   Left to right: The author, Liang Lijuan, He Zhenliang, and Tan Di (from Tsingtao Beer Company) in Qingdao, August 2005.

was translate it. My plan changed—the next day I asked him if I could translate his biography into English. It took most of my free time between 2002 and 2006. It was published in 2007 by Beijing Foreign Languages Press as *He Zhenliang and China's Olympic Dream*.

Through the process of working with Mr. He and Mrs. Liang to translate this book, I came to better understand what the Olympic Games mean to China. These are two people who grew up along with China. Their story is also China's story, from the creation of a new government in Beijing in 1949 to the Olympic Games in Beijing in 2008. They joined the Communist Revolution because they were motivated by the social injustice that they saw everywhere around them, to which they believed the Nationalist regime was turning a blind eye. They were members of the Shanghai student underground and were brought to Beijing, "the Great Crucible of the Revolution," in 1950 when the new central government was being formed. For thirty years they fought for international diplomatic recognition of the new China by the "free" world, which seemed to be pretending that the most populous nation in the world did not exist while extending recognition and support to what the Chinese perceived as the Nationalist renegade outpost on Taiwan. There is a certain irony in the fact that for the twenty years of his presidency from 1952 to 1972, the American IOC president, Avery Brundage, stifled He Zhenliang's voice with his prohibition against "talking politics." Half a century later in 2002, another American offered to translate Mr. He's biography because she wanted his voice to be heard. Such are the tides of history. The story of China's relationship with the IOC is told in chapter 5.

I felt a heavy responsibility to history, a responsibility to make this story known to the rest of the world. There were times when I was typing my translation with one hand and wiping tears from my eyes with the other. Like so many Chinese with Western contacts, Mr. He and Mrs. Liang were imprisoned, interrogated, and sent down to the countryside to "labor with the peasants" during the Cultural Revolution. The leading figures of the sports world suffered greatly because Chairman Mao's wife Jiang Qing had a special vendetta against the State Sports Commission, which was placed under the control of the military.[12] In addition, sports cadres were attacked either because they had been celebrities and anyone who stood out was a target or because many of them had Western connections. It is this intersection of personal histories with the history of the nation that underlies the passion that so many high-ranking sports officials feel for the Olympic Games; they are collective redemption for the national suffering of the past century. Perhaps China's rise as a world sports power gives them hope that their sacrifices for the revolution and their personal suffering during the Cultural Revolution were not in vain. Many of these people who suffered such violations of their own human rights now feel that Western attacks on Chinese human rights are interference in China's internal affairs and a hypocritical pretext used to prevent China from taking its place as a world power.

"ONE WORLD, ONE DREAM"

The official theme of the Beijing Olympic Games is "One World, One Dream." According to the official website of BOCOG, "In spite of the differences in colors, languages and races, we share the charm and joy of the Olympic Games, and together we seek for the ideal of Mankind for peace."[13] With war no less likely in the new millennium than it has been in the 2,770 years since the first Olympic Truce was declared in ancient Greece, it is especially important that we remember the idealism of the quest for world peace that produced the modern Olympic Movement. And after 111 years during which the IOC has brought together often hostile nations on sports fields, let us delve beneath superficial stereotypes and devote more effort to increasing mutual understanding between nations through the channel of the Olympic Games.

In my twenty-two years of engagement with China and particularly in the course of translating *He Zhenliang and China's Olympic Dream*, I have often encountered anti-American sentiments. I believe that, whether one agrees with them or not, it is important to treat these sentiments with respect. As He Zhenliang put it, "If you love your country, you respect the love that others have for their countries."[14] While translating the book, I was impressed by the frequency with which I ran into the word *gongzuo*, "work." It made me realize that international diplomacy is not easy. Cross-cultural understanding doesn't just happen. World peace will only be the result of hard work. This book is my contribution toward the work that it will take in order for China to eventually take its place as a full partner and positive contributor to global politics. By writing a book about what the Olympic Games mean to China, I would like to make intelligible the apparent differences between "us" and "them" and by so doing reveal our common humanity.

NOTES

1. "China Rises: Party Games," segment on Ai Weiwei. Four-part documentary and interactive website produced by the *New York Times,* the *Discovery Times*, The Canadian Broadcasting Corporation, ZDF, France 5, and S4C, written and directed by Neil Docherty (2005), www.nytimes.com/specials/chinarises/partygames (July 4, 2007).

2. "China Rises: Party Games," segment on Ai Weiwei.

3. Zhang Yimou is a member of the so-called Fifth Generation—the fifth cohort of film directors after the founding of the PRC—which was the cohort that first began

to produce films deviating from the traditional party line after the beginning of the era of reform. He directed *Red Sorghum*, *Ju Dou*, *Raise the Red Lantern*, *To Live*, *Hero*, and others. *Red Sorghum* was the first PRC film to win a major foreign film award, the Golden Bear award for Best Picture at the 1988 Berlin Film Festival. In 1990, *Ju Dou* became the first PRC film to be nominated for an Academy Award for Best Foreign Language Film. *Raise the Red Lantern* became the second film to be nominated in 1991.

4. The following account of He Zhenliang's conflict with the leaders of the State Sports General Administration is recounted in Liang Lijuan, *He Zhenliang yu wuhuan zhi lu* [He Zhenliang and the Road of the Olympic Rings] (Beijing: Beijing Foreign Languages Press, 2005), 326–29, 331–37. It was omitted from the English translation, *He Zhenliang and China's Olympic Dream*, published in 2007, because by that time the leadership of the Sports General Administration had changed, He Zhenliang had played an active role in the successful bid, and it was not felt that petty Chinese politics would be interesting to the outside world.

5. Alain Lunzenfichter, "*Jeux Olympiques, CIO: Curiosité tardive*" [Olympic Games, IOC: Belated Curiosity], *l'Equipe*, May 4, 2003, 17.

6. Ma Tongbin and Qin Yuanyuan, *Beijing 2008—Shen Aode taiqian muhou* [Beijing 2008—Before and behind the Scenes of the Olympic Bid] (Beijing: Beijing University of Physical Education Publishing House, 2001), 35.

7. "Olympic Education" is the term used by the IOC to refer to the teaching of "Olympic values," such as mutual respect among nations, fair play and sportsmanship, nondiscrimination, and so on. There are many countries that have implemented such content in the public school systems. Since its first bid in 1993, China has had a large Olympic Education program, and the program developed for 2008 is the largest in the world; before the Athens 2004 Olympic Games, Greece also instituted one of the world's most comprehensive programs. Germany and France are also quite active. The United States, on the other hand, is notable for the absence of such programs, and the U.S. Olympic Committee has been seen as single-mindedly focused on gold medals and corporate sponsorships, not on "values."

8. Richard C. Cortner, *A "Scottsboro" Case in Mississippi: The Supreme Court and Brown v. Mississippi* (Jackson: University Press of Mississippi, 1986).

9. Chu Zi, "*Rexin Zhongguo tiyude Meiguo guniang*" [The American Girl Who Warmly Loves Chinese Sports], *Tiyu bolan* [Sports Vision], March 1987, 27.

10. Susan Brownell, *Training the Body for China: Sports in the Moral Order of the People's Republic* (Chicago: University of Chicago Press, 1995).

11. Tan Hua and Dong Erzhi, *Suyuan—Dong Shouyi Zhuan* [Long-Cherished Wish—The story of Dong Shouyi] (Beijing: People's Sports Publishing House, 1993).

12. The State Sports Commission was the organ of the central government responsible for sports, physical education, and mass fitness, with a status equivalent to that of a ministry. In 1998 its name was changed to the State General Administration of Sports.

13. BOCOG official website, www.en.Beijing2008.com (July 2006).

14. He Zhenliang, speech given at the closing ceremony of the Fifth World Forum on Sport, Education and Culture, organized by the International Olympic Committee's Commission on Culture and Olympic Education, Beijing, China, October 25, 2006.

Chapter One

Europe and the People without Sport History, or What Hosting the Olympic Games Means to China

Chinese people's desire to host the Olympic Games is nearly as old as the modern Olympic Games (the first modern Games were held in Athens in 1896). As early as 1907, patriots in the Chinese YMCA promoted a campaign linking physical education to national strength that asked three questions:

1. When will China be able to send a winning athlete to the Olympic contests?
2. When will China be able to send a winning team to the Olympic contests?
3. When will China be able to invite all the world to come to Peking [Beijing] for an International Olympic contest, alternating with those at Athens?[1]

The first two questions would be answered at the 1984 Los Angeles Olympic Games and the third at the 2008 Beijing Olympic Games, 100 years after it was first asked. These questions were often recalled in the context of Beijing's successful bid for the 2008 Olympic Games. They are an example of a plotline typical in the telling of Chinese national history. It begins with tales of national humiliation at the turn of the nineteenth century and ends with China's return to power in the twenty-first century, made possible by the Communist Revolution. I do not mean to make light of this plot by suggesting that it is merely official propaganda: as stated in the previous chapter and further developed in chapter 5, this plot echoes the actual life histories of many Chinese people. When athletes, officials, and sport diplomats recite the above three questions, they are moved by the belief that the respect that is now accorded to China in the sports world is the result of over 100 years of hard-fought battles and sacrifices.

Why has hosting the Olympic Games been so important to China for a century? The answer is found in the importance of the body, sports, and gender in China's encounter with the West over the past century.

THE PEOPLE WITHOUT SPORT HISTORY

[T]hey count the monotonous beat of the pendulum of time, but time contains nothing for them; they possess a chronology, but no history in the full sense of the word."[2]

Thus did the eminent German classicist Ernst Curtius, who was the first to carry out large-scale excavations at ancient Olympia, describe the civilization of Egypt at the start of his great three-volume work *The History of Greece.* By contrast with the Egyptians and other peoples of the Orient, he described the Greeks as a people who had left behind the other peoples of the world in their restless westward expansion and "chained the course of history to their steps."[3] His view was typical in the nineteenth-century West, which was in the throes of rapid and traumatic social changes wrought by colonialism and the Industrial Revolution, giving the appearance that historical change was happening in the West to a greater degree than in the rest of the world. Western intellectuals sought to understand the driving force behind historical change, assuming that whatever it was, the rest of the world must lack it.

In his classic *Europe and the People without History*, Eric Wolf observed that the Western intellectual tradition tended to view Europeans—the "people with history"—as the driving force of historical change and "primitive" societies as pristine, unchanging survivals from the past—the "people without history." He argued that if we looked more carefully at the interconnections between the world's peoples, then we would understand that "the global processes set in motion by European expansion constitute *their* history as well."[4] This chapter outlines how China got written out of the history of sport in the Western scholarship of the nineteenth century, with the result that when it reentered the international sports world in the 1980s, it was one of the "people without sport history." It was the desire to be counted among the driving forces of history and among the "people with sport history" that motivated the pursuit of Olympic Games and medals.

China's case is contrasted with that of a much smaller and poorer nation—Greece—which got written into the history of Western civilization from the eighteenth century on, acquiring in the process a large body of international scholarship on its ancient sport history. This difference is significant in the way Athens and Beijing represented themselves in the 2004 and 2008 Olympic Games. Both Greece and China used their sport histories to symbolically position themselves in the world system of nations.

Today, Greece has a population of 10.7 million. China, the most populous nation in the world, has a population that is nearly 100 times larger—1.3 billion.[5] Both Greece and China have large diasporas outside the homeland that historically played important roles in the creation of national identity: Greece's is approximately 5.5 million, or about half the number of those inside the boundaries of the Hellenic Republic.[6] China's diasporic population is about 34 million,[7] with the combined populations of Hong Kong, Macau, and Taiwan adding another 30 million,[8] but the 64 million Chinese living outside the mainland equal only 5 percent of its national population. The first Greek writing system (Linear B tablets) and the Chinese writing system (Shang oracle bones) occurred at approximately the same time: 1400 B.C. The first Greek histories (the Homeric epics) and the first Chinese histories (records of the Zhou dynasty) date to around 750 B.C. Their written histories are equally ancient, but between the modern nations that claim to be the heirs of those histories, China is now 100 times more populous than Greece, and so we might expect that there would be more books on ancient Chinese sports than on Greek, but this is not the case.

If we compare the number of books in European languages on ancient Greek and Chinese sports, we can see that until the mid-1980s, China was literally almost completely "without sport history." Thomas Scanlon's *Greek and Roman Athletics: A Bibliography* lists 186 books and articles on the ancient Olympic Games published between 1752 and 1984. Of these, 100 were in German, six were in Latin published in Germany, and thirty-six were in English, thirteen in French, ten in Italian, and the remainder in Danish, Dutch, Hungarian, and Russian. The quantity of scholarship that has been devoted to ancient Greek sports in general is indicated by the total of 1,345 sources on all aspects of ancient Greek athletics listed in Scanlon's bibliography.[9]

The Online Computer Library Center (OCLC) is the world's largest bibliographic database, representing 52 million records in 400 different languages contained in libraries worldwide. At present, it is the most advanced database for identifying the location of books in libraries worldwide. Although it is far from comprehensive and is biased toward North America and toward English-language sources, it might be viewed as a rough measure of the worldwide accessibility of information on a topic in English. In 2005, the OCLC contained several hundred entries on the ancient Olympic Games and the site of ancient Olympia in multiple languages. The history with the widest distribution was M. I. Finley's and H. W. Pleket's classic *The Olympic Games: The First Thousand Years* (1976), which was listed in 1,089 libraries.

In 2005, there were just four books on ancient Chinese sports in the OCLC database, all of them in both English and Chinese printed side by side. The earliest was published in 1984. The book with the largest distribution was listed as owned by eighteen libraries worldwide. More books on ancient Chinese sports existed than those listed in the OCLC—but not many. The first history of sports in China was written in 1919 (Guo), but in the half century after that, only a handful of books dealing with ancient sports were published in China, Taiwan, the Philippines, and other parts of East Asia. Beyond the books listed in OCLC, I was able to identify eleven more books on ancient Chinese sports that were published before 2006; the oldest was published in 1983 (Xu 1983).[10] As the Beijing Olympic Games approached, several more books were published in China as a result of increased scholarly interest and funding.[11] I have considered only books here; the number of articles and chapters in books would still amount to a fraction of the 1,345 articles and books on ancient Greek sports listed in Scanlon's bibliography. Furthermore, the vast majority of the articles were published in Chinese, particularly in the journal *Tiyu Wenshi* (*Sport History*, now *Tiyu Wenhua Daokan, Journal of Sport History and Culture*), which has been published bimonthly by the State General Administration for Sports since the late 1980s. Much more has been written about Chinese martial arts (especially in the *Journal of Asian Martial Arts*) than about other ancient sports.

In an independent development, scholarship outside China had reached the point in 2004 that Allen Guttmann, who had coauthored a book on Japanese sports and was keenly aware of the previous omission of Far Eastern sports from world sport histories, was able to devote as many pages to premodern Chinese and Japanese sports (eight pages combined) as to ancient Greek sport in his comprehensive overview of world sport, *Sports: The First Five Millennia*. It was probably the first book in English to achieve such parity.[12]

The point is that the amount of paper that has been devoted to ancient Chinese sport history is miniscule compared to the reams of pages devoted to the history of the ancient Olympic Games and ancient Greek athletics. In his world history of sport, Richard Mandell observes, "The claim might be put forward that the Chinese throughout their long history practiced more sports than any other people." However, because of the paucity of sources, he is able to devote only five pages to them, which he says is "a description so brief as to be possibly disrespectful of a culture of great age and enormous cultural creativity."[13]

Why is there so much history of ancient Greek sports and so little history of ancient Chinese sports? And why, in the 1980s, did it become important for Chinese historians to start writing one? And why, in the lead-up to the

Beijing Olympic Games, did the number of books on ancient Chinese sports surge again?

CLASSICISM, ORIENTALISM, AND SPORT HISTORY[14]

To answer these questions, it is necessary to understand the attitudes toward ancient Greece and China that characterized the complementary academic disciplines of classicism and orientalism and how they led to biases on the topic of athletics. It might seem strange to begin a book on the meaning of the 2008 Olympic Games with a discussion of two rather archaic academic disciplines, but, as will be seen, their legacy is still being played out today. In its day, a classical education formed the common language that unified elite men in the West via the notion of a shared "Western civilization" and a common ancestor—ancient Greece. The neoclassical revival was the driving force behind the Olympic revival and was the starting point from which Western sinologists and physical educators sought to make sense out of China. As YMCA missionaries educated their Chinese students in sports, they simultaneously inculcated the biases that they had acquired from classicism.

The first book on the history of the ancient Olympic Games was published in the Netherlands in 1732.[15] In 1875, the first full-scale excavations at ancient Olympia were begun by Ernst Curtius from the University of Berlin. German books on the Olympic Games already started to be published in the late 1830s, then there was a rapid increase through the 1880s and 1890s. In 1936, the German Institute of Archaeology began systematic excavation of Olympia, which still continues.

There was also English interest, indicated by several publications and papers starting in 1865. A number of English books were also published in the 1890s, though they were not as numerous as the German books. The start of the 1900s saw the publication of more English books in the period leading up to the 1908 London Olympic Games.

The publication of books on the Olympic Games was only one small part of the huge neoclassical revival that was going on in Europe and its current and former colonies. In the fifteenth to seventeenth centuries, Europe's movement out of the dark ages in the Renaissance was lent momentum by the rediscovery of ancient Greek texts, and neoclassicism played a central role in the Western European Enlightenment of the late seventeenth century. The close of the neoclassical age was marked by an interest in the Orient. Much of eighteenth- and nineteenth-century orientalism was shaped by Europe's rivalry with the Ottoman Empire, Great Britain's colonization of India, and

France's colonization of North Africa. China existed on the margins of orientalism; it was assumed that since it was the most extreme geographically, it must also be the most extremely "oriental."[16] Greece and China stood on opposite sides of the divide; Greece was embraced by classical studies and China by Oriental studies, with very different consequences for national identity as well as for the writing of sport history.

Classicism and orientalism emerged and developed in tandem as complementary opposites; classicism was the West's way of defining "who we are," while orientalism was the West's way of defining "who we are not." Classicism preceded orientalism, with the result that stereotypes about the East had been laid even before systematic inquiry had begun. Those assumptions were found in the classical Greek texts themselves, and classicists repeated them and began to elaborate on them from the eighteenth century on. Herodotus, Hippocrates, Aristotle, and other ancient authors had already set out some of the main themes of orientalism: Asian rulers are despotic and excessive, Asians do not care about individuals, and Asians are faceless hordes of people who live in conditions of servitude.[17] Plato and Aristotle were the earliest to associate Asia with despotic political systems.[18] Hippocrates wrote, "Europeans are also more courageous than Asiatics. . . . Where there are kings, there must be the greatest cowards."[19] The notion of the clever but physically weak and lazy Asian went as far back as Aristotle, who wrote,

> Europeans are full of spirit but wanting in intelligence and skill; Asians are intelligent and inventive, but wanting in spirit, and so are always in a state of subjection and slavery; but the Hellenic race is situated between them, is intermediate in character, and is high-spirited and intelligent.[20]

As the famous sport historian Carl Diem phrased it, "Sport is a grandchild of the Renaissance, a child of the French Revolution."[21] Neoclassicism occupied a central role in the French Revolution, which propelled sports toward greater visibility. The glory of ancient Greece was taken as an inspiration for the construction of new social forms to take the place of the rejected forms of the Middle Ages. Rousseau, one of the foundational thinkers of the revolution, mentioned the ancient Greek Olympic Games in 1771, and other leading figures of the revolution, such as Robespierre and Mirabeau, also mentioned the ancient games. The first known call for a revival of the ancient Olympic Games appeared in 1790 in France.[22] In their search for forms to replace the medieval Christian practices associated with the toppled monarchy, revolutionary thinkers looked to the pagan practices of ancient Greece. They developed the concept of the "civil religion," in which worldly abstractions like reason, equality, liberty, and nature were raised to the level of the sacred and celebrated in art, architecture, monuments, and other civic symbols—and with newly invented festivals that later served as models for the modern Olympic Games.[23] Thus, in the French Revolution, ancient Greek sports and their revivals came to be associated with democracy and civil religion. Furthermore, eighteenth-century revolutionary thinkers, particularly Montesquieu, utilized the stereotype of Oriental despotism in opposition to their ideas of freedom and democracy.[24] Because sports were identified with democracy and reason, they were believed to be incompatible with "Oriental despotism."

Ernst Curtius

This link was further elaborated by nineteenth-century classicists such as Ernst Curtius, whose words began this chapter. Curtius (1814–1896) not only led the early excavations at ancient Olympia but also had spent 1836–1840 in Greece as a tutor for a well-to-do family, and his three-volume *Griechische Geschichte* (1857–1867) (translated into English as *Greek History* in 1868) was the first major history of Greece by someone who had actually been there. He was probably the most widely read and influential historian of classical antiquity in the second half of the nineteenth century. Martin Bernal identifies Ernst and his brother Georg as the "most likely candidates" in promoting the Aryan model of Western civilization in the 1840s and 1850s.[25]

One of Curtius's key ideas was his claim that an essential trait of the Aryan people was their "competitive lust for action" (*Wetteifernde Tatenlust*), a legacy of the ancient Greeks. He stated that one word separates Hellenic life from all others: "wreath" (*kranz*). He illustrated this point with one of his favorite, oft-repeated stories from Herodotus—a story that Herodotus used to illustrate the opposition between Hellenes and barbarians: As the Persian soldiers of Xerxes reach the Thermopyle pass, the gateway to Greece, a deserter from Arkadia is brought before the king and asked what the Greeks are doing. He answers, "They are celebrating the festival of the Olympics; they are spectating at the contests and chariot games." Xerxes, expecting to hear that they awaited him with trembling and fear, was shocked to hear this answer and asked for what prize they were competing. "For the olive wreath," replied the Arkadian. Xerxes cannot restrain himself from exclaiming, "Good grief, Mardonius, against what kind of men have you led us, who do not hold contests for gold and silver, but for the virtue of men!"[26] Curtius argues that this was shocking and demoralizing to the Persians because this revealed to them a new valuation of life, "a view that sought the value of human existence not in comfortable possessions, in quiet pleasures, but in wrestling and striving, and this view, they felt, must indicate a wholly unique kind of heroism."[27]

This false view that the Greeks competed for honor, not for material wealth, became one of the foundation myths of amateurism in Olympic sports, which was debunked in the academic world by David Young in 1984 in *The Olympic Myth of Greek Amateur Athletics*. Although there were other factors contributing to the maintenance of this myth in sports, such as the British class structure, one of the original sources of the myth was an attempt to define Western civilization as rejecting the pursuit of material profit as opposed to the materialistic East. This was also linked to Curtius's devout Christian beliefs[28] as well as to the Protestant ethic of frugality that characterized Muscular Christianity (the ideology of the British and North American sports missionaries of the late nineteenth and early twentieth centuries).

Furthermore, Curtius argued that the form of the contest permeated all aspects of Greek life. "It was not only in Delphi and Olympia, not only on the gates of the running tracks, that the Hellenes held their contests; their entire life, as it lies before us in the history of the people, was one great contest."[29] In correspondence elsewhere, he stated that the Greek "agonistic character" was "in opposition to the life of pleasure of the Orient, the excessive valuation of possessions and holdings."[30] Moreover, the Greeks were aware that this set them apart from others: the more conscious they became of their difference with barbarians, the more loudly and distinctly did they develop the idea of competition.[31]

The Hellenic competitive lust for action also advantaged them over Orientals in the great contest between the human races.[32] For Curtius the Orient was unchanging, with "no history in the full sense of the word," because one regime might replace another, but this was followed by complacency so that true revolution never occurred. He argued that the Greeks and their heirs were completely different.[33] Because of the mountainous terrain and sparse soil, Greeks were forced to work hard and live in independent, circumscribed communities that "prevented oriental somnolence, and instead of the nameless masses of people being driven by the whims of a despot, here a people rose up toward spiritual freedom, for which it was created."[34] Curtius even implied that it was a special mission of the Hellenes and their descendants to spread their competitive lust to other peoples. "Because it was not just for themselves, but also for all the races to come that the Hellenes brought the barbarians of old and new times face-to-face with the light of Truth, that it is not possessions and pleasures, but wrestling and striving that are the only true source of joy at the end of the human career."[35]

Curtius was a key figure in the developments in Britain and Germany that led to the notion that civilizations should be racially pure, that more recent civilizations were superior to older ones, and that strong races would triumph over weak ones.[36] Germany had engaged in a troubled search for its own national identity since the seventeenth century as a result of its political fragmentation and economic backwardness in comparison with its rival France and its relatively late emergence as a unified nation-state in 1870. This search motivated the interest in Greece as a common ancestor to unify German identity. Curtius was one of many to argue that Germans had a special affinity with the ancient Greeks, and he explicitly discussed the lessons of ancient Greece for modern Germany. Thus, the German dominance of nineteenth-century scholarship on ancient Greek athletics was in large part due to the symbolic role played by ancient Greece and ancient athletics in the construction of German identity. The work of Johann Joachim Winckelmann, who introduced Germans to Greek art starting in the late eighteenth century, was an inspiration for German romantic notions of ancient Greece, and his work would later shape Hitler's notion of the Aryan race in Nazi Germany.[37] Germany was the world center for classical studies in the last two-thirds of the nineteenth century, and even Great Britain and the United States recognized the superiority of German *Altertumswissenschaft*, so its brand of nationalistic classicism strongly shaped the thoughts of many of the men who were involved in the Olympic revival. This included the first International Olympic Committee (IOC) member in the United States, William Milligan Sloane, who received a Ph.D. from the University of Leipzig in 1876. Classical symbolism in the modern Olympic Games often manifested the German tradition, reaching its height in the 1936 "Hitler" Olympic Games in Berlin.

In sum, Curtius's description of the essential character of the Greeks as competitive lovers of freedom allowed the ancient Greek Olympic Games to stand as an emblem for the essence of Greek civilization and of the European civilization that was its heir. This emblem also justified the dominance of Western civilization over other civilizations, including Chinese.

Jacob Burckhardt

Jacob Burckhardt (1818–1897), who succeeded Curtius as perhaps the most influential classicist of his time, carried this trend even further. He developed the concept of the "agonal principle" (from Greek *agon*, "contest") in the 1880s. He made the agonal principle one of the main characteristics of Hellenic culture, reaching its heights in Greece in the sixth century B.C., the "agonal age." "The agon was a motive power known to no other people—the general leavening element that, given the essential condition of freedom, proved capable of working upon the will and the potentialities of every individual. In this respect the Greeks stood alone. . . . In the Asiatic cultures, despotism and the caste system were almost completely opposed to such activities."[38] Burckhardt argued that the Greeks made everything into a contest: drinking songs, philosophy, legal procedure, wooing (of both the opposite and the same sex), cock- and quail-fighting, even sausage selling.[39] For Burckhardt, athletics were the quintessence of the agonal principle, and over one-third of the essay "The Agonal Age" is devoted to athletics and the Olympic Games.[40] Although it has been debated, this notion has been widely influential in classicism and is accepted to some degree even by contemporary scholars such as Thomas Scanlon and Michael Poliakoff.[41] The concept of Greek agon was carried to an extreme by Victor Ehrenberg in his 1935 work *Ost und West* (East and West), in which he stated, "To the Orient [the agonistic principle] remained alien and antipathetic."[42] Well into the twentieth century, *agon* played a role in racist scholarship that denied the existence of competition and of sport to non-Aryan races.[43]

Philhellenism

The American Revolution, the presence of the Ottoman Empire to the east, and the explosion of pilgrimage and travel contributed to the emergence of a pan-European identity. The romantic fascination with ancient Greek culture created a radical wing of the romantic movement called philhellenism, which became wrapped up in the Greek struggle for independence from the Ottomans that began in 1821. The war helped to solidify stereotypes of East and West: it was seen as a conflict between a youthful, European, Christian civilization that was on a dynamic path to progress, against an old, Asiatic, heathen civilization that was stuck in a pattern of decadence, corruption, and cruelty. The war ended in 1828, and an independent Greek state was established in 1832. Otto I was installed as king in 1833. He was the son of Ludwig I, the King of Bavaria, himself a philhellene, whose capital in Munich was a center of philhellenism. The Great Powers (England, France, Bavaria, and Russia) determined the form of government of the new state. It was common that new states were heavily determined by the existing nation-states because they were concerned with maintaining a balance of power with each other.

Neoclassicism and philhellenism were intellectual trends that led to the construction of what we now call "the history of Western civilization." They also led to the formation of the modern Greek state and the establishment of the modern Olympic Games. The key figure in the revival of the modern Olympic Games, Baron Pierre de Coubertin, was a classically educated and self-proclaimed philhellenist. After their revival, the Olympic Games served as a symbol of a continuous line of descent from ancient Greece to the contemporary West—and membership in this lineage constituted the people who *have* history, including sport history.

ORIENTALISM AND CHINESE SPORT HISTORY

China existed on the margins of orientalist scholarship, which was more concerned with Japan, India, Egypt, and the Ottoman Empire. China did not
come into the scholarly field of view in a big way until the end of the nineteenth century, when the number of Western observers and scholars writing
about China began to rapidly increase. In searching for late nineteenth- and
early twentieth-century Western accounts of Chinese sports, the fundamental
assumptions of orientalism are evident: accounts of sports are extremely rare
because competitive athletic activities were assumed to hardly exist due to the
stereotype of the noncompetitive, overintellectualized Oriental. In addition,
there was a stereotype that, because of the tradition of Oriental despotism, an
Oriental would rather order someone else to do physical exertion on his behalf than to engage in it himself.

One of the few sinologists to say anything at all about sports was Herbert
A. Giles. He began an article, "Football and Polo in China," with the remark
that "it was on the 9th of November 1905, while watching the Cambridge
University team make their splendid stand against the famous 'All Blacks,'
that I began to wonder if anyone would take an interest in, or even believe,
the fact that football was played by the Chinese several centuries before
Julius Caesar landed in Britain."[44] In *The Civilization of China*, meant for
"readers who know little or nothing of China," Giles included a chapter titled
"Philosophy and Sport." The combination of these two topics in one chapter
might seem unusual until one realizes that it was based on a dichotomy of
mind and body and involved an implicit comparison with the ideal of a
"sound mind in a sound body" attributed to the ancient Greeks. After his
overview of the main strands of Chinese philosophy, he discusses the history
of hunting and fishing but then observes, "Many sports were once common
in China which have long since passed out of the national life, and exist only
in the record of books."[45] These included horn butting, boxing, wrestling,
football, and polo. Giles's 1906 article on polo may be the first article ever
written on ancient Chinese sports by either a Chinese or a Western scholar.
For Giles, the historical decline of sports meant a loss of manhood: "The age
of manly sport, as above described, has long passed away; and the only hope
is for a revival under the changing conditions of modern China." He states
this even though it is followed by a list of "some few athletic exercises" that
have survived.[46]

According to Andrew Morris, the first sport history written in China was
Xu Yibing's 1909 essay "The History of Physical Culture," which acknowledged that China lacked Western sports but argued that it had its own rich

traditions. Other efforts tried to incorporate premodern Chinese sports into a progressive, linear history that culminated in republican sports in the 1910s.[47]

From the turn of the century on, the ancient Confucian tradition had been criticized for its contempt for physical activity and respect for the intellect. "Those who work with their brains rule; those who work with their brawn are ruled" (*laoxinze zhi ren, laolizhe zhiyu ren*) as the saying went. Since that time, the received view of Chinese history has been that since the Song dynasty (960–1279), written examinations had been the standard method for selecting government officials. The Imperial Examinations required memorization of the classics, which occupied many years of study. *Zhong wen qing wu*, "esteem literacy and despise martiality," became the elite ideal. The rise of intellectualism in the Song and the decline of Tang martiality is said to have led to the virtual disappearance of sports in Chinese society. According to Morris, this argument was outlined in the first book-length treatment of sports by Guo Xifen (1919), which attempted to explain why the superior form of modern sports never evolved in China; his conclusion was that it was due to the lethargy imposed by Confucian culture. Morris also observes that this effort to link ancient Chinese and modern Western sports was very important for the construction of the identity of the new republican nation.[48] The idea that Confucian culture was responsible for stunting the development of sports is still the prevailing one among Chinese and Western scholars writing about sports in China. As recently as 1985, Liu repeated it in an article about polo in the imperial courts:

> The non-aristocratic scholar-official class, refined, urbane, and genteel, cared little for the vigorous sports they viewed as inappropriate, pointless, harmful, and even risky. Under their influence, court circles gave up such games as polo. In fact, this negative attitude permeated the entire culture and persisted until the early twentieth century when modern sports were newly introduced from the West and Japan, as if China had never had them or their equivalents at all.[49]

In the stereotypes of Chinese and Greek civilization, the Imperial Examinations occupied a position similar to that occupied by the ancient Olympic Games: both embodied the essence of their respective civilizations, and both were used as emblems to stand for the ways of life and worldviews of a people. One scholar made this comparison explicit in an essay titled "The Influence of the Literary Examination System on the Development of Chinese Civilization": "No Olympic victor in the days of ancient Greece was ever more honored than the victor in the final examinations in Peking. Great processions met the returning hero. All the honors society could give were his, with official banquets and great feasts."[50]

For Western writers, the dominance of intellectual ideals in Chinese culture was perceived as effeminization. After a six-month tour of China, the prominent sociologist Edward Alsworth Ross wrote a thick book titled *The Changing Chinese*, in which he complained that the military spirit in China was long gone: "Chinese lads quarrel in a girlish way with much reviling but little pounding." He complained that spectacled scholars had been the trendsetters to the point that young men imitated the stooped shoulders of the scholar and wore broad-rimmed glasses even when they didn't need them so that they could look like scholars. For him it seemed to be a negative thing that there was no admiration for martial virtues, civilians did not carry weapons, soldiers were from the dregs of society, the duel was unknown, there was no shame in surrender, and it was not shameful for a man to weep. And he almost seethes at the fact that the young men played tennis like girls: "[L]issome young men with queues were skipping about the tennis courts, but they wore their hampering long gowns and their strokes had the snap of a kitten playing with a ball of yarn."[51]

In short, the West could be personified as a manly athlete, while China was an effeminate intellectual.

The orientalist portrayal of the "somnolent" Orient—as Curtius had put it—was also evident in Ross's book. "Perhaps the Young Men's Christian Association with its slogan so inspiring to the young, 'all-round development—physical, intellectual, moral, and religious—for myself and for others' is the best physician for the lethargy that lies like an evil spell on the energies of the yellow race."[52]

Ross also alludes to a story that attained mythical status among Western physical educators and the Chinese students they educated at the turn of the twentieth century. This story is also told by Webster,[53] and it was known to the Chinese people who were Western educated, such as Wang Zhenya. As Wang tells it,

At the end of the Qing, in the English consulate in Tianjin, there was a consul who once invited the highest official in the Tianjin administration—the Daotai—to dinner. After the meal, the consul wanted to play tennis to show his guest. This Daotai had never in his life seen tennis, and he was very curious, responding with enthusiasm. It happened to be a time of scorching hot weather, and although the players were wearing shorts and singlets, they were still streaming with sweat. After the demonstration, the consul asked his guest: "How do you think I played?" This Daotai shook his thumb back and forth and said: "Good! Good! Good! It's a pity that you worked so hard; you are so tired that your whole body is covered with sweat. It would be much better if you could hire a man to play in your place."[54]

Clearly this legendary story owes something to the image of Oriental despotism in the figure of the government official who would order someone else to work in his place.

The Western orientalist view was internalized by Chinese reformers and revolutionaries, including the man who would later lead the Communist Revolution to victory. In his first published article, "A Study of Physical Culture" (1917), Mao Zedong complained that "exercise is important for physical education, but today most scholars are not interested in sports." He stated that this was because they had no personal experience of exercise, felt no need for it, and therefore had no interest in it. They were influenced by the Chinese traditions of "respect for learning" and "a good man does not become a soldier."[55] He also attacked the practice of "quiet sitting" (*jingzuo*), a combination of Confucian tranquil study, Buddhist meditation techniques, and Taoist life-cultivation practices that was practiced by the elite.[56] He argued against its advocates, who believed that vigorous movement could damage the health. Throughout his political career, Mao held to the concept that *yundong*, which means "activity" or "movement," was the remedy for the passivity and weakness that ailed China. *Yundong* is also one of the words that can be used for sport. *Yundong* was also the word used to label the endless political "campaigns" of the Maoist period. These debates reveal the orientalist stereotype of the quiet, still (*jing*) East, which could become a strong nation only by getting into motion like the active (*dong*) West.

Traces of orientalism are evident in the writings of Coubertin, who was surprised by his first trip to Athens in 1894 because he expected to find the Greeks "reduced to Albanians, orientalized" but instead found that "the Greek resurrection seemed to me such a miracle that it imposed respect."[57] In 1906, he stated, "Hellenism . . . has the numbers, the prestige of history, and the excellence of biology on its side. No other Eastern people has such prerogatives to the world's confidence."[58] He later recalled, "Sport is the prerogative of all races. It is not so long since Asiatics were actually considered excluded by nature."[59] He was enthusiastic about the potential for the spread of sports in East Asia, but his attitude was clearly colonialist and imperialist, believing as he did that the "'yellow men' seem to us to be admirably prepared to benefit from the athletic crusade that is taking shape."[60]

There was one dissenting voice. On the question of the presence of the competitive spirit in China, Marcel Granet went against the grain of orientalism with his theory that the spirit of competition led to the origins of the state in China. He developed a hypothetical reconstruction of the origins of Chinese civilization from ancient ritual songs. Johan Huizinga, a medieval historian and author of a creative book about the roots of culture in play, did not completely agree with Granet's argument but was impressed enough by his evidence to argue against Burckhardt and Ehrenberg and to say that

> we must admit that he has demonstrated in an altogether masterly fashion how the agonistic principle plays a part in the development of Chinese civilization far more significant even than agon in the Hellenic world. . . . For in ancient China almost every activity took the form of a ceremonial contest; the crossing of a river, the climbing of a mountain, cutting wood or picking flowers.[61]

Addressing one of the stereotypes of the noncompetitive Chinese, Huizinga observed that the emphasis on politeness, humility, and "yielding" (*rang*) in China should properly be recognized as a competition for honor, a courtesy match. "We might call it an inverted boasting-match, since the reason for this display of civility to others lies in an intense regard for one's own honor."[62]

SOCIAL DARWINISM

At the time that Western sports were introduced into China, all the Western intellectual trends described in the first half of this chapter had already occurred. Neoclassicism and romanticism had waxed and waned, the notion of international sporting events as a way of bringing together different peoples was already established, and nationalist thinking had moved away from the Enlightenment tradition and toward new theories of sociology and universal education. Sports did not carry the heavy classical symbolism that they had had in Europe, but they did carry a heavy load of internationalism. This is one reason that the first regional games held in the world (beginning in 1913) were the YMCA-led Far Eastern Games, which initially formed a rival with the Olympic Games.[63] Although neoclassical and French revolutionary ideas were still in the air, the most influential theory in shaping Chinese nationalism and sports was social Darwinism—a view, inspired by Darwin's recent theory of biological evolution, that echoed the nineteenth-century classicists writing about the supremacy of the Greeks in the great competition between races. In social Darwinism, nations were seen as biological organisms struggling for survival among other like organisms. Social Darwinism had two links with sport.

First, it gave urgency to the orientalist stereotype of the absence of the competitive spirit in China because the absence of competitiveness could be seen as a cause of national weakness. The Buddhist ideal of "no contest with the world" (*yu shi wu zheng*) was identified as a traditional mind-set that must be changed. The reformist intellectual Liang Qichao proposed that China needed to learn from Japan and to recover the *bushido* ("way of the warrior") spirit that it had once had.[64] Like the idea that China had almost no sports since the Song dynasty, the notion that China never had a competitive spirit is still around today. The discussion revived at the beginning of the reform era in the late 1980s, when the competitive spirit was considered necessary for the economic reforms leading toward a competitive market economy. Lu Yuanzhen, a prominent social critic and sport scholar, wrote in a newspaper article,

> In traditional Chinese culture, Confucian thought advocated, "If only man would not contend, then all under heaven would not contend," respectful humility, a yielding and shrinking national spirit, and a social attitude of diluting competition, denigrating competition; this is extremely disadvantageous to a market economy society and the education of young people in a modernized society. In a sense, competitive sport not only has actual significance in stimulating the national spirit, but also has a deep value in shaping the character of a new generation of the people.[65]

Second, Herbert Spencer argued that moral, intellectual, and physical education shaped strong citizens for a strong nation. Above all else, physical education began to be perceived as a means of building a militarily strong nation—which was disappointing to YMCA educators who believed in sports as a means of moral education. Eugene Barnett, national director of the YMCA in China, was frustrated that Chinese were overly concerned with "national salvation" and not enough with "personal salvation" (i.e., Protestant Christian beliefs).[66]

THE SICK MAN OF EAST ASIA

Within the context of social Darwinism, the negative stereotypes about the weak Chinese body crystallized into the label of the "sick man of East Asia" (*dongya bingfu*). For a century, this phrase has loomed in the Chinese imagination as an insulting label applied to China by Japan and the West. The phrase was perhaps derived from the mid-nineteenth-century characterization of the Ottoman Empire as the "sick man of Europe." Xu Guoqi believes it originated with Yan Fu (1853–1921), who first translated the social Darwinists T. H. Huxley and Herbert Spencer into Chinese; he called China a "sick man" in 1895.[67] While it is true that images of Chinese opium addicts were popular in the West—the 1893 World's Fair in Chicago featured an opium den with "real" Chinese opium smokers—it is not clear whether the phrase originated in the West or in China. Wherever it originated, it always had more currency among reform-minded Chinese than it did in the West.

A common item of rhetoric states that the hosting of the Olympic Games will finally erase the label of "the sick man of East Asia" once and for all. This is so despite the fact that the stereotype of the sickly and effeminate Chinese is probably no longer the dominant one among Western youth because of the perceived rise of the "China threat," the popularity of Chinese martial arts since the 1960s, and film heroes from Bruce Lee to Jackie Chan to Jet Li. Kam Louie even argues that Chinese martial masculinity is now influencing global images of masculinity.[68] However, because Chinese children are still taught a history that emphasizes national humiliation, most Chinese believe that the "sick man of East Asia" is still a widely held image in Japan and the West.

As the Beijing Olympics approach, China still defines its identity in relation to Japan and the West to a degree that is not true in the reverse direction. Despite its growing national confidence, a true shift in the global order will have occurred only when China no longer defines itself in terms of how the West and Japan perceive it.

HOW BEING ORIENTALIZED DEPRIVED
CHINA OF ITS SPORT HISTORY

The preceding discussion has outlined the orientalist assumptions; at this point, let me show how these assumptions blinded authors to the world that actually lay around them.

"Sport" became a thing that had a "history" in Europe (with England as its core) only in the nineteenth century, when it emerged as a cultural category used to describe a set of activities. The ancient Greeks did not share our modern concept of sport and thus did not write their own sport histories, and neither did the Chinese, ancient or modern, until they were introduced to the English concept of sport. The history of ancient Greek athletics did not spring fully formed onto the page but was accumulated through years of analysis of texts and museum artifacts and archaeological excavations. It has been painstakingly pieced together for over 200 years now. While a wealth of sources has now been found, it took time to find them. There are actually only two main textual sources: the Odes of Pindar and the travel guide by Pausanias. Most of what we know has come from over a century of archaeological excavation, mainly carried out by Europeans and Americans. Systematic excavations have been carried out at ancient Olympia for 127 years, and they are still far from complete. The entity that is today named "Greek civilization" occupied a smaller territory and lasted a shorter time than that occupied by the entity called "Chinese civilization." Relative to its size, archaeology has never been conducted in China on anything close to the scale it has in Greece. Furthermore, since ancient athletics occupied an important place in classicism, archaeologists deliberately sought evidence for athletics. Sports have not been as important in Chinese archaeology. In short, it is no surprise that the evidence for sports in ancient China may seem sparse by comparison with ancient Greece. At this point, we can only wait for future developments in Chinese archaeology to find out how important the role of sports might have been in ancient times. When I have discussed this question with prominent sinologists, some feel that sports simply were not as important as in ancient Greece, and therefore we will never find evidence for sports in China that is comparable to what has been found for Greece; others feel that it is still an open question.

However, even despite the slight attention given to its collection, there was still a great deal of textual, art-historical, and archaeological evidence for many different kinds of sports in ancient China for those who had cared to look. For example, in 1941 the German sport historian Carl Diem was able to write thirty-seven pages about equestrian sports in China even though he was unable to read the Chinese texts; he used the few available sources in English and German and studied objects in museums. What is even more remarkable is that these pages were part of a larger book on *Asiatische Reiterspiele* [Asiatic Equestrian Games], which also discussed the rest of the Near and Far East.[69]

Sports arguably occupied an important a role in Chinese political systems. Mark Edward Lewis describes how the ancient form of soccer, "kick-ball," served as a simulacrum of the well-regulated state and argues that horn butting (*jiaodi*) and kick-ball were associated with the charter myths as new forms of the state emerged out of the Zhou dynasty in the Warring States period (403–221 B.C.).[70] Kick-ball playing fields were a standard feature of palace complexes as early as the Han dynasty (206 B.C.–A.D. 220). Polo was important in the Tang imperial courts, and wrestling was important in the Song and all subsequent imperial courts.

Turn-of-the-century observers could easily have looked around and noted the variety and importance of sporting activities, but perhaps because they did not conform to Western definitions of sport, they were ignored. Dragon boat races were popular throughout much of China and were held on a large scale in many places. Although sinologists and observers wrote about them, they did nothing to contradict the orientalist stereotypes about sport because they were classified as "religious festivals," not sports. Wrestling was important in

Mongol and Manchu culture generally and was also an important form of entertainment and public display for the Qing court, which maintained a special guard of skilled wrestlers in a system similar to Japanese imperial sumo— which by now has been well documented in both English- and Japanese-language books, while the Chinese version has not. The Manchu also displayed their horses and finery in races held outside one of the western city gates of Beijing.[71] In the sections of any major city devoted to street entertainment, such as the *Tianqiao* district of Beijing, a spectator could easily observe acrobatics, wrestling, and feats of strength and prowess. And, of course, the concept of the effeminate, intellectual Chinese is strongly contradicted by the martial arts tradition, which constitutes something of a subterranean history because it flourished among classes that ranked below the educated elite who wrote the official histories.

Moreover, the Imperial Exams were a kind of competition. If they were to be viewed as one of the central organizing institutions of Chinese civilization, then it should be acknowledged that this institution revolved around a notion of excellence through competition, and the Chinese were every bit as concerned with ensuring the fairness of the exams as the Greeks were in ensuring the fairness of their sporting events. Why wasn't this considered an expression of "agonal spirit" while contests of physical prowess were?

In short, there was ample observable evidence that could have contradicted the notion of the noncompetitive, intellectualized, effeminized Chinese with no sports of their own, but their preexisting views did not predispose westerners to see them, and, seeing themselves through Western eyes, reform-minded Chinese people echoed the Western views.

WHY IT BECAME IMPORTANT TO CHINA
IN THE 1980s TO HAVE A SPORT HISTORY

As the era of reform got underway in the 1980s, sport historians began to write the history of ancient Chinese sports and to portray continuity between modern China and its ancient sports. An article in the English-language magazine *China Sports* actually argued that Confucius promoted physical education and participated in sports himself.[72] One historian lamented the loss of China's own sports history:

> Because of various reasons, particularly because they lack a knowledge of history, people think that ancient Chinese society in fact had no sport activities: since ancient China never even heard of this word "sports," how could it have

had sport activities? . . . —I hope that this little book can contribute some material to the understanding and research of our nation's ancient sports by the broad masses of educators and physical educators.[73]

Why did China's sport history begin to be written in the 1980s? There were two reasons, one domestic and one international. First, the "seeking roots" movement began to reestablish links with China's past in reaction against the excesses of the Cultural Revolution (1966–1976). China started to reconcile its modern national history with its ancient past some 150 years after Greece did. The writing of sport history was part of this reconciliation, as it had been in Greece.

Second, in addition to the creation of a *national* imagined community, China also desired to take its place in the *global* imagined community. China rejoined the IOC in 1979 after twenty-one years of exclusion during the Cold War. In that year, Premier Deng Xiaoping was already thinking about hosting an Olympic Games.[74] China took part in its first post–Cold War Winter Olympics in 1980 and Summer Olympics in 1984. Many of the new sport histories were in English, targeted a foreign audience, and were published by the Chinese Olympic Committee and other government organs. As discussed in chapter 2, Chinese martial arts were promoted with the goal of including them in the Olympic Games. These histories expressed a desire to demonstrate that China had a long and illustrious sport history to contribute to the international sports world, a history every bit as legitimate as the Western one. This goal came into sharper focus with Beijing's first unsuccessful bid for the 2000 Olympic Games in 1993 and its successful bid for the 2008 games in 2001.

In June–October 1999, leading up to the second bid, China's senior IOC member, He Zhenliang, organized an exhibition on "5000 Years of Sport in China: Art and Tradition" at the Olympic Museum in Lausanne, Switzerland, the headquarters of the IOC. In his preface to the catalog, he wrote, "What was special about sport in ancient China was the way it was permeated by the characteristics of Oriental agricultural civilization, blended with the monist philosophy of *qi* (vital energy) and the ethical and aesthetic concepts of Confucianism, Buddhism, and Taoism." He claimed for the Chinese sporting tradition some of the traits that had been perceived as unique to the Western tradition, such as an emphasis on balance and harmony, attention to the process rather than the results, and the idea that sports embody an entire civilization. "Each object, like a dragon's scale, enables later generations to conjure up a picture of the whole Dragon, the symbol of China, and to draw inspiration from its vitality and noble spirit." He explicitly stated his goal in overseeing the exhibition:

[S]port has created a universal language. . . . It has become a new form of international communication. It is precisely for this reason that I would like, in my capacity as Chairman of the Cultural Commission of the International Olympic Committee and Honorary President of the Chinese Olympic Committee, to express my heartfelt gratitude to the Olympic Museum . . . so that the visitors, while taking delight in art, can gain a better knowledge and understanding of China.[75]

As China reentered the global village, leaders like He Zhenliang wanted to show that China is not one of the "people without sport history."

THE 2004 ATHENS OLYMPIC GAMES
AND THE 2008 BEIJING OLYMPIC GAMES

The result of the late nineteenth/early twentieth-century ideologies of classicism and orientalism was that when they were newly established, the nation-states of Greece and China viewed their own sport histories in very different ways. In the lead-up to the hosting of the Olympic Games in 2004 and 2008, these differences were brought into sharper focus. Both China and Greece labor under "the heavy burden of ancient glory."[76] Greece portrays itself as the fount of Western civilization, and China portrays itself as the fount of Eastern civilization. Both nations are struggling to establish themselves as worthy nations in the modern world system of nation-states. Greece emerged as an independent nation-state in 1832, China in 1912. Less than a century (sixty-seven years) after its independence, Greece moved from semicolonial status to being a central meeting place of the world's nations in the 1896 Olympic Games, and the world met again in Athens in 2004. In 2008, when Beijing hosts the Olympic Games, it will have been almost a century (ninety-six years) since a modern nation-state was declared on Chinese soil (1912) and China finally became a global meeting place.

Greek intellectuals saw themselves through the eyes of the West and adjusted their self-image to conform to Western standards, leading to what has been called "the problem of too much history."[77] Greeks have felt a duty to live up to the standards of their glorious past as it was portrayed by European classicism and have often found themselves deficient. In this sense, Greece had "too much sport history."

One of the slogans for the Athens Olympic Games was "Coming Home."

The long journey of the Olympic Games began more than 2,700 years ago. Records of Olympic history show that the ancient Olympic Games were held in

Greece as early as in 776 B.C. It was then that the basis of the Olympic Movement began to evolve into a philosophy of life: exalting and combining the qualities of body, will, and mind in a balanced whole. Out of this philosophy the Olympic Ideals were born, placing noble competition, sport, peace, culture, and education at the very core of Greek civilisation. In 1896 the first Modern Olympic Games were held in Athens and since that time have been on a journey around the world for more than a century. Now, at the dawn of the 3rd millennium, the Games are returning to the country of their birth and the city of their revival. In 2004, Greece will be called upon to empower the Olympic Movement once again, placing sport at the service of peace.[78]

When it reentered the Olympic Movement in 1984, however, China found that it had "too little sport history." In today's world, having a sport history is a mark of a modern nation. Nearly 100 years after Herbert Giles wrote his article on ancient Chinese polo and football, very little information on Chinese sport culture is available in the West. For 200 years, Western scholars have been fascinated with studying ancient sports as part of their "own" history but have shown almost no interest in the sports of non-Western "civilizations." This now provided a challenge for the cultural programs surrounding the Beijing Olympics since the basic material for museum exhibits, textbooks, documentaries, and other cultural products hardly existed. As a result, the Beijing Olympic Games have stimulated scholarship where previously there was none.

A 2001 book describing Beijing's bid illustrates how China portrayed itself as the fount of Eastern civilization and the originator of alternative traditions to the dominant Western one.

In 2008, when the "Olympic flag" waves over Beijing—the city with a 3,000 year history, the ideal representative of traditional Chinese culture—Eastern and Western cultures will achieve their greatest fusion, revealing to the whole world the enchantment of Eastern culture. A new Beijing, vigorously developing under the reforms and opening-up, will contribute to the world an Olympics unlike any other; its opening ceremony of exceptional splendor, its warm and friendly people, its rich culture, will propel the Olympic Movement to become a truly transcultural, transethnic, transnational, global cultural system.[79]

In comparing Greece and China, one cannot help but note the strength of the idea of "Western civilization" in the making of Greek and Chinese national identities. Western classicists praised the ancient Greek past, so Greek nationalists embraced it. Western orientalists criticized the ancient Chinese past, so Chinese nationalists rejected it. Both Greece and China underwent revolutions to throw off what was perceived as an oppressive oriental yoke: in the case of Greece, it was the Ottoman yoke, and in so doing it reclaimed

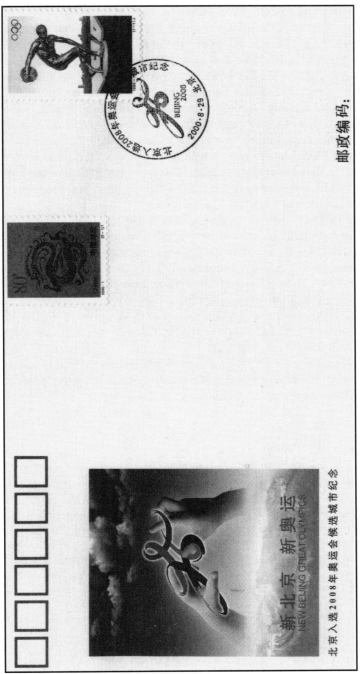

Figure 1.1. Souvenir envelope with stamps from Beijing's bid in 2001. Note the combination of symbols of the civilizations of China (dragon, five rings in the shape of a t'ai-chi practitioner, traditional string game) and Greece (discobolus, Olympic rings) and the English "New Beijing, New Olympics" versus Chinese "New Beijing, Great Olympics" (see chapter 7). Property of Susan Brownell.

its Western heritage; in the case of China, it was the oppressive yoke of the Manchu and of its own Confucian heritage—which meant that Chinese nationalists rejected connection with the past, unlike Greece, which retained a connection with at least part of its history (the most distant part).

Greece's inclusion in the Occident produced a problem of national identity that has tormented it ever since. Greece later had to reconcile the pagan past that it gripped so strongly with its Byzantine Christian heritage.[80] "Westernization" and the loss of Greek customs have increasingly been perceived as a problem over the past century. It is not so clear that the inclusion of Greece in the national histories of Western nations caused *them* the same amount of torment; rather, the idea of Greece seemed only to strengthen national identities in Western Europe, and to that extent, both classicism and orientalism reinforced the primacy of the West.

Since the 1980s, China has begun to reestablish links with its own glorious past, but it remains to be seen how it will ultimately be reconciled with the thirty-year interval in which that past was vehemently rejected. Unlike Greece, China considers itself a representative of an alternative tradition to the one embodied in the Olympic Movement. In the symbolism and rhetoric surrounding the 2004 Athens Olympic Games, we saw images of a single line of descent from ancient Greece to the modern world. In Beijing in 2008, we will see images of the coming together of the separate civilizations of East and West.

In both Greece and China, sport history has been an important segment of national history, making the hosting of the Olympic Games into a particularly powerful symbol of the place of the nation in the world.

NOTES

1. The phrase "alternating with those at Athens" refers to the Intermediate Olympic Games, which were planned to be held in Athens in the middle of the Olympiad. The first one had just been successfully held in 1906, but it was the last because of Greece's instability. The questions are in C. H. Robertson, "A Plan for Promoting Missionary Activity among Association Boys," *Annual Reports of the Foreign Secretaries of the International Committee, October 1, 1909 to September 30, 1910* (New York: International Committee, YMCA, 1910), 192; see also Andrew Morris, *Marrow of the Nation: A History of Sport and Physical Culture in Republican China* (Berkeley: University of California Press, 2004), 1–2.

2. Ernst Curtius, *The History of Greece*, vol. 1, trans. Adolphus William Ward (London: Richard Bentley, 1868), 15.

3. Ernst Curtius, *Althertum und Gegenwart: Gesammelte Rede und Vorträge*, vol. 1 (Stuttgart: J. G. Cotta'sche Buchhandlung Nachfolger, 1903), 133.

4. Eric R. Wolf, *Europe and the People without History* (Berkeley: University of California Press, 1982), 385.

5. "Greece" and "China" in *CIA World Factbook*, www.cia.gov (June 19, 2007).

6. Website of the General Secretariat of Greeks Abroad, www.ggae.gr/gabroad/ organosi.en.asp (June 19, 2007).

7. www.library.ohiou.edu/subjects/shao/databases_popdis.htm (June 19, 2007).

8. "Taiwan," "Hong Kong," and "Macau," in *CIA World Factbook*, www.cia.gov (June 19, 2007).

9. Thomas F. Scanlon, *Greek and Roman Athletics: A Bibliography* (Chicago: Ares Publishers, 1984), 55–65. These numbers are based on a count by the author.

10. The first book in Chinese on Chinese sports was Guo Xifen, *Zhongguo tiyushi* [The History of Chinese Sports] (Shanghai: Shangwu Press, 1919). Works in English include Ren Hai, "A Comparative Analysis of Ancient Greek and Chinese Sport" (Ph.D. diss., University of Alberta, 1988); No author/editor, *Sports and Games in Ancient China* (Beijing: New World Press, 1986); Olympic Museum, ed., *5000 Years of Sport in China: Art and Tradition* (Lausanne: Musée Olympique, 1999), is an art book in English and French with some essays. Large-format art books with captions and some commentary in both Chinese and English include Shao Wen-liang, ed., *Sports in Ancient China* (Hong Kong: Tai Dao Publishing, 1986); Xiong Xiaozheng, Liu Bingguo, and Zhang Tianbai, eds., *Illustrated History of Ancient Chinese Sports* (Beijing: Yanshan Publishing House, 1990); Liu Ji, ed., *5,000 Years of Physical Culture and Sports in China* (Beijing: Beijing University of Physical Education Publishing House, 1996); and Cui Lequan, ed., *Album on Ancient Sports Art in China* (Beijing: Zhonghua Shuju, 2000). Books in Chinese include Bi Shiming, ed., *Zhongguo gudai tiyushi* [The History of Ancient Chinese Sports] (Beijing: Beijing Institute of Physical Education Publishing House, 1990); Ren Hai, *Zhongguo gudai tiyu* [Ancient Chinese Sports] (Beijing: Shangwu Press, 1991, 1996); Ren Hai, *Zhongguo gudai wushu* [Ancient Chinese *wushu*] (Beijing: Shangwu Press, 1991, 1996); Ren Hai, *Zhongguo gudai wushu yu qigong* [Ancient Chinese *wushu* and *qigong*] (Beijing: Shangwu Press, 1996); and Xu Yongchang, *Zhongguo gudai tiyu* [Ancient Chinese Sports] (Beijing: Beijing Shifan daxue chubanshe, 1983).

11. Bing Mazhao, *Zhongguo chuantong tiyu* [Traditional Chinese Sports] (Beijing: Capital Normal University Press, 2006); sections in Lou Xiaoqi et al., eds., *Aolinpike yu Zhongguo/Olympic and China* (Beijing: Civilization Magazine, 2005); publication of revised editions of Ren Hai, *Zhongguo gudai tiyu* and *Zhongguo gudai wushu*.

12. Allen Guttmann, *Sports: The First Five Millennia* (Amherst: University of Massachusetts Press, 2004).

13. Richard D. Mandell, *Sport: A Cultural History* (New York: Columbia University Press, 1984), 90–95.

14. This chapter is shaped by Edward Said's notion of orientalism as a style of thought based on a fundamental distinction made between "the Orient" and "the Occident." He argued that Oriental studies arose out of the experiences of colonialism, particularly of Britain and France, whose colonies in India and Egypt were the major colonies of the Near East before World War II. After World War II, America dominated the Orient in the same style. Orientalism was shaped by the fact that the Orient

was a cultural rival adjacent to Europe and the site of Europe's oldest and richest colonies. As such, the Orient served as an image of the Other to Europe; it helped the West to define itself by providing a contrasting image. His most radical point is that this intellectual distinction is part of the Western style of "dominating, restructuring, and having authority over the Orient" (3). Said does not believe that academic texts are "merely decorative"; they are a form of cultural domination that complements political domination (25). Through studying the Orient, the colonial powers were better able to control it; by dominating the production of knowledge about the Orient, they ensured that the natives could read about themselves only through the lens of European scholarship. The West dominated intellectual discussions with the scholarship made possible by its wealth and power; furthermore, the West trained native intellectuals in Western European universities and Western ways of thought, so they saw their own culture through the eyes of the West. In Said's view, orientalism benefited European culture by strengthening its sense of identity, while it weakened Oriental culture by limiting what Orientals could think about themselves (3).

Said's model tends to assume that the West's ideologies are imposed on a largely passive East. Other scholars have observed that its colonized subjects internalize these ideologies in a process of self-orientalism—the process in which the East comes to see itself through the eyes of the West and to judge itself inferior by Western standards. In the case of Greece, we might want to coin the term self-occidentalism. The example of Greece complicates Said's conception of orientalism as the West's way of dominating the East through classifying it and treating it as an Other. Greece was classified on the "right" side of the divide as "one of us," but this was also a way in which the West dominated Greece. Edward Said, *Orientalism* (New York: Vintage Books, 1978).

15. Antonides, Theodorus, and Meinart Antonides, *Olympia, dat is, Olymp-speelen der Grieken* [Olympia and the Olympic Games of the Greeks] (Netherlands: Te Groningen, 1732).

16. Andrew L. March, *The Myth of China: Myth and Theory in Geographic Thought* (New York: Praeger, 1974), 34.

17. March, *The Myth of China*, 27–28.

18. Franco Venturi, "Oriental Despotism," *Journal of the History of Ideas* 24, no. 1 (January–March 1963): 133.

19. March, *The Myth of China*, 29.

20. March, *The Myth of China*, 30.

21. Carl Diem, *Weltgeschichte des Sports* [World History of Sports], vol. 2 (Stuttgart, 1971), cited in Otto Schantz, "Französische Festkultur als Wegbereiter der Modernen Olympischen Spiele" [French Festival Culture as Precursor of the Modern Olympic Games], *Stadion* XXI/XXII, special issue on *Studien zur Geschichte der Olympischen Spiele* (1998): 64.

22. Schantz, "Französische Festkultur," 66.

23. Schantz, "Französische Festkultur," 66–74.

24. Venturi, "Oriental Despotism," 135.

25. Martin Bernal, *Black Athena: The Afroasiatic Roots of Classical Civilization, vol. I: The Fabrication of Ancient Greece 1785–1985* (New Brunswick, N.J.: Rutgers University Press, 1996 [1987]), 332–36. While this statement may be true in

historical hindsight, Bernal does not do justice to the actual content of Curtius's work. His concept of race was not the kind of rigid, biologically determined racism that we now associate with the concept of the Aryan race; instead, he moved rather freely between biological descent, learned culture, and environmentally determined traits in a way that one might expect in an era before evolutionary theories of race had yet to take hold. Furthermore, he stated emphatically that Greek civilization had borrowed a great deal from Semitic civilization, and he viewed these as the two great foundations of Western civilization (Christian Bachhiesl, "Ein 'deutsches' Griechenland: Zum Bild der Griechen bei Ernst Curtius" [master's thesis, Institut für Altgeschichte und Altertumskunde, Karl-Franzens-Universität Graz, 2001], 3, 8, 25, 55–65). At one point, Curtius wrote, "I cannot remove the impression that in the rejection of Oriental culture is to be seen a certain antipathy, which dims the detachment of judgment" (*Gesammelte Abhandlungen*, vol. 2 [Berlin: Wilhelm Hertz, 1894], vii).

26. Curtius, *Gesammelte Abhandlungen*, 9.

27. Curtius, *Althertum und Gegenwart*, 134.

28. Bachhiesl, "Ein 'deutsches' Griechenland," 5, 43–46.

29. Curtius, *Althertum und Gegenwart*, 134.

30. Friedrich Curtius, ed., *Ernst Curtius: Ein Lebensbild in Briefen*, vol. 2 (Berlin: Julius Springer, 1903), 4.

31. Curtius, *Althertum und Gegenwart*, 141.

32. Curtius's racism was not as rigid as the concept of the Aryan race that emerged decades later. The German word is *Stamm*, which can be translated as "tribe" or "race." *Althertum und Gegenwart*, 134.

33. Curtius, *The History of Greece*, 12.

34. Curtius, *Althertum und Gegenwart*, 83.

35. Curtius, *Althertum und Gegenwart*, 144.

36. Bernal, *Black Athena*, 28–32.

37. Yves-Pierre Boulongne, "The Presidencies of Demetrius Vikelas (1894–1896) and Pierre de Coubertin (1896–1925)," in *The International Olympic Committee, One Hundred Years: The Idea, the Presidents, the Achievements*, ed. Raymond Gafner (Lausanne: International Olympic Committee, 1994), 34; Bernal, *Black Athena*, 212–15.

38. Jacob Burckhardt, *The Greeks and Greek Civilization* [Griechische Kulturgeschichte], trans. Sheila Stern (New York: St. Martin's Press, 1998 [1898–1902]), 162.

39. Burckhardt, *The Greeks and Greek Civilization*, 166.

40. Burckhardt, *The Greeks and Greek Civilization*, 160–213.

41. Thomas F. Scanlon, *Eros and Greek Athletics* (Oxford: Oxford University Press, 2002); Michael B. Poliakoff, *Combat Sports in the Ancient World: Competition, Violence, and Culture* (New Haven, Conn.: Yale University Press, 1987).

42. Victor Ehrenberg, *Ost und West: Studien zur geschichtlichen Problematik der Antike* (Brünn: Verlag Rudolf M. Rohrer, 1935), 93–94.

43. This history is dealt with in Ingomar Weiler, "'Aien Aristeuein': Ideologische Bemerkungen zu einem vielzitierten Homerwort," *Stadion* 1, no. 2 (1975): 199–227.

44. Herbert A. Giles, "Football and Polo in China," *The Nineteenth Century and After* 59 (April 1906): 508.

45. Herbert A. Giles, *The Civilization of China* (London: Williams and Norgate, 1911), 151.

46. Giles, *The Civilization of China*, 159.

47. Morris, *Marrow of the Nation*, 42–43.

48. Morris, *Marrow of the Nation*, 43–44.

49. J. T. C. Liu, "Polo and Cultural Change: From T'ang to Sung China," *Harvard Journal of Asiatic Studies* 45, no. 1 (1985): 204.

50. Paul F. Cressey, "The Influence of the Literary Examination System on the Development of Chinese Civilization," *American Journal of Sociology* 35 (1929): 254.

51. Edward Alsworth Ross, *The Changing Chinese: The Conflict of Oriental and Western Cultures in China* (New York: The Century Company, 1911), 339.

52. Ross, *The Changing Chinese*, 309.

53. James B. Webster, *Christian Education and the National Consciousness in China* (New York: E. P. Dutton, 1923), 207.

54. Wang Zhenya, *Jiu Zhongguo tiyu jianwen* [Information on Sports in Old China] (Beijing: Renmin tiyu chubanshe, 1987), 15.

55. Mao Zedong, "*Tiyu zhi yanjiu*" [A Study of Physical Culture], *Xin qingnian* [New Youth] 3, no. 2 (April 1917): 7.

56. Kunio Miuria, "The Revival of *Qi*: Qigong in Contemporary China," in *Taoist Meditation and Longevity Techniques*, ed. Livia Kohn (Ann Arbor, Mich.: Center for Chinese Studies, 1989), 334.

57. Pierre de Coubertin, *Un Campagne de 21 ans* [A Campaign of 21 Years] (Paris: Librairie de l'Éducation Physique, 1909), 112–13.

58. Pierre de Coubertin, "The Philhellene's Duty" [1906], in *Olympism: Selected Writings*, ed. Norbert Mueller (Lausanne: International Olympic Committee, 2000), 250.

59. Coubertin, "Legends" [1930], in Mueller, *Olympism*, 748.

60. Coubertin, "An Olympiad in the Far East" [1913], in Mueller, *Olympism*, 697. See Otto Schantz, "Pierre de Coubertin's Concepts of Race, Nation, and Civilization," in *The 1904 Anthropology Days and Olympic Games: Sport, Race, and American Imperialism*, ed. Susan Brownell (Omaha: University of Nebraska Press, 2008).

61. Johan Huizinga, *Homo Ludens: A Study of the Play Element in Culture*, trans. Johan Huizinga (Boston: Beacon Press, 1950 [1944]), 55.

62. Huizinga, *Homo Ludens*, 66.

63. Abe Ikuo, "Historical Significance of the Far Eastern Championship Games: An International Political Arena," *Bulletin of the Institute of Health and Sport Sciences, University of Tsukuba* 26 (2003), 37–68.

64. Liang Qichao, "*Zhongguo zhi wushidao*" [China's Bushido], in *Yinbingshi quanji* [Collected Writings from the Ice-Drinker's Studio] (1916), vol. 44 (Taipei: Wenguang tushu gongsi, 1959), 43–49.

65. Lu Yuanzhen, "Renlei jiben jiazhi guanniande hongyang" [The Spread of Basic Human Values], *Zhongguo tiyu bao* [China Sports News], September 30, 1988.

66. Eugene E. Barnett, *My Life in China, 1910–1936* (East Lansing: Asian Studies Center, Michigan State University, 1990), 189.

67. Xu Guoqi, *Olympic Dreams: China and Sports, 1895–2008* (Cambridge, Mass.: Harvard University Press, 2008), chap. 1.

68. Kam Louie, *Theorising Chinese Masculinity: Society and Gender in China* (Cambridge: Cambridge University Press, 2002), 140–65.

69. Carl Diem, *Asiatische Reiterspiele: Ein Beitrag zur Kulturgeschichte der Völker* [Asiatic Equestrian Games: Toward a Cultural History of Peoples] (Berlin: Deutscher Archiv-Verlag, 1941).

70. Mark Edward Lewis, *Sanctioned Violence in Early China* (Albany: State University of New York Press, 1990), 146–50.

71. Sidney Gamble, *Peking: A Social Survey* (New York: George H. Doran Company, 1921), 229.

72. "Confucius as Physical Culture Promoter," *China Sports*, February 1983, 24–27.

73. Xu Yongchang, *Zhongguo gudai tiyu*, vii–viii.

74. Liang Lijuan, *He Zhenliang yu Aolinpike* [He Zengliang and Olympism] (Beijing: Olympic Publishing House, 2000), 124–25.

75. He Zhenliang, "Forward," in *5000 Years of Sport in China: Art and Tradition*, ed. Olympic Museum (Lausanne: Musée Olympique, 1999), 12–13.

76. The phrase "the heavy burden of ancient Greek glory" occurs in David C. Young, *The Modern Olympics: A Struggle for Revival* (Baltimore: Johns Hopkins University Press, 1996), 2.

77. Keith R. Legg and John M. Roberts, *Modern Greece: A Civilization on the Periphery* (Boulder, Colo.: Westview Press, 1997), 9–24.

78. Website of the Athens Organizing Committee, www.athens2004.com (February 2004).

79. Ma Tongbin and Qin Yuanyuan, *Beijing 2008—Shen Aode taiqian muhou* [Beijing 2008—Before and behind the Scenes of the Olympic Bid] (Beijing: Beijing University of Physical Education Publishing House, 2001), 36.

80. Michael Herzfeld, "Hellenism and Occidentalism: The Permutations of Performance in Greek Bourgeois Identity," in *Occidentalism: Images of the West*, ed. James G. Carrier (Oxford: Clarendon Press, 1995), 218–19.

Chapter Two

The Clash of Cultures
Martial Arts and Olympic Sports

Western sports were introduced into China beginning in the late nineteenth century and were rapidly incorporated into programs for national reform and modernization. At the same time, there were competing efforts to incorporate the indigenous martial arts into modernization programs. The history of sports in China is an important realm for looking at issues of tradition versus modernity, East versus West, Chinese versus foreign, and so on as they have played out over the past century. This chapter compares the histories of the martial arts and Olympic sports, asking the following questions: Why did the martial arts increasingly become a source of national pride in the 1990s, while the effort to incorporate martial arts into nationalist programs was largely unsuccessful earlier in the century because they were a symbol of national backwardness? Why didn't the International Olympic Committee (IOC) accept wushu into the official program of the 2008 Olympics, and would it have been a good thing for wushu if it had? The answer to the first question is found in the shift in China's position in global culture in the past century. The answer to the second question illustrates that the IOC, a Western-dominated organization, is slow to respond to these trends.

THE CLASH OF BODY CULTURES

In conceptualizing the role of sports in Chinese nationalism since the turn of the twentieth century, I have found it useful to place sports within a larger framework that describes the relationship between the body and the nation. In doing this, I have utilized the concept of "body culture." I define body culture as the entire repertoire of things that people do to, and with, their bodies and

49

the elements of culture that give meaning to their actions. Body culture can include daily practices of health, hygiene, fitness, beauty, and dress and decoration; postures, gestures, manners, and ways of speaking and eating; and ritual, dance, sports, and other kinds of bodily performance. It includes the methods for training these practices into the body, the way the body is publicly displayed, and the meanings that are expressed in that display. Body culture is embodied culture.[1]

The Body in Empire and Nation

Concepts of the body differ between different formations of the state. The two particular formations of the state that are relevant to this chapter are that of empire and nation. Although constructions of empire and nation vary across time and cultures, they also tend to share features in any given time period because, as part of the world system of states, they have near or distant dealings with each other. Here, the empire that concerns us is the late Qing Empire (1644–1911), and the nations are the Republic of China (1912–1949) and the People's Republic of China (1949 to present). These constructions are relevant to the topic of sports because the imperial body formed the basis for the practice of martial arts, while the national body formed the basis for the practice of Olympic sports.

As has been observed for empires elsewhere, the Qing Empire tended to be imagined as a "civilizing center" with porous borders, in accord with what Geertz calls the "doctrine of the exemplary center": "the theory that the court-and-capital is at once a microcosm of the supernatural order . . . and the material embodiment of political order."[2] The cosmos was envisioned as a hierarchy organized according to principles encompassing all of its constituent parts, including the divine, heaven, the ruler, earth, the people, and the bodies of the people. This "moral encompassment"[3] differs from the central organizing principle of the nation. Nations tend to be constructed as discrete entities with very clear boundaries—territorial, political, cultural, and so on. Nationalism is "possessive"—the use of the female body as a symbol of Chinese national territory is discussed in chapter 4.

Empires and nations demonstrate correspondingly different constructions of the body. The Qing culture of the body was based on the classical Chinese medical tradition, which had become highly sophisticated and systematized over its several-thousand-year history. The *Yellow Emperor's Classic of Medicine*, the central canon since at least the Han (220 B.C.–A.D. 206), assumed a linkage between the body and the cosmic hierarchy, as exemplified in the concept of *tian ren he yi*, "humans and nature as one." The body and its surrounding environment were permeated by essences that circulated throughout the cosmos, the most important being *yin* and *yang*, which were the source of the universe, of life and death, and of health and illness in the individual parts of the body.[4] Fluids also flowed through the body and the universe: the "three rivers" were *jing* ("seminal essence"), *qi* ("vital breath or energy"), and *shen* ("spirit"); sometimes *xue* ("blood") is added. Of these three substances, *qi* occupies the most important place in the three related traditions of medicine, religious meditation, and martial arts. In medicine, the conduits that channel *qi* throughout the body form the theoretical basis of acupuncture. Acupuncture needles are inserted into the points (*xue*) at which the conduits meet the surface of the body, where *qi* is interchanged between the body and the environment. *Qi* is equally present inside and outside the body; the lungs form the main point at which it goes in and out, and the early morning hours are the best ones for absorbing environmental *qi* to benefit the health. The mouth and digestive system mediate between the internal and outside worlds. Food is the main means for incorporating outside substances into the body, and diet is an important means of regulating the body's internal balance. The line between food and medicine is unclear.[5] The Taoist and Buddhist meditational traditions involve learning to control the body's flow of *qi* so that it can be directed to the three reservoirs, or "cinnabar fields" (*dantian*), which are located in the forehead, behind the sternum, and just below the navel. Proper focusing of *qi* energy leads to enlightenment and immortality (note the absence of a mind–body separation in this religious tradition). The martial arts traditions tend to concentrate only on the lower cinnabar field below the navel; by developing the ability to concentrate *qi* in that area, the master becomes able to perform astounding feats. By directing *qi* to other body parts, the master is able to make them hard and impervious to injury. By redirecting an enemy's *qi* against him, the master is able to repel attack.

In sum, *qi* is an all-purpose essence that can be used to cure illness, attain enlightenment, and achieve success in combat. It is the sine qua non of Chinese concepts of the body. Although Western doctors are now using acupuncture and Western students are now learning Chinese martial arts, it is not clear whether these practices can be completely mastered without first mastering the theory of *qi*. And *qi* represents a very different understanding of the body, derived from alternative traditions from those of the modern nation and Western biomedical science.

If we examine the classical conception of the body in general and the concept of *qi* in particular, it becomes clear that Chinese body culture assigned more importance to the subjective experience of the body than does the Western medical body culture. In comparing the two, Shigehisa Kuriyama notes that by the second century A.D., in the writings of the Greek physician Galen, the emergence of what was to become a fundamental split had already started to appear: the schism between voluntary action and natural processes and ultimately between mind and body.[6] In the sixteenth century this would lead to Cartesian dualism in philosophy, and in the twenty-first century it would manifest itself in a Western medicine that relies on instruments and machines to treat a body that is in many ways viewed as separate from the person who inhabits it.

Mind–body dualism was never as clearly articulated in Chinese culture. At one level, this is reflected in the vocabulary used. Like many languages, Chinese has several words that may be translated into English as "body." The two most common characters in the language of the body are *shen* and *ti*. *Shen* and *ti* are similar to the German *Leib* and *Körper*, respectively. My discussion of the Chinese words is inspired by works on the history of the German words. Lippe argued that one of the important developments in Europe's modernization was a shift in the conception of the body. He outlined a movement away from the conception of a living, experiential, subject-body ("the body that one is"—*Leib sein*) toward a dead, instrumental, object-body ("the body that one has"—*Körper haben*). *Leib* was the word used in the phrase for "the body of Christ." A *Leib* was a *Körper* plus a soul. It implied purity, morality, and identity.[7] But by the turn of the nineteenth century, it was being supplanted in discussions of health and fitness by a concern with the *Körper*, which implied animality, immorality, and instrumentality.[8] The difference between the two is illustrated in two words for physical education. *Leibeserziehung*, "physical education," implies moral cultivation as well as physical training and was the word more commonly used in West Germany before 1989. *Körperkultur*, "physical culture," the science of human physical exercise, became the word commonly used in East Germany, but after the fall of the Berlin Wall the old system was attacked and a new effort initiated to recuperate the body from the grip of the state.

It is possible to trace a somewhat similar development in China. Sinologists have noted that the Chinese word *shen* connotes a living, experiential, subject-body. Sun Lung-kee observes that in thinking about themselves and their relationships with other people, Chinese people use the word *shen* rather than concepts like "personality" or "individual."[9] Mark Elvin adds that "in most Chinese phrases that translate into English phrases where the ideas of "person," "self," or "lifetime" are used or implied, the word *shen* appears." Examples are the common phrases *an shen* (lit. "to make peaceful one's body" = "settle down in life") and *zhong shen* (lit. "body's end" = "to the end of one's life").[10] Before the introduction of Western science and physical education, references to physical training tended to take moral character and life force as their target. An old phrase for self-cultivation, *xiu shen*, used the word for body but primarily implied the cultivation of moral character. *Yang sheng*, "to cultivate life," referred to the Taoist physical exercises that were supposed to make the body immortal. After the era of reform, it became popular again and was used to refer to a range of self-cultivation exercises.

Ti, not *shen*, is the character that became most common in the language of modern sports. "Physical culture" or "physical education" was translated as *tiyu*, which in turn was derived from the Kanji for the Japanese *taiiku*. Other common words included "physical exercise" or "gymnastics" (*ticao*) and multiple words for "physique" (*tizhi, xingti, tixing, tipo*). In other contexts, *ti* refers to an individual unit or a closed system; that it is inanimate is indicated by its frequent use in combinations that translate abstract Western scientific phrases like "system," "particle," and so on. Another important reference is to calligraphy types. Although the Chinese words do not contain as strict a subject–object dualism as the German (attributable at least in part to the absence of the Western Cartesian mind–body dualism), it appears that with the introduction of Western medical science and physical education, the language of the body became much more detached, objective, and instrumental than it had been.

The eclipse of subjective bodily experience, particularly after the communist takeover, had some foundation in the philosophy underlying Western modes of physical development. The cultivation of *qi* gives primacy to bodily experience: *qi* can be felt within the body through sensations such as heat or tingling, which signal to the practitioner that he or she is succeeding in focusing his or her *qi*. Success in the cultivation of *qi* is primarily measured by the subjective feelings of the practitioner rather than by any objective standards, such as the measurements of time, distance, points scored, and so on, that characterize the notion of success in Western sports. Another important point is that *qi* is not the possession of any single individual body that is a closed system but flows between the body and the environment and between one body and another. Yasuo Yuasa takes the usages of *qi* in healing as the foundation for an argument that *qi* constitutes a "third term" mediating between the psychological and the physiological that cannot be understood from the standpoint of Western mind–body dualism. In reviewing scientific evidence for the existence of *qi*, he argues that the activity of *qi* is some kind of correlative relationship between psychology (mind), physiology (life), and physics (matter).[11] In other words, on philosophical grounds he wants to argue that the notion of *qi* is revelatory of an entire conception of the self and its relation to the outside world that is very different from the Western conception with its dualisms of mind–body and subject–object.

This brief outline suggests some of the ways in which the classical Chinese conception of the body differs from the Western scientific conception and also sketches some of the links between this conception of the body and larger views of empire and cosmos. Keeping this contrast in mind, then, we can examine the relationship between sports, body, and nation that became dominant in later time periods.

FROM QING TO REPUBLICAN CHINA

Handler has called nationalist ideology one of "possessive individualism."[12] Nations possess individual objects and people that—in contrast to other kinds of state formations such as the Qing—are not constituent parts of a universal moral hierarchy; rather, they belong to the nation because they are discrete and equivalent entities united by the fact that they share a similar essence, a national character. National bodies tend to have impermeable borders, and because they are seen as inviolable entities, the connections with the larger cosmos and environment are almost absent.

When Western sports were introduced into China, they were called "new physical culture" (*xin tiyu*) or "foreign physical culture" (*yang* or *xiyang tiyu*). Reformers and revolutionaries emphasized their newness and foreignness in their attempt to break with the traditions of the imperial past. Modern sports were conceived in opposition to the martial arts, which were hailed by traditionalists as quintessentially Chinese and attacked by reformers as outmoded and "feudal." Although the boundary lines between the two and the politics of the debate have shifted in the past century, this opposition has remained. The earliest forms of physical education were introduced by Japanese and Germans, who were themselves developing new conceptions of the body that would serve the cause of national strength. German physical education was moving away from the body as subject toward the body as object. The development of physical education in Europe was inseparable from the rise of modern nationalism after the French Revolution.[13] By the time the ideas first gained a purchase in China, a new conception of body and nation had been developing in Europe for a century. In Europe, beginning in the late eighteenth century, national physical education programs were designed, popular political movements centered around rationalized physical training became powerful (e.g., the Turners and the Sokols), and by the end of the nineteenth century the first modern Olympic Games were organized. Physical education as a way of linking individual bodies to the welfare of the nation is a historically recent phenomenon that went hand in hand with the rise of the nation-state as the dominant political form in Europe. In China, it developed alongside efforts to turn a dynastic realm into a modern nation-state according to the political ideas of the times.

The first physical education program in China was instituted in 1875 at the Nanking Military Academy, and other military schools soon followed suit. In

1890 the first modern sports event, a track-and-field meet, was held at St. John's University in Shanghai. In 1912 the first Boy Scout troop was established, with its highly militarized practices. Military discipline and sports comprised two channels of Western influence on body techniques.

Transformations in Chinese body culture occurred in the context of heated intellectual debates about the nature of the Chinese nation and nationalism. The key figure in this development was Yan Fu, who translated Huxley's *Evolution and Ethics* and Spencer's *Principles of Sociology* into Chinese at the turn of the century. In Spencer, Yan Fu encountered the image of the nation as a biological organism struggling for survival among other like organisms. As Yan Fu summarized it in a later essay, "a country is like a body" (*shen*).[14] Schwartz argues that the analogy between the social and biological organism was new to Yan Fu. He notes that in the West the analogy goes back to the ancient Greeks, but it is not clearly evident in the Chinese literature. The classical Chinese tendency was to conceive of the body as a state rather than the state as a body. In Taoist and medical traditions, the human body was often portrayed as organized like a state, with departments and bureaus. This metaphor indicated a concern with nourishing the life of the individual rather than ordering the state. Schwartz concludes that "Spencer's biological metaphor, particularly within its Darwinian framework, strikes Yan Fu with all the force of a blinding revelation."[15]

Yan Fu and the other leaders of the Constitutional Reform Movement of 1898—Kang Youwei and Liang Qichao—frequently used the body as a metaphor. Liang argued that the Chinese sense of nationhood consisted mainly of loyalty to the emperor. Because Chinese individuals did not identify national interest with self-interest, they failed to realize that "when the head is attacked all four limbs must respond; when the stomach is stabbed, the whole body must suffer."[16]

Spencer had discussed the three types of energy necessary for social survival: physical, intellectual, and moral. Translating these into Chinese, Yan Fu advocated the cultivation of *minli*, *minzhi*, and *minde*. Spencer's conception of a tripartite physical, intellectual, and moral education eventually became central in Chinese Marxist theory about the role of education in the formation of the socialist person. Sometimes a fourth term, "aesthetic education" (*mei*), was added. In courses on educational theory, Chinese students were taught to rattle off "*de-zhi-ti (mei)*" (moral, intellectual, physical, and aesthetic) as the guiding principles of socialist education. However, Yan Fu was vague on the subject of how to cultivate the "people's physical strength" and had much more to say about intellect and morals. In an 1898 article, he urged the abolition of opium and foot binding. He also urged a change in attitudes toward physical fitness, comparing China to an idle man unused to labor whose death is hastened when he is suddenly forced to exercise.[17] Like Kang

Youwei and Liang Qichao, he advocated physical education for women because healthy women produce strong children. He opposed early marriage,
believing that sexual excess at a young age weakened the seed and led to the
degeneration of descendants.[18] When Yan Fu spoke of physical education, he
tended to use the words for "strength" (*li, tili*). It was not until later that *ti* became the focal concept in discussions of physical education. And so, while
the idea of physical training appealed to Yan Fu and the other reformers, they
represent something of a transitional stage between the late Qing body culture
and the rationalized body culture that was eventually to develop in republican
and, especially, communist China. The science of physical education was
necessary to complete this link.

OLYMPIC SPORTS AS AN "EMPTY FORM"

John MacAloon argues that contemporary international sports have become
an "empty form." By this he means that they have been emptied of the cultural and historical content that characterized them in their original (often
Western European or North American) context. "As pure, that is purely empty
forms for the constitution of intercultural spaces, they present themselves to
the human groups interconnected by them for refilling with diverse cultural
meanings."[19] In China, we can observe how sports practices that were originally classified as foreign nevertheless came to have a strong hold on the
emotions and self-conceptions of everyday people. What made sports
"empty" enough that Chinese people could find their own meanings in them
at a local level? The example of China further clarifies MacAloon's point and
illustrates that "empty" is perhaps not the right way to visualize sports. While
it calls up a useful mental image, the concept of the "empty form" is unsatis-
factory because it creates an artificial distinction between form and content,
making it seem theoretically possible that sport and scientific practices can be
completely emptied of their original local (in this case Western) cultural content in a mechanical process not unlike turning a bottle upside down to spill
out its contents before refilling it. This image does not do justice to the intense attachment that people can feel for "their" sports and their consternation
at what might happen to them in the hands of others. This will be discussed
further below with respect to the question of the internationalization of Chinese wushu. In Chinese nationalist ideology, the concept of "nation" went
hand in hand with two other concepts: those of "democracy" and "science."
Just as arguments about nationalism were central to developments in sports,
arguments about democracy and science were also central. The reason that
democracy and science were central is that they are the forms that, when
grafted onto sports, made them appear empty of local cultural content and

feudal superstition. This "emptiness" is something of an illusion because sports were not, in fact, "empty" of meaning; rather, they were attached to universalist ideas of nationhood, democracy, and science, which transcended local practices and loyalties in order to construct a larger, homogeneous political entity called a "nation."

Sports and Democracy

Both Western educators and Chinese reformers recognized that sports served as a leveler between social statuses. One of the ways that particularly engaged both Chinese and Western observers was that they erased the class-based dress code. In the late Qing, dress was an important signifier of social class: men of high status wore long gowns with long sleeves that covered the hands, publicly demonstrating that they did not do manual labor, because the gowns would have been too restrictive. Men of the working class wore a short jacket with sleeves that exposed the hands, over pants. The long gown so vividly crystallized the ethos of the scholar-official class that they were sometimes called the "long gown class" (*changshan jieji*). In his 1917 article "A Study

Figure 2.1. Photo taken in 1945 by John Latimer, an American serviceman stationed in Chengdu, Sichuan Province, during World War II. The man in the center was Latimer's assistant; his brother is on the left, and his father is wearing the traditional gown on the right. In the background are nationalist soldiers. The photo was given to the author by Latimer, a friend of her grandmother.

of Physical Culture," Mao Zedong noted that one reason that men did not like to exercise was that people respected and admired a flowing gown and leisurely movements so that a man was embarrassed to appear without them, showing his hands and feet in public. He thus had no choice but to exercise within the privacy of his own room.[20] In the scholar-official view of the world, sports were an activity for the lower classes. Around 1914, Eugene Barnett, director of the Hangzhou YMCA, wrote, "The spectacle of mandarins, department chiefs, and clerks, tearing in scanty attire after a basket or volley ball over the yamen law [*sic*], persuades me that Old China is passing away."[21]

Barnett was one of the key Western figures to aid the passing of Old China, and he believed that he was doing so, in part, by using sports to introduce the notion of democracy. In 1913 he organized an interscholastic soccer league. It was a new sport in Hangzhou, and instruction began from scratch. Barnett recalled,

> More difficult to inculcate than the skills and rules were the meaning and the requirements of team play and sportsmanship, whether in victory or defeat. Team effectiveness rather than the display of individual prowess was a norm which had to be learned. It was not uncommon in the early days for the losing team and its schoolmates to seek retrieval of their lost face by launching bodily assaults on the winning team and its supporters! "A sound mind in a sound body," "team play," and "good sportsmanship" were exciting new ideas, not tired cliches, and we saw more clearly than ever before the relevance of the qualities they connoted to good citizenship in a democratic society.[22]

Sport was also something of a leveler between genders. In the late Qing, the vast majority of Chinese women had bound feet. This was perhaps a more visible marker of gender difference than was dress because women as well as men wore their gowns over trousers. Because bound feet made it difficult or impossible to engage in sports, the sight of sportswomen running freely across the sports field became a symbol of women's liberation. In 1935, Eugene Barnett wrote after observing the Sixth National Games,

> No single feature of the opening parade, or of the contests which followed, was more symbolic of the social revolution which has taken place in China than the presence of the girl athletes, dressed, some in bloomers, some in slacks, and some in shorts. For these girls to travel distances requiring weeks of time (as was necessary for those coming from such places as Yunnan, Szechuan, and Sinkiang [Xinjiang]), and for them to compete before spectators numbering tens of thousands, is a far cry from the bound feet and the accepted seclusion which prevailed among women and girls less than a generation ago.[23]

Despite the role attributed to sports in the liberation of women, however, on the whole it was clear that sports were not envisioned as a complete democracy and that women were second-class citizens. As Andrew Morris documents in his summaries of the rhetoric that surrounded the 1915 Second Far Eastern Games, it was to be athletic *men* who would lead the nation into a new era of strength. In his opening address at the games, Foreign Ministry Representative Yang Cheng, representing President Yuan Shikai, told the participants,

> You are representing the best men of your nations, and it is reasonable to suppose that in time you will become the representatives of your nations and will take your places in the world's conferences to solve the great problems of mankind. . . . I wish you success in the development of the highest type of manhood.[24]

As Morris notes, it had to be young *men* who would carry forth the banner of nationhood because they were called on to replace "the queues and robes that had kept alive the dreaded image of a feminine China in a world of men and their nations."

Science and Sports

Western biology and physiology were invoked in a myriad of ways to justify physical training methods that, in turn, would strengthen the nation. Another way in which science penetrated sports was in the increasing rationalization and objectification of sports through measurements and record keeping. In the 1920s, standards were established for bodily measurements, evaluations of fitness and skill levels, teacher skill levels, and sports ethics.

Martial Arts: Chinese Tradition versus Western Science

By comparison with Western sports, the martial arts seemed to be bastions of local allegiances and irrational superstitions and were regarded as "unscientific." However, there were nationalists who attempted to empty them of their localism and superstition and remake them in the model of Western sports. The old martial terminology—words like *quanyong* ("courageous fists") or *wuyong* ("martial courage") were replaced with more modern-sounding phrases like *wushu* ("martial skills or arts") or *quanshu* ("skills of the fist"). In the 1920s, the martial arts (wushu) were renamed the "national arts" (*guoshu*) and reshaped to fit the Western model of sports. With respect to rhetoric, the emphasis shifted from self-protection and attack toward fitness and health, conceived more in Western medical terms and educational terms.

Advocates called for their inclusion in physical education curricula. For example, this kind of advocate would discuss not the martial artist's cultivation of *qi* but rather of morals, physique, and aesthetic appreciation. In 1931, a book titled *A Scientized Wushu* was part of an effort to remove "the formidable realm of 'science' from the foreign and place it back in Chinese history, language and culture."[25] However, the concept of *qi* remained central in the conception of martial arts training, as it still is today.

The importance of martial arts as representative of China's backwardness is evident in the attention given to them by key advocates of modernization. Author Lu Xun wrote an essay against the "New Martial Arts" in which he argued not that he was opposed to Chinese martial arts per se but that he opposed the way educators picked them up as the latest fad. Further, he stated that the feudal superstitions that were promoted along with the martial arts were downright dangerous.[26] Mao Zedong criticized the technique of quiet meditation (*jingzuo, jinggong*) in his 1917 article, arguing that quiet meditation was not an effective means of physical training, and he attacked the view of its advocates that vigorous movement could damage the health.

Reformers also tried to develop and promote unified, homogeneous forms that would transcend the multifarious styles with local roots and allegiances that had previously characterized martial arts. Around 1918, the New Martial Arts were developed by Ma Liang, a commander under the Northern Warlords, a Japanese puppet government. They included boxing and kicking, wrestling, cudgel, and sword skills. The government promoted the New Martial Arts among the troops and in the schools under their control, hailing them as "national essence physical culture" (*guocui tiyu*). They were said to promote traditional martial virtue and valor, and their association with nationalism was evident in Ma Liang's claim that among all the nations of the world, no martial artists could surpass the Chinese. National Essence proponents argued that foreign training methods had no effect on Chinese bodies.[27]

A national meet was held in 1923, and men's martial arts were included in all the National Games beginning with the third Games in 1924; women's martial arts were included in the fifth and subsequent Games. The National Martial Arts Hall was established in 1928, and national tests were held in 1928 and 1933. In brief, the martial arts were categorized, bureaucratized, scheduled into mass displays, and stamped with an official ideology that explicitly linked them with republican nationalism. However, one reason that the martial arts were never able to take the place of Western sports in promoting nationalism is that the organizers themselves could never overcome their local factionalism and unite in the nationalist project.

The first National Test, for example, stimulated the traditional rivalries between martial arts schools, provoking heated animosity. The test consisted of sparring matches. Participants registered and then drew lots to determine the order. The winner of two out of three bouts was the victor, and an elimination series determined the final rankings. There were no restrictions on the blows that could be struck with hand or foot, with points awarded for blows landed and knockdowns. The fighters wore metal screen face protectors. Because the rules and safety measures were inadequate, there were many serious injuries, including broken bones, knockouts, and gouged eyes.[28] The second National Test included other tests and divided the sparring into different types, but the same problems cropped up in the sparring tests. In the preliminary rounds of the fist (*quanshu*) division alone, over sixty people were injured; in the weapons divisions the injuries were even more serious, but a clampdown on the press prevented their documentation.[29] In the end, sparring was never successfully "sportized," and this was attributed in part to the enduring allegiances to local masters and schools that led to unsportsmanlike attempts to injure others and to challenges outside the context of legitimate competition. Today, wushu includes two types: sparring (*sanshou*) is scored by judges who award points as in boxing, and forms (*taolu*) are judged on a ten-point scale, as was formerly used in gymnastics.

Even with the "sportization" of martial arts, the debate over martial arts as opposed to Western sports as a way of strengthening China was not resolved. In the 1930s, the conflict between those who supported each type of training intensified again. As in other areas of culture, this conflict was labeled the "conflict between the indigenous and the foreign" (*tu yang zhi zheng*). The traditionalists consisted of members of the national *guoshu* association and some journalists, while the reformers consisted of Chinese students returned from studying overseas.[30] In his speech marking the establishment of the National Martial Arts Hall, Zhang Zhijiang argued,

> If we want to quickly train our skills, *guoshu* is the path to start upon. . . . Only with a strong body, a strong race, a strong nation will our national spirit develop and expand, and only then will there be hope for world peace.[31]

Reformers countered,

> In cultivating the skills of running, jumping, scrambling, and climbing, indigenous physical culture is completely ineffective.[32]

And again,

> Our nation to this day still has a serious habit of exaggeration, posing as the best in the world at everything, as if our ancestors from the past few thousand years have hogged all of the limelight; even though we unfilial descendants have been

like dead dogs after three generations of heroes, we still feel proud. This so-called enriching of our great store of knowledge is nothing more than systematizing a pile of trash.[33]

In summary, sports, like the nation-state, arrived in China with the appearance of being an "empty form" governed by (seemingly) universal principles like democracy and science. Chinese people embraced modern sports, as they did the form of the nation, because of their desire to take their place on the global stage of modernity. Although the indigenous martial arts had their supporters, they were never able to challenge Western sports as the predominant technique for training bodies for the nation. On the surface, the main reason was that their local and traditional meanings were simply too strong and evident. On a deeper level, I have argued that the martial arts were grounded in a different conception of the body from that of Western medical science and that they entailed a different relationship of body, self, and nation from that which was then dominant in nationalist ideologies.

The Return of Local Culture

However, by the 1980s, the nature of global nationalism was beginning to undergo a transformation. John MacAloon argues that the "emptying process" in modern sports has three aspects.[34] First, Western histories of sports are appropriated by rival groups and reinvented. Second, sports are naturalized when their foreign—frequently imperial and colonial—origins are forgotten or neutralized. Third, sports forms of different origins are mixed, as when East Asian martial arts are popularized in the West.

In 1980s China, the history of sports was subtly rewritten so that contemporary sports were not so clearly presented as a clean break with the imperial past. This version of history acknowledged that the phrase "physical culture" had first appeared in the "modern" period of Western contact at the end of the nineteenth century. However, it emphasized the continuities between modern and historical sports rather than the revolutionary break with the past.

Many of the new histories targeted a foreign audience.[35] These histories expressed a desire to demonstrate that China had a long and illustrious sports history to contribute to the international sports world, a history every bit as valid as the Western one. Martial arts, in particular, were extolled with the goal of promoting their spread worldwide and their inclusion in the Olympic Games, a stated goal of the State Sports Commission. As one history put it,

[Ancient Chinese sports] have enriched our society and Chinese martial arts constitute a glamorous pearl. . . . Through efforts made by the new Chinese government, ancient sports are being unveiled, re-arranged, reformed and improved, then given a new lustre that attracts the world so much so that people around the world are studying and practising Chinese ancient sports.[36]

By the late 1980s, the martial arts were positioned to occupy a central place in Chinese nationalism that they never occupied in the early nationalism. This was made possible by two developments: the global and domestic turn toward a search for the local "authentic" cultural forms that had seemed to disappear under the homogenizing march of capitalism, and China's strengthened position in the world political system.

The mid-1980s saw the emergence of the "seeking roots" movement in China, in which the fascination with the modern West began to wane and cultural producers began to look toward rural China and non-Han minorities for practices that could "revitalize" Chinese culture. In the aftermath of the Tiananmen Incident of 1989, intellectuals and policymakers began to search for a kind of "cultural nationalism" that could evoke a sense of national pride in the populace. These groups had different reasons for doing so: intellectuals were part of a regional East Asian movement that involved a search for alternative modernization models to the Western one, and party-state officials needed a way to inspire patriotism while avoiding the now-discredited Marxist slogans that had formerly accomplished this goal.[37]

The Recuperation of the Subjective Body

This return to the local in Chinese nationalism was also reflected in a subtle shift in the relationship between the body and nationalism. In the first-ever national physical culture policy (*quanmin jianshen zhengce*) that was issued in 1995, the time-worn Marxist "mass physical culture" (*qunzhong tiyu*) was replaced by "fitness-for-all" (*quanmin jianshen*, lit. "building the bodies of the entire people"), which was inspired by the concept of "sport-for-all," a label popular in capitalist nations that have national sports ministries and policies, such as Canada and Great Britain. One of the members of the committee that drafted the policy told me that actually the change was a last-minute one, such that the document itself did not contain the phrase "fitness-for-all," which was found only in the title. And so in 1995, the instrumental object-body (*ti*) began to be replaced with the less alienated *shen*, a change that is emblematic of the recuperation of the body from the grasp of the totalitarian state, which has been evident in many different realms. Although the official vocabulary change might have been rather spur-of-the-moment, it captured a feeling that was widespread. When I asked a well-informed friend of mine who was not himself involved in sports what had happened to the old "mass physical culture," he responded, "Let's just say it's no longer politically correct. It has an unpleasant sound to it." With the social change of the early 1990s, *tiyu* fell into some disfavor as "mass physical culture" began to evoke unpleasant reminders of Maoist-era mass calisthenics and the rigid, militarized body culture that formed the larger background for them. In addition, beginning with the 1990 Asian Games in Beijing, mass calisthenics fell out of favor as the preferred performance genre for opening ceremonies at major sports games and were replaced largely by more free-form performances, such as ballet, opera, aerobic dancing, and—of course—Chinese martial arts. *Yang sheng* was also revived and is used to refer to a whole range of health-preserving practices that, as argued by Farquhar and Zhang, are frequently a response to the social pressures brought by the market reforms.[38]

Qigong and *Falungong*

At the local level, one of the surprising developments of the post-Mao era was the tremendous growth in qigong as a popular movement in China. Qigong is an eclectic collection of techniques that revolve around the cultivation of *qi*, mainly through breath control, meditation, and mild bodily movements. The first use of the word qigong in its current sense is not documented until 1934. By the 1950s and 1960s, qigong techniques had become familiar to a large part of the population.[39] In the 1980s, qigong became a popular movement of astounding proportions, and several of the most popular qigong masters were arrested and jailed.

From the Western perspective, it was hard to understand why the Chinese government would feel threatened by these practices. For Chinese leaders, the chaos created by "heterodox sects" in the previous century, such as the Boxer Rebellion of 1900, is historical evidence that such groups can seriously threaten state power. There is also a mythology that waves of popular heterodoxy are an omen of dynastic fall.

Falungong was a form of qigong developed by Li Hongzhi in China in the early 1990s that quickly attracted followers all over China and, after Li's emigration to the United States in 1997, in major cities around the world. In June 1999, it gained international attention when tens of thousands of adherents to *Falungong* held sit-down demonstrations in Beijing and other cities, protesting a government crackdown. *Falungong* emerged as a point of contention in criticisms of China's record on human rights and religious freedom by Western governments. Most Chinese people view *Falungong* with the same sort of skepticism with which an American might regard nonmainstream religious sects with somewhat extreme practices, such as Pentecostals who become possessed by the Holy Spirit and speak in tongues. Since most Chinese people are not clearly committed to the Western notion of "religious freedom" but rather adhere to the traditional wariness of "heterodox sects," they are not necessarily outraged when *Falungong* practitioners are harassed or detained. While *Falungong* practitioners claim that they are nonpolitical, it should be noted that claiming to be nonpolitical as strategy for political action is common in Chinese culture: examples include the qigong and "old people's disco" fads of the 1980s and "self-cultivation" practices.[40] This strategy is also similar to Gandhi's "passive resistance." The assertion by *Falungong* practitioners that they are "nonpolitical" and the readiness of Western liberals to believe them reveals differences between Western and Chinese interpretations of "political."

Falungong was often in the public eye during Beijing's bid for the Olympic Games in 2001, when the fax machines and e-mail inboxes of IOC members were flooded with so many messages opposing the bid that machines had to be shut down and e-mail inboxes closed. In advance of the IOC Session in Moscow that decided the host city for the 2008 Olympics, Moscow Mayor Luri Lujkov promised the Beijing bid committee that during the two weeks of the session, only "the voice of Beijing" would be heard and not that of the "falungong fanatics." The Moscow police were very vigilant against demonstrations against Beijing, and a protest organized by *Falungong* practitioners in front of the IOC assembly hall was promptly dispersed.[41]

At the Athens 2004 Olympic Games, there were nearly daily *Falungong* demonstrations in Syntagma Square, the central meeting place for the Games. These were wordless demonstrations expressive of the *Falungong* position that their goals are not political.

Why would the end of the militarized, Maoist culture of the body correspond with a rapid explosion of qigong practices? This chapter has sought to ground such practices in a different conception of the body and its relation to the nation, a conception that gives more importance to subjective experience and diminishes the alienating, mechanical relationship between body and nation. Qigong was one way of reclaiming the body from the Maoist instrumental use of the body as a tool for revolution; it was also a reaction against the withering state health care system, which left many people feeling that they had no choice but to heal themselves.[42]

Wushu, the Olympic Games, and the Future of Western Domination in International Sports

In the popular Chinese imagination, the martial arts are considered to be truly Chinese, firmly anchored in ancient Chinese history, and an important means of defining the Chinese identity. Ironically, the strength of this belief may arise out of the long decades in which modernizers sought to portray martial

Figure 2.2. "Magpie balancing on a twig" position in wushu. From a collection of sports postcards published for international consumption by the People's Sports Publishing House in 1964.

arts in polar opposition to Western sports and to brand them as backward. In fact, most of these techniques are not as ancient as is commonly believed. Of the styles of martial arts practiced today, about 70 percent originated in the Ming (1368–1644) and Qing (1644–1911).[43] Nevertheless, wushu methods are believed to continue an ancient, authentic Chinese tradition.

Internationally, Chinese martial arts have grown by leaps and bounds as increasing numbers of practitioners have emigrated from China and started their own schools and as increasing numbers of schools in China have opened their doors to foreigners. The reasons for young Americans and other westerners to take up the martial arts are complicated, but they are not dissimilar from the Chinese effort to recover the body from the disciplined grip of science and nationalism since their link with Eastern philosophy offers an alternative system of meanings. Chinese martial arts have been included in the Asian Games program since 1990, although there has been grumbling at China's domination of the medals.

There are only two sports of clearly non-Western origin on the Olympic program: judo was added for the 1964 Olympic Games in Tokyo and taekwondo for the 1988 Olympic Games in Seoul. After the beginning of the era of reform, the Chinese State Sports Commission began an attempt to promote wushu worldwide with the eventual goal of seeing it included in the Olympic Games. There was always an assumption that since Japan and Seoul were able to have "their" sports added to the Olympic program when they hosted the Games, if China ever won the right to host the Olympic Games, this would also be the moment that wushu became an Olympic sport.

However, Beijing was awarded the Olympic Games at the same IOC Session at which Jacques Rogge was elected president. One of the planks in his platform had been the control of gigantism in the Olympic Games. Actually, the main motivation for this initiative was one that was intended to benefit the Third World: because of the huge size of the Olympic Games, only a few cities in the world were capable of hosting them, and it was becoming ever more difficult for cities outside the developed West to aspire to host them, particularly in Africa, which had never hosted an Olympic Games. President Rogge established the Olympic Programme Commission in 2002 to study the sports on the program with the goal of reducing their number. The commission established thirty-three criteria for inclusion in the Olympic program, on the basis of which they decided to consider five sports in addition to the twenty-eight sports already on the program: roller sports, squash, golf, karate, and rugby. Further information was sought from the international federations governing these sports. Thus, as early as 2004, wushu had been eliminated from consideration as an Olympic sport. Adding insult to injury, from the Chinese perspective, the Japanese martial art of karate was preferred over wushu. One of the arguments for karate was its popularity: the World Karate Federation was established in 1970 and had 173 affiliated national federations in 2007, while the International Wushu Federation was established in 1990 and had 112 affiliated national federations.[44] Compared to judo, taekwondo, and karate, wushu deviates most from the Western model of sport, and if included it would be the least westernized sport on the Olympic program. People who had contact with IOC members at wushu competitions noted that there were some IOC members who did not feel wushu was enough of a "sport." An example of this attitude was a prominent German Olympic scholar who observed to me after seeing wushu for the first time, "It is nice, but it is not Olympic."

At the 117th Singapore Session in July 2005, the IOC membership voted to retain twenty-six of the sports on the Athens program, to remove softball and baseball after 2008, and to consider adding two different sports for the 2012 London Olympics. The Olympic Programme Commission presented the five sports to the membership for a vote. After seven rounds of elimination voting, karate won with fifty-four votes, and squash came in second with thirty-eight. These two sports were then presented to the membership for a yes/no vote, but both were turned down. Karate was rejected by a count of thirty-eight for and sixty-nine against, with a two-thirds majority necessary for inclusion on the program.[45] The 2008 Olympic program was finalized in April 2006.

The decision not to include wushu also had implications for another strategy that China might have been pursuing. While I have never been told that this was the case, I hypothesize that the career of South Korea's Kim Un Yong served as a model for Chinese sports officials. He had served as the president of the World Taekwondo Federation since 1973 and in 1986 became president of the General Association of International Sports Federations. He was the Vice President of the Seoul Olympic Organizing Committee and was in charge of the television rights negotiations. He was co-opted as an IOC member in 1986 and was elected to its Executive Board in 1988, the same year in which taekwondo debuted as an Olympic sport. He became chairman of the IOC Radio and TV Commission in 1989.[46] Because of the importance of television rights in Olympic finances, he was very influential. In 1992 he was elected as an IOC vice president. In 2001 he launched a bid for the presidency of the IOC, and although he was defeated by Jacques Rogge, his surprisingly strong candidacy put him two votes ahead of Canadian Dick Pound.

China's second member, Yu Zaiqing, was co-opted as an IOC member in 2000, before which he had experience as an administrator in cycling and rowing but not wushu. In 2003 he was elected as the president of the International Wushu Federation, which is Chinese-dominated with its headquarters in Beijing. He was put forward for election to the IOC's Executive Board in 2003 and was finally elected in 2004. Thus, in 2004 he had been positioned to begin a career trajectory like that of Kim Un Yong, and the inclusion of wushu in the Olympic Games would have suddenly increased the power and prestige of the Wushu Federation. That wushu was not included was also a setback to the strategy to increase the status of a Chinese member within the IOC. In 2004, Kim Un Yong was convicted of embezzling 3.8 billion won (US$4 million) from the Taekwondo Federation and other organizations, and it was rumoured that the embezzled money had been used to buy the IOC votes that almost made him president. Presumably this was *not* part of China's strategy for Yu Zaiqing.

China fought a hard battle over wushu inside the IOC, and its exclusion was received with a great deal of popular discontent. While in some previous Olympic Games there had been a category of "exhibition sport," the IOC had eliminated this category. After many heated debates, it was agreed that wushu will be contested under the auspices of the Beijing Organizing Committee for the Games of the XXIX Olympiad in 2008 as a "local organizing committee sport" but would not be an official sport. Even this was a concession on the part of the IOC.

The future of wushu is a hotly debated topic in Chinese sports circles. Traditionalists feel that its cultural background is richer and more complicated than the other Olympic sports and that its continued internationalization and inclusion in the Olympic Games would lead to a loss of its Chinese character. They complain that proper wushu training requires years of the cultivation of *qi*, which cannot be scored by judges, and that international wushu has become too similar to gymnastics. Some radical thinkers consider the Olympic Games themselves to be a form of Western cultural domination, and for them wushu is a symbol of an alternative non-Western sports tradition that must be preserved against the onslaught of the West.

Ironically, the same forces that led to the rise of Western sports as the main nationalist sports technique in China are now producing a shift in the winds, leading to the rise of martial arts as the sport with the deepest nationalist associations. The reason is that global nationalism has undergone changes, and China's position within the global system of nation-states has undergone changes. While the first step for China has been admission onto the playing field of international sports, even if it means playing by Western rules, the second step will be for China to start to change the rules. If China's influence in the world system of sports increases, it could initiate a fundamental change in the definition of what constitutes an "Olympic sport."

NOTES

1. See Susan Brownell, *Training the Body for China: Sports in the Moral Order of the People's Republic* (Chicago: University of Chicago Press, 1995), 8–21. This concept is drawn from the work of Henning Eichberg, who uses the notion of *Körperkultur* to look at the body primarily as cultural, emphasizing the multiple roles of the body in social process and historical change. The concept is undergirded by a political agenda that has the goal of recuperating the body/self from the fragmenting effects of professionalized, competitive sports that characterized the use of *Körperkultur* in the East German sports regime before the fall of the Berlin Wall. It thus seeks to reconstitute the field of practices from which sport was historically singled out by the East German regime, which made high-level sports accessible to an elite few and

made unpleasant, militarized physical culture drills (such as mass calisthenics) mandatory for the masses. The revitalized concept of "body culture" is useful to a sinologist and anthropologist for two reasons. First, a similar critique of elite sports and "mass physical culture" took place in China in the late 1980s and 1990s. Second, the concept encourages us to look at the relationship between sports and other kinds of body techniques; from this perspective, sports are no longer a separate, peripheral topic of study but are linked with everyday practices such as table manners or bodily decorum (to name only two of the infinite possibilities) as well as with other kinds of bodily performance, such as ritual, theater, and so on. As Eichberg puts it, "Body culture as the new paradigm places sport in the context of *culture*." This, then, has the effect of placing sport firmly within the dominant paradigm of cultural anthropology, offering the possibility of using an interpretive approach to situate body practices within a system of meanings and symbols. See Henning Eichberg, "Body Culture as Paradigm: The Danish Sociology of Sport," in *Body Cultures: Essays on Sport, Space and Identity*, ed. John Bale and Chris Philo (London: Routledge, 1998), 111–27.

2. Clifford Geertz, *Negara: The Theatre State in Nineteenth-Century Bali* (Princeton, N.J.: Princeton University Press, 1980), 13; see also Benedict Anderson, *Imagined Communities: Reflections on the Origin and Spread of Nationalism* (London: Verso, 1991).

3. "Moral encompassment" was a concept outlined by Louis Dumont, *Homo Hierarchicus: The Caste System and Its Implications*, trans. George Weidenfeld and The University of Chicago Press (Chicago: University of Chicago Press, 1980 [1966]).

4. Patricia Buckley Ebrey, ed., *Chinese Civilization and Society: A Sourcebook* (New York: Free Press, 1981), 36.

5. Judith Farquhar, *Knowing Practice: The Clinical Encounter of Chinese Medicine* (Boulder, Colo.: Westview Press, 1994), and *Appetites: Food and Sex in Postsocialist China* (Durham, N.C.: Duke University Press, 2002).

6. Shigehisa Kuriyama, *The Expressiveness of the Body and the Divergence of Greek and Chinese Medicine* (New York: Zone Books, 1999).

7. Rudolf zur Lippe, *Vom Leib zum Körper: Naturbeherrschung am Menschen in der Renaissance* (From [Subjective] Body to [Objective] Body: Control of Human Nature in the Renaissance) (Hamburg: Reinbek, 1988).

8. Henning Eichberg, *"Der Dialogische Körper: Über einen dritten Weg der körperanthropologischen Aufmerksamkeit"* [The Dialogical Body: On a Third Kind of Attentiveness in the Anthropology of the Body], in *Körpersprache: Über Identität und Konflikt* (Body Language: On Identity and Conflict), ed. Knut Dietrich and Henning Eichberg (Butzbach: Afra, 1993), 265–66.

9. Sun Lung-kee, *Zhongguo wenhuade "shenceng jiegou"* (The "Deep Structure" of Chinese Culture) (Hong Kong: Jixianshe, 1983), 20.

10. Mark Elvin, "Tales of *Shen* and *Xin*: Body-Person and Heart-Mind in China during the Last 150 Years," in *Fragments for a History of the Human Body, Part 2*, ed. Michel Feher (New York: Zone Books, 1989), 275.

11. Yasuo Yuasa, *The Body, Self-Cultivation, and Ki-Energy*, trans. Shigenori Nagatomo and Monte S. Hull (Albany: State University of New York Press, 1993), 137.

12. Richard Handler, *Nationalism and the Politics of Culture in Quebec* (Madison: University of Wisconsin Press, 1988).

13. Eichberg, "*Der Dialogische Körper*," 63.

14. James Pusey, *China and Charles Darwin* (Cambridge, Mass.: Council on East Asian Studies, Harvard University Press, 1983), 64.

15. Benjamin Schwartz, *In Search of Wealth and Power: Yen Fu and the West* (Cambridge, Mass.: The Belknap Press of Harvard University Press, 1964), 57–58, 255.

16. Schwartz, *In Search of Wealth and Power*, 70–71.

17. Schwartz, *In Search of Wealth and Power*, 73.

18. Pusey, *China and Charles Darwin*, 86, 213.

19. John MacAloon, "Humanism as Political Necessity: Reflections on the Pathos of Anthropological Science in Pluricultural Contexts," in *The Conditions of Reciprocal Understanding*, ed. James Fernandez and Milton Singer (Chicago: Center for International Studies, University of Chicago, 1995), 234.

20. Mao Zedong, "*Tiyu zhi yanjiu*" [A Study of Physical Culture], in *Une étude de l'education physique*, trans. Stuart R. Schram (Paris: Mouton). Originally in *Xin qingnian* (New Youth) 3, no. 2 (April 1917): 7.

21. Eugene E. Barnett, *My Life in China, 1910–1936* (East Lansing: Asian Studies Center, Michigan State University, 1990), 89.

22. Barnett, *My Life in China*, 89.

23. Barnett, *My Life in China*, 248.

24. "The Far Eastern Olympic Games," *North China Daily News*, May 17, 1915, 8, quoted in Andrew Morris, *Marrow of the Nation: A History of Sport and Physical Culture in Republican China* (Berkeley: University of California Press, 2004), 25–26.

25. Morris, *Marrow of the Nation*, 218.

26. Lu Xun, "*Suiganlu (sanshiqi)*" [Random Thoughts (33)]," *Xin Qingnian* [New Youth] 5, no. 5 (October 15, 1918): 514–15, quoted in Morris, *Marrow of the Nation*, 193–94.

27. *Renmin tiyu chubanshe* (People's Sports Publishing House), *Zhongguo jindai tiyushi* [History of Sports in Modern China], general use text for physical culture departments (Beijing, 1985), 79–80.

28. People's Sports Publishing House, *History of Sports in Modern China*, 131; Wang Zhenya, *Jiu Zhongguo tiyu jianwen* (Information on Sports in Old China) (Beijing: People's Sports Publishing House, 1987), 117.

29. Wang Zhenya, *Jiu Zhongguo*, 117.

30. Xie Lingzheng, *Shixi Zhongguo jindai tiyushishangde "tu yang zhi zheng"* (A Preliminary Analysis of the "Conflict between Indigenous and Foreign Physical Culture" in Modern Chinese History) (master's thesis, Beijing Institute of Physical Education, 1988), 7.

31. Xie Lingzheng, *Shixi Zhongguo*, 6.

32. Wu Wenrui, "*Lun 'jinhou Guomin tiyu wenti' shuhou*" [Postscript on "Past and Present Problems" in National Physical Culture], *Dagong bao* (Tianjin), August 23, 1932, quoted in Xie Lingzheng, *Shixi Zhongguo*, 7.

33. Xie Siyan, "*Ping 'Dagong bao' qiri sheping*" [A Critique of the Editorial in "Dagong News" on the Seventh], *Tiyu zhoubao* [Physical Culture Weekly] 30 (August 27, 1932): 1, quoted in Xie Lingzheng, *Shixi Zhongguo*, 7.

34. John MacAloon, "Interval Training," in *Choreographing History*, ed. Susan L. Foster (Bloomington, Indiana: Indiana University Press, 1995), 34.

35. For example, "Sports in China Has Ancient History," *Beijing Review* 29, no. 5 (April 1986): 32–22; New World Press, *Sports and Games in Ancient China* (Beijing, 1986); People's Sports Publishing House, *Sports in Ancient China* (Beijing, 1986).

36. New World Press, *Sports and Games in Ancient China*, 6.

37. Ben Xu, "'From Modernity to Chineseness': The Rise of Nativist Cultural Theory in Post-1989 China," *Positions: East Asia Culture Critiques* 16, no. 1 (1998): 210.

38. Judith Farquhar and Qicheng Zhang, "Biopolitical Beijing: Pleasure, Sovereignty, and Self-Cultivation in China's Capital," *Cultural Anthropology* 20, no. 3 (August 2005): 303–27.

39. Kunio Miuria, "The Revival of *Qi*: Qigong in Contemporary China," in *Taoist Meditation and Longevity Techniques*, ed. Livia Kohn (Ann Arbor, Mich.: Center for Chinese Studies, 1989), 343, 335.

40. Brownell, *Training the Body for China*, 265–88; Farquhar and Zhang, "Biopolitical Beijing."

41. Liang Lijuan, *He Zhenliang and China's Olympic Dream*, trans. Susan Brownell (Beijing: Beijing Foreign Languages Press, 2007), 490.

42. Nancy Chen, *Breathing Spaces: Qigong, Psychiatry, and Healing in China* (New York: Columbia University Press, 2003).

43. Gu Shiquan, "Introduction to Ancient and Modern Chinese Physical Culture," in *Sport in China*, ed. Howard G. Knuttgen, Ma Qiwei, and Wu Zhongyuan (Champaign, Ill.: Human Kinetics, 1990), 7.

44. "Karate," "wushu," official website of the International Olympic Committee, www.olympic.org (June 2007).

45. Report on the Singapore Session, official website of the International Olympic Committee, www.olympic.org (June 2007).

46. James F. Larson and Heung-Soo Park, *Global Television and the Politics of the Seoul Olympics* (Boulder, Colo.: Westview Press, 1993), 74–75, 185.

Chapter Three

Symbols of State Power
Stadiums and National Identity in Beijing

It has become fashionable in the lead-up to the Beijing Olympic Games to ask, Will the Games be used by the Communist Party to symbolically legitimize its regime? This chapter makes two main arguments relevant to this question. The first is that major sports events have symbolized state power in China since at least 1900, a strategy that China learned from the West and interpolated into its traditional state symbols. The history of sports stadiums in Beijing from the end of the Qing dynasty to the 2008 Beijing Olympic Games maps the history of state power.[1] The locations, architecture, and occasions for use of Beijing's stadiums inscribe state power onto space and time. The changes in their architectural forms also map the changes in national identity as China moved from the imperial to the republican to the communist to the postsocialist state. The symbolism surrounding stadiums and their architecture is thus fruitful for analyzing the symbolization of state power. The second point is that this analysis shows the complexity of such symbol making and reveals that the question as posed is too simpleminded.

Although this chapter is concerned only with one small though important element of Olympic symbolism—the symbolism of the stadium—it will be seen that even this limited segment involves a complicated web of meanings. On the one hand, as was described in the introduction, the symbol makers themselves have complicated political pasts. These included the artist who worked on the stadium, Ai Weiwei, and the designer of the ceremonies, Zhang Yimou. On the other hand, the symbolism itself involves a complicated interplay between symbols of tradition and modernity, China and the West, the Chinese nation and the global community, overseas and mainland Chinese identity, and more.

THE SYMBOLISM OF SPACE IN IMPERIAL BEIJING

At the end of the Qing dynasty (1644–1911), the layout of Beijing conformed to the ancient principles dictated by feng shui and cosmology. It was made up of five walled districts, three of which were concentric. The symbolic and literal heart of the city was the Forbidden City, where the emperor and his court lived, surrounded by a wall and a moat. Around the Forbidden City lay the Imperial City, where the lesser members of the court lived. Surrounding this was the Inner or Tartar City, where members of the ruling Manchu ethnicity lived. The legation quarter, a small district in the southern part of the Tartar City, was given over to official representatives of foreign countries (site of the Boxer siege of 1900–1901). Below this series of three boxes was the Chinese City, occupied by the Han Chinese subjects of the Manchu. The entire city was laid out on a north–south axis according to the principles of feng shui, which dictated that north was inauspicious and south auspicious. Thus, there were fewer gates in the north walls, and the main gates were in the south walls of each district. Streets did not pass straight through any district because that would make the way easy for evil spirits. The center was the most auspicious location because it was the source of prosperity and fertility. The palace of the Emperor of the Central Kingdom,[2] Son of Heaven, was located there (see figure 3.1).

Urban landmarks also functioned as a map of the Qing state. The state religion divided official sacrifices into three types: Grand, Middle, and Common. Grand Sacrifice was conducted by the emperor himself at the temples in the capital and its suburbs. Middle Sacrifice was conducted by the emperor or delegated officials in the imperial and lower-level capitals. Common Sacrifice was performed by local officials at all capitals.[3]

The Grand Sacrifices were most important to the maintenance of the cosmic-social order. There were four of them: to Heaven, Earth, the Imperial Ancestors, and the Land and Harvest. The most important ritual of state was the emperor's worship of Heaven, which he performed on the winter solstice at the Temple of Heaven in the southern suburb of Beijing. Earth was worshipped on the summer solstice at the Temple of Earth in the northern suburb. The Imperial Ancestors were worshipped on an auspicious day in the first month of each of the four seasons and at the end of the year in the Temple of the Ancestors within the walls of the Forbidden City. The Land and Harvest were worshipped in the middle month of spring and of autumn at the Temple of Land and Harvest in the western suburb.

In sum, the timing and location of the sacrifices imposed a distinct order onto time and space. Temporally, they marked important moments in the lunar calendar that governed the practice of agriculture. Spatially, the temples structured the landscape of Beijing, as they still do today, functioning as ma-

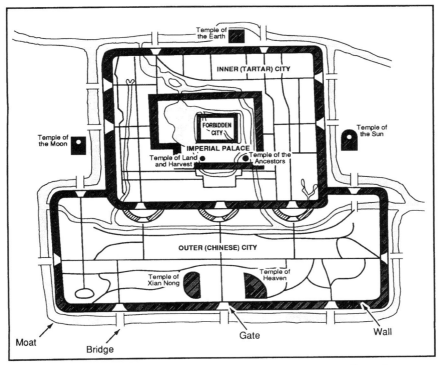

Figure 3.1. Layout of Beijing in the late Qing dynasty, with city walls, major streets, and important temples (adapted from an old map). Map by Susan Brownell.

jor landmarks. Blending space and time, the sacrifices moved from south/winter (Temple of Heaven) to east/spring (Temple of the Ancestors) and west/spring (Temple of Land and Harvest) to north/summer (Temple of Earth) to east/fall (Temple of the Ancestors) and west/fall (Temple of Land and Harvest) and finally started over again in the south.[4]

Sports occupied only a minor role in the religion and architecture of the imperial state. Kick-ball and polo stadiums had been a standard feature of ancient palaces up until the Song dynasty (A.D. 960–1279), but by the Qing they no longer made up an element of palace architecture. Before the introduction of Western sports, the one large-scale spectator sport seems to have been horse racing. These races had been an occasion for the Manchu nobility to display their horses and finery before the fall of the Qing dynasty in 1911.[5]

A site known as the "International" racing grounds was located at a recreation center in the south of the city, just outside the wall of the Temple of Xian Nong, god of agriculture. The temple had been the location of one of the emperor's Middle Sacrifices. From the 1910s on, the temple was a major recreation area. In 1918, the South City Amusement Park, a group of concrete buildings with theaters and restaurants, was built in the northeast corner of the temple.[6] In later decades, sports fields and a sports institute were built on the grounds. Finally, as will be discussed, it became the site of the first major sports event in the People's Republic of China (PRC) and the training center of the Beijing Municipal Team.

Horse racing seems also to have been the major large-scale spectator sport for the foreigners in Beijing at the end of the Qing. Six miles west of the city was a Western-style racecourse accessible from a stop on the railroad named the "Racehorse Track" (*paoma chang*) station. A golf course was also located nearby. A hand-drawn map from 1936 marks the racetrack with a cartoon drawing of empty liquor bottles and turned-over glasses.[7] One of the first events of the Boxer siege of 1900–1901, when "Boxers" trained in traditional martial arts and meditation surrounded and attacked the foreign legation quarters in Beijing, was their burning of the grandstand at the international horse-racing course. According to the British reporter Henry Landor, it was with this outrage that "all the young men of a sporting disposition in Pekin began to realise how serious matters were getting. . . . They could hardly believe that Boxer villainy could reach so far."[8] The Boxers may have been more conscious of the significance of their act than we might think: surely they were able to recognize the international horse races as events that, like the Manchu races, displayed aristocratic privilege and power. Their attack was no doubt motivated by this recognition, just as the international outrage was.

When troops from the Eight Powers (Great Britain, the United States, Italy, France, Germany, Austria, Japan, and Russia) arrived from abroad to relieve the siege, they had their revenge. The Temple of Heaven was occupied by the British relief troops and the Temple of Xian Nong by the American troops. The troops bivouacked on the temple grounds "for want of a better spot" because of the open green areas and the fresh well water. Once they were inside, they were quite aware that they had penetrated the sanctum sanctorum of the Qing. The temple complexes were looted, furniture was destroyed for firewood, and grass was used for grazing horses. At the Temple of Agriculture the soldiers used the emperor's throne as a barber's chair until their commanding general took it into his own possession.[9] Sports were common in garrison life, and the British instituted regular field hockey, polo, and gymkhana events on the grounds at the Temple of Heaven that drew participants from several of the other Eight Powers.[10]

To my knowledge, the occupation of the temples at the end of the Boxer siege was the starting point for the use of these sites as areas for the practice of Western sports. Because Beijing's temples were surrounded by large tracts of land, they were the logical site for sports fields in a densely populated city.

Beijing's few parks are landscaped according to traditional principles, with paths winding beneath trees along twisting, man-made lakes and canals, so there are not usually many large open fields for sports in these areas. Thus, two of the first stadiums were located near the Temple of Heaven and at the Temple of Xian Nong, as discussed below, and in preparation for the 1990 Asian Games, arenas were built at the Temple of the Moon and the Temple of Earth (see figure 3.2).

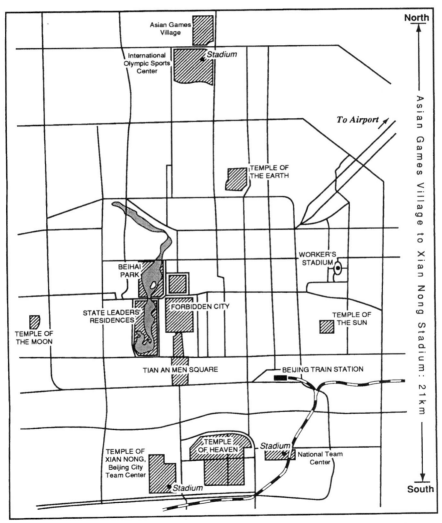

Figure 3.2. Locations of former Qing dynasty temples, major streets and highways, landmarks, and stadiums in Beijing after the 1990 Asian Games. Map by Susan Brownell.

STADIUMS IN THE REPUBLIC OF CHINA (1912–1948)

In 1914, the second Republican National Games in Beijing attracted over 20,000 spectators in two days.[11] They were organized by the YMCA and held inside the walls of the Temple of Heaven, outside the Hall of Fasting, with spectators seated in temporary bleachers.[12]

Beijing lost its importance as the center of state power when the nationalist regime established its capital in Nanjing from 1928 to 1948. For the National Games in Shanghai in 1935, the Nanjing regime built what was the first large-

Figure 3.3.   Doorway in the Hall of Fasting near the location of the 1914 National Games in the Temple of Heaven. Photo by Susan Brownell, 1994.

scale modern stadium in China, the River Bend (*Jiangwan*) stadium. Wang states that it seated nearly 100,000 spectators, but this must be an exaggeration. At the end of the War of Resistance against Japan in 1944, the stadium was utilized as a military barracks and for munitions storage and was badly damaged from an explosion. It was later poorly repaired for the seventh and last Republican games in 1948, when there were three separate incidents involving collapsed railings, and many people and even athletes were injured.[13]

The first modern stadium in Beijing was built at the Xian Nong Temple in 1937, with a capacity of 10,000 and a dirt soccer field in the center. From the historical record it is difficult to establish the nature of stadiums because the Chinese language uses the same word (*tiyuchang*) for a simple playing field with one small bank of concrete steps for sitting on, a huge stadium that seats tens of thousands, as well as everything in between. Before the founding of the PRC in 1949, there were only thirteen stadiums with permanent seating in the entire country.[14]

Sporting events marked the transition away from a dynastic empire and toward a modern nation-state. A very interesting point is that many of the important sporting grounds were located on the ancient temple grounds where the major state rituals had been held during the Qing. The 1914 National Games were held inside the Temple of Heaven; sports fields, a stadium, and a racetrack were located in and near the Temple of Xian Nong, and another racetrack was located near the Temple of the Sun. There seem to have been two reasons for this: first, the temples were surrounded by large tracts of open land; second, they fell into disrepair after the establishment of the republic, and the regime seemed uninterested in managing them, much to the consternation of some westerners who wanted to preserve the dynastic landmarks (even while others looted them). Thus, the land was available for use by westerners. Still, one can't help but marvel at the implications of westerners setting up sports fields on the sacred grounds of the Qing state religion. As discussed by Hevia, the Eight Powers came to perceive their occupation of the Qing sacred sites as a way of demonstrating their superiority over the Qing court and destroying the traditional reverence for the throne; their parade through the Imperial Palace after the Boxer Rebellion was quelled was a calculated display of power.[15] One can also imagine that by playing sports on the temple grounds, the victorious international troops had their revenge on the Boxers and the Qing court that, it was believed, had covertly supported them. We can also imagine that the YMCA physical educators who organized the 1914 National Games consciously believed that in so doing they were supplanting the traditional state religion with a Muscular Christianity that would help modernize China, and in that sense it was a kind of "religious" and not "military" occupation of sacred space.[16] If some Chinese were distressed by

Figure 3.4.   Morning recreation in the Temple of Heaven. Photo by Andy Miah, 2006.

the playing of Western games on temple grounds, modern Chinese sport histories do not provide any insight into the matter because they are written by authors more interested in recording the "progress" in the development of their sports. Today, the Temple of Heaven is one of the main spaces for recreation in Beijing, and beginning in the early morning hours (for which Beijing residents can get a cheap monthly pass), one can see people of all ages engaging in recreation and exercise, everything from tai chi to Beijing opera to kite flying to exercises on workout stations installed for that purpose.

The division between the sacred and the profane was never drawn in Chinese culture as it is in Western culture: "temple fairs" (*miaohui*) that combined markets with entertainment were formerly one of the staples of Chinese social and cultural life. The Christian view that marketing activities inside a temple constitute an abomination was not held in China. Thus, the practice of recreational activities in a temple has a cultural tradition. However, the sites of the four Grand Sacrifices were different because they were reserved for displays of the power of the emperor. From this perspective, the Western occupation of these spaces after 1901 expressed China's transition from an imperial state to a modern nation-state.

THE MAOIST PERIOD (1949–1978)

With the establishment of the PRC in 1949, Beijing became the national capital once more, and the relationship between the stadium and the state became more direct. Immediately after liberation, the new communist government funded the construction of three small stadiums around Beijing. The stadium at Xian Nong Temple was enlarged to a capacity of nearly 30,000, lights were added, and the infield was covered with grass. The first large-scale sports event of the PRC, the First National Workers' Games, was held there in 1955.[17] In order to celebrate the tenth anniversary of the PRC in 1959, the Workers' Stadium was built. This remained Beijing's largest stadium until the construction of the main stadium for the Beijing Olympics. It occupies over 70,000 square meters and seats 80,000 people. In 1959, the opening ceremony of the First National Games of the PRC was held in the Workers' Stadium, which was also the site for the opening and closing ceremonies, track-and-field events, and soccer for the National Games of 1959, 1965, 1975, and 1979. After two absences in 1983 (Shanghai) and 1987 (Guangzhou), the National Games returned in 1993. Unlike every other stadium discussed in this chapter, the Workers' Stadium is not located in a significant space according to the traditional principles of feng shui. It is in the southeastern quadrant of the city outside the old city walls. But perhaps this is not surprising when we consider that it was built during the period when the "feudal" past was most strongly rejected.

The Workers' Stadium was refurbished to serve as the central site for the Asian Games of 1990, which marked another turning point in the relationship of the stadium and the state: after this event, the stadium was expected to support itself, and state and city subsidies were ended, except for those needed for large-scale competitions such as the National Games. It opened its own businesses, including a fleet of taxis, a hotel inside the stadium with over 1,000 beds, a karaoke bar, a hair salon, an air travel service, and advertising, food, and furniture companies. With revenue from ticket sales, it began to support itself.

STADIUM ARCHITECTURE AS A MIRROR OF STATE POWER

Stadiums serve as an imposing backdrop for ceremonies of state, and certain architectural features enable them to do so effectively. The opening ceremony of the National Games constitute the biggest national celebration in China apart from a few National Day festivities. Chairman Mao and Premier Zhou Enlai attended every National Games held during their lifetimes. Although

Deng Xiaoping was not present at the 1987 Games, Premier Zhao Ziyang was, and Premier Li Peng was present at the subsequent Games in 1993. Newspaper articles about major sports events always begin with a list of the thirty or more state officials, in order of importance, who sat on the rostrum at the opening ceremony to review the parade of athletes.

The opening ceremony of the Chinese National Games consist of the elements that have become common internationally: a parade of athletes, welcoming speeches by state leaders, raising of the flag and playing of the national anthem, athletes' and officials' oaths, and a cultural performance. Until the 1990 Asian Games, the cultural performance typically consisted of mass calisthenics with a placard section as background, a genre raised to its highest form by the socialist nations. Much of this performance is oriented to the state leaders sitting in their own territory in the stadium. Typically, their space is located in the best viewing spot: the center of one long side of the stadium about halfway up. It consists of several flat areas terraced upward. Long tables are set up on each area, covered with a white cloth, and provided with hot tea and refreshments. State leaders sit in padded chairs behind these tables. This area is literally called the "chairman's platform" (*zhuxi tai*), that is, a rostrum or reviewing platform. When the athletes march onto the field, their performance is directed primarily toward the high officials, who review the performance just as they review the military displays of soldiers. When I was training with the Beijing City College Team for the 1986 National College Games, we had a dress rehearsal in which Beijing's deputy mayor, Chen Haosu, reviewed our marching to make sure it was up to standard (he was the highest municipal official charged with overseeing our preparations). In the socialist genre, the athletes shouted slogans as they marched. The placard section was located on the opposite side of the stadium so that it was visible to the officials, as if presented for their approval.[18] Spectators on the same side as the placard section could not see it, even less so those students who were sitting under the placards held over their heads. Thus, there was a decided hierarchy, with one side of the stadium much more prestigious than the other. In midsize stadiums, the lower-status side might not have a roof. All the Chinese stadiums that I photographed have some sort of chairman's platform. Even in open-air stadiums, the platform is still covered, often by a roof supported by high pillars that lend a stately air (see figure 3.5). At the Workers' Stadium, the platform leads back to a large room inside the building with carpeting, paintings on the walls, and padded chairs. The wide staircase that exits this room leads to the stadium entrance that is opposite the main gate to the stadium grounds, thus giving easy access to dignitaries in their limousines.

Because the Chinese social order takes on a different shape from the Western capitalist order, its spatial manifestation in stadium architecture is also

Figure 3.5. The "Chairman's Platform," Beijing Forestry University Stadium, decorated for the 1994 Beijing City College Track and Field Meet. Photo by Susan Brownell.

slightly different. If we take the Workers' Stadium as an example, the most striking difference from Western stadiums was the absence of glassed-in luxury boxes. As of yet, Chinese stadiums do not possess luxury boxes; when they first appear (as they undoubtedly will), it will certainly be a sign that the egalitarian ideals of the Revolution are finally dead and that capitalist class difference has taken their place. But for the moment, high-ranking officials sit on the chairman's platform out in the open air with everyone else (see figure 3.5). This seems to imply that Chinese leaders do not fear assassination by sniper, as is the case in the United States.

For the 1990 Asian Games, fifty glassed-in "observation booths" were added in a row on either side of the chairman's platform. These booths were used by commentators, security and communications personnel, and some reporters—but not by dignitaries. A more clearly demarcated social hierarchy was evident in changes made to the seats. The original seating consisted of wooden benches that were very narrow, enabling the stadium to seat 80,000 people. For the Asian Games, the wooden benches were replaced with individual fiberglass seats, the most desirable of which were on either side of the chairman's platform and had backs. Many of these were occupied by foreigners, who paid almost twice the cost of the most expensive tickets available to the Chinese. The prices of seats decreased the farther they were from the chairman's platform. Thus, for an international soccer game in May 1994, I was quoted the following prices: 500 yuan (then US$60) for foreign guests below the chairman's platform, 280 yuan for the seats with back supports near the chairman's platform, 160 yuan for seats with no backs further from the chairman's platform and above it, 120 yuan for the seats further from the center, 60 yuan for seats on the ends of the stadium and near the players' entrance, and 40 yuan for students (see figure 3.6).

Another architectural feature of Chinese stadiums is their exclusivity. They are surrounded by walls and are relatively inaccessible, even to sports teams who want to train in them. When I was a member of the Beijing City collegiate track and field team in 1986, the team leaders constantly had to negotiate with the manager of the Xian Nong Temple stadium to get access for us, even though we were backed by the Municipal Education Commission. My coach quoted a Chinese pun, *xianguan buru xianguan*, which literally means "the county official can't measure up to the person immediately in charge." This sort of insularity is characteristic of most administrative units in China and is spatially expressed in the walls that surround them.

At major sporting events, this exclusivity extends to the difficulty in obtaining tickets for the most popular events—the opening and closing ceremonies and the soccer finals. For example, the 1990 Asian Games placard section required that 20,000 seats be reserved for the local students who held

Figure 3.6.   The "Chairman's Platform" and observation booths installed for the 1990 Asian Games, Worker's Stadium. Photo by Susan Brownell, 1994.

up the cards. The same number were reserved for journalists, distinguished guests, and fund-raising officials.[19] A large area of the stadium, as mentioned, was occupied by high officials. Over 20,000 seats were sold to foreigners, leaving only 10,000 tickets available for the Chinese. For such major sports events, many of these tickets are distributed through the "back door": officials, members of the organizing committees, and others distribute tickets to their families, friends, and their political network, leaving only a small number of tickets to be sold publicly. Many thousands of people may congregate outside the gates to the sports complex on the night of the opening ceremony hoping to buy scalped tickets. The ability to get tickets for exclusive events is an important means of cementing *guanxi* in China, and the "gift economy" perhaps shapes the distribution of tickets as much as the "market economy" of paying spectators. Ultimately it is a result of the fact that large-scale sports events are designed primarily to display and consolidate power; earning a profit is a secondary consideration. During a discussion of opening ceremonies with a Chinese sports sociology professor, I commented that one reason we do not have placard sections in the United States is that the 10,000 students involved do not buy tickets; in fact, they are a net drain because they also receive subsidies for lunch and other expenses during the several-month training period. This was of great interest to the professor, who turned to his wife and commented, "You see, *they* pay attention to economic efficiency."

I should not exaggerate the difference between China and the West too greatly, however, since Olympic Games are notorious for the large numbers of the most desirable seats that remain empty at any given sports event, the reason being that the tickets have been distributed to corporate sponsors and dignitaries who are not actually interested in attending.

In sum, the stadium serves a representative function, revealing an important character of state power in China: on public occasions, state rulers represent their power *before* the people rather than *for* the people. This "representative public sphere" is tied to the personal; it is created by the presence of state leaders.[20] Chinese leaders *must* personally appear at major events; presence in the same personal space is the way in which a sense of a relationship between "leaders" and "the people" is created in China. An example of this attitude is the opening paragraph of the chapter titled "By the Side of the Leaders" in the biography of He Zhenliang:

The long years of bitter struggle and incredible hardship of the Chinese Revolution forged a generation of proletarian revolutionary leaders who became legendary. With their great talent and bold vision, they led the Chinese people in composing a magnificent revolutionary epic on so grand a scale that nothing in the world could compare with it. The leaders warmly loved their people, and the people respectfully loved their leaders. Zhenliang was fortunate. In the fifties and sixties, not long after he entered the ranks of the revolution, he had many opportunities to stand beside the nation's top leaders, to see up close the dignified demeanor of these leaders whom he had admired for so long, to hear their familiar and friendly voices, and even to directly receive an important Marxist education from their diplomacy and negotiations.[21]

NATIONALISM, INTERNATIONALISM, AND STADIUMS

In 1990, China hosted its first Asian Games, and the facilities were constructed with an eye toward China's bid in 1993 to host the 2000 Olympics. The Workers' Stadium was renovated, a second 40,000-seat soccer stadium was built at the sports center in Fengtai just outside the city, and a new 20,000-seat soccer stadium was built in the "National Olympic Sports Center" nine kilometers north of Tiananmen Square. The name "Olympic" expressed China's aspiration that this complex could be used to bid for the Olympic Games. It later became popularly known as the "Asian Games Village," but the official "Olympic" moniker finally became appropriate when the area was incorporated into the main complex for the 2008 Games. The chief architect of the center, Ma Guoxin, was Chinese. He stated that he attempted to include "national characteristics" in the design.[22] Beginning in the 1990s, greater attention was paid to "Chinese characteristics" as part of the effort to define a distinctly Chinese national identity (see figure 3.7).

Figure 3.7.　The stadium in the Asian Games Village complex. The sloping roof was considered to exhibit "Chinese characteristics." Photo by Susan Brownell, 1994.

This was not important at the time the Workers' Stadium was built in 1959, when generic, Soviet-inspired architecture symbolized that China was becoming "modern"—and that was all that China aspired to be. I remarked to one of the managers of the Workers' Stadium that the new Asian Games complex was said to have "Chinese characteristics" and asked if the Workers' Stadium had any. She replied that it did not—it was built according to a commonly used international standard; they didn't pay attention to this issue in the 1950s: "It's not like the Olympic Sports Center, which has curved roofs that look like an airplane. At least I think it looks like an airplane." She did note, however, that the cauldron that was added for the Asian Games torch was held up by two large dragons, which are very Chinese (see figure 3.8).

As she thought for a moment, she recalled a final "Chinese characteristic": the two electronic screens that were added for the Asian Games were the largest in Asia and were built by a Chinese company. Her comment illustrates the way in which measurable scientific/industrial achievements are taken to represent a nation in the same way that traditional cultural elements do. It is common in China that "Chinese characteristics" can refer to either traditional Chinese cultural elements or cutting-edge contributions to global culture by people defined as "Chinese."

Figure 3.8. Dragons and cauldron added for the torch of the 1990 Asian Games, Worker's Stadium. Photo by Susan Brownell, 1994.

The greater internationalization of China was reflected in the support of overseas Chinese. The natatorium for the Asian Games was funded by Hong Kong developer Henry Fok (Huo Yingdong) and named the Ying Tung Natatorium. For China's unsuccessful bid to host the 2000 Olympic Games, Fok offered US$300 million to build the Olympic stadium if it was named after him. I. M. Pei, the Chinese American architect, agreed to design it. The Ying Tung Natatorium will also be a venue for the 2008 Beijing Olympic Games, while Henry Fok's son Timothy has succeeded his father as a leading figure in the Chinese and Hong Kong sports world and is the current president of the Hong Kong Olympic Committee.

THE BIRD'S NEST STADIUM AND THE
OPENING CEREMONY OF THE BEIJING OLYMPICS

Major sports events still mark the rhythms and energy flows of state power. National Games, Asian Games, and now Olympic Games have taken the place of the Qing Grand Sacrifices as the major occasions on which Chinese state power is represented before the people. While the National Games show little of the cyclical, agrarian spatiotemporal orientation that governed Qing rituals, major sports events are scheduled to mark what the state considers transitional moments in national history, and many of them take place at the sites dictated by feng shui. It is useful, then, to analyze the symbolism of space and time in the Beijing 2008 Olympic Games.

The Structure of National History

The transitional moments in Chinese national history that were marked by the building of stadiums and major sports events were the following:

1955: First National Worker's Games (Xian Nong Stadium)—the establishment of the PRC
1959: First Chinese National Games (Workers' Stadium)—the tenth anniversary of the PRC
1990: XI Asian Games (Asian Games Village)—China's emergence as an Asian power
2008: XXIX Olympic Summer Games (National Stadium and Olympic Green)—China's emergence as a world power

The Structure of Time

The opening ceremony for the Beijing Olympics will begin on the eighth evening hour of the eighth day of the eighth month of the year 2008. "Eight" is an auspicious number in traditional Chinese culture. The Eight Taoist Immortals were the traditional Chinese equivalent of today's Western superheroes.[23] The pronunciation of the word for "eight," *ba*, sounds like the word *fa*, which is the first character in the words for *fazhan*, "development," and *facai*, "to become wealthy." Needless to say, these two words have defined China's engagement with modernity in the past century: *In Search of Wealth and Power* is the title of the book by the prominent sinologist Benjamin Schwartz on Yan Fu, China's leading reformist intellectual of the late nineteenth and early twentieth centuries.

The Structure of Space

The opening ceremony will take place in a stadium that is located on the northern end of the north–south axis of the city of Beijing. On roughly the same axis, as one moves south, are the Asian Games Village, the Forbidden City, and the Temple of Heaven. Since ancient times, Chinese cities have been laid out on a north–south axis according to the principles of feng shui.[24] Since the auspicious power (*qi*) of the famous monuments will flow upward from the south—which is the most auspicious of the Four Directions—toward the Olympic Green, which will face them, the location of the stadium and Olympic Park on that sacred axis should not only ensure a successful Games but also help channel good fortune into the city of Beijing for the future. The Beijing Municipal government had been retaining that choice spot for the Olympic Park since Beijing's first Olympic bid in 1993. Urban development had increasingly encroached near the site because the location of the Asian Games Village to its south, combined with the knowledge that this was to be the Olympic site, had created a feeling that this part of the city possessed an auspicious future. It had become prime real estate, and it was generally thought that if the bid for the 2008 Olympics were unsuccessful, the government could reserve that space no longer and must begin to develop it.

The Stadium Architecture

The stadium in the Asian Games Village had been designed by a Chinese architect, and the stadium for the unsuccessful bid for the 2000 Olympics was to have been designed by a Chinese American architect, but by 2001 China had given up the idea that the designer had to be "Chinese" and instead held an open competition for the best architects in the world, whether Chinese or not. The design for the National Stadium was awarded in 2003 to a joint proposal by the Swiss firm of Herzog and De Meuron with China Architecture Design Institute[25] in a competition judged by a panel of thirteen experts from five countries. Seating 91,000 and occupying 258,000 square meters, it finally

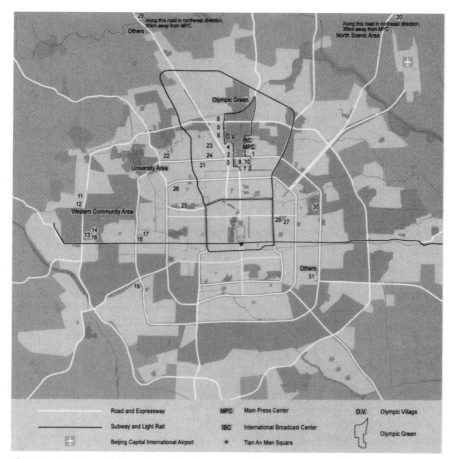

Figure 3.9. **Map of the venues for the 2008 Beijing Olympic Games, showing the location of the Olympic Green on the city's north–south axis. From Beijing Organizing Committee for the Games of the XXIX Olympiad,** *Beijing Olympic Venues,* **4. Key: 1. National Stadium, 2. National Indoor Stadium, 3. National Aquatics Center, 4. Fencing Hall, 5. Olympic Green Archery Field, 6. Olympic Green Hockey Field (7–10 are the old Asian Games Village venues): 7. Olympic Sports Center Stadium, 8. Olympic Sports Center Gymnasium, 9. Olympic Green Tennis Center, 10. Ying Tung Natatorium, 27. Worker's Stadium, 28. Worker's Indoor Arena.**

surpassed the size of the Workers' Stadium (80,000 seats and 70,000 square meters).[26] It became popularly known as the Bird's Nest Stadium because of its unusual design of interlaced steel girders reminiscent of the twigs of a bird's nest. Jacques Herzog and Pierre De Meuron collaborated on the design with avant-garde Chinese artist Ai Weiwei, who was introduced to them by a former Swiss ambassador to China. Ai, the son of Ai Qing, one of China's most famous modern poets, had lived from 1981 to 1993 in the United States, and his art and interests often dealt with the shattering of Chinese tradition and the collection and reconstitution of its fragments "to show how destruction can bring new meaning."[27] Reportedly, the idea of a bird's nest shape was his. The idea of a bird's nest was said to be Chinese because it is reminiscent of bird's nest soup, a Chinese delicacy that is believed to be good for the health. Accolades for the design did not point out that bird's nest soup is rather infamous in the West as one of those Chinese foods, along with dog meat, that westerners find disgusting in concept if not in actual taste. About the collaboration, Jacques Herzog said, "You cannot just walk into China and do what you have always done. We like to learn from other places, and China is the oldest civilization on the planet. With Ai Weiwei, we find contemporary lines of energy from that tradition."[28]

In a 2005 documentary, Ai described the stadium's Chineseness with reference to its Zen Buddhist character rather than to its physical shape:

Lots of people are attracted to its oriental appearance. This kind of design reflects how the Chinese tradition views a single object. There is always this desire to capture an entire worldview, a vision of the whole universe in a single

Figure 3.10. Artist's rendition of the Olympic Green with the National Stadium in the foreground. From Beijing Organizing Committee for the Games of the XXIX Olympiad, *Beijing Olympic Venues*, 9.

piece of work. So actually the stadium is more than just a stadium. It reflects the ambitions of our time, the dreams of our time. They may fail, they may disappoint, they still say a lot about China at this moment, its hopes and how it would like the world to see it.[29]

Revealing a difference between the Western and Chinese uses of space to express hierarchy, the design of the VIP reception area had to be modified: originally designed to accommodate 1,500 VIPs, the Chinese wanted it to accommodate 11,000.[30] Furthermore, it did not include a conventional chairman's platform. While this was still under discussion in 2007, it was felt that it would be best to first meet the requirements of the Olympic Games and then to modify it later if necessary.

In the spring of 2004, the project received a setback when a group of senior academics in China wrote a letter to Premier Wen Jiabao challenging the practice of hiring foreign architectural firms to create outlandish and potentially unsafe designs that they would have difficulty getting built in their own countries. A senior professor of architecture at Qinghua University (presumably one of the signatories of the letter) explained to a *New York Times* reporter, "They couldn't do this in their own country, so they are taking advantage of the Chinese psychology that European thinking is better. They are using the Chinese as their new-weapons test field." Ai Weiwei criticized this group by saying, "They never tell the truth but always try to build up this so-called nationalism against foreigners who open up society. They lost prestige when society opened up. For 50 years they never made a single object that is countable as valuable."[31] Eventually the project was examined for its engineering soundness, scaled back, and resumed.

The incident revealed an ongoing public debate in China that it would be inaccurate to describe as a conflict between a conservative, nationalist old guard and innovative, open-minded future talent. The debate was more complex, and the battle lines were not so clearly drawn. In fact, it was probably valid to say that these designs could not have been built in the developed West, so the real question was whether that was a good thing or a bad thing for China. Even Herzog had said, "They have the most radical things in their tradition, the most amazing faience and perforated jades and scholar's rocks. Everyone is encouraged to do their most stupid and extravagant designs there. They don't have as much of a barrier between good taste and bad taste, between the minimal and expressive. The Beijing stadium tells me that nothing will shock them."[32] The opposition to the stadium design was part of the larger public debate about what it means to be Chinese and whether anything distinctively "Chinese" will remain as China plunges headfirst into the international community. The sides of this debate do not simplistically break down into conservative/progressive factions.

WILL THE OLYMPIC GAMES BE USED BY THE COMMUNIST PARTY TO SYMBOLICALLY LEGITIMIZE ITS REGIME?

The history of stadium building in China serves as a map of the development of national state power and its relationship with the outside world. The first stadiums were the product of Western influence. The fact that the two most important stadiums in Beijing were located in the grounds of two major Qing temples exemplified the process by which a nation-state inspired by the Western model was superimposed over the ruins of the Qing dynasty. Generic architecture that was nothing more than "modern" and not intentionally "Chinese" was the rule until the 1990 Asian Games. The desire to build a stadium utilizing "Chinese characteristics" to represent a nation with an ancient history that has much to contribute to modern world culture entered its most recent stage with the design of the Bird's Nest Stadium for the Beijing Olympic Games.

Will the 2008 Beijing Olympic Games strengthen the Chinese Communist Party by convincing Chinese and non-Chinese alike that it—and it alone—is qualified to lead China? This analysis has demonstrated that this will actually

Figure 3.11.　The countdown clock for the Beijing Olympic Games, Tiananmen Square. Photo by Andy Miah, 2006.

not be the core symbolic point of the Beijing Games. Rather, the more important symbolism will concern the place of Chinese culture and the Chinese nation in the modern world. It will be multifaceted and open to various interpretations. It will mix such things as feng shui and avant-garde architecture, the art of *guanxi* and VIP reception rooms. The handful of top leaders who govern China will occupy a very small and not very determinative role in this massive and tangled symbolism, for which the Bird's Nest Stadium offers a fitting visual image. The legitimacy of the current regime will be measured by how well it manages this tangle—but the symbols of power will be so complex that no one will end up as a clearly "legitimized" winner. Rather than providing a definitive answer, instead even more debate will be stimulated in the outside world as well as inside China.

NOTES

1. For a more theoretical treatment of Chinese stadiums that pre-dated China's successful Olympic bid, see Susan Brownell, "The Stadium, the City, and the State: Beijing," in *The Stadium and the City*, ed. John Bale and Olof Moen (Keele: Keele University Press, 1995), 95–110.

2. *Zhong* means "center," *guo* (国) means "country" or "kingdom," and *Zhong-guo* (中 国) means the (central kingdom) and is the name by which Chinese people have typically known their country. The contemporary debates over this name in the context of China–Taiwan relations are described in chapter 5.

3. Stephan Feuchtwang, "School-Temple and City God," in *The City in Late Imperial China*, ed. William Skinner (Stanford, Calif.: Stanford University Press, 1977), 585–86.

4. Angela Rose Zito, "Re-Presenting Sacrifice: Cosmology and the Editing of Texts," *Ch'ing-shih Wen-ti* 5, no. 2 (1984): 59.

5. Sidney D. Gamble, *Peking: A Social Survey* (New York: George H. Doran Company, 1921), 29.

6. Gamble, *Peking*, 29.

7. Frank Dorn, hand-drawn map of Peking printed on silk scarf (Yale University Library Map Collections, 1936).

8. A. Henry Savage Landor, *China and the Allies* (New York: Charles Scribner's Sons, 1901), 19.

9. Landor, *China and the Allies*, 253, 248, 267.

10. Richard A. Steel, *Through Peking's Sewer Gate: Relief of the Boxer Siege, 1900–1901*, ed. George W. Carrington (New York: Vantage Press, 1985), 63–67.

11. Wang Zhenya, *Jiu Zhongguo tiyu jianwen* [Information on Sports in Old China] (Beijing: People's Sports Publishing House, 1987), 131–39.

12. Rong Gaotang et al., *Dangdai Zhongguo tiyu* [Contemporary Chinese Sports] (Beijing: Chinese Academy of Social Sciences Press, 1984), 479.

13. Wang Zhenya, *Jiu Zhongguo*, 159, 161.

14. Wang Zhenya, *Jiu Zhongguo*, 184; Rong et al., *Dangdai Zhongguo*, 479.

15. James L. Hevia, "Making China 'Perfectly Equal,'" *Journal of Historical Sociology* 3, no. 4 (December 1990): 379–400.

16. I have done only a cursory overview of this time period, but I suspect that a thorough examination of the sources will turn up explicit expressions to this extent by YMCA organizers. In general, they were hyperaware of the contrast between "traditional, non-Christian" China and the "modern, Christian China" (as they saw it) in whatever they did. As described in chapter 1, this exaggerated East–West distinction is the fundamental characteristic of orientalist thinking.

17. Rong et al., *Dangdai Zhongguo*, 478; Zhou Yixing, ed., *Dangdai Zhongguode Beijing* [Contemporary China's Beijing], vol. 1 (Beijing: Chinese Social Sciences Press, 1989), 260.

18. Although placard sections were not common in the West, the 1984 Los Angeles Olympic Games organizers borrowed this quintessential socialist genre and added a twist during the second consecutive boycotted Olympic Games at the end of the Cold War. Instead of a specially trained placard section of nonpaying students (a problem for the generation of ticket revenues), the choreographers gave a placard to every spectator in the stadium, and at the appointed moment all the spectators raised a placard over their heads to form a continuous bank of the flags of the participating countries. Instead of symbolizing socialist discipline, it was made to symbolize an open, democratic global society. Beating the socialists at their own symbolism, it was the largest placard section of all time.

19. *Beijing Review*, "XI Asian Games: Beijing, 1990" (1990), 7.

20. Jürgen Habermas, "The Public Sphere: An Encyclopedia Article," *New German Critique* 1, no. 3 (1974): 51, 51 n. 4.

21. Liang Lijuan, *He Zhenliang and China's Olympic Dream*, trans. Susan Brownell (Beijing: Beijing Foreign Languages Press, 2007), 63.

22. *Beijing Review*, "XI Asian Games," 11.

23. The Eight Immortals (*ba xian*) are the following:

Immortal Woman He (He Xiangu)—the only female, a virgin; tools are a lotus flower and a flute, bamboo ladle, or fly whisk

Royal Uncle Cao (Cao Guojiu)—brother of an empress who left court life in disgust at its corruption; tools are castanets and a jade tablet

Iron-Crutch Li (Li Tieguai)—represents the sick; tools are a crutch and a gourd

Lan Caihe—of androgynous gender, is eccentric and a drunk, represents the poor; tool is a flower basket

Lü Dongbin—of aristocratic descent; tools are a fly whisk and a magic sword

Philosopher Han Xiang (Han Xiangzi)—represents the philosopher; tool is a flute

Elder Zhang Guo (Zhang Guo Lao)—represents the elderly; tools are a bamboo drum and drumsticks and a donkey that can be folded up like paper when not in use

Zhongli Quan—leader of the group; represents the soldier, is fat; tool is a fan

The issues that concern the Eight Immortals are more varied and reflective of real life compared to the mission of stopping evil would-be world dominators that typically concerns Western superheroes. If today's Western superheroes owe anything to Friedrich Nietzsche or minimally to the cultural context that also produced Nietzsche, we might recall the history of "Western civilization" recounted in chapter 1 and note that, according to Ingomar Weiler, Burckhardt's ideas about *agon* and Western civilization influenced Nietzsche's ideas about ruthless competition and the *Übermensch*. The two of them were friendly in Basel, and Burckhardt invited Nietzsche to sit in on his lectures on the topic. See Ingomar Weiler, "*'Aien Aristeuein'*: Ideologische Bemerkungen zu einem vielzitierten Homerwort," *Stadion* 1, no. 2 (1975): 204–7.

24. This is a distinct difference from ancient Greece, which had no such fixed practice of aligning cities and temples with the four directions. In China, even today, the sentiments about the four directions are so strongly held that it is inconceivable that one could ignore them for an event as important as the Olympic Games.

25. Chinese law requires foreign architectural firms to cooperate with a local design institute. The legal requirement of foreign firms to form collaborations or joint enterprises with Chinese partners is to prevent foreigners from extracting wealth from China without making any long-term contributions to local development—a lesson learned from the history of Western and Japanese imperialism before the communists took over. This will come up again in chapter 7, which touches on the creation of a Sino–foreign joint enterprise for broadcasting the international feed for the Olympic Games.

26. "Venues," official website of BOCOG, www.en.Beijing2008.cn (June 2007).

27. "China Rises: Party Games," segment on Ai Weiwei, four-part documentary and interactive website produced by the *New York Times*, the *Discovery Times*, the Canadian Broadcasting Corporation, ZDF, France 5, and S4C, written and directed by Neil Docherty (2005), www.nytimes.com/specials/chinarises/partygames (July 4, 2007).

28. Hugh Pearman, "Iconoclasm Rules: How Herzog and de Meuron Work with Conceptual Artist Ai Weiwei on Beijing's New Olympic Stadium," in *Gabion: Retained Writing on Architecture* (March 5, 2007), www.hughpearman.com/articles5/weiwei (June 2007), 1–2.

29. "China Rises."

30. Arthur Lubow, "The China Syndrome," *New York Times Magazine*, May 21, 2006, www.nytimes.com (June 2007), 10.

31. Lubow, "The China Syndrome," 9.

32. Lubow, "The China Syndrome," 1.

Chapter Four

What Women's Sports Mean to China

In the early hours (Beijing time) of May 8, 1999, three American bombs ripped into the Chinese embassy in Belgrade during NATO's air strikes against Yugoslavia.[1] Twenty people were injured, and three people, all journalists, were killed. The dead were forty-eight-year-old female Shao Yunhuan and a young married couple, thirty-one-year-old Xu Xinghu and his twenty-eight-year-old wife Zhu Ying. They were quickly hailed as "revolutionary martyrs." The incident sparked mass anti-U.S. demonstrations, apparently led by university students, in cities across China, including Beijing, Shanghai, Guangzhou, Chengdu, Chongqing, Shenyang, Nanjing, Changsha, Xiamen, Lanzhou, Hefei, Jinan, and Hong Kong. The demonstrations before the U.S. embassy in Beijing were particularly vitriolic, with as many as 100,000 students and residents shouting slogans; holding up photos, placards, and banners; pasting up posters; throwing objects; and harassing and spitting at foreigners.

Two months later, U.S.–China relations returned to civility during the finals of the Women's World Cup Soccer Tournament in Pasadena, in which the United States defeated China 5 to 4 on penalty kicks after a hard-fought scoreless game and overtime play.[2] Why would a women's soccer game assuage the anti-American emotions ignited by the bombing of the embassy and restore polite public communication between the Chinese and American presidents?

The central point of this chapter is to claim that gender must be taken into account in understanding popular nationalism in China because the gender issues evoke deeper, more visceral emotions than any others. A widespread, generally unstated assumption tends to be that "nations" are abstractions that do not have a gender and that their affairs are conducted mainly by male heads of state, military forces, and businessmen who are too busy conducting important affairs to think about their own masculinity. This chapter argues that gender constitutes a fundamental structure in Chinese nationalism that is often overlooked and is particularly evident in the world of sports. This chapter understands gender in a broad sense as a system of cultural beliefs about manhood, manliness, and masculinity as they exist in complementary opposition to womanhood, womanliness, and femininity. Nationalism is also understood in the broad sense as a system of cultural beliefs about a certain kind of social grouping—the "nation-state"—and the sense of identity that emerges among those who feel that they belong to it. Nations are different from states: "state" refers to a complex form of social organization revolving around a centralized government, encompassing both agrarian empires like Qing dynasty China and industrialized nations like the contemporary People's Republic of China (PRC). The modern nation-state is a relatively recent state formation that emerged in Europe and its colonies in the late eighteenth century and was introduced into China in the late nineteenth century.[3]

If you scratch the surface of almost any relationship between self-consciously "Chinese" people and others, gender is not far below—and in this, Chinese people are no different from any others, including Americans. In reality, nations are only abstract categories, and the relations between them actually consist of interactions between living people who must ultimately sit together at the bargaining table. Grasping these self-concepts must be the starting point for any real mutual comprehension. This chapter outlines how the meanings of being a "man" and being "Chinese," along with the meanings of being a "woman" and being "Chinese," have changed since the start of the era of reform and how sports have played a role in expressing and defining Chinese gender-in-the-nation. It also touches on how this has affected Chinese people's views of their place in global politics.

NATIONAL HUMILIATION, MALE IMPOTENCE, AND FEMALE SUFFERING

As European ideas about nationalism were introduced into China in the late nineteenth century (often via Japan), Chinese intellectuals and statesmen began to come to terms with a new conception of the state. Yan Fu and the other constitutional reformers (Kang Youwei and Tan Sitong) argued that a key reason for China's weakness lay in the physical weakness of Chinese women, who were kept bound footed and in a condition of virtual servitude. They contrasted the Chinese woman with women from Western nations, who were said to be strong, natural footed, and nearly equal with the Western man, if not in some ways superior. Thus, physical education and sports for women became linked with nationalist ideology. However, despite the importance attached to women's sports in reform efforts of the early decades of the 1900s, it was clear that China must ultimately prove its worth as a nation through manly exploits on the sports field that would erase the dread label of the "sick man of East Asia" and the effeminate image of the scholar in his robe and queue.[4] And despite the successes of China's sportswomen in the 1980s and 1990s, it might be argued that the same sentiment still exists.

In reformist thought, the "oppressed Chinese woman" became a symbol of China's backwardness and weakness as a nation. From its beginning, then, Chinese nationalist ideology was intertwined with gender ideology.[5] The category of the backward woman in need of modernizing emerged in tandem with the category of the modern man who was going to lead her. However, a theme that was to repeatedly recur in Chinese nationalist ideology until the 1990s was the inability of Chinese men to take the lead. Instead, scholars have shown the prevalence of a theme of Chinese male impotence to right the wrongs done to Chinese women by Japanese and Western men. In short, nationalist ideology might draw on images of the suffering, self-sacrificing Chinese woman, but it was really all about men: women suffer because men are impotent to right the injustices done to *men* through their women. Male impotence is the thing that really needs to be fixed.

The theme of the rape of Chinese women was a common one in nationalist literature, used to symbolize the rape of the Chinese nation by Japan and the West.[6] If the nation was like a body, then the occupation of the nation was like the rape of a female body. China as a nation thus became female relative to the more powerful Japanese and Western imperialist nations, which became male. If the early history of the Chinese nation had been one of sovereignty and expansion, then perhaps the male body would have dominated nationalist allegories. However, the suffering and violated female body seemed to be a more potent symbol for China's national humiliation at the hands of others. This theme of female suffering and male impotence continued until the 1990s.

THE MAOIST PERIOD:
EMASCULATION AND MASCULINIZATION

With the founding of the PRC in 1949, the assumption was that national liberation had also liberated women. The Maoist period and particularly the Cultural Revolution period (1966–1976) were for a long time said to be characterized by "socialist androgyny"; gender politics were largely replaced by class politics. Between the Yan'an period in the early 1940s and the late 1970s, clothing was essentially the same for men and women, and women wore their hair either bobbed or tied back in braids or pigtails. The covers of women's magazines were decorated with images of women in plain working clothes engaging in manual labor, and women who did difficult men's work such as oil drilling or coal mining were called "iron maidens." Women who tried to look "feminine" were criticized for their improper attitudes.[7] However, feminist scholars are now realizing that it is not accurate to say that gender was "erased" or that sex was "androgynous" during this period. Rather, women were on the one hand forced to conform to a male norm and on the other still subordinate to men in many ways.[8] While women were encouraged to enter the workforce and take on dangerous jobs, men were not encouraged to do more housework and child care. "Equality" actually involved forcing women to conform to the male norm.

During the Cultural Revolution, for example, female Red Guards invariably dressed as male soldiers. In her analysis of their violence, Emily Honig notes that in the popular culture of the early and mid-1960s, everyday life was permeated with images and practices designed to promote military effectiveness, a result of the highly hostile nationalism that characterized China in this time of Cold War oppositions. In this atmosphere, girls recognized that in order to make a contribution to the nation, they most follow the new models of militant women. In doing so, they were contesting old gender conventions in a way that men did not have to, so that in some ways they felt under more pressure than men to demonstrate their "redness" through violence. However, analysis of the treatment of female violence in popular culture also indicates a male uneasiness toward this female contestation of gender roles, with the result that female violence is increasingly contained within structures of male authority from the 1940s through the 1970s. For example, in the historical records of the events portrayed in the famous revolutionary ballet and film *Red Detachment of Women*, which took place on Hainan island in the 1920s, the peasant women were organized by a militant female commissar and taught themselves to use rifles. In the 1960 ballet version, however, they are led by a handsome male commissar. In the 1970 film, they are given guns by men, trained by men, and led by men into battle.[9]

GENDER AND NATIONALISM IN THE 1980s

The Chinese women's volleyball team's victory in the 1981 World Cup in Tokyo was the turning point in the revival of national pride and patriotism after the end of the Cultural Revolution. Along the way, they defeated China's main global rivals: the Soviet Union, the United States, and finally Japan. It was front-page news in all the major newspapers—the headline in *Tiyu bao* [Sports Daily] was outlined in red—and any Chinese person who was in China and even mildly aware of national affairs will recall the event as a momentous one. I have discussed the victory with dozens of Chinese people over the years, and all have responded with strong emotion to my questions. Everyone could remember where he or she watched the game and how it was celebrated afterward. In Beijing, people flooded into the streets, setting off firecrackers, and openly weeping. A graduate of the Beijing Institute of Physical Education recalled that the students started a bonfire that got out of control and partly burned a classroom building.[10] The team went on to win five consecutive world and Olympic titles, and they were far and away China's most visible national heroines. In political study sessions and public speeches nationwide and in all kinds of settings, people were exhorted to "learn from women's volleyball." In the official rhetoric surrounding the volleyball victories, the dominant theme was that the team had realized the long-held revolutionary dream of erasing the label of "the sick *man* of East Asia" (*dongya bingfu*—the male bias is present in the original Chinese *fu*).[11]

The victory would probably not have had nearly the same impact if it had not been viewed in a live television broadcast by millions. The central government in China had previously regarded television so lightly as a propaganda tool that there was not even a national broadcasting station until 1980, when China Central Television (CCTV) was created out of the Beijing Television Station that had been serving as the national broadcaster. In 1981, CCTV did not plan to broadcast the volleyball World Cup games live, but viewers called in to demand it for the China–U.S. semifinal match. Frenzied inquiries finally produced a link with Pacific Satellite only moments before the China–U.S. semifinal game appeared on the screen.[12] The telecast made sports commentator Song Shixiong's name a household word. It was Song who provided the words that attached meanings to the television image of the team that was broadcast across China. In an interview, he told me that beforehand he had carefully prepared the image that he would propagate.[13] In order to more fully understand them, he watched them practice. He described their training as "very bitter." He saw them cry, yell at the coach, sweat, and fall to the floor. He saw them when they were so tired that they couldn't climb up stairs. He also "learned from women's volleyball," and it inspired him to work harder at his own job. I asked him how he felt when the team won the championship. He said that when they played the national anthem and raised the flag, he was very moved. I asked him if tears came to his eyes. He acknowledged that they did, "but I still had to exercise restraint." Song's portrayal of the team was clearly shaped by his own nationalism, which reflected

the popular Chinese nationalism of the time. He was a man, and, as I will argue below, the popular nationalism was essentially masculine.

Television was only one of the myriad channels by which public opinion
about the 1981 victory was expressed and shaped. Over 100 groups and individuals sent them gifts, including Young Pioneer scarves, Youth League pins,
school badges, commemorative badges, valuable food items, embroidery,
metalwork, and fresh flowers. Famous artists sent them a seal, calligraphy,
artwork, and statues created in their honor. More than 30,000 letters were
mailed to the team members; star spiker Lang Ping alone received over 3,000.
Thousands of letters were written to editors of newspapers and magazines and
sports departments of television and radio stations. Newspapers carried front-
page headlines in red; magazines devoted entire sections to day-by-day accounts of the victory and the diaries of the athletes. Artists dedicated musi-
cals, poems, and paintings to them; a book was written about them. The vast
majority of these artists and authors were men. One notable exception is the
feature film *Seagull* (*Sha ou*), which was directed by Zhang Nuanxin, a female. It will be discussed further below.

How did these *young women* come to stand for national unity and honor? In
the current of patriotic fervor, their gender was subsumed by their Chineseness. Indeed, the thing that was remarkable about the official discourse of that
time was that the team's gender and women's liberation were not emphasized
to the degree one might expect. They were Chinese first and women second.
An example is one letter sent to the team by Chinese students studying abroad
in West Germany that mentions the team's gender only to quickly subordinate
it to their Chineseness:

> You have simultaneously demonstrated before the eyes of the world the modesty
> and goodwill of the Chinese people, the traditional virtue of Chinese women, the
> fighting spirit of today's young people, and superlative ball skills. You've told
> the world, "These are the Chinese!"[14]

By far the more prominent theme was that the team had realized the long-
held revolutionary dream of erasing the label of "the sick *man* of East Asia."
When specific people were named as the dreamers of this dream, they were all
men: Premier Zhou Enlai, who had first invited a Japanese volleyball coach to
China to help the women train; Marshal He Long, the popular first director of
the State Sports Commission; and Ma Qiwei, one of the key figures in the introduction of Western sports to China and the first women's volleyball coach
after the founding of the PRC national team in 1950. The welcoming speech
made by an elderly high official at the airport was typical:

That your victory stirred the heartstrings of one billion people has deep historical roots. . . . When we were young, people from the outside world cursed us as
"the sick men of East Asia." . . . This time, when we saw the five-star flag of our
ancestral land rising up to the solemn accompaniment of the national anthem,
we old folks could not stop the hot tears from rolling down. Only under the leadership of the Chinese Communist Party was this day made possible.[15]

While millions of women were inspired by their victory, I have also observed that the most active and visible fans seemed to be male, many of
whom were college students. Young men seem to dominate the newspaper
and magazine photos of crowds at the "welcoming ceremonies" (*huanying
yishi*) held at airports, college campuses, and elsewhere when the team returned home victorious. In public appearances at celebratory ceremonies after major victories, the team was usually surrounded by a bevy of male officials who read out congratulatory letters to them and often spoke for them.

However, although they were often used as spokespeople for male Party
officials, they were also a source of personal pride for Chinese women. An
example is a young Beijing university student who told me that she and her
friends found glee in challenging sexist statements from male students by
asking, "So what's wrong with the *men's* volleyball team?"

The women who made up the team had their own dreams, and some of
them were fulfilled after their victory. It is a common practice to appoint star
athletes to political positions; this is said to demonstrate that "the state has not
forgotten." The first-string team members were appointed as delegates to the
National People's Congress and other political positions; three of the women
were given high positions in the Sports Commission system and one in the
People's Liberation Army.

However, the person whose political star rose most rapidly was Yuan
Weimin, the male coach who led the team to its first three victories. Almost
immediately after retiring as the team coach in 1984, Yuan was appointed
deputy director of the State Sports Commission (in 1998 renamed the State
General Administration of Sports), and from 2000 to 2004 he served as director. In 2000 he became chairman of the Chinese Olympic Committee, and
in 2004 he became executive president of the Beijing Organizing Committee
for the Games of the XXIX Olympiad, positions he still held in 2007. In the
mid-1980s when the market reforms were just getting underway and people
with ambition were still stifled by the lack of mobility and opportunity in the
state-planned economy, Yuan was admired because he was perceived as
someone who had succeeded on his own hard work and talent. His rapid rise
in sports administration was believed to be due to the same competence that
had made him such a successful coach. He was also attractive to women: in

a 1985 survey of women at China's top liberal arts university, Beijing University, he was most often named as the ideal male.[16]

The emotions that compelled ordinary people to write the team are expressed in the multitude of letters, poems, and songs that were published in newspapers and magazines. Only a few of the letters mailed to the team were ever published. In 1996, when I tried to track down the letters sent to the team, I was told that the bags had been thrown away sometime in the 1990s; several people told me that it was probably because no one considered that they might have historical significance. However, it is also the case that, when a Chinese sports scholar requested to look through the letters in the early 1980s, she found that she was able to gain access only by pulling connections and promising to return all the letters when she was finished. The reason, she was told, was that many of the letters were written in blood (a customary way of expressing deep emotion). A vast number of them were also love letters and proposals of marriage from young men. The implication was that making public examples of such extreme emotion could be potentially dangerous.

The letter writers published in the media often linked their own pain to national humiliation. A recurring narrative goes as follows: the women's volleyball team endured extreme physical and psychological pain, persevered against overwhelming obstacles, and finally succeeded in their long quest, in the end redeeming their own suffering and China's national humiliation. The traumas of the Cultural Revolution had only officially ended in 1976. This narrative offered hope to average people that their own suffering was not meaningless and could also serve to redeem China's past humiliation. Thus, the overriding emotion provoked by the 1981 victory was grief and its redemption. "Scar literature" had already begun to give public expression to this grief in the form of novels and short stories; the women's volleyball victories provided not just a catharsis but also a vindication of sorts. A letter written by a middle school teacher in Hunan to *Sports News* [*Tiyu bao*] echoes my analysis:

> Women's volleyball's tears of victory and the inspired tears of the hundreds of millions in the TV audience—what do they mean? They mean that victory doesn't come easily, they mean that the Chinese people need victory, they need the sweet dew of victory to moisten the spirit that was wounded in the past.[17]

ZHANG NUANXIN'S *SEAGULL (SHA OU)*

The "bitterness" of their training constituted one of the enduring aspects of their story. The interlinked themes of personal and national pain were dramatized in a rather extreme way in a popular feature film, *Seagull*, filmed in 1981 before the World Cup victory. Cowritten (with Li Tuo) and directed by Zhang Nuanxin, a prominent Fourth Generation director and a woman, this film was an exception to the rule that the popular images of the volleyball team were orchestrated by men.

Seagull portrays the bitter life of Sha Ou, a member of the national volleyball team, who is played by an actual second-string team member. The film opens as she and her teammates skip across a grassy field toward the camera in their red "China" uniforms. Sha Ou's voice explains, "Every person has her dream. My dream was to defeat the Japanese volleyball team and to be the champion." The year is 1977, the Asian Games are three months away, and she is twenty-eight years old and nearing the end of her career. Her voice recalls, "If only we could win, I was willing to pay any price and make any sacrifice. But I didn't know that the sacrifice was that great, the price that high."

The story then begins as she is pulled out of practice to go to the team clinic, where she is told that she has a serious back injury and that to continue playing will risk permanent paralysis. We are thus introduced to the tragic mood that pervades the film from beginning to end. Through most of the film, Sha Ou is sullen, stubborn, sobbing, and suffering. When she wins only the silver medal in the 1977 Asian Games, she is so disappointed that she tosses the medal into the ocean on the boat back from Hong Kong while seagulls soar in the distance. However, her sadness is briefly allayed when she reads in the newspaper that her boyfriend, Shen Dawei, a member of the mountain-climbing team, has successfully conquered Mt. Everest. Everything seems beautiful for a moment: she tells her mother that she is happier than if she had succeeded herself and that she will now retire, go through with her oft-postponed wedding, and devote herself to being the "head of the support team" (*houqin buzhang*) for her husband. Her brief happiness is shattered when an avalanche kills Dawei on the way back down. Her will collapses like the crashing snow of the avalanche. In her lowest moment, she recalls a time when they visited the Yuan Ming Garden (Old Summer Palace) ruins together. Dawei, who is older, wiser, and a mentor, explains to her that the palace was burned by the imperialist powers. "Whatever could be burned was burned. Only these stones remain."[18] These words echo through her mind, drawing a parallel between her own personal loss and China's most poignant symbol of national loss. The allegory motivates her to return to the national team as an assistant coach. In the airport before Dawei left, Sha Ou had recounted that her most ruthless coach had been a woman in her thirties, whom Sha Ou had once called "Tiger Yu" in a fit of temper. Coach Yu had vowed not to marry until she had won a world championship. When she was finally unable to make the international traveling squad, she had no choice but to marry, but she put her hopes on the younger women. Like her, Sha Ou now mercilessly pushes the next generation of women to greater performances.

The wedding party of her friend and former teammate Lili highlights the film's recurring conflict between marriage and the pursuit of national honor. Lili, who had never been as tough and single-minded as Sha Ou, was always a bit of a flirt—but she has now achieved happiness. Dr. Han, the team doctor who had always harbored strong feelings for Sha Ou, attends the wedding and is now a widower with a young daughter. The daughter follows Sha Ou into Lili's bedroom, picks up one of Lili's trophies, and says, "Look at me—I'm a world champion. Auntie, are you a world champion?" Sha Ou answers sadly, "No. Auntie isn't a world champion. Auntie is nothing." The little girl tells her not to be afraid, that one day she will be a world champion. Dr. Han enters the room, and it soon becomes clear that he is about to propose marriage, and it looks like Sha Ou has decided that marrying him will make her into something, and she will accept. Her dead boyfriend Dawei had asked Dr. Han to look after her just before he left to climb Everest, noting that "girls will inevitably have their weak moments," and so one man had essentially handed her over to another. Unfortunately, just at this moment she tries to pick up the daughter, collapses, and knows that she will never walk again.

The movie ends with her in a wheelchair in the hospital. She has just heard that the women's volleyball team has won the world championship. Although she had refused to watch, she agrees to go to the TV room to watch the end of the broadcast. She arrives in time to hear the voice of Song Shixiong, the television commentator, saying, "The people thank you. The nation (*zuguo*) thanks you." As she wipes tears from her cheeks, Sha Ou's voice concludes, "Friends say being an athlete is too bitter. . . . Not me. If people could really change things, if I could live it all over again, I'd still want to be an athlete, I'd still want to play ball, I'd still want to be a world champion." The final scene shows a new generation of young volleyball players bouncing across a field toward the screen in their red "China" uniforms.

This film could have been made by a man in that it echoes the elements of Chinese nationalism that are constituted from a male point of view. The feminist critic Dai Jinhua criticized films such as this, made by women about women, because they were still made from a male point of view.[19] *Seagull* is, for the most part, an example of this trend. The women clearly have to choose between marriage and volleyball, so that their main sacrifice is their womanhood (with the implicit assumption that wifehood and motherhood are what makes a woman a woman). And after all, the one who ends up happy and healthy is the married Lili, not Sha Ou. Sha Ou achieves her success under the tutelage of a male coach, a doctor, a boyfriend, and even at one point a male cook. They are all concerned and supportive, while the most ruthless person is the female Coach Yu, whose place Sha Ou later takes. Coach Yu and her own mother are also the only people whose authority Sha Ou openly defies.

However, there is a small space for feminism if we compare this film to the official rhetoric discussed above. There, the women's volleyball team realized the hopes held by several generations of men. This film, by contrast, is very much about a female lineage, extending from the bitter thirty-year-old coach Yu to Sha Ou to Sha Ou's students to Dr. Han's daughter. The people most strongly committed to national honor are women. Only the woman coach has the nerve to tell Sha Ou that her problem is not physical but lack of willpower. It is often the men who try to dissuade them from putting themselves through such suffering. Sha Ou has "traded the second half of her life for a game," as Dr. Han had pleaded with her not to do, and the film leaves no hint that her future holds anything other than a wheelchair in a small room. The extremely tragic tone of the movie offers the possibility of understanding this film as a criticism of the cruel self-sacrifices made by women who are ultimately tougher than the men whose honor they serve.

This fictional story was lived out in reality by the female gymnast Sang Lan, who was paralyzed from the neck down while warming up for the vault event at the 1998 Goodwill Games in New York. American journalists who met her and wrote about her were amazed by her willpower, optimism, and apparent view that this sacrifice for the nation had been justified, a view that was also echoed by her parents.

LOVE AND COUNTRY (BUT NO SEX)

In the years following the women's volleyball victory, female athletes generally had greater success in international sports than males, and so they became the symbolic figureheads in the revival of Chinese nationalism.

As a member of the Title IX generation in the United States, I remember that there was much discussion of whether sports turned girls into lesbians, whether muscles were attractive on women, and a whole range of questions about the relationship between sports and sexuality. The pressure on a young girl like myself in the formative years of her gender identity was intense. The PRC had established a sports system in the 1950s that essentially gave equal sports opportunities to men and women. This was seventeen years before American women began to achieve legal equality in school sports with the passage of Title IX, but Title IX had no effect on the huge professional sports industry, where women were greatly underrepresented. Since China had no professional leagues until the mid-1990s and sports were state funded, there was a state-mandated equality between men and women. When China stepped onto the world stage in the 1980s, Chinese sportswomen achieved immediate success.[20] The Chinese women's volleyball team were the super-stars of the 1980s, followed by the "Ma Family Army" of long-distance runners in the 1990s. Most of the Chinese women volleyball players and long-distance runners were considered relatively unattractive in China when judged against the feminine ideal, but they were national heroes anyway. As was earlier done to the Soviet and East German sportswomen, in the United States the successes of the Chinese women were neutralized by accusations of a lack of femininity and masculinization due to drug use. For example, in an NBC television segment broadcast in 1995, six-time Olympic gold medalist Amy Van Dycken, an American, is featured, saying,

> We were in the locker room, myself and another US swimmer, and we were talking and having a good time, putting on our swimsuits, getting ready for our races. All of a sudden we have our suits up about around our knees, we hear these really deep voices. We freaked out and [gasp] grabbed our towels and put them around us really quick, and it was just two Chinese women.[21]

The centuries-old Chinese tradition of the woman warrior provided an archetype of a woman who sacrifices herself or wins glory for the nation through physical pain and prowess. In the 1980s, China's star female athletes were described with classical phrases like "headdress heroines" and were likened to China's most popular woman warrior, Hua Mulan. Woodblock prints of Mulan from the eighteenth through the early twentieth centuries generally depict her as thick bodied with a big nose—unattractive by the standards of the time—but she was a popular figure because of her loyalty to her father and family (see figure 4.1). The label "Ma Family Army" was a play on the title of the sixteenth-century Ming dynasty novel *Yang Family Generals*, in which a matriarch and her daughters-in-law take up arms to avenge their male kin. Looking back over my own athletic career after exposure to the Chinese tradition, I felt deprived. I wondered what it would be like to grow up surrounded by women warriors, and I wondered why they were so ever-present in Chinese popular culture and not in U.S. popular culture at that time. If I had had access to cultural images of the woman warrior, it would have given me a richer and more positive understanding of myself as a female athlete. Joan of Arc simply did not fulfill this need since she got burned at the stake for aspiring to male martial glory. The gender politics in the United States after World War II and through the women's movement were not conducive to the woman warrior until the mid-1990s, when the woman warrior reemerged in

Figure 4.1. Hua Mulan, woodblock print from Wei Xiyuan, *Xiaoxiang gujin xiannü zhuan* [Illustrated Biographies of History's Virtuous Women], vol. 1 (Shanghai: Jicheng tushu gongsi, 1908).

U.S. culture in a big way when *Xena: Warrior Princess* appeared on television in 1995. Xena's emergence also happened to be the year before the 1996 Atlanta Olympics, the "women's Olympics," in which gold medals by the U.S. women's softball and soccer teams over the Chinese were widely considered to mark the coming of age of women's sports in the United States. It marked the emergence of women from sports previously stereotyped as masculine— such as soccer and basketball—as popular national celebrities. As the woman warrior fad continued in the United States, producers of popular culture turned to China for the heroines that the United States lacked: Disney released the animated feature film *Mulan* in 1998, and the Chinese/Hong Kong/Taiwan joint production *Crouching Tiger, Hidden Dragon* won the Academy Award for Best Film in 2001.

Thus, the image of the female athlete as a national heroine in China and the United States converged from opposite directions. In China, the sports system had been highly militarized until the 1990s. Displays of femininity were considered to indicate a lack of dedication to the sport. This began to change with China's increasing engagement with global culture. The militarized rules on sports teams were relaxed to the point that Chinese women now commonly wear long, loose hair in the Parade of Athletes in the Olympic Games opening ceremony, which would have been completely shocking throughout most of the 1980s. In the United States, the sexualization of female athletes subsided as women's participation in sports became common, and China and the United States met in the middle. The East–West hybrid figures of the woman warrior such as Disney's Mulan or the heroines in *Crouching Tiger, Hidden Dragon* finally provided the archetype that young American girls needed.

In Chinese pop philosophy, it is common to say that Western culture is an "oppositional culture" (*duikang wenhua*) that allows only for rigid, unchanging oppositions. The Chinese philosophy of yin and yang, in which opposites complement each other and are always in motion relative to each other, allows for martial heroines who combine *wen* (gentle, literary) and *wu* (fierce, military) traits in one persona. Chinese people note this with a feeling of superiority. And sometimes they may be right.

But what kind of women were the Chinese national heroines? In the 1980s, sportswomen were still the product of a sports system that subjected boys and girls to the equalizing effects of a uniform military discipline, intentionally erasing gender differences. Removed from their families and put into sports boarding schools, they were trained into military-style discipline from a young age. Sports team rules were especially draconian with respect to gender and sexuality. The provincial, municipal, and national teams administered by the State Sports Commission forbade athletes to have romantic relationships with members of the opposite sex, and sex segregation was strictly enforced in the dormitories. Violation of these rules could result in expulsion from the team. Until the late 1980s, athletes were allowed to be engaged only after the ages of around twenty-four (for women) and twenty-six (for men) and were not permitted to marry while still competing. This contrasted with the minimum legal ages for marriage of twenty (for women) and twenty-two (for men) for the general populace. In the late 1980s, it became possible for star athletes in their late twenties or older to negotiate with their teams to allow them to marry; second-tier athletes who wanted to marry felt their only

Figure 4.2.   Women's middle-distance running event at the National Team Center in Beijing, 1985. Photo by Susan Brownell.

option was to retire from sports first. In an influential article that criticized the sports system, "Superpower Dream," Zhao Yu commented that "not a few leaders and coaches of professional sports teams stand guard against love as if they were standing guard against a flood."[22]

The dress code on sports teams forbade women to wear long hair hanging loose over their shoulders. Until the mid-1990s, sportswomen were required to wear their hair short or tied back in public, including in competitions. If tied back, the ponytail or pigtails should be low on the head because a high pony-tail was considered too provocative. When Florence Griffith Joyner won two gold medals in the sprints in the 1988 Olympic Games, Chinese audiences were as amazed by the full hair streaming behind her as they were by her speed. The popular press frequently reported approvingly that several famous male coaches required their female athletes to cut their hair and forbade them to wear face cream, makeup, or high heels.[23]

"Love" occupied an important role in the women's volleyball phenomenon in the form of love letters and love of country. An example is a letter written to the team by a university student who had been brought back from the depths of despair:

> You have aroused again the love of country in the bottom of my heart. . . . [You] have lit the flame of my love which had already died out. . . . In ten years this was the first time I felt my heart beating—along with the strong rhythm of the pulse of the nation; in ten years this was the first time I felt the honor of being human—China's pride.[24]

However, personal love was subordinated to love of country. This sheds some insight into why figures of women occupy such prominent roles in Chinese nationalism. For if the primary audience is actually a male audience, what better figure to symbolize the nation—the object of his love—than a woman? In the 1980s volleyball furor, she is a marriageable young woman; in the 1990s anti-NATO demonstrations, she is a daughter or a mother.

Articles were also careful to emphasize that sportswomen who might appear aggressive during competition were in fact gentle females. A judo player was described as "a shy, demure-looking girl, but on the training mat she becomes as tough and aggressive as any tomboy."[25] It was often as if reporters felt compelled to find something to mark sportswomen as female and the efforts became more desperate if the women were engaged in stereotypically male sports like judo or soccer or if they were physically large. A member of the national women's basketball team who was 2.07 meters tall undoubtedly stood out among Chinese women, but that didn't matter because, "with a pair of fan-like palms large enough to grab a basketball, she is nonetheless as dexterous at sewing and knitting as any other girl on her team. She is also fond of singing and has taken the stage on many occasions."[26]

The point is that the masculinized sportswomen of the 1980s were presented in ways that never truly threatened the sex/gender code. Their sexualities were strictly controlled by the rules on appearance and behavior on sports teams. Potentially threatening images of aggressive females were defused with comments about obedience to boyfriends, demureness, sewing, and knitting. As Evans notes, the radical changes in public images of women since 1949 masked many continuities; founding assumptions about gender distinction were already well established, and the seemingly radical changes in women's status could be misleading.[27] Chinese nationalism of the 1980s continued the themes of Chinese nationalism over the past century described above: female suffering and self-sacrifice were above all a sign that men were unable to protect their women. Men who feel impotent are likely to feel threatened by sexually aggressive women, but they can accommodate passive women who are more victimized than they themselves feel.

THE YIN WAXES AND THE YANG WANES?

This kind of male–female dialectic was revealed in the decade-long discussion of why Chinese women had more success in international sports than men did. The aphorism "the yin waxes and the yang wanes" (*yin sheng yang shuai*), which harkens back to competitive Taoist sexual practices in which one partner could suck the life force out of another, was invoked to describe the situation. In attempting to formulate an explanation for the situation, many reasons were given. However, one reason seemed to prevail more than the others in both media discussions and in my interviews and conversations with sportspeople. Women were said to be more "obedient" than men. They were better able to "eat bitterness and endure hard labor" (*chi ku nai lao*) than men, and their physical suffering and pain were much emphasized in press accounts. They were more likely, it was said, to do what the coach told them to do. This obedience, it should be noted, was usually to male coaches and cadres. Yuan Weimin, of course, was a man.

The concern with the relative backwardness of Chinese sportsmen as compared to the women seemed to reveal a feeling that such a state of affairs was not desirable or even natural. The underlying assumption seemed to be that the men really should be the ones to carry the national banner and that they eventually would catch up, given enough time and effort. For, as much as people loved the women's volleyball heroines, they would also admit that if the Chinese men's soccer team ever got its act together enough to win a major world title, *then* there would be a celebration like none before.

In the 1980s, sportspeople and fans were quite frustrated with the failure of men's soccer to reach the finals of the World Cup or Olympics and the generally poor showings of men's sports in the international arena. This is the flip side of the strong sportswomen who led the resurgence of Chinese nationalism. Meng Yue argues that the images of strong women arose not so much out of the party's struggle to end sexism as out of the party's desire to create dominated men.[28] The fact that it succeeded to some extent is evident in that, after the end of the Maoist period, a great number of literary and film works by men began to express just how dominated men had felt. Recent reassessments of the Maoist period have suggested that many men experienced it as a period of emasculation and impotence. Scholars have noted that urban men will use the term "castration" (*yan'ge*) or "eunuch" (*taijian*) to describe the situation of men in the Maoist era.[29]

The string of volleyball victories in the 1980s occurred at a time when, despite the repression of femininity on sports teams, the bodies of sportswomen had become the first site for the reassertion of sexuality in the popular media. This was probably due to the fact that the clothes worn by women in many sports reveal the body more than typical street clothes do. This baring of the body was permitted by the state because of its promotion of top-level sports. Hence, calendars, magazine covers, playing cards, and postcards at that time often featured gymnasts in leotards, swimmers in bathing suits, tennis players in short skirts, and so on, while Western-style swimsuit calendars were still banned as pornography. When, after a heated debate, the State Council allowed the State Sports Commission to approve the wearing of bikinis by women bodybuilders in 1986, women bodybuilders quickly became a favorite image in these media, and their photos could be seen on the fronts and backs of magazines having nothing to do with sports.

In the 1990s, the expression of gender difference became common in urban society at large, but change was slower to come to sports teams. Athletes who grew up in this atmosphere often experienced a kind of awakening when they retired and began to look for a husband. For example, a former basketball player decided to take a modeling class in the early 1990s after she graduated from the Beijing Institute of Physical Education and her boyfriend, a teammate, broke up with her. She told me,

> On the sports team when I was younger, we were forbidden to dress up. Long hair over the shoulders was forbidden. We always wore our hair in a ponytail or pigtails. All the Chinese athletes did. . . . I didn't even have the idea of make-up in my brain until I took the modeling class. . . . I had short hair like yours and an athlete's demeanor . . . the way I moved and carried myself, and my hunched back. . . . I learned to have confidence in my appearance, to improve my posture, and to carry myself like I'm somebody. . . . I did find another boyfriend. . . . I got into fashion modeling because I thought it should be a kind of aesthetic appreciation, it should be elegant.

As a fashion industry emerged and began to grow in the 1990s many, perhaps most, of China's runway models were former athletes who had been chosen to do sports because of their height. In the first half of the 1990s, industry insiders criticized the sports background because they noted that sports teach a completely different way of carrying the body from runway modeling, and they said this accounted for the lack of grace, musicality, and

**Figure 4.3.   Models onstage during the 1995 Elite Look Supermodel Contest in Beijing.
Photo by Susan Brownell.**

femininity in the movements of Chinese models, which was inhibiting
China's ability to produce an international "supermodel"—a widely held
national ambition.

Yan Yan Zhang, whose 1.78-meter (5-foot 11-inch) height had led to her recruitment as a high jumper, studied modeling and later moved to the United
States, where, among other accomplishments, she was the "Oscar girl" at the
2001 Academy Awards who escorted the winners of the Best Film Award for
Crouching Tiger, Hidden Dragon on and off the stage. In 2001, I asked her

about her life at the Beijing Institute of Physical Education, where I had met her in 1987. "Now, you're living in Los Angeles, and you're a model, and you've learned to appreciate beauty in your life. Was there any beauty in your life then?" She replied (in English),

> I know, that's really amazing when you think about that. Ahh, unbelievable, it's amazing! When I was at Beijing P.E. Institute, the first two years I didn't even know what beautiful things should be. I didn't even dress up myself nicely. It was ugly, you know. I didn't know what fashion was, even. Even though I had the chance to read books in the library at the P.E. Institute, all kind of books, I didn't even pay attention to magazines!

This transformation, which was occurring at a very personal level among urban Chinese women, was also reflected at a national level in public performances, and it was also linked to broader issues of the body, gender, and nationalism. In 1981, the women's volleyball team had neither the opportunity nor the social context for this awakening. They were the products of a militarized disciplinary regime in which a masculine appearance symbolized the proper fighting spirit.

GENDER IN BEIJING'S BID FOR THE 2000 OLYMPIC GAMES

On September 23, 1993, the host city for the Olympic Games to be held in 2000 was decided by a vote of the International Olympic Committee (IOC). The winner was Sydney, Australia. This was the first year that a PRC city had bid for the Games, an event that attracted global media attention. Beijing campaigned zealously to host the 2000 Games and appeared to have a very good chance of winning; it led the vote counts until it lost to Sydney in the last round, when it was apparent that one part of the Western bloc shifted its vote from Manchester, England, to Sydney.

The World Championships of track and field were held in 1993 in Stuttgart a month before the IOC was to vote on the host city. Six Chinese women runners, whose average age was about twenty, unexpectedly dominated the women's long-distance events by taking six of the nine medals in the 1,500-, 3,000-, and 10,000-meter races. Perhaps the location of the World Championships in a reunited Germany contributed to the accusations against the Chinese of drug use, which were much more open than had ever been the case in the Cold War era. China was said to be picking up where the former East Germany had left off. The women were described as masculinized because of their acne, facial hair, lean bodies, short hair, and unprecedented endurance.

Less than three weeks later, in China's Eighth National Games in Beijing, seven women shattered the world records in all three events. The Games were scheduled to conclude just before the IOC vote on the Olympic host city and were to showcase all that was best about Chinese sports. The Chinese sports world hailed the women's breaking of the world records as a way of attracting the world's attention and demonstrating China's contribution to world sports. Instead, the victories worked against Beijing when Western sportspeople cited the suspicion of centralized state doping as one more reason that Beijing should not get the Games.[30]

The amazing thing about China's women runners was that they had performed well beyond what had been conceived as possible even for Soviet, German, or American women who were on steroids. One of the world records that was broken belonged to a Soviet who had herself tested positive for steroids several years after setting the record; it is not unlikely that steroids had aided her record performance.

The gender stereotypes that emerged from Western accusations and Chinese responses exemplify the different attitudes toward female athletes in the United States and China that were previously discussed. The American *Track and Field News* asked, "Why are the women suddenly so good while the men remain so average? . . . because anabolic steroids work better on women than men."[31] The deputy secretary-general of the Chinese Association of Sports Medicine explained, "The Chinese female athletes can withstand hardships better than the men."[32] Their coach, Ma Junren, was the latest in a by now well-established line of male coaches who recruited their best athletes from peasant stock. Playing into the martial arts paradigm that I have already discussed, Ma's athletes were called the "Ma Family Soldiers." He said, "All the runners I chose are from rural areas. They are used to enduring difficulties. Otherwise how could they bear to run a marathon a day at the high altitude of 2,236 metres? Who else in the world does this?"[33] The assertions by the Chinese that their women could train harder than men were met with disbelief by Western sportspeople and in letters to the editors of *Track and Field News*. I would argue that this was because different perceptions of gender and nation got in the way. Western sports fans could not accept the Chinese assertion that their women could train harder than their men because they were blind to the issue of hierarchy that underpinned it: women train harder than men to compensate for their social inferiority.

The outrage that the Western sports world expressed was probably also enhanced by revulsion at the thought of sacrificing *female* bodies for the nation. It has been widely known for almost a decade now that steroid use can have potentially fatal long-term effects, but until the tightening of drug controls in track and field in the past few years, many athletes took their chances. In my experience, Western men were more willing to take those chances, and the risks were regarded more lightly for men—after all, if they sacrificed their bodies for national glory, it did fit a certain cultural logic. But in the United States, the idea of women sacrificing their bodies for national glory was more disturbing than appealing. The specter of a communist state that carried the egalitarian principle to its extreme was evoked by the sight of "Ma's soldiers," whose bodies might be sacrificed for national glory in a way that Western cultural logic would reserve only for men. Unlike in the West, the financial rewards for these women's sacrifices would have been the same if they were men. And unlike in the West, these women's sacrifices had a certain mythological potency for their compatriots.

GENDER, SPORTS, AND THE FORCES OF THE MARKET

In the 1990s, the state control of the sports system loosened, and market forces began to influence female athletes. While this change liberated some female star athletes from the disciplinary rigor of the state, it subjected them to the even more inevitable forces of the market. The relative equality in financial resources devoted to men's and women's sports was shattered in the mid-1990s with the commercialization of men's soccer and basketball and the formation of corporate-funded professional leagues. Men's basketball and soccer were judged to have the potential to earn money; women's basketball and soccer were not. This was true even though the women's teams were among the top five in the world, while the men's teams were not. One of the key arguments in support of this capitalist-style professionalization was that it would improve the level of competition and propel Chinese *men* toward Olympic gold medals.

However, the market also brings its own kinds of freedom. By 1995, Ma Junren's star runner Wang Junxia had led a rebellion of the Ma Family Soldiers. They had left his tutelage and started their own team, complaining that he had kept large portions of their prize money and claimed the three Mercedes cars they had won at the 1993 World Championships. Wang told Reuters, "We simply couldn't take it any longer. We had absolutely no freedom. We were all on the brink of going crazy. The pressure was too intense; we couldn't take it."[34] Wang found herself another coach and went on to two outstanding performances at the 1996 Olympic Games, where she won one gold and one silver medal.

After many years in the United States, Lang Ping, the spiker who had led the volleyball team to its string of victories, returned in 1995 to take over as the national coach of the women's volleyball team in preparation for the

1996 Atlanta Olympic Games. The team quickly turned around its eighth-place finish in the 1994 World Championships and became a medal contender. When the Chinese team toured the United States shortly before the Atlanta Games, Lang Ping received raucous standing ovations from the Chinese members of the audience, much to the surprise of many American spectators, who had no idea what a national icon she was. The team won the silver medal in Atlanta. Members of the Olympic delegation told me that this rapid turnaround was due not to her skills as a coach but rather to her presence as an inspiring symbol.

Quite a lot of discussion was stimulated by another transformation: Lang Ping had, since she was last in the limelight, become quite attractive, to the point of being nearly unrecognizable. Despite the tremendous admiration and even love that was felt for her as an athlete in the 1980s, it was generally agreed that she was not very pretty. At the 1996 Olympic Games, she sported stylish glasses and a shoulder-length, bobbed haircut. Her formerly heavy-lidded eyes now seemed larger, and indeed her entire face seemed different. The rumor among the Chinese Olympic delegation in Atlanta was that she must have had cosmetic surgery to have changed so much. Since cosmetic surgery had become quite popular, especially the "double eyelid" operation to make the eyes seem larger, this was not improbable. However, after comparing her photos from the 1980s with the official team photo in 1996, I concluded that she had not necessarily undergone surgery. The difference could have been that between a woman in her twenties with short, boyish hair whose life revolved around a volleyball court and a cosmopolitan thirty-plus woman who had learned to use makeup and hairstyles. Lang Ping's metamorphosis is truly a sign of the changes in Chinese women's self-presentation. This is where the economic reforms are leading Chinese women: if even Lang Ping's appearance is subjected to such harsh scrutiny and her team's success attributed to her value as a symbol rather than her skills, then surely no woman is free from the tyranny of stereotypical feminine beauty.

THE RETURN OF MALE POTENCY

The prominence of debates about female sexuality in the 1980s and 1990s was something of a foil for the largely unnoticed reshaping of male sexuality. Can it be that during the 1980s and 1990s male sexuality was quietly reshaping itself in relation to a more assertive female sexuality, slowly recovering its potency? If life imitates art, then the plotline that has featured so strongly in so much literature by Chinese male writers over this century may finally be reaching its climax (pun intended). In the 1990s, sensual female bodies began to take their place at the forefront of popular culture. The plot-line demanded sexual women for the recovery of male potency. Chinese men are recovering their potency domestically and in the world political/economic arena, where Chinese leaders are now flexing their muscles on issues like human rights, the North Korean nuclear crisis, Taiwanese sepa-ratism, and so on. After the professionalization of men's soccer and men's basketball, hordes of eager male fans could consume their favorite mascu-line images, while the feminine images no longer occupied center stage as did women's volleyball in the 1980s and the Ma Family Soldiers in the 1990s. Even the brief moment in the limelight of the women's soccer team in 1999 was dimmed by the fact that no sponsors had yet signed up for the abbreviated (compared with the men's league) eight-team, two-month pro-fessional women's league in China. Although the Chinese Football Associa-tion had encountered difficulty in finding sponsors in the past and had been forced to subsidize the league with 1 million yuan each year, this was the first year that no sponsor had come forth at all.[35]

THE MAY 8 DEMONSTRATIONS

We have now returned full circle to the anti-U.S. demonstrations that began this chapter. With a fuller understanding of the symbolism of gender-in-the-nation in China, we can see the logic behind the restoration of polite com-munication between two presidents during the Women's Soccer World Cup.

Two of the three journalists killed in the Belgrade bombing were women, and they died on the day before Mother's Day, May 9. Shao Yunhuan was a wife (her husband, a diplomat working in the Belgrade embassy, was seri-ously injured in the attack) and a mother (her son had been studying at a Yu-goslavian university until the bombing began and he returned to China). Zhu Ying had been married only a year before, and while she was not yet a mother, reports portrayed her as soon to be one: fellow journalists reported that dur-ing her last talk with her husband fifteen minutes before the bombing started, she had mentioned her plan to have a baby during their vacation this year. On the whole, the major newspapers devoted much more attention to the two fe-male deceased than to the one male.[36] This attempt to present the event with the strongest possible moral outrage gives us insight into the Chinese con-cepts of morality that formed the context for the outrage. Particular outrage was attached to the images of murdered mothers and daughters. The front-page editorial commentary in *People's Daily* on May 10 denounced Ameri-can hegemonism with the words, "Because of this violent action, completely lacking in humanity, on this Mother's Day three Chinese mothers lost their children, and a Chinese child lost his mother." Popular reactions echoed these official statements. For example, *China Daily* quoted one Web user on the large Chinese website netease.com who posted notes reading, "Today is mother's day, but NATO's airstrike has claimed a mother from her child, and has taken many children from their mothers." Another posting (not reported in the Chinese media) suggested, "We'll blow up their mothers, too!"

Women's organizations were particularly active in the demonstrations. On March 26, the Capital Women's Journalists Association had been the first Chinese journalists' organization to oppose the NATO bombings. In a letter to the editor of *China Daily*, the vice director called the bombing a barbaric act of "flagrant violence against women and human lives and violation of human rights."[37] She recalled Shao Yunhuan as "a filial daughter and a caring mother, but mostly a responsible journalist. . . . NATO murderously deprived her of her life, her son of his mother, her husband of his wife, her parents of their daughter. What a present they have given to a Chinese family on Mother's Day!"[38] She further observed that Chinese women journalists had learned from the West to monitor domestic violence, only to have Western hypocrisy exposed by this "relentless international violence against women." Over 500 women gathered at the Women's Activities Center in Beijing, and the Women's Federation issued a statement containing the exhortation, "In the names of mothers, wives, and daughters, we cry out: peace-loving women of the world, mobilize!"[39] These are only a few examples of the multitude of references to mothers and familial relationships that permeated media coverage of the events.

Jeffrey Wasserstrom, a historian and an expert on student demonstrations who happened to be in Beijing and Shanghai at the time of the demonstrations, observed that by far the dominant television image of those days was that of Zhu Ying's father weeping over her body when he arrived in Belgrade to retrieve it.[40] He was reported to have repeatedly tried to wipe a bloodstain off her face, murmuring, "Daughter, dad is here to take you home." A vivid still photograph of this event appeared on page 1 of the May 10 *China Daily* and page 4 of the *People's Daily*, and a different version appeared on page 3 of the *Guangming Daily*. In the first photo, Zhu Ying's body lies in the foreground on a steel gurney, covered with a sheet that is pulled back to reveal her head. Her face, in profile, seems to have a sad, peaceful expression, but there is a large dark stain over her left eye. Standing behind her, Zhu's father's face is twisted in grief, his right hand stretched gently and protectively across her body. Two unidentified men, whom we might guess to be officials on the mission to Belgrade, stand behind him on each side. The man on his left has a firm, supportive grasp on Zhu's father's forearm and looks at him with a hard, straight-lipped expression. The man on his right has eyes downcast with uncontainable emotion. The photo seems to convey the bitter grief of three men for the single fallen young woman whom they were unable to protect. To an American audience, this public presentation of a father's grief and the television and photo images of the dead bodies (including in situ photos of the couple's twisted, blood-covered bodies in the debris of the embassy) might seem like a sensationalization of "private" moments. However, such emotions are not quite so "private" in China, where, as was discussed in chapter 3, the merging of the personal, the familial, and the national has characterized popular Chinese nationalism.[41] It is also evident in the common practice of publishing diaries (such as the unfinished "War Diary" of Xu Xinghu and Zhu Ying, which was rapidly published after their deaths), letters from people involved in national events, and letters or telegrams from state leaders to individuals.[42]

Several of these letters were published after the May 8 bombing. Shao Yunhuan's bedridden, seventy-six-year-old father and Zhu Ying's younger sister wrote open letters that were published in newspapers. Of particular interest are the letters written to President Clinton by Zhu Ying's father, Zhu Fulai, and Shao Yunhuan's son, Cao Lei, that were also published in whole or part. While in Belgrade to retrieve the bodies, Zhu Fulai wrote to President Clinton as one father to another, recalling his own happy memories of his daughter and family, imagining that Clinton felt the same when he was together with Hilary and Chelsea. "What did my daughter and her husband ever do to you?" he asked.[43] This letter was reprinted in full in the *Guangming Daily* under the title "A Letter to Chelsea's Father, American President Clinton," and it was signed, "Zhu Ying's and Xu Xinghu's father, Zhu Fulai."[44]

The image of Bill Clinton as a man played a key role in the protests. On the one hand, Zhu Fulai's letter appealed to Clinton's conscience as a father and a husband. In other contexts, however, Clinton's sex scandals and impeachment hearings were invoked to draw parallels between his sexual insatiability and American hegemonism. Jeff Wasserstrom saw one poster at Beijing University, in English, that accused Clinton of being a "bi-raper" because first he had ravished Monica Lewinsky and then, unsatisfied, set out to rape the world. In one of the Beijing demonstrations in the embassy district, he saw a very large, very phallic model of a cruise missile. He was also told of a placard that appealed to Monica to "use her mouth" to distract Clinton from interfering in the Balkans. Wasserstrom notes that his observations fit the theme already discussed: in China over the past century, in time of national crisis, there has been a tendency to focus on the damage done to female Chinese bodies by foreign men and the passivity or impotence of Chinese men.[45] In reaction to this feeling of impotence, one of the angry reactions on the Chinese website netease.com suggested having sexual relations with several generations of Clinton's family as an effective revenge.

The gender images that dominated the protests were ones that appealed to the righteous anger of the father or son whose daughter or mother has been brutally taken from him. Much more media attention was devoted to the grief of Zhu Ying's father, Zhu Fulai, and Shao Yunhuan's son, Cao Lei, than to any other relatives, including the mothers, sisters, and husband. This was symbolically reinforced by the ceremonies accompanying the return of the cremated ashes to their homeland. Zhu Fulai and Cao Lei went to Belgrade to retrieve the ashes, and when the mission returned to the Capital Airport in Beijing, their exit from the plane was covered by the media. Following a special guard of two uniformed soldiers holding bayonets, Cao Lei descended first, carrying the box of his mother's ashes draped in a Chinese flag. Then Zhu Fulai followed, heavily burdened with a small casket of ashes cradled in each arm, one for his daughter and one for his son-in-law, both draped in flags. *People's Daily* carried a photo of nineteen-year-old Cao Lei in the waiting room at the Belgrade airport, bent over the casket of ashes in his lap, "silently weeping."[46]

Thus, the primary victims in the media coverage were women, and the primary bereaved were men: a father and a son. That the grief is portrayed from the positions of fathers and sons is not surprising if we pay attention to the composition of the protesting crowds, which appear to have been mostly male. In the photos of protesters that accompanied these reports, the ratio of clearly visible male faces to female faces is roughly ten to one. Such gender imbalance is typical of public gatherings in China, including sports spectatorship, and was also typical of the Chinese fans at the Women's Soccer World Cup. The appeal to fathers and sons would have resonated with this male audience.

THE THIRD WOMEN'S SOCCER WORLD CUP

Almost exactly two months after the embassy bombing, on July 10, the Chinese and American women met in the final game of the third Women's Soccer World Cup. This was the latest stage in a rivalry that went back to the first World Cup, held in China in 1991, which was won by the United States while the Chinese lost in the quarterfinals. In 1996, the United States had taken the first-ever women's soccer Olympic gold in Atlanta, while China settled for silver. In 1998, China had lost to the United States in the Goodwill Games held in New York. In 1999, China had defeated the United States, 2 to 1, in contests leading up to the World Cup and entered the final game as the favorite. Seven Chinese players had been named to the tournament all-star team, while only five U.S. players were. Sun Wen had tied for the title of top scorer of the tournament. "It is very, very important that we win now, for ourselves and for China," she told Xinhua news agency.[47] Sun Wen was followed by the same kinds of mobs as Mia Hamm, the U.S. star, and Chinese fans were obviously in attendance at all of their games. During the semifinal match with Norway, some fans held up placards reading, "Little Sisters, when it's time to kick, just kick" (*meimei ni gai chujiao shi jiu chu jiao*). The night before the final game, the team had received a phone call from President Jiang Zemin, who told them, "You have demonstrated fully the aspiration to win honours for our motherland."[48] Millions of Chinese awoke in the early morning hours to watch the live broadcast, which started at four in the morning, Beijing time. Security around the U.S. embassy in Beijing was tightened. During the finals in the Rose Bowl, the Chinese fans unfurled a huge five-star flag in the stadium and held up placards with such slogans as "Glorious little sisters" (*meimei guangrong*). Minutes after the game, Vice Premier Li Lanqing called to express congratulations for their efforts. Later, a team photo was taken with President Clinton. Soon after the final, Clinton sent a letter to President Jiang Zemin expressing congratulations. Jiang returned a reply on the same day and congratulated Clinton on the victory, praising the skills, sportsmanship, and friendship of the American women. On their return to the Capital Airport, the Chinese team was met in the drizzle by 200 fans who unfurled a sixty-square-meter Chinese flag. On July 13, they were heralded in a grand ceremony at the Great Hall of the People, attended by President Jiang, Li Peng, and other high officials (Premier Zhu Rongji sent a letter in his absence). In his address to the team, Jiang observed, "The team displayed well our nation's long-cherished virtues: unity to combat differences, independence, self-confidence, hard work and a spirit to go all-out to make ourselves strong."[49] There were no reports of riots or aggressiveness against the U.S. embassy. Although there were some Chinese complaints of unfair treatment, the Chinese team and spectators were generally resigned to the results. Both Sun Wen and Coach Ma Yuan'an attributed the American victory to luck.

In May, when Clinton had tried to place a direct telephone call to Jiang immediately after the embassy bombing, it had been refused—while Boris Yeltsin's call was not only accepted, it was front-page news in the May 11 *People's Daily*. That Clinton had tried to call was not even mentioned, although an article on page 6 conceded that he had sent a letter to Jiang on May 9. After the World Cup, however, these symbolic exchanges of letters were reported in a timely and front-page fashion. The attention paid to the event by both Clinton and Jiang would seem to indicate that they recognized its deeper importance. Thus, China–U.S. relations returned to something of an equilibrium after the May 8 bombing, with an image not of Chinese women as passive victims of cruel American aggression but rather of strong Chinese women nearly holding their own against a superpower that, ultimately, was just a little bit stronger and luckier—this time.

NOTES

Some of the descriptive sections of this chapter were presented elsewhere within different conceptual frameworks. See the following publications by Susan Brownell: "Gender and Nationalism in China at the Turn of the Millennium," in *China Briefing 2000: The Continuing Transformation*, ed. Tyrene White (New York: M. E. Sharpe in cooperation with The Asia Society, 2000), 195–232; "Strong Women and Impotent Men: Sports, Gender, and Nationalism in Chinese Public Culture," in *Spaces of Their Own: Women's Public Sphere in Transnational China*, ed. Mayfair Mei-Hui Yang (Minneapolis: University of Minnesota Press, 1999), 207–31; "The Body and the Beautiful in Chinese Nationalism: Sportswomen and Fashion Models in the Reform Era," *China Information* 13, no. 2/3 (autumn/winter 1998–1999): 36–58; "Representing Gender in the Chinese Nation: Chinese Sportswomen and Beijing's Bid for the 2000 Olympic Games," *Identities: Global Studies in Culture and Power*, special issue on "The Nation/State and Its Sexual Dissidents" 2, no. 1 (1996): 223–47.

1. The official explanation was that the bombing was a mistake due to the use of an outdated map.

2. I wish to express my thanks to Jeff Wasserstrom for drawing my attention to the role of gender in the May demonstrations and Tyrene White for asking me to take a look at the women's World Cup in soccer.

3. See James Townsend's definition of modern nationalism in "Chinese Nationalism," in *Chinese Nationalism*, ed. Jonathan Unger (New York: M. E. Sharpe, 1996), 8.

4. Andrew Morris, *Marrow of the Nation: A History of Sport and Physical Culture in Republican China* (Berkeley: University of California Press, 2004), 26.

5. Tani Barlow argued that "woman" did not exist as a unitary category until the term *nüxing* (lit. "female sex") entered usage during the May Fourth Movement (1919). In imperial China there was no generic category of Woman; there were daughters in the family (*nü*), married wives (*fu*), and mothers (*mu*). Gender occupied a different place in the nation, and the neologism *nüxing* helped accomplish that shift: it made "woman" into a sign that could be used in the attack on Confucianism and "Chinese culture." See Tani E. Barlow, "Theorizing Woman: *Funü, Guojia, Jiating* (Chinese Woman, Chinese State, Chinese Family)," in *Body, Subject and Power in China*, ed. Angela Zito and Tani Barlow (Chicago: University of Chicago Press, 1994), 254, 265.

6. Prasenjit Duara, *Rescuing History from the Nation: Questioning Narratives of Modern China* (Chicago: University of Chicago Press, 1995), 11–12.

7. There was a brief interlude when femininity appeared in public images in the mid-1950s, when women were urged to withdraw from the labor force to help lower the level of urban unemployment, and an interest in feminine fashion encouraged. See

Harriet Evans, *Women and Sexuality in China: Female Sexuality and Gender since 1949* (New York: Continuum, 1997), 137.

8. Yang, *Spaces of Their Own*, 45–46; Dai Jinhua, "Invisible Women: Contemporary Chinese Cinema and Women's Film," *Positions: East Asia Cultures Critique* 3, no. 1 (1995): 255–80; Emily Honig, "Maoist Mappings of Gender: Reassessing the Red Guards," in *Chinese Femininities/Chinese Masculinities: A Reader*, ed. Susan Brownell and Jeffrey N. Wasserstrom (Berkeley: University of California Press, 2002), 255–68.

9. Honig, "Maoist Mappings of Gender," 263–64; Mayfair Mei-hui Yang, "From Gender Erasure to Gender Difference: State Feminism, Consumer Sexuality, and Women's Public Sphere in China," in Yang, *Spaces of Their Own*, 43.

10. For an official Chinese history, see Rong Gaotang et al., eds., *Dangdai Zhongguo tiyu* [Contemporary Chinese Sports] (Beijing: Chinese Social Sciences Press, 1984), esp. 197–200, 429–30. For the sports coverage, see the front-page headlines outlined in red in *Tiyu bao* [Sports News], November 17, 1981, and numerous articles from then through mid-December; see also *Xin Tiyu* [New Sports], December 1981.

11. Although people often *said* that the women had erased the label, people's sentiments of national humiliation remained, and twenty-six years later people were expressing the hope that the 2008 Beijing Olympic Games would *finally* erase the label. This demonstrates how slow national mythologies can be to change, especially when they serve the ruling political interests.

12. *Xin Tiyu* [New Sports],"*Kan nüpai duo kui huaxu*" [Tidbits from Watching Women's Volleyball Seize Supremacy], December 1981, 22.

13. Susan Brownell interview with Song Shixiong, China Central Television Station, Beijing, May 21, 1994. The interview was in Chinese and is translated by the author.

14. Cao Xiangjun, *Tiyu Gailun* [General Theory of Physical Culture] (Beijing: Beijing Institute of Physical Education Press, 1985), 139.

15. Rong Gaotang et al., eds., *Dangdai Zhongguo tiyu* [Contemporary Chinese Sports] (Beijing: Chinese Social Sciences Press, 1984), 429.

16. Xie Baisan and Zhang Ming, "*Nüdaxuesheng bitan nanxingmei: Meixue xinli diaocha*" [Female College Students Discuss the Masculine Ideal: A Psychological Aesthetics Survey], *Beijing daxue xiaokan* [Beijing University School Newspaper], vol. 91 (October 1985).

17. Wang Mingjun, an open letter to the public, in *Tiyu bao* [Sports News], December 11, 1981.

18. The Yuan Ming Garden ruins carry a heavy load of tragic symbolism in China; a section of the Summer Palace built in 1709 was fashioned out of marble imitating the neoclassical buildings then popular in the West, but it was burned and looted by French and British troops in 1860 in the second Opium War, when China was forced to accept British opium imports and open its ports to trade. It is now a popular tourist site. China's International Olympic Committee member He Zhenliang told me that he had never visited it because of its unpleasant associations.

19. Dai Jinhua, "Rewriting Chinese Women: Gender Production and Cultural Space in the Eighties and Nineties," in Yang, *Spaces of Their Own*, 195–99.

20. Dong Jinxia argues that what appeared to be sudden success actually built on a foundation that had been laid starting in the 1950s, that government investment in women's sports had continued throughout the 1970s, and that the Cultural Revolution was not as disastrous at lower levels as it was at the elite levels. See Dong Jinxia, *Women, Sport and Society in Modern China: Holding Up* More *Than Half the Sky* (London and Portland: Frank Cass, 2003), 73–96.

21. "1995 Pan Pacific Games—Drug Piece," produced by Richard Brenner for NBC Sports, 1995.

22. Zhao Yu, "*Qiangguo meng*" [Superpower Dream], *Dangdai* [Contemporary Times], February 1988, 182.

23. Xu Yongjiu, "*Zai jian, jingzou!*" [Goodbye, Racewalking!], *Tiyu bao* [Sports news], January 29, 1988, 1.

24. Cao, *Tiyu Gailun*, 137.

25. Zou Xia, "China's Women 'Judokas,'" *China Reconstructs*, March 1984, 38–39.

26. Xie Kainan, "Giant Cagerette Chen Yuefang," *China Sports*, April 1983, 6–7.

27. Harriet Evans, "Past, Perfect or Imperfect: Changing Images of the Ideal Wife," in Brownell and Wasserstrom, *Chinese Femininities/Chinese Masculinities*, 335–60.

28. Meng Yue, "Female Images and National Myth," in *Gender Politics in Modern China*, ed. Tani E. Barlow (Durham, N.C.: Duke University Press, 1993), 134–35.

29. Yang, *Spaces of Their Own*, 51; Judith Farquhar, "Technologies of Everyday Life: The Economy of Impotence in Reform China," *Cultural Anthropology* 14, no. 2 (May 1999): 168; Everett Yuehong Zhang, "Rethinking Sexual Repression in Maoist China: Structure, Ideology, and the Ownership of the Body," *Body and Society* 11, no. 3 (2005): 1–25.

30. None of Ma's athletes ever tested positive, but when a test for EPO was developed just in time for the 2000 Sydney Olympic Games, most of his team was kept home when their hemoglobin levels were found to be excessively high. It might be noted that at least one top U.S. runner withdrew at the last moment, too, while others showed precipitous drops in performance.

31. "Chinese Raise Questions," *Track and Field News*, November 1993, 74.

32. "Chinese Official Denies Drug Accusations," *China Daily*, September 8, 1993.

33. "Star Coach Reveals His Secrets," *China Daily*, September 13, 1993.

34. "Ma's Army Disbands," *Track and Field News*, April 1995, 59.

35. Yu Yilei, "Official Hopes World Cup Success to Ease Plight," *China Daily*, July 12, 1999, 10.

36. The discussion of the Chinese media coverage and popular reactions to it is based on a survey of *China Daily*, *Renmin ribao* (*People's Daily*, overseas edition), and *Guangming ribao* (*Guangming Daily*) from May 10 to May 13, 1999. The English-language *China Daily* is obviously intended to sway an Anglophone audience; the *People's Daily* is the official mouthpiece of the Communist Party; the *Guangming Daily* targets intellectuals and was particularly significant in this case since two of the deceased were its reporters. In addition, the archives of the websites of H-Asia (www.h-asia.msu.edu) and China News Digest (www.cnd.org) (including

Huxia wenzhai, the Chinese-language digest) were surveyed. The H-Asia archives surveyed included David Cowhig's summaries of postings from the Chinese-language website netease.com.

37. Capital Women's Journalists Association, "Cowardly, Barbaric Act," letter to the editor, *China Daily*, May 10, 1999, 4. Interestingly, a report on the association in the May 10 *People's Daily* omits the mention of violence against women and calls it simply a "trampling of human lives." The *People's Daily* did not foreground gender as much as the other two papers surveyed, which is consistent with its position as an official party medium that is less reflective of popular sentiment than other media.

38. Xiong Lei, "NATO Killing of Innocent Feeds Silent Hypocrisy," letter to the editor, *China Daily*, May 10, 1999, 4.

39. "Zhongguo xinwenjie tongdao xunzhi tonghang" [Chinese Journalism Circles Sadly Mourn Colleagues Who Died in the Line of Duty], *Renmin ribao* [People's Daily], May 10, 1999, 2.

40. Jeffrey N. Wasserstrom, "Student Protests in Fin-de-Siècle China," *New Left Review* 237 (September–October 1999): 52–76.

41. This merging of the personal and the political is probably traceable to the Confucian conception of the patriarchal family as a microcosm of the state. A strict separation of the private/domestic from the public/state realms is said to be a characteristic of the West since the eighteenth century.

42. It is also common to publish the diaries of celebrity athletes, coaches, and officials attending major international championships. He Zhenliang published two diaries for the 1993 and 2001 IOC Sessions at which China presented bids for the Olympic Games.

43. Bian Ji, "Journalist's Father Writes to Clinton," *China Daily*, May 11, 1999, 2.

44. "Zhi Qieerxide fuqin Meiguo zongtong Kelindunde xin" [A Letter to Chelsea's Father, American President Clinton], *Guangming ribao* [Guangming Daily], May 11, 1999, 4.

45. Wasserstrom, "Student Protests in Fin-de-Siècle China," 68.

46. "*Hui Jia*" [Coming Home], *Renmin ribao*, May 13, 1999, 3.

47. "Sun: A Student, Poet, Singer, Scorer," *China Daily*, July 9, 1999, 10.

48. "Women's Soccer Team 'Marvellous,'" *China Daily*, July 12, 1999, 1.

49. Jiang Yu, "State Accolade for Heroines," *China Daily*, July 14, 1999, 1.

Chapter Five

Mixing Sport and Politics

China and the International Olympic Committee

The International Olympic Committee (IOC) is a particularly unique institution, and because it is so unusual, it is not especially well understood, but this is precisely what makes it so significant: it offers an alternative to the usual modes and channels of international politics. There is a widespread mythology that "sports should be separate from politics" and that the IOC's official policy is to "keep politics out of sport." Based on this mistaken belief, in the intensely political atmosphere surrounding the Beijing Olympic Games the question was often raised, Why have sports "suddenly" become so political? China was frequently blamed for politicizing the Olympics. Actually, national politics had been a part of the Olympic Games at least since the 1906 Intermediate Olympic Games in Athens, only the fourth modern Olympics and the first at which athletes marched behind national flags in groups organized by National Olympic Committees and three national flags were hoisted for the medal winners. Peter O'Connor, the silver medalist in the triple jump, climbed the flagpole to wave the Irish flag in protest over the British Union Jack that had been raised for the ceremony since the British Olympic Council had monopolized the Irish entries and he had been unable to register as an Irish athlete.[1] The presidents of the IOC during the Cold War—Sigfrid Edström, Avery Brundage, and Lord Michael Killanin—began using the admonition "don't mix politics with sport" as a way of preserving the Olympic Games amidst the irresolvable political oppositions of the time, but there has never been an official policy explicitly forbidding members to engage in "politics." The closest thing to an official policy has been the Fundamental Principle in the Olympic Charter, first added in 1949, stating that there shall be no discrimination on the grounds of color, religion, or politics.[2] When Beijing was bidding for the 2008 Games in 2001, that article in the

Charter had been watered down and the word "politics" erased to read, "sport practised without discrimination of any kind and in the Olympic spirit, which requires mutual understanding with a spirit of friendship, solidarity and fair play."[3] This was modified in the 2004 Charter, the one in effect in 2007, to name "politics" again. Fundamental Principle #5 stated, "Any form of discrimination with regard to a country or a person on grounds of race, religion, politics, gender or otherwise is incompatible with belonging to the Olympic Movement."[4]

In short, there is no official policy within the IOC against "mixing sport with politics," and the politicization of the Beijing Olympic Games will continue a 102-year-old Olympic tradition.

On the other hand, it is true that sports often provide an alternative channel to mainstream diplomacy that may have reached a dead end. Because of its alternative character, sports diplomacy has played a particularly important role in the diplomatic history of the People's Republic of China (PRC) since its founding in 1949, and in 2008 we will be seeing the results of decades of complex interactions between the foreign policies of the IOC, China, Taiwan, the United States, and other countries being played out on the Olympic playing fields. This chapter tries to represent the mainland Chinese view of this period of history—a view that is not generally known or understood in the West.

THE "CHINA PROBLEM" IN THE IOC

The PRC was established on October 1, 1949. The defeated Nationalist Party (Kuomintang) headed by General Chiang Kai-shek fled to the island of Taiwan, also known in the West as Formosa, taking with them the name of their defeated regime, the Republic of China (ROC). The two governments each claimed to be the legitimate government of all of China and remained in a state of mutual hostility. Direct contacts were forbidden. From the point of view of the mainlanders who had taken part in the revolution, the island was being used as a renegade outpost from which to challenge the authority of the Chinese Communist Party, which had won a brutal civil war. It was an illegitimate and corrupt regime that survived only because it was propped up by the United States and Western powers. Its continued existence was—and is—a challenge to Chinese national territorial sovereignty. At first, most nations retained diplomatic relations with the regime on Taiwan, which held a seat in the United Nations until the PRC's admission in 1971. In both the PRC and the ROC, the policy was guided by the "one China principle," which tolerated no expression of ethnic Taiwanese separatism and held the goal of reunifying

China under one regime. In the PRC, with respect to membership in international organizations, the guiding principle was "first expel, then we enter." In other words, an international organization must first expel the "Chiang Kai-shek clique" before China would apply for admission.

The biography of He Zhenliang, China's senior sports diplomat and the PRC's first member in the IOC, is an insider account of the history of the PRC's relationship with the IOC. Written by his wife, Liang Lijuan, a journalist, it was first published in 2000; a new edition was published in 2005, and the English translation by myself was published in 2007.[5] From He's biography, it can be seen that foreign sport policy was largely created and implemented by the International Department of the State Sports Commission through communications with top leaders. "Guiding principles" were handed down by top leaders through policy documents, speeches, occasional meetings, and other channels. The members of the International Department were keenly sensitive to these guiding principles and monitored their own affairs accordingly. When they encountered particularly difficult problems in their work, they held group meetings in which a "Request for Instructions" (*qingshi*) was produced. Sometimes the Ministry of Foreign Affairs was involved in generating these documents. These documents were an outline of a problem, an assessment of possible solutions, and a request for a decision from the top leadership. This system is essentially the one that is still in place today.

From 1949 to his death in 1976, Premier Zhou Enlai was most frequently the top leader who received the Request for Instructions. He was the leading influence on Chinese sport foreign policy from the founding of the republic, and his views continued to shape policy after his death. He was most frequently the state leader who met with national teams before and after their competitions abroad, he gave instructions to the Chinese sports diplomats and officials about how to deal with foreign countries, and he clarified policies toward Taiwan in the realm of sports. He was the figure identified by He Zhenliang, who would later become China's leading sports diplomat, as his model.[6] Zhou was a firm advocate of the "one China principle" in sports, and it was this stance of Zhou that shaped Chinese sport diplomacy.

The PRC sent its first Olympic delegation to the 1952 Helsinki Olympic Games at the urging of the Soviet Union, which had joined the IOC in the previous year and was hoping to strengthen the socialist presence at its first Olympic Games. At the 47th IOC Session in Helsinki on July 17, 1952, two days before the opening ceremony of the Helsinki Olympics and after a long discussion by the IOC membership, a compromise proposal was approved in which neither of the national Olympic committees of China and Taiwan was formally recognized, but each was allowed to compete in the sports in which its national governing body was recognized by the respective international federation. Taiwan boycotted the Olympic Games, and after being apprised that they would do so, the mainland delegation only arrived just before the closing ceremony because of the difficulty in traveling imposed by the fact that most countries did not have diplomatic relations with the PRC. This was the first time that the national flag of the PRC had been raised at the Olympic Games, and as He Zhenliang stood with the team for the flag-raising ceremony in the Otaniemi Forest Olympic Village (where China had been separately housed with the other socialist countries at the request of the Soviet Union),

> he felt extremely proud and elated. At that moment Zhenliang absolutely did not imagine that from that point on, he would end up spending the years of his youth waging a nearly thirty-year battle with the forces within the IOC that were hostile toward China, in order that the red five-star flag would rightfully be raised over the Olympic Games again.[7]

In 1954, at Soviet initiative and with no representatives from Taiwan or China present, the Athens IOC Session recognized the "Olympic Committee of Democratic China" (i.e., the PRC but mistakenly called by a different name) by a vote of 23 to 21.[8] In the IOC Minutes, these committees were generally called the "Chinese Olympic Committee having its seat in Peking" and the "Chinese Olympic Committee having its seat on Taiwan." There were then two Chinese national Olympic committees claiming jurisdiction over one national territory. This was used by the mainland Chinese and their supporters for the next twenty-five years to argue that the IOC had violated its own Olympic Charter, which stated that only one National Olympic Committee could be recognized in a country.

This state of affairs was unacceptable to the PRC because of the "expel the Chiang Clique" guiding principle. At IOC meetings in 1955 and 1956, the Chinese felt that their legitimate request for recognition and the expulsion of Taiwan was not heard and that the other socialist nations were not standing up for what was right because they were more concerned with their own agendas. At the 50th IOC Session in Paris in 1955, the Soviet member Constantin Andrianov discouraged the Chinese member Dong Shouyi from speaking and even physically restrained him from standing up when he tried to do so because he feared that China would negatively influence the status of the newly admitted socialist nations within the IOC and might get itself expelled for being too "political."[9] This was in the time period when the Chinese were beginning to feel that the Soviets were too conciliatory to the West, before the Sino–Soviet split flared publicly in 1960.

When China's advance group arrived at the Melbourne Olympic Games in 1956, it discovered that Taiwan had already entered the Olympic Village, registered under the name "Formosa, China," and the "illegitimate national flag" of the ROC had been raised. The mainland Chinese declared that they were pulling out of the Games. In Liang's analysis,

> The fight on the sports frontline reflected the battles in international politics. The imperialist elements who were hostile to the revolutionary victory of the new China had a bottomless bag of tricks with which they propped up the fallen Chiang Kai-shek clique, and at every stop they obstructed China's legitimate right to recover its place on the international stage. It was like that in the United Nations, and it was like that in the international sports organizations. At the time, our enemies within the IOC were relatively strong and we were weak. . . . At that time there were very few Asian and African members within the IOC, and even those few were influenced by the West, to the point that some of them did not themselves belong to Asian and African countries, such as Kenya's member, Reginald Alexander, a white Briton who had been mayor of Nairobi and who was also a colonial plantation owner. On the contrary, more often than not they echoed the conservative, reactionary political views of the West. There was simply no reasoning within the IOC: the Charter and resolutions could all be arbitrarily tampered with, and this state of affairs could not be changed in a single day.[10]

At the 52nd Session in Melbourne in November, the IOC decided that a letter should be sent to the Peking Chinese Committee expressing "displeasure [at its] repeatedly raising political questions which have no place in IOC discussions." Dong Shouyi expressed opposition to the assertion that these were "political" discussions in a letter written to President Avery Brundage in December 1957 contesting the minutes. This was the beginning of the end of China's relationship with the IOC. The rise of "extreme leftist ideology" in China at that time was reflected in the tone of the letters exchanged with Brundage. Brundage contested the PRC's view of its own history. Dong wrote a fierce reply to Brundage (the letter was drafted by He Zhenliang) that included this paragraph:

> As for your remark "There is a seperate [*sic*] Government in Taiwan," Mr. President, you must not forget how this situation is brought about. . . . That these traitors are able to survive in Taiwan until today is due to the political, economic and military aid openly given by the U.S. Government and open interference in the internal affairs of our country by the U.S. Government.[11]

Brundage's reply on June 1 continued to insist, "The IOC has nothing to do with politics. It does not recognize nor deal with governments," and threatened to request his resignation.[12]

"SPORT AND POLITICS DON'T MIX"[13]

Brundage, who was president from 1952 to 1972 and is the only American to have held that position, frequently used the ban against "mixing politics and sport" or "talking politics" to silence opposition, even threatening to expel IOC members if they continued to bring up "political" matters. In this he continued a tradition already begun by the previous president, Sigfrid Edström (1942–1952), and strengthened by his own stance against boycotting the 1936 "Hitler" Olympics in Berlin. Allen Guttmann argues that Brundage shared Pierre de Coubertin's vision of the Olympic Games as nonpolitical and was never able to understand that calling for freedom from government interference was ipso facto a political position.[14] In his January 8 letter to Dong Shouyi, he even claimed that "one of the fundamental principles [of the Olympic code] is that there shall be no politics in sport."[15] As mentioned previously, the Fundamental Principles of the Olympic Charter did not state that there shall be no politics in sport. That the IOC members believed Brundage is indicated by Andrianov's admonition to the Chinese in 1955, mentioned above. Of course, Andrianov was probably not well versed in the nuances of parliamentary procedure in the second year after the death of Stalin. Nor was Brundage the keen political thinker that the later president Juan-Antonio Samaranch would be (1980–2002), but he was clever and domineering enough to ram his desired results through the Session by utilizing tactics that had the appearance of being legitimate but were probably violations of the Charter and bylaws.

China prepared to withdraw from all international sports organizations that "practiced 'Two Chinas.'" Representatives from friendly socialist countries were called to Beijing in August in order to discuss this decision; the Soviets supported it while warning that this would severely curtail China's international sports exchanges because of the contamination rules in the international federations (i.e., members who competed with non-members were subject to expulsion). On August 19 the Chinese Olympic Committee issued a press release stating that it was suspending all relationships with the IOC.[16]

Dong also wrote to President Brundage and the IOC members expressing his resignation and accusing Brundage of being "a faithful menial of the US imperialists bent on serving their plot of creating 'two Chinas.'" And further, "To uphold the Olympic spirit and tradition, I hereby declare that I will no longer cooperate with you or have any connections with the IOC while it is under your domination."[17] China thus began the period of twenty-one years of exclusion from the IOC, along with internal chaos. The economically disastrous Great Leap Forward began in 1958.

GANEFO AND PING-PONG DIPLOMACY

After China's withdrawal from the IOC, its diplomatic efforts turned toward Asia, Africa, and Latin America. The 1962 Asian Games were held in Indonesia, with which the PRC had established diplomatic relations. The Indonesians privately assured the mainland Chinese that Taiwan would not compete, but they were unwilling to take a public stance. In the end, the identity cards mailed by the Indonesian organizers to Taiwan mysteriously disappeared in the mail, and the team was unable to enter Indonesia. The IOC withdrew its patronage of the Asian Games and threatened sanctions, which angered Indonesia's President Sukarno. Inspired by the success of the 1955 Bandung Conference, which had led to the formation of the Non-Aligned Movement in 1961, he led the establishment of the Games of the New Emerging Forces (GANEFO). The First GANEFO in Djakarta in 1963 attracted forty-eight nations. It also marked China's first full-scale participation in a major, international, multisport event. In Liang's assessment, "It was not until after that fierce attack that the international sport organizations, including the IOC, gradually paid attention to the voices of the developing nations and changed their own courses toward democratic management and the genuine meaning of 'universalism.'"[18] A coup d'etat in Indonesia and the Cultural Revolution in China put an end to GANEFO.

Because of the Cultural Revolution, China had stopped taking part in international sporting events until a personal entreaty from Koji Goto, the head of the Japanese Table Tennis Federation, persuaded Chairman Mao to send a team to the 31st World Cup in Table Tennis in Japan in March 1971, where they had friendly contacts with the U.S. team. The American team was officially invited to visit China from Japan, which it did in mid-April. The Americans returned the invitation and a Chinese team visited the United States in April 1972. These exchanges were known as "ping-pong diplomacy," and in China it is said that "the little globe moved the big globe."[19] Ping-pong diplomacy paved the way for China's admission into the United Nations in October 1971. In 1971, the Asia-Africa Table Tennis Invitational was held in Beijing, followed by the 1972 Asian Table Tennis Cup and the 1973 Asia–Africa–Latin America Table Tennis Invitational. Over eighty nations and territories, many of which did not have diplomatic relations with China, participated in the latter three-continent event. It became a launching pad for the establishment of diplomatic relations.[20] Premier Zhou oversaw much of the diplomacy that surrounded these tournaments. At the conclusion of each, the premier received the athletes and participants.[21]

This tournament was also notable for the fact that, at Zhou's suggestion, a contingent of Taiwanese living in the United States and Japan took part under the name "China, Taiwan Province, Overseas Compatriots Table Tennis team."[22] After Zhou's death, this would be remembered and offered as a solution to the "China problem" in the IOC, with a stamp of legitimacy provided by the belief that Zhou would have approved.

At the initiative of Iran, the host of the 1974 Asian Games, and with the support of Japan, China was admitted to the Asian Games Federation in November 1973. This was the first time since 1959 that China had succeeded in being admitted to a major international sport organization and having Taiwan expelled. Liang observed,

> This victory reflected new changes in the structure of Asian politics. The friendly forces in Asia had already surpassed the conservative forces . . . although there were still many diehard conservatives in the international sports federations, they could not oppose all of Asia.[23]

Lord Killanin followed Brundage as IOC president in 1972. In contrast to Brundage, from the very start he expressed his friendship and support to the Chinese, while he was considered antagonistic by the Taiwanese.[24]

The China problem heated up before the 1976 Montreal Olympics. Canada had recently formed diplomatic relations with the PRC, and Prime Minister Pierre Trudeau declared that Taiwan could compete only under the name "Taiwan." Taiwan did not accept Trudeau's conditions and withdrew at the last moment.[25]

The Cultural Revolution officially ended in 1976. Chairman Mao died, Deng Xiaoping rose to power, and in 1978 the Era of Reform and Opening Up began.

It was not until January 1, 1979, nearly eight years after ping-pong diplomacy, that China and the United States announced the establishment of diplomatic relations and, as the major precondition, the United States acknowledged the PRC as the sole legitimate government of China. In March at the Executive Board meeting in Lausanne, Killanin observed that the IOC was faced with a practical problem created by politics over which it had no control: "[The Taiwanese] have internationally become a non-people." They could not, for example, compete under their national flag and name in any of the countries of the members of the Executive Board seated around the table. "It's no good recognizing people who can't compete internationally."[26]

China also changed its official policy toward Taiwan's membership in international organizations, no longer insisting on the expulsion of Taiwan but allowing Taiwan to maintain its membership so long as it was denoted as a province of China and did not use the name "Republic of China." This policy was not openly communicated to the IOC, however, because the "battle strategy" was that the issue of Taiwan's changing its name would not be raised by the Chinese themselves.[27]

CHINA'S READMISSION TO THE IOC IN 1979

At the 80th Athens Session in 1978, the Soviet member Andrianov came out more strongly in support of China than he had in the past, and the Chinese felt this was because the Soviets were worried that a boycott might mar the Moscow Olympic Games; it was estimated that as many as thirty-four nations might boycott if Taiwan participated and China were excluded.[28] Killanin established a three-member committee to visit China and Taiwan and submit a report. The committee was made up of New Zealand's Lance Cross, Romania's Alexandru Siperco, and Jamaica's Roy Anthony Bridge. Killanin had assumed that Siperco would favor mainland China, Bridge would favor Taiwan, and Cross would be neutral; thus, the committee would be balanced.

Cross was later remembered with no fondness by either Lord Killanin or the mainland Chinese. Killanin had not expected that he would come out strongly in support of Taiwan and end up being Killanin's main opponent on the issue in the Executive Board. Probably Killanin had not done his homework on Cross before establishing the commission—in fact, Taiwanese member Henry Hsu's memoirs indicate that the Taiwanese had identified Cross as a friend as early as Hsu's election to the IOC in 1970.[29] When Killanin visited Taiwan in 1977, he arrived to find Cross awaiting him and wanting to accompany him, an offer that he declined. He later recalled that at that point, "I had made a mistake in the composition of my Commission."[30]

Cross, a quick-talking radio announcer, had become an IOC member in 1969. The IOC member in New Zealand whom he succeed, Sir Arthur Porritt, opposed his election to the IOC and wrote to Lord Killanin that he was not a suitable person because he was a professional sports broadcaster. Cross's stance against mixing sport and politics was no doubt strengthened by the African boycott of the 1976 Montreal Olympic Games over the visit of a New Zealand rugby team to South Africa. He had argued that the boycott was unjustified since rugby was not an Olympic sport and was not under the control either of the New Zealand government or the IOC.[31] During the visit to China, the mainland Chinese felt that Cross was particularly antagonistic. They also protested the visit of the committee to Taiwan after it left China. Cross and Bridge went to Taiwan anyway, and because of Cross's later friendly stance toward Taiwan, the mainland Chinese perceived that he had become even more outspoken in favor of Taiwan and suspected that the Taiwan side had "worked" on him.[32] This viewpoint reflected the common view in the mainland that Taiwan had a habit of using bribery to achieve its political goals. This view was reinforced by Killanin, who, as described below, implied to the Chinese that Lance Cross had been "bought off."

At the Executive Board in Lausanne on March 10, 1979, Cross, as head of the China Commission, argued vigorously for an arrangement under which both the PRC and the ROC changed their names, claiming that "geographic" designations would sidestep the "political" problem: "That's why I tried to avoid political determinations because the IOC cannot be involved in a political decision. Let the political people make those decisions."[33] The Executive Board received a Chinese delegation at this meeting. He Zhenliang answered the discussion questions, and Lou Dapeng[34] acted as his interpreter. He Zhenliang had begun his career as a French interpreter for top Chinese leaders and since French is an official language of the IOC could have dispensed with using an interpreter, but this was a tactic to allow him time to collect his thoughts before speaking. In He's recollection, Cross was the only Executive Board member to "persist in being unreasonable." Cross asked, "It is a fact that there are two regimes existing, both claiming control of respective areas and this has been existent for 26 years without the respective governments reaching a solution. Why is it felt that the IOC should solve it?" He Zhenliang replied in Chinese and Lou Dapeng translated into English, "This is an interesting question. The IOC is a non-political body that considers questions from the interest of sports."[35] He Zhenliang's biography recalls with some relish that he gave a slight smile with his answer because he felt he had used Cross's favorite aphorism—"don't mix sport and politics"—against him. Cross had raised the political question, and He could use only politics to answer him. Cross was—for once—rendered speechless.[36]

At the 81st Session of the IOC in Montevideo in April 1979, the mainland Chinese conceded that after their "rightful place" was restored, they could allow Taiwan to remain in the IOC as a local Chinese organization. This was in accord with the change in the Taiwan policy that had occurred after the restoration of Sino–U.S. relations. The "one China principle" was still in effect, however. The prerequisite would be that Taiwan could not use the written words "Republic of China" or the word "Taiwan" alone, nor could it use the flag, anthem, or any other symbol representing the "Republic of China." This was the first time in an IOC meeting that the Chinese Olympic Committee had made such a concession. However, the Session was unable to reach any resolution.[37]

After the Session, the Executive Board continued meeting through the night into the early morning of April 7, when they proposed to offer to the Session a draft resolution. While maintaining some degree of neutrality, Killanin felt that they had already established that the PRC would not change its

name, flag, or anthem and that, if they were asked to, it would end the negotiations. Cross stubbornly held the position that both Olympic committees
must be treated equitably—meaning that both must be asked to change their
names, flags, and anthems, not just the Taiwan side. He explained,

> There seems to me, Mr. Chairman, a very definite desire to create a superior and
> an inferior group, and the moment we do that we're playing politics. We decide
> on the rules and if people don't accept them they don't get in. I'm not being mul-
> ish about this. But I think my record is well-known. In the years I've been on
> the Olympic Committee, I have fought very hard to free the IOC and its deci-
> sions from any political connotations whatsoever and I'll go on fighting to have
> the IOC establish itself in the eyes of the sporting world as an organization that's
> led the way in divorcing politics from sport.
>
> Killanin: I think on that basis we should decide to recognize neither.
>
> Cross: You're already got one, you can't do that.[38]

Despite Killanin's opposition, the Montevideo Session produced a resolution
requiring both sides to change their names.[39] The mainland Chinese issued a
statement that they could not accept this resolution but were willing to engage
in further discussions with the IOC. According to Liang, in a meeting with the
Chinese delegation Killanin said, "Even though I have worked very hard, I
still suffered defeat—apparently Taiwan has bought off more than a few people."[40] As mentioned, Lance Cross was one of the people whom the Chinese
thought had been bought by the Taiwanese.

The Montevideo Session had elected a new Executive Board in which the
balance of power was more in China's favor. In June, the Executive Board appointed a three-person working group consisting of First Vice President Mo-
hammed Mzali of Tunisia as the head and including Siperco and Cross. They
drew up a draft resolution:

1. To confirm the recognition of the Olympic committee located in Peking [Bei-
   jing] under the name of "Chinese Olympic Committee."
2. To maintain the recognition of the Olympic committee located in Taipeh
   [Taipei] under the name of "Chinese Taipeh Olympic Committee," on the
   condition that the latter adopts an anthem and a flag which are different from
   those of the "Republic of China" used until now.[41]

Because of Cross's obstruction, the Executive Board was unable to pass the
resolution but did solicit more support and confirm the resolution at its October meeting in Nagoya.[42] Since there was not enough time to take the resolution to the IOC Session before the Lake Placid Winter Games, through
a postal vote, the IOC membership approved the resolution by a count of

62 to 17, with one abstention.[43] At that point the mainland Chinese Olympic Committee agreed to the resolution, but the Taiwan side refused, claiming the Executive Board had overturned the decision of the Session and opposing the use of a postal vote. Taiwanese member Henry Hsu filed suit against the IOC in a Swiss law court—the first time that an IOC member had initiated a suit against the IOC. A second lawsuit was filed on behalf of Taiwanese athletes in a Lake Placid court. These were unprecedented actions that stimulated an ongoing process of the rigidification of the IOC's rules as protection against litigation.

Afterward, the "Olympic formula" was used to settle the question of the use of national symbols in other organizations and international settings. China is known as the "Olympic Committee of the People's Republic of China" and competes under the national anthem and flag of the PRC. Taiwan is known as the "Olympic Committee of Chinese Taipei" and competes under the anthem and flag of its Olympic committee. Liang writes,

> It was a tremendous victory with profound significance for us in international sports organizations. Beginning in 1951 with the preparations to participate in the 1952 Helsinki Olympic Games, this fight to maintain China's legitimate rights in the world of international sports, and uphold state sovereignty and territorial integrity, was fought for fully 28 years.[44]

In 1981, He Zhenliang was co-opted[45] as the first IOC member in the PRC.

THE IOC'S IGNORANCE ON THE CHINA QUESTION

During these thirty years, the Western-dominated IOC showed a striking insensitivity to the question of national names. Although the names used to designate the different Olympic committees were at the center of the China question for thirty years, the IOC rarely managed to get the names right. In the minutes of the 1952 through 1955 Sessions, the People's Republic of China was called Democratic China, and in 1956 it was called the Democratic People's Republic of China. Dong Shouyi protested this misnaming at the 1956 Session, but the Session minutes did not reflect it, so he wrote a letter asking that the minutes be corrected to reflect the official name of his country. Brundage finally approved the correction in the letter written to Dong in 1958, but Chancellor Otto Mayer does not seem to have gotten it right in his correspondence until around 1964. While it was under Killanin's leadership that the name question was resolved in 1979, in his 1983 book he misnames the PRC as the People's Democratic Republic of China. Cross's insensitivity was illustrated in his statement at an Executive Board meeting that he had once suggested to Taiwan that it call itself by the ancient name "Cathay," but they never took up his suggestion.

In Olympic matters the ROC was often designated with the label Formosa, a Portuguese word first applied to the island by Portuguese sailors in the sixteenth century. It is not a Chinese word and is not used by Chinese speakers. The Nationalist Chinese themselves rejected it because it was associated with the native Taiwanese independence movement; in 1959 ethnic Taiwanese wrote to Brundage in the name of the Formosan Olympic Committee, requesting him to recognize them as representing the people of Formosa and not the Nationalist Chinese.[46] Even as late as the 1979 Montevideo Session in which the China question nearly achieved resolution, the Taiwanese member Henry Hsu had to explain that the ROC had never called itself by this appellation.[47]

Personal names were also consistently misspelled. Dong Shouyi (Shou-yi Tung) was almost never spelled accurately in the minutes, and in his book, Killanin misspelled it as Shou Yi-tung.[48]

The mistakes in names were symptomatic of broader ignorance. The major figures in the IOC did not understand the history of China and Taiwan. Avery Brundage thought he did by virtue of his status as one of the world's foremost collectors of East Asian art, but as a dilettante and an outsider his understanding was very different from the national narratives in which Chinese and Taiwanese were invested; Brundage was too dogmatic to understand this.

THE 1993 AND 2001 BIDS

The period of China's absence from the Olympic Games from 1958 until its return at the Lake Placid Winter Games in 1980 and Los Angeles Summer Games in 1984 is often remembered as a boycott in the West, but this is not a fair assessment. Olympic diplomacy has played a key role in Chinese foreign policy since 1952. Except for the worst years of the Cultural Revolution, China always keenly desired "recognition" on the world stage. During this time the China problem was on the agenda of almost every IOC Session, but because the IOC was unwilling to expel one of its members (Taiwan) and because of the "one China principle" in Taiwan and China, it could not be solved.

As early as 1907, Chinese YMCA patriots asked the famous question, "When will China be able to invite all the world to Peking for an International Olympic contest?"[49] In 1946, the Chinese National Amateur Athletic Federation decided to bid for the 1952 Games, but the outbreak of the civil war prevented it.[50] In February 1979, when China had not yet recovered its seat in the

IOC, Premier Deng Xiaoping had said to a Japanese visitor that when the situation was ready, "We can undertake to hold the Olympics in China." In July 1990, during the preparations for the Asian Games, Deng came to inspect the construction site and asked the accompanying members of the State Sports Commission, "Have you made up your minds to bid for the Olympic Games yet?" Demonstrating the importance in Chinese politics of such seemingly casual statements, these two statements by Deng were a source of great encouragement to the Sports Commission. In October 1990, during the closing ceremony of the Asian Games, a banner was unfurled in the stands with the characters "successful Asian Games, the people look forward to the Olympic Games."[51] In 1991, the central government approved China's bid for the 2000 Olympic Games. China lost to Sydney by two votes at the Monte Carlo Session in 1993. In the IOC corruption scandal that erupted in 1998, it was revealed that the president of the Australian Olympic Committee had offered 50,000 Australian dollars to the national Olympic committees of the IOC members in Kenya and Uganda on the eve of the vote, which might have tipped the balance in Sydney's favor.

The hostility toward China and the failed bid were recalled with some bitterness by He Zhenliang in his "Monte Carlo Diary":

> Recently I was moved by a talk by a student representative from Beijing University, Sun Haiyan. She said that the two-year long bid process made her classmates understand a lot of things. She enumerated the groundless allegations trumped up by certain Western nations, from the so-called gift of terra cotta soldiers to the IOC, to the so-called boycott of the Atlanta Olympic Games if the bid did not succeed, which reveals the hostile attitude towards us and the opposition towards China's strength in Western countries; and it reveals that they do not want China to increase its international influence through hosting the Olympic Games, nor to increase the pace of its progress towards establishing itself as a world power.
>
> There's nothing that makes one happier than a young person who sees the true face of the West. Our young people have indeed become much more mature.[52]

Because of the anger and disappointment in China toward this loss, it would be five more years until the central government would approve a second bid for the 2008 Olympic Games, which was to be decided at the 2001 Moscow Session. As He Zhenliang recalled, this bid was a stronger one from the start:

> In Beijing's first bid eight years before, neither the international environment surrounding China nor the competition between the bid cities was as favorable as this time. That time, it was Beijing that was striving to chase down the other bid cities, running almost neck and neck with Sydney at the end; this time, however, Beijing was the favorite from the start, and it was the other cities that

were chasing Beijing. But the situation still had its complexities. Internationally, there were still political powers that were attempting to use "human rights" and other problems as an excuse to interfere in Olympic affairs and oppose Beijing's hosting of the Olympic Games. Moreover, their oppositional activities were better organized.[53]

How to deal with the human rights issue was debated by BOBICO as the content of the final bid presentation was finalized in meetings in Moscow. As described by He Zhenliang, there were

> different opinions about whether or not to mention that Beijing's hosting the Olympic Games could promote the cause of human rights in China. I and many others all advocated a direct answer. I advocated pointing out that human rights are a common cause of concern for every country, but because the economic development and cultural background of each country are different, or they are at different stages of development, each country has a different order of priorities for those problems related to human rights. China's human rights situation has already had great development, but there is still much work to be done. If the Olympic Games are held in China, it will aid China's opening up and reform, and the establishment of a democratic legal system, thereby further promoting the development of our human rights. BOBICO had a few leaders, however, who advocated not mentioning "human rights," but emphasizing "benefiting all-around human development;" moreover, they were very persistent.

Beijing Mayor Liu Qing invited the members of the working group and the Press Office of the State Council to meet with Vice Premier Li Lanqing to discuss how to handle the human rights question. The Press Office proposed that Vice Premier Li should add a statement in his address to the Session stating that "if the Olympic Games are held in Beijing, it will benefit China's opening up and reform, etc., and it will benefit the development of our human rights." Li felt that it was enough that his draft included the statement that the games would promote "social progress" and that a statement about human rights would not change anyone's mind. He Zhenliang then proposed that Mayor Liu could add a sentence to his presentation stating that the Olympic Games "will benefit development of our human rights." Li said that he would think about it, and later Liu was able to secure his approval when he rode with Li in the same car to a meeting.[54]

This account suggests that the attitude toward human rights among top leaders is so restrictive that it was not considered fitting that a top leader should even mention human rights, and even one sentence from the Beijing mayor had to be negotiated. The account also suggests that while those members of the working group who had daily contact with the international community were convinced that mentioning human rights could make the difference in the vote, the vice premier did not agree. Perhaps this indicates an underestimation of the importance of the topic to the international community by a top Chinese leader.

At the Moscow Session, He Zhenliang gave the final speech of Beijing's bid presentation before the IOC membership. Opening in English, he said, "No matter which decision you make today, it will be recorded in history. However one decision will certainly serve to make history. With your decision here today, you can move the world and China toward an embrace of friendship through sport that will benefit all mankind."[55] He then switched to his more fluent French and said,[56]

> Almost 50 years ago, I took part in the Olympic Games for the first time; it was in Helsinki. Since then, I have become deeply attached to the Olympic spirit. And like so many of my countrymen, I am convinced that the Olympic values are universal and the Olympic flame lights up the way of progress for all humanity.
>
> For many years, the Chinese people have tirelessly pursued the Olympic Ideal, with an unwavering faith in Olympism like your own. It has been a dream of mine throughout my career to find a way to bring the Olympic Games to China. I, too, want my countrymen and women to experience the eternal beauty of the Olympic dream in our homeland.
>
> By voting for Beijing, you will bring the Games for the first time in the history of Olympism to a country with one fifth of the world's population and give to this billion people the opportunity to serve the Olympic Movement with creativity and devotion. Dear Colleagues, the message you send today may signal the beginning of a new era of global unity.
>
> Dear colleagues, if you honor Beijing with the right to host the 2008 Olympic Games, I can assure you that, in seven years from now, Beijing will make you proud of the decision you make here today.
>
> Thank you.

Beijing won in the second round with fifty-six votes, with Toronto coming in second with twenty-two votes. When a journalist asked He Zhenliang what he felt when the bid was announced, he said, "I am proud of my country, I am proud of my people."

China's top leader, Jiang Zemin, invited the members of the Politburo to watch the live broadcast with him. He was so moved by the throngs of people celebrating in the streets that he made a rare spontaneous appearance, first at the Millennium Monument and then at Tiananmen Square, where he climbed onto the rostrum of the Gate of Heavenly Peace and led the crowd in singing the "Ode to the Ancestral Land."[57] He flew to Moscow the next day, where he met with the IOC president, four vice presidents, and the secretary-general. At that meeting, IOC President Juan Antonio Samaranch requested a five-minute private meeting. He used those minutes to suggest to President Jiang that China had a golden opportunity to change its international image and that it should seize the moment. He suggested that President Jiang should declare a general pardon. While the account of this request does not specify, it appears that he was referring to a general pardon for political prisoners. This request was received politely and ignored. He Zhenliang, who had repeatedly advised him not to make this request, observed, "Apparently he was excessively self-confident and did not clearly understand Chinese politics."[58]

THE POLITICAL IS PERSONAL

China's emergence as a world sports power was built on the backs of individual people who worked very hard to achieve goals that had great personal meaning for them. Many of them had endured war and poverty under the nationalist regime and the Japanese occupation and risked their lives for the Communist Revolution. The PRC was one among the wave of new nations that started to emerge after World War II as former colonial empires collapsed and their colonies gained independence, a world transformation that the international sports world was slow to accommodate. To break the "death grip" of the powerful Western nations over international sports, they cultivated personal networks of support among Asian, African, and socialist nations. This was a very human process, and the politics were often very personal. Because I want to do justice to their sentiments (which are not and cannot be my own), let me allow the words of He Zhenliang to end this chapter. In his speech in the ceremony celebrating Beijing's victorious bid, before an audience of nearly 10,000 in the Great Hall of the People, He Zhenliang said,

> After it was announced that Beijing had won, the entire Congress Hall thundered with applause. Dozens of members lined up to come embrace me with warm congratulations. My wish of many years had finally been fulfilled and I could not hold back the tears of joy. When the Chinese Taipei member Wu Ching-kuo embraced me, tears covered both of our faces, and he said to me, "I am so happy, so elated, that the Chinese people have gained the right to hold the first Olympic Games in over a hundred years. Our common wish has been realized." I believe that at this moment there were far more Chinese people than just the two of us who were crying tears of elation, including our compatriots in Taiwan, Hong Kong, and Chinese people around the world. Because everyone understood that the implications of the successful bid far surpassed the realm of sports.[59]

NOTES

The first version of this chapter was written for the 41st Otago Foreign Policy School conference on "Sport and Foreign Policy in a Globalizing World," June 23–26, 2006, University of Otago, Dunedin, New Zealand. I am grateful to the Foreign Policy School for its commitment to such a high-level international conference devoted to sport and to Steve Jackson and Steve Haigh for the invitation to take part in the conference and their excellent organizational skills. Funding for the research on which this project is based was provided by a Research Award from the University of Missouri–St. Louis and a Fellowship in the Center for International Studies, University of Missouri–St. Louis. For their help in various aspects of the research I am grateful to Ren Hai, director of the Olympic Studies Center at the Beijing University of Physical Education, who provided facilities and help; Xu Guoqi, who gave me Henry Hsu's book and shared opinions with me; Philippe Blanchard, director of the Information Management Department of the IOC, who approved access for my research in the Olympic Studies Center; and Nuria Puig and Ruth Beck-Perrenoud of the Olympic Studies Center, who made the concrete arrangements.

1. Mark Quinn, *The King of Spring—The Life and Times of Peter O'Connor* (Dublin: Liffey Press, 2004).

2. Karl Lennartz, "The Presidency of Sigfrid Edstrøm (1942–1952)," in *The International Olympic Committee: One Hundred Years, The Idea—The Presidents—The Achievements* (Lausanne: International Olympic Committee, 1995), 40.

3. *Olympic Charter* (Lausanne: International Olympic Committee, 2001), 9.

4. *Olympic Charter* (Lausanne: International Olympic Committee, 2004), 9.

5. Liang Lijuan, *He Zhenliang yu Aolinpike* [He Zhenliang and Olympism] (Beijing: Olympic Publishing House, 2000); *He Zhenliang, wuhuan zhi lu* [He Zhenliang and the Road to the Olympic Rings] (Beijing: World Knowledge Publishing House, 2005); *He Zhenliang and China's Olympic Dream* (Beijing: Beijing Foreign Languages Press, 2007). I completed a rough draft of the translation, which was then "polished" by a committee at the press. I did not see the final proofs, and awkward usages ended up in the final version. Therefore, I use my own translations in this chapter.

6. Liang, *He Zhenliang, wuhuan zhi lu*, 45–52.

7. Liang, *He Zhenliang, wuhuan zhi lu*, 19.

8. Minutes of the 1954 49th IOC Session in Athens, 24.

9. Liang, *He Zhenliang, wuhuan zhi lu*, 29; Tan Hua and Dong Erzhi, *Suyuan—Dong Shouyi Zhuan* [Long-Cherished Wish—The Story of Dong Shouyi] (Beijing: People's Sports Publishing House, 1993), 135.

10. Liang, *He Zhenliang, wuhuan zhi lu*, 33.

11. Letter from Dong Shouyi to Avery Brundage, April 23, 1958 (IOC Archives).

12. Letter from Avery Brundage to Dong Shouyi, June 1, 1958 (IOC Archives).

13. For a more detailed analysis of the prohibition against "mixing sport with politics," see Susan Brownell, "'Sport and Politics Don't Mix': China's Relationship with the IOC during the Cold War," in *East Plays West: Essays on Sport and*

the Cold War, ed. Stephen Wagg and David Andrews (London: Routledge, 2007), 261–78.

14. Allen Guttmann, e-mail communication, March 10, 2006.

15. Letter from Brundage to Tung, January 8, 1958 (IOC Archives).

16. Liang, *He Zhenliang, wuhuan zhi lu*, 34.

17. Letter from Dong Shouyi to Avery Brundage, August 19, 1958 (IOC Archives).

18. Liang, *He Zhenliang, wuhuan zhi lu*, 59–60.

19. For the first account to utilize all of the relevant archives (but for the Chinese State Sports General Administration Archives, which were closed), see chapter 6 in Xu Guoqi, *Olympic Dreams: China and Sports, 1895–2008* (Cambridge, Mass.: Harvard University Press, 2008).

20. Liang, *He Zhenliang, wuhuan zhi lu*, 62–66.

21. Liang, *He Zhenliang, wuhuan zhi lu*, 50.

22. Liang, *He Zhenliang, wuhuan zhi lu*, 65.

23. Liang, *He Zhenliang, wuhuan zhi lu*, 79.

24. Liang, *He Zhenliang, wuhuan zhi lu*, 90–91; Hsu Heng [Henry Hsu], *Xu Heng Xiansheng fangtanlu* [Conversations with Henry Hsu] (Taipei: National Historical Archives, 1998), 67.

25. For a very well-researched account of these events that utilized the Canadian government archives that were just declassified, see chapter 5 in Xu Guoqi, *Olympic Dreams*.

26. Audiotapes of Executive Board meeting, Lausanne, Switzerland, March 10, 1979.

27. Liang, *He Zhenliang, wuhuan zhi lu*, 104–5.

28. Liang, *He Zhenliang, wuhuan zhi lu*, 107.

29. Hsu, *Xu Heng Xiansheng fangtanlu*, 62.

30. Lord Killanin, *My Olympic Years* (London: Secker and Warburg, 1983), 113–14.

31. *Dictionary of New Zealand Biography*, www.dnzb.govt.nz/dnzb (June 18, 2006). The original version of this biography was published in the *Dictionary of New Zealand Biography*, vol. 5 (1941–1960) (Wellington: Ministry for Culture and Heritage, 2000).

32. Liang, *He Zhenliang, wuhuan zhi lu*, 108.

33. Audiotapes of IOC Executive Board Meeting in Lausanne, Switzerland, March 10, 1979.

34. Lou Dapeng is currently a vice president of the International Association of Athletics Federations (IAAF).

35. Audiotapes of IOC Executive Board Meeting in Lausanne, Switzerland, March 10, 1979.

36. Liang, *He Zhenliang, wuhuan zhi lu*, 115.

37. Liang, *He Zhenliang, wuhuan zhi lu*, 119.

38. Audiotapes of the Executive Board Meeting in Montevideo, Uruguay, April 7, 1979.

39. "Decisions," page 39 of the minutes of the 81st Session of the IOC, Montevideo, April 7, 1979.

40. Liang, *He Zhenliang, wuhuan zhi lu*, 121.

41. Minutes of the Executive Board meeting in San Juan, Puerto Rico, June 18, 1979, 33.

42. Liang, *He Zhenliang, wuhuan zhi lu*, 122–23.

43. Minutes of the Executive Board meeting, Nagoya, Japan, October 23–25, 1979, 103.

44. Liang, *He Zhenliang, wuhuan zhi lu*, 126.

45. IOC members are chosen and voted in by the IOC in a process called "co-optation." They are not elected by their home countries, and they are not considered to be representatives of their home countries to the IOC. Rather, they are ambassadors and trustees of Olympism to their home countries.

46. Letter from Frank Lim to Avery Brundage, July 8, 1959 (IOC Archives).

47. Audiotapes of the 81st Session of the IOC, Montevideo, Uruguay, April 7, 1979.

48. Killanin, *My Olympic Years*, 109–10.

49. C. H. Robertson, "A Plan for Promoting Missionary Activity among Association Boys," *Annual Reports of the Foreign Secretaries of the International Committee, October 1, 1909 to September 30, 1910* (New York: International Committee, YMCA, 1910), 192; see also Andrew Morris, *Marrow of the Nation: A History of Sport and Physical Culture in Republican China* (Berkeley: University of California Press, 2004), 1–2.

50. Tan and Dong, *Suyuan*, 93.

51. Liang, *He Zhenliang and China's Olympic Dream*, 403.

52. He Zhenliang, "Monte Carlo Diary," in Liang, *He Zhenliang yu Aolinpike*, 400–401. The diary was deleted from the English translation because of the already long length of the book.

53. He Zhenliang, "Moscow Diary," unpublished manuscript. A different version of the diary was published in China in serial form during the 2001 Moscow IOC Session. This version was given to the author for translation but was not included in the published translation of He Zhenliang's biography.

54. He Zhenliang, "Moscow Diary."

55. He Zhenliang, "Moscow Diary."

56. "Mr. He Zhenliang's Speech," Official Website of the Beijing 2008 Olympic Games http://en.beijing2008.cn/spirit/beijing2008/candidacy/presentation/n214051424 .shtml (October 5, 2007).

57. He Zhenliang, "Moscow Diary."

58. He Zhenliang, "Moscow Diary."

59. He Zhenliang, "Meeting to Report on the Successful Olympic Bid" in the Great Hall of the People, sponsored by the Central Propaganda Department before an audience of nearly 10,000, Beijing, July 23, 2001. Liang, *Wuhuan zhi lu*, 352–56. Translated in Liang, *He Zhenliang and China's Olympic Dream*, 500–507.

Chapter Six

"China Bashing" at the Olympic Games

Why the Cold War Continues in Sport Journalism

On July 14, 1996, when China entered the stadium during the NBC telecast of the opening ceremony at the Atlanta Olympic Games, anchor Bob Costas said,

> The People's Republic of China. One-fifth of the world's population. With an economy growing at the rate of about 10% a year, every economic power, including the United States, wants to tap into that huge potential market, but of course, there are problems with human rights, copyright disputes, the threat posed to Taiwan. And within the Olympics, while they have excelled, they were fourth in the medal standings in Barcelona with 54 medals, 16 of them gold, this after a 30 year absence which ended in 1984, they've excelled athletically, they're building into a power, but amid suspicions, Dick, especially concerning their track athletes and their female swimmers, possibly using performance enhancing drugs. None caught in Barcelona, but since those Olympics in 1992, several have been caught.

After the telecast, the Chinese community in the United States, led by members of the Berkeley Chinese Students and Scholars Association, mobilized to protest Costas's comments. Thousands of signatures were collected, a letter of protest was sent to NBC, and tens of thousands of dollars were raised to purchase a full-page ad in the *Washington Post* and a quarter-page ad in the Sunday *New York Times*. Heated letters were exchanged on the Internet through the listserv *China News Digest*, and mainstream American media—such as the *Boston Globe*, *Chicago Herald-Tribune*, *San Francisco Examiner*, *New York Times*, and *USA Today*—editorialized about it. Jay Leno invited Costas to *The Tonight Show* on NBC to talk about it. The protesters demanded an official apology from NBC and from Costas. This was never given, but a vice president of NBC Sports did write a private letter that was later made public stating that NBC did not intend to hurt anyone's feelings.

I have been following American media coverage of Chinese sports for over twenty years now, and I have felt all along that the image of Chinese sports is generally negative—in fact, Costas's comments in the opening ceremony are quite mild by comparison with many other reports. So there are three questions I would like to address: Why is the coverage of Chinese sports so negative? Why did Costas's comments in the opening ceremony incite such outrage among the Chinese community in the United States? Finally, is cross-cultural understanding possible through Olympic journalism?

THE NEGATIVE IMAGE OF CHINESE SPORTS

Reports on the Chinese sports system commonly highlight the same negative aspects: state-supported sport as a machine that produces automatons; the sport school system as state-supported, systematic child abuse; and suspicions of centrally organized doping. As the story goes, China has a former Soviet-style, communist sports system in which children are removed from their parents, sent to government-supported sports boarding schools, given performance-enhancing drugs by a centrally administered sports medicine system, and trained to win glory for the nation. These stereotypes are almost never contextualized within the entire system of Chinese culture and society, and the reader is often left with the impression that negative aspects of the sport system are simply due to the fact that they are communists. The fact that the West shares many of the same abuses and problems is not considered. Moreover, the language that is used is often very extreme—much more extreme than one would find if the same issues were being reported for the United States or a European country—and the resulting impression in some cases becomes a science-fiction–like parody.

THE STATE-SUPPORTED SPORT MACHINE

A sample of the language often used to describe China's sports system includes "sports factories," "communist sports machine,"[1] "finely tuned sports machine,"[2] and "assembly line of pain."[3] This language refers to the fact that Olympic sports are based on a state-supported system of sports boarding schools and training centers. Given the generally low standard of living in China, the lack of popular access to sports facilities, and the centralized economy, this was the only possible way to provide opportunities for talented children to attain a world-class level. Until recent years, individual households could not have afforded even the food for their children in hard training. For example, in 1988, an athlete at the National Team Training Center in Beijing ate 600 yuan worth of food per month at a time when the average monthly urban wage was around 100 yuan. Without government support, there would have been no top-level sports at all in China. After being exposed to the wonders of capitalist sport at the 1984 Los Angeles Olympic Games, in 1984 the State Sports Commission issued a document calling for the "societization" of sport, which meant the shifting of economic support from the state to society. However, this was easier said than done. It took one more decade until in 1994 a professional soccer league and in 1995 a professional basketball league were created. If government sports factories are unacceptable to Western critics, then perhaps they would be more sympathetic to these more capitalist arrangements. However, they have brought along their own set of problems, such as corruption and cheating. One Olympian complained to the journalist Sang Ye,

> I don't know why they think it's a "reform." It's really bad news. We haven't gotten anything out of it. The state's still there putting pressure on you to "win glory for the nation," but now you've got pressure from those capitalists as well, expecting you to be successful so you'll make their companies famous. They're even worse than the government, because they pump up the pressure even for local meets, not just international ones.[4]

In addition, *men's* soccer and basketball were professionalized, and those women who were "holding up half the sky" soon had comparatively fewer opportunities to do so than the men.

The Insufficiency of Government-Supported Sport

In the buildup to the Beijing Olympic Games, China's quest to top the medal count is often followed by statements about government-supported sport that assume that the Chinese government is pouring huge amounts of money into sport that (the implicit assumption seems to be) far exceed what is going into sport in capitalist countries. While it is true that the Chinese government puts more money into elite sport than, say, the U.S. government does, it is not true that this means Chinese sports as a whole are comparatively better funded. When sports are an integral part of social life as they are in the United States, then they are funded by so many sources that it is not a fair comparison. The majority of Olympic team athletes in the United States have benefited from training in universities. Almost any top NCAA Division I university has superior sports facilities to the National Team Training Center in Beijing. There are forty-five member universities of four of the top conferences (Atlantic Coast Conference, Big 10, Big 12, Pacific 10) of the NCAA's Division I alone. There are thirty-two provincial and municipal team centers in China, which generally have inferior facilities to the National Team Training Center. The infrastructure of American sports is far, far larger than that of Chinese sports—and that doesn't even take into account that China's population of 1.3 billion is more than three times larger than that of the United States. This is the reason that ultimately China aspires to develop a sports system that is much more like the American system than the one that it now has.

Automatons Competing for National Honor

Chinese athletes learn from a young age to say that they are competing for the honor of the nation, but to some extent this is a formulaic response. They also compete for themselves, but in China it is not acceptable to emphasize this. Because they are tracked into sports boarding schools where their education may be neglected, there is a general complaint in China that athletes are not very well educated. For this and many other reasons, Chinese athletes do not generally give good interviews—Chinese sports fans complain about this as much as anyone. For U.S. media the interviews are also done either in Chinese with poor translators or in the athletes' poor English. None of this helps the stereotype of Chinese athletes as robots. In addition, as shown in this book, national honor in sport means something to Chinese people that is hard for the average American to understand because the United States has never experienced the kind of national humiliation that China has. The result is that Chinese patriotism is not perceived favorably by American reporters, and it further contributes to the stereotype of the Big Red Machine that turns out robotic athletes for the state.

Genetic Engineering

A book about Yao Ming, the Chinese superstar in the National Basketball Association, made much about the fact that he was the product of a "genetic conspiracy" in which the marriage of his tall parents, both basketball players, had been arranged by officials in the Shanghai Sports Commission eager to have their child as a basketball player.[5] If more fully contextualized, this story might not seem so sensational. Eugenics was introduced into China from the West in the late nineteenth century, but because it never developed into the excesses found in the West, it was never discredited there as it was in the West.[6] With the implementation of the One Child Policy, eugenics gained greater emphasis because the policy is justified by the slogan "fewer births, superior births." In 1984, a Chinese sport sociology article took "eugenics and the influence of the social environment as the starting point to suggest concrete methods of encouragement for allowing a couple in which either the mother or father or both are Master Sportspersons or above to give birth to a second child."[7] This idea was well received in the sports world, though sport sociologists noted that one obstacle was that, as indicated in academic studies, athletes did not want their children to become athletes because of the "bitter" life. Furthermore, in the period in which Yao's parents were married, a "dating culture" did not exist in China, and most marriages were arranged through introductions by friends, family, or coaches. It was considered difficult for a very tall woman to get married, so it was necessary for those concerned to find her a very tall man. Finally, the common belief was that "doors and windows should match" in a marriage—the spouses should be of the same social status—so athletes most frequently married other athletes.[8] The path to marriage of many athletes was similar to that of Yao's parents, and probably many of their children are now athletes in China's sports system.

Another example was the marriage of a 5-foot 9-inch former national softball player with a 6-foot 1-inch man, which produced the three-time Olympic gold medalist swimmer (in 1988 and 1992) Yang Wenyi and her older brother Yang Wenyong, an Asian champion in fencing. Their marriage was described with the exaggerated language:

> One might assume the government—which scours the countryside and playgrounds for youngsters with growth potential—took one look and demanded, "Give us your young."
> That's not too far off.[9]

One problem with Western coverage of Chinese sports is that Chinese people are not good at putting their own practices into context for westerners since they are immersed in their own culture and take it for granted that their practices are logical to others. One could imagine a Chinese person's response to a westerner's views on Yao or Yang: "His mother, who might have had a difficult time finding a mate, was matched to a man suitable in both height and social status—was this not a good thing? They had children who brought honor to Shanghai, their families, and China—is that not every parent's dream? If you Americans held a more pragmatic attitude toward marriage and childrearing, maybe you'd have a lower divorce rate and less juvenile delinquency." In China these are stories that are generally admired as an illustration of what families are all about.

STATE-SUPPORTED, SYSTEMATIC CHILD ABUSE

The problem of child athletes has received increasing attention worldwide over the past thirty years, sparked in 1976 when Nadia Comaneci won Olympic gold in gymnastics at the age of fourteen. Sports such as gymnastics and figure skating slowly instituted minimum age limits for world and Olympic competitions. This is a worldwide problem, not just a Chinese problem. However, much journalistic coverage implies that the exploitation of Chinese athletes is a distinctly Chinese problem; perhaps they find it particularly offensive in China because they think that Chinese children are being exploited in the name of the state and that this is somehow less acceptable than when they are exploited by their own families.

Figure 6.1. The caption on this postcard reads "Budding sportsmen/*Florissante prospérité.*" It was published for foreign consumption in 1964 by the People's Sports Publishing House.

One example is *The Ultimate Athlete*, a documentary directed by Scott Hicks and aired on the Discovery Channel in the month before the 1996 Atlanta Olympic Games and several times thereafter. The opening trailer has a scene of a Chinese gymnastics hall with empty rings swinging in the foreground and a slogan on a large banner in the background. The voice is that of John Hoberman, perhaps the most vocal critic of Olympic sports in academia. Hoberman's voice says, "What are the human costs? How much suffering is too much?" Later, his voice is heard while shots of young female Chinese gymnasts are shown:

> There's no question in my mind that some of the stresses and schedules to which small children are subject in the gymnastics business, for example, do constitute child abuse. How much suffering is too much? Which sorts of procedures are more than civilized people should tolerate? At what age should children be sucked into a high performance factory under the tutelage of adult coaches whose one purpose really is to produce that perfect little machine?

In a phone interview in 1996, I asked Hoberman if he had been speaking specifically of Chinese gymnasts when he made these statements. He replied, "It was not a specific critique of the Chinese. It was a critique of global sports in general." I had provided some of the background research materials for the portrayal of China to the director, including my book. I had discussed Chinese sports with the researcher over the phone for over an hour. I was also interviewed for this documentary and am shown elsewhere in the film. Hoberman is not a China expert. I was the China expert who was flown to Austin, Texas, and interviewed for the project.

Why wasn't my voice used in the opening introduction to Chinese sport? Evidently I had not said the things that Hicks wanted to juxtapose against the images of Chinese gymnasts. Instead, he chose to juxtapose John Hoberman's radical criticism of *global* Olympic sports with shots of *Chinese* athletes—not with shots of sprinter Carl Lewis or cyclist Lance Armstrong, for example, who were featured elsewhere in the film. When I discussed this juxtaposition with Hoberman, he clarified the point he had tried to make in his interview with Hicks:

> What you see around the world is people ratcheting up the pressure . . . and the Chinese happen to be one of them because they want success. . . . I have mixed feelings about the famous Bob Costas thing. . . . I think that what is valid about the Chinese complaint is shit; why pick on us? [. . .] The other point to make is that nobody ever accuses the Chinese of ever having special racial aptitude—it's always drugs.

The United States and China: Not as Different as You Might Think

I was on the Board of Directors of the St. Louis Skating Club from 2001 to 2007 and its president from 2004 to 2006. In the period that I was on the board, there were eight skaters who appeared to have enough talent to aspire to be top national competitors. Of those eight, only two remained at home with their families in St. Louis to train without disrupting their family lives, and only one of them stayed in the regular school system, while the other was homeschooled. The remaining six relocated to cities regarded as centers for skating: three of them left their families to live with host families (the youngest was thirteen) and were homeschooled or attended a special school for children in the performing arts; in two cases the entire family uprooted and moved, and the children were homeschooled; and in one case the mother moved with her child. In many sports this scenario is repeated by countless families across the United States who remove their children from the regular school system and sometimes send them away to live in other cities in order to provide them the best opportunity to fulfill their potential. At the top levels of U.S. sport, the vast majority of athletes will have moved from their hometowns to another location, although generally after the age of eighteen. Although they begin training at the same young ages that Chinese athletes do, they generally do not leave home until later. This is because the grassroots infrastructure in U.S. sports is sound enough to allow child athletes to develop their potential in their home environment for a longer period until they must seek out better coaches and conditions to continue to improve. China lacks this grassroots infrastructure.

The willingness of Americans to disrupt family life for a child athlete is widespread even though U.S. "family values" do not condone this practice as much as "Chinese family values" do. In China, there is a saying that parents "hope their children become dragons" (*wang zi cheng long*), referring to the high hopes that parents place on children. For this reason it is quite common for parents to send a child to be raised by a grandparent or relative in another city where there might be more opportunities for the child. It is also done if both parents work and feel unable to take care of the child. The residence permit system increases this tendency because it restricts access to the desirable cities in China and makes it more difficult for whole families to move. Since children who are selected for training at provincial team training centers gain residence permits in the major city where the center is located, parents are often eager for children to join the teams and gain this lifetime benefit. Parents and children usually talk about how much they miss each other, but families do not seem to define themselves by whether they live together, and so the practice does not weaken the notion that they are still a "family"—on the contrary, making this kind of sacrifice for the good of the family is believed to demonstrate the highest commitment to the family by giving the family "face."

Yet reporting on Chinese child athletes seems to assume that "they" are completely different from "us." I was interviewed for a segment on child rearing in National Geographic Television's *Taboo* series. The segment on Chinese child athletes who live in sports boarding schools appeared along with a segment about children from the Mentowai tribe raised in the tropical forest of Indonesia with little supervision by their own parents and children raised in prisons in India so that they could be with their imprisoned mothers. The advertisement for the DVDs describes the show with the sensationalistic words, "Witness stunning stories from the first two seasons about rituals and traditions so shocking that you can't help but be attracted to them."[10] The show was introduced with the lines,

> Throughout the world some people raise children in ways others might find extreme. Would you let your child run wild in the forest and smoke cigarettes at age six? Do you think toddlers should be raised in prison? Would you give up your only child and send them off to endure . . . this? [shot of a young boy doing a Russian split with his ankles propped up on blocks of foam and a small teammate pressing down on his back]

This piece was rather typical in that it featured an image of a gymnast doing flexibility training. Flexibility training is often selected to illustrate the "brutality" of Chinese training methods with an attention-getting image of a body twisted into seemingly unnatural positions.[11] Extreme flexibility training is limited to only a few Olympic sports (gymnastics, diving, and figure skating) and is hardly representative of training methods in China or elsewhere. It is by nature painful because in order to increase flexibility, the body must be pushed past its normal range of motion until a physiological response is induced by the pain that causes the muscles to relax further. Since gymnasts from other countries are as flexible as Chinese gymnasts, it is likely that their training is no less painful than the Chinese training.

During the 2004 Figure Skating World Championships, NBC aired a "fluff piece" about the pair skaters Xue Shen and Zhao Hongbo. Peter Carruthers introduced it by noting that they were "two skaters who grew up in conditions few of us could imagine." Jim McKay's narration elaborates that these conditions included Zhao's moving to a sports boarding school at the age of six, while for Shen, living in the "crumbling ancient slums of the city" of Harbin, "sport represents her family's best hope for escaping dire poverty," and her mother went eight years without buying any new clothes because their money went for skates. They trained outdoors in the cold and wind, Shen competed with an injury that required cortisone shots, and it was a long journey of ten years before they won China's first-ever world pair skating title. McKay observes, "Shen and Zhao could endure hardship. As the Chinese say, they could 'eat bitterness.'" "Training could be brutal." He concludes, "It may be hard for a Westerner to comprehend how much the Chinese endured to become great."

This is an exaggeration. The lives of Shen and Zhao as portrayed in the segment could have been those of many American figure skaters except that the overall standard of living in the United States is higher than in China, American skaters generally stopped having to train outdoors sometime in the 1970s (even Peggy Fleming, gold medalist at the 1968 Olympics, sometimes skated figures in the cold at night), and an American would probably be living with a host family rather than in a dormitory. But many American skating mothers go without new clothes to pay for skates, and American training is just as "brutal." American athletes can also "eat bitterness," but the media have a tendency to downplay it, particularly in figure skating, which is cast as a glamorous sport. In China, "eating bitterness" is praised as an admirable ability, but journalists should also remember that "speaking bitterness" (*su ku*) has been cultivated as an art by the Communist Party ever since its formation. This refers to the consciousness-raising sessions that the party organized among oppressed peoples (such as poor peasants and women) to make them see the sources of their oppression so that they would be motivated to join the Communist Party's fight to throw off their chains. The standard plotline for any athlete's life story entails an account of the "bitterness" he or she has eaten. The tendency to emphasize the ability of Chinese people to suffer may make for a good story, but the subtext seems to be that they will threaten American preeminence in sports because Americans cannot. This not only does not do justice to the difficult lives that many American athletes are living, but also it dupes American parents and children into thinking that a sports career is an easy path to a pot of gold.

Bob Costas, who was hired by NBC sports in 1980 and has anchored NBC's coverage of the Olympic Games since it first bought the television rights in 1992, is one of America's most popular sports commentators. He is also known for his ability to speak intelligently about more than sports, and in 2001 he was hired by HBO network to host a talk show in which he talked about topics inside and outside the sports world and was able to exercise his investigative skills. In an interview with me in 1996, Costas observed,

There's a lot of heroic stuff that happens at the Olympics. It's at least heroic in a sports sense, and sometimes it's heroic in a human sense. But we will always go for that—when I say we, I mean television in general—we will almost always go for that as opposed to any dark side stories. If you're looking to the network that's carrying the Olympics for an evenhanded journalistic look at the downside of women's gymnastics, you're probably looking in the wrong place. If they ever decide that they want to do that, I'm first in line to do it. Not because I want to attack the gymnastics establishment, not at all, but because I'm always interested in an evenhanded look at what's an interesting issue. But we would show a hundred features about Kerry Strug's[12] puppy dog before we would do a single piece about whether or not it might be dangerous for some of these kids to do gymnastics.

American journalists have been more willing to pass harsh judgments on the training of Chinese child athletes than on American. Moreover, the problem of the overinvolved parent is the major problem for youth sports in the

Figure 6.2.   Young competitor at the 1986 Haidian District Middle School Track Meet, Beijing. Photo by Susan Brownell.

United States today: it is often questionable whether the parents have the best interests of the child at heart, and the psychological or even physical abuse of children by adults, whether their own parents or those of a rival, is relatively common. Why do we assume that a system that removes the children from potentially overinvolved parents and places them under the tutelage of trained administrators and coaches is a less humane system?

CENTRALLY ORGANIZED DOPING

The first major journalistic piece on post-Mao Chinese sport, a 1984 *Sports Illustrated* article about high-jump world-record-setter Zhu Jianhua, contained an amusing but telling account of the reaction by Wu Zhongyuan, director of China's Olympic press committee, to a question about conjectures that Zhu's world record of 7 feet 8¾ inches had been aided by doping: "We wish we had this kind of drug in China, but unfortunately we have not."[13] The use of steroids and other drugs was certainly known by 1988 when I was doing my Ph.D. research. The use of stimulants was discussed in a controversial exposé of the sports system, Zhao Yu's "Superpower Dream."[14] China merely joined the trend that was already common in the outside world.

In the Western press, the idea of the People's Republic of China as the heir to East Germany had begun to congeal at the 1992 Barcelona Olympic Games when the extremely muscular Chinese women had suddenly dominated the swimming events. In a 1995 NBC Sports segment, U.S. Olympic medalist Janet Evans called it "the whole thing starting again. The East Germans took so much away from our women."[15] As described in chapter 4, at the 1993 World Championships of track and field in Stuttgart, six Chinese women runners won six of the nine medals in the 1,500-, 3,000-, and 10,000-meter races. All but one trained on the Liaoning province team under Ma Junren and not on the national team. Perhaps the location of the World Championships in a reunited Germany contributed to the accusations against the Chinese of drug use, which were much more open than had ever been the case in the Cold War era. China was said to be picking up where the former East Germany had left off. Less than three weeks later, in China's Eighth National Games in Beijing, seven women shattered the world records in all three events. Eleven Chinese athletes had positive drug tests during the 1994 Asian Games in Hiroshima: seven swimmers (four men and three women), two canoeists (male), a cyclist (female), and a hurdler (female). Chinese swimmers had won all fifteen titles in Hiroshima. This and a spattering of other positive drug tests initiated the stereotype of a centrally administered doping system.[16]

However, the parallel was not accurate. The Chinese sports system was never centralized to the degree that the East German system was. There are intense rivalries between provincial teams and the national team center, and the autonomy of the provincial teams has increased with the economic reforms as they can seek sponsorship from local corporations and rely less on central government funding. In addition, the quadrennial National Sports Games pit provincial teams against each other, and their government funding depends on their placement.

Ma Junren was an outsider viewed as a "country bumpkin" (*tu baozi*) by the sports establishment in Beijing because he had no formal education at a physical education institute. He was regarded as unstable and sometimes violent, and many people did not approve of the way he treated his female athletes. He publicly admitted to hitting them occasionally. He also displayed an almost obsessive dedication to his coaching, experimenting with different methods over the years, reading Chinese translations of Western sports medicine articles, and educating himself in Chinese medicine. These methods were detailed in a report commissioned by the State Sports Commission in 1994. The commission asked some of the most renowned experts in the principles of sports training to interview Ma and write a report that was for internal circulation only. One of the authors was Guo Jiaxing, who had been my adviser during my Ph.D. research at the Beijing Institute of Physical Education in 1987–1988. He later gave me a revised version of the report that detailed Ma's training methods and the multiple herbal medicines that he gave his athletes but made no mention of steroids or other drugs. Professor Guo commented to me that he believed in the efficacy of the traditional Chinese medicine and the training methods[17] and that he did not think the Ma Family Soldiers had used steroids. Since this report was commissioned by the State Sports Commission, I assume that if Ma were using banned substances, the commission did not know about it. It is also telling that the leaders in Beijing even felt compelled to send someone to find out what Ma was up to in the first place.

Ma Junren openly discussed his training methods in press conferences. Showing how far the sports world has moved from the days of the East German state secrets, he said he could not discuss his methods in detail *because he wanted to patent them!* The *Beijing Evening News* reported that he had sold a secret formula to the Today Group, a maker of health drinks, for 10 million yuan (US$1.15 million).[18] The point is that Ma Junren was no straight-line party man and his athletes were not simply cogs in a socialist sports machine. On the contrary, it was the loosening of state control that made it possible and lucrative for an ambitious man like Ma to exploit female athletes to benefit himself (and them—at whatever cost). This was not centralized socialism run rampant—it was free enterprise run rampant. However, in general, sports journalists were not interested in highlighting the ways in which the market economy facilitates doping in sport but were more interested in perpetuating old Cold War stereotypes.[19]

During the NBC broadcast of the 1996 Olympic women's gymnastics, a six-minute segment on Chinese women athletes, narrated by Hannah Storm, was aired. The piece is divided into segments marked by a close-up shot of a calligraphic brush writing of Chinese characters: "China," "sacrifice," "woman," "eat bitterness," and "glory." A sample narrative follows:

> But over the past four years, their women have excelled in the two sports requiring strength and stamina. In Barcelona, female swimmers ruled the pool so suddenly that defeated rivals suspected steroid use, suspicions borne out over the following two years when 11 swimmers were caught and banned for using drugs. A year later, rivals made similar but unproved charges against runners like Wang Junxia, who shattered the world record in the 10,000 m. Her coach, Ma Junren, gave his runners exotic elixirs, had them run a marathon a day, and so subjugated them that he even drove away their prize Mercedes.

I had several discussions over the phone with the producer of this segment when he was planning the content to be filmed during the camera crew's trips to China. He had a copy of my book. I was in China when they were there and had several discussions with the NBC Beijing Bureau and with their liaison with the Sports Commission. Other sections of the segment did emphasize sociological reasons for the successes of Chinese sportswomen, such as their ability to "eat bitterness," over the theory of performance-enhancing drugs. However, sensationalistic language such as that used in this segment tends to leave a stronger impression than attempts to create a deeper sense of social context.

WHY THE COLD WAR CONTINUES IN SPORT JOURNALISM

My point is that directors and reporters are not simply presenting a neutral reality to their audiences. Journalists come to their investigations with *some* preconceived notions about China that are negative. Where do these notions come from? They are drawn from limited sources because there is very little information on Chinese sports in English. When what they know about China does not suffice, they draw on what they know about the former Eastern bloc. One important source of their preconceptions is other journalists. Journalists hang out together at sporting events, read each other's writing, and exchange opinions. In the absence of other reliable information, once stereotypes are generated they gained a life of their own.

Furthermore, the Chinese side has little understanding of how to use the media to promote a positive image. In the 1980s and 1990s, reporting on China was often very difficult even after journalists had gained official approval. Their cameras were confiscated at the airport, interviews were interrupted by an official when sensitive questions were asked, and so on. The Sports Commission bureaucrats assumed for decades that if only China wins Olympic gold medals, then a glowing national reputation in the global arena will be the inevitable result. They have failed to understand and respond to the negative stereotypes that have accompanied their sports successes.

Finally, the negative stereotype of Chinese sports is located within a larger negative stereotype left over from the Cold War. Americans never understood much about socialism and Marxism, and they still do not. How could it be otherwise? In the McCarthy era the teaching of Marxism was almost erased from American universities, and after the fall of the Berlin Wall it no longer seemed necessary to understand it, so it is not easy to get a short course in Marxist philosophy in the United States. This will be dealt with further in the following chapter.

Figure 6.3. Image of Chinese soldiers over the Olympic rings at the closing ceremony of the Beijing 4th Olympic Cultural Festival, July 2006. An example of a combination of symbols that Chinese choreographers might not realize could be seen as inappropriate or even threatening by non-Chinese. Photo by Andy Miah.

I have emphasized the negative distortions because I believe they are the more numerous. Not all of the reporting on China is this negative, and sometimes distortions occur in a positive direction. An issue of *Sports Illustrated* devoted to China in 1988 contained an article on divers that, against the stereotype, emphasized that they dove because it was fun.[20] Another article by Rick Reilly on a young gymnast, Liyin, depicted her happy family life. I was working as a translator for Reilly and overheard Liyin's parents say that they had temporarily dressed up their apartment with new decorations that they planned to return to the store the next day. I also overheard Liyin's father comment that he hoped she was accepted into the sports boarding school because both he and her mother worked and it was hard to take care of her. I duly reported these comments to Reilly, but he chose to ignore them to emphasize the warm family scene.[21]

There are also a few journalists in the United States who have specialized in reporting on the Olympic Games for many years, so they have a deeper knowledge base from which to draw when the Olympic Games roll around—such as Alan Abrahamson of NBC Sports, Elliott Almond of the *San Jose Mercury-News*, and Philip Hersh of the *Chicago Tribune*.

This is the bigger picture behind the controversy over Bob Costas's commentary in the opening ceremony. Let us now return to it.

THE OPENING CEREMONY COMMENTARY

Why did the generally negative sports coverage leading up to the Olympic Games attract no outrage, while Bob Costas's comments did? Obviously, the opening ceremony attracts a huge audience, including people who do not normally follow sports. While not the largest viewing audience during the Games, the opening ceremony audience probably attracts more attention from foreign nationals living in the United States than the other sports events. Of course, people from around the world bring different expectations to their viewing of the opening ceremony. What did the Chinese protesters expect? The advertisement published in the *Washington Post* and the *New York Times* was accompanied by an image of the head of a statue of Apollo and read,

Costas Poisoned Olympic Spirit
Public Protests NBC

We strongly protest the irresponsible remarks made by Mr. Bob Costas of NBC regarding international athletes, including members of the Chinese team, during the Olympic coverage.

Mr. Costas's frequent and incendiary comments on alleged drug use by foreign athletes were unprofessional and biased. The Olympics are no place for prejudice. Athletes from all nations are under the same scrutiny of IOC in drug testing—no more, no less. Mr. Costas's gratuitous remarks only tarnished the outstanding efforts of all athletes.

The Olympics are a grand celebration of common ideals where athletics overcome politics, friendship overcomes hostility, and camaraderie overcomes difference. It is a unique opportunity for the host country to extend a warm welcome to all guests. At such an auspicious moment, the arrogance and inhospitality of Mr. Costas alienated millions of faithful viewers, deeply offended the international community, and greatly embarrassed the American public.

Mr. Costas should have the courage and decency to issue a sincere and public apology.[22]

I was invited to give a talk on the controversy at the Institute of East Asian Studies of the University of California, Berkeley, where I met and had dinner with the two graduate students, Li Yi and Chen Kai, who had spearheaded the protest. Chen Kai explained to me the reason he had been so enraged by Costas's comments. He had high expectations going into the broadcast. He felt that China still lacked democracy and that it was still economically backward, but the one area in which it had achieved success in which he could be proud was Olympic sports. When he felt that this had not been recognized, he became very upset and vowed to take action. He also felt that the statements about China were unfairly negative and that things were said that Costas would never say about the United States, for example. This criticism was not entirely accurate because Costas did say positive things about China's economic growth and achievement in sports, and when the U.S. team entered the stadium, he did discuss drug use by American athletes when he mentioned the steroid suspension of 400-meter-runner Butch Reynolds.

Nevertheless, it is accurate to say that his commentary was political in a way that was not then acceptable in Chinese Olympic broadcasts. In 1994, I interviewed China's most famous sport commentator, Song Shixiong, about the commentary on Olympic opening ceremony. He said,

> Announcing the opening ceremony is the most troublesome part of the Olympic Games. China pays a lot of attention to the ceremony because the audience is very large; in fact, the two things that Chinese people are most concerned with are the opening ceremony and the performances by Chinese who win medals. The opening ceremony is an important opportunity to spread the Olympic spirit and display a people's culture and history.[23]

He said that he learned the main principle behind his commentary from Premier Zhou Enlai, who told him to "be the eyes and ears of the sports fan" and to use "fewer adjectives." In his commentary, Song aimed to "seek the truth from facts." Value judgments, political criticism, and even humor were out of place. At the 1992 Olympics, Song Shixiong's commentary was very formulaic: he repeated phrases like "Swifter, Higher, Stronger," "Peace, Friendship, Progress," "World Peace," and "The important thing is to take part." He made no political commentary about nations, instead stating only the name of the country in many cases; in other cases he gave the size of the team and its medal hopes. An example of his style is what he said when China entered the stadium in Barcelona.[24] This would have been the most recent Olympic broadcast seen by those mainland Chinese students who were studying in the United States in 1996:

> Now it's the team of the People's Republic of China in the stadium. The flag-bearer for the team is Song Lingang. The Chinese team has 381 people, among them 251 athletes. They will participate in 28 sports and 105 events. The athletes will use their entire hearts and apply their thoughts, be confident, compete with style, compete to potential, strive to achieve good performances. They will express the aspirations of a rich popular culture, express Chinese people's mental attitude, win glory for the nation.[25]

In a twenty-seven-nation study of the 1992 opening ceremony telecast around the world, Miquel de Moragas found that the Chinese telecast contained less information than any other telecast.[26]

This seems to be the approach that the Chinese protesters were advocating. Of course, it is understandable that they would bring expectations to their viewing based on the ceremonies they had watched in China. In China, the opening ceremony is regarded as a "solemn" (*longzhong*) event. In his interview with me, Costas said, "To make a solemn statement about all 197 teams, you'd end up with a totally solemn broadcast." I noted to him that this was precisely the way that opening ceremony is described in China, and I asked if he felt the American audience could accept it. He replied, "The American audience doesn't want it."

At the same time that Song's commentary was being broadcast to China in 1992, Bob Costas's commentary was being broadcast to Americans on the other side of the world. When China entered the Barcelona stadium, he said,

> Bob Costas: The People's Republic of China, so very strong in the diving competition. Gao Min and Fu Mingxia are names we'll be hearing a lot of.

> Dick Enberg: Men's and women's—they might sweep it. They're going to take a lot out of the diving venue.

> Costas: Most populous nation in the world, moving up on 1.2 billion inhabitants. And they might be the closest thing to an old-style East German sports machine,

closed society, very efficient, taking young athletes, putting them in sports schools and using who knows what methods in their pursuit of Olympic medals.

[shot of U.S. athletes under the stadium]

Enberg: The Chinese will also be motivated by bonuses if they should win medals here.

As is apparent, this commentary was even more strident than his commentary in 1996, which had already toned down the Cold War imagery.

Some of the NBC protesters seemed to feel that Bob Costas must have a personal vendetta against China, to which Costas offered this counterargument:

Who in their right mind wants to insult countries? Or use the Olympics to make little political points? It would be stupid even if you were so inclined. It would be stupid to do. Because it would diminish your broadcast. It just wouldn't be appropriate. Now, inevitably, what your sensibilities are and your sense of what's dramatic or admirable or not gets into everything you do, but that's true of every report. And so the sense of what should be emphasized that someone from France has is different from someone from South Africa or someone from Canada or the United States. So in that sense, there probably is a political or personal judgment involved that I'm not aware of when I'm doing it. But in terms of any overt political stuff, it would just be ridiculous to use the Olympics for some kind of a soapbox.

I asked Costas why he chose to say what he said at that particular point. He replied,

I wasn't singling China out, except in this sense: there's a handful of countries that you wouldn't exactly have to be Henry Kissinger to figure out are more important on the international landscape than others. And China would be in that category, simply by virtue of its size. [. . .] And so—given its population, given the type of discipline its top athletes are willing to subject themselves to—China can be an international sports juggernaut, and so I think they deserve more attention both for achievement and missteps than some other countries might. And, by the way, the same thing is true of the United States. [. . .] [A] lot of people thought—whether they were right or wrong—that what was happening with the Chinese swimmers in '92 in Barcelona—a lot of the female American swimmers who had competed against the East Germans said that this mirrors it. This is an echo of everything that we saw and experienced there. Now even if that couldn't 100% be proven, it was an interesting enough story to pursue. . . . [S]o that's the reason for the athletic comment. The political comment, mild and general as it was, was just to kind of indicate to the general audience that this isn't closed-off China that didn't even participate in the Olympic Games for 32 years. . . . So anyway, my point is kind of that, okay, everyone wants a piece of this market, big United States interests which are in there tentatively, but there are obstacles, it's not just like "open up the door, boys, and here we come." And so I clicked off a few of the obstacles, and in truth I could have mentioned more, like exporting suspicious nuclear materials to Pakistan and whatever else. [. . .] I thought of it that way too, that it wasn't intended as a bash, it was intended as an even-handed, factual thing, very broad, which is all that the time allows, and plus I never—even in sports—present myself as an expert on something that I'm not an expert on. [. . .] [A]lthough I hope that I'm a reasonably well-informed citizen, I would never declare that my area of expertise is international relations or international economics. But I have enough of a grasp of it that I can make an appropriate, pertinent, general comment in the few moments that the parade of the opening ceremony allows.

Costas's commentary echoed the perceptions of China that are common in sports journalism, which I have already discussed. I asked him where he found the information on China that he used in preparing for the opening ceremony, and he explained that for the 1992 and 1996 Olympics, he had spent several months reading about the sports, the competitors, the host country, and the history of the Olympics. Then, a night or two before the opening ceremony, he sat down with the NBC researchers and went through the notebook

Figure 6.4. Inside the International Broadcast Center (IBC) at the 1996 Atlanta Olympic Games. Photo by Susan Brownell.

they had prepared. He spent a total of six to seven hours preparing for the opening ceremony but later felt that this was not enough.

He showed me the pages out of the binder that he referred to during the ceremony, which included typed entries provided by the NBC researchers, with his own handwritten notes in the margins. Only a small fraction of this information can be used during the broadcast because, as Costas described it, "you're watching what's on camera, you're listening to what the other person said, you're anticipating what's on next, and in a snap judgment you're deciding how much, if any of this, fits here, or should I say something that just occurs to me off the top of my head?" He said,

> I don't think it's worth it just to say, "so here comes India, which remains torn between democratic secularism and religious fundamentalism," unless there's some way that that impacts on the Olympics, even if it's true. Because there are two possible reactions: One is, we don't need Bob Costas to give us a high school history or global politics lesson—and there's some merit in that observation. Or two: Why did he say that about India but he didn't say it about Pakistan? And the real reason about that may simply be that Dick Enberg said something and then they said in my ear, "Throw it down to Hannah Storm." But people don't think of those kinds of mundane aspects. They think that each thing is some kind of exalted decision made with either affection or malice for the country.

In a follow-up phone interview in 2003, he also complained about the pressure to say *something* and felt that a different format in which there was either a choreographed commentary from a host in the stadium to go along with the ceremony, which could be tapped into, or graphics to provide information might reduce the pressure on the commentators. He observed that the IOC establishes a certain protocol that limits the possibilities but that the IOC is not in the best position to determine "what plays in Peoria," as the saying goes.

Costas said he had come to realize that commentating on an opening ceremony is unlike the sports commentating he normally does. Olympic Games do not happen every weekend, and NBC had bought its first Olympic broadcasting rights in 1992. He had first anchored the 1992 opening ceremony in Barcelona; Atlanta was his second time. He described the opening ceremony as a "hodgepodge of pageantry with political overtones and fact and fantasy"; "half show biz schlock, half National Geographic. It's like Las Vegas on the World stage"; "half somber international gathering and half Macy's Thanksgiving Day Parade—it switches back and forth almost instantaneously."[27]

> You know, leaving aside right or wrong, I think that in the American perspective, my defense is airtight. [. . .] But still, even though I feel like there's obviously nothing to apologize for, there's obviously nothing that I feel was amiss,

at the same time, you don't want to needlessly hurt people's feelings. If there's something larger at stake, an important thing you have to report or something that has to be said, then you do it. But I think there's probably ways you get more and more sensitive to these different perspectives and you realize that the Olympics are simply different. You know, the Chinese sports fan who's watching the Superbowl—he's not watching *his country* represented. And I think especially in this case, because it was in the United States, people had the antennae up to see what the American response is going to be to our country on their soil. And they look at me—wrongly—as some sort of representative of some sort of larger American feeling. . . . I'm not going to avoid controversy, but without sacrificing any integrity, any pertinence, any entertainment value, I could still avoid some of these pitfalls. And it isn't a case of right or wrong. [. . .] It's sort of just a case of that if this offends someone, or runs the risk of being so grossly misinterpreted, how can I avoid this or express myself differently so as to minimize that risk. I don't think of that as surrender or backing down, because on this issue I'm 100% not backing down. On the other hand, if to a substantial number of people, any mention of their country during the opening ceremony carries extraordinary symbolic weight, then you're better off not recklessly courting misunderstanding.

THE SLOW EVOLUTION IN
OPENING CEREMONY COVERAGE

In the broadcast of the 2000 Sydney Olympic Games ceremony, Costas limited his commentary only to topics related to sports and contextualized his statements about suspicions of doping:

> Next the large delegation from China, which includes their outstanding divers, gymnasts, the women's soccer team that took the United States to overtime in last year's World Cup final. But another part of the story is the 27 Chinese athletes who are *not* here. Those 27, including many swimmers and track athletes, were dropped just prior to the games and the Chinese made no secret that the reason in most cases was concern over the possibility of positive drug tests. The IOC has stepped up its drug monitoring effort for these games, and many athletes from many countries come here under a cloud of suspicion, or others have been left behind because of that. China, though, has more at stake than most nations do. They're determined to be the host of the 2008 Games. Most people think Beijing has the inside track, the decision will be made next summer and Chinese officials don't want to run the risk of anything happening here that will tarnish their image and diminish their chances.

In the NBC telecast of the 2002 Salt Lake City Olympic Winter Games opening ceremony, Katie Couric, not Costas, ended up talking about China.

A morning talk show host at that time, she had been added at Costas's suggestion because she appealed to a female audience:

Katie Couric: The summer Olympics are coming to China, the world's largest nation, for the first time in 2008 and those games will be in Beijing. We'll have much more ahead in the Parade of Nations right after this. [commercial break]

The NBC telecast of the 2004 Athens Olympic Summer Games opening ceremony repeated some of the same old themes — the repetitive pattern drives home how simple are the images of nations presented in the Olympic Games:[28]

Bob Costas: Holding the flag highest of any nation just because he's seven and a half feet tall, Yao Ming of the Houston Rockets and the *Chinese* basketball team.

Katie: In four years perhaps we'll be doing this in Beijing, Bob.

Bob: They're emerging, as we all know, as a world economic power, and also becoming a world sports power. They won fifty-nine medals at the last summer Olympics, third best behind the United States and Russia. They expect to eclipse that total here, and their goal ultimately is to rise to the top of the medal standings when they host the 2008 Olympic Games.

Katie: In Greece they bring the best men's gymnastics team, best diving team, they're gold medal favorites in women's volleyball and, as always, tops in table tennis.

Bob: That's Dell Harris, longtime NBA head coach and assistant coach. He is actually coaching the Chinese basketball team and marching with their delegation.

Katie: Looks like he's having a pretty good time doing it. We'll be back with more in a moment. [commercial break]

With the addition of news anchor Brian Williams to the NBC telecast of the 2006 Torino Olympic Winter Games opening ceremony, some substantive political content was returned to the commentary as compared to Katie Couric's chatty commentary:

Brian Williams: Interesting, you look at the Chinese team, the largest winter Olympic team they have ever sent, seventy-six members, of course home to 1.3 billion, the fastest-growing economy in the world. We will be there in two years for the Summer Games. First time their flag's been carried by a female athlete, Bob, there is so much to say on this front, so much developing while we're here, and it will be interesting to see what kind of China we encounter.

Bob Costas: We know that on the athletic side they've become an Olympic power — in Athens they won thirty-two golds just behind the U.S. haul of thirty-five, and they have a huge push going on for supremacy in the Summer Games when they host in 2008 in Beijing.

Brian: Under a lot of pressure around the world, issues like environment, human rights, politics will be in the air during the Olympic Games.

Bob: And the large Chinese delegation is followed by the tiny group from Cyprus.

It is possible to trace a slow evolution in the way in which NBC covered Olympic opening ceremonies in the ten years after the uproar over the Atlanta coverage—there was a slight shift toward the Chinese model emphasizing respect for nations and the Olympic ideals, with less political content. Because of several protests that had occurred when viewers in the United States were angered that their home countries had been deleted from the opening ceremony coverage because of a commercial break, NBC eventually, in 2004, began to quickly recap the countries that had entered during the break when they returned to the air. CCTV had always covered every country out of respect for the participating countries, even though the likelihood that a large number of foreign nationals were watching the broadcast in China was much less. In this respect, NBC finally approached the Chinese model eight years after the 1996 controversy. Obviously, it was not a direct result of the protests. On the other hand, it was probably at least an indirect result of a greater sensitivity to patriotism in other countries, which was forced onto NBC's radar screen in 1996.

In 2003, seven years after my interview with Costas about the 1996 controversy, I followed up with him and asked him how his thoughts about opening ceremonies had changed. He noted that in retrospect, he had realized that the Chinese were used to national television and had perhaps linked him with the U.S. government. Since the Atlanta Olympics were a U.S. Olympic Games, they had felt as if the government itself as the host had welcomed them and then started criticizing their country.

Since 1996, Chinese sports telecasting has become more open, and Song Shixiong's adjectiveless vocabulary no longer sets the standard. However, in 2006 there was a nationwide outburst when China's most popular sports commentator, Huang Jianxiang, demonstrated a preference for Italy in its defeat of Australia in the Soccer World Cup, and the Chinese audience felt he had lost the objectivity that they had come to expect of reporting on international matches. His somewhat lengthy diatribe concluded,

Hiddink . . . lost all his courage faced with Italian history and traditions. . . . He finally reaped fruits which he had sown! They should go home. They don't need to go as far away as Australia as most of them are living in Europe. Farewell!

Huang later issued a public letter of apology for "attaching too much personal feeling" to the match.[29]

IS CROSS-CULTURAL UNDERSTANDING
POSSIBLE THROUGH OLYMPIC JOURNALISM?

In 1996, the NBC protesters finished their "International Press Release Letter" by saying,

> The purpose of this protest is not to foment hatred or to provoke a confrontation. Rather, our purpose is to initiate dialogue and build consensus among people of different backgrounds regarding what forms of behavior are acceptable within the context of the Olympic Games. Moreover, we hope to prevent similar unfortunate situations from happening again.[30]

While the sentiments expressed in this letter are admirable, there are structures underlying sports journalism and Olympic coverage that stand in the way of dialogue. Television images may appear to float toward us off of the television screen, but in fact they are grounded in real and complicated structures that limit the shapes that the images can assume. The media industry and international stereotypes operate according to their own rules. They are not greatly affected by the voices of individual people or academic specialists. There is a handful of international scholars who have researched the Olympic Games since 1984 and who have documented the particular difficulties in cross-cultural translation that are presented by the opening ceremony. In an attempt to provide journalists with a richer background for the Atlanta ceremony, John MacAloon of the University of Chicago helped the Atlanta Committee for the Olympic Games (ACOG) write the media guide for the opening ceremony, and he presided over a press conference with academics who were experts on the telecasting of opening ceremonies and how to interpret them. ACOG made an unprecedented effort to help the press and broadcasters understand the content of the opening ceremony, but the reaction was lukewarm if not antagonistic. The press conference was sparsely attended by about forty journalists; Bob Costas did not attend. *Sports Illustrated* described the opening ceremony as containing "symbolism only an anthropologist could understand." I was one of the academics in attendance, and as we left the press briefing room we were almost trampled by the stampede of journalists coming to the press conference for the U.S. basketball "Dream Team" that followed us.

Let me conclude with Bob Costas's argument for the importance of occasional depth and complexity in sports journalism:

> I think that in general sports broadcasting is not and should not be 100% journalistic—that it's a combination of information, entertainment, drama, and journalism, history, context, perspective. And how much of each is required differs from situation to situation. [. . .] But there are times when issues come up where

you should be able to interview in as straightforward a fashion as if it were a newscast. Or where you need to report and do investigative work as if it were just the same as a news story. . . . If we did it more often, I think that (a) it would be interesting, (b) it would be responsible, and (c)—and I think sometimes the executives don't understand this—it would lend greater credibility to a thinking person when someone says, "You know what, this is exciting, it's moving, it's emotional, it's heartbreaking, it's dramatic, it's touching, it's thrilling"—if you said all that amid a presentation that included journalistic elements, included a recognition that not everything is always peachy-keen, I think it would have more credibility to it. I think we strike some of the same notes too often, and that a little bit more history, a little bit more commentary, a little bit more journalism, would give more texture to it.

EPILOGUE

I was contacted by National Public Radio's *All Things Considered* before the Atlanta Olympic Games about doing a piece on China and the Olympics. By the end of the Games, my contact had become interested in the "China bashing" that had gone on in the press and asked me to write a commentary on it. I did so and faxed it to her the morning after the closing ceremony. Her executive producer rejected it, saying that the Olympics were over and that they had moved on to other things—the Republican convention was coming up.

NOTES

All opening ceremony transcriptions in this chapter are my transcriptions of videotape recordings. I am grateful to Nancy Rivenburgh for providing me with the tape of the 1992 Barcelona Olympic Games.

1. Brook Larmer, "The Creation of Yao Ming," *Sports Illustrated*, September 26, 2005, 66.
2. Elliott Almond, "'The Crooked Shadow': Chinese Swimmers, under a Drug Cloud, Today Are Expected to Be Banned from Pan-Pacific Championships," *Los Angeles Times*, February 12, 1995.
3. Hannah Beech, "The Price of Gold," *Time Asia Magazine*, August 16, 2004, www.time.com/time/magazine/article/0,9171,678686-1,00.html (July 14, 2007).
4. Sang Ye, "Unlevel Playing Field: Confessions of an Elite Athlete," in *China Candid: The People on the People's Republic*, ed. Geremie Barmé with Miriam Lang (Berkeley: University of California Press, 2006), 175.
5. Brook Larmer, *Operation Yao Ming: The Chinese Sports Empire, American Big Business, and the Making of an NBA Superstar* (New York: Penguin Books, 2005).
6. Frank Dikötter, *Sex, Culture and Modernity in China* (Honolulu: University of Hawaii Press, 1995), 109–16, and *The Discourse of Race in Modern China* (Stanford,

Calif.: Stanford University Press, 1992), 169–95. The current Marriage Law does contain some strictures against marriage by certain categories of people, but—contrary to popular belief in the West—forced sterilization is not mandated by law as it was in some states in the United States in the 1920s and 1930s and in Nazi Germany, to name two examples.

7. Ma Mingshan, "The Spiritual Requirements and Satisfaction of a Selection of China's Top Athletes—A Survey of 68 National and World Champions," *Tiyu shehuixue wenji* [Collected Sport Sociology Papers] 1 (Tianjin Institute of Physical Education Dean's Office, February 1982): 109–117, cited in Kong Xiang'an, Niu Xinghua, and Qiu Bo, "A Summary of Sport Sociology Research in the PRC," trans. and ed. Susan Brownell, *International Review for the Sociology of Sport* 25, no. 2 (1990): 101.

8. Susan Brownell, *Training the Body for China: Sports in the Moral Order of the People's Republic* (Chicago: University of Chicago Press, 1995), 231–32.

9. "Hopeful Parents Give Up Prize," *Atlanta Journal and Constitution*, April 18, 1994, D10.

10. "Taboo: Childrearing," National Geographic store website, http://shop.nationalgeographic.com/product/238/1757/128.html# (June 2007). Aired January 6, 2004, and repeatedly thereafter; it was still being aired in 2007.

11. It is also featured in Rick Reilly, "Here No One Is Spared," *Sports Illustrated*, August 15, 1988, 75; Beech, "The Price of Gold"; "The Ultimate Athlete: Pushing the Limit." Discovery Channel documentary, directed by Scott Hicks, produced by Ultimate Pictures, 1996.

12. Kerry Strug was a member of the gold-medal-winning U.S. Olympic gymnastics team in 1996 who "nailed" the landing on a high-scoring vault with an injured ankle and then collapsed and was carried from the mat.

13. Gary Smith, "The Great Leap Upward," *Sports Illustrated*, July 18, 1984, 529.

14. Zhao Yu, "*Qiangguo meng*" [Superpower Dream], *Dangdai* [Contemporary Times], February 1988, 163–98.

15. "1995 Pan Pacific Games—Drug Piece," produced by Richard Brenner for NBC Sports, 1995.

16. For more detail on doping in Chinese sports, see Susan Brownell, "Comparative Analysis of Doping Scandals: Canada, Russia, and China" (jointly written with Bruce Kidd and Robert Edelman), in *Doping in Elite Sport: The Politics of Drugs in the Olympic Movement*, ed. Wayne Wilson and Edward Derse (Champaign, Ill.: Human Kinetics Press, 2001), 153–88.

17. Ma's training methods included strategic use of altitude training before competitions, and a "many meals, small meals" schedule that he pioneered. This referred to the fact that his athletes trained four times per day and ate four meals per day. Those skeptics of the fact that his runners ran "a marathon a day" were not considering that this averaged to only six and a half miles per training session. This principle was later perfected and disseminated throughout China's sports system. It did not become common among European and North American distance runners until some years later. They, of course, were hampered by the fact that they had other time commitments in their lives besides running.

18. "Get Faster Quick!" *Track and Field News*, April 1994, 60.

19. An exception was Alexander Wolff, "The China Syndrome: Chinese Athletes and Coaches Are Increasingly Subject to the Ills and Temptations That Afflict Sports in the West," *Sports Illustrated*, October 16, 1995, 84–93.

20. Robert Sullivan, "A New Twist in Diving," *Sports Illustrated*, August 15, 1988, 78–84.

21. Reilly, "Here No One Is Spared," 70–77.

22. *New York Times*, September 1, 1996, National section, 17; *Washington Post*, August 14, 1996. The advertisement listed the organizations that had donated funds for the campaign: New York United Federation of Chinese Associations; Chinese Students and Scholars Associations (CSSAs) at Harvard, UCSF, Stanford, Columbia, and UMCP; Tongji Alumni Association; Silicon Valley Chinese Engineers Association; Foundation for U.S.-China Relations, Inc.; Chinese American Business Association; CSSAs in New York, Chicago, and Washington, D.C.; Federation of Chinese Students and Scholars in Canada; and about eighty other organizations and countless individuals worldwide.

23. Susan Brownell interview with Song Shixiong, China Central Television Station, Beijing, May 21, 1994.

24. A fuller analysis of CCTV's broadcast of the Barcelona opening ceremony, along with background information about the history of sport television broadcasting in China, is found in Susan Brownell, "Cultural Variations in Olympic Telecasts: China and the 1992 Olympic Games and Ceremonies," *Journal of International Communication* (special issue on "Olympian Communication") 2, no. 1 (1995): 26–41.

25. This is my translation of a videocassette of the Chinese telecast of the Olympic ceremony. This videocassette was very generously provided to me by Nancy Rivenburgh and was collected as part of the international research project headed by James Larson, Miquel de Moragas, and Rivenburgh, titled *Global Television and the Olympic Games: The Experience of Barcelona 1992*.

26. Miquel de Moragas Spà, "Olympic Values and the Television Broadcast of the Inaugural Ceremony at Barcelona in 1992," in *Olympic Centennial Congress Bulletin* (Lausanne: XII Olympic Congress Media Ad Hoc Committee of IOC, 1993), 42–48.

27. Susan Brownell interview with Bob Costas, September 24, 1996; phone interview with Bob Costas, April 2003.

28. Nancy Rivenburgh demonstrated the lack of "richness" in the national images presented in U.S. Olympic broadcasts in "National Image Richness in U.S.-Televised Coverage of South Korea During the 1988 Olympics." *Asian Journal of Communication* 2, no. 2 (1992): 1–39.

29. Reuters, "Chinese Commentator Sorry over Anti-Socceroo Rant," *Sydney Morning Herald*, June 28, 2006, www.smh.com.au/news/aussie-update/i-dont-like-australians-indeed/2006/06/28/1151174235245.html (July 15, 2007).

30. Protest NBC Fundraising Committee, "International Press Release Letter," August 31, 1996.

Chapter Seven

Will the Olympics Change China, or Will China Change the Olympics?

One hundred years have passed since the question now famous in China was asked, "When will China be able to invite all the world to Peking [Beijing] for an International Olympic contest?" In 2008 the Olympic Games will be hosted by the least westernized nation in the world to yet host them. It will mark a pivotal moment when the Olympic Movement begins to attain an unprecedented universalism, expressed in the slogan "One World, One Dream."

But the past century has left a legacy that must be overcome. On the one hand, Western governments still deeply mistrust communism, a leftover from the Cold War. On the other hand, the age of Western colonialism and imperialism is not that far behind us, and neither is the idea that the West represents the pinnacle of human civilization that the rest of the world should imitate. These are beliefs that have changed slowly as the peoples of the world have come to know and understand each other, and they will continue to change in the future. As shown in previous chapters, the Olympic Movement has played a role in promoting this change, and we can hope that the Beijing Olympic Games will help improve the lack of understanding of China that still exists.

The Beijing Olympics have widely been touted as the harbinger of a new age of Eastern imperialism and the rise of the "China threat." But a less paranoid and more measured assessment of the past 100 years as well as projections for the future reveal that global politics and culture are still Western-dominated and will continue to be in the near future. The International Olympic Committee (IOC) has been numerically and politically dominated by Western European countries since its inception. From its founding in 1894 to 2006, as the total number of members has increased from fifteen to 114, the percentage of European members in the IOC has decreased from 80 to 42 percent, with Western European members moving from 67 to 33 percent—a

Figure 7.1. The theme slogan of the Beijing Olympic Games at the Badaling section of the Great Wall. Photo by Diana Grande, 2007.

decrease of 34 percent. However, most of the increase outside the West has been in the number of African members (from zero to 18 percent) since 1960, while the proportion of Asian members has remained relatively constant since World War II. In 1945, Asia constituted 18 percent of IOC membership with ten members; in 2006, it constituted 20 percent of IOC membership with twenty-three members (see table 7.1).[1] When the People's Republic of China (PRC) was founded in 1949, there were three IOC members in China. In 2007, there are four Chinese members: two members in mainland China, one in Taiwan, and one in Hong Kong.

The changing composition of the organization is only part of the picture because there is also the question of whether its ideas have or have not changed. With the West generally and Western Europe in particular still dominating the IOC numerically, the *ideas* that rule the Olympic Movement could well be slower to change than the numerical *composition* of the organization itself. This will be dealt with further below.

Although China was a strong supporter of the Olympic Movement before the revolution, its relationship with the IOC was characterized by a great deal of misunderstanding after the founding of the PRC. At that time, over 50 per-

Table 7.1.   Numbers of International Olympic Committee Members by Continent and Percentage of Total Membership

Region	1894	1920	1945	1960	2006
Europe	12 (80%)	35 (66%)	31 (55%)	30 (47%)	48 (42%)
Western	10 (67%)	27 (51%)	23 (41%)	24 (37%)	38 (33%)
Eastern	2 (13%)	8 (15%)	8 (14%)	6 (9%)	10 (9%)
Asia	0 (0%)	2 (4%)	8 (14%)	7 (11%)	17 (15%)
Africa	0 (0%)	1 (2%)	0 (0%)	2 (3%)	20 (18%)
Middle East	0 (0%)	1 (2%)	2 (4%)	6 (9%)	6 (5%)
South/Central America	1 (7%)	6 (11%)	9 (16%)	11 (16%)	13 (11%)
North America	1 (7%)	6 (11%)	4 (7%)	4 (6%)	5 (4%)
Oceania	1 (7%)	2 (4%)	2 (4%)	4 (6%)	5 (4%)
Total	15	53	56	64	114

cent of the IOC membership came from Western Europe, North America, or Oceania. The main reason that a better understanding of China could not be reached was that productive conversation was impossible because of the IOC's unofficial policy against "mixing politics and sport." On the one hand, this policy is understandable since the IOC was caught in the middle of the Cold War, and so the ban on "talking politics" prevented political conflicts that were not under IOC control from tearing it apart. Probably Edstrøm, Brundage, Killanin, and other IOC leaders sincerely believed that this policy was the best thing for sport. However, they could not see that the effect of this policy was to silence the voices of the new nations formed in the wake of World War II while allowing the West to talk, which was itself a political act.

If China's experience provides the IOC with a lesson for the future, it is that in difficult situations mutual understanding can be achieved only through hard work on both sides, and the dialogue must be characterized by what Pierre de Coubertin called "mutual respect."

I would like to address three questions:

1. Can the Olympics really bring about social change?
2. Will the Olympics change China?
3. Will China change the Olympics?

CAN THE OLYMPICS REALLY BRING ABOUT SOCIAL CHANGE?

Leading up to the Games, Western politicians, human rights groups, and media commentators will each use the Olympic Games as a platform for their own political agendas. Probably they will criticize the Olympic Games for failing to live up to their promise to "contribute to building a peaceful and better world." The founder of the modern Olympic Games, Pierre de Coubertin, had a vision that still shapes the Olympic Movement today, but in this age people expect concrete proof that a vision is being carried out. In previous decades, with some notable exceptions, scholarship on the Olympic Movement tended to consist of chronicles of events and celebrity athletes rather than comprehensive analysis. In recent years, much of the public perception of the IOC has been shaped by the investigative journalism of the British journalist Andrew Jennings and the Salt Lake City Olympics scandal.[2] It is a necessary part of democratic society that U.S. congresspeople and groups like Human Rights Watch use the Olympic Games as a platform to gain media attention. However, this is an instrumental use of the media and a cynical use of the Olympic Games by people who do not understand the inner workings of the Olympic Movement. We need well-researched journalistic and social scientific analysis to help us understand the possibilities and limitations of the world of sport, which has its own rules that are different from those of mainstream politics and economics. In order to get beyond the superficial exploitation of the Olympic media platform, we should better understand those rules. Since the job of investigative journalism is primarily to uncover what is being done wrong, others must discover what is being done right. In the past decade scholars have begun to fill in the void with increasing numbers of studies by economists, media scholars, historians, and others.[3]

In recent years, the IOC itself has recognized the need for a more scientific understanding of itself, particularly on the question of "legacy," which refers to all those things that are left behind after the Olympic Games have come and gone. The IOC is not currently in a good position to respond to criticisms of the Beijing Games because it lacks solid scientific evidence to back up its claims that the Olympic Games can bring about positive social change. As described in the *Olympic Review*,

> Hosting an Olympic Games has a significant impact on the Host City and its community. From tangible infrastructure construction, such as competition venues and transport construction, through to the evolution of the image of a Host City, the event acts as a vehicle and catalyst which leave a lasting mark on the city, host country and its people through its economic, urban, social or historic influence. To what extent, with what results, and to what benefit have been a long-lasting debate.[4]

Beijing will be the first host city to produce a full Olympic Games Impact (OGI) report. The local organizing committee signs a contract with a university in the host country, and both work together with the IOC to collect information on 150 economic, social, and environmental indicators.[5] Collection of the information for OGI begins when a city's candidacy is announced and concludes two years after the staging of the Games, a period of eleven years. Beijing will be the first host city to carry out a complete OGI for the entire eleven-year period; it is being done by the Humanistic Olympic Studies Center at the People's University. While this is one of the top universities in Beijing and in China, there was a feeling among academics that the contract was awarded to the People's University because historically it was the university with the closest links to the Communist Party. Beijing University, China's top liberal arts university but with a history of radical student protests, was bypassed. However, the People's University's close connection with the government has advantages since it will facilitate access to statistics required by the IOC that are normally difficult to acquire.

This is a big step toward understanding the Olympic Movement as a complex social phenomenon, but the OGI is composed largely of quantitative measures of economic and sports development, such as improvements in water quality, increases in sports participation, increases in open-air leisure spaces, or increases in hotel infrastructure. It is much harder to measure more abstract social and cultural changes, which will be especially interesting in the case of China. In particular, OGI will not assess the cultural fields that are uniquely significant for China. For example, it will not measure the effects on cultural heritage, such as the preservation of cultural practices, artifacts, and monuments to enrich the Olympic cultural program versus the destruction of historical sites for new construction; the growth of traditional exercises like qigong and wushu versus their replacement by Olympic sports; the effect of the Olympic Games on traditional cultural beliefs; and so on. While OGI will attempt to measure some political changes, this will remain a realm that is largely opaque to measurement and thus public knowledge.

WILL THE OLYMPICS CHANGE CHINA?

The Legal Legacy

One of the most fundamental changes that might occur because of the Olympic Games will be the "legal legacy" of the Games. While social change can occur when a nation is pressured by international media scrutiny, enduring change is most likely to occur when it is reinforced by the rule of law. Since international law is one of the main ways of pressuring countries to conform to the Western-dominated international standards in today's world, it is important to understand the legal foundations of the Olympic Movement. These are not very well understood by the popular audience because they have been swiftly changing over the past two decades and because this is one area where the world of international sport tends to "play by its own rules," compared to

Figure 7.2. Facing the main entrance of the Beijing Sport University, a sculpture of a sprinter in the blocks, constructed in the 1990s, is running down a statue of Chairman Mao, whose back is turned, constructed in the 1950s. Photo by Susan Brownell, 1994.

other international organizations that may be linked into larger legal systems (e.g., the sports world has its own Court of Arbitration for Sport).

The Olympic Charter

The Olympic Movement is guided by the Olympic Charter as its fundamental document, but this document is concerned with the world of sport and does not directly address many of the issues that concern people pushing political agendas. The only human right recognized in the Charter is found in Fundamental Principle #4, which states, "The practice of sport is a human right."[6] The right to participate in sport has not been upheld as a human right either in international law or even in the United States.[7] Nondiscrimination is also enshrined in the Olympic Charter, and the Olympic Movement has been fairly effective in improving racial and gender discrimination through sport. However, overall, the Olympic Charter cannot serve as the legal basis for changing the human rights in any nation, China or otherwise.

Manual for Candidate Cities for the Games *and the Host City Contract*

For a legal foundation for the issues that concern journalists and politicians, we have to turn elsewhere than the Olympic Charter. One place to turn is the *Manual for Candidate Cities for the Games* and the associated host city contract.[8] The bid process itself puts the host city under a great deal of pressure to conform to Western standards, and this pressure intensifies if the city is awarded the Games. The 2008 candidature file was a very detailed, legally binding document requiring the bid city to respond to seventeen categories of questions about its economic and political structures and its social and cultural traditions. It also required the submission of thirty signed covenants or guarantees by the relevant authorities. The host city contract is based on the candidature file and is also legally binding, but it is not made public.

Requirement of English and French

To begin, all bid documents must be in the two official languages of the IOC, English and French, which placed a particularly heavy burden on China. The painstaking process of translating Chinese drafts into English kept many people awake into the early hours of the morning whenever deadlines approached. It made the selection of the emcee for the bid presentation difficult—finally the female news anchor Yang Lan was selected for her years of reporting for Chinese English-language television and was widely considered to be a huge success. Vice Premier Li Lanqing joked about his English in his bid presentation in Moscow. Those officials in the Beijing 2008 Olympic Games Bid Committee (BOBICO) and the Beijing municipal government who did not speak English were at a disadvantage in dealing with the almost weekly visits from the IOC and the International Sport Federations. Beijing Vice Deputy Mayor and BOBICO member Wang Wei, who had received an M.A. in English literature from Rutgers University, quickly rose in the hierarchy as he became the most visible spokesperson for BOBICO. He later became executive vice president and secretary-general of BOCOG and vice chairman of the All-China Sports Federation.

Environment-Friendly Construction

Forced evictions for the construction of venues are one accompaniment of the Olympic Games that sometimes gets attention (in Atlanta as well as Beijing), and it was stridently protested by Human Rights Watch in the context of the construction of the Olympic Green. The most relevant guarantees in the candidature manual are found in the sections on competition sites, the Olympic Village, and the media centers. These sections require guarantees of the agreement of the owners to allow the use of the property. In the section on "Environmental Protection and Meteorology," the manual states outright that "Environmental Protection is an area where Candidate Cities often experience tough public scrutiny and opposition."[9] The IOC has emphasized environmental protection, but it is reluctant to interfere in the urban planning of the host cities.

Media Guarantees

Facilities for the media are the subject of some of the important guarantees in the manual. The candidature manual estimated that for the 2008 Games the IOC would request accreditation for 17,000 members of the media. Later the number was increased to 21,600. Freedom of the press is dealt with in the statement that "media accommodation must be provided to all accredited media representatives who apply for it in accordance with the procedure set up in agreement with the IOC and within the set deadlines."[10]

Freedom of Travel

In one case the IOC considers itself above national laws, and that is in the question of freedom of travel. The immigration and customs guarantee states that "notwithstanding any regulations in your country to the contrary,"[11] all holders of the Olympic identity card (referring to the large numbers of people involved in organizing the Olympics) will be authorized temporary entrance into the country and will be allowed to import and export goods for the IOC free of all customs duties. This was in violation of China's constitution, customs, and censorship laws and caused much stress among the members of BOBICO. They presented the problem to the top leadership, the State Council, saying, "Look, this is what the IOC requires. If we bid for the Games we must do it right. Do we bid or not?" And the answer came back: bid.

Limitations of the Candidature Manual and Host City Contract

So it is possible for the IOC to demand conformity to its own standards, and conceivably a host city contract could add requirements banning forced evictions, media censorship, and so forth, but the IOC does not make such demands because they are considered "political," and, as was discussed in chapter 5, the IOC tries to define itself as a nonpolitical organization. The bid process is supposed to be concerned only with technical matters; if individual IOC members choose to vote for a host city on the basis of political factors, that is an individual choice.

In certain areas, the legal system of China is being changed in order to comply with international standards in order to make possible the organization of the Olympic Games.

Intellectual Property Rights

The protection of the Olympic marks was a very big concern of the IOC from the beginning. China also sees this as an opportunity to educate people about intellectual property rights, considered important for the development of the Chinese economy as well as its international relations, because fake imitations of famous brands have been a big problem for domestic as well as for foreign brands. BOCOG hired the New York–based legal firm Morrison &

Figure 7.3.   The five "Fuwa" mascots at the Beijing Olympics Souvenir Shop on Wang-fujing Street, Beijing. There have already been problems with mass counterfeiting of Fuwa without licensing. Photo by Andy Miah, 2006.

Foerster LLP to oversee its legal affairs. As a result, the IOC was generally satisfied with protection of the Olympic marks. Large-scale production of knockoff products did take place, but they were dealt with when exposed. However, the understanding of intellectual property that was disseminated was very limited because people understood that the Olympic marks could not be freely used, but pirated CDs, for example, were still available everywhere. In addition, the character *ao,* the first character in the Chinese word for "Olympic," *aolinpike,* became extremely popular in names of companies, restaurants, and products, which could have been considered a kind of "ambush marketing," but because of the language difference it slid under the IOC's radar screen, while Chinese people were unaware that it could be considered problematic.

Beijing Olympic Broadcasting Company

Chinese law does not allow direct foreign investment in Chinese television, but central approval was given to form a foreign–Chinese joint enterprise, Beijing Olympic Broadcasting Company (BOB), to broadcast the international feed. Media publicity has avoided stating that this meant that the State Council made a decision to set aside a law that was considered very important for national security. The problem began when the IOC decided to set up its own in-house broadcasting agency, the Olympic Broadcasting Service (OBS) as the Official Broadcaster for the Olympics (OBO) for Olympic Games, starting with the Olympic Games of 2008, not imagining that this might conflict with any country's national laws. A compromise was reached, and the website for BOB carefully worded the compromise as follows:

> Beginning with the Olympic Games of 2008, the International Olympic Committee (IOC) has created Olympic Broadcasting Services (OBS) to serve as the Official Broadcaster for the Olympics (OBO) for future Olympic Games.
>
> The IOC has requested that the Beijing Organizing Committee for the Olympic Games (BOCOG) use OBS as the OBO for the Games.
>
> BOCOG and OBS have determined that, rather than have OBS serve alone as the OBO for the Games, the functions and responsibilities of the OBO, in the case of Beijing, can best be carried out through a Sino-foreign Cooperative Joint Venture, established under PRC laws, managed by OBS in accordance with the Cooperative Joint Venture Contract, the Articles of Association, and the Master Operating and Management Agreement. Accordingly, BOCOG and OBS have established Beijing Olympic Broadcasting (BOB) as a cooperative joint venture to perform the role of the OBO.[12]

The chief executive officer of BOB was Manolo Romero of OBS, and its chief operating officer was Ma Guoli, the former director of the Sports Bureau at China Central Television. The president of the Board of Directors was Jiang Xiaoyu, executive vice president of BOCOG, while IOC Coordination Commission Chairman Hein Verbruggen was the vice chairman. Among the executive management, the department heads, and the Board of Directors, there were ten IOC personnel and twelve Chinese personnel, assuring numerical dominance by Chinese people.

The Nagoya Resolution

For China and Taiwan, another important legal document is the IOC's Nagoya Resolution of 1979, which readmitted China to the IOC under the "Olympic formula." In all IOC events and publications, China is known as the "Olympic Committee of the People's Republic of China" and competes under the national anthem and flag of the PRC. Taiwan is recognized as a branch division of the Chinese Olympic Committee and is known as the "Olympic Committee of Chinese Taipei" and competes under the anthem and flag of its Olympic committee. Taiwan is not allowed to use the name of the Republic of China or its national flag and anthem. The "One China Principle" of Chinese foreign policy allows no expression of the existence of the Republic of China as a sovereign state. It is also a precondition in all of China's diplomatic agreements with the United Nations and the 168 national governments of the world that extend diplomatic recognition to China that they will not allow the symbols of the Republic of China to be shown in venues controlled by them. This is an extremely important political issue in China, and it is unlikely that there will be a change in China's position. Thus, any move toward independence by Taiwan could provoke a military reaction in Beijing that would disrupt the Olympic Games. Taiwan is more important to China than the Olympic Games because it is considered a question of national sovereignty.

How Long Will It Last?

It might be said that the IOC currently has its "foot in the door" of Chinese law. The question is how far the door will open and how long it will stay open. Most of the legal changes mentioned here are temporary. The freedom from customs and censorship restrictions for holders of the Olympic identity card, the freedom of reporting for foreign journalists (discussed below), and the Sino–foreign joint enterprise in television will probably all disappear a few months after the Olympic Games. However, during their existence, many Chinese people will have had a chance to work and communicate more closely with foreigners, and they will have become more familiar with international practices and standards. Intellectual property protection will remain, and the system for enforcing it might be a bit better than before.

SOCIAL PROCESSES

While significant, the realms in which the legal legacy might be felt are quite limited. It is not primarily through legal means that the Olympic Games could effect broad-based change; rather, it is through long-term processes that will be unlikely to make headlines. At the 2002 Symposium on the Legacy of the Olympic Games organized by the Olympic Museum and Studies Center and the International Chair in Olympism of the Autonomous University of Barcelona, it was pointed out that there is an "intangible legacy" and that culture is the ultimate source of all other legacies.[13]

IOC as a Teacher of Democracy?

He Zhenliang was present when the flag of the PRC was raised for the first time over an Olympic Village in Helsinki in 1952. He was twenty-two years old. It would be twenty-eight more years until it was raised again at the Lake Placid Winter Games and thirty-two years until it was raised over the Los Angeles Summer Games. He Zhenliang had spent the golden years of his youth working for the sports diplomacy that finally led to China's readmission to the IOC in 1979. He was co-opted as an IOC member in 1981 after he had spearheaded China's readmission. IOC Sessions and Executive Board meetings are run according to parliamentary procedure, which may be new to people from countries that do not have democratic political meetings. He had no choice but to become a master of parliamentary procedure during his years of arguing that the IOC had violated its own charter in admitting two Chinese Olympic Committees—in essence, he learned to use the IOC's own rules against it. President Samaranch praised him for his loyalty to the charter in his foreword to He's biography.[14] Between 1988 and 1996, he was a member of the Seventh and Eighth Chinese People's Political Consultative Conference (CPPCC), which is one of the two representative assemblies in the Chinese central government. During much of this time, the CPPCC followed parliamentary procedure in name, but all the proposals presented to it were unanimously approved, and so it was not actually democratic process in action. He took his IOC experience back to the CPPCC, where he initiated lively debates on national sport policy and was part of a general trend toward a more legitimate democratic process.[15] Today, proposals in the CPPCC are actively debated, votes are not unanimous, and sometimes proposals do not pass at all.

Cynics might find it hard to believe, but it is conceivable that the IOC teaches democratic process to members from countries where it is not the rule, and they then take that process back to their home countries. The Department for Relations with the National Olympic Committees has as one of its mandates the goal of ensuring that elections in National Olympic Committees are conducted according to proper procedure, and they are sometimes called in to act as election observers.

The Most Important Legacy: People and Culture

The 94 percent approval rate that was calculated by the Gallup poll commissioned as part of Beijing's bid in 2001 showed that Beijing residents had a high level of confidence in the promises of the Games. Yet their hopes and dreams do not occupy the prominent place in the Western imagination that is occupied by the question of human rights. The changes that the West hopes will be brought to China by the Games are not exactly the same changes that the Chinese themselves hope for. Beijingers are concerned largely with whether the preparations for the Games will improve their quality of life. The infrastructure that is being put in place for the Olympic Games will change the face of Beijing with new monumental architecture, roads, environmental improvements, and sports facilities. The investments in controlling air and water pollution and reforesting the area, in particular, should improve the basic quality of life of a large segment of the populace. Additionally, as was previously discussed, Chinese people hope the Games will present an image of a healthy and flourishing China to the world and erase the stereotype of the "sick man of East Asia." We can hope that the hopes and dreams of average Chinese people will not be forgotten in the media coverage of the Games.

The greatest legacy of the Beijing Games will be its human and cultural legacy. There are three themes for the Olympic Games: the high-tech Olympics, the green Olympics, and the *renwen* Olympics. *Renwen* is difficult to translate. Blending people and culture, it is formed of the characters for 人 *ren*, "human," and 文 *wen*, "literature, culture." Normally it is the translation for the academic "humanities," and thus it is sometimes translated as the "humanistic Olympics." Actually, it has two facets, one of which might be translated as the "people's" Olympics, and the other as the "multicultural" Olympics. The "people's" Olympics means that the Games will provide an opportunity to train Chinese people for a globalizing world. The "multicultural" Olympics means it will promote a blending of Chinese and Western culture, enriching both Chinese and global culture.

Hosting the Olympic Games will require China to—as a currently popular phrase puts it—"link up with international standards" (*yu guoji jiegui*), accelerating the process that began over 100 years ago. The changes that occur will not be those forced on China by others but will be those that China voluntarily seeks out so that it may play a key role in the global society of the twenty-first century.

Olympic Education and Volunteer Training

Confucian tradition holds a strong faith in education as a means for creating a harmonious society. One of the main ways in which the "people's" Olympics will be realized is through "Olympic education" on a scale never seen before. There are academic and professional conferences, textbooks and courses for public schools and universities, educational television and radio shows, magazine and newspaper essays, Internet training, and more. BOCOG and Olympic scholars see the enthusiasm of volunteers as an opportunity to improve the public educational level and morality with education in Olympic history and values, traditional Chinese culture, Beijing history, public etiquette, international customs, foreign languages, and lifesaving first-aid skills. Originally, 100,000 volunteers were slated to receive training, but after assessing the potential for shaping the next generation, BOCOG decided to multiply that number up to 500,000. Because of the importance of foreign language skills and the goal of shaping the next generation, most of the volunteers will be college students.

Intense International Media Scrutiny

During the Games it is expected that 21,600 accredited media and around 10,000 unaccredited media, or a total of nearly 32,000 media, will be swarming around Beijing. Journalists being what they are, we can be sure that they will not all be looking for whitewashed stories. Dissidents and critics will gain more media attention than they would otherwise have had. For two weeks China will be open to the world as never before.

In late 2006, several new restrictive measures on journalists in China were announced. After an international outcry, the Ministry of Foreign Affairs enacted a temporary law guaranteeing media freedom to foreign journalists researching the Olympic Games and "related matters" from January 1, 2007, to October 17, 2008. This law has been criticized because it does not guarantee Chinese journalists the same freedoms. In addition it has been reported that foreign journalists are being harassed by officials in local areas who are either not familiar with the law or who feel that the journalists are looking into topics not related to the Olympic Games.

Academic studies have shown that Western media coverage of the Beijing Olympics has been more dominated by political topics than coverage of other Olympic Games.[16] Chinese regard the politicization of the Western media as hypocritical since the West has constantly criticized Chinese media for their political bias, and since 1978 the reduction of the political content of Chinese media has been considered one of the accomplishments of the policy of opening up to the outside world.

Chinese culture places a great emphasis on respect for the dignity of people and nations. There is a highly refined protocol between a host and a guest; this also extends to Chinese conventions for the expression of mutual respect between states, which historically was more highly developed than that of the West.[17] As was seen in the previous chapter, in 1996 the Chinese audience in the United States interpreted Bob Costas's comments about China during the opening ceremony as the host country criticizing its guest. Negative media reporting during the Games will probably make some Chinese people angry because it is as if a host invited a guest to his home and the guest then criticized the host. In the Chinese tradition, host–guest meetings are highly ritualized and are not supposed to be occasions for straightforward debate. There is a general feeling that the Western media are not interested in the new construction, the rising standard of living, or the economic achievements of the past decades—the things that matter most to Chinese people. Reporting that serves the West's appetite for "curiosities," highlighting China's differences with the West rather than its commonalities, is considered disrespectful to China and to the Olympic ideals. Chinese beliefs echo Coubertin's notion of "mutual respect." He recognized that it is possible to learn from another culture only if one regards it with a basic attitude of respect. China's desire to learn from the West is an expression of this respect, but it is not so clear that the West approaches Chinese culture with similar respect. It is also true that negative reporting could spur new and sometimes painful levels of self-reflection as China sees itself through the eyes of the rest of the world.

The Promotion of Cosmopolitanism and English

The general command of English in the city will rise as everyone from volunteers to hotel employees to taxi drivers is expected to study it. While some people might question whether the learning of a little English might have any lasting effects, it is actually part of a larger process in which everyday people start to see themselves as members of a global community. The need for foreign languages is a challenge for BOCOG. Many BOCOG employees are studying English. It is easier for the top leaders of BOCOG with a good command of English to deal with their non-Chinese counterparts. Many of these leaders also hold positions in the Beijing Municipal government. As they deal with members of the international sports community on a regular basis, they will not only reach a better understanding of their international counterparts but also learn about international standards in such areas as corporate sponsorship and intellectual property protection. The next generation of Beijing's top leaders—and perhaps even leaders of the central government—will be more cosmopolitan because of the Olympic Games.

International Networks Formed by Corporate Sponsorships

In the summer of 2005, I was in Qingdao (Tsingtao) for the Tsingtao International Beer Festival. Tsingtao Beer was also celebrating the fact that it had just been designated the domestic beer co-sponsor, with Yanjing Beer, for the Games. I was surprised to find that our hotel in Qingdao was full of Americans from my home city of St. Louis, the headquarters of Anheuser-Busch Beer Company, the makers of Budweiser beer. The Americans were there because Anheuser-Busch, the global beer sponsor of the Beijing Games, is a partner of Tsingtao Beer. I learned that most of my Chinese hosts had already visited St. Louis many times. They told me that they felt they had much to learn about how to use American marketing techniques to maximize the sponsorship. Olympic sponsorship helps China "link up to international standards."

Chinese people are proud that the Chinese personal computer company Lenovo is the first TOP sponsor that is a Chinese company,[18] although there are some who think that because the other sponsors are from developed countries, the TOP Program helps the rich nations get richer—a problem the IOC may have to confront in the future. Lenovo is also working with a foreign partner to learn how to maximize its sponsorship.

WILL CHINA CHANGE THE OLYMPICS?

People in Beijing are talking about the Olympic Games as an opportunity for China to learn knowledge and practices from the West that will benefit China's development. They are not paying as much attention to the question of whether China can teach anything to the West. Likewise, OGI will assess the impact of the Olympic Games on China and not China's impact on the Olympic Games. Although Chinese people believe that the result of the Games will be a "combination of East and West," if the Olympic Games are only a one-way process in which China learns from the West, then the cultural exchange will not be truly mutual.

The second goal of the "humanistic Olympics" is to display Chinese culture to the world and propel the Olympic Movement to become a truly transcultural, transethnic, transnational, global cultural system. Actually, there is a great deal that Chinese philosophy could contribute to the philosophy of Olympism, such as respect for human dignity; the search for world peace or *datong*, "the Great Harmony"; *he er bu tong*, "harmony among those who are different"; and *tian ren he yi*, "humans and nature as one." Wushu expresses the traditional concept that "humans and nature are one"—linking humans with the environment through *qi*, it teaches a "green" sports philosophy that could be a new contribution to Olympism.

Chinese culture will be expressed in the forms of hospitality toward guest nations, the exhibitions of the traditional sport of wushu, the starting time of the opening ceremony (8:00 P.M. on August 8, 2008), the cultural performances in the opening and closing ceremonies, the layout of the Olympic Green along the north–south axis of Beijing according to the principles of feng shui, and in other ways.

However, it is not easy for a non-Western nation, even one with such a strong cultural heritage as China, to propel the Olympic Movement to become universal. The IOC's decision not to include wushu as an Olympic sport even after two decades of effort by the Chinese government to promote

Figure 7.4.   Guo Liang, a national champion martial artist in the 1980s. Photo taken by Susan Brownell at Beijing University, 1985.

it internationally is one example. China's difficulty in promoting its own traditions within the context of the Olympic Games illustrates how slowly change comes to an international organization like the IOC and the global cultural event over which it presides. If China cannot increase its presence in global Olympic culture, then the prospects are even worse for other non-Western nations.

As recalled in He Zhenliang's biography,

> European sports developed comparatively early, and the majority of previous Olympic Games were held by European nations. The IOC was founded in Europe, its headquarters are in Europe, and European members outnumber those of other nations. Therefore it is unavoidable that inside the IOC there exists a certain degree of Eurocentrism. In his dealings with the IOC, Zhenliang experienced this problem early on. After being co-opted as a member, Zhenliang established that he would fight for the dissemination and globalization of the Olympic Movement. [. . .] Nevertheless, perhaps because old habits die hard, [Western IOC members] still consciously or unconsciously reflected this problem in their ways of thinking.[19]

He Zhenliang initially encountered difficulties in promoting Chinese sport culture as a part of "Olympic Culture." The Olympic Museum at the IOC headquarters in Lausanne, Switzerland, largely features exhibits from the modern Olympic Games, along with a modest collection of ancient Greek sports art. After the establishment of the museum in 1993, He proposed that it should introduce the "sport cultures of different civilizations," but some members of the Executive Board disagreed, stating that it should display "things relevant to Olympism." He argued,

> Times have changed; the participants in the ancient Olympic Games were limited to the various city-states in the area of Greece, in the later periods it expanded to various places along the Mediterranean sea. Even in the modern Olympic Games, the first participants were limited to a dozen European and North American countries. However, participants in today's Olympic Games come from every corner of the world. They represent different cultures and what they have introduced into the Olympic Games is completely different from the past, and needless to say the meaning of the modern Olympic Games is completely different from the ancient Olympic Games, too. Can we only transmit Greek sports culture to the nations of the world and should we not at the same time introduce the sport cultures from different sources?[20]

In 1999, leading up to Beijing's second bid for the Olympics, He Zhenliang organized an exhibition on "5000 Years of Sport in China: Art and Tradition" at the Olympic Museum, mentioned in chapter 1 as part of China's effort to create a sport history. Later the art of other non-Western peoples was also exhibited there, and the resulting catalogues were published by the IOC.

BOCOG considers the opening ceremony to be the most important opportunity to show Chinese culture to the world. It is widely agreed that the opening ceremony at the Athens Olympic Games were very successful. But the rest of the world was already familiar with the history of "Western civilization," so the images in the Athens ceremonies were easily understood. China faces the challenge of presenting cultural symbols to a global audience largely unfamiliar with them. There was discontent with the Beijing segment choreographed by the famous film director Zhang Yimou for the closing ceremony in Athens because many Chinese felt it catered to Western stereotypes. Particular disapproval was expressed toward the musical performance by women playing traditional Chinese instruments and dressed in the iconic traditional dress, the *qipao*—but with a twist: the *qipaos* displayed the traditional mandarin collar and side-closing frog buttons, but they had extremely short miniskirts. This was felt by some observers to sacrifice authenticity to a blatant use of eroticism. In addition, the child sitting on top of the great red lantern that rose out of the stage was said to be an advertisement for his own film, *Raise the Red Lantern*. In the summer of 2005, the ceremonies were opened up to a bid competition. Zhang Yimou's film company applied as well as that of another famous director, Chen Kaige, and others. Eventually Zhang Yimou was redesignated as the choreographer along with a series of "advisers" who included Chen Kaige and Steven Spielberg. BOCOG perceived a dearth of Chinese people with the ability to communicate their own Chinese traditions to a wider audience.

Some people, however, recognized that maybe westernized Chinese culture can be better appreciated by non-Chinese, akin to the phenomenon that westerners tend to prefer westernized Chinese food over the more authentic version, which is more heavily flavored and may consist of things that westerners do not usually eat.[21] There was also discussion about how "Chinese" the cultural segments should be. The result was a serious public reflection about what exactly "Chinese culture" is, which will help shape a new vision of it for the twenty-first century. Since China's top leaders were at least aware of Zhang's choreography and perhaps officially approved it, in light of the ensuing public discontent, they are probably reexamining their own conceptions too.

ARE WE READY?

Few people are seriously asking the question, Will China change the Olympic Games? In the West, there is more concern with the question, Will the Olympic Games change China? Why is the West so concerned about changing China and not concerned about China's changing the West? Chinese people hope that the West can learn something from China through the Olympic Games. Can it?

The Chinese slogan for Beijing's bid, *xin Beijing, xin Aoyun*, "New Beijing, New Olympics," was translated into English as "New Beijing, Great Olympics." Members of the bid committee felt that non-Chinese might not understand how China could create a "new" Olympics. China hopes that it will help to make room in the Olympic Games for different cultural traditions, but is the West really open to that possibility? Are we truly ready for "One World, One Dream"?

NOTES

1. Figures drawn from Allen Guttmann, *The Games Must Go On: Avery Brundage and the Olympic Movement* (New York: Columbia University Press, 1984), 263–71, and "Members," www.olympic.org (June 18, 2006).

2. Andrew Jennings and Clare Sambrook, *The Great Olympic Swindle: When the World Wanted Its Games Back* (London: Simon & Schuster, 2000); Andrew Jennings and Vyv Simson, *The New Lords of the Rings: Olympic Corruption and How to Buy Gold Medals* (London: Pocket Books, 1996); Vyv Simson and Andrew Jennings, *The Lords of the Rings: Power, Money and Drugs in the Modern Olympics* (London: Simon & Schuster, 1992).

3. Examples with a global scope include Miquel de Moragas Spà, Nancy K. Rivenburgh, and James F. Larson in cooperation with researchers from twenty-five countries, *Television in the Olympics* (London: J. Libbey, 1995); Holger Preuss, *The Economics of Staging the Olympics: A Comparison of the Games 1972–2008* (Cheltenham: Edward Elgar, 2006); Christina Koulouri and Konstantinos Georgiadis, eds., *The International Olympic Academy: A History of an Olympic Institution* (Athens: International Olympic Academy, 2007); John Bale and Mette Krogh Christenson, eds., *Post-Olympism? Questioning Sport in the Twenty-First Century* (Oxford: Berg Press, 2004); Boria Majumdar and Sandra Collins, eds., "Olympism: The Global Vision: From Nationalism to Internationalism," special issue of the *International Journal of the History of Sport* 23, no. 7 (November 2006).

4. "What Is the Olympic Games Global Impact Study?" *Olympic Review: Official Publication of the Olympic Movement*, June 2006, 1.

5. "Measuring Global Impact," *Olympic Review: Official Publication of the Olympic Movement*, June 2006, 2.

6. 2004 Olympic Charter (Lausanne: International Olympic Committee, 2004), 9.

7. James A. R. Nafziger, *International Sports Law*, 2nd ed. (Ardsley, N.Y.: Transnational Publishers, 2004).

8. *Manual for Candidature Cities for the Games of the XXIX Olympiad 2008* (Lausanne: International Olympic Committee, 2001).

9. *Manual for Candidature Cities*, 39.

10. *Manual for Candidature Cities*, Theme 16: Communication and Media Services, B: Media Operations and Services.

11. *Manual for Candidature Cities*, Theme 18: Guarantees, Question 3.1, 3.3.

12. Official website of Beijing Olympic Broadcasting, www.bob2008.com/about.html (July 15, 2007).

13. "Conclusions and Recommendations," *International Symposium on Legacy of the Olympic Games: 1984–2000*, Joint Symposium of the IOC Olympic Studies Center and Olympic Studies Center, Autonomous University of Barcelona, November 14–16, 2002 (Lausanne: Documents of the Olympic Museum Collection, 2003), 2, www.olympic.org (June 2007).

14. One of the members of the Culture and Education Commission, which He Zhenliang chairs, described him as "the most democratic person in the IOC."

15. Liang Lijuan, *He Zhenliang and China's Olympic Dream*, trans. Susan Brownell (Beijing: Beijing Foreign Languages Press, 2007), 510–11.

16. Dong Xiaoying et al., "*Aoyunhui yu guojia xingxiang: Guowai meiti dui sige aoyun juban chengshide baodao zhuti fenxi*" [The Olympics and National Image: An Analysis of the Themes in Reportage on Four Olympic Host Cities in Foreign Media], unpublished manuscript, Beijing University.

17. See, for example, James Hevia, *Cherishing Men from Afar: Qing Guest Ritual and the Macartney Embassy of 1793* (Durham, N.C.: Duke University Press, 1995).

18. TOP stands for The Olympic Partner Program. It is awarded to eleven corporations that acquire the only sponsorship with the exclusive worldwide marketing rights to both the Winter and the Summer Games.

19. Liang, *He Zhenliang and China's Olympic Dream*, 389–90.

20. Liang, *He Zhenliang and China's Olympic Dream*, 383.

21. At the opening banquet of the IOC's Fifth World Forum on Sport, Culture, and Education in Beijing on October 23, I was surprised to find that the food that was served was bland and generally not very good. But when the Greek and German guests at my table starting picking gingerly at the wood-ears (*muer*), not a particularly exotic food, and asking what they were, I realized that we were being served westernized Chinese food and that even this toned-down version was testing the limits of tolerance of my fellow table-mates.

Selected Bibliography
of English-Language Sources

Abe Ikuo. 2003. "Historical Significance of the Far Eastern Championship Games: An International Political Arena." *Bulletin of the Institute of Health and Sport Sciences, University of Tsukuba* 26: 37–68.

Bale, John, and Mette Krogh Christenson, eds. 2004. *Post-Olympism? Questioning Sport in the Twenty-First Century*. Oxford: Berg Press.

Barnett, Eugene E. 1990. *My Life in China, 1910–1936*. East Lansing: Asian Studies Center, Michigan State University.

Brownell, Susan. 1995. "Cultural Variations in Olympic Telecasts: China and the 1992 Olympic Games and Ceremonies." Special issue of *Journal of International Communication* 2, no. 1: 26–41.

———. 1995. *Training the Body for China: Sports in the Moral Order of the People's Republic*. Chicago: University of Chicago Press.

———. 1996. "Representing Gender in the Chinese Nation: Chinese Sportswomen and Beijing's Bid for the 2000 Olympic Games." Special issue of *Identities: Global Studies in Culture and Power* 2, no. 1: 223–47.

———. 1998–1999. "The Body and the Beautiful in Chinese Nationalism: Sportswomen and Fashion Models in the Reform Era," *China Information* 13, no. 2/3 (autumn/winter): 36–58.

———. 1999. "Strong Women and Impotent Men: Sports, Gender, and Nationalism in Chinese Public Culture." In *Spaces of Their Own: Women's Public Sphere in Transnational China*, edited by Mayfair Mei-Hui Yang. Minneapolis: University of Minnesota Press, 207–31.

———. 2000. "Gender and Nationalism in China at the Turn of the Millennium." In *China Briefing 2000: The Continuing Transformation*, edited by Tyrene White. Armonk, N.Y.: M. E. Sharpe in cooperation with The Asia Society, 195–232.

———, Bruce Kidd, and Robert Edelman. 2001. "Comparative Analysis of Doping Scandals: Canada, Russia, and China" In *Doping in Elite Sport: The Politics of*

Drugs in the Olympic Movement, edited by Wayne Wilson and Edward Derse. Champaign, Ill.: Human Kinetics Press, 153–88.

———. 2007. "'Sport and Politics Don't Mix': China's Relationship with the IOC during the Cold War." In *East Plays West: Essays on Sport and the Cold War*, edited by Stephen Wagg and David Andrews. London: Routledge, 261–78.

Chen, Nancy. 2003. *Breathing Spaces: Qigong, Psychiatry, and Healing in China*. New York: Columbia University Press.

Coubertin, Pierre de. 2000 [1913]. "An Olympiad in the Far East." In *Olympism: Selected Writings*, edited by Norbert Mueller. Lausanne: International Olympic Committee, 695–97.

Cui Lequan, ed. 2000. *Album on Ancient Sports Art in China*. Beijing: Zhonghua Shuju.

Dong Jinxia. 2003. *Women, Sport and Society in Modern China: Holding Up* More *Than Half the Sky*. London: Frank Cass, 73–96.

Elvin, Mark. 1989. "Tales of *Shen* and *Xin*: Body-Person and Heart-Mind in China during the Last 150 Years." In *Fragments for a History of the Human Body*, part 2, edited by Michel Feher. New York: Zone Books, 266–349.

Fan Hong. 1997. *Footbinding, Feminism and Freedom: The Liberation of Women's Bodies in China*. London: Frank Cass.

Farquhar, Judith. 1994. *Knowing Practice: The Clinical Encounter of Chinese Medicine*. Boulder, Colo.: Westview Press.

———. 1999. "Technologies of Everyday Life: The Economy of Impotence in Reform China." *Cultural Anthropology* 14, no. 2: 155–79.

———, and Qicheng Zhang. 2005. "Biopolitical Beijing: Pleasure, Sovereignty, and Self-Cultivation in China's Capital." *Cultural Anthropology* 20, no. 3: 303–27.

Giles, Herbert A. 1906. "Football and Polo in China." *The Nineteenth Century and After* 59 (April): 508–13.

Guttmann, Allen. 1984. *The Games Must Go On: Avery Brundage and the Olympic Movement*. New York: Columbia University Press.

———. 2004. *Sports: The First Five Millennia*. Amherst: University of Massachusetts Press.

Killanin, Lord Michael. 1983. *My Olympic Years*. London: Secker and Warburg.

Knuttgen, Howard G., Ma Qiwei, and Wu Zhongyuan, eds. 1990. *Sport in China*. Champaign, Ill.: Human Kinetics.

Kolatch, Jonathan. 1972. *Sports, Politics, and Ideology in China*. Middle Village, N.Y.: Jonathan David Publishers.

Kuriyama, Shigehisa. 1999. *The Expressiveness of the Body and the Divergence of Greek and Chinese Medicine*. New York: Zone Books.

Larmer, Brook. 2005. *Operation Yao Ming: The Chinese Sports Empire, American Big Business, and the Making of an NBA Superstar*. New York: Penguin Books.

Larson, James F., and Heung-Soo Park. 1993. *Global Television and the Politics of the Seoul Olympics*. Boulder, Colo.: Westview Press.

Liang Lijuan. 2007. *He Zhenliang and China's Olympic Dream*. Translated by Susan Brownell. Beijing: Beijing Foreign Languages Press.

Liu, James T. C. 1985. "Polo and Cultural Change: From T'ang to Sung China." *Harvard Journal of Asiatic Studies* 45, no. 1: 203–24.

Liu Ji, ed. 1996. *5,000 Years of Physical Culture and Sports in China*. Beijing: Beijing University of Physical Education Publishing House.

Majumdar, Boria, and Sandra Collins, eds. 2006. "Olympism: The Global Vision: From Nationalism to Internationalism." Special issue of the *International Journal of the History of Sport* 23, no. 7 (November).

Mao Zedong. 1917. *"Tiyu zhi yanjiu"* [A Study of Physical Culture]. In *Une étude de l'education physique*. Translated by Stuart R. Schram. Paris: Mouton. Originally in *Xin qingnian* [New Youth] 3, no. 2 (April). Excerpts in English translation are found in Fan Hong, *Footbinding, Feminism and Freedom*, 313–17.

Miuria, Kunio. 1989. "The Revival of *Qi:* Qigong in Contemporary China." In *Taoist Meditation and Longevity Techniques*, edited by Livia Kohn. Ann Arbor, Mich.: Center for Chinese Studies, 331–62.

Moragas Spà, Miquel de, Nancy K. Rivenburgh, and James F. Larson in cooperation with researchers from 25 countries. 1995. *Television in the Olympics*. London: J. Libbey.

Morris, Andrew. 2004. *Marrow of the Nation: A History of Sport and Physical Culture in Republican China*. Berkeley: University of California Press.

Nafziger, James A. R., and Li Wei. 2004. "China's Sports Law." In *International Sports Law*, 2nd ed. Ardsley, N.Y.: Transnational Publishers. Also in the *American Journal of Comparative Law* 46, no. 3 (summer 1988): 453–83.

New World Press. 1986. *Sports and Games in Ancient China*. Beijing: New World Press.

Olympic Museum, ed. 1999. *5000 Years of Sport in China: Art and Tradition*. Lausanne: Musée Olympique.

People's Sports Publishing House. 1986. *Sports in Ancient China*. Beijing: People's Sports Publishing House.

Preuss, Holger. 2006. *The Economics of Staging the Olympics: A Comparison of the Games 1972–2008*. Cheltenham: Edward Elgar.

Pusey, James Reeve. 1983. *China and Charles Darwin*. Cambridge, Mass.: Council on East Asian Studies, Harvard University Press.

Ren Hai. 1988. "A Comparative Analysis of Ancient Greek and Chinese Sport." Ph.D. diss., University of Alberta.

Rivenburgh, Nancy. 1992. "National Image Richness in U.S.-Televised Coverage of South Korea during the 1988 Olympics." *Asian Journal of Communication* 2, no. 2: 1–39.

Sang Ye. 2006. "Unlevel Playing Field: Confessions of an Elite Athlete." In Sang Ye, *China Candid: The People on the People's Republic*, edited by Geremie Barmé with Miriam Lang. Berkeley: University of California Press, 166–80.

Shao Wen-liang, ed. 1986. *Sports in Ancient China*. Hong Kong: Tai Dao Publishing.

Smith, Gary. 1984. "The Great Leap Upward." *Sports Illustrated*, July 18, 522–33.

Sports Illustrated. 1988. "Sports in China: The Birth of an Athletic Power" (special report). August 15, 36–88.

Wolff, Alexander. 1995. "The China Syndrome: Chinese Athletes and Coaches Are Increasingly Subject to the Ills and Temptations That Afflict Sports in the West." *Sports Illustrated*, October 16, 84–93.

Xiong Xiaozheng, Liu Bingguo, and Zhang Tianbai, eds. 1990. *Illustrated History of Ancient Chinese Sports*. Beijing: Yanshan Publishing House.

Xu Guoqi. 2008. *Olympic Dreams: China and Sports, 1895–2008*. Cambridge, Mass.: Harvard University Press.

Yasuo Yuasa. 1993. *The Body, Self-Cultivation, and Ki-Energy*. Translated by Shigenori Nagatomo and Monte S. Hull. Albany: State University of New York Press.

Zhang, Everett Yuehong. 2005. "Rethinking Sexual Repression in Maoist China: Structure, Ideology, and the Ownership of the Body." *Body and Society* 11, no. 3: 1–25.

Index

Note: Page numbers in italic type indicate figures.

A Scientized Wushu, 60
Abrahamson, Alan, 164
acrobatics, 37
acupuncture, 51
agon, 25–27, 28, 33, 40, 96n23; agonal
principle (or spirit) 27–28, 33, 37;
agonistic character, 26. *See also*
Burckhardt, Jacob; Curtius, Ernst;
Ehrenberg, Victor; competition,
notions of in China
Ai Qing, 2, 90–91
Ai Weiwei, 2, 73, 90–92
Alexander, Reginald, 133
Almond, Elliott, 164
Andrianov, Constantin, 132, 134, 137
Anheuser-Busch Beer Company, 192
archaeology: Greece, in, 23, 35–36;
China, in, 36
Aristotle, 24
Armstrong, Lance, 155
Aryan race. *See* race
Asian Games, 88, 105; 1962 Djakarta,
135; 1974 Tehran, 136; 1990 Beijing,
64, 67, 77, *77,* 81–84, *84,* 86–89, *86,
87, 90,* 93, 142; 1994 Hiroshima, 160
Asiatische Reiterspiele, 36

Australia, 142, 172. *See also* Olympic
Games, 2000 Sydney
Autonomous University of Barcelona,
188

Bandung Conference, 135
Barlow, Tani, 125n5
Barnett, Eugene, 34, 58
basketball, 1, 109, 112, 114, 118, 120,
151, 152, 171, 173
Beijing Institute of Physical Education,
see Beijing Sport University
Beijing City Team Center, 10
Beijing Olympic Broadcasting
Company, 186–87
Beijing Olympic Games (2000), bid for,
17n7, 38, 65, 86, 88–89, 116–8,
128n42, 142, 196
Beijing Olympic Games (2008): bid for,
1, 3, 14, 19, 38, 40, *41,* 65, 89,
128n42, 129–30, 142–45, 170,
183–86, 189, 194, 196; corporate
sponsorship in, 191–92; cultural
programs for, 40, 181, 189–90; and
democracy, 188; English language in,
5, 41, 183, 191–92, 196; and

About the Author

Susan Brownell is professor of anthropology and chair of the Department of Anthropology and the Department of Foreign Languages and Literatures at the University of Missouri–St. Louis. She has lifelong experience in the world of sports, beginning with equestrian events at the age of two, followed by a career as a nationally ranked U.S. track-and-field athlete (in pentathlon/heptathlon) from 1978 to 1990, including her experience as a national champion college athlete in China in 1986, and continuing with medals in the U.S. National Adult Figure Skating Championships in the past decade. She was president of the St. Louis Skating Club and a member of the organizing committee of the 2006 U.S. Figure Skating Championships in St. Louis. In 2007 she was inducted into the Washington County (Maryland) Sports Hall of Fame.

Her first book, *Training the Body for China: Sports in the Moral Order of the People's Republic*, was based on her experiences as a member of the Beijing University track-and-field team during 1985–1986. It was among the first ethnographic works based on intensive fieldwork written after China opened up to foreign social scientists. She is also coeditor with Jeffrey N. Wasserstrom of *Chinese Femininities/Chinese Masculinities: A Reader*, and editor of *The 1904 Anthropology Days and Olympic Games: Race, Sport, and American Imperialism*. Since 2000 she has been a member of the postgraduate grant selection committee for the Olympic Studies Center of the International Olympic Committee. In 2007–2008 she was a Fulbright Senior Researcher at the Beijing Sport University, doing research on the 2008 Beijing Olympic Games.